I0453366

THE
APATHETICAL
MAN

The Apathetical Man
by Gregory M. McLeod

"Today all of my Hopes point me to God's principles and his Son's Words."

Author McLeod has lived through many remarkable events, sharing them here so others may learn to seek and find such a miraculous purpose for themselves. He recounts a childhood drawn from prodigious memory, raised in a quiet rural atmosphere but within a dysfunctional family grouping. Early on, he fell into experimentation with lust and later into the pit of drug addiction, the latter leading to rehab facilities and more dependence on the drugs provided by the medical profession. He resisted counseling in favor of the palliation of drugs but was finally diagnosed with depression and bipolar disorder. Those challenges were overcome by his gradual conversion to strong Christian belief. He had unusual experiences. For example, he once lost a very valuable chain of keys and, being urged by an inner voice to keep looking, drove out in the dead of night and found the keys shining in the moonlight alongside a highway miles from home. Such happenings deepened his faith and encouraged him to record his experiences for others.

McLeod states that his life changes came through choice, and offers lengthy, often highly perceptive, metaphors and fables to support that assertion, all relating to his Christian convictions. He writes with energy and a personable style that frequently includes the phrase "no kidding," as though he and the reader were in a one-on-one conversation. His unique visions and communications with God have enlivened his duties as a part-time preacher and a powerful confessor among many congregations. The book contains many scriptural references vividly explored and explained. His work covers subjects such as the sins of idolatry, witchcraft, and emulations, and there are numerous comparisons to machinery that the author has encountered in his working life. This book focuses on hard-won faith and could provide engaging guidance for group discussion and personal seeking.

-The US Review of Books

THE
Gregory M. McCleod
APATHETICAL
MAN

ARPress
45 Dan Road Suite 5
Canton MA 02021
Hotline: 1(888) 821-0229
Fax: 1(508) 545-7580

Ordering Information:
Quantity Sales. Special discounts are available on quantity purchases by corporations, associations, and others. For details, contact the publisher at the address above.

Printed in the United States of America.

ISBN-13   Paperback   979-8-89389-034-1
                      eBook   979-8-89389-035-8

Library of Congress Control Number: 2022904709

Contents

Dedication

To MY PARENTS WHOM HAVE SUFFERED GREATLY THROUGHOUT their life, but steadfast in Love toward all us children.

To my brothers and sisters whom have also suffered with me throughout my life and have encouraged me to live.

To my dear daughter whom I love dearly and gives me a hope for the next generation.

To All my family throughout the Great USA.

To All whom is suffering from Mental Illness and from Addiction to Drugs and Alcohol.

To All the Doctors whom have charity within their heart to help those with these problems.

To all my In-Laws, before and after.

To all those whom have came into my pathway of this Life on earth and gave to me a piece of their life and gave me hope when I had lost my hope.

To all the Pastors and Teachers of the Gospel of Jesus Christ.

Last and most, to my dear Honey, Sylvia, my wife, which is like Honey to my Soul. Thank you honey for showing me the longsuffering of a man's hand. Thank you for suffering with me and staying with me with patience throughout my trouble days.

INTRODUCTION

L IFE THE WAY THAT I PERCEIVE IT TODAY is a matter of "Understanding". Have you ever thought these things to yourself or said to another man, *"I just don't understand."* or *"I just don't believe that man understands."* or *"You don't understand what I'm going through!"* Have you ever thought this to yourself, *"This life is like a dream that I cannot awake from. Is this life real? Am I who I really think I am, or not? Could there be something greater beyond my imagination to this life, much more than, I really understand?"* Maybe you have never asked these questions to yourself or maybe you have given up about these matters in your life, because the understandings of these matters seem to be too great to conquer. Maybe you have said, *"This Life just doesn't make no sense!"* Listen closely my friend; if I thought that this physical life on this earth was all there was to Life, then I would be a man most miserable and without nothing. My past life was surrounded by these thoughts daily, and I gave up on these matters. I was a man without a true understanding of my Life's Purpose, much more so, the Purpose of All Life. I suffered greatly of not having confidence in Life and failed many times, because of not understanding Life in its trueness. Today my friend, a have been given a greater confidence in the matter of Life in completeness or its trueness and I have a great passion to give this confidence to you. Once I began to understand somewhat the mystery of Understanding, I asked God, "God Please tell me what I need to do." My God was quick to answer me back with a gentle, yet powerful magnificent voice, and he said to me, "Give your Life Away."

Today, I am confident that I can do nothing of myself, except to live, but I couldn't breathe without the air from my God and Creator of All. These writings that follow are not of what I have created but was built from the foundations of others and things of this life. Surely, I wrote the writings on paper for the eyes to see, but I take no glory. My life would not exist, if it wasn't for others in my life: For an example; If it wasn't for my Father, Mother, grandfather, grandmother and my God, I wouldn't exist, and you perhaps would not be reading these particular writings now. My life is not of my own and I'm confident today that there is something greater than of myself. Would you ever think that you or I could create ourselves?

I would think not, and much more so, would I think that I could have the power to create an ant?

My friend, there is something greater of Life, much more than, that of my own life. Would a clay vessel have "will" over the potter that made it? Or can an infant just from the mother's womb be Commander and Chief over a Great Nation? Understanding is mysterious in the same as the Creator of All Life is Mysterious. But, we today as mankind have a Holy Book right before are very eyes to grasp onto the mystery of understanding. We may say God is mysterious and hides things from us, but How can God hide himself from you? My friend, just look into the mirror at yourself, look to heavens of his marvelous works, look at the oceans and mountains, look at the living creatures, the flowers, the foods and trees of his great handy work. God has given his all to mankind to know him, which is, the greatest purpose of Life, if only a man would seek him. This Book, that I am talking about, is the Holy Bible. I believe the Word of God is the Holy Bible and it is the Understanding of God, as he reveals himself to the World and into an individual man's Life. I believe that if a man doesn't understand the Word of God and letting God revel himself to a man would be that of not letting go and letting God. For an example: "Can an ant stand in the way of an Amtrak train?"

Of Course, I believe an ant can stand in the way of an Amtrak train. An Ant has the right to travel on the tracks of a train, just as we can travel by a train-Pause- What? Could I think an ant could stand in the way of an Amtrak train? Maybe, if the train isn't moving, follow me? If I would have written this; "Can an ant stand in the way of an Amtrak train traveling at a speed of 70mph be able to stop the train?", then my answer would had been much more of, not. My friend, that was just for an example of how we as mankind maybe fast to think without understanding. We would read something and be quick to judge the writings, before understanding the writing in its trueness.

I believe today with a greater confidence that "NOT" Understanding Life in its trueness will stop a man dead in his tracks, such as, a man would be in the way of an Amtrak train traveling at a speed of 70mph. I believe that Understanding is Life and All Life was established by Understanding. And if a man is without the Understanding of Life, that man would be dead from Understanding Life.

Today I believe that I can do nothing of my own, except make choice. Surely there are inventors, but there is only one Creator. Everything that you could hold with your hands or see with your eyes or hear with your ears are from another and not of yourself. All things have purpose, except nothing. Your complete existence was created for purpose and this Book is based on that purpose which is Life. Purpose? Life? I believe that purpose is the Effect of Understanding Life. If, it wasn't for purpose you and I surely would not be reading these writings at this moment.

My friend, I will say this with confidence: I don't take any glory from any understanding or comprehension of the writings of this book; for I have only built upon of what I have been given of the purpose of Life. Just for starts: if I wasn't taught by a teacher to read and write in grammar school, again, you may not be reading these writings at this moment.

I wrote this Book from the foundations of what was given to me by others that were led by the understanding of Life's Purpose. Now, I have a great passion to share this purpose with you.

Life is a matter of understanding and if we could understand just this one purpose, we would be well: All life Is built on the foundations of our ancestors or even as far back to Adam and Eve. If it wasn't for Adam and Eve mankind would not exist today, follow me? Life isn't all about me; it is about us and all that is among All Creation. Would something as simple as an ant have purpose or would it just want to exist? Today, we as mankind may boast and may say that we have great wisdom or even great knowledge, but, if it wasn't for others, you and I would have nothing. Even though we have Presidents and Governors over us, great Scientist, great Doctors, great Pastors of the Fold, great Teachers, Masters, Servants and even Fathers or Mothers, but, if it wasn't for others, we would have nothing. Therefore, we as mankind only build upon the foundation of Understanding Purpose of Life from others and that Is why I say, "I can't live without others, and I take no glory for any of the writings."

When I truly began to Understand somewhat the Truth of Life, I was in a Rehabilitation Center willing to Understand the Matter and was desperate for a Change in my Life. I was near physical death and my spirit man was being quench from understanding life by my own self will living. I did have knowledge of one thing during this time at the Rehab Center and it was this; "If I don't get help on this matter, I was going to die." It wasn't a matter of "If" I would die, it was a matter of "when" I would die. Institutions and jails had already past my life, and I knew there was only one matter left for my life and it was, death. I've never spent time in a prison, but institutions and jails had past my time, and I didn't judge and think any different.

There at this Rehabilitation Center one particular day, I was suffering much and was seeking Understanding of Life. I was seeking desperately of how to live a much more abundant or normal. I went to a counselor that was there for me at this Rehab Center and I was desperate for help on the matter of Understanding Life in it trueness.

I told this counselor this, "I want to leave from the care of this rehab center, because you or no one else here can help me. I've been through the program many times, but I have always ended up right back in this same position. It's always the same blob, blob, blob. You just don't understand what I'm going through!" This counselor looked at me and knew something was greatly burdensome on me and he gently closed the door and said this to me, "I know your history, but please don't give up. Please tell me what is wrong, so that I can Understand." As soon as this man said this to me, I began to discern this man and knew he honestly wanted to help me. Not only did I discern the truth of this man's intent, I also knew I didn't even understand the word understand, no kidding. For the very first time in my life that I can remember those words from the mouth of that man touched me where only God himself had ever touched. I felt an awesome power of love and compassion in my heart and my life immediately began to change. I began to have hope in this Life again and told him what I believed to be the truth of my Life. I got honest for the first time in a long time with this man and it was if weights had drop from my heart. I told him this matter; "I know deep within my heart that I will die, if I don't get help with this matter now. I want to live a normal life and I do not want to die the way that I was living. I want to live for Life and not die in the Horrors that I was living for such a long time. I'm sick and tired of the way that I'm suffering and also the way I've cause my family and others to suffer for me." So, we sat there for hours and he began to understand my past and he understood the truth of my desperate call for Life. Together we began to seek help for the matter. I know this with confidence; if another man, such as a Doctor or Counselor, doesn't know the truth of a matter in your life, then that man cannot help you in the matter.

When I was willing to give this man my understanding of my life with honesty, he did somewhat understand the severity of my life. This man knew that he had to seek more counseling for me.

This man told me that he was willing to help me, if it took bringing in special Doctors into this Rehab Center at their expense, no kidding. It was at this very moment that I began to understand that I was almost at the end of my thread of Life. For the first time in my life, I was truly beginning to Understanding the severity of my life when the counselor said this to me, *"Please tell me, so that I will understand."*

In my past life, I had always thought that everyone knew and understood my problems and illnesses, especially the Doctors, but they really didn't understand. If they really understood the severity of my life during chances that came my way, would they come to my rescue? When this Counselor said this to me, I began to understand the Doctors really didn't understanding that I was going to die, if I didn't get help on this matter. I had no doubt of that understanding and I was desperate for change and I made a choice to fight for my life.

I believe Understanding is somewhat like the game hide and seek, but Understanding is everywhere. Speaking of myself, Understanding sleeps with me, walks with me, eats with me, talks to me, and is even inside me, but I still couldn't grasp onto it in my past dead life. Understanding can be in the physical where the fleshly eye can see it, and it is also Divine or Spiritual where you can't see it. I thought that I had been giving great Understandings of Life during seasons of my life, even from the time I was but a child to this very moment. God had revealed many things to me through his Word, Visions, Revelations and by his Spirit. But, it seemed to me as if the understandings had a lock upon them and I just could open the Truth of the Understandings.

Today I am confident that All Understandings that are given to a man are for purpose of Life and are for appointed times or seasons in a man's life. I also believe that Understanding can be given to a man and if the man isn't willing to break the Locks of self-will from the doors of his heart, then the Understandings would never become to manifest into the man's life. During my past dead life, I would seek with my fleshly eyes for something that I could put my finger on at that very moment and if I couldn't get it right then, I just gave up on getting it.

During these times of my past life, I would quench may the Spirit of God from my Life and my spirit man would not grow in the Great Understanding of Life. This quenching was that of a fear from deep within my heart of what I thought was the Truth of Life. I would become much void and empty of the Understanding Life as I would continue to quench my inner man from growing through and by the Spirit of God's Word, Visions, Revelations. Today I have a much greater confidence is this matter: "Understanding is Life. All of Life is Established by Understanding. God is Life. God is the Understanding of Life. I believe that Understanding is Divine and it is giving to them that want to Live. Understanding dwells with Life and not Death."

Given Understanding to a dead man is somewhat liken to this question; "Would you take a dead jack ass, lying and bloated beside the roadway, hold it in your arms, and then try to give it mouth to mouth resuscitation, so that, the dead jack ass would have a chance at life again? Would you want it to Understand Life?" My friend, I know that question was somewhat strong, but this life is serious; for it is a matter of Life or Death. Even though, if it was someone that had died that was as close to you as your own child, wife, husband, mother, father, brother or sister you would grieve greatly to bring them back to life again. But, you would know deep within your heart and see with the eyes of reality liken into a slap upon your face, with no doubt, that their works and rewards were finished in this physical Life on earth. Therefore, Understanding is given to a man that is Alive only.

My friend, I believe this with all my heart today: If a man wants to Live this Life much more Abundantly and wants all things that would make his Life much more abundantly, then that man will seek

Understanding of the God of Life. I am confident today, that if a man is willing to seek, ask, knock for Understanding in the right places, he will live a Life much more abundantly and have a greater confidence of Life in its Trueness. But, if the man gives up on living or quenches the divinity of understanding for a life much more abundantly, I'm confident that man would be void of Understanding the Truth of Life and would possibly die a death void of Life. Remember this; "God can't help a man, if the man stands in the way." Even though we were once sinners and maybe still are, God did knock at our hearts to help us. Standing in the Way of God would be in the same likeness as this:

"Standing in the way of an Amtrak Train, traveling at a rate of speed at 100mph loaded with passengers." Would you ever think that you could stop God? You may survive, but it would not be good. It is written in God's Word, *"Trust in the Lord with all thine heart, and lean not unto thine own understanding." (Proverbs 3:5-6). "The fear of the Lord is the beginning of knowledge: but fools despise wisdom and instruction." (Proverbs 1:7)* I believe that this life is liken into a Boot Camp or a Great School of Learning and Training for a Journey. I believe the Great Creator has given mankind all things to "Live" and "Survive" here on this earth and the Life to come. I believe God has given mankind everything you could think or imagine in the physical man and the spiritual man of Understanding the Truth or Reality of the Trueness of his Great and Marvelous Purpose. I believe that the Creator has provided physical and spiritual gifts or senses to every man under the heavens to grow in this physical life and the True Life of Eternity to come. I believe with a greater confidence today this; The Great Creator has given mankind All senses to grow in Life and to come to an Understanding of Him and we as mankind has no excuses (blame). I believe that the Creator has given the senses, such as that of sight, hearing, feeling, tasting, smelling, and thought to come to a choice of Understanding him.

I believe the Creator has given every man severally of the spiritual senses, such as *The Word of Wisdom, The Word of Knowledge, Discernment, Faith, Prophecy, tongues, interpretation of tongues, the gifts of Healing, the gifts of Miracles and the gift of Charity*, to grow in his Understanding of "All" Life's purpose. Today, I'm confident that mankind has no more excuses of not Living a Life much more Abundant on this earth and to have a greater chance at entering through the Straight Gate and Narrow Way of the Kingdom of the Great Creator of All Life. There are other spiritual things somewhat liken to the physical senses, such as sight, hearing, taste, feeling of touch, smell, and thought. I will expand much more on the spiritual senses and physical senses later in the writings. All of these physical and spiritual gifts or senses are given, so that, a man may grow in the spiritual Understanding and Wisdom of the Great Creator of All Life and have a greater Hope and Trust in him, with all the body and soul. For an example: if a man would have the spiritual gift of Discernment and exercise the gift by the Spirit of God in his life, then that man would have a much more understanding of good from evil. The man would have a much more ability to sense Chance, Choice and Change in his daily life as it comes to him like the wind. Oh Yes my friend, there is a great difference between the words right from wrong and good and evil. I will expand on these 4 words throughout the writings of this book.

"Go by your gut feeling!" Have you ever done anything wrong or just didn't make the right choice, even though, you thought not to do it in the beginning? This gut feeling is the spiritual sense of discernment which is a spiritual gift and not a fleshly judgment. There is a night and day difference between discernments and judgments. I will expand of these *Discernments* and *Judgments* throughout the writings of this book.

I believe that Understanding is the ability to see all things in their true relationships with the Creator's Spirit's Eyes and grasping on to them with greater confidence and a greater hope with our complete Life, physical and spiritual. I believe and have great confidence in this understanding today:

Chance is The Season that comes in a man's Life,

Choice is A divine gift or decision giving to man for acting on Chance. The willingness of a man's intent for his life.

Change is The effect and growth of a man's life from their choice of Understanding Life. It is also the manifested choice a man makes at the chances he would get in this life.

I believe that these three matters our engulfed into Understanding and it is what we do with these matters that will determine the way we live our life here on earth and how we end are life after at our appointed time. After the appointed time has manifested in our life, then what? Chance, Choice and Change comes into our lives unexpected like the wind. *These matters aren't a matter of "IF" it is a matter of "WHEN" they come to a man.* Remember this my friend: *"Life is not all about what we know in the Matter of Understanding, it is what we do with what we know of Understanding of Life that will determine the way a man lives his Life and ends his Life on this earth."*

The Purpose or Intent of this Introduction and the complete book from the beginning to the end, is for you to grasp onto what I believe to be the truth of the Understanding of Life as I give my life away to you. This introduction is given, so that, you will become familiar with my Life and to discern and understand me, if you make a choice to continue to read the writings. The writings are giving to you on what I believe to be the truth of Understanding Life in its Trueness. I am in no way intending you to follow me. The True intent of this book are written for only one purpose, *"Change."*

It is by Chance, Choice and Change that you are beginning to read this book. "I don't believe in coincidences". I believe all things have a reason for the chance that happens in a man's life. I also believe that not having the understanding of these matters hinder a man from making the right Choice at the Chance to Change for their self and all that is among him. In the Holy Book of Ecclesiastes 3, verses 1-9 will clearly give you an understanding of why I don't believe in coincidences in my life. I believe every man under the Heavens have been given Chance after Chance, Choice after Choice and Change after Change to better their ability to Live and has no more excuses. I believe a man has one chance to live, one chance only my friend and the choices that a man makes will determine how that man lives.

Life is Good and Well today for me, because I understand how to understand. It took me almost 28 years just to begin to understand how to understand the word "Understand", no kidding. I will say this with confidence; The way that I once lived I chose to live that way at the Chances that came like the wind in my life. I will say this with confidence also: in order for a man to begin to Understand Life he must understand the word "Understand". Would you think? I thought I understood all about the Matter of Understanding in my

Life in the past, but I didn't even have the Understanding of the word "Understand" at these times.

There once was an Old Slave that Prayed a Prayer like this: *Father, I ain't what I want to be, I ain't what I ought to be, I ain't what I'm going to be, but, Thank You Father, I ain't what I used to be.* Somewhat like the Old Slave Praying, I'm confident we all may have been there in that same position during a chance in our lives, praying, hoping and asking in something that could or would change our life. I'm sure as the Old Slave was praying, he was discerning reality in its trueness of purpose, with understanding. He was looking in the past, future and present at chances, choices and changes that he could or would make differently in his life at that very chance. Maybe he was thinking this; "If Only I had another chance at what I wanted to become in this life, would I make the right choices to change?" But, he also turn his thoughts to accept for who he was when he was praying at that chance. The old slave was well with that moment of chance he had been given at that very moment. He had the knowledge of understanding of who he was for the present chance. He must have sensed that living the way he was living for that day was much better than, that of his past time choices. He also must had been discerning that he was a slave at the present time and he had no control of his life for the future. "But", he had a confidence in something greater than that of his self. I am confident that this is a sense that a man needs to have knowledge and understanding of; *Discernment.* I believe it is the keeper of a man's life here on this earth and the Life to come. I've come to realize that the chances, choices and changes that I have control of, is *One Day at a Time.* I have to accept who I am for today and examine myself daily, sometimes minute by minute and second by second. If I'm happy and well, then that's great, but, if I'm not happy and well then, I have to examine myself to find out what is causing my sufferings.

Even though, I may think I understand the cause of my suffering from the past, there is nothing that I can do to change the choice of my past. But, If I am still breathing there is hope and I can change for today.

If I'm sensing sufferings in my life for today, then I must be still alive and I have another chance for change and I must be happy for that, or am I?

Chance, Choice and Change comes to us all, if we are still alive physically. If a man is still alive and is not dead physically, the man can Change for the better, if he is _willing_ for change. Today I can say this with a greater confidence; if a man is still alive physically, then that man has a chance for a much more abundant life on this earth. But, if the man is dead physically then that man's chance is vanished away as a vapor. That man has no more rewards on earth; for he is dead and his work is finished.

In the Holy Word of God it is written in Ecclesiastes Chapter 9 verses 4-6, *"For to him that is joined to all the living there is hope: for a living dog is better than a dead lion. For the living know that they shall die: but the dead know not anything, neither have they any more reward; for the memory of them is forgotten. Also, their love, and their hatred, and their envy, is now perished; neither have they any more a portion forever in anything that is done under the sun."* Today, change is the hope that I live for every day and I do not *want to live in the Horror that I lived in for nearly 30 years. Today, I understand with a greater confidence this; I must change and I have no more excuses but to change, if I want to live life much more abundantly. Not long before I started the writings of this book, I accepted the chance that came my way in this life. I made the choice for a change to the much more abundant life on earth and it was a great miracle in my life. The miracle was, "Resurrection".* I was Resurrected from a dead man walking, to now, a son of the Living God. Today I can say with confidence, "I Live! I live, because God purpose lives in me." I now anticipate every day, minute by minute, second by second, change in my Life.

Today I know life is all about change or growth in my physical and spiritual life. The world around me is changing, second by second and I must accept change to better my understanding of myself, my God, and all that is among me. Chance, Choice, and Change still comes like the wind in my life, but like the wind, I can hear it coming now, whereas, I didn't for a long time.

I believe a Man has 3 different dimensions of himself. I also believe that All Life Spiritual and Physical, has the witnesses of the God of Life. I believe that the witness in the spiritual things is that of God, the Son (Jesus Christ), and the Holy Ghost (The Holy Spirit). I believe that the witnesses of the physical on earth is that of blood, water, and the spirit of a man. Let me explain. God is the Operator, the Son is the Administrator, and the Holy Ghost is the manifestation of the witnesses of God in All Life. God is the Creator of All things. The Son of God (Jesus Christ and God's Christ) is his Administrator of All of the God of Life. The Holy Ghost manifests the things of God, through his only begotten Son, only. I believe the Holy Ghost manifest all things in a man's life severely and accordingly to God's Will or Purpose. I believe that the Holy Ghost is the witness of all God's Will. The witnesses of the earth is that of blood, water, and spirit. Today, I believe with a greater confidence that the blood running throughout a man's veins and heart, contains Life and it is the witness of a man. I believe that I had the witness of Life through the blood of my mother's womb when I was just an embryo, but I became God's property as soon as his breath Life came into my nostrils when I took my very first breath of air and received my living soul. When I received my soul as an infant, I received the witness of Life at that very moment of the God of Life and God marked (to know) me. I will explain throughout this book this Mark of God and some other Marks. I was God's property and God made me in his Image in his likeness. I believe that water also contains Life and it is also the witness of the Life on earth.

I believe also the spirit of a man is the witness before the Living God, of a man, on this earth. I believe that God's searches a man's Life (his spirit man or soul) by his Holy Ghost (Holy Spirit), and judges that man's life. I believe a man contains the witnesses within himself of the Spiritual and the Physical, and man has no excuses (blame or to be ashamed). I believe the witness are here of the Spiritual and Physical, so that, mankind has the Love of God within them to make his own choice in Life, without excuse (blame or to be ashamed). I believe a man has a soul, a body, and a spirit. My friend, I am in no way leading you to believe that I know all things of these mysteries of the Living God, but, I know what I know, and that, I know. I don't know that mystery in its completeness, but I do know that I can't even breath without the Living God giving me breath. My friend, this entire book is confirmed through God's Living Word by his Holy Ghost. There are things I've written in my past or shared with another man that was given to me where I thought that I knew it all, but later, the understanding that I had at the time, was just the beginning of a greater understanding. I will say this with confidence and then I will go forward. Today, I do know that I wasn't present with God in the beginning, when he said, *"Let us make man in our image, after our likeness:"* So, how would I know anything, except it be a witness to me by God's Spirit?

Now, the following writings will help explain this matter of the different dimensions of a man: *First-The Soul.* The soul is the inner man or spiritual man. I believe the soul is in the Image and likeness of the Living God. I believe it is the soul of a man that God has great passion for; a passion beyond a man understandings. In the Holy Book of Genesis 1:26 it is written, ***"And God said, Let us make man in our image, after our likeness: and let them have dominion over the fish of the sea, and over the fowl of the air, and over the cattle, and over all the earth, and over every creeping thing that creepeth upon the earth."*** I believe that a man has a soul in the likeness after the God of All Creation, but the creatures don't have a soul.

The reason I believe this to be true, is that of, mankind having dominion over all the living things of the earth. I believe that all living has a spirit, but not a soul. I believe that God can work through all the things of the World by his Spirit, but man has the soul in his likeness. The Soul is Eternal in the likeness of the Living God. I believe when I first took my breath out of my mother's womb, I received my soul. In the Holy Book of Genesis 2:7 it is written, ***"And the Lord God formed man of the dust of the ground, and breathed into his nostrils the breath of life; and man became a living soul."*** The soul is a replica body in the likeness of our fleshly body, but the soul doesn't die a death in the likeness of the fleshly body. The Soul is somewhat liken looking into the mirror and seeing yourself in the body, but from deep down in your heart you just feel that isn't you in the reflection, but only a reflection of your body. After the fleshly body dies the earthly death the soul of a man goes back to the Eternal God whom made it. It is somewhat in the likeness of a locust shedding its skin. The soul has a Mind somewhat like the brain of the earthly body. The Mind stores our understandings of this life on earth for eternal purposes. The mind stores the eternal understanding of a man and will determine a man's eternal Life, if it be Life or death. The Mind is the storage of our Soul and stores our intents and understandings of Life, such as these good things by God's Spirit; discernment, hope, joy, compassion, truth, love, patience, longsuffering, gentleness, love, forgiveness, and faith. I also believe the Mind is the gateway or the Door to the spiritual and it is here in the mind that you can imagine and dream. I believe it is here in the mind of the soul that the enemy, Satan, entices a man away from God's purpose for their life.

I believe the mind can be either good or evil. The Mind is the conscience of our soul, and the mind and soul are in one accord in the same likeness as our fleshly body and brain are in one accord. A man cannot function correctly without the eternal mind or conscience and the man cannot function correctly without the fleshly brain.

The Mind and Soul are a replica of our Fleshly Body and brain. I believe the Mind and Soul is the complete eternal intent of a man. I believe that the mind will only store those things which are eternal and has no other fleshly intent. I believe if a man's soul and mind is void of God's Will and is evil, it will be destroyed when it goes back to the Creator. I also believe if the mind is full and not void of the Creator, then the Creator knows that man and receives him back for his Glory. It is somewhat like this: If you plant a grapevine and only a few branches of the vine produced grapes and some branches where dead, what would you do? First, you would cut away the dead branches and cast them into a fire. If a certain branch would produce only one grape, what would you do? I would probably take it away from the rest of the vine and take care of it like pruning it, so that it would produce much more fruit. I also believe the mind is the gateway or door to our spirit man.

Second-The Body. The body is the Puppet or vessel and it contains the living organs, such as the heart, lungs, eyes, mouth, brain, bones and reflects an image in the mirror, so that the man has no excuse. I believe the body is a self-living creature and can make decisions on its own. I believe the Fleshly Body is a gift from the Creator God for Choice, such as learning, growing, grasping the Creator's Glory and Grace while living here on the earth. The Fleshly Body has a brain, which is in the likeness of the Mind, but the brain goes back to the earth and rots where the worm does crawl. Whereas, the mind goes back to Creator and does not die. The Fleshly Body's brain is the intelligence of the fleshly body and acts somewhat the same way as the Mind is for the Soul. The Brain stores feelings, such as, pains as if you hit your finger with a large hammer, past experiences (memories), judgments, fear and doubt.

The fleshly body also contains a heart which is located in the center of a man's body. The heart pumps life throughout a man's fleshly body. I believe that the fleshly life of a man is contained in the blood and the heart pumps this life throughout the body. I also believe that the blood contains the complete physical Life of a man, such as, the intents and thoughts of the man. I believe the blood is the complete Life and intents of the man. I believe Life is in the blood and the blood pumps through every living part of a man's physical body to keep it alive. I believe the blood of a man holds the completeness of the man's life; for the blood is life. I believe that the blood picks up the intentions and thoughts of a man's brain and they enter the heart. I believe it is at this moment when the heart receives the intents and thoughts of a man's brain mass, it enters all his body. It is somewhat like this: If I thought that I was going to die all the time, then that thought would enter into my blood and my whole complete body would not feel too good. If I would think this all the time, I would certainly not be well or die before my appointed time. I believe the Fleshly Body is a self-contained Intelligent being and can live on its own here on earth, by its memories and judgments stored in its brain, but will die the death without the Spirit. I believe also that the fleshly body is the weaker vessel of a man. I also believe it is here in the flesh that a man is weak and the enemy tempts a man to be led by his evil spirit. I believe that that body was made in the Image of God and when God made man's body he said, *"It is good."* I believe that the body is good and not evil, but the body can be abused by the sinful nature of mankind. I also believe the body to be the Temple of God for a man's life.

Third- The Man's Spirit. The man's spirit is who we really are and is the strength and effect of both our eternal soul and fleshly body. The spirit of a man is the intelligence or Effect (Power) of both soul (spiritual man) and fleshly body. The man's spirit is somewhat like a self-contained power reactor that gives power to both the fleshly body and spiritual soul.

It gives power to the fleshly body, so that the fleshly body can talk, eat, see, hear, smell, taste, move, think and stores these experiences in the body's brain mass. The Spirit then discerns, not judges, the heart which contains the life of a man and then stores understanding (confidence) in the Mind or conscience of the soul whether it be good for eternal purposes. These eternal experiences are how our spirit grows or matures in statue in the Creators Glory and Grace. It is somewhat like going to school for our very first time and after we have graduated, we would have the knowledge of things. But, we wouldn't have wisdom only knowledge. After we begin to grow and learn by experiences of life, we then begin to receive wisdom of Life. I believe the spirit of a man is the eternal intents and is who the man really is. I believe if a man's intent is sinful then that man's spirit is evil. I believe if a man's intents are good then that man's spirit is good. I believe if a man's spirit is evil then that man's spirit is being led by the evil spirit of Satan. The evil man is willing to do what is evil, such as Adultery, fornication, Idolatry, witchcraft, strife, seditions, heresies, wrath, murder, thefts, envying, drunkenness, and such like. I believe if a man's spirit is good then that man's spirit is being led by the Holy Spirit of God and is willing to do that which is good such as love, joy, peace, longsuffering, gentleness, goodness, faith, meekness, temperance and against such are not held by or under the law of the Creator. I believe all creatures under the heavens contain blood and have a spirit. I believe only a man has a soul or spiritual man and conscience. I believe the spirit can be either a good spirit or an evil spirit and it is somewhat like the darkness of the night from the Light of the Day.

I believe the Creator of Life creates all his creatures with a Good Spirit in the beginning, but that spirit is void. I believe it is void, so that it will grow in His Amazing Grace and Glory and get to know him much more and go back to him without void. I also believe the reason a man's spirit is void in the beginning is for the divine choice of the man to make while he is living under the sun.

I also know that there are evil spirits that can possess a man's spirit and keep the man bound from growing in the Creator's Love, Grace and Glorious Creation. I believe that there is a spiritual realm that the spirits are always struggling to do good for a man or evil for the man.

I believe a fleshly body and the man's spirit can be possessed by an evil or good spirit. I also believe that these spirits are the keeper or loser of a man's soul. I believe that if a man's spirit is possessed by an evil spirit, then that man is in danger for his eternal soul. I also believe that if a man's spirit is possessed by the Good Spirit of the Creator of Life, then that man wants to do what is well and is not in danger of his soul. I believe that when a man's spirit is possessed by an evil spirit and dies the death in the fleshly body, then that man's soul and spirit goes back to the God of Creation void of Understanding. I believe when a man dies the death in the fleshly body the Spirit of God discerns the man's Life to see if it is void or not of him. If it is void of God, then that man's soul is cast into fire, somewhat like the dead branches on a grape vine. I also believe that if a man chooses to be led by an evil spirit then that man after he dies the fleshly death, will go stand before God's Great Judgment Throne and will face an eternal judgment without any excuses, because of a void Life. I believe The Eternal Judgment is the eternal torment for the evil souls and all that are led by an evil spirit.

The Spirit of God is the Understanding and the Light of God (Life and witness) and the evil spirits are from the Darkness of Satan, which is, man's enemy and rebels against God's Good Spirit. I believe that the God of Life has given a man the Choice to choose between the two and choice is a gift from God; for God is Freedom and Liberty for all the Living. I also believe if a man's spirit is led by the Good Spirit of God and wants to do what is well then, his spirit is well and will not face the Great Throne of judgment.

I believe that if a man's spirit is Led by the Spirit of God then that man has already faced the judgment of God on this earth and has been tried to be found worthy of God's Love and Grace and Understanding. I believe this to be true, because, if a man is led by God's Spirit then that man is doing which is good and has found Grace in God's Eyes and his Life is not void of God. I believe that when a man makes the choice to receive and be led by God's Good Spirit then that man has already faced the judgment and will not experience eternal death (torments). Remember Enoch? But, the unbelievers and those that rebel against God's Good Spirit will be accounted as unworthy and be judged after their works on earth are done. I believe all that have rebelled against God and have not repented (changed) will enter torment.

I will say this with confidence with no shame; I once was being led by evil spirits. But my spirit which God had given me in the beginning as a newborn child cried out to him, "ABBA, FATHER! Please save me!" Even though, I was being led by evil spirits for so long during my past dead life my spirit man didn't want to be led by these evil spirits and be cast into the eternal torments. I was without understanding of Life, because the evil had darkened the light that my Life had at one time. But, I cried out loudly within my inner man and called on the Father of Light to shine into my Life and bring Life back to me. The Creator of Life was faithful and just to come into my life and the Creator cast out the darkness of horrors, misery and void.

I remember when I was but a child this principle from God's Holy Word. God's Spirit brought it back to my remembrance and it reads as written John chapter 3, *"There was a man of the Pharisees, named Nicodemus, a ruler of the Jews: The same came to Jesus by night, and said unto him, Rabbi, we know that thou art a teacher come from God: for no man can do these miracles that thou doest, except God be with him.*

Jesus answered and said unto him, Verily, verily, I say unto thee, Except a man be born again, he cannot see the kingdom of God. Nicodemus saith unto him, How can a man be born when he is old? can he enter the second time into his mother's womb, and be born? Jesus answered, Verily, verily, I say unto thee, Except a man be born of water and of the Spirit, he cannot enter the kingdom of God. That which is born of the flesh is flesh; and that which is born of the Spirit is spirit."

I believe also that the Body will eventually die without the Spirit and the Spirit will leave the Body if it is dead. Please keep reading, the points are coming. For who can understand all of The God of All Existence? The more I am willing to be led by his Holy Spirit the more life grows much more abundantly in His Marvelous Grace and His Infinite Understanding. The experiences that I've been through in my life have led me to believe and have Greater Hope and Confidence in this Matter of Life. I believe a man can be physically alive, but spiritually near death. I also believe a man can be near physically death, but spiritually alive. I also know that a man can be both physically near death and spiritually near death at the same time and this is what I will call, *Horror.*

The writings of this book are based on Spiritual Principles and I've taken Man's pen and let go and let my Higher Power's Spirit work though my Spirit and lead me throughout these writings. The writings do not force my Higher Power on anyone; for my Higher Power is Love and he knocks only on the man's heart (Life), so that he can come in and Love them and show them what Loving and Living is all about. I also will share with you what I believe to be the truth of the Difference of Love and Lust and also, some consequences of my choices throughout these writings.

The writings are to share my Higher Power with you and share some of his principles (His Will) with you. I have a great passion deep within my spirit man to share his principles with you with a fervently. I have this passion, because of the change they made in my Life. My Higher Power changed me from a dead man walking, to now, a son of the Living God and now, God is my Spiritual Father.

I please ask that you don't judge me that I'm being very preachy in these writings, but feel with me and not for me as I share my life with you. Please be patient with the writings, because the writings didn't come to me over night. Even at this very moment, I am still receiving understandings of Life.

I know with confidence; the writings of this book are a part of God's Will for me to get this book to you. I know today that this Life is about the one chance and choice over Life or Death. I have chosen life over death and this matter, I would like it greatly with a passion to share this matter of Life and Death with you. There maybe some or a lot of the writings that you possibly may want to feel for me or even judge me, but I ask you please to keep one thing on your heart as you read this book and that is, *"What is God's Holy Spirit saying through me?"* I ask if you possibly can or will to let go of your judgments of the fleshly intents and let your spirit discern the writings. I will be sharing with you many of God's principles throughout these writings, because if it wasn't for them in my life, you would not be reading these writings now. If it wasn't for God's Written Word I would be still dead and lost into the depths of emptiness and void or complete death. I would be empty of Life.

I'll try not to be very preachy, but I know today what God has done for me. My friend, it is my purpose and passion how God's Principles resurrected me from spiritually and near physical death. *Today I also know that my life isn't a matter of "Why" it is a matter of "How".*

In my past dead life, I was somewhat like a zombie, but today I say with a greater confidence; "I am Alive and I will Live! I am now a son of the Living God! He made me, surely he will save me." Today I can say this with a greater confidence; *"It's not I that Lives, but He that Lives in me, is why I Live."*

The writings will not demand you what to do or insinuated you must do in anyway anything to change, but if you sense at anytime that these writings are speaking directly to your inner man, I am not sorry for it. I know today with confidence that it was by God's Word that I was resurrected from death, to now, a son of the Living God. I know that you and I and all mankind has choice and it is a divine gift from God in this life and I have no right or power to try to control it in any way.

I will share with you some Wisdom that I have been blessed with throughout my life for nearly 30 years. Most of all this Wisdoms were revealed to me through the Written Word of God, Visions, Revelations and some through men that were led by God. But I will say this with confidence; it was by the Spirit of God that confirmed these understandings by the Written Word of God. I have been blessed with many and I may not share all of them with you. But, my God is the pilot throughout these writings and if it be so, it will be done. I believe there are two types of Wisdom: Faith Wisdom, comes only from God and Experience Wisdom that comes from the experiences of this life on earth.

During the time of my resurrection, I asked God, "Lord God what must I do? Please Lord! Tell me what I must do to Live?" God answered and said to me, "Give your life away. ". I will give my life to you from that very wisdom of God throughout the writings of this book. This book is not my book; for It is our book to keep and share for the rest of our lives here on earth, if we are willing to do so.

My Hope is with you, whether or not you read this book. Once I was willing to give my life away I did just that, and now, it is yours also. My friend, if you find only one word that quickens your Spirit throughout these writings hold fast to it for the rest of your dear life on earth.

These writings have no respect of persons either, age, origin, religion, gender, rich or poor, sick or healthy, converted or not; for my God is not a respecter of persons. My God Loves the Whole Wide World as One. I will share with you in the writings how God saved me and resurrect me from my horrors, Void-ness, Emptiness and eternal death. My God's name is I AM. I AM is the Good Shepherd of my Life, my Spiritual Father and Creator of all Life. My God's principles also pointed me toward another Higher Power and his name is *Jesus Christ, The Son of God and my Lord.*

I also ask that you try to remember this as you read the book; Christ Jesus never concludes he is a god or he is God, but The Son of God. He and God are in One Likeness somewhat like a fleshly father has a firstborn Son and the first born inherits all that his father has. I believe that Jesus Christ came from heaven and from his Father's Throne and was incarnated into the flesh of a man to administer to all mankind his Father's Riches. He came to leave with mankind a better understanding of God the Spiritual Father's Will, so that we as mankind could live life much more abundantly here on earth and receive Eternal Life. I believe in all that he did here on earth over 2000 years ago and every Word that he has left for us in the Holy Bible today. Christ Jesus became Lord and Savior of my life, because his Words directed me to the Father God of all Living. By the Power of Jesus Christ's Words resurrected me from near total death.

Today all of my Hopes point me to God's principles and his Son's Words. Jesus Christ Words pointed me to God's Will for my Life and His Will saved me from the Horror and near complete death. He is the example that I follow today to keep the Greater Hope that lives in me today. In God's Holy Book, Matthew Chapter 6,verse 33 clearly states what I had to do to change. It Reads Like this, ***"Seek ye first The Kingdom of God and His Righteousness; and all these things shall be added unto you."*** When I read this and truly understood it, I had the chance for Life right before my very eyes at that very moment. I made the choice and the changes came to my life immediately. I knew when I read this principle that I had to seek God First before any change could happen in my life. I had to seek his righteousness and What is Righteousness? His principles and His Will for my Life which is his Son, Jesus Christ. Then it reads, *"and all these things shall be added unto you."* These things from God are just a few: Love, Joy, Peace, patience, a Good Job, a Good husband or Wife, Wisdom, Understanding and

Everlasting Life. Before I sought God this last time of desperation I would had ran from this principle, because I always thought living a Good and Abundant Life was not free, but today, I can tell you with confidence, It is Free! The Price of all these things have already been taken care of and all I had to do was believe it with honesty and be willing to accept God's Will for my Life and live it. God's principles give me greater Hope in something much greater than my own self will understanding and I have found Life since I put my Hope in my God's Principles.

At the Chance I gave my will and Life over to the care of God as I understood Him the only hope that I had was to survive though the day, minute by minute. This only hope was all that I had within me and I call it, *"The Hope of Survival."* I didn't even know I had this hope within me. This hope came from somewhere deep in my spirit crying out at desperate times, "GOD! Please Help Me! Save me from the Horror and from facing death before my appointed time!" I was spiritually dying and near physically death. I was lost, empty and void. I was dead in the sinful nature, without the true understanding of life. But, when I cried out loud to God he heard me and said, *"Son, Where have you been?"*

It was at this time the Finger of God touched me and gave me a Greater Hope than just to survive. He then pointed me to his written Word and I remember reading, ***"For whosoever shall call upon the name of the Lord shall be saved."*** This principle led me to my first step back to God as I understood him at the time. He immediately took full control of my will afterwards, because I was willing for change with honesty.

The writings of this book is intended for change. I have a great confidence in what I'm going to share with you in these writings changed my life. Life is worth living today and I have a greater confidence in what my purpose here on earth is and most of all, who I am. I now know where I'm going, where I am today, and where I have been. I am not ashamed anymore about my past, because my past is dead and I have been forgiven for my past dead life. Today, I know that I do have purpose here on earth and so do you! I believe life isn't by coincidence; for it is a gift from the Creator of Life for me and you to get to know the Creator more abundantly and have Life much more Abundantly on this earth and to have a greater chance to become a son or daughter of the Living God. It is somewhat like this: Do you remember when you were conceived? Do you remember when you were in your mother's womb as an embryo? Do you remember being born as a helpless innocent little baby? Do you remember the very first step you took on your own as an innocent little baby? Do you remember eating and drinking without your mother there as you were learning as a little baby? Do you remember your first sunrise, as an older child? Do you remember your first time seeing flowers bloom, as an older child learning? Do you remember having your first pet as an older child learning with responsibility? Well, I could go on and on, but the matter is this: God gives us life, so that we can get to know him much more abundantly and grow in our spirit and mature much more abundantly in his Loving Grace.

But, if we are not being lead by his Spirit or we quench his Spirit from teaching us the True Understanding of Life, then we will look over the blessing of Life and miss the growth (understanding of Life) that God wants for us to have. I know that every child that is born on this great earth is a gift from the Creator of Life. I also have great confidence that it is God's Will for every child to have Life and grow in his Understanding and Loving Grace. You and I are God's Life. He made us in his image and surely he will save us! But, I also know this with confidence, "God cannot help a man, if the man stands in the way." Remember this my friend, *"Life on earth is somewhat like Boot Camp. Training for a Journey."*

Today, I can Love and be Loved. Before I gave my will and Life over to my God, I thought I knew love, but it wasn't true Love. This Love of my past was only the lust for the things of this world to fulfill my own self will pleasures. When I was reborn and started to put my trust in my God I began to get Honest with myself and others. *Honesty* is where my spiritual Resurrection started and Honesty requires willingness, the action of letting go of my self will and let God take complete control of my Complete Life. I admitted I was powerless over my own will and actions and God was the only answer that I could trust in. Once I began to get Honest with God and myself, I began to feel again and sense life in reality and my Mind and Spirit where becoming stronger.

This strength was *"Faith"*, which is, a gift from God's by his Holy Spirit. Honesty is a principle of God's Will for you and me. Honesty opened Pandora Boxes after another in my life. The more that I would get honest with God the much more God's Spirit was checking (discerning) my life and heart. It seemed to me as if I was battling dragons after dragons. It was as if God's Light would shine into the dark crevices of the hidden places within my heart and the dragons came flying from within the hidden dark places of my heart. It was a very spiritually and physically tiring time of my life. But today, I'm much stronger than before. God's Spirit was changing the intents of my heart to become a son of the Living God during this time. Honesty is a spiritual intent to draw closer to God's Will for our lives. God already knows our intents; for his Word is written in Hebrews Chapter 4 verse 12, ***"For the Word of God is quick, and Powerful, and sharper than any two-edged sword, piercing even to the dividing asunder of Soul and Spirit, and of the joints and marrow, and is a discerner of the thoughts and intents of the heart."*** God's Word is Life changing; for it is a divider between the Soul, Spirit and Body. When God's Word came into my Life completely it was like a two-edged sword searching and cutting right through from my spirit, soul and straight to my bones and marrow as would a bright light that would shine in the darkness. It was somewhat like if you shined a bright light in a dark closet and then seen with your eyes bugs fleeing from the light.

When I was separated from my God, because of living the sinful natured man. He could not work through my spirit man, because the sinful nature man had me bound. My spirit man had no control of the intents and thoughts of my heart or mind; for I was living in the flesh (self will, sinful nature) and by my brain mass of the experiences of my past life and leaning on my own understandings of Life My sprit man was in the likeness of being bound by chains. My heart was only pumping blood and I was living by past experiences and that was about it. I had a friend that told me one day, "I don't think that you have a heart. You only have a thumping gizzard." No kidding my friend, that is what he told me. I was living for the flesh and by compulsive behaviors from my brain of my past experiences and my spirit man was weak and was somewhat leaving my body. I had quenched the Spirit of God from working through my spirit man to give me Life and I was bound by the sinful nature of this world.

When I finally got honest with God, I began to believe him for who he was and that was a miracle in itself. My Faith in God was getting stronger from hearing and reading God's Principles. Believing in something I did not see took a little bit of *Faith* at the time. Again God's Loving Spirit brought another principle to my mind and it was this; ***"God is a Spirit: and they that worship him must worship him in spirit and in truth."*** Not only did I have to get Honest with God, I also had to believe in Him for who he is. God's Word is written in Hebrews Chapter 11 verse 6, ***"But without Faith it is impossible to please him: for he that cometh to God must Believe that he is, and that he is a rewarded of them that diligently seek him."*** This was the beginning of my Faith in God: It is written ***"The fear of the Lord is the beginning of knowledge: but fools despise wisdom and instruction." (Proverbs 1:7)*** First, I had to fear (revere) God for Who he is. After I started revering God for Who he is at that chance of my life, God was faithful and answered my prayer. He pulled me out of the Horrors I was living. I started revering him more so and believe he was able and willing to do for me what I couldn't do for my self. God did save me out of the horrors and from my belief in him. *Believing* is an intent of willingness from a man's spirit, willing to change for the good. Second, God in return rewarded me with Faith Wisdom (His Spirit) and He did reward me by his Word. Now, God's word reads in Hebrews Chapter 11, verse 1, ***"Now faith is the substance of things hoped for, the evidence of things not seen".*** When I began to believe God for the saving of my Life he touched me with His Holy Spirit and gave me hope. When I began to hope in God for the keeping of my Life, he then rewarded me and planted the incorruptible seed of the gift of faith into my spirit. Today my seed of faith grows stronger everyday. I will say this with confidence the seed, that God planted in my heart, was the *Seed of Glory, The Word of God, which is Jesus Christ his Son.*

I believe that God is the Great Husbandman and Gardener of my life and he has the Incorruptible Seeds of all Life. Remember the Garden of Eden? Everything that had Life or has Life, such as all the heavens, all the plants, all creatures and all mankind, God, the Great

Husbandman, planted those seeds in the beginning, so that all can Live and grow in His Marvelous Grace. God and his Son Christ is my Faith and Hope today and I'm living life the way God wanted me to live it in the beginning, just like a new born child. God the Father and his Son Jesus Christ has planted the incorruptible seed, which is The Word of God, in my life and my life is much more abundant than my past life. I am producing much more good fruit in my life today. These good fruits are joy, peace, patience, love, gentleness, goodness, and such like. My life today as a child and son of the Living God is great and I wouldn't have it any other way my friend.

I know today with a greater confidence that there is a night and day difference between Loving and Lusting. I've also came to the understanding that Desiring and Lusting after the things of this world led me to the Horrors for so long. I will share with you some consequences that I had to live with, because of lusting after things of this world more than the things of God.

I will share some choices I made by Lust and self will and where God forgave me at the spare of my breath. I will share that there is a difference between Loving, Desiring, lusting and actual sin. I have much more of an understanding of what the consequences of Lusting, then Sinning, to acquire my own fleshly self will intents. My life isn't worth a nana-second in self will pleasure and out of God's Will for my Life. Today I know that this life live, is a matter of Life or Death. I now can say today, I Lust and my heart pants after God's Will for me, because I want to Live and not Die.

I will also share with you that there is an enemy that is always trying to entice mankind to do wrong against Gods will for their Life. In the Holy Bible in the Book of Genesis Chapter 3, God's Word explains in detail the enemies intents and mans intents. I have lusted and desired a lot of things in this world and after lust had conceived, sinned, and after sinned had conceived, I was facing death many times. But, I don't know with a confidence I would have ever made the choice to die on my own. Satan knows a man's weakness; for it is the man's flesh. The flesh is of the physical man and it desires those things that it can put its finger upon at that very moment it desires. Satan didn't go to Adam and try to entice him to sin, he went to the weaker vessel and enticed her to sin. My friend, I'm not saying here now that a women is weak, but Satan knew that she was desiring the fruit of the tree of good and evil, and *Satan discerned her weakness*. Satan is of Ancient and he is extremely crafty in his devices, but today I have confidence and I have authority over that devil. I tell you now, being led by God's Spirit and walking daily in his Will gives me a greater confidence of Life's Purpose. I can now smell that filthy maggot (Satan) a mile away coming towards me riding upon a fly's eyelash. Not only can I discern today when that devil is trying to entice me, God's Spirit is around me, in me and God's Spirit is like a Cherub with flaming swords covering my ever step in his Will and protecting me when I can't help myself.

Today I know by living by self-will pleasures and being drawn (enticed) away from God's Principles in my life by that devil, led me to the horrors for so long. I have the right of choice, but Satan is always trying to kill and destroy what God's Will is for me. It was definitely an act of an enemy to kill me and Satan (that devil) enticed me to commit sin. Satan knows after sin had manifested in my life, it would had been death before my time. But today, I know his devices of enticements. Satan doesn't want me or any man to have a abundant Life here on earth or peace with God and neither does he want any man to receive Eternal Life from God.

Satan has already been Judge and Sentenced by God and he received eternal death and is void of God, the Creator of all Life. I will say this with confidence, Satan would like it greatly if all mankind would go to Hell with him and his followers. I was spiritually and physically dying for a long time from the void and emptiness of this understanding. But today, I have a greater understanding that Satan exist and he wants me spiritually dead and physically dead and to go to Hell with him, that God has prepared for him and his followers at the appointed time. Like night and day, Jesus Christ has great passion for all mankind to have eternal Life and go to Heaven, but Satan, has great passion to carry mankind to eternal death and Hell. I will share with you more on this Enemy throughout the writings of this book.

My God has forgiven me today for living by my self will intents for so many years of my life and most of all; He has forgiven me for all that I did against Him and others in my past dead life. I believe God forgives a man immediately when the man honestly believes God to Save him out of his Life's Horrors. But, I also know today that forgiveness is a Life and we must forgive to receive the full forgiveness from God. Today I can say this with a greater confidence; "A man that doesn't forgive his neighbor or brother would be the same as sin, in God's eyes." Forgiveness is God's Will for all mankind. I ask this question my friend, "If God could sacrificed his only begotten Son on the Cross of Calvary and as he was dying the fleshly death said to the Father this; *"Father forgive them, for they no not what they do."* Would you think that we as mankind could forgive another man, for less than, murdering us?

My friend, God is always on time, if you get a chance to call on Him. In the Holy Book of Luke chapter 23 verses 32-43 clearly gives the example to mankind that it doesn't matter what position you are in, God and his Son Jesus Christ will save you, if you believe God to do so.

In this following principle, Jesus, the son of Man and the Son of God and his Christ was led away to be crucified on the tree and with him were two other malefactors. As these three were nail to their own crosses at the place of Calvary and then raised upon their crosses, Jesus Christ was in the middle of these two other malefactors. As these three men were hanging upon their own crosses and suffering the fleshly death, one of the malefactors railed on Jesus saying, ***"If thou be the Christ, save thyself and us. But, the other malefactor rebuked this malefactor and said to him, Dost not thou fear God, seeing thou art in the same condemnation? And we indeed justly; for we received the due reward of our deeds: but this man hath done nothing amiss. And he said unto Jesus, Lord, remember me when thou comest into thy kingdom. And Jesus said unto him, Verily I say unto thee, To-day shalt thou be with me in paradise."*** My friend, look closely with your heart at the words again and see the malefactor with <u>disbelief</u> when he said, *<u>"If thou be the Christ"</u>* and then look at the other malefactor with *Belief* when he said, *"<u>Lord</u> remember me when thou comest into thy kingdom."* Who would you think went with Jesus Christ to paradise? If you chose the man with belief that Jesus Christ was Lord then you are right. Even at this malefactors last breath he called on Jesus to save him from eternal damnation with belief, because he feared God. My friend, look closer at where the malefactor was at during this time of Salvation. He was crucified on a cross suffering and dying and on his "own" cross. In these writings, I will share with you some points on forgiveness and how Jesus Christ saved me and forgave me at the spare of my breath.

My friend, today I will say this with great confidence, I will not be on my death bed calling on him to save me anymore. Jesus Christ is the Lord of my life and Keeper of my Life and I have life much more abundantly than in my past dead life. Thank you Jesus Christ for remembering me as I was suffering and dying from the consequences of myself will intents (Sinful Nature) on my "own" cross.

God and his Christ was always there when I was suffering and dying. But, they couldn't intervene until I feared God and believed them to save me from my horror at the times. I made a choice to sin and was suffering the consequences. So, I had to make a choice not to sin and the only way that I couldn't sin was to believe Jesus Christ as Lord of my Life and the keeper of my Life to keep me from sin. I will expand on forgiveness throughout the writings of this book.

When my Horrors were progressing sometimes I didn't know if I would live to see another sunset or sunrise. The horrors that I was living in gave me a sense from deep down within my heart that physical death was definite. But, deep down from somewhere I just did not want to die the way I was living. I have my whole life panted after a normal life and God's Will for my Life and I just wanted the Horrors to stop! I never wanted to live the way that I was living, but, because of living by the sinful nature and without God's Will in my life, I suffered greatly for these matters. Often times I thought that physical death would be just for me, because of all the sufferings myself and others. I had giving up hope and would think, that God would not hear me if I called to him with a load trumpet sound. I had suicide thoughts almost every day, but again, I just did not want to give up and die the death that way. It was that Hope of Survival coming out way deep within my spirit man, wanting desperately to live and to grow in God's Grace. I was so empty and void and would think that anything I did in life did not matter anymore, either it was a good intent or a bad intent. I was dead in sin and was a servant to sin without understanding of the trueness of Life's purpose. I had numbed myself from Life purpose by alcohol, drugs, pornography and many other sinful natures.

Chances, choices and changes kept compounding my Horrors and I did not know who I was or where I was going. Yes of course I would see a face in the mirror occasionally, but I did not want to face him; for I was ashamed of him.

The sinful natures became my gods and I was without the Living God. I was worshipping my own self will pleasures and being led by evil spirits without understanding of the consequences. I began to trust in Drugs and Alcohol and many other things of this world, much more than trusting God and suffered greatly the consequences. I was a man without much feelings and emotions, except anger for a long time. I had lots of anger, especially when I wanted something and could not get it. If I couldn't put my finger on it, I just didn't want it. I did not know who I was at times, and was told by many that they wanted me back and I would just shake my head and say,

"I don't know what you are talking about, want me back!" I was without understanding of the matter and was in denial of my Life for many years. I will share with you the confidence that I have been given by trusting in my God (I AM) and His Son Jesus Christ (I AM's Will) for my Life.

I have a greater confidence in *Who I am*, rather than, *Who am I?* I will share more of the *"Who I Am"* in the writings. I have found serenity with myself and my God, like never before. Since I have given my life and will over to my God and his Christ, I can finally rejoice and be glad; for the Horrors and misery is over! I will share with you in the writings the night and day difference from suffering consequences of the sinful nature and suffering for God's Will in my life. I will also share with you what I know to be the truth of _Trust_ and _Dependency_ on the things of this world more than, God. I still remember the Horrors of my past form the scares they have left on and in me. I don't dwell in the past, because there is nothing that I can change that is dead in my life. I do reflect where I have came from every day of my life and what God has done for me. I know it's a miracle that I'm where I am today and these writings are my testimony to you of how I was changed from a dead man walking, to now, a son of the Living God.

It is a part of My Strength of my Salvation and I'm confident that it was all because of God's Love, Mercy, and Grace that I can Live today. My life is much peaceful and much easier since I know who is in control. In my past living I would always have God as my co-pilot and I would only call on him, if I needed him. But today I know this with confidence; "My God is my Pilot and I'm only a passenger on his ship and life is much, much, better. I know now, I don't have to live in the Horrors and misery that I once lived in for so many years and I can now live a normal life. I now know today with confidence that the manipulative way that I once lived, is not the way I want to live. The pain I feel today is a good pain and it is great to be able to feel love and compassion for others and not the consequences of myself will living. I have Love for myself and others and feel great compassion for people today like never before and I have joy in this suffering. I can finally say this with confidence, *"I have let go and Let God!"* Today I can weep when I'm sad, I can laugh when something is funny, and I can surely feel my body's pain from the scares of my past living.

Before in my past life, I didn't know what to feel, because of living a sinful natured and numbed life. The pains I feel today in my physical body are pains from living by myself will for many years and having the Rod of God upon me for a long time. But I will say this with confidence, I much rather suffer these pains today in my body and do God's Will, than to suffer the pains of self will over again. The choice that I have today is somewhat like this, "Go back into the horrors and miseries of your past life of self will living or be shot by a firing squad". My friend, I would choose the firing squad.

I do not claim by any means I've got a perfect life today; for I'm still in my fleshly body and God is still Disciplining, or let's say, *"Training me for the journey home."* Satan is trying many different devices to lure me away and separate me from my God.

But, I will say this with confidence today, I am pressing towards the prize of perfection in my life and that prize is God's Perfect Will, which is, Life Everlasting and Life much more abundantly.

Today I will say this with great confidence, "I much rather have God's Staff around me anytime than to have his Rod on me." I will share this matter (disciplining) with you in the writings. My life is so much better and peaceful than before, even when God is Disciplining me; for his discipline is for my profit and his Glory. In the Holy Book of 2Corinthians Chapter 12, Verse 7-9, The Apostle Paul wrote to us, ***"And lest I should be exalted above measure through the abundance of the revelations, there was given a thorn in the flesh, the messenger of Satan to buffet me, lest I should be exalted above measure. For this thing I besought the Lord thrice, that it might depart from me. And He Said unto me, <u>My grace is sufficient for thee: for my strength</u>***

is made perfect in weakness. Most gladly therefore will I rather glory in my infirmities, that the power of Christ may rest upon me." What? The great Apostle Paul had a thorn in his flesh? Today I have thorns in my flesh and will probably always have them. One of my thorns is a mental illness. I will say one thorn is Lust and another is addition. I will cover more on these thorns in the writings later in the section of, *"What Sufferings are you Talking About?"*

I had prayed to God to bless me and others in many ways, such as deliverance from my fleshly thorns, but God's answer to me was this; *"Give Your Life Away".* By his saving Grace I'm alive today and it is sufficient for me to Live. When I'm suffering with these thorns, God's Grace and Love always strengthens me and it is because I call on him and I become stronger day by day through his Amazing Grace. *Amazing Grace how sweet the sound that saved a wretch like me! Twas grace that taught my heart to fear, and grace my fears relieved; How precious did that grace appear that hour I first believed!*

Thru many dangers, toils and snares I have already come; Tis grace hath brought me safe thus far, and grace will lead me home. When we've been there ten thousand years, bright shining as the sun, we've no less days to sing God's praise than when we first begun. My friend, all Life is engulfed by God's Amazing Grace. In my past life I would let the lust become sin, but I can say with a greater confidence today, I call on God for his strength and his Grace that he has shown toward me helps me through the suffering times. God does give me rest from the thorns, but as for now, they are still there. There is a prayer from the Alcoholic and Narcotics Anonymous society that I've embedded in my mind that reads: *"God, Grant Me The Serenity, To Accept The Things I Cannot Change, Courage To Change The Things I Can, And The Wisdom To Know The Difference".* Peace from God is my strength. Please give yourself what you deserve, Peace from God, if you do not have it already. Today I will say that this peace that I have is somewhat like a battle to keep every moment of my life, but the battle is easy, and the burden is light (Life). I will also share a lot of the matter of what I know to be the truth of these matters throughout the writings.

Like I said before times, I still have troubled times and good times and I still make wrong decisions, but nothing like I was making without God's Will in my life. I'm still growing in my spirit and I continually to press forward for the Mind of Christ and will always, until I take my last breath on earth. I hope these writings will be a hope for you or someone you know. Again my friend, remember this; *"Life here on earth is like Boot Camp, Training for a Journey."* I truly believe the fleshly life here as a man on God's Earth is only a vapor and what we do here on earth will determined our everlasting Life, where we go, after we lay our fleshly body down to the dust it came from. We don't even have a day here on earth compared to eternity and I have loved ones that are suffering and dying from the pains of self will as you read this word.

We have a chance at this very moment to better my own self, so that I might be an open book for the suffering and dying to read.

Please, even if you decide not to further your reading of these writings, help someone that is suffering from self-will. Always Remember this my friend as you reach out and share your life to someone suffering; "God is Love and He only knocks on a man's door (heart) with a passion of Love to come in. God and his Son Jesus Christ never forces His Will on any man. It is the individual's choice to change for the good or evil, but I always hope for the good. One more to remember; "Play with the swine long enough, you will certainly smell like one." Today I have a greater understanding of this also; "Life is not only about what you know, it is what you do with what you know."

I Hope these writings will quicken your spirit and may you find want you are looking for, if you are seeking something. My friend, please don't give up before your blessing. Seek and you will find, knock and it shall be opened unto you, ask and it shall be given to you; for that is God's Promise for me, you, and the Whole Wide World. In the Word of God it is written, *"But as it is written, Eye hath not seen, nor ear heard, neither have entered into the heart of man, the things which God hath prepared for them that love him."* The blessing of Life is worth finding and we can not afford to do any better work in our life than to seek Life over Death, which is, God's Perfect Will. Remember always; the things of this world are temporary and will pass away just as your flesh will pass away, but the blessing of Life (God's Word) will never pass away. *"For what is a man profited, if he shall gain the whole world, and lose his own soul? Or what shall a man give in exchange for his soul?"* God wants us to have all things and he will give you your heart's desire, if you are found worthy to have them.

We as mankind just can't afford to put the lust of the things of this world in our hearts, before we put the Love and Trust of God's Spirit into our hearts.

I will share with you in the writings many times in my past as I would get an understanding of what God wanted to give me and then I would lose it, because of my self will intents. God would try me with a blessing, but then I would lose it, because of not being worthy of the blessing. God will try a man to see if he is worthy of something, such as money and spiritual gifts. If, a man isn't found worthy of the things from God the man would have those things for a short time, but it could be taken from him as quick as it came to him. And then, he would suffer greatly the consequences of his self will intent. I now know today that when I was converted in my past life as a teenager; God wanted to bless me with all things my little heart desired, but I was without understanding of this matter for a long time.

Most of the times I did not get what I wanted at the time when I asked God for something and I would wait and wait and then just give up on it and start to loose my hope in the matter. You see, God already knew my intent and I wasn't worthy to be blessed with those things at the time. God would have to give me first understanding of the matters before I could even begin to be found worthy of one thing. I will share with you in the writings many times that I just gave up on God for material things and went back to my self will pleasures; for they were my intent the start with, no kidding. I will share with you in these writings about the Trials of God, the Judgments of God and the Blessings from the Trials or the Consequences of Trials. Today I know that if I want something from God, I will be tried from God to be found worthy or not for the blessing. God is the husbandman, and he will prepare a mans heart in order for his blessing to grow, because he holds all the incorruptible seeds. I will forever thank God for his righteousness and that he only tries a man's heart for the man's own profit. Today, I Know when I'm being tried that God is wanting to bless me. Today, I count it as Joy and wait patiently for the promise without no doubt.

I will say this, during some of past life living, it was as if I was playing Russian Roulette with my life; for I didn't have all the understanding, but only wanted a part of the understanding to fulfill my own self will intents.

My friend living and thinking that way was extremely suicidal and dangerous for my life. Today, I pant after God's Will for my Life and I desire with a great passion his Will perfected to my last breath; for I know it is Life or Death. Today I know that the chance that God has given me is not a game; for this life is serious and I have no doubt that it is a matter of Life or Death. I will say this also; "I thank God for not finding me worthy when I wasn't worthy at times for his riches, because you would not be reading these words right now."

These writings are in no way fiction or imagined from my brain mass and are in truth to the best I can remember. The only thing I use my brain mass to do through these writings are the skills of writing the words on paper. Sometimes I'm still amazed at being able to read and write, because I held a C- in reading and writing class in school. Every writing in this book is from my Life and not in any way have I distorted them, but the men, women and place's names and such like, that is a part of my life in the writings, have not been enter, because it is not the point of this book. They all have been deleted to protect their names.

Now Father God, please bless the reader of these writings with your Abundant Grace, Love and Understanding of the True Life. In Your Most High and Precious Son's Name, Jesus Christ, the Lord and Savior of the World.

FORWARD

NOW, I AM GOING TO SHARE WITH YOU some of my life's struggles from a child with a passion, trying desperately to grasp onto the understanding of Life, to now, a son of the Living God with an understanding of Life. I will pass a lot of details to get to the points of the matters. Even if I tried to write all the details it would take me 30 years to write them and for you 30 years to read them and I don't have that much time here on earth to share the details with you. Even if I had all the time in the world, all the details just would not matter; for It's all about the point of the matter that quickens the matter of the understanding. With God as my pilot and I as the co-pilot, God's Holy Ghost will lead me through these writings and get to the points. Like I have said before, I've taken man's pen and let God's Spirit work the writings through me, but I'm still in the flesh my friend, and I ask that you to forgive me for anything that you may think that I'm writing from my flesh. As I have asked before in the Introduction, please try not to judge me, but let go and let God help and lead your spirit to discern the writings, if you are willing to do so. I can tell you now with confidence, God's Holy Ghost, which is my Great Comforter, keeps me safe through these writings and I know and have great confidence that it is the truth, and I am not ashamed of any of what I have and what I will share with you.

I have been judged and have been told by many men of my past and also of recent times that I had an attitude, but my friend, it isn't an attitude, it is my Life and I will not take it in any other way, even if a man thinks I have an attitude or not. For an example: I have left Jobs because men thought I had an attitude and plotted against me to remove me from there life, even though, the only attitude I had at the time was to live a honest and good life before them and my God.

But, these men plotted against me anyhow, because they didn't understand me and they didn't like someone as honest and fearing God around them; for today I know they were without understanding of Life. I have Honestly prayed this prayer for all of them; "My Father, which is in Heaven, Forgive them for they know not what they do." Today I have a greater understanding that the Life I'm living today is much more abundant than my past dead life. I also know this with confidence; This season of my life here on earth is only a vapor and I want to live and not live in the horrors that I once lived.

Today I know that this life is a one time chance and my choice to live and this chance and my choice that I make will determine my life here on earth and my everlasting life when I lay this body that I'm in back to the dust where it came from. Today I know this with confidence; A man has only one chance for life and it is also one chance to choose to live or die. My chance that I have today to live and my choice that I have made to live, I have counted it all for the suffering of God's Will in my life and I will tell you my friend, I have great joy in these matters. I may have an attitude, but I mean it not in anyway a evil attitude; for I call my attitude, a righteous attitude towards Life. I am a much more serious Man today, than I was in my past dead life and maybe I do have an attitude, because I don't want to die and go to Everlasting Torment or Hell. I will stand with God before I stand with any man and be lead away again into the horrors and miseries that I once was a servant to. What I'm saying does not mean that I will not help a man, it only means this; Before I loose my peace and Life that I have received today, I will stand with my God before I would stand for any man; for today I want to live and not die, whereas, I didn't understand life for a long time. This life is a choice and now I ask this question; "Would you think while Jesus Christ was here on earth, that he may of had an attitude?" I would think that he did have an attitude, a righteous attitude for Life, and not death <u>for all of God's Creation.</u>

+Jesus Christ knew the severity of man's will and it was then and still today carrying mankind straight to Eternal Destruction. But, God and his Son Jesus Christ suffered greatly for mankind and doesn't want anyone to go to Hell. Jesus Christ left us as mankind the Keys to Eternal Life and Life on earth to live much more abundantly, if only a man is willing to believe the matter. Man did think Jesus Christ had an attitude and mankind Crucify and killed Jesus Christ on a Cross for his attitude, but they were without understanding of the matter of Life at the time; for Jesus Christ was their understanding of Life. Jesus Christ said as he was giving up his Spirit back to the Father of Life on the cross, *"Father, Forgive them; for they know not what they do."* So, I ask this question; "Would you have a choice to make on the matter of Life or Death?" There where many times in my past dead life that when I was being tried by God to receive an understanding of Life or I was suffering the consequences of my fleshly self will intents, I would curse, use drugs, blame others and fly off the handle and do things that was destructive for my life and even destructive for others. I would just give up and quit what I was doing or run and try to hid from God without understanding of the matter. But, today I know I was without understanding of life then and I had no control of my life and I was living a dead course of destruction. Have you ever thought to yourself, "I wish I could be born again as a newborn child, but have the wisdom I know today as a grown man." Maybe you have thought that or maybe not, but My friend, please listen with your heart, "You can be born again just like a newborn child, if you are willing to do so." I have been resurrected and born again with a new life and feel as if I'm an young child of age in my spirit. I live today as if I'm a young child of age with a great passion for God. I live today again with humbleness, meekness, shyness, watching and discerning all things around me. I have a greater understanding of Life and Death today and I just keep my trap shut as I would when I was a shy child.

I will open my trap once and awhile when I know that God's Spirit is leading me to do so, and he gives me the understanding of the words to say to a man; for any other way could be life or death for me or the other man. Today, I understand that Life and Death are in man's tongue and I must bridle it at all cost.

My fleshly body hasn't changed in statue, maybe a little more weight in my belly, but I do feel very much better in my body. My mind is much clearer and my intents are always on God and every now and then, someone will say this to me, "You look good, how do you do that?" I will always tell them, "I have been Resurrected from the dead by the same Power that arose Jesus Christ from the Dead." And then they would giggle and just walk away.

As you read the writings, I ask that you please don't think or judge me that I'm telling you or any man what to do through these writings; for I know today man has a choice and that is a gift from God. Like I've said before, The God of Life and his Son Jesus Christ only knock on man's door of their heart to come in to it and doesn't knock their door down. But, sometimes looking into my past dead life, it may have seemed if they did; for they have great passion to save me from Destruction and Death. I will say this with confidence; When God was knocking on my door of my heart during my past dead life, he started with His Finger gently and then his Staff and then it ended with his Rod upon me with a great passion for my life. I know today that God and His Son Jesus Christ are my Good Shepherds. Let me explain: A Good Shepherd of a flock has both a Staff and a Rod. The shepherd would use the Staff to lead and save a wondering kid that would try to wonder away from the flock, because the shepherd had the understanding that the kid would be facing danger away from the flock. The shepherd would pull the kid back into the flock fold with his Staff.

When the kid would get older and would still try to wonder away from the flock without understanding of the dangers, such as high cliffs, hunter traps, wolfs and even men, it would be at that very moment the Good Shepherd would discipline it with his Rod, such as a slap upon its behind. I believe that God would had broken every bone in my body to keep my soul from burning in the Lake of Fire. I know my friend you may think I am exaggerating, but I am confident he would had. Not just because he wanted to make a point of discipline to me, but that is how much of a passion he has for my soul.

As I mentioned in the Introduction, I will quote many of God's Principles throughout these writings, because I do know and understand the value of these principles for the keeping of my Soul and my complete Life on earth today. I also know for today, if it wasn't for God's principles I would be still living a dead life without understanding of the matter of Life and you would not be reading these words from me now. I would still be on this earth as a dead man walking, zombilized without emotions or any type of attitude, if it wasn't for the Life that God's Principles have given me. Today I can shout this with great joy, "I LIVE! I live today not of myself, but I live because, The God of Life lives in me."

I ask that you think not that these writings are in any way a war story. But, I consider it a "good fight" as a son of The Living God. It is a good fight to know God's perfect Will for my Life with confidence. It is a good fight, so that, I can enter Eternal Life, rather than, Eternal Death. It is a good fight to live a Life here on earth much more abundantly. It is a good fight to keep my peace with my Spiritual Father. It is a good fight to receive the godly things from God through Christ Jesus. It is a good fight between good and evil.

Now, this good fight has already been won by my Lord and Savior Jesus Christ at the Cross of Calvary and he left mankind these great examples to follow.

Jesus Christ has left for me and the whole wide world the understanding of these matters of Life. But, I now know today with a greater confidence, I will fight the good fight of my faith in my God and his Christ until after, I take my last breath on this earth. Christ Jesus defeated self will (sin, the fleshly intents, sinful nature of a man's heart), and Satan (an evil intent, death, destruction, consequences of sin) by the Power he had in him, which was the Power of Life from his Father God and which is, the Creator of all Life.

I now know today and have a greater understanding of this matter: God and his Son Jesus Christ is The Way, The Truth and The Life and the Great Resurrection for all mankind. Christ Jesus was made the greatest example on the tree of Calvary as God's Will for me and the Whole Wide World to follow, if only a man will follow him. Jesus Christ had the power to resurrect himself from the grip of death and rose and defeated death over 2000 years ago and today holds the keys to hell and death. There were witnesses of his resurrection and also there were witnesses when he resurrected a man that had been physically dead in a tomb for several days. This physical resurrection of this man by Jesus Christ was for mankind to have a great understanding of a man living a dead life to be resurrected to a Living life. Not only to leave that example, but to leave a greater faith for mankind to build upon. This resurrection was the Hope that every creature under heaven had groaned for since the beginning of the fall of mankind to sin. Jesus Christ, the Son of God wanted mankind to have a greater understanding that a man could be resurrected from a dead life to a much more abundant life, if the man believed. I now have an understanding of what Resurrection is all about and it is this; "Power over Death." Christ Jesus reveals himself as the Resurrection as he stands at the tomb of the physically dead man, Lazarus. Lazarus had been dead for several days and I'm sure the smell was beginning not to be too pleasant.

In the Holy Book of John chapter 11, verses 24-25 it is written, *"Martha said unto him, I know that he shall rise again in the resurrection at the last day. Jesus said unto her, I am the resurrection, and the life: he that believeth in me, though he were dead, yet shall he live: And whosoever liveth and believeth in me shall never die. Believest thou this?"* Jesus Christ did use the power he had within him and called out to this dead man, "Lazarus, Come Forth!" Lazarus did come forth from the death and was resurrected from the death of the flesh. All that were there at the time witnessed the resurrection of Lazarus and were all amazed. Since I have been Resurrected from my dead past life and converted over to the care of my God and his Christ, I do believe and hope in this matter with great confidence. I was resurrected from complete emptiness and void to now a son of the Living God. I was spiritually near death and near physical death, but my God resurrected me from that horror. Today I can say with confidence, I do not fear death and Death is swallowed up in Victory thru Jesus Christ my Lord and Savior. For God's Word reads in the Holy Bible, 1Corinthians chapter 15, verse 55-57, *"O death, where is thy sting? O grave where is thy victory? The sting of death is sin; and the strength of sin is the law. But thanks be to God, which giveth us victory through our Lord Jesus Christ."* Jesus Christ ask Martha, which was Lazarus's sister this very powerful question, <u>*"Believest thou this?"*</u> When I believed that Jesus Christ could and would resurrect me from my past dead life he did just that! Do you believe this? Trust me my friend, Jesus Christ did resurrect me from my dead life that I was living. Today, I Live! I live today, because Jesus Christ lives in me

You will sense, if you choose to continue to read the writings, that I didn't fear death when I was walking by my rebellious, sinful nature for many years. This fear wasn't the same fear as I know of today. When I was walking by the sinful nature in my past dead life, I was without understanding of life and this matter did lead me to the horrors in my past dead life.

The "No Fear" of death intent that I once had in my past dead life was suicidal thoughts almost everyday and sometimes worse. But for today, I can say this with a great confidence, "To be out of my body is to be with my God and his Christ" and that is the difference and intent I want to live today from not fearing death. Today I have a better understanding of the Proverb that is written, "*The fear of the Lord is the beginning of knowledge: but fools despise wisdom and instruction." (Proverbs 1:7)*

When I began to get honest with my Lord and started to fear him, or let's say, started to reverend him, then I began to have much understanding of his Holy Words. God's Word became the keeper of my soul and I eat of his Word daily and have no hindrances of understanding his Word. Sometimes I think that I understand it to its fullness, but God's Spirit is quick to show me the real understanding and I count it as a reward or a pearl in my life. Now, I will share with you a little key of Understanding God's Word that I have received today. In the writings I will share many times that I thought that I understood God's Word, but I know today that I only understood it to my own understanding in my past life. I would judge God's Word for my own self will intents and I would only search the scriptures that would only comfort me at the times of my sufferings. Now, is good to read the Word of God by all means, but if you are just reading it to try to measure up to yourself, you may be surprise that you may just shrink and wither away.

Today I do understand God's Word with a greater confidence and I would like to share this little key that I have found with you. But first, let me asked you a few questions my friend: "Have you ever tried to read God's Word and just gave up on understanding it, because it seemed too difficult to understand or you just didn't like what you may had just read?," "Have you every tried to listen to the Gospel from a minister and you couldn't perceive it and maybe you didn't like what he said?,"

"Have you ever asked God to give you an understanding of his Word and you just didn't like the outcome of what God may had given to you?" Just a couple more questions my friend for the point is coming.

"Where is your Word of God?," "Is it on your night stand, your kitchen table, your vehicle's dash, or do you have the Word of God anywhere?" Or, "Is God's Word in your Mind and Spirit?" Trust me my friend, I have many times thought these questions to myself in the past and please let me share with you now a little key to help unlock the door of understanding of God's Word that I have received today. Ready? <u>God's Will not Self Will</u>. Seems pretty simple doesn't it? "God cannot help a man, if the man stands in the way." If I didn't know the Author of a Book then I probably would not understand the book. Unless, I would judge the book from my own self will intents, imaginations and then start to lean on my own understandings of what I would think that the Author must be saying throughout the writings of his book. But, later I would find out quickly that the Author meant for something different than what I thought I had just read to be the truth and then maybe I would stop reading the book, because I felt ashamed of my self. In my past dead life, I would judge the Word of God and by judging the Word of God, I was judged and was greatly ashamed afterwards. We must put ourselves in the Authors Life and the Author in our Life in order to really understand the real meaning of the Book from the Author. So, how do we get to know an Author of a Book, especially an Author like the God of Life and his Son Jesus Christ, so that, we could see much more clearer the understanding of their Book? This is the only way that I know of today my friend and I have a great confidence in this matter: Ask the Author to come into your Life and show you the understanding of his Book and wait patiently for the understanding without any judgments from your brain mass, which is judgments and doubt.

In the Holy Book of Hebrews, it is written, ***"WHEREFORE seeing we also are compassed about with so great a cloud of witnesses, let us lay aside every weight, and the sin which doth so easily beset us, and run with patience the race that is set before us, Looking unto Jesus the author and finisher of our faith; who for the joy that was set before him endured the cross, despising the shame, and is set down at the right hand of the throne of God."***

Therefore, God's Word is not complex. Today, these great Words give mankind the understanding that Christ Jesus is the Author and Finisher of a man's Faith. The man must believe that Christ Jesus is able to do for him what he cant do for himself, which is, LIVE!. That great and marvelous principle also tells us not to judge (*let us lay aside every weight*), but look to Jesus as the Author of our Life with patience. The Holy Book of Hebrews clearly defines faith and the witnesses of the faith and the rewards of having the faith in Jesus Christ. We as mankind must lay aside every thought and imagination from our fleshly brain masses and start to believe with our heart that Jesus Christ is the Author and finisher of our Life. God and his Son's Words are written as you see it in his Holy Bible and Jesus Christ warns about changing his Words in the Holy Book in Revelations chapter 22, verses 18-19. I have got to ask this question, "Why would God try to hide Life from us?" Or, "Would God use his Word and code it for a man that believes in his Word only and hide it from a sinner or a lost child?" Not! For God is Life and he can't hide himself from us, because his testimonies are forever around and in us and he wants all mankind to have understanding of him; for that is the Will of God. Remember this my friend; Gods Great Wheel (Will) makes the World Go World. Here is just a few of his testimonies for all mankind; The Waters, The Heavens, The Stars, The Earth, The Flowers, The Trees, The Living Creatures and most important, you, me and all mankind. Just look into the glass my friend and see what he has done for you, me and all mankind.

"Would you think that all this life is just a coincidence?" Or perhaps, "Thought that life all like came from a big bang or a monkey? My friend, I may have came from a big bang, but I can say this with confidence; I didn't come from no monkey. "Even if I came from a big bang, where did the big bang come from?" "Did it come from another big bang and then another and another and another and so on?" My friend, the God of Life is Eternity and He is the same yesterday, today and tomorrow and it is our choice to get the fullness from God at his Will. Oh yes! While I'm still on the subject of the big bang, let me just throw this bang at you: "Do you know what an atom is?" I will confess, I'm not a Doctor in Science or Physics, but bare with me as I try to explain. An atom is in every thing that your eye can see. All mass that your eyes can see contains atoms. An atom consist of a nucleus, which is the energy of the complete atom, and sits in the center. From the nucleus there are valences that circle the nucleus and the valences contain other elements, such as photons and electrons. These other elements circle the nucleus and holds the atom together in perfect harmony, please follow me the bang is coming. The way I look at life today my friend, is just like looking at an atom. For an example: The Galaxy that we live in is just like an atom. The galaxy has a nucleus, which is the Sun and full of energy beyond your imagination. The planets circle the Sun just like the photons and electrons circle an nucleus of an atom in their own valences or orbits, and holds the complete atom together in orbit in perfect harmony. Your body may contain billions of atoms and I believe that this galaxy that we live in, is just one atom in God's Great Body, follow me? And I have to ask this question; "If, perhaps this galaxy is just one atom in the God of Life's Great Body, would you ever think you will exhaust God great body." Or, "Understand God in fullness?" One more question my friend; "Why do you think that the first Life of mankind was given a name like Adam?" Somewhat ironic isn't it, Adam or Atom? Today I know this with confidence; If I'm every going to know the Creator God whom has put all things into orbit in perfect harmony, then I must let God into my life. Today I have a better understanding of why Jesus Christ said this; *"I am in the Father and the Father is in me."* Oh yes! I cant leave the monkey part out. Please let me ask this question my friend. "Why would I have the intelligence to take care of a monkey, if a monkey could take care of me?" Follow me the monkey is coming and he is just a swinging. "Can a monkey feed a man, clothe a man, wipe a man, heal a man, marry a man, have children with a man, save a man from death!" <u>NOT!</u> I will say this with confidence; God made me as a man to care for a monkey and not for the monkey to care for me. Some may think they came from a monkey, but I was made as a man. Have you every heard the saying, *"As a man thinks, so he is!"* Some may think they came from a monkey, but I know with a greater confidence that I came from a man and that man was, Adam.

Oh yes! While I'm still on the monkey business please let me ask you some questions for you to ponder upon. In the Holy Book of Genesis, God created man and women correct? Adam was the man's name and Eve was the women's name. Adam and Eve lived in the Garden of Eden and then got ran out of the Garden of Eden by God because of sin, correct? Now, Adam and Eve gave birth to two boys, whose names where Cain and Abel. Cain killed Abel and then God cast Cain to another part of Eden called Nod. Cain found a wife. What? Found a wife? Where did the wife come from if Adam and Eve only had two boys? Was his wife a monkey? My friend, this maybe the answer. It isn't written that God made only Adam and Eve, follow me? Search the scriptures my friend. When God made man and women he not only made Adam and Eve, he also made other men and women all over the earth at the same time. Now, that is my theory and isn't written in the Holy Word, except that he made man and women.

When God made Adam and Eve he also made other men and women throughout this beautiful earth and that maybe where Cain got his wife in the land of Nod. It was Adam and Eve that he set in the Garden of Eden to care for it. Just a thought to ponder on. I have always desired the Sciences of searching Life, but I know this; if a man doesn't have The Great God of Life in his Life then that man will never understand Life in it's trueness. We may think we know, but do we really know the truth?

I will say this with confidence; God doesn't know a man that doesn't believe in him, because there is no witness to God for that man. My friend the point is close. When a man gets converted by his belief in God and calls to him with a true and honest heart then God is faithful and hears that spirit man crying out to him, "Abba, Father, save me!" God is faithful to save a man and then that man is saved from the horror and begins to receive a greater understanding of Life. The fear (revering) of the Lord is the beginning of Knowledge (Proverbs 1:7). God is faithful and just to save a man from their horrors, if the man will believe God for who he is and to save him from himself. Himself? Yes, I believe the greatest horror that a man lives is fear of himself. After the man is saved from the horrors of his Life, God will start rewarding the man with faith according to his will, if the man is willing to walk with God and <u>do</u> his Will. God's Will is Life for us and his Word is the great understanding of Life and that is what he wants to give all mankind here on earth and Eternally.

I believe if a man doesn't understand God's Word then that man's self will, or lets say, the man's doubts and judgments would be hindering the man from the true understanding of The Book of Life. If self will is hindering a man from understanding the Book of Life (The Holy

Bible) then God's Perfect Spirit, which is man's perfect Teacher and Comforter of Life cannot do what he will for that man. Self will works as a firewall against God from entering a man's life. Self-will is rebellion and sin in God's Eyes.

If self will is present in a man's life then God's Will cannot work perfectly in that man's life for his Life. God's Will is Perfect and self will is not. Self will has doubts, judgments. If a man would read and be willing to understand God's Word then the man must not doubt or judge one Word of it. If a man does doubt or judge one word of God's Written Word then he will not understand the truth of God's Word of Life. The man is still letting self-will judge, rather than, letting go and letting God's Holy Spirit teach him the True Reality of Life.

Today I know I must have the complete Holy Bible, which is The Old Testament and The New Testament. I know with confidence today that I must have the Old Covenant (Old Testament. The Laws and Prophets for Mankind) and the New Covenant (New Testament. The complete fulfillment of the Laws and Prophets for Mankind through Christ Jesus) to begin to understand God's Will for myself, mankind and all God's Creation. In order for me to understand something that has been fulfilled, then I must understanding what has been fulfill.- Pause- A man needs the Understanding of the Complete Word of God from the Beginning of Genesis to the Last word of Amen in Revelations to ever fully understand God's Perfect Will for him and all mankind. I can't afford to leave the Law out of my understanding, because if I do leave the Laws out of my understanding, then I would still be dead in sin and would suffer greatly for the matter. Please keep reading, for the point is closer. Today I say this with confidence; I do understand God's Word as I read it daily and I have let go of my self will and let God's Holy Ghost come into my heart and it is that simple. If I ever do stumble in any of God's Words I began immediately to examine myself. I ask this to myself; "Have I let go and let God's Spirit?" Oh Yes my friend, "Quench not the Spirit!". I will say today with confidence that I have got to let go of my self-will (sinful nature) and let God's Holy Ghost come into my complete life and teach me his Word. God's Holy Ghost is our Teacher and Comforter and is willing to teach us "all things".

In the holy Book of John Chapter 14, verses 23-26, Jesus Christ left this understanding for us and it is written, *"If a man love me, he will keep my words: and my Father will love him, and we will come unto him, and make our abode with him. He that loveth me not keepeth not my sayings: and the word which ye hear is not mine, but the Father's which sent me. These things have I spoken unto you, being yet present with you. But the Comforter, which is the Holy Ghost, whom the Father will send in my name, he shall teach you all things, and bring all things to your remembrance, whatsoever I have said unto you."*

My friend, if you can grasp onto anything out of these scriptures, please grasp this; if you and I keep and love God's Complete and fulfilled Word then both the Father and Christ will come unto our life to live. But, if we as mankind don't love God's Word we will only know what the Father has said in the Old Testament (The Laws) and we as mankind would still be without understanding of the matter of The True Reality of Life. If a man doesn't love Jesus Christ's words and follow them, then Jesus Christ can not set the man free from the curse of the Law. The man will still be under the curse of the Law and be empty of understanding Life. Please let me also share this great wisdom with you from God's Word. In the Holy Book of John chapter 1, verses 1-2 reads, *"In the beginning was the Word, and the Word was with God, and the Word was God. The same was in the beginning with God."* If you would read the following writings of this scripture in the Gospel of John, the Word of God reveals himself as The Son of God, Jesus Christ. Please read this Book completely sometime soon now if you will. If we don't love Jesus Christ Words then we reject Jesus Christ from our life and then we will only know the Law, which the Father had sent in old times. Let me go into somewhat more detail on this matter: In the beginning, God cursed the serpent, the earth, and mankind and this was called the curse, because of sin.

Then later, The Father God of all Life sent the Law of the Old Testament to Moses to give to his people for the understanding of sin that mankind was perishing from. Mankind was without understanding of sin before the Laws were set in stone for mankind to have in their hand and hearts to read and follow. God sent the Commandment, so that, if they did the commandments mankind would understand sin and would not do sin. God would call these people that did his commandments, His People. In the Old Testament times God had given mankind a map (the Commandments), so that, mankind could have a chance to have a relationship with him, because mankind was separated from God, follow me? Then Later, God sends his Word (Jesus Christ) into this world and his Word became flesh and his Word dwelt among mankind and mankind beheld his glorious Word (the glory of the only begotten Son of the Father full of grace and truth. John 3.) God sent his only begotten Son (The Word of God in incarnated Into Flesh) to the earth so that mankind would have examples of how not to live In sin and be free from sin.

Now, today with his Word (Jesus Christ) with all mankind we have the chance to live life more abundantly without sin and be free from the curse of the Law. Mankind also has a 100% chance to be with God the Father eternally, if only a man will follow his Only Begotten Son's Examples. Please read the entire Holy Book of the Gospel of John sometime soon and it will enlighten your understanding of this matter greatly. Jesus Christ (The Son of God. God's Will for mankind) came later to fulfill the Old Testament, so that we as mankind would be free from the curse of the Law of the Old Testament that was written and to give mankind a much more greater understanding of the True Reality of Life.

In the Holy Book of Matthew chapter 5, verse 17-18 it is written, *"Think not that I am come to destroy the law, or the prophets:*

I am not come to destroy, but to fulfill. For verily I say unto you, 'Till heaven and earth pass, one jot or one tittle shall in no wise pass from the law, till all be fulfilled." Jesus Christ also gives examples of the laws and prophets fulfilled in the following scriptures here in His Holy Word of the Gospel of Matthew. Please read it sometime soon. If a man does not love Jesus Christ's Words and follow them then I would say that man is still under the curse of the Law of the Old Testament. Before I go any further, please let me explain the difference between the laws and the prophets. Jesus said that he came not to destroy the laws and the prophets. So, what does the laws and the prophets mean? First, the laws were given to mankind from God, so that mankind would grasp onto why they were perishing. The laws were given to mankind, so that, if mankind would do the laws and revere them mankind could have a relationship with God. Now, the prophets were men that were led by God's Holy Ghost and the Holy Ghost would manifest certain revelations and visions to them, such as the coming of a Messiah to set mankind free from the laws. Not only did the prophets receive understanding of that mankind would be free from the laws, they also receive revelations and visions that mankind would be able to receive the Great Promise, which is, Eternal Life with the Father God. There were many prophetic revelations of these things given to the prophets from God as they were led by the Spirit of God (The Holy Ghost) and the prophets would give this great hope to all mankind. The prophets would write these great hopes in writing for all mankind to see with their eyes, until the prophesies were fulfilled. So, when Jesus Christ said, ***"Think not that I am come to destroy the law, or the prophets: I am not come to destroy, but to fulfill. For verily I say unto you, 'Till heaven and earth pass, one jot or one tittle shall in no wise pass from the law, till all be fulfilled.",*** he was saying that he was the one and only and would fulfill all of the laws and what the prophets had said before time, follow me?

Now, if a man is still under the curse of the law then Christ is not in his heart to set him free from the Law of the Old Testament. If a man is still under the Law then he is still walking in self will (the flesh) and not by the Spirit of God. There are three that bare witness in Heaven: The Father God, The Son of the Father and the Holy Ghost. The Father, the Son and the Holy Ghost must be in unity in a man's life for the complete understanding of God's Will to be fulfilled in a man's Life. It is like this; You can't get to the Father God, except through Son. You can't get any understanding of Christ unless it is by the Holy Ghost sent from God in Christ name. But there is a High calling for all mankind and God will honor it. This High calling for all mankind is repentance. My friend I know you must be tiring about now, but hold on, the point is nearer than before. So, Mankind was separated from God because of sin. God later sent his Laws that mankind must follow in order to Live a relationship with him on earth. God sent these Laws that Man must live by in order to have a True relationship with him. Mankind was held by these Laws in the Old Testament times, before the coming of Christ Jesus to the world. These Laws where given for Instructions of Living a life free from sin from God, but man was still captive by the law; for man was lost in sin before the Law was given and they didn't understand what sin was and was perishing from the lack of understanding sin.

Therefore, God gives mankind a Law book of understanding (The Ten Commandments), and if a man one would break one of the laws, then that man would suffer the consequences of breaking the Laws, such as death. Oh yes! Before I go any further, let me share this with you this. Today people are in anguish concerning this, "Why are the children killing each other in schools and on the streets? Why is there so much murder and sin in the world?" I can say this with confidence; mankind has taking the laws from the children. When I was just a small boy in elementary school we did have the Ten Commandments on the walls.

We would read and study the Bible at least 2 times a week and I would always looked forward to that time as a small child. Then the next year, the Bible and the Commandments were took from the school. I was but a child and had no understanding of sin, but the Ten Commandments were teaching me what sin was and I would revering them to the best of my ability at the time. Sure, I was still going to church with my family during this time, but what about those that didn't go to church and wasn't being taught what sin was? I remember that school was good at this time and you would had never heard of such killing among children.

For today, I know that the children are crying out to God for understanding of this matter, sin; for they don't know sin and they don't have a teacher to teach them what sin is. We teach many things in the schools to our children and that is great and is well, but we are leaving the most important thing out, which is, the instructions of how to live a honest and good life. If we continue to leave these instructions out of our children's lives then who will build the Nation up, if all are dead, follow me? Sure, there will be a few that endure because they believe, but what about those that have never heard the understanding of the Laws? Can we as grown adults that know right from wrong afford to rob this understanding from the hearts of our children? I'm sure that some have said things such as, "Well, I don't believe in that matter and I don't think it should be taught in this Schools. No one should push this matter on anyone, even a child." I will ask this today;

Where is that man or woman that said this? Are on the Throne of God? Are they well today or are they dead? My friend, I will say this with confidence; some leaders have strayed from understanding of this matter of sin and we all will feel the consequences, if these leaders don't change the way of this matter for our children very soon. In the Great Nation of the United States of America it is written on our currency, "In God we Trust." I asked this question, Do you trust God? The God of all Life and his Son Jesus Christ is well today and will forever be well and alive. So, who do we put our trust in, God or man?

The United States of America was established by a firm understanding of God's Word and is favored in God's Eyes. But my friend, if the leaders don't start teaching the children and quit being ashamed of what they believe to be the truth the enemy will continue to enter our camp at the watch of our leaders' eyes and continue to remove God and his Son Jesus Christ from this great Nation or even worse. If any man that enters this country tries to entice or convert a child from the Love and Grace of God, that man is an enemy towards this Nation and God. We need to put God back into our children's daily life's or we will feel the consequences severely. If a family comes to this nation with a different belief and doesn't want what this Great Nation has then let them build their own schools somewhere else. I'm not a radical religious freak my friend and neither have I marched the streets to try to lure or entice another man from their beliefs, because like I've said before, choice is divine and I have no right to change it. But, when I know something to be good for another man and it would keep another man from going through so much horror, I believe it is my responsibility to tell him so. I also will do as the prophets did as they were led by God's Spirit, prophesy. I will stand firmly in what I believe to be the truth behind this matter, but I don't have murder in my heart to make someone believe it. I just let my God take care of it at his will. I have discerned from the top of my mind through the depth of my spirit and soul that taking God Laws out of the schools was a horrible choice and I am greatly burden on this matter for our children. I will say this with confidence; Taken the Laws out of our public schools was a evil intent to destroy our children and destroy this great Nation of the United States of America. I say that it was an evil intent, because any intent that isn't good, is evil.

For the God's Holy Word reads as it is written, ***"Train up a child in the way he should go: and when he is old, he will not depart from it."*** I will say, the blood of our children is on the hands of our leaders, but what is so ironic, they have the power to change the matter. It is never to late for change; for life is all about change.

But, we must put our beliefs and hope in God's Principles for the keeping of our Lives. I will also say this, If a man believes Gods Word, then that man will keep God's Word in his heart and will do them. But, if a man doesn't believe God's Word, then that man will stray from God's Word and suffer greatly the consequences, follow me? I will pray this prayer now with passion, *"Father God, forgive them; for they know not what they do. Father anoint every leader of this Great Nation and every Leader in this World that is Willing to do your Will by the Power of your Holy Ghost. Lead them all by your Spirit in your Will and Understanding of Life. In the Name of your Precious Son, Jesus Christ, Amen."*

Now, after that year when Satan enticed man to remove God's Laws from our schools, it did hurt me greatly in my little heart, because I loved God with a passion as a child and I felt as if I had a large empty hole through my heart. My life became worse at an early age of 12 and I will ask this question, "Can we as a Great Godly Blessed Nation or any Nation afford to take God from our children?" Do we hide and say to ourselves, "Their parents will teach them the Laws and there are churches everywhere. They will find their self someday."

A man that knows to do right and chooses to do which isn't right, will suffer the consequences of their choice. A man that knows to do good and does it not, to him it is sin. It isn't a matter of "IF" the man will suffer, it is a matter of "When" the man will feel the consequences.

Today I believe this with confidence; If a man rebels against the Laws of Life then that man rebels against God and if the man rebels against God, that man will be in the State's custody some day and it isn't a matter of "IF" it is a matter of "WHEN". When my parents began to believe that they had no control of my life when I was young in age, they turned me over to God and then God turned me over to the State for discipline. I faced judgments many times from the State and it was not good at times.

Sometimes the consequences of myself will intents where too great for me to bare and then there were times that the State would save my

Life. There were times that I did something wrong, such as drinking and driving and I would suffer for it. There were times that I didn't even know I had done anything wrong and still suffered the consequences. It seemed like to me during these times of my life that the State had a special agent assigned to my life to discipline me. It seemed as if the State was on my back constantly. But today I will say this; I love the State that I was raised in and I thank God for giving me this chance for living in such a wonderful State. I will share this matter of discipline much more later with you.

I Loved my parents and family during these times of my life, but I rebelled against them and God. I suffered and they also suffered for me. I can say this with confidence today; we that know the Law are responsible for those children that don't know the law and God will hold the blood of these children at our account. I must ask this question now also, "Can we afford today to sacrifice the blood of our children for our own self will intents? Do we say we Love them, but still don't teach them, LIFE? Do we that know the consequences of sin just set back and just say in our hearts, "<u>They will understand one day</u>." I know this with confidence today also; if we only think that way and not do something about it, our children will continue to die. Life isn't about what a man knows, Life is what a man <u>does</u>. I would rather a man to tell me with his mouth what he believes to be the truth, rather than, just sit and think that I will know someday the truth. Sure, I did finally get an understanding of the truth about Life after 30 years, but I almost died in sin without the understanding of Life. I know today this; man is still without understanding of this matter.

I know that I'm just a man and I don't have any control over the power of the leaders, except my voice in the ballet box, but I will say this with passion, "I'm praying within my heart daily and I believe that God's Laws will be given back to our children with a great confidence." I know that Gods Laws are for righteousness and are rewarding for our children and a man has no right to rip them from their hearts and make an empty hole. Today my heart cries out for the children of this great Nation and the World and I know we are now starting to feel the ripple through the waters from taking God's Laws from our children.

Remember Moses? Remember Elijah? God would only use Men that was willing to be led by his Spirit and were full of Faith and understood the Consequences of not living by the Law and these men where Kings, Judges and Prophets throughout the Old Testament. God would put his Holy Spirit on these men and tell them what to say to mankind concerning the Laws and visions from God. Mankind was separated from God because of sin, but God sent the Laws to mankind, so that, they could understand what sin was. God also had given mankind a greater Hope that he would send his Christ (Messiah) to deliver them from the Laws completely one day. This greater Hope was that mankind would be delivered from the Laws and could have a Messiah to stand in the gap, between God and the Law as a Mediator and then all mankind could be restored to God the Father again as from the beginning of Creation. Let me now share with you just one of the Laws that was fulfilled when Jesus Christ was here in the flesh over two thousand years ago. This fulfillment is a very important part of the Laws of the Old Covenant being fulfilled to its fullness and it is also a testimony to mankind of the sacrifice of the great sin offering from Jesus Christ for mankind's cleansing from sin. This fulfillment of a Law is about a leper man that was healed by Jesus Christ. When the leper was healed he would now be able to enter the tabernacle of God that he desired with a passion, since he was but a child. But, there is much more than meets the eye in this scripture my friend. A leper during these times where considered an outcast from the rest of God's people. A leper was considered as an unclean being and sinner and didn't have much of a life within the congregation of God's People. A leper was not to dwell with any of God's People and would stand outside the congregations and were looked down as unclean. I believe that during these times the lepers were very ashamed of themselves, shy, and were humiliated by other men to a point that a leper was the example of being plagued by God, because of sin. But, Jesus Christ came to heal and to fulfill all the laws of the commandments of Moses. Jesus Christ came to heal any man from sin, even a leper that may had not sinned. Jesus Christ came to set any man that is willing free from the curse of the Law. The scripture reads as it is written: Matthew chapter 8, verses 1-4, "***When he was come down from the mountain, great multitudes followed him. And, behold, there came a leper and worshipped him, saying, Lord, if thou wilt, thou canst make me clean. And Jesus put forth his hand, and touched him, saying, I will; be thou clean. And*** *immediately his leprosy was cleansed. And Jesus saith unto him, See thou tell no man; but go thy way, shew thyself to the priest, and offer the gift that Moses commanded, for a testimony unto them."* Jesus Christ immediately made that leper clean and set him free from the shame and reproach of other men. If we look closely at what the leper said as he approached Jesus, we will see with the eyes of our heart that the leper was somewhat ashamed when he said to Jesus, *"Lord, if thou wilt, thou canst make me clean."* The leper was willing and recognized and reverend Jesus as Lord. But, because the leper had been put down all his life and was ashamed of his appearance he said, *"If thou wilt,"*. I believe that when the leper approached Jesus and believed Jesus to cleanse him from the leprosy, Jesus did just that for him.

I believe that the leper was shy and ashamed, but he asked Jesus Christ in humbleness anyway and by him asking and believing that Jesus was Lord, Jesus Christ was faithful and healed this leper immediately. Jesus also told this leper after he was healed from the leprosy not to tell any man, but to go straight to the priest and show himself for a testimony for all lepers. During this time in order for a leper to be considered back unto the fold of the congregation, the leper would have to offer certain gifts unto the priest for a sin and trespass offering (Leviticus 14). Not only did the leper have to offer blood sacrifices to the priest he would still have to do many different things, such as shave all his hair from his body, wash continuously in water, tarry in front of his tent for certain days until he was considered to be clean again. But, when Jesus healed this particular leper he was restored immediately to God. Jesus did tell the leper to go the priest and offer the gifts to the priest, but the point was that Jesus wanted to tell all lepers and the priest that he was here on the earth. Not only did Jesus want to be recognized, he also wanted the priest to understand that the laws of the leper had been fulfilled at that very moment. Bear with me my friend, the point is coming is here. All the rituals that the priests had to do in order to consider a leper to be joined back to the congregation of God's people were not needed anymore, because Jesus Christ had come to fulfill the Laws of Leprosy also. Boy, I bet the priest thought that Jesus was firing them from their jobs, uh?

Now, Jesus Christ came and fulfilled all the Laws, so that, we can be free from sin completely and we could have Life on earth more

Abundantly and have Life Eternal. This fulfillment of the laws was the Faith and the Hope of mankind of The Old Testament times. Jesus Christ promised that after he had fulfilled the Laws and all righteousness (God's Will) of God the Father here on earth, God the Father would send his Holy Ghost in his name to the believer, also known as the *Comforter*, to teach and to console the believer of "all things."

Not only does mankind have the Laws of Understanding Sin, God sent his only begotten Son to fulfill the Laws, so that mankind could be free from the Laws, if only mankind would believe in the Only Begotten Son of God and follow him. Today, because of Jesus Christ fulfilling the Laws and Prophets, mankind can be free from the Law on earth and live Life much more Abundantly and Enter Life Everlasting, if only mankind is willing to believe on the Only Begotten Son of God and follow him. My friend, mankind has no more excuses not to be free and free indeed. Today God shed his blood for mankind and What greater Love is known to mankind, than that of which was shown through the sacrifice of his Only Begotten Son, Jesus Christ? None.

I will say this with confidence; In my past life the reason for me not understanding God's Complete Words from the Beginning of Genesis to the Amen in Revelations was because I still had self will intents in my heart. This self will intents were quenching the comforter from entering my life and teaching and consoling me on all things. But today, I do have understanding of this matter and my spirit man is growing day by day and is not dead and rotten anymore.

Today, I have no more excuses not to live a life much more abundantly. "I Thank You God the Father for sending the sweet Comforter to help me understand this matter today, in your Son Jesus Christ name, Amen."

In my dead past life, I thought as I would read the Word of God, that it would be saying this or that and I would judge his Word and would pull bits and pieces out of context to fulfill my own self will pleasures, but I will say, I was in danger of Eternal Hell Fire (Torments and Horrors). My friend, God's Word is written and framed and hanging upon his Throne in Glory. Why should we try to change it? I know today with confidence why I didn't understand God's Word in the past; for it was entirely because of self will and the true understanding of sin and its consequences.

God's Word is the Map of Life and if we desire what God has promised to us then we must understand his Word. God's Holy Ghost can work through my spirit man today and God's Holy Ghost is my Teacher and Comforter of his Holy Word. <u>God's Will not Self will and it is that simple my friend.</u> I can honestly say for today with confidence; I'm not under any of Spiritual Law or curse; for I am walking in God's Will and walking in and by his Spirit to the best of my ability as a new born child. I'm finally walking in God's Spirit and not the flesh (self will) or being led by an evil spirit, but I battle the flesh daily and have to put it in submission (Crucify It) daily and this is my part of my good fight of my Faith for the promise of Life from my God. I will say this with confidence; since I do have the Holy Ghost as my teacher and Comforter, I am well today. Having the Sweet Holy Ghost in my Life today is somewhat like this; I know that I didn't live 2000 years ago when Jesus Christ walked this earth, but with the Holy Ghost with me as my Teacher and Comforter, it is if I'm there in the Spirit and I witness those times, because the Holy Ghost was there from the beginning and he knows all things, follow me? In the Holy Book of John, chapter 14 clearly gives in detail the promise of the Comforter to any man that Loves Jesus Christ.

In John chapter 20, verses 24-31, gives the blessing of Life from the mouth of Jesus Christ to any man that believes in him and Loves him for there life. There was a disciple that was told by his friends that they had seen the Lord Jesus Christ after his death and resurrection. This disciple, whose name was Thomas, doubted somewhat. Thomas said to his friends, ***"Except I shall see in his hands the print of the nails and put my finger into the print of the nails and thrust my hand into his side, I will not believe." Later after all the disciples were together with Thomas, Jesus came into them again. Jesus said to Thomas, "Reach hither thy finger, and behold my hands; and reach hither thy hand, and thrust it into my side: and be not faithless, but believing."***

And Thomas said unto the Lord, "My Lord and my God." Then Jesus said to Thomas, "Thomas, because thou hast seen me, thou hast believed: blessed are they that have not seen, and yet have believed." Before Jesus Christ was Crucified on the tree and arose from the death, he had promise something to anyone that Loves him. This promise was the Holy Ghost, which Jesus called the Comforter. In John Chapter 14, verse 26 reads as written, ***"But the Comforter, which is the Holy Ghost, whom the Father will send in my name, he shall teach you all things, and bring all things to your remembrance, whatsoever I have said unto you."*** I will say with great confidence today my friend; the Holy Ghost is real to any man that believes and Loves God's Only begotten Son, Jesus Christ. I am a witness today of Life, because I believe and love Jesus Christ with my Life and the Holy

Ghost comforts me on my faith. I will share more on the matter of the Great Comforter later throughout these writings. Today I am not under the Laws of the Ten Commandments or the curse, because I'm walking in the Spirit and I'm free from the law and curse.

Now, there is a great difference from God's Laws and Man's Laws, but I will say, they are in the same likeness. Today I do respect man's laws; for it is also a law of understanding and all laws are given for instructions and discipline. If God had not given man, the Ten Commandments we as mankind would then be all dead in sin and we would not know how to stop committing sin and would be continually suffering death as the consequence. If God would have not engraved the Commandments into stone for mankind to see with their eyes, we would all be dead in darkness without existence. For the Law was given for instruction to man and understanding of God's Will, which are the Laws and Commandments of God. Here is a Example of a Man's Law: If I'm traveling down the interstate at a high rate of speed and chose to drive above the posted speed limit, then I would say, I am under the law and would possibly get a ticket, if I'm caught or worse.

But, if I'm driving the posted speed limit and revering the law, then I'm not under the law. The law works the same way with the spirit and flesh. If then I know to do right, but choose to do wrong, then I'm under the law of the flesh, because that would be a choice I would make and then I would be under a fleshly law and probably would have to suffer the consequences. I tell you today my friend, there is no joy in that. But, the Spirit is not under the law, because it is of God and free from the law and always wants to do what is right in God's Eyes. If we are free from the law, then I can say that we have crucified the flesh (self will, the sinful nature) and are walking in the Spirit of God and if we suffer because of walking in the Spirit of God, then there is great Joy in that matter my friend. It is a good fight between the flesh and spirit and they are always fighting and I know today that there is only one thing for me to do for this matter and it is this: Do God's Will, so that I will not be under the law or curse of the flesh. But also remember this my friend, you are still in the fleshly body are you not? Oh yes!! Let me clear this one thing up while we our still on the matter of our flesh. Our bodies, which is flesh, is not sin! What? Not sin? Then why would Jesus Christ come and want to crucify his flesh, if the flesh isn't sin?

My friend, your bodies are the temple of God and when God made your bodies he said, *"It is good!"* Therefore, your bodies are not sin, it is the sinful nature of mankind that is sin, follow me? The flesh is the weaker vessel and it is in the flesh where we are most vulnerable. It is in the flesh that we are wanting and desiring the things of this world more than the things of God. This is where the sinful nature of mankind comes in.

Just like Satan, when he desire to be as God, his sinful nature cast him out of God's Glorious Kingdom and now he has to pay the price, which is death eternally. Just a question for you to ponder on; Who was here on the earth first? Was it mankind or Satan? Well, we've ponder enough; Satan was on earth first.

By the rebellious spirit of Satan would be the true reason why mankind fell to sin. But, mankind made the choice to eat of the tree of knowledge of good and evil. Satan is the sinful nature. If a man is living by the sinful nature, he is no doubt being led by the one and only sinful spirit of Satan.

Now, if we are still in the fleshly body, then we will have to fight against the flesh daily in order to do what is right. Therefore, this is the good fight. The flesh is always wanting to do what is sinful and the Spirit is always wanting to do what is good in God's Eyes. Here is a example of this good fight in my life one day. After my Resurrection to my new Life, I had a matter to happen to me and it goes like this: I went to work and I was trying to do what I was suppose to do according to what I was asked to do on my Job and I can say this with confidence; I always did so to the best of my ability. I was told to repair a machine by my co-worker and was told by this man that he had already looked at it, but he couldn't fix it. So I went to work on this machine and had to order parts just to get the machine to fire and heat the water. It was a large oil fired water pressure washer. I worked on it when I got a chance to do so; for I was busy doing other responsibilities at this facility. I will say this machine wasn't working at all when I first checked it out for repairs. I will say there where many matters that I repaired at this facility that where just left as is, because of no one there at the facility had the skills to repair the matters, but I did have the skills and fixed them quickly; for that is the reason the owner hired me.

So one day, I knew I had to order another part for this machine. When I finally got this machine to fire and work, I noticed that the thermostat wasn't working and I knew there was danger for others, if I didn't order this new part. So, I went to this man, which was my leader, in meekness and humbleness; for I knew he was a angry man and ask that I order this part and he curse me and said, "_-_-_-_, I cant believe that that machine needs all these parts _--_--_-_, get out of my _- -_-_ face!"

I thought to myself, been there, done that, I even have the hat on my shelf. This man had many problems in his life and was an angry man toward me and life, and he thought I was a threat to his position. But, I wasn't plotting no sort of matter against him or his brother; for I just did my job that I was asked to do for him and for others. I committed myself to my job to the best of my ability and had great compassion for each one at this facility, as if I would never see them again. I began to have good friends there at the facility and sometimes they would just make an excuse to call me to them, so that we could just talk about life in general. I was walking in God's Spirit to the best of my ability and had the understanding of the matter of self will and I had made my mind up at the time, that nothing such as a job, a man, my house, my land, my family, my daughter, all this world can throw at me, was not going to separate me from the Love of God that I had; for it is my peace and Life.

Before this man cursed me this last time, I had told this man a month before in humbleness and meekness, after he had cursed me in anger another day before, "If you curse me or talk to me this way again, I will leave this job. Man, you or any job are not going to take the peace from my heart that I have received at this time. It has taking me my whole life to get this peace and I am here to help you and the owner and I've done nothing wrong. And if I did something wrong, you shouldn't curse me like that." I had walked to my vehicle that day and was going to leave this job and he ran to me to apologize and he begged me to stay. He apologized somewhat for being so angry towards me and told me he wouldn't do it again and made an excuse that the owner was putting to much on him, but at the time, I knew what the real problem was and I had understanding of the matter.

Today I know what the matter was all about and it goes like this: I had repaired so many things at this plant that had been left untouched for so long and no one could or would fix them at the plant, including this man and his brother. I believe that they both felt that I was threatening their jobs. Most everyone there at the facility knew this also, that this man was an angry man and neither did didn't they have the skills. They would not call this man and would call me to fix their problems with machines and would ask me for understanding of certain things. That particular day before I left this job, I noticed the owner had given him and his brother a small project to do for him. That morning I had ask him this, "If you need any help with anything, you know that you can ask me, OK?" and he would say, "_-_-_ No! I can do this myself. You work on something else!" I thought at the time, "Been there, done that and I have the hat on my shelf."

So, I stood back and worked on my project, singing melodies in my heart and then I began to hear the tools flying and the cursing and such like that I would see and hear every day. This man and his brother didn't know how to do this project and they would not ask me or anyone for help and I knew this matter, but kept it to myself, because of what he had said earlier to me; for he had cursed me and was an angry man. I believe this man and his brother were thinking I was making them look bad, because I would fix something in a few minutes, where it may had took them weeks or just left it without repairs. I do remember one particular day that this angry man yelled at me and said, "What are you trying to do, take my job?!!" But I will say, that wasn't my intent. I was just doing what I was told to do and would try to help them as much as they would let me and wanted much just to have a great day. Sometimes this man had no choice, but to ask me for help because of the production and I would fix it quickly, like I had made the machine. I would discern during these occasions that this man would stand near me and look at me with anger in his eyes and I knew at this moment what his intent was.

I knew and discerned in my spirit man that this man was holding this angry in his heart towards me, but I pressed forward and said nothing.

So, this man and his brother that worked at the shop with me; for it was just us three in the Maintenance department, started to plot against me. But, they didn't know that I already knew there intents at the time; for God had already reveal this matter to me a time before. The reason I had not already left this job was because, I had compassion and felt that I was committed to this job and I just didn't want to quit. I knew that these two men were trying to plot against me and to try to make me break and curse them or worse and get fired, but I felt saddened for them, because I knew their intents were evil.

After this man had curse me for the last time, I looked at this angry man with meekness and said to him, "You don't have to talk to me this way. I will leave from this Job, because I will not let a Job or you or anything take my peace that I have." and I did leave from this job. As I was leaving out of the shop, I heard some mumblings from him under his breath and I felt greatly saddened for the whole matter. He and his brother had not known that I had already spoken to the owner months earlier concerning these matters and about trying to work under those conditions. The owner had opened his ears that day somewhat and agreed somewhat with me that he understood, but didn't want me to quit and for me to try to work with them for awhile. He also knew this man was a angry man; for he told me this when he had hired me 1 year before. I left the shop and went to pickup my last check at the office there at the plant and I felt saddened about the situation, how a man can be so angry towards me for doing only good. I will say this wasn't the first time, it was these conditions almost every day, if not towards me it was towards almost everyone at the plant and it was beginning to burden me greatly.

Before I went back to this job after my Resurrection, I had already discerned that I will not let anything stand in my way and be led again by self will intents and I meant every word, because I knew that my life was on the line; for it was Life or Death now.

So, I chose to give up this job, because it was hindering God's Will in my life. Most of all the other jobs I had ever been given in my past, I had lost them due to self will pleasures, drugs and drinking, but this time, I did begin to discern it was the right thing for me to do. So, I went through the office door at the plant to get my check, the owner met me and ask how I was doing. I told him I was leaving and wanted to resign from my duties. He looked at me and said, "I don't want you to quit!" But I will say, he really didn't understand the matter and he insisted to called these two men in a meeting between us. I had already discerned there intent and it was to plot against me and to try to make the owner think it was all my fault. They didn't know I had already talked with the owner several months before on this matter somewhat. These two brothers came into the office where me and the owner were sitting and looked over at me as if I had killed someone in there family. There eyes and their faces were red and I was beginning to think that they were dragons, no kidding. The owner ask the angry man, "So tell me, What is the matter with you and this fellow?" I just didn't believe what this angry man would say next. He opened that trap of his and began to lie about things and tell the owner this or that and that everything I had worked on was working before I started to work on it and that was the reason he was mad at me. And then he said, "You ask my brother! He will tell you!" And his brother opened his trap and also lied about the matters and told the owner that I wouldn't listen to his brother and I had an attitude. I just couldn't open my mouth. I just could not believe the craftiness of these two men's plot towards me. I set there calmly as a child without saying anything hurting deeply in my heart.

After they quit spilling their bellies out the only thing I did say after they had plotted against me was this, "These things they have said concerning me, are not true." And then the angry man said as he looked at me and then to the owner, as if he had a concerned look in his eyes and voice, "I don't want you to quit, I just want us to work together and for you to listen to me when I tell you what to do!" And then I said to the owner, "Sir, I thank you for the chance for this Job, but I resign from my Duties." and the Owner was somewhat discourage about the matter, but he knew I was ready to leave from this situation and that

I had made my mind up and then the owner said, "Boys! Its over. You go back to work."

Now, after I went home I began to feel the flesh trying to rise against these men for plotting and lying against me; for they where not good thoughts. I laid down on the bed and began to ask God understanding of this matter and wept over the matter; for my heart was troubled and I didn't want these thoughts in my heart and I was saddened greatly and began to weep within my heart over this matter and then I fell asleep in the bed. The next morning I got my understanding of the matter and I was grateful and thanked my God the Father for the understanding and this understanding goes like this: I knew that I couldn't have anything in my life that would hinder me from having God's Will perfected in my life. I had been already warned and had the understanding of this matter, but it just had not manifested completely yet in this situation. I was reading God's Word and then the understanding came to me like the wind would come, quickly. I had finally did something right for my life, such as giving up something like this job in order for God's Will to work still in my life. I suffered for the good, rather than, an evil sinful intent. I really wanted the income at the time, but I knew that the income wasn't going to get me where I needed to go in my life.

So, I gave the job up willingly for God's Will to still work in my life and that my friend, was great joy. I began to listen to the Spirit and to have understanding of this matter and God then put a peace in my heart and it was joyful. I finally discerned I had done something right about a matter in my life and suffered for God's Will and not self will. But, my flesh kept trying to rise and put bad thoughts and intents in my mind. Here is the point and a little key for you on this matter: The whole weekend after this incident, my flesh would start to flare over this matter like a fire. I prayed fervently and ask God to remove these thoughts from my mind, because I didn't want to think of those men the way I was thinking; for they were evil thoughts.

So, after these thoughts would hinder me from sleeping well at night, I finally got out of bed, went out side, and prayed to God and said with my heart and mouth, "God, Please help me with this matter. I trust you God with my Life, but I feel as if I'm still without understanding of something, because I'm still having these bad thoughts from within me. Please God! Please give me the understanding of this matter." I did get the understanding of this matter and it goes like this: For I still have a fleshly body and the sinful nature of my flesh is always fighting against my spirit man to do what I don't want to do. My flesh is of the sinful nature of this world, and my spirit man is from Creator's Breath. Faith and Works my friend is the answer. I never asked God to take this matter into his hands by speaking it with my mouth. I always thought that God would read my mind, because he is spiritual. I thought also that God already knew what I need, so then, why should I ask? I will say he does know what my needs are before I ask, but he is like a Father to me and he likes to hear it coming from my heart out of my mouth.

Today, because of that incident, I have a greater confidence in that particular matter. This confidence is this; In order for my faith to have action or any effect (Power) in my life, I must put my faith in action by my works. I must put my faith into action and how do I do this?

By speaking faith into life with my mouth and there is no other way. I could had been tormented by these evil thoughts for ever, if I didn't put my faith into action by doing this. Faith and Works are explained entirely with all facets that a man may look into in the Holy Book of James. Please read it now if you like. I also prayed this prayer, *"Now God, have mercy on those men for offending me and give them understanding of the matter. God take the bad thoughts from my mind and forgive me for my trespasses, in Jesus Christ Name, Amen."* When I truly gave this matter to God, I crucified the sinful nature of my flesh and it was crucified. I have never had any bad thoughts on that matter, ever again; for Faith and Works is the key. I didn't just think this prayer in my mind. I prayed out load with my mouth and doing this, my spirit spoke through my flesh and I had crucified my sinful nature of the flesh by my spirit man. Oh yes! Did Jesus Christ while he was here on Earth ever walked around and said, "God knows my intents and I don't have to do or say anything to you, because he reads my mind and my heart."?

My friend, Jesus Christ always put his faith into action by works and speaking it into life with his mouth. I know that this is another reason we have a mouth, but be careful my friend; for there is Life and Death in the tongue. I asked God to give me understanding and he did and then I asked him to have mercy on these men and give them understanding of the matter and I trust him to do so.

As of today, I have no thoughts on this matter, because God has taken it completely out of my life. Today, I have the understanding that Life isn't all about what you know, it is what you _do_ with what you know.

Speaking of Jobs in my past dead life, almost every day while I was at work on most of my past jobs, there would be something that came up suddenly and turn my apple cart over and would make me angry. I would let compulsive behaviors or my sinful nature take over and do things that I would regret later.

There were many times that I would just curse badly, say something or do something to someone in anger or just quit and give up on a job and leave without notice, blaming the job for my problems. I would feel bad about the cursing and leaving my job later and couldn't go back to the job, because I would be ashamed at what I had done. Then I would repent and ask God this, "Why God did I do this bad thing? Why God am I suffering again? I thought for sure God that this job was your Will for me." Today I know the true reason; for I wasn't walking in God's Will, even though I thought I was living a normal life. But, I was still walking in my own sinful nature or self-will (Fleshly) and I didn't have the understanding of the matter of the true life that God wanted for me. I do know for today that I must bridle my tongue and keep my trap shut also and crucify the sinful nature of my flesh daily when it tries to rise up against my spirit man by God's Word.

It is written in the Holy Book of Matthew chapter 15 verses 16-20, *"And Jesus said, Are ye also yet without understanding? Do not ye understand, that whatsoever entereth in at the mouth goeth into the belly, and is cast out into the draught? But those things which proceed out of the mouth come forth from the heart; and they def ile the man. For out of the heart proceed evil thoughts, murders, adulteries, fornications, thefts, false witness, blasphemies: These are the things that def ile a man: but to eat with unclean hands def ileth not a man. "* Jesus Christ knows all about the flesh and it's sinful nature and that is why he came to give to us the understanding of this matter. He crucified the sinful nature of mankind, by crucifying the flesh on Calvary and I ask this, "What could be any other greater example of crucifying this sinful nature of the flesh, than that of Jesus Christ on his own cross?"

Now, God's principles (His Holy Word) clearly give all the details for walking in the spirit and not by the flesh. Please read the complete Book in God's Word of <u>Galatians</u> for understanding of this matter greatly, sometime soon.

I and the Whole Wide World now have a better chance of understanding God's Will and have a 100 percent chance at having Life here on earth much more abundantly and to enter the gates of Eternal Life. If only a man will follow God's Will for his life, will he ever find peace and understanding of Life. God loves all mankind; for God sent his only begotten Son to crucify the death of man's sinful nature, which is sin, so that we as mankind could live. Please read John 3:16-21 sometime soon. I also know today this; not only can we as mankind have eternal life, we can also start here on earth with life more abundantly. In John10:10 it is written, ***"The thief cometh not, but to steal, and to kill, and to destroy: I am come that they might have life, and that they might have it more abundantly."***

I know this with great confidence; I must follow God's Will to have this Life here on earth more abundantly and Life everlasting. Today there is no greater love for mankind than that which God has showed toward us through his Son Jesus Christ. Today I know with confidence this one fact; If a man dies the death by his sinful nature, it isn't because God didn't try, it is because that man did not Love God and follow his Son Jesus Christ with his life. Oh yes! Please let me share with you another eye opener: In God's Holy Word, Jesus Christ clearly states the reality of mankind dying the death of sin. In the Holy Book of Matthew 7:13-14 it is written, ***"Enter ye in at the strait gate: for wide is the gate, and broad is the way, that leadeth to destruction, and many there be which go in thereat: Because strait is the gate, and narrow is the way, which leadeth unto life, and few there be that f ind it."*** I will share much more on the straight gate, the sinful nature of mankind, and trying to live a normal (consistent) life on this earth later in the writings. The man that dies the death of his sins, chooses his will over God's Will and has refused God to come into his house to establish it. I know this with confidence; God doesn't want not one man to be lost to sin. My friend, I hope that this little key opened a big door for you on the matter of Understanding God's Word.

Remember, "God's Will not Self Will. How can God help a man, if the man stands in the way?"

In the following writings, I will share with you experiences that will point out God's Love for me, his Discipline Rod upon me, and the consequences of not heeding to the knocking from God on my heart for almost 30years. King David to wrote in Psalms 23, *"The Lord is my Shepherd; I shall not want. He maketh me to lie down in green pastures: he leadeth me beside the still waters. He restoreth my soul: he leadeth me in the paths of righteousness for his name's sake. Yea, though I walk through the valley of the shadow of death, I will fear no evil: for thou art with me; thy rod and thy staff they comfort me. Thou preparest a table before me in the presence of mine enemies: thou anointest my head with oil; my cup runneth over. Surely goodness and mercy shall follow me all the days of my life: and I will dwell in the house of the Lord forever."*

God and his Son Jesus Christ grieves when one is lost and dies the death of the sinful nature. God wants to enter every man's heart on the face of the earth, so that His Perfect Will may enter our hearts and show us how to live here on earth. Not only does God want to show us how to live much more abundantly here on earth, he wants to give us a sneak preview of what he has for us in his kingdom in heaven, if only we will follow God's principles for our lives.

Today I know my God is also my Good Shepherd and he watches over me day and night. I know today how God, my Good Shepherd, used his Shepherd's Staff and Rod on me throughout my life and had shown me his mercy and grace, even though I was still without understanding of His Will. In the Holy Book of Matthew, Chapter 16, verses 24-26 clearly comes alive within my spirit man of what I had to do to keep my soul and life from eternal death.

It is written, *"Then said Jesus unto his disciples, If any man will come after me, let him deny himself, and take up his cross, and follow me. For whosoever will save his life shall lose it: and whosoever will lose his life for my sake shall f ind it. For what is a man prof ited, if he shall gain the whole world, and lose his own soul? Or what shall a man give in exchange for his soul?"* Jesus Christ speaks to me through his words and urges me that I must deny myself (Give my will to him), take up my own cross (Bare my own sufferings), and follow him (Doing God's Will). Doing God's Will in my Life is the only way that I can enter God's Kingdom on Earth and Heaven. For today, I'm still breathing and living, and then something must matter; for I have a chance to change from Death to Life.

Today, I know we are living under the loving Grace of God by His Christ. Before Christ had come to this sinful world, God had repented that he had even made man, because of their sinful nature. He sent a Flood over the entire World to destroyed it and cleanse it from this awful mess that man had done to it. Only for Noah and his family had found Grace in the eyes of God and God gave Noah the wisdom of this matter. God sent the flood and all was cleansed from the Earth, all mankind and all creatures. Only Noah and his family and the creatures which God had commanded for Noah to save on the Ark, where saved by God's Loving Grace. Today, Christ is the Grace for mankind and all creation. If we follow Christ, we can enter the Ark of the Covenant of God's Loving Grace and there is no other way. My friend, Hear what the Spirit is saying; For Christ is the Ark of the Covenant for mankind today and if you want to be saved from Death, you must be in his Ark. I know this with a greater confidence; I must follow Jesus Christ in order to have the Understanding of God's Grace which he has shown toward us. This is the only chance I have today and it is the only chance I will get for Life. This is my chance of Hope for Life and if I don't hasten to it, I will die the death of destruction.

For it is written in God's Word, ***"For to him that is joined to the living there is hope: for a living dog is better than a dead lion."***

There is a lot I don't know and understand about God's Perfect Will for me here on earth; for God is still training me for my journey home. But God, through his Son Jesus the Christ, has left me and the Whole Wide World Keys to Unlock the closed Doors of a man's heart on this matter and left us a map to Life Eternal. I know his Will for me and the World is for all mankind to enter his Gates of Eternal Life and not Eternal Death and also have life here on the earth more abundantly. That my friend, is my Great Hope I have today. I don't know the complete details of how to get to Eternal Life from here on Earth, but I do have a map, which is God's Holy Word. I know I am living today more abundantly than in my past dead life and these principles are showing me day by day to the straight gate of Eternal

Life. Today I know I have entered into the Ark of the Covenant and if I press forward to the Mark of my High calling, which is, Life. This is also my good fight to keep the Faith in God and his Son Jesus Christ, so that they will give me a better understanding of how to keep my life and soul from eternal death. This is also my good fight, so that the Holy Ghost would teach me "all things." In the Holy Book of II Timothy Chapter 4, verse 7-8, the Apostle Paul wrote to us, as his departure from this earth was approaching, ***"I have fought a good fight, I have finished my course, I have kept the faith: Henceforth there is laid up for me a crown of righteousness, which the Lord, the righteous judge, shall give me at that day: and not to me only, but unto all them also that love his appearing."*** Today I do understand that this fight is a minute by minute fight and I will continually to fight it until my departure from this earth draws to the end. But, it is a good fight and I have much more joy in the matter.

The greatest example of this good fight is that of Jesus Christ as He was near physical death on the Cross of Calvary. His last fight was to fulfill all righteousness of God's Will while He had breath in his fleshly body. He knew that this must be done in completeness in order for God's Perfect Will to have any effect in our lives today. As Jesus Christ was on the cross dying the death of the sinful nature of mankind, he said this; *"Father, forgive them; for they know not what they do."* Even though, man had crucified him, persecuted him, spit on him, beat him, plotted to kill him, humiliated him, Christ still interceded for man and ask God to forgive mankind for all those things. Christ left this example for us to follow; that no matter what man has done to you and I, in order for God's Perfect Will to work in our lives, we must not hold one imperfect self will intent in our heart. God's Will is Perfect and it will not work in a man's life with a self will intent in his heart, such as not forgiven someone, because self will quenches the Spirit of God from entering a man's heart.

Today I can say this with confidence, I know my course I'm taking and what course I've taken in the past and I know what is waiting for me on the other side of the finish line and I am willing to get there at any cost. Let me share another principle from God's Word with you and believe it or not, here it is. In the Holy Book of Matthew Chapter 10, verse 37-38 it is written, ***"He that loveth father or mother more*** *than me is not worthy of me: and he that loveth son or daughter more than me is not worthy of me. And he that taketh not his cross, and followeth after me is not worthy of me."* Wow! What do you think about that principle my friend? To not love your family more than Christ? That is a hard one, isn't it? It is a hard one alright and I should know, because I lived my past dead life accordingly to my self will for nearly 30 years. I never thought on this matter at any time, until God's Will came into my life and gave me understanding of this matter today. Please let me share this matter with you.

What Christ is saying in this principle is this; if you love <u>anyone</u> more than him, then you are not worthy of him. He picked the closest to us as the example and he meant every word that is written. I do love my family today and have always loved my family, but I will say I do not love them more than God and his Christ. The reason is this; My family will not get me to eternal life and they had not the power to resurrect me from my past horrors and death that I was living in for so long. My family want get me to Life Everlasting, only doing God's Will to my last breath will get me there and that my friend, is what I believe Christ is saying in this principle. Now, Christ isn't saying you cant love your family, but if you love them more than him, you are not worthy of him or his riches.

In my past life, living by self will pleasures, I did love things of this world more than God. I left God for those matters and was without understanding. I now know today, no matter who you are, I will walk with my God before I walk with you. If I don't walk with God first in my life, then I'm telling God that I don't love him and I will be headed back on a road of destruction. I would be fulfilling my own self will pleasures and I don't want that anymore and I now know today, there are not any exceptions to this matter, if I want to Live. I will stand with my God before I stand with any man, but a man can stand with me and my God. That my friend, would be wonderful. My thought today on this matter is this; God is always first, Family is always second, and then Work is always third. I must follow God and His Son at all cost, if it means giving up my family and my work, but I will say, God does want us to have all things. I am confident that we can have them, if we put him first in our life; for it is good to have all these things with God.

Remember this as it is written, *"But seek ye first the kingdom of God, and his righteousness; and all these things shall be added unto you."*

In my past life, it seemed as if I lost all that I put first before I put God first in my life and today I have the understanding of this: if I put anything first before I put my Father God, I will loose it and suffer for it greatly. I don't want that anymore and I know it is much better, if I just put God first in my life; for his burden is light for me. This is just another part of my good fight of my faith in God today and this is the way I'm trying to live. Today I am much happier and excited about the matter. There were many times in my past life that I had put others and things first before I would God and it was disastrous for me and them. I always think of the Tortoise and Hare when I read these principles of God, as they raced toward the finish line. The good fight is not about how fast or slow and how many short cuts you take to get to the finish line, but crossing the finish line and what is waiting for me at the finish line is all that will matter at my appointed time. In the Holy Book of Hebrews Chapter 9, verse 27 it is written, *"And as it is appointed unto men once to die, but after this the judgment:"*

Today, I know also that It takes patience in this life and patience is the keeper of our souls. In my past living, I had no patience and I always wanted things then and now. When I didn't get them then and now, I would quit trying to get them and would be led away in my own desires, by searching with the intents of my heart or by self will. But, today I know that God knows my patience and if I don't have any, he sure will give it to me. In my dead past living, I was without understanding of patience for so long and even when I thought I had understanding of this matter, I was still without understanding. I still got angry when I couldn't get it when I wanted it. I thought I was running the course of Life the way I wanted to run it was a right course, but that course would always lead me back to the Big Hole and the horrors time after time.

I tried running the race of life the way I thought was right from my own self rebellious will and from my own understanding from the experiences of my brain mass, but I suffered greatly the consequences. As you read these writings you may sense that I was without understanding of how to live a normal life and it may seem as if God had given me the understanding of living a normal life, but I just couldn't perceive it.

Please let me explain this one thing, so that when you read the writings you will not think that I was an idiot when God would give me certain understandings for Life. Now, let's get started with the book.

CHAPTER ONE

TAKEN OF THE TREE
OF KNOWLEDGE OF GOOD AND EVIL

LET ME START, BY SHARING WITH YOU A portion of my childhood. I was born on a Christmas Day, December the 25th around 9:00am of that morning. What a Christmas present, hey? I was born the fifth child of eight siblings. At the time of my earthly birth, I was the forth boy and I had one older sister. After I was born, there came along the other three siblings, one girl, and two more boys. There were eight children that came forth from my father and mother.

I honestly believe that my father and mother took the verse of Genesis 2:28 with a fervent passion.

Genesis 2:28, *"And God blessed them and God said unto them, Be fruitful, and multiply, and replenish the earth, and subdue it:"*

I believe this with confidence; when I took my first breath out of my mother's womb, it was at that split second that I received my living soul. In the Holy Book of Genesis 2:7 it is written, *"And the Lord God formed man of the dust of the ground, and breathed into his nostrils the breath of life; and man became a living soul."* At the very moment when I took my first living breath, I received the witness of Life and God marked (to know) me with a living soul. At that very moment when I received my soul, I became God's property. In the Holy Book of Genesis 1:26 it is written, *"And God said, Let us make man in our image, after our likeness: and let them have dominion over the fish of the sea, and over the fowl of the air, and over the cattle, and over all the earth, and over every creeping thing that creepeth upon the earth."* What? *"Let us make man in our image, after our likeness:"* I am made in the likeness of God and so are you, unless you are a talking and reading monkey having a eternal soul. Not. I honestly believe the "Image" part of that scripture, is your soul. Surely an unborn child in the mother's womb has a spirit, blood and water, which is, the witness to God of a child. But, does the unborn child have a living soul in the likeness of God in the womb of the mother?

My friend, I will confess that I am not a "Soul Professional" and neither do I understand God in fullness, but, I am confident that God knew me in my mother's womb. When I ask myself that question above, I must trust God for the answer: for he made me and you, did he not? Every time I think of that question, "He made me didn't He?", I think of a potter with his clay. All throughout the Holy Word of God is clearly written that God formed man in the mother's womb from the dirt of the earth. My friend, I honestly believe this one thing and I am willing to share this with you; and it is my great hope.

I also hope it may help you to start to grasp onto that miracle of God's Creation. But, I am in no way insinuating for you to believe what I am going to tell you with all your being; this is just a starting point. I will never know the mystery of my complete being in fullness, until after my soul is free from my body. So, I believe this; God formed me in my mother's womb from the water and blood and I received my spirit or effect of life in my mother's womb, to live for God. After I was taken from my mother's womb, then at that very moment God breathed a Living Soul within my body; then I became a living soul in the likeness of God.

I believe when I was conceived and took the witness of the water and blood in my tiny body as a embryo in my mother's womb, I received a spirit from God of effectiveness or power to live. I believe that all living things that have blood running through its veins has a spirit or an effect of God. This effect is a willingness to live and God gives all things a spirit to live; for God is life and all that contain a living spirit, "Lives." But, I believe it is only mankind that has a Living Soul for God's Purpose for eternity. Now, I believe the Soul is a growing process, just like a fleshly body is a growing process. When I received my little soul through my little nostrils at birth, I received a little soul in my body's likeness and in the eternal likeness of God. I believe the soul is in a likeness of water. I believe the soul is transparent, just like pure water is transparent, but it is in the shape or a replica of my fleshly body. If you could shape pure water into a man, then you would understand the likeness. I believe that the blood, the water, and the spirit that was within me at my birth, is a witness of both physical and spiritual. Either way, I was made in his likeness of God and it is certainly not my flesh. Even though I am my parent's child by the witness of the blood, but I became God's property when I received my eternal soul at the very moment that I received the breath of Life, through my little nostrils.

Today, I have a greater confidence that I am not of my own; for I am God's Property. My parents still today tell me the story of a time that I liked to had died as a infant, because I was somewhat sickly. I caught pneumonia as an infant and went into convulsions, but I pressed on to live and came out of that sickness by the Grace of God. My parents say to me still today, "It grieved us badly that you were so sick, because we thought we were going to loose you honey." My friend, even at this early age the enemy knew that God had marked me with a living soul and he tried his best to kill me and my family in a whole, but by the Grace of God, we live. Being born into this sinful nature of mankind as a infant, like to had took a toll on my existence here on earth. I didn't choose to be born into the sinful nature of mankind, much more, the sinful nature of the enemy of Satan, but Life chose me; and I am grateful for that.

Today, I have a greater confidence and a great chance to live in the Creator's Marvelous Creation, Love and Grace; and I have a great purpose to live life, much more, abundantly. This great purpose is for me to grow in my spirit man (Soul); for God to receive me back to him with a Living Soul with knowledge of Him for his Glory, and eternal purposes.

As an infant, I didn't even know how to breath on my own, until perhaps, the Doctor may had slap my little back to get my little lungs to start moving air. Even though, I honestly believe that I would had popped out like a jack in a box from my mother's womb, but thanks be to God for the special trained Doctor that helped my mother and myself with the delivery. Myself and all of my other siblings were born in a hospital, but my baby brother was born in a car in the parking lot of a hospital, no kidding. My baby brother must had wanted out faster from the dark hole, much more than, I and my other siblings. Even at my birth, I had to depend on someone to help me breath, and to take me from my mother's womb.

When I was born as an infant and even as a young child, I couldn't discern from my left hand or my right hand. When people would tell that I wasn't right, I would agree with them, because I'm left handed.

My friend, If perhaps I was born as an infant and already had the wisdom of a old man of age, then what purpose would my life have today? I believe the truth would be that of learning to choose from good or evil and to make the right choices. I believe that the birth of a child is just the beginning of knowing the "Great I AM". I believe with all my soul and body today, that we as mankind have one greater purpose than any other. I believe that the birth here and the life here on earth is just a vapor in the wind compared to eternity. But, the "Great I Am" gives us the choice to choose between the narrow line of good and evil. I believe the purpose of a man's life is to get a taste of the reality to come after our appointed time calls us to the grave. This life on earth is to me like a dream that I can't awake from. But, when I'm called to the grave at my appointed time, will eternity be the true reality? Yes, I honestly believe it will be with no doubt. Everything that your eyes can see, ears can hear, and fingers can touch are the testimonies of God's Love for mankind. I believe mankind has no excuses not to grow into God's great Love and Grace. But, mankind has the choice to choose to either grow and trust God or trust the things of this world. I believe choice in a divine gift given to mankind and God can not make the choice for you. God has given his all and all for mankind to make the right choice. But, do we make the right choice?

There is a great difference between the words of right and wrong and good and evil. I believe it would be appropriate at this time to share a quick story with you from God's Holy Word of his Wonderful Grace and Mercy.

In the Holy Book of Jonah chapter 4 verse 11, God said to Jonah his prophet, ***"And should I spare Nineveh that great city, wherein are more than six score thousand persons that cannot discern from the right hand and their left hand; and also much cattle?"*** The point is this my friend: as an infant or a person that has never known good from evil (taken of the Tree of Knowledge of good and evil) honestly, God will spare them and give them the chance at Life by his Grace.

I honestly believe that the purpose of the birth of a child, is for that child to grow into God's Love and Grace; and get to know him for who he is. How will we understand the purpose? Choosing between good and evil and to know the difference between the two will give us understanding of the Great purpose of Life. I honestly believe the purpose holds true to what we choose to do in this life, rather it be good or evil. But, mankind's enemy knows when a child is born, and knows the child has the mark (living soul) of God and he will surely try to kill it. Even as of today that serpent is trying to kill and destroy me, but I have a advocate to the father; and this advocate protects my whole complete Life. Remember Baby Moses, Baby Jesus and how the Kings wanted to kill the first born? Do you understand "why" these Kings sent out soldiers to kill the first born? To sum the answer up would be this; Satan hates mankind, and if he knows that one such child has been chosen to bring peace and joy to mankind, that serpent, Satan, will certainly try to kill it. My friend, that serpent is still at work today trying to kill all of the children of God, even the infants of the firstborn. Even as of this very moment and being born into God's family, by and at, his Table of Grace, I'm confident that Satan is roaring as a lion to kill and destroy me. But, God and his Christ protects me from that enemy just as they did when I was a new born child, innocent.

My father and mother were dedicated Christians and so were us children; being born into the Faith and the Grace of a Christian family that is. We were at Church every Sunday and Wednesday nights that I can remember. My whole family had a great passion of the Love for the Church during this time when I was a young child and still today. Still today, I also have a great passion to go to Church, even if I am a sinner in remission. Even as of today when I smell a crayon, it brings back the remembrance of coloring those little Bible Book stories pictures, such as David and Goliath, Noah and his Ark, The little animals on Noah's Ark, Jacob wrestling the Angel of God, Abraham and Isaac. I remember making a drawing from my little hand of a Turkey or coloring a picture of pilgrims and a picture of the Last Supper during the Thanksgiving Season. I remember coloring the pictures of the Three wise men, A Christmas tree, or making a snow flake ornament with small scissors for the tree during the Christmas Season. I still remember the Christmas Programs we would have at Church during the Christmas Season and myself being as a little lamb, or, a little drummer boy in the Christmas programs. I still today participate in Easter and Christmas programs or at least going and seeing one at a Church during these seasons. These Seasons of Easter, Thanksgiving, and Christmas were holy to me then, and are much more, still today.

I still today like drawing pictures from the Holy Bible or a Vision and Revelation that God blesses me with. I remember coloring little chicks, a Cross and a empty tomb on paper and coloring real eggs at home with my mother during the Easter season. I can still remember the Easter egg hunts we would have at Easter time at Church and home. I still today like to hide and find Easter eggs, but I will say this today; "I do not hide lucky eggs, but blessed eggs, and whosoever finds them, are blessed, not lucky." Nevertheless, the Easter Season was somewhat confusing during my childhood. I believe the reason would be that of maybe that of the Easter Bunny. Even as a child, I shunned from believing a rabbit would hide eggs, much more, could lay eggs. I would think things like this; "I wondered why he would hide eggs, if he even had them. Why wouldn't the Easter Bunny just give the eggs away to us children like Santa Claus just gives away his stuff at

Christmas?" I would look at the Easter Bunny as a mean person and think he was somewhat sneaky, no kidding. I definitely didn't look at the Easter Bunny in such a way as I did Santa Claus.

During my early childhood at Easter egg hunts, I would try to find eggs, but other kids would find more eggs than I. When the other kids would find more eggs than I, they would somewhat get a reward, such as, a piece of money. At the time I didn't think it was right for someone to get a reward and would think things like this; "Shoot! I looked hard for those eggs too and worked just as much as the other kids looking for those eggs. The ones that found the most eggs were peeping anyway. So, why don't I get a reward also?" I remember several times being as a child when other kids would be bragging of finding more eggs than myself, I would get somewhat frustrated and take my one or two eggs and then go hide from them. Then after a few moments of being alone, I would say to the other kids that were bragging, "I bet you can't find those eggs that I hid." The other kid or kids would say, "I bet I can!" Then again, I would say, "Then go find them Mr. Big!" I would be walking around in the shadow snickering and giggling and watching the other kid getting somewhat frustrated of not finding those eggs that I had hidden. Then it seem like all the kids would get involved in finding them eggs too. When the other kids would get involved, they too would get somewhat frustrated and then they would say, "You haven't hid no eggs. You are just mad, because we found more eggs than you." Then I would walk up to the first kid with a stern face and my jaws puffed out and say, "See, I knew you couldn't find them. I never hid them out there where you could find them anyway. I just ate them and hide them in my stomach with some of your eggs too. I also hid the eggshells in the trash. Go look if you don't believe me!"

There were times I never told them that I had eating them eggs either. As my family and I were driving away from the Easter egg hunt, I would watch them still looking for them eggs; the eggs that they thought that I had hidden. But, today I don't play that Easter Bunny Trick on no one, especially a child. Even today, I honestly don't really like going to any Easter Eggs hunts, because I don't like to see the children get discouraged.

Nevertheless, I will manage to go to my father's and mother's home during the Easter Season and watch the grandchildren Easter egg hunt.

Sometimes I will help hide those eggs and hide the eggs where the kids can find them, rather than, in such a place like my stomach and then say, "Go find them eggs that I hid, Mr. Big." Sometimes after the egg hunt, I will take a large bag of candy eggs and throw them in the air, and when they hit the ground, all the kids get a chance at the candy eggs. If, I had the power to change the thoughts of a parent's mind on the Easter Bunny, I would make the Easter Bunny liken to Santa Claus.

Just today, I came from a Hospital for my medication refills and as I and my wife walked into the gift shop, I noticed how the respect of the Easter Bunny has changed today dramatically. I looked into a glass show case of merchandise for sell and I see a ceramic rabbit dressed as a chicken, no kidding. The Rabbit was holding an Easter basket and also wearing a Easter bonnet (hat) with its ears somewhat stuck through the top of the bonnet. The rabbit had a pecker (beak) upon its face, wings and feathers, but the funniest was that of, it's chicken's feet. My friend, this Easter bunny looked like he just came from the operating room at that hospital and had chicken parts surgery grafted onto it's body' as an experiment or case study. I looked at it with my eyes somewhat as silver dollar sizes and said to my wife, "My God honey! Look! What in this world is it? If that rabbit scared me, I am sure it would scare a child. I hope a child don't see it, because they will start crying and their parents want know why the child would be crying. It is near Easter, isn't honey? It's not Halloween?" Now, I know that hiding chicken eggs or candy eggs works a child's brain to find them, but it will surely discouraged some; if they don't know the truth of the purpose of hiding the eggs. If, perhaps you are a parent or a child that still believes in the Easter Bunny, just try given the Easter Eggs away, rather than, hiding them. If you still want to hid them, know the truth behind the "hiding" part, and tell your child this truth. ***"Seek" and you will find. "Ask" and it shall be given to you. "Knock" and it shall be opened.*** If you want to know where that is written, seek the Scriptures of God's Holy Word and you will find the True Easter Egg of Life. *(Hint-Look in The Gospel of Matthew.)* Now, today I have a greater understanding of the Easter Bunny and the Easter Egg; and there is a great difference of the two. First, the Easter Bunny was something that I enjoyed as a pet. My father raised rabbits for meat and I never seen a rabbit lay an egg or sneak one away from my father's chickens and hide it. Surely I would see little baby rabbits in my father's rabbit cages, but that just seemed normal to me. I never seen a rabbit lay a little rabbit or see a little rabbit come from an egg. I would see the little rabbits just somehow being there when I would look into my father's rabbit cages. I remember that my father would call me to him and say, "Look son at the baby rabbits." and then I would say, "Where in the world did they all come from daddy!?" My father would snicker and walk away, and I would be standing and looking at the abundance of little bunnies in amazement, but somewhat confused also. Something just didn't make no sense to me, because I knew that the little rabbits had to come from somewhere.

As a child, the little rabbits would give me a hope and excitement of the abundance of life. But, "Where did all those little rabbits come from in just one night?" Last but not least, my father raised chickens0 and would call me to him and say, "Look closer son and watch." and he would point at a certain spot on the egg. About that time as I would look closer under the chicken hen's under side, I would see a little hole start to break away from the egg. I would say to my father, "Daddy it's coming out! It's coming out daddy! It's alive daddy, It's alive." In just a moment, the eggshell was broken into many pieces and there sat a beautiful little chick and I was amazed.

As the little rabbits would just pop up from somewhere, and the chicken eggs would hatch into a little chick, would be always near the Spring Season. I remember seeing everything blooming around our home, such as the flowers and the trees and I would be greatly amazed. The resurrection of all that was around me gave me a great amazement and excitement. The hatching of a chicken egg represented something even greater than that of a new birth to me. The birth of a little chick from a chicken egg represented a new life to me then and still today. During this egg hatching season as a child, it would be almost every time during the Spring and Easter Season. The Spring Season has always been a Holy time during my life. It is filled with the Life of the Testimonies of the Creator right before my eyes, with no doubt. I love to see God's Creation come back to life during this particular equinox and season.

Now, I love the Easter and Spring Season as a little child; and still today as a big child. I love to see the flowers start to raise from the earth and begin to bloom, the trees begin to bud out and began to leaf, the tender plants struggling to break through the earth's surface to live and produce fruit. I even can feel within my spirit man, people, and even animals getting excited about the warmth of the near approaching season.

My friend, this particular season that I am editing this particular chapter is one month before the Easter Season, and I am coming alive, no kidding. Just last night, I watched the Lunar Eclipse of the Moon and it was amazing to see the Moon turn into an orange. My wife and I have been watching a blue ring around the Moon for several nights, and we knew something was up and it wasn't the moon. I felt something was about to happen and it did. I haven't been watching the news much lately and my wife came home from work and said, "They say we will have a Lunar Eclipse tonight." and we did. Maybe we will have an early spring this year. Nevertheless, if we don't have an early spring, I still have a great confidence that we will have a spring season. I have always been excited as a child during the Spring and Easter Season, just as a child would be at Christmas. Now, there is a poem that I wrote over 14 years ago when I experienced a true meaning of Easter. The poem is called, "A Holy Time" and it goes like this:

There is a time that is Holy to me; when I received my soul and Grace indeed. There is a time that is Holy to me; when I feel the Spirit of Life growing within me. There is a time that is Holy to me; when I see all the life God has given to me. There is a time that is Holy to me; when I think of the Time that Christ died for me. There is a time that is Holy to me; when Christ defeated death on the Cross of Cavalry. There is a time that is Holy to me; when Christ Resurrected to give me Victory. There is a time that is Holy to me; The time Christ said, "I will be back for thee." There is a time that is Holy to me; The time my soul will be soaring through the air, to join Christ and my loved ones in that glorious Affair. There in Heaven in my Savior's side; Where I will live forever and never die. Holy, Holy, Holy!

Now, there is one particular time of the year that I really didn't care much about during my childhood and still don't much today. This time seemed to me a dark time and I didn't like this dark time as a child. This particular time of the year is called, Halloween.

I remember clearly times that I was fearful of this particular time of year. I thought that everything of the earth was being taking over by aliens from different worlds. The goblins, the gargoyles, the witches, the monsters, the mummies, and the ghost, made this time of year in my life fearful. I didn't like it as a child and still today don't like it. If, I have offended you my friend by saying this, forgive me, but I am not sorry for saying it. First, let me explain why this time put a fear in my life when I was but a child. I was a very shy child and I would shun from what I thought was evil or the things that I would fear. I was already being enticed to do things that were not good, and Satan, that serpent, was causing things to be imagined from my brain at this early age. When I would see a monster at Halloween, I would run and hide. I wouldn't come out from my hiding place, until I knew that monster was gone. I had major problems of sleeping, even as a child, because I was somewhat paranoid from things that I had already experienced. I would have nightmares of the monsters, gargoyles, witches and they would seem real to me in my dreams. But, later in life as I grew in stature, I did experiment with such things as I have mentioned before; and I suffered greatly for the evil in my life and I will share those things with you later. I honestly believe that this Halloween time, that is celebrated today, is a gateway for Satan to come into the mind of a child; if the child doesn't understand the truth of Halloween.

Today, I celebrate this time of Halloween by thanking God for his all and all for me, such as the fall season of harvest for the great abundance of food. Just to let you know, "Hallow" originates from the word "Holy" and the "Een" part, originates from the word "Evening." So, if we put the originated words together we would have a "Holy Evening." My friend, Halloween isn't a time to put fear into a child's mind by deception. I know it looks funny as the kids dress in customs or such things, but times are worse than they were in my young days and you best be vigilant for your child's life here on earth and their eternal soul. I believe that Halloween can lead a child into the darkness of Satan's Realm; if the child isn't in the safety net of God and the parent's care. Remember this one thing my friend; a child learns from its father and mother. Everything that is in their little heart comes from trusting their parents, or, friends and family members of their parents. When a child grows up and begins to know of evil and good, the true matter would be this; What will the child trust in? Their parents, or, the things of this World? My friend, ***"Train up a child in the way he*** *should go; and when he is old, he will not depart from it." (Proverbs 22-6)*

I remember clearly a time that I went to a haunted house as a child. This place of the haunted house was friends of my father and mother and they set the program up to keep the older children off the streets, I do believe. My older brother was playing football at school during this time and this one particular Halloween evening. He had on his football gear and his skin was painted green being dressed as Frankenstein; he won the prize for the best custom also. During this particular time at this Haunted house, I was no bigger than one of Santa's smallest Elves at this time, and I would come up to my brother's belt in physical statue. My cousins and siblings were trying to encourage me to enter into this darkened hole. I wasn't hasty, but I trusted my kin folk and especially my siblings, so, I went in anyway. I remember as I walk into this dark hole, I was somewhat fearful. I remember someone grabbing my hand and somewhat leading me around in this dark hole and said to me, "Don't be scared. I will show you around." I was as blind as a bat and I wanted out of that place. But, this person said this to me with a soft voice in the darkness, "Put you hand in this bowl and tell me what you feel." This person somewhat led my little hand to a bowl and I felt some round tissue type objects. Then the person who was holding my hand, shouted out loudly like this, "Oooh! You just rubbed some eyeballs!"

Then every goblin (child) that was in this dark place, screamed also to the top of the voices. My friend, I jerked my hand from that person and I don't know how I got out of that place, but, I did. I believe that I crawled on my hands and knees, inch by inch, under my big brother's Frankenstein legs following just a crack of light through the bottom of the doorways, outside to a dim light upon a porch; and there I stayed somewhat in the shadow. I remember the children coming out of that dark hole saying, "Where is he? Where did he go? And then they would shout out as if they would be calling for me saying, "Its Ok. Come out, come out, where ever you are." I would just hide myself, much, much, more from those scary monsters and I would watched them as they would look for me. Then I would sneak inside the house where my parents would be and play inside where the light was. Then the older people would say, "Why aren't you out playing with the other kids?" and I would look at them and somewhat cry and run and hide in the house somewhere, listening to what they were saying 0also. I remember the older people would say something like this as I was near them hiding behind a couch or chair; "He likes playing hide and seek, doesn't he?"

Now, when the haunting was over at this haunted house and the lights came back on in that dark hole, the lights gave the whole thing away to me. I knew then that it was all just a hoax then. Some of the older children were telling me that there has never been no lights in that dark hole, because the boogie man would keep them out. I was desperate to know the truth about those eyeballs. So, I snuck back into that dark hole by my self and found those eyeballs and just as I thought, "Those aint (a southern little term for "are not") no eyeballs. They are just grapes in a bowl. They think they scared me, you just wait. They haven't seen scared yet." Then I would mash those grapes in the bowl with my hand and make juice out of them. Then I would run around putting mashed grapes and juice on the older kids, but they would laugh, even though, I didn't think it was funny.

Today, I treat Halloween as a time of giving, just as I would during the Christmas season, but Halloween doesn't have the same effect as it does at Christmas. I will share as I did get older later, how this Halloween celebration influenced my life. It brought my imagination out at Halloween, but it almost caused my life. Now, I have today bought a robotic Santa Claus from my favorite hangout, Wal-Mart, and it is deck out with a motion sensor, Red raiment and a cap with the little white fuzzy ball on its end.

This Santa sings Christmas Carols, as someone would walk by it and somewhat moves its body. During the seasons, besides Christmas, this Santa Claus changes his appearance though. I have it deck with dark sunglasses, camouflage military fatigues, a Jungle hat and other features, no kidding. My friend, Halloween can be a fun time of year, but if you don't know the truth of the real Halloween, you may be deceived.

During these times, I was a very shy child, but I had a great passion for God and the people at Church. I found it much easier to do things for the people that went to Church, more than, for the mean people that didn't go to Church. Now, that is was I thought at the time as a child, anyway. I was a very shy child while I was growing up and when people would want to touch me or talk to me, I would run and hide, especially from the little girls. I had a great passion of going to Church and I loved my parents and family very much. I didn't understand what love was as a child, so, how could I say that I loved God and my parents? My friend as a young child that had not eating of good or evil, I was innocent and God was in me and God is Love. The Sunday school teachers, my parents, and the good people at Church, would tell me much about Jesus Christ. But, some people would ask me things, such as, "Son, Jesus will come and live within your little heart, if you let him. Don't you want Jesus and God in your heart?"

I believe the strangest thing was that of already knowing that God and Jesus was already working in my heart at that time. After people would ask me this, the congregation would then sing a song called, "This little light of mine, I'm going to let it shine." I would sing that song standing on my tip toes, to the top of my voice, just to let those people know that I was letting my little light shine as much as possible.

Like I mentioned before, God and his Son Jesus were already working in my life as a small child, but I was a child without the understandings of dangers of spiritual enemy and his devices. I felt as if something just didn't make any sense in my little heart. Even as a child, I thought I was innocent of sin, but I knew that I was certainly born into the sinful nature of this world, because of things that were said and what I was seeing with my little eyes. I began to feel things already in my little heart that certain things just didn't make any sense. I felt like everyone was a lair, and I began not trusting no one outside my family and Church. I knew from somewhere that I didn't choose to be born into this sinful nature of mankind, but Life had chosen me.

Even as a child I knew that Life had given me a chance to live and I wanted desperately to know of the things of Life. I really didn't understand those things, but, that is the way I looked at things as a child. I knew coming from somewhere in my heart that there was more to life than my eyes were seeing and my heart was feeling, but I just didn't understand. When bad things would happen to me or someone in my family, I couldn't make sense of them. I was in a child's way of thinking, innocent, and I didn't think bad things should happen in my life or others, except, perhaps the mean people.

There were times that the good people that went to Church would say something to me and I would later find out it not to be the whole truth or they would do something to me and I wouldn't know what to believe and leave me somewhat confused.

There were times I would catch someone at Church doing something that I thought was wrong, such as, sneaking to the bathroom and smoking cigarettes. But, I was a shy child and I would just keep my trap shut and hold it in my little heart for a long time.

I do remember times that someone would ask me, "Does Jesus lived in your heart son?" I would just look at them with a stern face and my jaws puffed out, somewhat like a puff adder, run and hide from them, and think something like this; "I wonder if Jesus lives in their heart?" I really would think that, my friend. I would think that I had done no sin and I was a child innocent in God's eyes; even if I didn't understand sin. So, "why should I be judged like the other mean people?" Even as a child, I felt a judgment in my little heart and I didn't like it at all. It seemed to me when someone would ask me that question, the much more, I held a little anger in my heart towards them. I would start to be on the look out for these people that asked me that question, watching them, to see if God's Love was in their heart. I felt within my little soul and heart that God and Jesus were the only one's that I could trust in, beside my parents. I felt as if God and Jesus Christ were already in my little heart. So, why would people keep asking me those questions? But, there were some that I thought loved me; and they wouldn't ask me that question above. I felt like these certain people just loved me and would say this, "Isn't Jesus wonderful son. Aren't you glad he's in your little heart?" I would think they were the smartest people on the face of the earth and these people were the ones I drew closer to. When they would say that to me, I would get excited and smile. Even as a child, I thought that my greatest mission was that of wanting "much more" of God's Love and his Son Jesus in my heart. They were already in my heart as a innocent child and I wanted to now them more.

Now, Church was like a home away from home as a child. I honored God, my family, and the people at Church with all my little heart and soul could possibly do. There were times that I do remember, I didn't want to leave Church at the end of the Sabbath Day Worship. I felt a passionate Love as a child going to Church and the Love gave me a greater confidence of belonging within myself. I loved Church with all my little soul and heart. I will say this with confidence; Church and the Love that I felt of God was my first Love. Surely, I felt a great love at home, but this Love at Church was different. It was if the word "Love" was all I knew and I wanted to know much more of it, during my childhood. Most every time that I would hear the Sunday School teachers, a Preacher, big people or even my parents say the word "Love", I would open my ears, much more, to listen. As a child, I thought God's Name was Love and surely I am still confident that he is Love. When someone said the word love, I thought they were talking about God and I would get very excited. But, I soon found out that when someone would say the word "Love", the word became confusing. I would see the word love written in my older brothers or sister's school notebook, such as, I love this boy, I love this girl or I love you. When my father or mother would tell me that they loved me, it just didn't make no sense.

Even as a child I felt within my heart that it was much better when people would hugged me or do something for me; and that made me much more comforted or loved. I would get attached to people and family when I thought they loved me, just like the same love I felt at Church. Even at this young age I was beginning to take of that fruit of Love, but I also learned that Love had many different facets. These different facets of Love were very confusion to me as a child and I would search until I found out who Loved me or not through my little heart. But, even as a child I knew where I felt the true love within my heart and it was at Church.

My friend, when an infant child is born into this sinful natured world, neither discerning from his left hand or right hand, or knowing good from evil, would the child need God and his Christ in their heart? Yes, I do believe a child would need God and his Christ to live in their heart. But, as an innocent child without sin or not discerning good from evil, God and his Christ already lives in their heart. It is the sinful nature of mankind that separates a child from God and his Son, Jesus Christ.

As a child begins to grow and starts to take from the Tree of Knowledge of good and evil, it is at this very moment for a child to understand the need of truth between good and evil. Even as a child, I was separated from God from being born into this sinful nature of mankind, ignorant from the truth of Him, but God gave me the grace to live and to make the choice to get to know him much more and to grow in him. So, is a child separated at birth from God? We as mankind put a time on a child's beginning of discerning right from wrong or good from evil, which I believe is 12 years of age, but, would that be the truth?

I honestly believe that I began to discern right from wrong when I was just a child, 1 or 2 years of age to be exact. When my mother or father would say this to me, "Boy! Don't you do that again or I'm gonna" that would be all they had to say to me. I believe that I knew right from wrong as I was growing as a child, but I didn't know good from evil. Oh yes! There is a great difference between right and wrong and good and evil. Some children grow fast and some grow slow, and some neither ever can discern right from left and good from evil as a man of age, so, who can judge a child my friend? In the Holy Book of 2 Chronicles, chapter 24 leaves us today a clear example of how a child could be very wise. In this chapter, it is written that there was a child whose name is Joash and he was seven years of age. He reigned as king and judge over Jerusalem for 40 years. There is one purpose that God had for this child and it was to repair the Temple of the Lord.

I'm sure after battles after battles, the Temple of God was in ruins and the people of God were suffering of not having a place to worship God. But, God brought forth a child to comfort them and it is Amazing isn't it? God gave a child the wisdom and authority to do His purpose, even at the young age of 7.

Today, I have a very special cousin that is Autistic and is 44 years of age as of today. Today, he is a miracle right before my eyes, because he wasn't expected to live until his 20s. To me he is just as innocent in God's eyes as a new born baby, but does God know him and does he know God? He surely talks about God sometimes and his mother is a Christian and believer. When I visit or see him, I will say something like this, "Hey buddy. God knows everything." He will point at me, himself and then up to heaven and say, "God knows you and me." and then he would giggle somewhat, as if he is joyful. I truly believe this particular cousin doesn't know right from wrong, but he has the Love of God within his heart, I am confident. I truly believe his brain is not develop as a man's brain would develop, but his heart surely is.

He can't shave himself, cook for himself, or anything a man would do to support himself, but he is still God's property. He is innocent as a child and just as humble as one too. I believe his brain hasn't developed into a large piece of flesh and neither does he judge or doubt. He is still today as he was when he was a child, humble and shy and very loving.

Now, I know you may think this is somewhat Ironic, but his mother just passed away to be with Jesus, just as I am writing these words, no kidding. His mother was my first cousin and a great friend to me and my wife. She was like to me as a big sister and would be to my side at every second, if I had called her. She was the oldest daughter of my mother's oldest sister. She was raised and born in these parts where I live today, but she had moved to California with my aunt at a early age. She lived in California almost her whole life. She married a man from Washington State, which was a good man to her and her children, but she had lost her husband a few years ago and decided to move from California back here to her home State. They have lived here in her home State for almost 8 years and had settled down, but, she has passed away at 60 years of age from cancer. I just came from the funeral service today, no kidding. As I walk into the home of my Autistic cousin's sister's, my autistic cousin looked at me and pointed to heaven quickly, without much expression, except a smile and said to me, "Mama gone to heaven." His mother took care of him all his life and today he lives with his sister.

I truly believe the very first step of an understanding of that question of "innocence", would be that of "willingness." I believe that the water baptism is the beginning of the willingness toward the choice of good, rather than, evil. Some very young children understand the purpose of the water baptism, but it would take some men at or on their death bed to every come to the understanding. But my friend, it doesn't matter how old you are when you receive the understanding of that purpose and make the right choice. What will matter is this; if you have made the right choice in this life when your appointed time is called. What will matter is when you awake to the true reality of Eternity and where you will spend eternity. I believe with all my soul and body that the water baptism is the first step of choosing good over evil and the Spiritual Baptism of the Holy Ghost, is the first step of understanding between good and evil.

In the Holy Book of Matthew chapter 3, verses 13-15 it is written, *"Then cometh Jesus from Galilee to Jordan unto John, to be baptized of him. But John forbad him, saying, I have need to be baptized of thee, and comesth thou to me? And Jesus answering said unto him, Suffer it to be so now: for thus it becometh us to fulfill all righteousness. Then he suffered him."*

Jesus was without sin, even though he was born into the sinful nature of mankind. Yet he was without sin and blameless or innocent in all eyes. But, Jesus knew the importance of the Baptism of Water and commanded John to baptize him anyway. If Jesus didn't think it was an important purpose of God's Will for his Life and mankind, do you think he would have ever been baptized? I truly believe the baptism is a public profession of a man or child's faith in God, and it is a necessity to fulfill all obedience of God's Will on this earth. I can't remember how many times I wanted to be baptized as a child, but I didn't understand the importance. I just wanted it or I perhaps I just liked to be submersed in water. I remember many times when people were being baptized, I would walk up to the water, wanting to jump in with them. But, later in Life, I did receive the true understanding of the water baptism and I was baptized in a local lake by a minister of the Gospel and my life did change immediately. The Water baptism is not only the first step of obedience to do God's Will, but it is also the profession to man of knowing good from evil. It is a profession of faith, to do which is good, rather than, evil. It is letting the world know that you have chose to do that which is good in God's Eyes and Man's eyes.

In God's Holy Word, Jesus Christ shared something greatly with mankind and I have a great passion to "quote" it with you today. It is a great understanding of how to have a relationship with the Father God. It also explains how much more God loves his children. In the Holy Book of Matthew chapter 18, verse 1-6 it is written, *"At the same time came the disciples unto Jesus, saying, Who is the greatest in the kingdom of Heaven? And Jesus called a little child unto him, and set him in the midst of them, and said, Verily I say unto you, Except ye be converted, and become as little children, ye shall not enter into the kingdom of heaven. Whosoever therefore shall humble himself as this little child, the same is greatest in the kingdom of heaven. And whoso shall receive one such little child in my name receiveth me.*

But whoso shall offend one of these little ones which believe in me, it were better for him that a millstone were hanged about his neck, and that he were drowned in the depth of the sea."

My friend, Jesus Christ clearly tells us through this principle what a man must do in order to become a child of God, and also the consequences of offending one of God's children. My friend, just this one note: We as human beings are born in the likeness of God and we are his property, and Satan, doesn't like that at all. Satan, man's adversary, has already been judged and sentenced to eternal death at the Creator's appointed time for his rebellion. Satan has no chance to live and is greatly angry at God and mankind. Satan is panting to kill and destroy our children, even at their birth.

As a child just beginning to sense Life, and learning of the Creator of Life, was a wonderful and amazing time in my early childhood. But, I knew from something deeper within my little heart that something just wasn't right. I was surely desperate for answers, even though, I didn't know what I was looking for at times. I would search everywhere, under a brick, under a log, up a tree, under the tables at home, in the closet, in the hay barn, in the flower garden, in the dirt, in the sky, under my bed, studying the ants, even asking a pet, down a frogs throat, no kidding, but, I still could not find the answers to my questions. I really didn't know what I was looking for and I felt as if something just didn't make any sense in my little heart. I had a great passion to know of these things of God with my whole heart and soul. I thought that I had a purpose to be on this earth, even though, I just didn't understand it. I would look everywhere for God and that purpose, but he was already in every place, even if I thought that I couldn't find him. Everywhere that I my little eyes would fix upon, I would seek him, but, I truly didn't know why.

I loved to play outside in my father's flower gardens and watch the butterflies and other creepy crawling things. I would see which one had eyes, a mouth, ears, a body, legs and such. I would love to find praying mantis and just watch them in amazement as they would grabbed a grasshopper and just crunch and munch away at it. I would sometimes just lie in the dirt on the ground watching ants, as if they were little people. I would take little sticks and stick them in the dirt near the ant hills and act like they were trees. I would build little dirt houses near the ant holes just to see if they had any sense to go in my dirt houses. I would take little plastic army men and surround the ants, as if I was at war with them, just to see what the ants would do. Sometimes, I would catch a grandfather spider and hold him by the legs just to see how strong he was, if his legs would pull from his body. I would even take a small stick about the size of a broom straw and stick it in little holes in the earth that I would find, just to see if something was in there.

Now, it didn't matter where I looked in my little world; it just compounded my "not understanding" of the Great Creator of Life. I wanted to know of the purpose of my Life, and God, with a fervently passion as a child. But, everything that I possible thought was the answer, amazed me even more so. Sometimes, I would bring something to my mother inside the home, such as, a grandfather spider. I would be holding it by its legs, as it tried to struggle to get away. I would say to my mother, "Mama is this a spider or what is it?" Then my mother would say, "Boy you get that thing out of here. Now!" As I would hold the spider up to my mother a few of the spider legs would break away from its body between my finger tips and its body would land on the floor in the home. My mother would jump to the ceiling and say, "Kill it son! Don't you let that thing get away! Help me get!" Then, I would reach down with my little hand and cuff it's entire body and take it back outside. I would squat down somewhat watching the grandfather long leg spider walking limp to its side away, as it was missing two or three legs; and I would feel sorrow for it.

I would go inside the house and start to pout somewhat and say to my mother, "Mama that creeping crawling spider lost its legs and it's not going to make it out there." My mother would look at me and giggle somewhat and say, "Come here honey. That old spider will make it, but leave it alone! It will live outside and be ok. Don't you bring nothing like that back into this house or it want live." I didn't understand that those words either, and now, I wanted to find out what would live outside the house or in the house. I knew the grandfather spider lost its legs in the house, but what would live in a house?

During my childhood, my mother and father worked to support us children with a fervent passion and they did meet our needs to the best of their abilities at that time. Today, my parents suffer greatly in their earthly bodies and are in sorrow for their children. After the fall of mankind to the sinful nature of Satan, which is written in the Holy Book of Genesis, that we as mankind would suffer for the rebellion or sinful nature against God's Word. It is written in the Holy Book of Genesis chapter 3:16-19 clearly, and explains the sorrows of conception of children and the thorns and thistles a man will bare in this life from the earth. *"Unto the woman he said, I will greatly multiply thy sorrow and conception; in sorrow thou shalt bring forth children; and thy desire shall be to thy husband, and he shall rule over you. And unto Adam he said, Because thou has hearkened unto the voice of thy wife, and hast eaten of the tree, of which I commanded thee, saying, Thou shalt not eat of it: cursed is the ground for thy sake; in sorrow shalt thou eat of it all the days of thy life; Thorns and thistles shall it bring forth to thee; and thou shalt eat the herb of the field; In thy sweat of thy face shalt thou eat bread, till thou return unto the ground; for out of it wast thou taken: for dust thou art, and unto dust shalt thou return."* My God, and my God, how great and marvelous is your rebuke? How Great is thy Grace and Mercy Oh Lord? Sorrows, thorns and thistles shall I live with, until I return to the dust that I came from.

My friend, my parents, myself, my brothers, my sisters, my aunts, my uncles, my whole country and all mankind as of today still suffer greatly from the thorns of their fleshly bodies, because of the curse from the beginning. Not only do we suffer, we also wait for the appointed time to be called to the grave which is, another great suffering. Just that one particular suffering is enough to grieve about, but we have hope with no doubt, my friend.

Today my parents suffer greatly from raising 8 children and suffer greatly from vertebra disc disease (degenerative), arthritis, bursitis, osteo-arthritis in their shoulders, elbows, hip and knees, bladder and kidney illnesses and there are many more. My mother and father today have had surgeries after surgeries to try to correct these problems, but different problems just keep coming back. Having eight children was a hard time for my parents, but today, God has richly blessed them with much of Heavenly things and much more children also. Today my mother and father has 7 children (one brother has past away), 8 in-laws, 13 grandchildren (one grandchild has passed away), 6 great grandchildren and one more on the way. Yes, we have a civilization started just in my immediate family. We have all separate lives now, married, and have children of our own. Today, we love each greatly, just as close as a friend could ever have.

Today I know with confidence that we as mankind will suffer the thorns and thistles until our appointed time to the grave and God is not a respecter of persons. But today, we as mankind have received a greater promise of a great deliverance from the sorrows and thorns from our labor on earth. Not only deliverance from the thorns of the flesh, but also victory from the grave; and I will share much more on these thorns and sufferings later in the section of, "What Sufferings Are You Talking About?"

During my infant life and early childhood, my father worked with a Milk Deliver Company and my mother worked at a Candy Factory. I guess milk and candy were on their minds for us kids, hey? My father and mother worked with a fervent passion to make it in this suffering world for us children. My father later got a better paying job at a factory that made televisions and such. The company was Sylvania, to be exact. I do remember clearly a time that my family and I went to this factory. When we started to walk through the entrance doors of this factory, I looked and I could see my self on a television that was sitting on a conveyer at the entrance doors and I was stunned and amazed. It was about the time that Cam Recorders were making it's debuts. I just shut my mouth and stood there in the doorway looking at my self on television in amazement putting my little finger on my face in the glass. Then my mother grabbed me by the hand quickly and we went for a tour of the facility. I got somewhat discouraged, but I didn't struggle, because I thought, "I wonder what else is here at this place?" I don't remember clearly much of anything else of the tour of the plant, except of that television watching me in and through that glass and that was amazing! This tour was during a time of my father's Company having a summer cook out and celebration. My father carried my mother and us 6 children with him, and I will never forget it. My baby sister was born at this time and she was in the arms of my mother and I was holding her hand. My baby sister was 1 year old and was the youngest boy at this time of my family. My youngest sister and I, differ In 3 years of age. There were so many different things to do and see, and I was greatly amazed. But, their was one particular person that amazed me the most and the following writings will expand on this person somewhat. I called this person a funning looking man as a child, but today I know who he really was, a Clown.

I remember clearly one game that I will never forget that I got somewhat frustrated at. It was throwing little darts at little balloons

holding by strings on a sheet of plywood. I was so small, my father had me in up his arms, so that, I could see the little balloons. I would try to throw the darts at the little balloons, but I would miss the target every time.

I got somewhat discourage and a man with a very large red nose, a very big mouth with a smile, red bushy curly hair, very large feet, very colorful raiment upon him and a bell that would jingle somewhat, came over to me and my father.

This funny looking man said to me, "What's wrong son? You can't pop those little bad balloons? Let me show you how its done."

At first when I saw this funny looking man, I thought he was different than any one else. I thought that he was from a different world and I wanted to find out where he was from. I thought he was the only person there at this party that really wanted to play. He looked somewhat as an alien from another world, but he was persistent in everyone having fun, especially the kids at this party. That funny looking man took the darts and starting popping those little bad balloons. Those balloons were popping right before my little eyes, like pop corn would pop in a popper, and I was amazed. I began to laugh and get much more excited as this funny looking man and my father were laughing also. After the funny looking man had busted the balloons, he looked at me and said, "See son, those little bad balloons are gone. You can do it." Those balloons were busted in many pieces and were hanging on a sheet of plywood by small strings. I looked at this funny looking man and puffed my jaws out and thought within myself as I looked at him with a stern face, "There isn't no more balloons to pop you funning looking man." Then, this funny looking man began to wave at the little bad balloons, somewhat like as if he was waving to the little bad balloons, "good bye little bad balloons." Again, I was amazed.

Now, after this funny looking man wave to the little bad balloons good bye, he quickly went and hid behind the plywood stage for some reason and then I said to my father, "Where did the funny looking man go daddy?" About that time, I began to see little candle flames pop up above the plywood and I was greatly amazed.

I felt my father somewhat giggle and snicker as he was still holding me in his arms. When I began to see these little flames popping up, I was excited and was in a greater amazement. After there were a line of little candle flames above the plywood the funny looking man touch me on my little shoulder from behind. I jumped in my father's arms and giggled at the same time, and again, I was greatly amazed. The funning looking man gave me a small water pistol with one in his hand and said to me, "Can you shoot those little bad flames out with this? You don't think you can shoot out those little bad flames? Watch me son and let me show you how it's done." The funny looking man began squirting water at the little candle flames with his water pistol and quenched the flames of just a few. I began to squeeze the trigger of the water pistol and then I hit one of the little bad flames with water and the little bad flame went out. Then I jumped with excitement and said to my father holding me in his arms, "Daddy, I did it!" Yes, I shot one of the little bad flames out with that water pistol and I was much more amazed. My father and that funny looking man began to laugh as I began squirting water at all those little bad flames, as if I was in a contest or a fireman at a fire with a water hose. I began squirting water from my left to my right and if anyone walked up near the booth, they were watered down also. The funning looking man said to me, "See son? I knew you could do it!" He walked away from my father and I, somewhat skipping and dancing with those long feet and the bell just a giggling. I kept shooting the little bad flames out and glancing at this funny looking man as he was walking away in amazement. I was also glancing as where this funny looking man was going and what he was doing during my fireman experience. This funny looking man was going to all the kids there at this place and I got somewhat jealous in my little heart, no kidding. I guess I was thinking something like this; "After what that funny looking man showed me, I thought he was sent for me and not for the other kids. He was also playing with big people, and I thought that was even much more strange. Why would he play with the big people?" After I had shot out all the little bad flames with the little water pistol, my father with me still in his arms, left that game and he started walking around the grounds meeting his co-workers. I remember some big people as my father presented himself to his co-workers would look at my father and me and say, "Oh, he is so darling. What is your name little fellow." I remember not saying a word and I would just looked at them and then away, with a small stern look and my jaws puffed out upon my face. I believe I was thinking this to myself, "Don't you touch me you big bad person that took my funny looking man away from me." At this same time, I still had the water pistol in my hand and it was still half loaded with water, of course. I began to get a idea in my little brain and then I began to smile and giggle somewhat. I can still remember my father, as I somewhat squirmed like a worm in his arms, glancing in my eyes and knowing that I was up to something. But, I knew he thought something, so I just pretended everything was a O.K. As we were meeting his co-workers and walking around on the grounds, I began squirting water at the big bad people that I could get a shot at and then I began to enjoy the party, much more. Everyone that I would squirt with the water would laugh or giggle and my father would snicker somewhat under his breath. I did it much more, until I shot my daddy in the face with water also. I thought at the time that my father needed to laugh also, but my father took the little water pistol from me and I watched him place it in his pocket. He did laugh somewhat and I thought that was strange too. I got somewhat frustrated again and I began to cry or pout, because I thought it was a time to play, especially when the big people would laugh when I would squirt them with water.

When I refused to have any more fun and had that stern mad look on my face, I guess the funny looking man must had been watching me. He came back over where my father and I were and wanted to hand me some large balloons.

I somewhat shunned from him, because I had watched him play with other people and I was somewhat angry at him. These large balloons that the funny looking man wanted to give to me, were bigger than I was at the time. I believe those balloons were around 2 feet in diameter and I was somewhat afraid of the balloons. I would watch the other kids take the balloons and they would float away in the air, and I was amazed again. No, not the kids, the balloons.

Now, I was afraid of the large balloons, because I thought this; "if I took one of those big bad balloons, I would float away in the air." This funning looking man would somewhat act like he was going to give me a balloon, but he would release it quickly and it would float away into the heavens. I got somewhat again frustrated and started to squirm in my father arms. My father finally let me down out of his arms and I began to hold tight to his pant leg as I was watching this funny looking man in amazement. The funning looking man with the big bad balloons squatted down and said to me, "Are you scared of those big bad balloons." I finally took one of the big bad balloons from the funning looking man and I released it as quick as I got it. As I released the big bad balloon and watching this funning looking man, I was much, much, more amazed. It wasn't the big bad balloon that I was amazed at, it was the funny looking man that amazed me, much, much more. I watched the funning looking man point his finger at the big bad balloon as it was floated away into the atmosphere and then he would point at me. As the big bad balloon would float away into the atmosphere then the funny looking man would look as if he was crying and waving with his hand at the big bad balloon as if he was saying, "Good bye big bad balloon." This funny looking man surely made my day at this visit to my father's work place. Later that day, I would run around that place looking for every balloon that wasn't tied down to another kids arm.

When I did find a balloon that I could get my little hands on, I would grab it quickly and run and find this funny looking man to let the balloon float away, so that, I could see him cry and wave his hand "good bye to the big bad balloon."

Now, let me share this with you. I believe about or during this particular time of 4 years of age, I began to have little nightmares and guess who was the one in my nightmare? If you guessed the funny looking man, you guessed right. Today, I know what the intent was of those nightmares; the enemy was trying his best to put fear in me even at this young age of 4. He was trying to take a good thing in my life and scare me with it. I know that it was the enemies intent through my little mind to sow fear. The nightmares were real to me and were as if the funny looking man was trying to get me and hurt me in my sleep, somewhat like swallowing me with his very big mouth. During these times of my nightmares, my parents would carry us kids to a Christmas parade. I would look away from the funny looking men, hiding behind my parents, and looking up to my parents saying, "Daddy, mama, are the funny looking men gone? They scare me. Is it time for Santa's float to come?"

Today, I never look at a funny looking man in the same way as I did that day at my father's work place as a friend; I look at the funning looking men as entertainers or "Clowns." But, the funny looking men are surely creative in bringing out the imagination of a child's brain. I know also the nightmares were a warning sign to me; to be careful around funny looking men, because they could be a wolf in sheep's clothing and ready to eat me up like a lion. I am in no way saying all clowns are in that way, but without the proper disguise, a clown can be fearful in the eyes of a child.

Today, I still enjoy seeing clowns at parades and parties and I believe it is good to enjoy life and laugh. But as a child, sometimes a clown can put fear in their heart. Now, Professional Clowns are very creative and I believe it is good to have clowns at children's parties or such, but be sure you have the references of the clown that you are willing to put in the mind of your child. My friend, it doesn't take but one wrong word, to sow a seed of fear in a child's mind. God wants us as his children to be joyful and to laugh. My friend, God does laugh, and he is also much more humorous than a clown. If you don't believe me, carry your child to a zoo!

I remember clearly the day my mother carried me to the Candy factory where she worked. I remember not being in her arms, and as we walk near the entrance, I said to my mother, "Mama, I can smell the candy. Are we going get some mama?" I'm sure the language wasn't that pronounced, so, I wrote it for you to understand it. I remember this time, because my mother had broken her arm by falling on the concrete at this factory. My friend, when the doors opened at this Candy Factory, I shut my mouth and I was in amazement. There were large flats of candy rolling around on tables and a conveyor. The smell and aroma was heavenly. I thought I was at the North Pole, where Santa Claus's elves made all the goodies for all the children of the world, no kidding. I thought that I had seen something and been somewhere, where no other child had ever seen or been before, somewhat like the movie, Star Track. I will never forget the red and white stripped candy as the women folded it with their hands, and the smell of peppermint. My friend, it was a child's paradise. My mothers co-workers were dressed with a net over their hairs of their heads and wore a white gown. I thought that these people looked somewhat funny, and I began to giggle and smile in amazement. I remember standing near my mother in amazement of all that my little mind and body could sense. I said to my mother as I tug her by her hand and then her dress, "Mama is this where Santa makes all his candy?"

My mother looked down at me and said, "Honey, Santa has all kinds of candy. So, you best be good, or you want get any candy at Christmas." I shut my mouth at that moment and tug her dress again, wanting into her arms. I somewhat shunned away and hid behind my mother and it seemed as if all the women there, were looking at me. I thought they were Santa's Elves and I didn't want them hearing my mother get upset with me. I thought the party with my father was amazing, but this, I almost passed out with amazement right in the backside of my mother. Thinking back today, I think I did pass out, because I can't remember anything else of that day of the visit to the Candy Factory. Later, the Candy Kitchen was closed, and my mother had to find another job.

During the times that my mother would work at the candy kitchen, she would always bring home samples of different pieces of candy to us children. After the candy kitchen closed, I got somewhat mad at the people at the candy factory, because I couldn't get no more candy.

Today, I can still smell that Candy Kitchen when I go to my mother's and father's home. I can still smell that sweet smell of the candy kitchen as I go to a candy store or my favorite hang out, Wal-mart. My mother still today keeps her candy dishes with candies for her children. As of today, I still visit a local wholesale dealer that sells a particular soft peppermint candy that I like greatly. I also keep my candy dishes full of sweet peppermint candy, but I have them high where my Chihuahuas cant get to them. If you every get a chance to go to a candy factory, go! While I am on the subject of this particular candy, peppermint, please let me share with you today pertaining to it. I call this insert, *"The Candy Cane."*

THE CANDY CANE

During many times of my life, this one particular candy, the red and white stripe peppermint, has presented itself to me in many different ways. Just the taste of a sweet piece of peppermint candy somehow brings out the child within my heart. It has always and still today is greatly special in my life.

Every time I go to a Church, I smell this particular smell. Even at my mother's and father's home today, I smell this particular smell. I had a Vision once and this smell was the beginning of that particular vision. So, what is this sweet savoring smell? I truly can't explain it in perfection, but it is somewhat like mint and sweet herbs that have been perfected into a blend that embeds into the mind. To me, it so sweet that I cant get it out of my mind or senses, no kidding.

Every time that I smell this particular smell within my senses, I immediately think of Jesus Christ and the Church. The Spirit of God immediately brings my remembrance to the alabaster box full of precious ointments from a sinner that Jesus Loved greatly. In the Holy Book of Luke chapter 7, verses 37-50 and it is written, *"And, behold, a woman in the city, which was a sinner, when she knew that Jesus sat at meat in the Pharisee's house, brought an alabaster box of ointment, And stood at his feet behind him weeping, and began to wash his feet with tears, and did wipe them with the hairs of her head, and kissed his feet, and anointed them with the ointment. Now when the Pharisee which had bidden him saw it, he spake within himself, saying, This man, if he were a prophet, would had known and what manner of woman this is that toucheth him: for she is a sinner. And Jesus answering said unto him, Simon, I have somewhat to say unto thee. And he saith, Master, say on. There was a certain creditor which had two debtors: the one owed five hundred pence, and the other fifty. And when they had nothing to pay, he frankly forgave them both. Tell me therefore, which of them will love him most? Simon answered and said, I suppose that he, to whom be forgave most. And he said unto him, Thou hast rightly judged. And he turned to the woman, and said unto Simon, Seest thou this woman? I entered into thine house, thou gavest me no water for my feet: but she hath wiped them with the hairs of her head.*

Thou gavest me no kiss: but this woman since the time I came in hath not ceased to kiss my feet. My head with oil thou didst not anoint: but this woman hath anointed my feet with ointment. Wherefore I say unto thee, Her sins, which are many, are forgiven; for she loved much: but to whom little is forgiven, the same loveth little. And he saith unto her, Thy sins are forgiven."

Also in the Holy Book of Matthew 26:13 and it is written, *"Verily I say unto you, Wheresoever this gospel shall be preached in the whole world, there shall also this, that this woman hath done, be told for a memorial of her."* Jesus commands this to be a memorial of the Alabaster box of anointment for the forgiveness of sins. "Not" that the alabaster box will deliver a man from sin, but for a memorial of the forgiveness of sin, which is, a very sweet savor. This act of faith that this sinful woman did before Jesus' feet, is the memorial. I honestly believe in this one thing today; Jesus was anointed by this sinful woman and Jesus forgave her for all sins. He wipe her sins away, whiter than snow, just as she wipe his feet with her hair and tears. The sweet smell of that anointing ointment still holds true to the Resurrected Body of Christ as of today and forever; and is also a sweet savor for the remission of sin.

Now, peppermint or any of the mint family contains aromatic oils that can be blended to created a anointing oil. These anointing oils are Holy and are described in the Holy Book of the Laws, Exodus to be exact. These Holy anointing oils were used specifically for anointing the Tabernacle of God and any other use, would be death. "The Tabernacle of God." Does that ring a bell? Does, "You are the temple of the Lord" ring a bell? These anointing oils are used for specific purposes, such as, a healing, a blessing of oneself to God's Service, the sign of the remission of sins at a confession.

These mints, such as peppermint, has many purposes. Today, I personally use peppermint for heart burn or indigestion. I keep a large bowl of it on my supper table as of today. I even feed it to my little Chihuahuas and they are addicted to it. I don't feed it to them all the time, but maybe once a week; now they need something sweet too. There was a time my candy was starting to disappear form my coffee table at home. I almost had blamed my wife for eating all the peppermint, but I found the wrappers lying under the cushions of my sofa. Yes, my little Chihuahuas were sneaking my candy away from the candy dish sitting on the coffee table, while I slept at night. I had to hide the candy from them afterwards. I still don't know how they unraveled the paper off the candy either and how they knew to hide the wrappers under the cushions. I have one particular female Chihuahua as of today that is 13 years of age. If, she hears a wrapper crumpling, she will come panting up to me, to see if it is peppermint, no kidding. She doesn't like any other candy that I know of, except peppermint. Oh yes. I also have a new baby male Chihuahua, which is two years of age now, and he is also addicted to peppermint. Today, I have to feed everyone in the home with peppermint just to keep them happy, but it is a sweet pleasure.

The candy cane that is made specifically of peppermint is a very important candy in my life throughout the year. I try to buy candy canes during the Christmas Season and store them accordingly. I am not a hoarder of candy canes, but I buy enough during Christmas season, since I cant get candy canes during the other seasons. If I had a Candy Factory today, I would make candy canes all throughout the year and submit a request to the President of the USA to make it the Nation's Candy. There is a great story behind the candy cane and I would like now to share it with you. I will start here. The Candy Cane is formed into a "J", which is, the first letter of Jesus name. The candy cane is also formed into a staff, which I know today with confidence, who holds the staff of Life; Jesus Christ is the Good Shepherd.

In the Holy Book of Mark Chapter 6 it is written that Jesus came to his own, such as his brothers, sisters, kin, his people and country, but they were in disbelief. Jesus was surely without honor in his own household and country. I would think that his kin would honor him the most, but that isn't so then and neither today. Jesus says this, *"A prophet is not without honor, but in his own country, and among his own kin, and in his own house."* It is even written that his brothers and sisters were offended of Jesus preaching and healing with the works of his hands and Jesus marveled at their disbelief, no kidding. But Jesus had a plan my friend, and it went this way. He knew that he wouldn't be received in his own country, so, he called to his 12 disciples and commanded them to do something for him in his own country. It is written, *"And he called unto him the twelve, and began to send them forth by two by two; and gave them power over unclean spirits; And commanded them that they should take nothing for their journey, save a staff only; no scrip, no bread, no money in their purse: But be shod with sandals; and not put on two coats. And he said unto them, In what place soever ye enter into an house, there abide till ye depart from that place. And whosoever shall not receive you, nor hear you, when ye depart thence, shake off the dust under your feet for a testimony against them. Verily I say unto you, It shall be more tolerable for Sodom and Gomorrah in the day of judgment, than for that city."*

My friend, Jesus Christ was going to work in his own country, if it cause all his country kin to fall into the judgment. Jesus knew the severity of their disbelief and the saving of their soul. Jesus commanded the twelve disciples to carry only a saving staff and their feet shod with sandals to represent humility, which is a show of repentance. Jesus knew that his kin wouldn't accept him as the Savior of the World, much more, the Son of the Living God.

Jesus Christ gave his kin folk and country, a chance to receive him by sending his twelve disciples as witnesses of him, two by two, out into his own country. He also commanded them to wear only one coat, which I truly believe to represented nothing to give away, except the saving Grace of God, which was represented as the saving staff.

Now, there are other representations of the candy cane besides the saving staff. The candy cane is formed into a hard candy that you can break, which is in the likeness of the Rock of Christ and his body broken for us to eat. The red stripes in the candy represents the blood of Christ the he shed for the whole wide world. The White represents the purity and the righteousness of Christ and the Resurrected Body of Christ. The taste of the mint is the memorial of sweetness of Jesus Christ for the forgiveness to mankind from sin. Therefore, when you eat your next peppermint candy cane or mint candy, think on those things.

As a child, our table was never empty and all our needs were always met. My father and mother came from very large families and if we did lack anything, my father or mother's family were there with the truck loads to help. My father had 4 brothers (all of my father's brothers have passed away as today) and 5 sisters (1 of my father's sisters have passed away). My mother had 2 brothers (1 of my mother's brothers have passed away) and 5 sisters. One of my mother's siblings died as an infant with pneumonia. I'm' sure that grieved my grandmother and grandfather greatly. Now, there is one thing in particular I would like to share with you concerning my father's father. I never knew my grandfather on my father's side, because my grandfather died when my father was 4 years of age with a brain tumor. My father still as of today, tells me that there wasn't much the Doctors could do for that type of illness and that he had to watch his father just die in bed, in agony.

My father still tells me today that he remembers seeing his father lying in bed with a hole in his head, to relieve the pressure and pain that he was suffering with. It still grieves me today about my father knowing and seeing his father suffering in such away.

My father didn't have a father when he grew up and had to fight the good fight on his own and I respect my father greatly. My father was raised by his older brothers and sisters during that time. My father is the youngest of his family. My father was a stern and vigilant man fighting and struggling to make it in this life without a father here on earth. My father has so far endured, because God became his true Father and he surely trusted him greatly with his Life and with his Children. I'm blessed that I have a great earthly father as the one I have at this time. As of today, my father has lost all his brothers to cancer or malpractice. My father has also lost one sister.

During the time of my infancy, my father was called and chosen to the ministry of the Gospel of Jesus Christ. He tells me today how he received the Baptism of the Comforter (Holy Ghost) and how his life changed over 40 years ago. My father is an Ordained Minister of the

Gospel of Jesus Christ, but, he has since retired today from the hard labor and stays home with my mother. He will still today sometimes preach or teach at different Churches upon request, but he and my mother are tiring. My mother has the gift of singing with her voice. She has sung with many gospels groups and special singing at Churches, nursing Homes, Weddings, Funerals upon request, but today, she is tiring also. I will share much more of my earthly father and mother later in the writings and you will begin to understand the true reason of their tiring.

My mother and father will still today ask me, "Do you remember much of your childhood son?" I would say to them, "Yes! Of course I do. I can remember a lot of my childhood.

I remember so far back to a time of not being able to feed my self with a spoon or my fingers. I remember that I could even crawl and you would lay me upon a bed or upon a sofa during this time. I do remember an occasion that I felt that I was somewhat smothering in the crevice of a sofa. That's right! I remember that I rolled to my side in the crevice of the sofa and I cried out, because I was so small that I didn't have the strength to move by myself. Really! I felt as if I was smothering in the crevice of that sofa. No kidding! I remember being in a dark place that I could not get out of and there wasn't much room to move. I felt cramped and bound up for some reason and felt as if I couldn't breath. But, somehow I pushed myself out of this dark hole and I saw the light! And then I took a big deep breath of air and I was amazed. "My mother and father would laugh and giggle, but I was serious when I tell them this. My friend, it is the truth! I don't now how I could know those things without experiencing them, but I do remember them somehow.

I remember clearly the time when I was the only child home. I remember glancing out the window down the dirt road of our home where we stayed at this time. I remember watching the school bus roll up and my older brothers and sister would climb aboard. I would see all the other children on the bus through the windows. Some of the children on the bus would see me standing at the window looking out and they would wave at me through the windows as if they were taunting me. I wouldn't wave back, because I felt like I should had been on that bus also and I wanted to go with my brothers and sister.

I would start to somewhat cry, because I wanted to go with them. But, my mother would always comfort me and tell me, "Come here honey. We can go to school right here at home. "Then my mother would give me some scrap paper and some broken crayons and I would draw that school bus with my brothers and sister on it. I would watch them and I would become somewhat excited about the day that I would be boarding a school bus also.

I remember a time that I could not had been but about 4 years of age. We had a Winter Ice Storm, and the lights in our home went out for weeks. I would glance out the window and see all the trees bowing down with ice and hear the large limbs crashing down to the earth, night and day. I could hear the electrical transformers exploding down the dirt road and it somewhat frightened me. I would jump almost out of my underwear and run and hide. But, I was somewhat amazed at that sound and force of power and I would think, "I just wonder what could cause so much power to cause a fire ball to light up the night and to make me jump and run from it." Then I would sneak back to the window to go peek again and then my mother would tell, "Honey! You need to get away from that window before that fireball gets you!" About that time, another explosion would occur and I would see the flash from the explosion through the window. I would again run and hide under the blanket in bed, in amazement. I honestly believe the power transformers that would explode, wasn't what was amazing me; for it was the Ice Storm and how destructive it was; The Power of God is what made me fearful.

I do remember clearly times, especially Sundays after Church services, as my family would go over to my grandmother's home of my father side. I remember as I would walk through the door, from the old screen porch, I could smell the chicken and pastry that she had just cooked, and especially those old fashion homemade biscuits. I would always be excited about going to my grandmothers on my father's side for one particular reason that I can remember. This particular reason was that of my grandmother's homemade biscuits and molasses. I thought that those biscuits were the best thing ever known to mankind. I remember clearly my father's mother as if she was standing in the kitchen cooking those homemade biscuits. I can just about smell them now. I was small child at this time, and could barely stand on my tip toes to look upon the table where those biscuits where sitting.

When we would go to visit my grandmother, she would look down at me with those pointed rimmed glasses, as I was barely tall enough to look over the edge of the table. I know my grandmother knew what I wanted when I would stand on my tip toes panting after one of those delicious biscuits. My grandmother would take one of those delicious biscuits out of a plate in the middle of the supper table, and take her finger, punch a hole within it and then pour molasses syrup into it and say, "Here son. Eat this." I would grab that biscuit like a small tiger for meat, and run outside or find me a place alone and suck that biscuit down, as if I was starving to death. But, as I was running away from grandma eating the molasses biscuit, I would say this to my sweet grandmother, "Thank you grandma. I love you."

I didn't really get to know my father's mother much afterwards, because she dies when I was around 4 years of age. I remember my grandmother being at wake in her bedroom at the old home place, which is my father and mother's home today. She laid in a casket in the back bedroom for all to view and grieve for a day or two. I would go into the room and glance at the body of my grandmother, and she looked as if she was just asleep. This was the first physical death that I had experienced or remember during my childhood. I didn't understand the death and I just thought that my grandmother was asleep and we were just waiting for her to awake. I remember touching her face and it was cold. I knew at that very moment from somewhere, when I touch her face, that something wasn't just didn't feel right.

After the death of my grandmother we moved to her home. My father got the home place and a large acre of land out of the will. The rest of my father's brothers and sisters split the remaining land within themselves, which was about 25-30 acres. The house was built in 1940 and it wasn't in the best shape. But, my father loved his home place and he jump into the deed as soon as possible.

Later my father restored the old house and built onto it and it is still the old home place. The large grain, hay and mule barn still sets at the home place, but it also has been restored.

The only things that have changed somewhat in the landscape, are the Large Oak and Pecan trees that are missing. My father and us children loved those Large Pecan trees and we would help my father pick up bushels of pecans as children. But, on the Day of September 6, 1996, Hurricane Fran came for a visit through our State and took the large Pecan and Oak trees down. The pecans tree were around 75 years of age and the Red Oak trees were well over 100 years old. The trees survived Hurricane Hazel in the 1950's, but Fran was something different. My father wept for the loss of those trees and us children wept also. It wasn't because we wouldn't have pecans anymore, but those pecan and oak trees were like a land mark upon the old home place. Us children would play in those trees swinging from an old tire and rope my father would set up for us. It was if the memories were just beginning of the reality from the loss of those trees. One of the Larger Oaks was at least 4-5' in diameter. Those trees were there long before my father's birth and he told us story of playing in those same trees. But, today they are just memories. Today, my father has planted two pecans trees and some new oaks have been established in the landscape. He has planting many Cedars and White and Red Myrtle trees in their place and many flowers also.

Now, before my grandmother had died she had remarried, and this man was staying in the home with us during this time. My step-grandfather was an alcoholic. On the weekends, I and my older brother, which was 2 years older than I at the time, would sneak onto the front porch and laugh and giggle at my step grandfather. He would be somewhat jerking in his chair watching wrestling as he would be spilling his coco-cola from his hand and his false teeth were somewhat hanging from his mouth, no kidding.

I will say this with confidence; He loved his wrestling, Coca-colas and peppermint candy. His room smell like alcohol covered with peppermint candy and I can still smell that particular smell sometimes today. When he would see me or my brother peeping at him through the screen door, he would shout out to us, "Hey boys! What are you doing? Come hither. One of you boys run through the field to the store and get me a honey bun and a coca-cola and I will give you a big piece of that pepper mint candy." If it was me, which was most of the time, I would run barefoot like a deer through the corn fields to the small country store just about a 1/4 mile away from home. When I got back with the coca-cola and honey bun, he would give me a few pieces of peppermint candy and it was worth the run. My step-grandfather stayed for awhile after the death of my grandmother, but later he remarried and moved away. I loved that man, even though, I knew that he really wasn't my true grandfather at the time. He sure treated us children good and I also miss him today. He has also now passed away and lays beside my grandmother in the Cemetery Gardens, just a stone throw from my father's home place.

After we had moved to my father's home place, my father farmed some chickens and rabbits and also had about ½ acre garden, that we lived on quite a bit. I remember my Father taking chickens and chopping their heads off and the chickens would still run in the yard with no heads, and us children, would run after the headless chickens laughing and cutting up. I can still smell the steam from the water as my father would catch the headless chickens and throw them in a large foot tub, so that, we could de-feather the chickens much easier. I don't remember my mother much working the feathers from the chickens. My mother would only stay in the kitchen during the chicken slaughter and just cook the chickens. I believe that was an agreement between her and my father.

Now, I do remember there were times that I would just happen to be in the kitchen when my father would bring in the dead chickens for my mother to cook. My mother would shout this to my father, "You carry those dead chickens back outside, and clean all those stinking feathers off, before I touch them." There were sometimes that I would gently touch and look at one of the dead chickens as my father would say this to my mother, "What are you talking about honey? They are clean!" And then I would open my little trap and say this as I was standing near my father and those dead chickens, "I see a stinking feather right there, daddy." My father would then say this to me, "Get out of here boy and go back out and play." I would run out of that kitchen like lightning and hide and watch my father bring those chickens back outside and throw them back into the hot steaming water, somewhat mumbling something to himself. I would snicker somewhat under my breath and sometimes my father would catch me peeping at him from around one of the large pecan trees; and I would then help him clean those stinking feathers off those stinking chickens.

I can still remember the days as my older brothers and my father would go out to the rabbit cages and grab a large white rabbit from the cage. I knew what they were up to, but I also knew how good they tasted when cooked in gravy with some creamed potatoes on the side. I would watch my father kill the rabbit and he and my brother would gut and skin them. When I seen the rabbit flutter to his death, I would turn my eyes away. I just hated seeing the killing, but I loved to eat them. So, I somewhat forced myself to watch the rabbit's sacrifice for the meat. My father would raise the rabbit somewhat in the air and say, "Thanks to the Good Lord for the Meat." I can still remember the old barn with the rabbit skins tanning on the walls and doors. But today, no one knows where not even one of those skins are; and I think it is somewhat strange.

I can still remember as a small child out in the garden, which my father would plant, pulling weeds or grass. My father would work the grave yard shift and still come home and tend to his garden. But, sometimes he would depend on us children to take care of it while he would be so tire and would sleep some in the morning. I will say this with confidence; My father can plant a stick in the ground and later it would bud out to something beautiful. My father has a gift of gardening and he exercises this gift greatly. As of today, not hardly able to walk, he still tries to have a beautiful flower and vegetable garden. During this time, I was so small, some of the weeds in the garden were bigger than I, no kidding. My father would tell us children, "get to the garden and pull weeds and chop grass from between those crop rows and tender plants." I would go in the garden trying to find a weed that was small enough for me to pull up. I would tug and tug, until, I would cry and run and say to my father, "Daddy I cant pull no weeds." Then, my father would look at me in amazement and if I was crazy and say, "Boy, you go back out there and pull those weeds and grass or I'm gonna" My friend, that was all that he had to say to me, and I would run back outside, trying again to find a weed small enough to pull up and crying at the same time.

Later, after my father had gotten some rest from working all night at his job, he would soon come out to the garden, to check on the status of us kids in his garden. My older brothers would be chopping away at grass and pulling weeds and they were flying through the air.

No, not my brothers, the weeds and grass. But little ole me, I would be somewhat just walking through the garden, as if I was checking to see if everything was growing properly. I would squat down and hide somewhat from my father, and pretend to be pulling dead plants away from the rows. My father would see me and say, "Boy! What are you doing. Don't pull up the bean plants, son! What in this world is wrong with you? Come here. Look right here son, right in between those little plants. Do you see that little spade of grass trying to choke that tender bean plant's life out?

Can you pull that little piece of grass up son?" I would reach down and pop off the top of the grass spade from the root and my father would stand up and say, "My God! Son! You have got to pull the root up with the grass, or it will grow back." I would start crying or pouting and then my father would squat down to where I was and say this, "Watch me son." He would show me how to pull a little piece of grass up by its roots using his fingers and I was amazed. Then my father would say, "Can you do it now son?" And I would sniffle somewhat and say, "Yes daddy I think I can. I can pull these little grasses up, but not those big old weeds." My father would start helping my older brothers and then he would come back to check of me. But, to his surprise, I would had clean a whole row of beans from grass, as if a professional grass puller had been there himself. My daddy would giggle and laugh and say, "Now you are doing it son." I would start smiling and pulling grass like my older brothers were. But, I wouldn't throw my grass to the side, I would put it in a neat little pile in the middle of the row, so that, my father could see every little piece of grass and roots that I had pulled away.

Now, It seem to me as my family would go over to my mother's parents or my grandparents would keep me for a night, I would always play my favorite and secret game of possum. I would pretend to be asleep, but I wasn't asleep. I would do this, so that, I could hear people talking, especially the adults, and I would peep at what they where doing also. I would open my eyes, but I would somewhat squint them, every now and then. I heard a lot of good things and a lot of bad things. I remember the adults would always peep in the doorway to see if I was asleep, but I would not be asleep, just my eyes shut and a really pretended soft snore. I still like to play possum somewhat, just to hear what others will say or do. I don't know why I'm bringing this up, but I thought it was pretty crafty during my early childhood.

So, all you folks that thought I was asleep, I wasn't; and I remember many things today, clearly. Even away from my grandparents, I played possum. Sometimes when the elders thought I was asleep, they would leave the kitchen and I would sneak into the kitchen and smell the can of what my grandfather was drinking and still today, I still smell it sometimes. I would look at the ash trays to see what they were smoking, no kidding. I thought it was wrong even as a young child and I held this in my little heart for a long time. But, this wasn't an anger or madness that I held in my little heart; It was liken into this, "I wonder "why" question.

Now, my Grandfather and grandmother loved Jesus Christ and tried to live the best they could and follow the examples of Jesus. My Grandfather, my mother's father, was a minister of the Gospel and I know that his thorn of addiction to Alcohol buffeted him greatly. Even with this thorn of addiction, my grandfather still had the love of God in his heart and you would know it, if you would had met him. My grandfather and grandmother loved all their children and grandchildren greatly. He would never drink around any of his children, but I caught him while playing possum.

I do remember clearly a time that my family and I being at my mother's parents for a family reunion. My mother's parents lived in a large house in town. I had a cousin that was about 2 years younger than I was at this time. I was around 5 and he was about 3. My cousin threw a rock and the rock cracked someone's car window in my grandparent's yard. My aunt, my cousin's mother, came out and blamed it on me and said, "Don't you blame that on him. I saw you throw that rock." I remember getting somewhat angry at my aunt and my cousin, because my cousin didn't tell the truth. My cousin would stick his tongue out at me hiding behind my aunts backside, but I knew the truth. I held this anger in my heart for a long time, even at this young age of 5. Even at this young age I would think, "If I had a knife I would cut his nasty tongue out of his mouth. Maybe someone will put a rock in his mouth and break his teeth out."

I don't remember much of my mother's mother either, because just a few years after my father's mother's death, my mother's mother died also. I remember clearly the time of my grandmother lying in a casket at a funeral home. I remember looking up above the side of the large casket on my tip toes, wanted to touch her beautiful face. She was laying there with a smile upon her face, somewhat just as my father's mother looked.

I wanted to see if she was asleep and as cold as my father's mother was or just to see, if she was just playing possum. About the time I reach to touch her face, that same aunt that accused me of throwing a rock, slap my hand away from grandmother and said to me, "What are you doing!? You can't do that!" I didn't know what to do and went back to the seating area with my family and started to pout and cry. I guess everyone at the funeral home thought I was crying of grandmother's death, but that wasn't why I was crying.

Later, after my grandmother's death, my grandfather left and moved to California near my other aunt for many years. He marred a woman there and she died. Then he moved back to the old home place and remarried twice afterwards. He lost 3 wife's to the grave in his life. After he lost his last wife around 23 years ago, he moved in with my parents. I will share more of my grandfather's love for me later in the writings.

At or near the near the age of 5, I do remember going to a home for child care one day. I had not started public school yet and my mother had to start working to help my father support the needs of the ever populating family. I still remember a sense of taste that I had experienced eating for lunch that day at the child care; It was tuna cakes, macaroni with sharp cheddar cheese. There was an older and larger boy in the child care with me this day.

For some reason, it was the day for him to pick on me. He would try to get me to play with him all-day, as if he wanted to fight with me or wrestle. But, I just avoided him and kept my mouth shut. I was a very shy boy during this time and I tried to play possum as much as possible, but he would somewhat punch me in the arm and say, "Wat wrog wit you bo! You anit a leep!" I would still pretend to be dead, playing possum, until his punch got harder. When the punches would get harder, I would awake from my possum sleep and say, "Leave me alone! You are mean, Bo!" Then he would start laughing and mumble something and go away for awhile.

During this particular time at the child care, I would eat when it was time to eat, and then go back to my possum sleep, waiting and wanting my mother to come and get me. As my mother came to pick me up that same day, my oldest sister was with her. I would run out the door to meet them before they could get to the door. As we were walking to the car from the day care this young boy comes out and stands on the steps and hollered at me to stop. I and my oldest sister that was holding my hand turned around to see if he needed something. He look straight at me and spoke with a frog voice (his voice was changing) and called me a name. The name went something like this, "You are a bald headed NO!" and then he started laughing. At that time, I understood why he called me bald headed, but I didn't understand the "No" part of that sentence. My Mother and Father believed in getting their moneys worth from a haircut and the barber would skin my head once every 3 months. That name calling made me *angry* and I called him a "Bald Headed NO back" at him and then my oldest sister also said, "Don't you call my baby brother a bald headed no. You bald headed No!" He looked at me again and laughed at me, and at that time, I didn't think it was so funny. I felt as if he was laughing at me for some unknown reason or maybe I was just poorly looking.

I began to cry and *held an anger toward him in my little heart.* I told my mother when we were driving away from the child care that I didn't want to go back to where that "mean bald headed no" was at. For some reason, I never went back to that daycare again. I do believe I know the reason why he called me a name that day. The reason was that I would not play with him; for I was shy and I really didn't want to be there in the first place.

Growing up as children, my siblings and I didn't have much as far as material things of this world were concerned. But I can surely say for today with a greater confidence this one thing; we were richly blessed with the good things from God. I owe this to My Father and Mother for they knew what we needed and tried to give us what we wanted. Christmas was the time of getting such things as we wanted from Santa Claus. Our family was growing very fast; for now there where two more in our home, my baby sister and a baby brother and my youngest baby brother was already in my mother's womb. My parents didn't have the extra income for such things; for food and shelter seemed sufficient for them and us. I and my siblings did have things to play with, such as, paper, crayons, clay, little cars or little army men and my favorite, dirt. Dirt?

My friend, when I was a child, "Dirt" was my best friend. I could do many things with dirt. Still today, I like playing in dirt, no kidding and I have to play in the dirt at least once a week or I just don't feel just right. When I do gardening in my yard, if I don't get dirty, then I know something just isn't right. Let me share this with you before I continue. "Oh Dirt! How precious you are to me!."

Everything that your eyes can see, came from dirt. The Large Buildings, your home, the Large 18 Wheelers, the automobile, the trees, the grass, the roads, the animals, and even you and I came from dirt, did we not? Even the tip of you eye lash came from dirt. Even God likes to play in dirt; for he made dirt, didn't he?

Playing in dirt goes back all the way back to the beginning of Creation when God created the earth and man from dirt. I was amazed greatly as a child with dirt, and I am still today amazed at dirt. I remember being told that I came from dirt, and I would play in the dirt as if, I was being formed or created again.

During my childhood we didn't have much as material things of the world, such as toys, games on a computer, watching television or saying such things as this, "Mama I'm bored." I would always be outside playing in the dirt or inspecting things made from dirt. My friend, I really love dirt. Sometimes as a child, I would play in the dirt all day and my mother or father would have to spray me down with a water hose before going into the house and I would be amazed, no kidding. My body would be so blacken with dirt, that when the water would hit the dirt on my little body, my parent and I would laugh and giggle; seeing my self come to life again. My friend, right across from my father's home place was and still is today is a large gravel pit. When I got somewhat older, I would stay in the gravel pit from sun up to sun down playing in the freshly made dirt pits. I would see what kinds of dirt was way deep in the earth, such as clay. I would be in the deep pits looking for some type of good clay. I liked to go to the pit to get clay to make things with, such as a little bowl or cup, just to see if it held water. There were times that my older brothers or someone in my family, would have to come to the pits, and shout for me to come home to eat supper. When I came out to go home, I would have a handful of fresh clay to play with when I got home. I would play with that clay, as if it was my best friend. Sometimes I would hide the clay and make little clay balls and let them harden and if someone made me mad, I would throw that hard ball of clay at their knee, no kidding. I even believe I tried eating dirt and clay as a child, but eating it, didn't taste too good. Now, if anyone would every say this to you, "You are nothing but dirt!" then say this to them, "Why thank you. I'm glad that you understand that I am dirt."

Let me just share this scripture and principle with you that I am reminded of as I think of clay today. In the Holy Word of Jeremiah chapter 18, verses 1-6 it is written, *"The word which came to Jeremiah from the Lord, saying, Arise, and go down to the potter's house, and there I will cause thee to hear my words. Then I went down to the potter's house, and, behold, he wrought a work on the wheels. And the vessel that he made of clay was marred in the hand of the potter: so he made it again another vessel, as seemed good to the potter to make it. Then the word of the Lord came to me saying, O House of Israel, cannot I do with you as this potter? saith the Lord. Behold, as the clay is in the potter's hand, so are you in my hand, O house of Israel."*

Now, there were times I do remember clearly that I had to wear hand outs or used clothes, but at that time, it didn't matter to me, because the hand outs were better than I had at that time. Could you imagine buying new clothes for 8 children all the time? Most of the time, I would wear my older brother's clothes, as they would out grow them or my aunts would bring my cousins clothes. During these times, clothes were never an issue. To be exact, I believe I'm still today trying to get rid of some of those old clothes. As of today, I still don't know where all these clothes keep showing up from. I believe I have 2 Large 55 gallon Black plastic bags full of used clothes, no kidding. I think I will go through them and then, give them to Good Will or someone that needs them. Go through them! Shoot fire! That maybe the reason I still have them.

There were times I would go on field trips with my class, and my teacher would buy me a snack or soda, because I would be the only child with no money to buy things with. It wasn't because my mother and father didn't want me or my siblings to have any money; it was because they just could not afford it. I would certainly have my lunch money when I started school which was, a quarter then.

When us children would come home from that long day of school, we would all sit at the supper table, waiting patiently for that delicious meal. We would wait quietly as our father would sit at the head of the table and then ask Grace. We would be as quite as worms and wouldn't talk or even hardly move at the feeding table. My Mother was always home at this time, to prepare a big supper for us children and my father that would work hard to support all of us at this time. I will say this with confidence; We as children may not of had many things of this material world, but we had food, shelter, clothes, and great comfort from our parents as children.

There were many times that I would go with my parents to my cousins, and most of them would have lots of different games and toys to play with. I had one particular cousin that I loved dearly and I got attached to him as my own little brother during my childhood. I would go over to his house and spend the night a lot and we would play games and many other things. When I would spend the night with this particular cousin, he would always want to play his favorite game, which was, "Operation". I'm not sure if you every have play that game, but it goes like this: You have pieces made into the likeness of body parts. These body parts are placed in the specific areas, such as the arm bone set in the arm area. There is a cartoon of a man drawn for the body parts to lay into. The object of the game, would be to take the body parts out of the correct place from the cartoon man. You would take a set of steel tweezers and try to take the body parts out. If, you would hit the sides of the cartoon man's body with the tweezers, the cartoon man would flash lights and make a noise and then you would loose the game. My cousin would always amaze me, because of so good at that particular game and I would always loose. We would play this game all night, until we would play "Operation" on each others bodies, but not with a set of tweezers. I may had like it at first, because he showed me things that I would had never thought of, but I soon felt something tugging within my little heart; that this act just wasn't right.

After time passed I didn't want to go and stay with this particular cousin anymore overnight. Later, I would get an understanding from

God and people, that what I was doing, wasn't good. But, I still love my cousin as my own brother today and I have just chosen to go a different path. Before I go any further, let me just say and clear up these few things, please. I did not write the above writings or any writings in this book to accuse anyone of anything. I am writing these things for you to start to get a grasp onto how Satan, that deceiving serpent, was trying to kill and destroy me through the lust of this world, even as a very young child. He had already tried to kill me as an infant and now he was trying his best to lure me into a very destructive life of sin. He was now trying to sow a seed of confusion from God's Love and my first Love within my heart.

During this time as a young child, I would do anything to learn about myself, but Satan was already trying to entice me down a wrong path, because of my ignorance. He would use anyone to get to me, even if it was the good people that went to Church.

Even at my birth, that serpent, Satan, was there trying his best to kill me. The enemy knew that I was made in God's Image and he wanted me dead. But, I will say this with confidence; God protected me even as a young child; even if I didn't know right from my left or good from evil. As I was developing into a young child, I would experiment on myself, creepy crawly things and such things just to see what hurt me, or what made me feel good within my heart. I knew no better as a child, and, it was if I was already beginning to understand the difference between good and evil. I was certainly beginning to know the difference from boys and girls by there body parts, but I knew still within my heart, something just wasn't right. I will say this with confidence; Satan, that rotten, dirty, deceiving serpent was already trying to lead me away from the truth of Love. He tried to confuse me of what the truth of Love really was.

At times, if someone wanted me to do things for them, I would do things for them or to them, because I loved them or they said they loved me. But, I soon found out that this love wasn't Love; it was lust and sinfully natured. Time after time of different experiences from sexual activities as a child, I became somewhat ashamed of my self. I was already shy and now I was felt ashamed within my little heart and my life began to change.

Now, later as I grew and still ashamed, It seemed to me that every cousin that I would go to stay the night with, we would somehow check each other's bodies out. My friend, I know what you may be thinking at this point, but be patient with me; for the points are coming. I had different cousins that came into my life, after I somewhat didn't like my "Operation Champion" cousin. These cousins were females and we became somewhat kissing cousins, no kidding. I really thought that I loved them at the time and I wanted to check things out with them also. We would play with each other in ways that are not appropriated to write or talk about during these times. My female cousins were surely different than my "Operation Champion" cousin. I would even spend the night with certain cousins and play possum, just to see what they would do. The things that I would find out playing possum at certain places, I didn't like it and refused to spend the night with them too. I would hold these things in my little heart for many years against certain cousins. To be exact, you are the first to know that.

Now my friend, have we not been in a time of our life wanting and panting after a Love that would make us feel more comforted or well within our hearts? Have we ever desire a love that we could get, at all cost? Have we been there thinking that perhaps we were in love, and then the love would break our heart into many pieces, and the pieces would seem scattering throughout the universe? My friend, let me say this with confidence and then I will continue.

"True Love", will cast out fear or doubt, and, "True Love", doesn't take away, it just gives and gives without wanting anything in return. You could also call this Love, "Charity" if you like. I will share this "True Love" and "Charity" later throughout the book as I would get a much more understanding of it's trueness.

As a child, this "True Love", I had already found at Church and at home, which was the Love of God, but Satan, that deceiving serpent, was already trying his best to confuse me and to sow a disaccorded, deceiving, seed of love into my little heart. That serpent knows a child will always have the Love of God within their life with innocence and that God is their first true Love. But, he will certainly deceive a child from the "True Love", if the child isn't being taught the truth of God's Love. Even though my cousins made my body feel better, my heart wasn't feeling well deep within, because the serpent was leading me away from my first Love, which is, God. I will say this with confidence; God did intervene into my childhood and he took those devices of that serpent from my life, even at this early age of childhood without understanding of the matter. God had intervened and I am confident that He, and He alone, protected my little soul from the deception of that serpent's poisons at a very young age.

Today, I love my family and all my kin in a very different way. This love for them is not a lust: It is a fervent, passionate Love for God, and his Christ, to save their souls from that serpents poison. That foul serpent hates me much for that today, but it is a good fight, and I count this good fight as a great joy within my life.

Now, after I started to refuse to stay with many cousins, because of sexual experiments, I began to want to stay with older people, such as my Aunts or Uncles, much more than, my cousins. There are a few particular times that I would like to share with you of staying with my aunts and uncles.

First, I remember wanting to stay with my aunt and uncle on my father's side one night. This particular Aunt is my father's sister. Her husband at the time was a retired military soldier and had took tour in the Korean War. He was wounded and was relieved from service, due to injury. He had gotten a job at the same place my father started to work at this time, which was, Goodyear. My aunt is a homemaker and had one small child at home at this time. I believe it was a Friday night and I stayed with them from Friday to Sunday afternoon. My aunt and uncle had a child at this time, about 3 years younger than I, but I didn't go to play with him, I went because my uncle was like a child himself. Every time that my uncle would come to visit us at my father's home, he would have some type of toy, such as a robot, spinning toys, remote toy cars or trains, some type of glowing special lights, and such. He would amaze me every time that I would see him and I thought he was Santa Claus. He actually played Santa Claus one Christmas Season and came to our home when I was small. I look to my uncle as someone like a child and he loved Life, and to have joy and laugh. I still today look at my uncle in the same way.

Well, I did get my chance as a child, and off I go to stay the night with my aunt and uncle. Before we went to their home that night, we went to a retail store and my uncle bought me a car that would move fast as you would pull a plastic rope from a gear. I will never forget the excitement as my uncle showed me how to use the little car, right in the isle of the department store. My uncle and I played with toys right in the middle of the isle of that store and I was excited and amazed. So, we went home that night and it was late. Later that evening, I was even more excited. We went to a drive in movie and I was greatly amazed. I laid in the back in the vehicle with my little cousin, cutting up and watching a Bruce Lee movie (Karate Champion) on a City block sized television set. But, I don't remember much of the movie, because me and my little cousin just laid back in the hatch back of this vehicle, watching the moon and stars. We would lay back there and I would point and say to my little cousin, "See that star? I wonder what is there?" and my little cousin would just giggle. Now, that was a great feeling and I will never forget it. I felt a different Love than I had experienced earlier. I thought at the time my uncle and aunt loved me and they treated me to things, just as their own son.

Now, there is one thing that somewhat made me not want to go

back to me aunt's and uncle's home to stay the night. It wasn't because I didn't love them or they did something to me; it was because Satan again was trying to deceive me. I will share with you now an experience that I will never forget and is embedded within my mind.

Two things happened, but they both correspond in accord together. One is about a Large Garden Spider, and another is about a girl.

Before I explain those experiences that day, let me share this one with you. My aunt and uncle lived in a large city and they had a Large privacy fence in their back yard. That Saturday mourning I remember wanting to go outside to play. My aunt, as she would always say to her son, said this to me, "Son! Don't you get near that highway now!" I remember saying, "I want. I am just going out side to the back."

It was early this Saturday morning, maybe 7:30 - 8:30 am. I remember as I walk out the door I noticed a large garden spider in a large web fresh as if it just webbed it that night. I remember the dew on the web where I could see it well and the large spider setting in the middle of the web. As I was somewhat amazed at this Large spider and it's web, I somewhat backed off from it and kept my eye on it as I continued to walk to the back yard. My little cousin had a few toys in the back yard, such as, little steel Tonka dump trucks and loaders lying in the dirt hills that my uncle had made for him to play in. I remember squatting down and taking the Tonka toys and playing with them somewhat. About the same time that I was starting to get use of playing with the Tonka toys and playing with the dirt, I began to feel within myself that I was being watched. I just pretended or tried to quench this feeling, but I noticed in my sight, that someone was peeping at me through a crack in the fence. I didn't know who it was or what it was, but I kept seeing as if someone was moving and looking at me. I just pretended to act like I didn't see them and then, I jump up from the play ground and sprinted fast to the fence to see who it was. When I finally seen who it was, I was amazed and very excited. It was another child, a young girl that was the same size and maybe the same age of myself at this time. She had sandy blond hair, hazel green eyes, and wore a white flowery dress. When she seen me, she somewhat stood back away from the fence and I said to her, "Who are you? Do you want to play with me?" My friend, this little girl didn't say a word. She just looked at me and shook her head in the "No" gesture every time that I would ask her to play with me. After I had quit asking her to play with me and kept looking at her, as if I was in disbelief of what I was seeing, she said this, "Bye!" and that was it.

During this time as I was asking this girl this question of "wanting to play with me", she would get further away from me, as if she didn't want me to touch her. I felt something different in my little heart, but I just couldn't make no sense of it.

I do know that she didn't want to play with me, and it did somewhat hurt me in my little heart. Maybe she knew that we would start to play with ourselves and she didn't like that, I will never know. But, I do know that she was there for a purpose, and, I will never forget it.

After this experience with the little girl at my aunt's and uncle's home, I never wanted to play with a boy in the way that I had played with them before. I honestly believe that God placed this young little girl there at that particular place, at that very moment, for me to grasp onto this one thing; The way that I wanted to play, wasn't the way that God wanted me to play. Today, If I could say anything to this little girl, I would say this, "Thank you for being obedient and giving me something more than just a deception of Love." Not only did the little girl change my way of thinking, but I will say she changed my life that day. I will never forget the way this young girl looked at me and shook her head in the "No" gesture, as I would ask her to play with me. know my friend, you must be thinking I am some kind of nut by now. But, I felt a godly love within my heart when I seen this little girl that day. There was no lust, but the same Love that I felt when I went to Church. I thought she was the most beautiful being that I had ever seen with my eyes in my life. I never wanting to play with no one in the ways that I played with them, after I seen this beautiful little girl.

I honestly believe from the deepest of my soul, that God had place that girl there at that very moment for me to grasp onto a purpose of Life. I believe the purpose was for me to see with my eyes and give me a hope, that he was preparing me a wife, in the future. I call her today, *"The little Angel by the Fence."* Oh yes! Let me just share this with you at this appropriate time. My dear wife today was born near the Easter Season, the 23rd of March and I was born on Christmas Day, the 25th of December. We were born nearly or exact 9 months apart. Somewhat Ironic isn't? Sometimes, I look at my wife and say, "You know dear, If it wasn't for Easter, I wouldn't have a Christmas."

This particular time I am writing these very words, my dear wife's birthday, is on Easter Sunday.

Now, there is something else that I would like to share with you about that one particular visit to my aunt's and uncle's home. It is about the Large Garden Spider that was setting in it's web near the door outside my aunt's home. After the visit from the little angel by the fence, I started to walk toward to door to go back inside to ask my aunt about this little girl, because I was amazed. I wanted to know about this little girl and if what I had seen was real or was I dreaming, no kidding. Before I got to the door, my aunt was standing on the top of the stoop outside, looking at me as if she was somewhat mad. My aunt said this, "Son! Where is my Garden Spider? Did you kill my spider? That spider keeps the insects away and I let him grow here. What did you do with it?" My friend, I didn't know what to think. I thought that I had just seen an angel and now my aunt is mad at me for no reason that I had done. I said this, "Auntie, I just seen a little friend, do you know her?" My friend, this is what my aunt said to me, "What in this world are you talking about boy? There aint nobody living back there that I know of; and what did you do with my spider?"

Even as a child, as my auntie was saying this to me, I somewhat just closed my ears and began to just see her mouth move, thinking about that little girl by the fence. Then her voice was getting louder and I started to hear her again as she would say, "Do you hear me!?" and I said, "Auntie, I promise I don't know where that spider is. I promise you that I didn't kill it. I like spiders too. I just came out to play and I seen it there when I came out, so, its got to be here somewhere. It maybe hiding from us." My auntie somewhat snicker under her breath and said, "Well, if you promise me that you didn't kill it, it will show back up. Come on in and lets go eat some breakfast." We walked down a few streets to a I-Hop (a pancake house) and ate breakfast.

Later after we had eaten, we came back to the house and guess what? Yes, the large disappearing garden spider was setting in the middle of it's web again. I remember saying to my auntie, "See auntie? That big spider is back." As we got closer to the large garden spider my aunt said this, "You stinking little spider. Don't you hide from me no more." Then we laughed and she went in and I and my little cousin played outside. This visit to my aunt's and uncle's home was a visit that I will never forget. I learned more in a few days there, than I had learned in many years. The little girl by the fence, and the spider disappearing, were understandings of how God was preparing things for life for the future, as a child.

Now, during this time of my childhood, my father was working a good job and are needs were certainly met. My mother was also working to helped with the every demanding needs for all of us children. But, my father and mother manage somehow to have income budgeted for a vacation time during the summer seasons. My father and mother would take us children to many different places, such as, the mountains camping, the beach to swim and fish, Niagara Falls, and my favorite, the Grand Canyon. We would go to friends and family which live in different states, such as, California and Illinois. My friend, could you imagine having 8 children in a 6 seated car, going across the Nation from coast to coast? As we would make a pit stop, we wouldn't be amazed, but the people looking at us would be amazed. We were packed in the car like sardines in a can. When one of us children would come out of the car and then the others one by one, people would look at us and their eyes would grow in amazement, no kidding. I remember clearly as my brothers and sisters would giggle at their expressions on their faces. It took longer to get back into the car, than it was for us to do what we needed to do at the pit stop. Today, I can barely think of just myself and my wife going on a trip across the State, much more the Nation.

Nevertheless, we did mange to go on vacation many times during my early childhood; and those days I will never forget. I cant expand on many of those amazing trips, but there is one that I will expand on. This particular trip is giving to you, so that, you would get to know me somewhat better as a child. This particular trip was a time when my family and I went to my father's friend's home in Illinois. My father had met a man in his younger days in Illinois, when he was on a trip for job training. This man professed to be a Christian also. My father and this man became close friends; and are still today much closer. My father took us children to this family's home, and it was a trip I will never forget. It was during the summer season and it was very hot. My father had a Chevrolet Super Sport and there was barely enough of room to pack 6 people, much more, 8 children, 2 adults and the luggage.

During this trip in this vehicle, I do believe that I must had slept in the back window hatch, or possibly, between the legs of one of my older brothers. I am really not sure where I was sitting to be exact; I may had been asleep in a luggage case, but I just don't remember. But, I do remember when we hit an animal in the road way late at night as we were traveling to Illinois from North Carolina. I remember being awakened from my possum sleep, to an awful, rotten, foul smell. All of my family were somewhat hysterical. I remember them saying things like this, "My God! Who died!? What in the world is that awful smell." About that same time, I began to smell it and I almost past out completely, wherever that I may had been squeezed into. My whole family couldn't move, because of being somewhat cramped and we had to bare that awful smell for hours. We soon found out what the animal was and it was a skunk, no kidding. My friend, that smell wouldn't go away and it followed us almost the whole trip. I do remember my father having my older brothers and my mother to roll the windows down as he sped away at a high rate of speed, hoping to get fresh air through the vehicle.

Well, the smell finally went away as we stopped at a rest area off the Interstate and spent the night. We slept on the hood, the back trunk and the top of the vehicle, no kidding. Yes, those where the good old days.

Now, when we reach my father's friends home, we were somewhat amazed. Their home place looked somewhat like our home place, no kidding. But, their home was larger and was probably built in the 1940's or 50's also. My father's friend also had many children and when we all met in their front yard, it looked like a new civilization. This family consisted of one boy and many girls and I was amazed. When I seen those girls, I thought I was in heaven. They were the prettiest things I had ever seen with my little eyes, except maybe the little angle by the fence. The boy was about or the same age as my older brothers and I didn't have no one to play with, except those girls. So, I just stayed with the girls and played in the dirt outside with some of them and staying near my father and mother most of the time.

I do remember my mother making us kids a banana sandwich and one of my father's fiends looked at my mother as if she was crazy and said, "Fruit on bread? I have never tried fruit on bread, especially a banana with mayonnaise and peanut butter. Is it good?" I believe my mother and my father's friend wife started to laugh and giggle together and my mother said something like this to her, "Watch.". My mother gave myself and perhaps another one of my siblings a banana sandwich and we engulfed that sandwich down before theirs eyes, as if it was the best thing in the world. When my father's friend's wife seen us children eating those banana sandwiches, she and my mother made everyone banana sandwiches. My friend, I believe we forgot the main course meal and there were banana peelings all over that kitchen and all over the outside back yard, no kidding.

Now, I do remember after we had eaten those sandwiches, my father's friend said something like this to my father, "Hey buddy, I got something for all us kids in the refrigerator, and it has been chilling for us all to eat. When you told me you where coming, I went out and bought the biggest one that I could find." My father's friend took out a watermelon the size of a small sofa from his refrigerator, and placed it on a picnic table out in the back yard; and all us children were amazed big and small. We had seen watermelons grown in the South, but this melon, blew our minds away. I'm telling you my friend, if I remember correctly, the seeds from that melon where as big as my eyes at the time. We ate all that watermelon, until we all just laid around in the back yard, somewhat looking like stuffed turkeys. We children did try play the game, spit the seeds, but some of the seeds were so big, I couldn't get them in my little mouth and we all giggled and laughed together. Some of my older brothers and their older children, did mange to spit watermelon seeds as if they were in competition, but the seeds surely didn't go far. We really had a great time and it was a visit I will never forget.

I do remember the older boy of this family and some of my older brothers, going night crawler hunting. Yes, I know. What is night crawler hunting? At the time, I thought they were going to hunt for little evil men crawling in the night around their home, somewhat like trolls or monsters. I do remember wanting and pouting somewhat to go with them, but they told me that I was too small, and too young, and told me that the night crawlers might eat me. So they told me that it would be best for me to stay back, until they got back from the night crawler hunt; and they promised me that they would bring me some night crawlers back from their hunt. I waited outside at dark, until they came back from their hunt. I finally found out what an Illinois night crawler was too, my friend, and it surely wasn't no little troll. My father's friend's boy, pulled a worm out of a bucket, the size of a small snake; and it almost scared my shorts off, no kidding.

I remember saying, "Dat aint no worm. Dat is a nake." The older boys laughed and giggle when I said that, but I was serious and somewhat ran away from it. That night crawler was at least 12-14 inches long and fat like a small snake. If those were worms, I surely wouldn't want to see the size snakes that were growing around those parts. I somewhat put two and two together later, and figured out how those worms got so big. I thought that the large watermelons must had been their food and that, is what they were eating. They must had been eating the watermelons, so, that is why you go night crawler hunting in Illinois; to keep the huge worms from eating the huge watermelons.

Now, to the point of this trip. These people that my father had met were just like us country folk. The only difference was that of, they had just as many girls, as we had boys and vise versa. They had a passion for God and also their children. I felt a Love there at their home like I had experienced in Church. Oh yes just let me add this in too. That smell we talked about earlier, the sweet peppermint smell, was also in their home. I felt an unconditional Love that only God could give at these people's home; and as a child during this time, God's Love was all I knew. I truly didn't understand this marvelous, deep euphoria that I was experiencing was Love, but I knew that it was good within my little heart; and I panted after this godly Love, as a child. When my family was saying their goodbyes later that week, I somewhat hid and didn't want to leave from their home, no kidding. I remember my father's friend saying to me, "Son, you mother and daddy is waiting and you brothers and sister too. You need to get in the car and go with them." When he said that to me, I remember running and hiding again. My older sister and their girls would come to find me and callout to me and say, "Your mother and daddy is leaving. You don't want to be left, do you? Come on baby, we have got to go!" I remember seeing my father, mother and family act somewhat like they were driving away; and acting like they were crying for me to get in the car.

But, I just puffed my jaws out and refused to go with them as I stood by my father's friend. I remember my family actually getting on the Interstate, but then I would see then turn back the vehicle toward the home again. My friend this is the truth of why I didn't want to go back. I felt a true Love, like I felt at Church from their entire family; and I just didn't want to leave them. I didn't understand that my father had to get back home and go to work the next week. I just wanted to stay with them as long as I possible. The distance between North Carolina and Illinois certainly wasn't a trip you could take every day; unless you flew a jet. I believe I said, "They will come back and pick me up later. I don't want to go home right now. Can you carry me home Mr.?" I didn't want to leave that love that I had just found, and I was somewhat fearful that I would not see them again, no kidding. I did finally get in the car, after my father's friend said this to me, "Son, your family loves you and so do we. We will come and see you later and I promise that we will. OK?" When he said this to me, I had a hope that I would see them again. So, we left Illinois from these Loving people and I wept much of the way home for them.

Later this family did come and visited us; and we had a ball. We went to the beach and camp out and guess what? A ferrous monsoon came up while camping at the coast of the shore of North Carolina, no kidding. I bet they want forget that one. The point is this my friend, God is good and he gives friends. My father found a friend and now we are all friends. I love them today much more than I did before times. I haven't seen them in awhile, but I know that they are well. They write my parents and my parents write them, because they are tiring also and cant travel like they use too. But, God still brings us all together by the good memories of that one visit to their home in Illinois, when I was but a child. I will never forget the Love that these people showed toward my father, mother and us children.

Now, during this young age it wasn't uncommon for me to go and stay away at a home of my father's or mother' family. I didn't understand what I wanted or much more, what I needed. But, I was beginning to feel a love away from my own home as a child. I had experienced some bad things already during my childhood and I was searching and panting after this Unconditional godly Love. I was a very shy child and I guess my family thought something was wrong with me. I would go over to family and stay much more than my siblings. I guess they thought I needed Love. I had another aunt and uncle 0that wanted me to stay with them one weekend. This aunt is my father's older sister. I may had been around 7-8 years of age at this time. This visit is another I will never forget. I went to their home on a Saturday evening. My aunt and uncle had only one child, which is a daughter; and she is somewhat older than I.

During this time, I will never forget the love that she show for me as she was a teenager, and was already dating boys at this time. I remember seeing her in the bathroom brushing her teeth, putting makeup onto her face, looking into the mirror, and I said to her as I glanced into the doorway of the bathroom, "You are pretty. Are you going out for the night?" She looked at me and said, "I sure am, but tomorrow, we will do something together. Tonight you will be fine with mama and daddy. You said I looked pretty. Am I?" and then I said again to her, "You are beautiful. You must have a lot of boyfriends." And she said to me, "No, I don't have a lot. I only have one that I like, and we are just good friends. We are going out to eat! Speaking of eating, wait until tomorrow; and we will go over to grandmothers and eat, and you will love her food." I got excited, because I felt that she loved me in a different way than other people loved me; I felt it in my heart and it felt good. I just went back to the little room where my aunt and uncle had prepared for me; and went to sleep, with tomorrow on my mind.

My aunt, uncle, their daughter and myself went to church the next morning. My friend, I felt a great love from the people of their congregation as I always felt at Church. When we got back to their home, we went straight to my uncle's mother's home, for a Sunday meal. I was already panting after what my cousin had said to me the evening before, but the smell of that food changed my way of thinking. My uncles mother treated me just like if I was her son. We ate home grown vegetables she must had grown herself and chicken and pastry. There at my uncle's mother's home brought the remembrance back to my little mind of my father's mother's chicken and pastry. But, not only did we have chicken and pastry, we also had homemade buttermilk biscuits. I felt as if I was seating at my grandmother's table; and was amazed. The best thing that I remember eating, was homemade strawberry preserves that my uncle's mother poured over my biscuit. Oh my! I thought I was in heaven. I can still taste those strawberry preserves and those homemade biscuits as if it was just last night. My friend, I felt a love that only God could give during this visit to my aunts and uncles home. I was a child and they didn't want nothing back from me; they just wanted to love me and I was greatly amazed. I didn't even want to go back home again, no kidding.

Later, my dear uncle past away nearly 12 years ago and I miss him greatly. He was a car parts salesman and he really like his cars. But, his appointed time was called, even as he was standing under a tree in his yard, nearly 12 years ago. He died of a heart attack. My pretty cousin married her love and has one child, a daughter. My cousin is just as a friend to me today as she was standing in that bathroom nearly 35

years ago. Her husband became like a big brother to me and I love them all greatly. My aunt is well today and has remarried. She suffers greatly of arthritis and other such things, but she is just the same today as she was then in heart. I will never forget the Love that they gave away to me during this visit to their home.

Now, I know what you are about to read is somewhat ironic, but it is the truth; and I feel it to be appropriate to insert at this time. It is about strawberries.

During about this same time of the visit to this particular aunt and uncle's home, something happened afterwards. When I first tasted the strawberry preserves at my uncle's mother's home, I began to love strawberries greatly. One day as I was playing in the edge of the woods near my father's home, I found a wild strawberry patch in the woods. I told no one, until later, and I would go to this spot each year to eat fresh strawberries, alone. I was beginning to think that Indians had planted this strawberry patch, no kidding. But, later my father would tell me that people did there live in a home in that area before he was even born. So, I believe the strawberries were planted at this particular spot when there was a home in that area many years ago. But at the time, the strawberries just grew wild at the edge of the woods, hidden right beside a small creek.

During this same time of the strawberry's harvest, I went to the wild strawberry patch. I would go to the patch somewhat like a maze and checking to see if anyone was following and looking at me. When I got to the strawberry patch this particular time, I noticed that there wasn't not one strawberry to eat. I looked and I looked and couldn't figure out where the strawberries were and I just gave up and walked away. I walked a different way from the wild strawberry patch and ended up walking across my uncle's property towards home.

This particular uncle was one of my father's older brothers. This particular uncle passed away many years ago with bone cancer and I miss him greatly. My father stayed near John Hopkins hospital many days with my uncle giving life away to him, which was my father's bone marrow. My uncle's body took the bone marrow from my father, but later, the cancer was too aggressive and his time was called.

Now, as I was walking across my uncle's property, I met my cousin by their pond. My cousin, which is somewhat older than I, met at my uncle's strawberry patch. My uncle had hidden this patch of strawberries in the landscape, under his grape vines; and I didn't know it was there. I remember saying this to my cousin, "I didn't know you had a strawberry patch." My cousin and I started looking at some small strawberries that were just beginning to ripen. These strawberries were about the size of a large grape, but my eye got a glance at a particular strawberry, hidden under some leaves and I was greatly amazed, no kidding. My cousin walked over to me and his eyes got about the size of silver dollars, as I removed the leaves from this strawberry; and he was greatly amazed too. My friend, this strawberry was almost the size of an apple, no kidding. My cousin was hasty and said to me, "Stay here! I got to go get daddy, so that, he can see this strawberry. It is the biggest strawberry I have every seen. I will be right back with daddy. Don't you let nothing mess with it, until I get back with daddy." My friend, I did something that I knew no better to do. As I watched my cousin walk away from this enormous strawberry, I plucked that strawberry, hid it in my shirt, and ran across the road to my father's barn. There hidden in my father's barn, I ate the whole thing. My friend, at this time, I truly knew no better; for I just wanted that strawberry. I peeped out from the barn door at my father's home, looking and listening to my cousin getting somewhat mad and my uncle somewhat laughing.

I remember my cousin saying out loud, "I'm not crazy daddy! There was a large strawberry right there in that spot!" I think my uncle may had thought my cousin was crazy or something. At that time, it got silent and I seen my cousin and uncle somewhat glance over toward my father's home and then at the barn. But, at that moment when I seen my cousin getting upset and looking over at my father's home, I felt something deep within me that just didn't feel right in my little heart.

Even at this early age, I knew that I had just stolen; and I didn't feel to good afterwards either, deep within my little heart. I guess my uncle had to find the truth about the strawberry too. So, later that day he must had talked to my father about me and that strawberry. My father did ask me if I had taken that strawberry without asking and I said to my father, "Yes daddy. I did take that strawberry, but I was hungry. I didn't mean to do anything wrong. I thought that uncle wouldn't mind if I ate that strawberry." I seen my father get somewhat frustrated in his eyes and said, "Boy! Don't you ever take nothing that doesn't belong to you again without asking! Or! Do you understand?" I somewhat shook my head in the yes gesture and that was that.

Today, I am still reminded of that one strawberry that I had stolen from my uncle and cousin. Today, I am allergic to certain strawberries, no kidding. I can eat fresh strawberries right straight from the patch, but not from certain places. I remember the first time that I had a allergic reaction to some strawberries from a buffet bar at a restaurant. My mouth and tongue swelled to where I couldn't swallow, no kidding. Some people tell me that it is the preservatives in the strawberries that causes my allergic reaction; and that may be true. Nevertheless, I know what the problem is. I told my cousin not to long ago about this particular incident of strawberries; and we laughed together and had joy, no kidding. But, I know it is still today a reminder of not stealing no strawberry or anything from someone else's patch.

During around this same time as a young child, I went to the woods with my cousin's and my brothers to play. I would be able to go with them to build pine straw camp houses and do such things in the woods. There were sometimes that my older brothers and cousins wouldn't want me to go with them; and I would somewhat pout on the front porch of wanting to be with them. I do remember one particular time as I had permission to go to the creek behind my uncle's property with them. My older brothers and cousins had built a device that you could hold onto, and fly over the creek, high above the rocky creek; and I was amazed. I remember my older brothers and cousins taken hold of a steel pipe on a steel cable and holding onto it, as they would slide down a steel cable 100 feet across the creek. My older brother that was 2 years older than I, and has recently died, fell from the cable into the rocky creek, face first. I remember every one getting silent and my brothers and cousins where shouting at him as he was laying face first in the rocky creek, "Buddy get up! Oh my God! Are you ok? Buddy! Buddy! Get up!" We thought he was dead, no kidding. This cable was at least 30-40 feet above the creek and we knew he had hit the ground hard.

But, after about 1 minute and after my brother got his breath back, he stood up and said, "Yes I am Ok, but don't know one try that." He and all of us started giggling and laughing and I was relieved from the worse. I really thought my brother was dead at this time, but I, my older brothers, and cousins were relieved that he got his breath back, and was ok. We somewhat stopped the riding on the steel cable and pipe for some reason too. I believe my uncle found out about the incident and stopped the riding on the steel cable across the creek.

Now, my cousin that I stole the strawberry from has a brother that was about the same age as my brother, that has recently died. Them two, were like two peas in a pod, and were together all the time. I do remember one incident of them getting in some trouble. They had made themselves bows and arrows from reeds and tree branches. I believe the trouble was that of, my cousin and brother were target practicing with my uncle's chickens. After they killed one of those chickens with an arrow, they would hide it and carry it deep into the woods, clean it, and then cook it on a fire. I guess my uncle was noticing his chickens were starting to disappear; and he put a stop to their chicken target practicing.

I do remember one time that my brother and cousin left from my father's home toward the woods. I always wanted to be with my brother and cousin, but they demanded me to stay home, somewhat in a angry manner.

I felt sadden in my little heart, because I wanted to be with them in the woods, plus, I knew they were up to something and they weren't sharing the secret with me. I was sitting on the front porch of my father's home, pouting somewhat and watching them crossing the road and heading towards the woods. But, I knew they were up to something or hiding something; and I didn't stay on the porch. As I noticed them going into the woods, I jump from the porch, barefooted, and bolted across the road as lightening, straight into the woods from a different direction that I had seen them go.

I didn't know where they were, but I smelled smoke from a pine straw fire. I was hasty and followed my nose, no kidding, my nose.

As I was somewhat trotting through the woods, I would sense the smoke, either it was strong or less and just followed my sense of smell, until, I found something. My cousin and brother had a small pine fort deep into the woods, somewhat hid. When I reached the little forth they had built, I noticed that they had not even reached the forth yet. I went into the pine fort and set way back into the little pine fort hiding somewhat from them. I started hearing voices in the distance and knew it was my brother and cousin. At the time, I was hoping to get out of the fort and scare them from behind a tree or such, but they were to close; and I just stayed in the fort alone. I could see through the front of the opening of the fort as one of them put a little pine straw on the coals of the fire. My brother knelt down and blew into the fire coals to get the fire to start again and when he peeped into the fort, he seen me. I will never forget my brother's expression when he seen me in the fort. He walked to the opening and looked in and said, "My God!" and then he called to my cousin to come and look at me also. Then my brother said again, "My God! Cousin? Didn't we just leave him on the front porch?" My cousin and my brother were amazed and said to me, "How in this world did you get here before we did? How did you know where we were at?" I just sat back in the fort and said, "I know a secret too and I will share it with you if you let me be with you." My cousin and brother were amazed and started laughing out loud. After that translation from the front porch, to the hidden fort in the woods, my brother and cousin began to let me go with them to the woods. I remember a lot of good times with my brother and cousin. We would go duck hunting, rabbit hunting, squirrel hunting and such. I learned much from my cousin and brother, but who taught them about such things? I guess it was God, because I surely don't know how I amazed them that day; at their little hiding place in the woods. Now, there is one more remembrance during about this same time that I would like to share with you. My cousins and my brothers were at the creek one day by my uncles place and my cousins had built a tree house by the creek. I walked to where they were at; for I heard their voices and the hammering of nails, setting on the front porch of my father's home. As I was walking near the tree house by the rocky creek, my older cousin yell at me and said, "Don't move! Don't move! Just stand still. Whatever you do, Don't move!" When he said this to me, I didn't know what I had done and thought they were mad at me for some reason; and I somewhat started to pout. Nevertheless, I did stand still as my cousins and brothers were demanding me to do so. I notice as they were yelling at me, that they would somewhat glance or look near my front legs. When I looked down, I started to cry, much more. There was a large copperhead moccasin snake crawling at my feet with his head between my legs. I can still remember seeing his tongue sensing and hissing my every move. I thought the snake was going to bite me for sure, so, I just stood there like a stature and cried gently. My cousin went to his father's shed and got a shovel; and brother had a hoe. My God! It looked like they were going to war with that snake for me. They would tell me, "Buddy stand still and don't move. We are going to get that old snake for you. You just stand still." About that time, my cousins and brothers started yelling at the snake and somewhat trying to get it's attention from me. They were somewhat walking around me, hitting the ground with their weapons. But, that snake curled up right between my legs and somewhat stayed there for a minute or two and checking my brother and cousin's every move; and looking up and down my legs as if it was going to strike me. That snake finally curled down and slowly crawled from between my legs, hissing and sticking that tongue out, looking up and down at my legs as he went out from between my legs. My friend, that snake made the wrong choice that day and it should had stayed in between my legs or his dark hole where it would had been more safe.

My cousins and brothers beat the pudding out of that old snake and it was awful mess. It was so bad, it looked like that snake was shot with a machine gun and then ran over by a steam roller, no kidding. When the battle was over, my cousin held the snake up by the end of the shovel and he looked at me and said, "Now, do you know why we said, Don't Move?" I still remember the look on my cousin's and brother's faces as they were in amazement. I still remember that snake's tongue, somewhat hanging out of it's mouth, and it's eyes popped out from it's head and I said to the snake, "You poor ol nake. You want try to bite me again, will you?"

Now, I was very shy still at this time, but I wanted to be strong and have power like my brothers and cousins did over that snake. I did finally find something that made people run from me. This power that I had found, was a tooth that had been pulled from my mouth, no kidding. I would carry this tooth in a little bottle in my pocket everywhere that I would go, even Church. I remember that I would take it out of the bottle and scare other kids, especially the girls, with it. I would hold on to this power for awhile, and I would pull this tooth from my little hidden bottle at school and Church and some of the kids would run from me and say, "Oooh, that is naaaasty! Get away from me". I'm not sure what happened to this power tooth, but I think my parents may had snuck it from me and hid it, or, did the tooth fairy get it? Yes! I do believe my parents promised me that if, I would put that tooth under a pillow, I would have a reward the next day. I do remember getting a quarter for that power tooth the next mourning, and I wasn't to happy with the outcome. I sure wish I could find that power tooth.

During my childhood, I loved my family and kin with a great passion and trusted them more that any other. Let me just share with you one point of how much I did trust my family. When I was 9 or about, I remember doing something one of my older brothers had ask me to do.

He had even promised me that he would give me a million dollars, if I did it at the time. My older brother (my brother that has just past away) said to me," If you ride down the steps with your new bike, I will give you a million dollars." We were on the front porch of my parent's home and the steps are 6 steps high and are brick and somewhat steep.

I had taken my new bike my parents had got me for Christmas that previous year, onto the top of the concrete porch where my brother was at and I was somewhat showing it off to him. I remember saying to my brother, "You promise you will give me a million dollars if I do it?" and my brother looked at me and giggled and said, "Yes, of course! Would I lie to you?." So, down those steps I went, over the handle bars and the bike ended up on top of me at the bottom of the steps. I began to feel something wet on my right leg and looked down at it and liked to had passed out. At first, I really didn't feel no pain from my leg, but when I looked down at it, I began to be fearful and scared at what I was seeing; and began to cry out loud. My friend, the handle bar on my little bicycle had stuck into my right leg and plugged at least a 1" deep hole into my leg. My leg was bleeding badly and it looked liked ground hamburger. I began to cry and my brother came over and looked at me and seen the wound and rushed to get my mother.

We rushed to the hospital, but there was nothing that they could do for me, because it was a hole and the meat was gone. They cleaned the wound and packed it with gauze and told me and my mother that it would have to heal on it's on; for they couldn't stitch it. I had to live with the pain from this wound for several years, until it finally closed and healed over. I remember going to school for that year and the top of my boot would irritate this wound every day. There was times that I had to go home, because of the wound. Their were sometimes that the teachers would look at it and clean it themselves.

Now, my classmates knew I had this wound and sometimes they would come to me and say, "Show me your wounded leg. Let us see it." and I would pull my pant leg up, take the bandage somewhat off and then they would giggle and say, "Ooh! Ooooh! That is naaaasty!, and they would run from me. There were also times that I would chase after them and tempt them that I was going to show them this wound, no kidding. I had found something again that I could do, to put my other classmates a running; and I was proud of it, no kidding. This wound on my right leg stayed somewhat infected for almost one solid year, and my parents would always clean it and take care of it for me.

Later, I finally asked my older brother later where my million dollars was at and he said, as he would giggle, "You know I don't have a million dollars. You should have not believed me." Then I would say,

"But you promised me!" After that incident, It was a long time before I trusted anyone, especially my brother again. But, I know today when I was a young child then, that God was already knocking on my door; for I had put my complete trust in my brother for my life and it wasn't right. My friend, God the Father didn't hurt me, I hurt myself by doing something I had no business doing; for I wanted that money for our family, if it took getting money from my own brother. But, as a young child, I was certainly without the understanding of that matter. I will expand on the matter later.

I do remember one incident at this early age that hurt me deeply within my little heart and soul. I had a very good friend that we would do everything together at this elementary school. It was during the same time of my wounded leg; for we were in the same class together. I do believe that I drew close to him, because he and I had some things in common; being poorly I guess was one, and another, we both were somewhat shy.

It was Halloween night and that is all we were talking about that day, especially getting all that candy. My friend did tell me he and some others friends where going to a haunted house that evening and he wanted me to go with him. But, I knew I couldn't go with him, because our Church was sponsoring a little treat for the kids at the church and I knew my parents were taking me there. My friend, I just couldn't perceive or believe what I was told the next day at school. My friend was playing around at this haunted house and accidentally hung himself with a rope, no kidding. The others kids were saying the next day to me, that they thought he was just kidding or playing around, but he was dead. That hurt me pretty bad at this young age and all I could think about was my friend. I began to think that one of the other mean kids done this to my friend and I wanted to find out the truth and get revenge. Really, I thought this for a long time and this was just the beginning of anger and resentments in my little heart. After the death of my best friend, I would never seek or trust another friend for a long time; and somewhat calmed up more so.

Now, I was around 10 years of age and I had began to take from the Tree of Knowledge of good and evil, but I was certainly without understanding of the matter. I was already holding anger in my little heart and resentments against others in my life. I do remember another incident during this season of my life when I remember being looked at somewhat poorly at school or humiliated. I had an old pair of red converse tennis shoes that were given to me as a hand down and I wore them every where I went; for I was proud of them. I had two pairs of shoes, one pair of brogans (boots) and the pair of converse (tennis shoes). I was proud of these converse and wore them like they were glued to my feet. I would wear those tennis shoes to school, because everyone else would wear tennis shoes and not brogans (boots). I felt within my self that wearing those tennis shoes, made me somewhat fit into school.

So, one day I went to school and we went outside to play ball and one of my classmates wanted me to race him in a short run; and I agreed to do so. I was still somewhat a small child, but quick as a jack rabbit; and I had beaten a lot of my classmates in school short sprints and also had won first place in several outsides events. So, off we go and I was ahead and suddenly, one of the soles of my converse came loose and I had to stop running; for I was tripping over it. These tennis shoes had holes through the soles and sides, and you could see my socks, no kidding. Everyone started laughing at me and it hurt me deep in my heart and I felt humiliated. But, I didn't cry and I got somewhat angry and kept it inside my little heart, like a fire burning. Now, their were some of those kids that didn't laugh and somewhat walked away. But at the time, it seemed to me as if the ones laughing, had everything that a child would want, such as new tennis shoes, clothes, jewelry, braces for their teeth, fancy lunch boxes and all that other stuff.

Nevertheless, I went home that day from school and threw an angry fit towards my mother and father about this matter. I believe my words went like this, "Why do I not have new shoes, like everybody else has at school? Everybody in my class has new tennis shoes, and all I got are these floppy tennis shoes and stinking boots!" My father overheard me talking to my mother in that angry voice and his words went like this, "Boy! Go to the bedroom! I'll teach you to never talk to your mother like that again!" When I came out of that bed room, I wished that I would have had cried at school in front of all my classmates and let them humiliate me, laugh and spit on me, even more than, going though the lesson that my father had just showed me. My father also taught me that I had another pair of shoes, those stinking boots (brogans); and I was certainly going to wear them to school the next day. I never did ask my parents for another pair of tennis shoes throughout my whole life and I wore those old leather brogans for many years, until they just fell apart. Either they would fall apart or I would out grow them and my parents would have no choice, but to buy me new ones.

I will also say this; After that incident, it seemed to me that I had no other choice of picking out my type of shoe to wear to school, because I wanted leather boots always. I began to understand by experience that leather boots lasted longer than tennis shoes.

Today, I've had one pair of tennis shoes in almost 30 years, no kidding. I bought them almost 15 years ago, because I liked the name of the shoes which was, "No Fear". I bought them one evening, as I had a few of a youth group members with me at a shopping mall. I was a youth minister at a local Church during this time, and I thought the words were something for the youth group could see on my feet. Plus, I like where the words where located on the shoes, which was, the heel part. I would where these No Fear tennis shoes to the youth group meetings and the youth would say, "I like your "No Fear" tennis shoes." I would use these tennis shoes as a conversation piece. The conversation would be about having a "No Fear of Satan" and that we have the power to bruise his head with are heels. I still have those shoes also, but I have stored them in the closet. Still today, I still prefer to wear leather sandals and boots over tennis shoes.

Now there was a time while we are still on the subject of shoes that I remember being sorry for. Like I said before I liked leather boots and were proud of them. About this same time of my life, my parents had bought me a pair of Cowboy Boots (Pointed Toe Boots). My friend, I was proud of them boots! I walked around with those boots on like I was a prophet or apostle or preacher. If anyone made me mad, I would kick them right in the knee cap, no kidding. I do remember my older brother, the younger twin, saying something to me one day. I believe they were picking on me about my pointed toe boots. He wasn't the only one talking about my boots, but I chose him for an example. My friend, we were at the edge of a corn field, by my father's home, and the older boys were somewhat picking on me. They were saying things perhaps like this, "Hey little boy.

You think you'll tough? The only thing you could beat up is a roach in the corner with your pointed toe boots." and then they would laugh at me. I heard enough and didn't say a word and went toward my older brother that was laughing and looked straight up at him in his eyes, with my jaws somewhat puffed out, and said, "You made me mad!" At that same exact time, I kicked him just as hard as I possibly could in his knee cap with those pointed toe boots, and my big brother fell to the ground, lower than I was. Then I said this, "You made me mad brother." Then I ran back toward the house pouting, while my brother rolled on the ground hollering with pain. But, later that day, I felt saddened that I had kicked my brother and I told him that I was sorry for it. My friend, this is what my older brother said, "It's Ok little brother. I deserved it, I shouldn't had been making fun of you. But, My God! Please don't kick me again little brother, with those pointed boots on." After that incident, I kept those boots for that one knee kicking reason, especially when the older boys would make me mad. When the older boys would see me come out of the house with those pointed toe boots on, they would get silent and disappeared right before my eyes. Yes, I had found something again that I had power with and it even made the big boys to run from me.

Now, later at this age 10, I began to get very sick from infection. My deep leg wound was healing well, but I became very sick still anyhow. I remember going to the doctor's office with my mother and he checked my body to find what was causing my infection. He lifted my shirt and I somewhat try to hold it down from him looking, and then he said, "There it is." It was a wood splinter, just over a inch long, stuck into my right stomach and it was greatly infected. I remember getting the splinter by sliding down a wooden plank on my belly from a hay loft at my cousin's home one day. I was so shy at this time, that I wouldn't talk at all. There were some people that thought I was perhaps a mute. I didn't want anyone to know that I had the splinter in my stomach. I didn't trust no one and I didn't want to be around no one; for I was a extremely shy child.

I thought at the time also, that the splinter would come out on it's on and I would be ok later. But, that didn't happen, and I had to trust another person to help me with this matter.

So, the doctor lanced my right side, pulled the splinter out, put four stitches in my side and he looked at me somewhat amazed. He said to me at this time with a very soft and humble voice something like this; "Son, son, If anything like this happens again, you need to tell your mother, because you could die from this, and we all would be very sad."

About a month later I had to go back to the doctor again, no kidding. I was very sick and my parents thought I was starting to have convulsions again like I did when I was an infant. We went to the same doctor and he requested my tonsils were very infected and they would have to be removed. So, the surgeon removed my tonsils the next day and then I began to get somewhat better from this awful infection that I had to live with for nearly two years. Boy, that was a bad time in my young age. But, I know today with a greater confidence what those matters were and it was this; I was beginning to grow in my little spirit man through God, even as a very small child. I loved God, the Church, and my family with my whole heart. Even as an small child, I would always imagine and be wanting to be a man of God when I grew up, no kidding. I wanted to be like the preachers and the teachers from the Churches that I had grown to love with my heart. There was a peace that I desired and I knew at this time as a small child, I wanted this peace for the rest of my life. But, the enemy, which is that serpent, Satan, was already trying to kill me at this young age. That serpent wasn't only attacking me, but the rest of my family also. That serpent knew that we as a family loved God and Christ Jesus and we were living in his Love and Grace.

I could continual on and on with my experiences as a child beginning to take from the Tree of Knowledge of good and evil, and, I am confident that you have begun to see me as a child at this point of my life, and there is no further points to go much deeper. Even as a child and without discerning from my left hand or right hand, that enemy, which is Satan, was trying to take me out of God's Love, Mercy and Grace.

There is just a few more points I would like to share with you at this time, and I will close on this chapter of my life. My father had received the Baptism of the Holy Spirit and chosen to the ministry of the Gospel of Christ and trying to do God's Will to the best of his ability. My father and mother were trying their very best to direct and teach us children of God's good principles. But, during this early time of my childhood, this was just the beginning of the good fight in my family's life that I had experience. That serpent knew that my mother and father had a herd of children and his plan was to take us out one by one. But, I will say this with confidence; If it wasn't for my father and mother being obedient to do God's Will in this time of my life and having us children in Church when the Doors were opened, I would not be writing this words at this time. I am confident, that the way I was taught and was lead as a child by my parents to Jesus Christ, I wouldn't know God today. I honestly believe that I wouldn't be living today. It was a trying time in my life and my family, but, we have endured by the Grace of the Lord God Almighty. But, this time of my life that I have shared with you, is just the beginning of my Life, to Live Life. Today, I know with a greater confidence; "It isn't a matter of what I believe, It is a matter of what I do with what I believe."

CHAPTER TWO

A SEASON OF REASON

NOW, BEFORE I START WITH THIS CHAPTER OF my life, I want to share this with you what has been revealed to me about how to grow within your spirit man with God's Grace and Truth. I share this with you, because I know with confidence as you read the following writings you may have a better understanding of how God was my Husbandman and Spiritual Father throughout my life, and, as of today. This second chapter is for your to grasp onto a piece of the puzzle from my life. This season was just the beginning of the end of the beginning and the beginning of the end of many things. What? Could you please say that again?

Simply put; This season of my life was just the beginning of change in my life as a child and this season of my life was also the beginning of the end to many things in my life, as a child.

I know with a greater confidence today that I cannot even breath on my own will, and it was God's Will for me to live. I owe my all and all to God and his Son Jesus Christ for given me the will to live. Their will is sometimes painful, but their will even though it is painful at times, I still have great joy by living in his great and marvelous Will. I will expand more of the "Purpose" and "Will of God", later throughout this book. There will be an insert later in this book that will explain God's Will for Creation, man's purpose and such in a much more deeper way, as I got a much more of understanding of the matter. The insert is called, "The Wheels of God." For an example of God's Will in my life as a child and today as one of his sons chosen: It is written, *"Many are called, but few are chosen (Matthew 20:16)."* Remember this my friend, many are called to Salvation, but only a few will do God's Will. It is written, *"Blessed are the peacemakers: for they shall be called the children of God (Matthew 5:9)."* One more principle my friend and it is written, *"Not every one that saith unto me, Lord, Lord, shall enter into the kingdom of heaven; but he that doeth the will of my Father which is in heaven (Matthew 7:21)."* Those that do God's Will are the ones chosen as his own children. As long as I am doing his business or will, I will be one of his sons, follow me?

Now, when I began not to produce fruit (patience, goodness, love, faith, joy, etc.) in my little heart and soul, and, my little seed of Faith would not establish and grow, God would plow my heart and break my heart into pieces many times. I was beginning to feel the pains within my heart and making choices in my life without understanding of the matters. It is somewhat as we have already read in the first chapter about the potter with his clay.

My friend, I will say this; God's Hand is a long, longsuffering hand with Love for mankind; and it took nearly 30 years for me to understand that truth of God's Longsuffering Hand. I will call the plowing of my heart, *"Knocks from God."*

I will say this with confidence also; If any man would call on the Great Husbandman, the Father of All Life, to come into their life, that man will experience the techniques of Gardening. God is the Great Gardener of Life and God has by his incorruptible seed, planting Life into a Perfected Balanced Harmony (Please read Genesis Chapter 1).He planted every seed known to man and made every living creature under the heavens, even formed man from dirt. So, God planted life into existence, correct? Would you think he wants it to Live? If only a man will be willing to let the Gardener of Life into their Life will the man ever have Life much more abundantly on this earth. Not only Life on earth much more abundantly, but the man has a chance to Enter into the Strait Gate of Life Eternity. Understanding is the keeper of Life and I now know with confidence that when God plants his understanding into a man's heart, he will patiently wait with his longsuffering hand, eternally, for that understanding to mature in a man's Life.

Today, I am confident why my little seed of Faith stopped growing, and would not produce fruit when I was a child, and also later as I grew in stature. The reason my seed of Faith wouldn't grow was that of: as a child I had already began to loose my hope, my joy and passion to live as a normal child. It wasn't no one particular human for me to point my finger at, even though I could, but it was only one thing and it was, Satan. I had quenched the seed of Understanding of Life (Faith) to mature when I had began to set my eyes on the things of this world, more than, the things of God. I also had no patience, and I wanted to eat of my labor of my faith, before it was ready for harvest. I wanted things to happen then and now; and I suffered greatly without the understanding of patience.

Today I know with confidence and will say this; When God plants the incorruptible seed of Life (Faith) into a man's heart it will only grow, if, the man is willing to let it grow. But, if a man isn't willing, after God plants his seed of Faith into his heart to grow, the seed will lay dormant until the man gets willing. I've been told by my father and seen of television specials that there has been seeds that laid dormant for many hundreds of years. When the seeds were excavated they began to grow and the people were amazed, no kidding. Excavators have found plant seeds that have laid dormant for hundreds or perhaps, thousand of years under the ground. When they excavated that particular spot for a new building to be erected, the seeds would start to grow into beautiful and enormous flowers. I do believe it was because the seeds were exposed to the Sun Light and Water. The Sun gave the Seeds energy to grow and water gave them life. The seeds were laying dormant under the earth's surface, under old buildings, in total darkness and dry. But, when the excavators removed the buildings, and exposed the seeds by removing the earth's surface, the seeds of ancient started to grow again, amazing. The excavators called scientists of horticulture to the very spot and they are now studying the plants to determine what type of plant's they are in amazement.

Let me share this with you. I order some plant seeds from my favorite seed company, Terrestrial Seeds, and they where ground cover and flowers seed. I sowed the seeds 7 years ago and never seen a plant come up. It wasn't because the seeds were bad, it was because, I shouldn't had planted the seeds where I did. We lived in a mobile Home at the time and the seed washed under the mobile home and down the ditch out to the community. Every now and then. I will see flowers from the seeds I had sown, in the ditches in front of my neighbors. My community surely got a surprise with special flowers popping up during the spring season in the front yard, amazing.

Let me mentioned this also; when my wife and I bought our new home and the excavators dug the foundation and set the home up, I began to noticed the following year that I had a ground cover and flowers popping up all over near my home. I thought the birds may had dropped the seeds, or, someone like Johnny Apple Seed gave me a visit. But, it came to my remembrance when I seen the type of plants coming alive that it was the seeds I had planted nearly seven years ago, no kidding. I transplanted some and gave to my father and then others seeds came alive at my father's home place also. I thought that was amazing in it self; about those little seeds the size of a small needle hole coming alive after seven years, but, I now know what happen. I remember about this time we had a hurricane to give us a visit, and it's name was Floyd. Most of the seeds washed from my yard to my neighbor's ditches and some ended under my mobile home. I have never seen so much water come down at one time in my life and this water from the storm, washed my seeds away, but some laid dormant under my mobile home until 3 years ago, amazing.

Now, let me apply the above paragraph with the point. If, our seed of faith is never exposed to the Light (the Son of God) and has little or too much water (Holy Spirit) and then our seed of faith will just lay dormant and it will not grow. My friend, learning by experience and suffering throughout my life for 30 years, I will never let my seed lay dormant again. I don't want to suffer the way I suffered for nearly 30 years in my dark hole. If, I would had just let my seed of Faith grow in my past life, rather than, quenching my seed to grow in my Life, would I had suffered in the way that I had suffered? My friend, I don't even recall making that choice of not letting my faith grow, because I didn't understand it at the time. Nevertheless, I must had quenched my seed of faith from growing, because of ignorance, no kidding. But, the spirit of this sinfully natured world, which is, that rotten, dark serpent, lead me away from my first Love, which is, God the Father and his Son, which is, Jesus Christ and, the Light of this World.

That serpent, Satan, tried fervently to destroy me as a child without understanding. But, today, I know this with confidence; I must keep my faith sharpen as if you would sharpen a two-edged sword ready for battle, daily.

God had planted his seed of Faith into my heart earlier in my life, but I quenched God from my life and God couldn't establish my Life the way he wanted too. One way of not having the incorruptible seed of faith to grow and establish in your life, would be that of trusting in the things of this world, more than, God to help it grow. Remember this; "God cant help a man, if the man is in the way." Let me ask this question. If, you were preparing for a marriage, perhaps, for yourself and your mate, your daughters or sons or any one family or friend, how would you feel if a stranger came through the back door eating of your wedding goods, and then the stranger took your bride and groom's gifts? Well, I have heard many times of just that happening in society today. Yes, a thief coming to a marriage gathering without invitation and trying to destroy and steal from the groom and bride. My friend, listen, there isn't but one way to God and it is through the front door, invited. In the Holy Books of Matthew Chapter 22 and John 10, Jesus Christ gives great examples of someone trying to get to God the Father by another way than him; please read these great points sometime soon. My friend, no one will enter into the Table of Grace, but through the Grace, the Door, which is Jesus Christ. Any other way is liken into a thief that comes to steal and destroy at a marriage gathering. God's Christ is the Light of the World and the Door to the Father God. Only by and through Christ Jesus will we every get to know the true Father, God. Through Christ Jesus our seed of Faith can only grow by obedience to maturity. Through Christ, God's Only begotten Son and Heir to all things under and in the Heavens by God the Father, will we every get the Light of Life for our seed of faith to mature. I call the Light of Life, "Obedience" and I will share much more on Obedience later. God the Father of All, holds the incorruptible seeds of Faith in his hand and he is the Great Husbandman of it.

But, if a seed doesn't have Sunshine or Life, it will lay dormant and possibly rot.

Now, when I finally got willing to let my seed of Faith grow in my life, that God had planted many years before time as a child, my seed's roots are now getting well established and my life is producing much more fruit. Nevertheless, the roots from the seed of faith that God had planting in my little heart as a child, has experienced dry times and wets time, but the roots within my heart are much more stronger than they have ever been before and are still today growing deeper into God's Love and Grace. I believe it is because I got willing to let go and let God work in my life. I believe with no doubt it was because of this one thing God's Holy Ghost said through me and melted me away; "Give your Life Away." When I finally gave my all and all to the Creator of all Life through his precious Son, his Christ and the Savior of this World, the Son shined his Light into my dark hole. His countenance, and Brightness, that's full of Grace and Truth, drew me to the surface and today, my seed of faith is growing into the likeness of an Large Oak Tree planted by his Rivers of Water. My seed of Faith, since I got willing to let go and let God, has grown and it grows and grows, because of my willingness to let God do for me what I could not do for myself.

Would you think that you could plant a seed in dirt and just walk away and come back years latter without tending to the seed? Do you think it would every grow and establish, without care? Perhaps it would, but the probability would be quite slim. Perhaps the seed would be overtaken by weeds, or, perhaps dry up from the lack of water, or, a bird may sweep down and eat the seed. It doesn't matter what happens in my life today, such as trials, tribulations or temptations, my roots from that little seed of faith are deep and are stronger in my trust of my God and his Son, my Lord and Savior, Jesus Christ. I wait on my Lord for my Life, and I put my life in his total care and I have much more peace and patience in the matter of understanding of the matter.

Now I would like to share with you the "Techniques of Gardening."

TECHNIQUES OF GARDENING?

First, what is 'Understanding'? Most, if not all of my past life, I would had answered that question this way; "I just don't understand the question. Would you repeat the question please?" I really did not understand the word "understand" during my past life. I thought I understood everything in my past, but I really didn't understand the word "understand." It is impossible for me to exhaust the word of understanding, but I will try to define it as simple as possible. My friend, Who can understand God? Understanding God would be like trying to twirl the universe on you pinky finger tip. But, God does give understanding to his servants, without no doubt by his Holy Ghost or Holy Spirit. His Spirit moves upon the earth like a enormous Ship that sows seeds of understanding to whom God is willing to give understanding to, such as, his children.

Now, understanding simplified, is to have no doubt in what you would believe to be the truth in all things of Life. Understanding is without doubt or judgment. That is the most simplest definition that I know of today of the word Understanding. You will not find that exact definition in the Webster's Dictionary either my friend. But, I will say this also with confidence; The Webster dictionary is a great place to start seeking the word understanding, if you are seeking understanding. I am not ashamed to say that I started in the Word of God and his Word lead me to the Webster's Dictionary, no kidding. God lead me to another place than what I thought was right and it was to a definition of the word Understand as we know of it today in the Webster's Dictionary.

Once I finally got the word understanding through my thick skull and into my memory of my brain, I understood the word understand, amazing. The complete Holy Bible is engulfed in the trueness of the word "Understanding". I'm confident that the Worlds and Heavens were established by understanding. In the Holy Book of Hebrews chapter 11:1-3 it is written, ***"Now faith is the substance of things hoped for, the evidence of things not seen. For by it the elders obtained a good report. Through faith we understand that the worlds were framed by the word of God, so that things which are seen were not made of things which do appear."*** As you would read the following scriptures in this particular chapter, you would perhaps understand that through Faith comes understanding. Now let me ask a question and give the answer at one time. Ready? Here goes. It took thousands of years for men to write the Holy Bible, correct? One more question with an answer. How would you understand that question you just read to be the truth, if you do not believe that question to be the truth? I guess I would say this with an understanding; It is written in the Word of God and I must believe it without doubts or judgments.

Even though the scriptures are written and recorded in the Holy Book by elders of past times, how would you still understand that it would be the truth? My friend, there is only one way to know the truth, and it is through Faith. You will read much more on this matter of understanding all throughout the writings of this book, if you are willing to continue to read this book. I will also share understanding as it grows in a man's life and the training and discipline of it later in the insert of *"Strait Are the Gates."*

Now, let me share with you now this understanding of how a man receives understanding as I sense it, today. Before I go any further, I must say this with confidence; Understanding comes only from God. The understandings that we might think we get here on this earth, are only experiences. Today, I see God's Understandings as fertilizer given to a tender plant of a garden by a great husbandman. God being as the Great Husbandman, and a man as the tender plant in his garden. Also, the fertilizer you would put around the tender plants in the garden, as the understandings from God. God wants all mankind to have understandings, so that, we as mankind would grow in his Will, which is, his Love for mankind, much more, abundantly. His Love for mankind are broken down to many purposes or promises. I will say this with confidence; God wants all to have his Spirit within their life. His Spirit (the Holy Ghost) is for a particular purpose; to guide a man into his Truth (Righteousness) and Grace (Favor).

Now, there is also one important matter in Life and it is, "Water." The water to me represents the Holy Spirit of God given to all life to Live and he is a witness to God of the things of this world. My friend, without water nothing that your eyes could see would exist. Even in the beginning of creation it is written that the Spirit of God moved upon the waters of the Universe; given Life to All and All. If a man isn't willing to let go and let God's Spirit enter his life, then that man will only understand his own life and not the Life and Love of God for him.

If a man is not willing to receive the fullness of the Word of God, especially the Holy Spirit, which is, mankind's teacher, and consultant of the God of Life, then that man will not understand the truth of God's Will. If a man isn't willing to receive the fullness of the Spirit of God, then that man is quenching the Spirit of God to move in his life to teach him the Will of the father. It is written in Matthew 7:21, *"Not every one that saith unto me, Lord, Lord, shall enter into the kingdom of heaven; but he that doeth the will of my Father which is in heaven. Many will say to me in that day, Lord, Lord, have we not prophesied in thy name? And in thy name have cast out devils? And in thy name done many wonderful works? And then will I profess unto them, I never knew you: depart from me, ye that work iniquity."* I will share much more on the Will of God in the insert of *"The Wheel of God"* later in the writings. Also, I will be sharing much more on the Holy Ghost all throughout the writings of this book, because I am confident that is very important, if not the most important to have in a man's life. Therefore, if you at this time are not willing to let go and let God, then close this book now and go about your own business, because this book is about change; for God is about change. if you are not willing to change in any way then there is no purpose for you to continue to read this book.

I know without doubt that God, through and by his Holy Ghost has given me understandings throughout my life. But, God had to give me the understanding of the word understand first, no kidding. Today I will say this with a greater confidence: Understanding God's Will is the Power of God in a man's Life. What is the Power of God? God's great passion for all mankind to have the Physical Life on earth much more abundantly and have the Spiritual Eternal Life. God's Will is his only begotten Son, Jesus Christ. Only through Christ can we every begin to understand God's Will.

Yes, we can fly planes, go to space, invent great things, do brain surgery and greater things, but, are you doing God's Will?

God is in control of understanding and he gives it accordingly to a man at his Will. Understanding you could also say is a Reward from God, to a man from the Faith he would have in his Son, Jesus Christ. Yes, God is the Understanding of Life, but Jesus Christ is the only begotten Son of God and he holds all the rewards of God the Father in the palm of his hand, waiting patiently, longsuffering, to give to a man according to the man's faith in him. He knows when to give understanding, where to give it, and how much to give for the man's profit and his glory. I can't or imagine trying to exhaust the understanding of God's Will today, but I know that I do have much more understanding than in my past dead life.

Like I have said before, God's understanding to me is somewhat like fertilizer that a great husbandman of a garden would put around the tender plants in his garden, but there is much more to living than just getting fertilized. I will say this with confidence; When I thought I had a good understanding of the matter of my Life the Spirit of God changed my mind of my thinking. Now, this revelation came to me as I was planting a garden one spring day. I had been seeking God for an answer of understanding and my purpose in Life for many weeks during this time. My friend, God was faithful. Through and by his Holy Ghost he began to console or comfort me in the matter of understanding. The following wrings will explain the matter of receiving understandings of God. Like I had mentioned before, receiving an understanding from God would be in the likeness of this: "Planting a Garden." I began to till the land and then the Holy Spirit ministered to me on the matter of understanding, step by step. This is what happened:

First: I wanted to grow a garden and the place where I needed to grow the garden was growing wild with grass and weeds and the soil was packed and hardened.

I took my 5 horse gasoline powered tiller, and I broke the top soil away and remove the wild grass and weeds and the earth said, "That didn't hurt that bad!".

Second: After I had removed the grass and weeds, I subbed tilled the very deep soil and broke the soil apart deeply and the earth says, "Ouch! That did hurt man!"

Third: After I had broken the deep sub soil apart and it was soften I kept tilling the soil until the whole area was loose and it was ready to make a straight row for the seeds and the earth said, "Thank you very much; for I can breath much better now!"

Fourth: I make a straight row for the seeds.

Fifth: I make holes into the top of the rows and plant my seeds accordingly to the size and type of the seeds, and then I cover them with top soil.

Sixth: I water the seeds and wait for the seeds to grow into small tender plants.

Seventh: I keep a eye watch over my tender plants keeping predators from destroying them. I continue to water the tender plants as needed. I continually to remove any weeds or grass that may want to choke my tender plant's life away.

Eighth: After my tender plant's roots begin to establish and grow, I then start to fertilize my tender plants. I know where, when and how much to fertilize my tender plants. if I didn't know where, when and how to fertilize my tender plants, I could possible kill my tender plants.

I continually to watch over my tender plants carefully with patience as they grow. I continually to weed out the grass and weeds that wants to choke my tender plants life away. I continually to water my tender plants and fertilize them. Their roots get established and get larger in statue and start to produce fruit.

Next to last: I wait patiently for the delicious fruit from my garden and also keeping my eye watch on my fruit in the garden, taking away the dead fruit or branches and such.

When the tender plants have matured and have produced the delicious fruit, I then harvest the fruit.

<u>At last</u>: I sit at the Table of Grace and eat of them. After I have tasted and eaten of my fruit, I will say this, "It is good!" and then I rest from my labors.

Now, please let me apply what I have written to a man's life here on earth. When a man calls on God, which is the Great Husbandman of a man's Life, to save him from the horrors and death of this life, God will first get the man's heart ready for the *incorruptible Seed of Faith*. Yes! just like the earth cried out "it hurts!"; it is the only way that a seed will grow in good soil and it is for the man's profit. After the man's heart is ready for the incorruptible seed God makes his way straight like a row through disciplining. After the row is set straight God sows the incorruptible seed of Faith into the man's heart and covers it by the blood of his Son Jesus Christ. Then God will send the Holy Ghost in the name of Jesus his Christ into the man's life to water the man's heart with his tender love and care. Then he waits and watches over the seed that he planted into the man's heart, until it starts to grow. When or if it grows, he continually watches and removes things that could hinder him from growing in his loving Grace and Will. I will say this with confidence; if a man truly and honest calls on God to save him from life's horrors, misery or even death, God will continually too till and break the heart of that man until his heart is loosened and not hardened. My friend, I've been there and done that; and it wasn't to pleasant many times.

Reminiscing into my past life, I thank God continually for not giving up on me and continually to break my heart to plant his incorruptible seed of Faith. Now, after the man begins to grow somewhat in his spirit and mind, God will fertilize the man's heart with understanding.

God knows when, where and how to fertilize a man's heart with understanding and the seed of Faith begins to grow much, much more. God has been gardening for Eternally and as a gardener myself, I have learn how to fertilized a garden.

I will say this with confidence, if you don't know how to fertilize a tender plant, it will wither away and die. After God fertilizes a man's heart with understanding the man's life will become much more established and will grow in statue and start to produce fruit. God continues to watch over this man and protects him from any harm, as long as the man stays in the garden of God. Then after the man matures in spirit and in truth, God will fertilize and water the man's life until the man is ready for harvest. And when God receives a Man that has been planted and eats of the man's fruit he says, "It is Good. Well done thou good and faithful servant. Enter rest from thou labors."

Now as I began to grow somewhat, I was 11years old by this time, and I wasn't feeling the same as I had felt in the several years before as a child. I had experience some good things of life and some terrible things of life. I was beginning to hold anger and resentments deep in my heart at this early age. I began not to want to go to school and was becoming a little bit rebellious toward everyone, even my parents and the good people at church. Our household became more populated and the demand for more was necessary. School, Food and clothing became more demanding. My Mother had to start working a job during this time, to help with the every growing demand or need of us children. My Father and Mother had to work much more and they got really stressed. Situations were becoming disastrous in our household and there were a lot of bad memories from the stressful time from my families life during this time. But, I also remember a lot of good memories. My parents were working any shift job that they could hold down to get income for us children. They had to leave us younger children in the care of our older sister and brothers at night for a long time.

They had no choice but to work, and they both worked fervently to meet us children's needs.

I remember not being discipline much at all by my parents as a younger child, but now, discipline was continuously. At this time of my life, I had already felt rejection in my little heart and was holding anger and resentments deep within my heart. I was still a very shy child at this time and didn't talk much. I do remember the first physical discipline that I received from my father. My mother was at work this day and she was on a 2nd shift. My father was asleep from working all night; for he was on 3rd shift. One day after school, I do remember going over to a neighbor's house just a couple of country blocks below my home place. I liked going over to there home, because they had little games and toys I could play with. These neighbors were some kin to my father by marriage and I loved them just like my own family.

So, night was beginning to fall while I was at my neighbor's home and the neighbor asked me with concern upon their faces, "Does your father and mother know where you are, son?" And I said, "Yes. They said it was ok for me to come over for a while." I had not ask my parents anything of this matter at this time and I knew that they probably were worried already for my safety. My neighbors said, "We have got to go to the store. You go with us and when we get back, you go home OK." When they said this to me, I felt as if they didn't want me around and held this rejection in my little heart. I do believe I started to pout somewhat, so, they let me go with them to the store and then back, anyway. The store wasn't but about 2 miles down the road and when we got back toward their home, we didn't go back to their home. We went to a home just a ½ of a mile from the neighbors. They had to drop off something to someone else and it was cigars and wine. I believe they may had thought that my parents knew where I was at, and that my neighbors would take care of my welfare.

Now, as we walked in to the home of this other neighbors home just for a minute, one of the older men asked me, "Do you want to try one Boy?" After he had said this he started laughed. I felt as if he had tempted me and I felt another rejection and thought that he was laughing at me. But, he didn't let me smoke of that cigar, nor, drink of the wine and that, really made me feel rejected.

By this time of the evening, my neighbors had forgotten that I needed to get home for it was dark and late. As we where going out of the house, we seen headlights and dust flying down the dirt road where we were at, headed straight towards us. I knew who it was with no doubt; for it was my father. When my father reached the home and got out of his vehicle, he snatched me up by my shirt collar, throws me in the car, had a few words with my neighbors and then we went straight home, not saying a word. When we got home, my father said to me, "Son! Go to your bedroom, now!" I went to the bedroom and began to cry, I knew what was next. My father came into the bed room and taught me a lesson I would never forget and it makes me want to call him right now and tell him where I'm at. I never left the house again without telling my parents where I was going. I will say this also, the older man that tempted me later killed himself from carbon monoxide poisoning at his home in the garage. Also, the neighbors later divorced and moved away.

At this time of my life, I was beginning to seek ways of covering the hurt within my heart from the chances of life that had came my way. The following writings will give to you the beginning of my addictions to certain things. This chapter will help you understand how a child is very vulnerable to ways that don't seen to be harmful, but are harmful to a child. This chapter is the beginning of my addiction to drugs, sex, alcohol and other ways of covering the hurt that was deep within my heart.

I didn't know that I was hurting in such a way as a child, but looking back, I was hurting and I was already seeking ways to cover the hurt that I didn't understand. Some of the ways may not seem to you to be as bad as it may seem, but add the 1st chapter and this chapter together and then you may begin to understand the pain that I was suffering with. The following writings will somewhat speed up to get to the points, so, hang on for dear life, here they come.

Now, I do remember as I was walking the road way one day, looking down somewhat, and found a cigarette still smoking beside the road near my home at that time. I remember saying to my self, "I wonder why people smoke them and what does it do to them?" As a curious child would do, I picked that half smoked cigarette up and hid behind our barn and began to experiment with the cigarette. I did not know how to smoke it, but I had seen older people in my life at this time, do it. So, I tried puffing on it and I thought nothing of it, until I took a big puff and inhaled it. I started coughing really bad, but I felt something that I had never experienced before. Yes! I got high on a cigarette! I thought at the time, "Boy it sure makes me cough, but it makes me feel good."

So, as time went on, every time I had a bad day, I would seek and search the road way to find cigarettes and hide behind the barn to smoke to get that feeling. Sometimes I would even play hooky from school and church pretending to be sick just to search for and to smoke cigarettes. Please let me say this now, If you do smoke cigarettes, "please don't throw them out of your car window as you travel, because there could be a curious child walking the road way, and find the lit cigarette and get addicted to that poison. Not only will the child get addicted, it will open a gateway to worse things for his life and possibly death from the addiction.

I know you don't want God to hold you accountable for that child's life, do you?"

When I was near the age of 12, I was beginning to smoke cigarettes like a grown person and trying different ways of acquiring cigarettes and still hiding this from my family. One of my older brothers was already smoking and would have cigarettes hiding in his wardrobe. He was working on farms, as a farm helper, at the time and I knew he had cigarettes somewhere hidden in his room and could afford them. I looked around his room as he was at work one day, until I found the several packs of cigarettes and crafty took some from him without him knowing. I took the packs of cigarettes and took a knife and carefully opened them from the bottom of each pack. I took two or three cigarettes out of each pack and closed them with a very little amount of glue that was in the home. He never found out about it, but I figured that he thought, "Have I smoke that pack of cigarettes already?" So, I did this for along time until he started to hide them somewhere else and I couldn't find them. Today he has quit smoking and I'm thankful for that. I even had my own matches and lighters then and would hide them in the bricks under the barn, where I would hide and smoke.

Like I said, I would find ways of making money, like working on tobacco farms and doing little things around the neighborhood for money and to acquire cigarettes. I was even enticed to do things that I will not mention, but I will mention that I was enticed to do things for money, by older people, and those things made me very ashamed. *Yes I will share this with you: I was molested and enticed to do things for money and cigarettes and this was the beginning of my depression as a child.* My parents didn't know anything about this matter; for I was a very shy child anyways and I would hide the matter very crafty in my heart for 28 years.

Another reason I held these matters in my little heart at this time, was I couldn't tell them these things; for I thought at this time they would blame me or their selves and I would be disciplined for it or they would fight and blame each other. I do remember having nightmares at this age, due to the molestation and my mother would come to the room and ask what was I dreaming about, but I would always say, "it was a monster mama, and it was trying to kill me."

Now, at the age of 13, I was with some older boys, a gang from the neighborhood and I will call this gang, "The Old Fairground Road Runners". I was turned on to marijuana and beer. Again, I had been enticed to do these things and I did them without understanding of the consequences. I would sneak to there home while my Mother and Father was at work and started getting high almost every day of the week. I saw a lot of bad things during this time, such as deaths and seeing all those young men and women laid out on the floors from shooting drugs. Sometimes still I can smell the odor from this time, as if a pharmaceutical factory. I remember being with this gang for many years, until they just disappeared. Then my using went from the worse to the worst. Today, *Most of all these neighborhood boys and girls are either dead, missing limbs or paralyzed from car wrecks or other accidents, or, incarcerated today*. There are maybe two or three that I know of today out of about 25 or more, that made something out of their lives.

At the age of 14, I was already a full blown alcoholic and drug attic. During this time, I was beginning to experiment with a lot of drugs, such as, liquor, beer, marijuana, Quaaludes, valiums, LSD, fasten, preludes, and cocaine and such. Even at this young age I had began to use needles with older people and had shot morphine in my arm vein for the first time, and then I really started to lust for that feeling.

I do remember trying to overdose of pills one time at this early age. I took a lot of fasten and I somewhat went into a hallucigenic seizure. I tried to jump out the my bedroom window, no kidding. I guess I thought that the window was a door. I somewhat got cut and broke out the window panes and ended on the floor. My parents and my brother in-law rushed me to the hospital, where the Doctors pumped my stomach. They told my parents that I had a lot of pills in my stomach and I was close to death. My friend, I still remember those pipes that the ER Doctors pushed down my throat and that, wasn't too pleasant. This was my first suicide attempt.

Now, I was in the eighth grade at school. I began skipping school and drinking at the gravel pit near my home, hidden from everyone. I was drinking, using drugs and smoking at school, at home, or anywhere

I could drink or get high. I would even go to the grave yard that's just a stone throw from my home place and play and hide.

I do remember one particular time that I quit going to the graveyard as much. I and another young boy were getting high on Halloween night. We were drinking liquor and smoking pot. We decided to go treat or tricking and it wasn't to get candy. So, we went to the grave yard and we had a dozen of eggs. I had gotten six eggs from my home and he had gotten six eggs from his home and we hid in some bushes near the highway and we started egging cars, no kidding. I do remember that he would egg any car, but I would wait for particular cars to ride by to egg. I was ashamed of it afterwards, because of this; We egged one particular car really well, but the car came back a few moments later with the driver. When this particular car came back to where we were hiding in the bushes, the driver got out with something long in his right hand, and it wasn't a bag of switches my friend. This man had a long gun, a shotgun, and he meant business. He stood back as we seen the silhouette in the darkness of this man and he said, "You thank you can egg my car and get away with it!?

Come out of those bushes or else I am going to load you up with this bird shot that's loaded in this gun! Come out Now! I am not playing around and I know you are in there!" So, I and my friend began to shake like a leave in the wind and we somewhat crawled on our hands and knees from out those bushes and stood up near this elder man wearing coveralls and holding a shotgun. This man said, "What do you boys think you are doing? Did you think you could trick me? I've been around a long time boys, and this is the first time that I had to use my gun for tricking on Halloween. You know that I would had shot into them bushes, don't you boys?" I and my friend just stood there with tears following from our eyes and we both said at the same time, "Yes Sir." Then the elder man said this, "I will talk with you parents tomorrow about you washing my car or paying for any damage done to it. You boys go home and don't let me catch you back out here no more, do you hear me!?" I and my friend looked at each other and ran like jack rabbits to our home. We went out to trick or treat, but we got trick and it wasn't too pleasant. I somewhat felt like a worm after that incident and I can say, I never egged another car afterwards.

I remember also a time that I and the same young boy that I was with egging cars went back to the graveyard one night, but this time, we were high on LSD. This experience wasn't too pleasant either. I remember falling and screaming as if dead people were grabbing my feet as I would run through the grave yard. I managed to get out of the graveyard and the other boy ran home too. I was so disoriented that I climb upon a school bus that was parked at my parents that my older brother would drive during school days. On that bus is where I decided to never use LSD again. My friend, I thought I was seeing demons shaking their heads furiously in the no gesture, their faces were melting, and their teeth looked like a T- Rex Dinosaur, no kidding. I just laid in one of the seats, closed my eyes, and prayed that this LSD would wear off. I really thought that I was Overdosing on LSD.

At the time I thought it was getting worse, but when I began to pray, the LSD did calm down through my body, and I slept in that school bus that evening. I never used LSD after those incidents again and was somewhat afraid of it's effect. I will also mention, the young boy that was with me those nights, later got in a car accident and lost his right leg in the accident.

As time passed during this age, I started skipping school and would hide from my parents in the woods when I knew they had found out I had skipped school again. My brothers would come to the woods every now and then and yell for me to come home and they would tell me, "Mother and father said they were not going to whip you. Come home and eat." The next day I was at the principle's office with my parents about the matter, but I just didn't understand. I was already a full blown alcoholic and drug addict and I do not believe the principle or my parents knew this at the time. They just couldn't figure me out I guess.

I do remember one occasion, being so drunk and high one evening. It was a Friday evening around 11:00pm. I remember that I stumbled home and seen that my mother wasn't working that evening. I still had about 1 pint of wild turkey whiskey in my hand. I did not want my mother to see me like I was and I stumbled back down the road to where a corn field was and stumbled through it and passed out. I awoke the next morning around 6:30am with a chill and wetness upon me and I was cold.

There were many more times I would wake the next morning asking, "How did I ever get here. Did someone drug me and put me here?" My parents could only pray that God would intervene and help me though this trouble time. I was tearing there heart out at this time in my life and I wasn't being honest with them at this time and I would blame them for my problems. I was living my self will pleasure at any cost and Sex, Rock and Roll, drugs and alcohol became my gods.

That morning, I got up and started walking toward the plow rows in the corn field and I seen where I had stumbled and broke down many corn stalks that evening. I found the bottle of whiskey that I had earlier that evening, lying in the middle of a row. There was maybe a cup full left in the liquor bottle and I put the bottle in my front pants and started for the road. When I reached the road, I hid the bottle where I knew I could find it later. I was reserving the alcohol for later and I had no thought of quitting using at this time and I started walking toward home; for it didn't matter to me what my Father or Mother would do to me at this time, because I was hungry and cold. By this time my Father was home and I went to the door and he met me and to my surprise he didn't say a word, except in a calm sadden way said, "Son, go in there and go to bed. We have worried about you all night. We will talk about this later." My father had just got home from work and I knew he was tired and would be in the bed soon and as I walked by him towards my room, I heard my mother crying from the next room. I began to cry inside and felt my mother's and father's spirit saddened and I went to my room and laid down and slept for much of the day. I got up and my father was still asleep and my mother was in bed also and I left again, out the house and began my self pleasures over again.

At this time of my life, my Mother and Father realized that I was out of control and needed help, but they too were in a position that they just could not quit their jobs for me; for there were other children to care for now. I was so caught up in drugs and alcohol that I did not know what I was doing to myself and others in my family. I was already facing the Big Hole at the age of 14 and had no understanding of the matter. But, being still a child, my parents had the responsibility to intervene and try to save me from complete void and emptiness and soon, possible death. With chances, choices and changes that had already passed me by at this young age, I had forgotten my first Love, God the Father.

Everything that I possibly had ever learned in Sunday school and by the work of my parents had tried to teach me, I had rebelled against them and God. Shame, Anger, Drugs and rebellion had taken over my life and it was getting worse. At this young age I was already hiding the past in my heart and was living a course of emptiness, numbness and shame and most of all, "self will." My friend, while we are on the subject of self will, please let me share these understandings and revelations that God gave to me not long after my resurrection from my dead life. I'm confident it would be a good time to share it with you and I hope it will quicken God's Will in your spirit man. The title of the following writings is; *"Self Will A Road to Destruction."*

SELF WILLA ROAD TO DESTRUCTION

After my Spiritual Resurrection, early one cool morning, I and my wife was making ready for a journey out of town. We were going to see my wife's mother in the Nursing Home.

She had been sick for a long time and my wife had been there several times a week with her sister for the last year. Her Mother had been in the Nursing home over 9 months. Before we left the house, I ask my wife, "Do you know the way to the nursing home?" She replied, "Of course I do.". I thought nothing of it, because I knew she had been there many times in the past year. I had not been to see her mother at the Nursing Home since she had been in there, even though, she was dying. I was always in my self will of Life, living in the desires and lust of my flesh and was never at home most of the time. I had been one time since my Spiritual Resurrection and that was with My wife and her Sister. I knew how to get to the City where her mother was, but I didn't know where in the city she was located.

So, we began our journey toward the city. My wife said," I'm going to take a different route. I and my sister have been this way before and it is quicker." Again, I thought nothing of it, because my wife is an excellent Driver and I thought she had been that way before as many times as she and her sister had been to the nursing home. We got onto the Interstate and off we go. I noticed after about 30 minutes of Driving my Wife began to change Lanes quite often, and it grieved me. I asked her, "Are you ok? Why are you changing lanes so much?" She replied, "Of course I'm ok. I'm just a little anxious!" Again, I thought not much about the matter until she kept changing lanes in the middle of no where. But, then I had to ask again," Dear! Why are you switching lanes so much? Just stay in the middle lane and Drive straight ahead and the city is right there."

We were 40 minutes away from our destination according to the last time I went with my wife and her sister. Then as we got closer to the exit from the Interstate to the City, I sensed that my wife saying something and it went like this, "I, I ,I think this is this exit where I get off." I began then to think something was up, but, I didn't say a word and I just continued reading the book I had brought with me. After about 10 minutes of riding, I heard her again say something and it sounded something like this," I,I, think I'm going the wrong way." Then I really began to sit up in the seat and I looked at her and said, "I thought you knew the way to the Nursing Home." She looked across at me with one eyebrow raised and said, "I do know the way! I just missed my turn!" I didn't say another word for several minutes, but I knew that we were not where we should have had been. We were turning, going North, South, East and West and I could not help myself and it was like a fire burning within me and I had to let it out. Then I ask her in a very subtle voice," I know you know where you are going, but do you really know how to get there?" There was silence. I sensed at the time she knew where she was going, but was not confident in how to get there.

After I looked at her with my desperate eyes, she confessed that she knew the way, but wasn't confident how to get there and at that moment something amazing began to happen. I sensed at that moment, when she confessed, that she didn't know how to get there from a different way, and her self will lead us onto a different course than that of which we lead out to go. I also thought of all the times I shared with her what my self will had done to me and her in the past. I also thought that she should know and was able to sense when self will was beginning to take charge, but she actually didn't understand. I began to share with her how self will can lead us on the wrong course in life and how my own Self Will lead me to anxiety, destruction, and even the Big Hole many times.

So, we came to an Intersection approximately 15 miles north of our destination. Then, I began to help us out of the confusion that we were in. I said, "Do you know a main highway the Nursing Home is near?" and then she replied "Yes!" And she told me the name of the Highway and I said, "It is in the other direction. We are about 15 miles from that highway. We need to go back south." I knew my way around this City, because I use to Travel a bit in past jobs through this city and she knew that. We then turn the vehicle around and began to travel south until we reached the highway we were looking for. When we reached the highway I asked her, "Is this the highway? Is it familiar with you?" She looked at me and said," Yes! I knew it was here somewhere. I just missed my turn. I don't need your help now." And then she giggled somewhat. Again I sensed the self will of my wife and it grieved me within my heart. I began to sense within my spirit that God was showing us something and we were about to get the understanding of the matter. I gently ask her, "Can I share something with you? Will you please listen, not only with you ears, but with you heart?" She looked at me with that eyebrow raised and said," I said I will listen." It grieved my heart even more so the that way she responded to my question. It made me think she really didn't want to listen to me.

Nevertheless, I began to share with her again how self will can lead us to destruction, confusion, horrors, and even death! By the time I had exhausted my heart to her on this matter of how God had showed me the truth about self will, we were sitting in the parking lot of the Nursing Home, approximately 1 hour late. We were sitting in the vehicle silently, thinking about what just happened to us and then I asked my wife this question, "Do you really sense and understand what just happened to us and what I just shared with you?" And she said, "Yes! Self will is what lead me to my anxieties and confusion. If I would of took the course that I was confident with, then we would of saved 1 hour of time."

I sensed she was beginning to understand, but still, I ask God to put the words in my mouth that I might be able to quicken her understanding of the matter. I said to her, "No! It is not about the hour we could have saved. Its about your Hope of Survival kicking in. Its about your will or no will. Its about your self defense you have put up against me from all the horrors and misery that I had put you though from the past and you are fearful about tomorrow. Your Mother was dying, you thought that I was dying, and you were loosing your hope in me and everything we had ever worked for in our 20 years of marriage. It was hard for you to accept that I was killing myself and you didn't want to see me dying. So, you put up self defense in your life and let self will take over." Then I ask, "Now Do You Understand?" Tears began to fall from her and my eyes like a water fountain. We knew God was in this matter to make it better. We began to communicate better and listen to each other as if God himself was there among us with love and compassion and we both began to understood what it was all about. Self will, will surely destroy lives and self will had broken my wife and I from communicating. We were just talking and acting on our own compulsive behaviors, rather than, sensing and letting our spirits join together as one in marriage. But, because I had been spiritually resurrected to a new man, I was sensing matters in a different way. I Thank the God of all Understanding that day for showing us and delivering us from the power of self will and gave to us an understanding on the matter. God broke the power of self will with the Power of his Will. "Do you understand, what I have just shared with you?"

Now, Let me now share with you something that I wrote years ago concerning my life as I would live by my own self will. The title of the following writings is called, "Crazy Train. A Ride To Destruction."

CRAZY TRAIN. A RIDE TO DESTRUCTION

When I think of my own self will living, it is somewhat liken unto a Crazy Train. A train with only one destination; straight to destruction.

This crazy train has no engineer, but is alive wanting and panting for me as its engineer and to climb aboard for the ride of my life. When it sees me coming from in the distant, it calls out loud with its whistle calling, "All Aboard! Come for the Ride of your Life!" When it sees me starting to come near it, it begins to huff and puff, but has not much power. When I sense the engine of this crazy train, it comes alive, somewhat like a wild tornado and desperate for me to aboard. When I sense the engine began to start by the fuel of my own excitement, it rages and rages and gives me greater excitement, knowing I'm going for a ride of my life.

The more the engine rages and calls out for me, the more I sense that its all about me. I respond by my feeling of euphoria and I climb aboard the train for the ride of my life. I stand on the runner board still sensing maybe something is wrong, but soon the sense just vanishes away. The more that I stand still without any emotion, the more the engine rages and rages and shouts out with its whistle, "More! More! More! for the ride of your life!" I begin to deny that anything could be wrong, for it's a ride that I've always long. The sense I was feeling somewhat vanishes away from all the euphoria that was coming from my sense of me being in control. The crazy train begins to make me feel good and excited about being in control and soon I can ride the ride of my life. I climb on aboard into the engine cab and the engine calls to me and says, "Steer me and feel me and take me where you like for you are in control of the greatest ride of your whole life." But, when the train starts to moved and the Cab doors lock, I have a sense the ride may had been a trap, but its to late to sense anything, except to ride the ride of my life. The more euphoria of excitement I get, the faster I go of the ride of my life.

Now, the road becomes extremely rough and dangerous and very fast that I don't have time for my own escape, so I continue with the ride of my life. I try to look out of the cab's window to where I'm going, but I cant seen anything not even the tracks. As I get fearful of the ride of my life, I begin to hope I would make it back.

The more I am willing to try to steer my way, the more the engine feeds off my fear and faster it goes. The engines keeps consuming my every thought, even the hope that I once had sought. It keeps running faster as I change my thoughts to such things as my denial and anger that I never thought. The more I fuel it with my emotion of fear, the more suicidal it seems that it becomes. I try to look back to see the cars, but all those that where following were backing away and there was none let except me and the engine. The engine keeps whistling for "More! More! More! I began somewhat to close my eyes and just assume that it was a dream. But, soon awake by the screams of those who were braking away and some who had not made it, dead and laying by the wayside from this same ride. Every town that I could see out through the window seemed desolate liken into ghost towns, because of the destruction from this Crazy Train. I open my eyes to look out the cab and seen grave stones of all the ones who didn't make it on their ride of life. I could see out in the distance where some were lying and some were their on theirs knees, praying and screaming for me to jump from the cab, but they just didn't know the craftiness of this engine of its locked doors and shatter proof glass. I would try to stand to see if I could find away out, but there was no way out of this trap. By the time I began to sense these horrible things, I knew deep within me it's was too late and began to accept that this was the death of my life. I knew at this moment I had no choice, but to do one thing, to fall on my knees and cry out to the King. I fell to my knees and cried out loud to the King, "Please God! Please! Deliver me from this crazy train." I began to sense a hope coming from deep within me and I began too pray much louder to the King. I began to get hope and a sense of peace, and I was still praying that the Crazy Train would cease.

began to stand straight up as a man in battle, accepting that I had no control, but hoping in something better to take control. I looked straight ahead from the cab window below and began to see the tracks as this crazy train slowed.

I notice ahead there set an Beautiful Train that Shined as a brilliant diamond in the Sun. The Light from this train was too great to look upon, but I tried my best to keep my eyes on the Sun. I began to be afraid for what I was seeing for I was headed straight toward the Bright Train as if we would collide. I laid down low into the cab as I wept much more and cried even louder, knowing with no doubt I was going to die. But, the Bright Train ahead called out to the Crazy Train with a greater power and said, "Stop you Crazy Train and now be dead for the one on board, I heard what he said." The crazy train stopped as fast as it started and I heard a louder whistle from the train that stopped it. The whistle blew as a sound of an mighty trumpet saying, "Arise man! Arise! Come and climb aboard, for your Life!" As this crazy train died in its tracks, the doors unlocked and I jump for my life. I looked ahead toward the Light and seen the engineer standing by the train and he shined as the Sun. I crawled to him to give him thanks for saving me and he said to me, *"I am the resurrection, and the Life: he that beleiveth in me, though he be dead, yet shall he live: And whosoever liveth and beleiveth in me shall never die. Beleivest thou this?"* This engineer whose garments was white as snow, took me by the hand and said, "Son arise and follow me for your life."

Now, I will share and expand on what I believe to be the truth of this self will matter. I will say, be patient with me my friend, for this could be the ride for your life. *What is self will?* First, I will say with confidence that self will is the opposite of God's Will with no doubt. Self will is also the sinful nature of the enemy's will, Satan. Second, self will is the natural instinct of a man when the man has no other will to respond to in his life. Third and last, this self will is the sinful nature of a man and can be destructive or even cause death of a man's life before his time. Self will is a sign or fruit of a man that has no trust in God and is trusting in their own understanding rather than that of the Creator. Self will works from the heart of a man's life when things come up suddenly.

Self will can lead to things, just to name a few, impatience, denial, distrust, dishonesty, anger and resentments, compulsive behaviors, selfishness and even death before a man's time. Self will is a fire wall between a man and God in the same likeness as sin separates a man from God. I honestly believe that *Self Will is ignorance of not understanding the Reality of Life in it's Trueness.* How does a man remove such a will from their life, especially their own will they have live for so many years?

We as mankind have got to start somewhere, either it be by reading God's Word or going and hearing God's Word preached, if a man be willing to do so. Continuing with the ride, I will say this with confidence, there are 3 wills of life: The first is God's Will, which is Life eternal and much more of a abundant Life on earth. God's Will holds the keys to life and also holds these things that can lead a man to better things in his life. These things are what are called fruits of the Spirit, such as love, peace, faith, patience, joy, humbleness, meekness, temperance and longsuffering and the last, righteousness before God. What? Righteousness before God? Hold on my friend for the answer is coming. The second Will is Man's Will, which holds these fruits of his life; adultery, fornication, idolatry, uncleanness, witchcraft, hatred, variance, emulations, wrath, strife, seditions, heresies, envying, murder, drunkenness, revellings, and such like.

The last is Satan's Will, which is this fruit; death and destruction for mankind. Satan's will is to entice a man by the man's will or fruits. But, the greatest difference is that Satan's Will is to kill and destroy a man. Now I ask which Will rather you have in your life, God's Will, Self Will or Satan's Will? I would answer God's Will and I hope that you would agree with me that God's Will is much more of what a man would need in his Life. The only way that I know to day to receive a beginning of God's Will is this; Get to know his Word and then you will know his Will. "What if I don't believe in your God?" Then you want know my God's Will. "

"Is your God a respecter of a man, either a believe or not?" No. My God isn't a respecter of any person, but my God rewards his people which believe in him and loves him, with his understanding of his Will. "Can you give me a point of reason of how to know your God's Will, if I want to know your God's Will?"

My friend, the only way that a man will ever know and understand God's Will is by Faith and Faith alone. You can not work for it, because the work is finished from the foundations of the earth and God's Will is freely given to them that believe in him and love him. In simplicity, here is a Great Key to unlock the closed door of understanding God's Will. In the Holy Book of John chapter 14, verse 6, it is written, *"Jesus saith unto him, I am the way, the truth, and the life: no man cometh to the Father, but by me."* My friend, there is no other way to know and understand God the Father or his Will, except through Jesus Christ. Also in the Holy Book of John chapter 10, verse 9 it is written, "I am the door: by me if any man enter in, he shall be saved, and shall go in and out, and f ind pasture." Also in the Holy Book of Matthew chapter 7, verses 7-8, Jesus Christ said and it is written, *"Ask, and it shall be given to you; seek, and ye shall f ind; knock and it shall be opened unto you: For every one that asketh recieiveth; and he that seeketh f indeth; and to him that knocketh it shall be opened."* Therefore again, how can a man know God's Will? First I would say this to a man that would be searching for God's Will: Repent(change your mind) of your own will and seek God's Will, which is no other than, Jesus Christ the only begotten Son of God. Jesus Christ is the Will of God and Mankind and a man can not get to God except through Jesus Christ. More simply put, "Let Go and Let Christ!"

Now, even as far back as 4000 years ago, God blessed mankind with a pen and paper to write things upon the paper to keep for the man to read of his Word, such as the Word of God. Even when all mankind was living by self will (sin) and didn't have a pen or paper, God etched the Ten Commandments on a stone for mankind to live by. God knows the self will and sinful nature of mankind and strongly suggested that we would write his Will down deep within our spirit, soul, and body today. The Word of God clearly is written in stone and it is here for a man for instruction of how to know God's Will and do God's Will. The Ten Commandments where not only an understanding of what sin was, it was also the answer for mankind's life long question, "Why are we perishing before our time." We must be willing to let go of our self will and let God's Will into our life and my friend, there is no other way, except through the Jesus Christ. There is another great principle that is written in Matthew chapter 6, verse 24 and it is written, *"No* man can serve two masters: for either he will hate the one, and love the other; or else he will hold to the one, and despise the other. Ye cannot serve God and mammon."*

My friend, simply put, either you will love God or you will love yourself and the things of this world more than God. In the Holy Book of James chapter 1, verses 5-8 it is written, *"If any of you lack wisdom, let him ask God, that giveth to all men liberally, and upbraided not; and it shall be given him. But let him ask in faith, nothing wavering. For he that wavereth is like a wave of the sea driven with the wind and tossed. For let not that man think he shall receive any thing of the Lord. A double-minded man is unstable in all his ways."*

My friend, this ride is going to take off faster from here, so hold on. How does Satan's Will fit into all this? First I will say this; Satan was the sinful nature that enticed man away from God's Will in the beginning. It is Satan's Will to lure and entice a man away from God's Will and lead the man to destruction and then death before the man's time. Just as Satan's Will can take a mans life, so can Self Will. Self Will is the sinful nature of a man to rebel against God's Will for the man profit. When a man is in a Self Will state of mind, Satan is their panting to destroy the man at the chance he would get. I will try to explain as we go back to the beginning in the Holy Book of Genesis chapter 2, verses 16-17 it is written, *"And the Lord commanded the man, saying, Of every tree of the garden thou mayest freely eat: But of the tree of the knowledge of good and evil, thou shalt not eat of it: for in the day that thou eatest thereof thou shalt surely die."* Therefore, Adam had God's Word and commandment clearly at this time, but you know later, the man ate of this tree of knowledge and rebelled against God's Will for him.

There is something greater here than meets the eye; that a man would be willing to rebel against God's Word and it is this: Satan knows the desires of a man's heart, and if he can find away to entice a man away from God's Will through a man's Self Will, he will do it. As you would read in the 3rd chapter of Genesis, Satan did entice mankind away from God's Will in the 4-6 verses. It is written, *"And the serpent said unto the woman, Ye shall not surely die: For God doth know that in the day ye eat thereof, then your eyes shall be opened, and ye shall be as gods, knowing good and evil. And when the woman saw that the tree was good for food, and that it was pleasant to the eyes, and a tree to be desired to make one wise, she took of the fruit thereof, and did eat, and gave also unto her husband with her; and he did eat."* My friend, before this day, man was without sin and righteous before God. But when man ate of good and evil then their eyes were opened to the things that were evil, follow me? All of the Wills that we have just read about are engulfed in these few scriptures. God's Will was that of when he commanded man not to eat of the fruit of the tree of knowledge. Man's Will was that of desiring the fruit or lusting after the fruit. Satan's Will was that of enticing the man by the man's own will or lust to eat of the fruit.

So, we see much clearly with our heart of what man's will is and it was the fall of mankind to sin or rebel against God's Will. But, we also see that it wasn't all the man's will that man sinned against God's Will.

It was by Satan's Will, that serpent, coming to the woman and speaking deceit into her mind saying, *"Ye shall not surely die: For God doth know that the day ye eat thereof, then your eyes shall be opened, and ye shall be gods, knowing good and evil."* I believe that was a moment that Satan wished he had never done. Satan did entice man to eat of the tree by his enticing words, but Satan doesn't know God's Will for mankind either. He did know that a man wouldn't die at that moment, because he hadn't been destroyed yet, so he used this deception to lure man away from God's Will. But, like I said before, he didn't know the fullness of God's Will for mankind at that moment either. Satan knew that God was merciful and righteous and he knew that God would not destroy the man off the face of the earth. But, Satan doesn't know any truth, for he is the father of lies. Satan knew that God would punish man for the rebellion, but he just didn't know the beginning or the end of God's Will for mankind. Satan did tell the woman that she wouldn't die and that was ½ the truth. God did number the days of a man, but he also gave us a choice, because today with God's Will among us we can live eternity, if we are willing to do God's Will. I know with confidence that Satan surely didn't see that coming either. When Satan said to the woman that she would know good and evil, he didn't see that coming either. When Satan enticed mankind to crucify the Son of God on the Tree of Calvary, he didn't see God's Will being fulfilled for mankind either.

Today mankind does know the difference between good and evil and we have the power through Jesus Christ to bruise the head of that evil serpent. Satan didn't see that coming, would he? If I could put a picture on paper of this lying serpent, the picture would be half dark and half light which is not either the truth of one or the other.

I guess Satan should had left the man alone in the garden, hey? But, it is the rebellious will of Satan that he is forever trying to destroy mankind and entice a man from God's Will.

Because, we have been adopted as children in his kingdom by Christ Jesus, God's only begotten Son. Satan, because of his will, was judged and sentenced by God before mankind was even made on this earth. Satan's sentence was death and to be cast out of God's Kingdom, because Satan said, "I will be like God. I will set upon his throne. I will take charge over this kingdom. I will do what I want and I don't need God telling me what to do. I am mighty and I have great power just as God, so, I will be as God." I will say with confidence today, Satan's Will was the wrong Will. Still today, Satan looks at the Sun as a testimony of the Lake of Fire burning more fiercely day by day and getting ready to receive him and all that follow his will at the appointed time. I believe it is an awesome rebuke from God to the ones who would do his own will, rather God's Will. Sometimes, I look up at the flaming sun and this is what I pray, *"Oh Father God, please keep me from the fiery damnation and torments where there is no water to quench the thirst, and the worm never dies. Please God keep me safe in thy Will and from my own will that engulfs all those who rebel against your Will. Keep me safe in thy Will oh God, and teach me continually day and night the understanding of thy Will, so that I will not stray from it. Whatever it takes for me to know and to do your Will, do it unto me Oh God, for you Will is Life unto me, in you Son's name, Jesus Christ, amen."*

Today I have a greater confidence of one thing in my life and that is this: If, I would had continued living by my own self will, you would not be reading this now. I would be still dead in my own understandings void of knowing the truth and living still in my own miseries and horrors. But, the word "IF" is small, but packs a powerful punch my friend. The word "IF" holds Life and Death in it self. The word "IF" is man's choice and I have made my choice and it isn't a matter of "IF" anymore in my life; it is a matter of "WHEN".

Today I keep my mind on the things of God and I am learning day by day more about God's Will and I have a greater peace than ever before. I keep my mind on God's Word and read it every chance that I get. It is somewhat like this question, "Would you want to live by self will with a life of misery and horror or Would you desire to Live in God's Will with a Life full of peace, joy, faith, love, gentleness, patience and know with confidence, God holds you in the palm of his hand protecting your every step in the straightness of his Will? In my past life, it took a long time for me to count that cost, but today I count the cost no more, for I trust God with my every breath of my life. I have chose to do his Will at all cost and my life is much more abundantly today than the past and I would not have it no other way.

If, a man would desire to know and do God's Will he would have to start somewhere and the best place that I know of today is on his knees before God. The "on his knees" part is the kicker, because self will doesn't want to submit to anyone or anything, because self will is rebellious. But, it is the only way to repent and to show submission to God and his only begotten Son, Jesus Christ. God's Holy Word is there for any man that is willing to receive it and is waiting patiently for a man to come to it. Jesus Christ used many things such as parables to bring God's Will to life in a man while he was in the flesh on this earth, because self will or the sinful nature of man had bound mankind. These parables that Jesus would use was a great way of resurrecting a man's mind to change from his own self will thinking.

Today I have a greater confidence, that The Word of God is the Key to God's Will and it is the Way, the Truth, and the Life for any man to receive, if the man is willing to receive it. By now we have stirred the mind up somewhat on the 3 wills of life and we have read of Satan's Will and Man's Will, but I would like to define the Wills in simplicity. Satan's Will is defined in two words, destruction and death.

A Man's Will is much more complex, because we as mankind not only battle against spiritual wickedness, such that of Satan, but also the things of the flesh. The Man's Will has Choice where Satan has no choice and I will expand on it later. God's Will is defined as Life; for God is Life.

Now, I have expanded somewhat on Satan's Will for mankind, but there are a few points I would like to expand on, concerning Man's will.

I would like to share with you the effects of a man's life by living his self will rather than submitting to the one and only Will, God's Will. I will also expand on God's Will later, but for now, Man's Will. First, I will say that man's will is the opposite of God's Will. Mans will consist of many different natures such as, disobedience, self-righteousness, deception, denial and ignorance.

Man's will can be just as destructive and deadly as Satan's Will, but it is not Satan's Will. Even though, Satan knows the weakness of a man's will, Satan can not make a man live by his will. It is the man's choice to live by his self will, rather than, God's Will. Satan is their waiting for the man to desire the things of this world and at that moment when a man begins to lust, Satan is diligent to entice that man away from God's Will. Man's Will is extremely weak and if Satan can find a way into the man's life, he will do it and it isn't a matter of "if", it's a matter of "when".

Self Will can boast itself way above of which the man really is. Self will can lead a man to self righteousness. This self righteousness of a man can lead to other defects of character of a man, such as denial. I will try to explain much more on other defects, but for now self righteousness. In the Holy Book of Romans chapter 3, verse 23 it is written, *"For all have sinned, and come short of the glory of God;"* Also this one in the Holy Book of Isaiah chapter 64, verse 6 and it is written, *"But we are all as an unclean thing, and all our righteousnesses are as filthy rags: and we all do fade as a leaf; and our iniquities, like the wind, have taken us away."*

One man might say he hasn't sinned; but, if he would think this in his heart, then he would make God a liar. Please hold on my friend. There is just one more bump to cross, before the straightness of the point. In the Holy Book of 1 John chapter 1, verses 5- 10, God's Word clearly defines this truth and I ask that you read it now, if you are willing to do so. *"If we say that we have not sinned, we make him a liar, and his word is not in us."* My friend there is no man righteous before God, but a man can put on righteousness and not of any work the man does, but by the righteousness of Jesus Christ. If we are willing to follow Jesus Christ and do God's Will by the faith we have in Jesus Christ, then we are county worthy and righteous before God and there is no other way. Righteousness comes only by the exercising of our faith in Jesus Christ.

Now, Self-righteousness is a great destructive nature of Man's Will. Self-righteousness can be puffed up in a man's life, deceiving the man from the truth of the Word of God. Not only can self righteous deceive a man from the truth, the man will also be bound by another defect, which is denial. It is at this point of a man's life when denial has manifested in his life, that Satan has the moment at the chance to lure a man away from God and destroy the man completely. Satan was self righteous when he said this before God, "I will do it! I will be greater than God. I will set upon his Throne. I will have great power and God's Angels will bow down to me!" That just didn't happen, even though, Satan believed it to be so. God judged and sentenced Satan at that very second and cast Satan and his Will out to the darkness and from his Kingdom. "I Will" is a very destructive way of life.

Today if a man would even ask if I would be willing to do something for him, I don't say I will do it on my own. I will say, through Christ I am able to do it or be quick to say, If, the Lord be willing to do for you and I, I am willing to let God do it for me.

I remember many times as someone one ask me to do something for them in the past and I would be willing to do it for them. When the time came to do the job, it was if my mind and memory would go blank, in less than a split second and I would hardly know at that time my left hand from my right hand. Then, the man would look at me as if I was crazy and say, "I thought you knew what you were doing. You don't want to do it for me do you?" I would be stunned somewhat from the blankness of my mind and brain. But, as soon as I would pray and ask God to help me out of the trouble, I would do it for the man. Not only would I do the job for the man, God would give me the understanding of how to do the job somewhat perfect before the man in amazement and apply the understanding to my life. In my past life there were times that I would puff up things in my life and be so self-righteous, that no one else knew anything any better than I, except maybe those that were nuclear physics, no kidding. At the time I couldn't even make a fire cracker without someone making the powder, follow me? Today I may not have the knowledge of building a Nuclear Bomb or even a Nuclear Reactor, but I have All Power looking over me at all times. Self-righteousness can lead to destruction and it can lead straight to death.

Now, mankind's self Will engulfs these fruits of his life; adultery, fornication, idolatry, uncleanness, witchcraft, hatred, variance, emulations, wrath, strife, seditions, heresies, envying, murder, drunkenness, revellings, and such like and I will expand of this matter later. In the Holy Book of 2 Peter chapter 2, verses 9-22, clearly shows the destructiveness of a self will man. And I ask you to please read it sometime soon. Self will of a man can engulf his entire life in deception, leading a man to believe that what he is doing is the right thing, but will learn later it was the wrong thing and suffer the consequences. Self will can lead a man into deception such as I was lead many times in my life. These deceptions would be things, such as this; "I'm not feeling to good. If I could drink just one beer, I might feel somewhat better.

I'm living normal and have been clean for a long time, surely God will forgive me, if I drank one beer. I'm not wanting to get drunk or anything like that only to drink one beer. I'm just going to drink a beer to help my pains in my body and I know that beer can help with the pain. So, that is what I will do; go get me a beer." Later I go to the store and look into the beer cooler desiring the alcohol. I then begin to say to my self this, "Well, I can by a forty ounce just as cheap as a 16 ounce. Shoot! I may as well get a six pack, that way I will have some for another day." My friend the story ends at another Alcohol and rehabilitation Center almost dead from not only using alcohol, but also using drugs. Today I have a better understanding of this; *"One is too many and a thousand is never enough."*

There is something that a minister shared with me one day as I was in a Rehabilitation Center battling for my life. I went to a church service there at the facility one evening and this minister gave this example of Denial and he said this; "Do you remember when God caused so much grief on the children of Egypt when the Pharaoh of Egypt refused to submit to the God of Moses. I'm not saying that God did the awful to Egypt, because he had nothing else to do at the time. He had already pleaded with the Pharaoh many times to let his people go, but the Pharaoh continued to rebel against the Word of God from the mouth of Moses. Now, there is one part that I would like to share. Remember when God turn the water into Blood? At this time the Pharaoh walked into the river and screamed to the top of his voice saying, *This is not Blood, this is only a trick that Moses and those Hebrew people have pulled on us.* And about that time there were some of Pharaohs own people sitting by the River and they stood up and shouted at the Pharaoh this; "He's in De-Nile!" Just as the Pharaoh was in denial and his life lead by his own understanding and being deceived by his own thoughts, so can a man today be lead away by his own deception. I will say this with confidence today, when deception comes to a man it just doest happen. I've heard in my entire life this, "I don't know what happen. I don't know why I would do that. I didn't want to start using again, but I don't know why." My friend even when these people would say things like this to me, they were still in denial. When deception comes to a man, it is when a man is desiring or lusting after something of this world, follow me? Deception is a device of Satan and feel with me my friend, he is there in the shadow of darkness, panting with a passion to use this device on you, even when you sleep. When deception has conceived into the heart of a man, denial becomes the shadow of his life. When denial takes over a man's life, the man is headed straight to destruction with no doubt. When people would say such things as this to me, "I don't know why I use. I don't want to use, but I always end up in the some mess. I really don't know why I use." My friend, that "I don't know why" part, is deception. I didn't know why I use either in my past and always ended in a mess, but I soon found out that it wasn't a matter of "WHY", it was a matter of "HOW".

Today I know why I did drugs and drunk alcohol like a fish, and the other self will pleasures that I aren't really appropriate to mention. It was because of one thing and one thing only my friend, which was this; I wanted to do it and my flesh desired it and lusted after the feeling of euphoria, but deception had me blind from the truth of the consequences.

When I would started to lust with my eyes or my fleshly heart for something, such as drugs, alcohol or sex, Satan was there quicker than "Flash Gordon" in my ears, whispering deceit. My friend Satan is still working today, as he did in the Garden of Eden when he enticed mankind to sin. Today, I never say, "I don't know Why I did it", because of this understanding. Today I always ask, "How did that happen. Where was my weakness that that filthy devil could come into my life? I got to exercise that part of my life much more." My self will living in the past was a matter of why I did it, it was always a matter of how I did it.

Let me now share another example of deception my friend and Please hold on, because this one may get a little bumpy. Smoking cigarettes is a deception of mankind the reason I believe this to be true is this: Some may say, "Well cigarette smoking is not a sin to death and neither does smoking a cigarette hurt no one, except the one that chooses to smoke. Not only that, the poor farmers need the income to feed their family." My friend let me say this with confidence. The man that would say such a thing, is deceived by his own thoughts. Cigarette smoking may not be a sin to death, but sooner or later the man that smokes will have complications with his health and the "neither does smoking cigarettes hurt no one" part is a lie. Let me ask this, "Would you give a cigarette to a child and tell him it is good to do?" I had a man to tell me one day this; "Cigarette smoking may not carry you to hell, but it sure will get you to heaven faster!"

I believe this with confidence, cigarette smoking is a deception and smoking can lead a man further into deception and destruction. When I was 11 years of age I seen a half lit cigarette lying by the roadside and as any child with curiosity would do, I picked it up and smoked that buzzard. When I introduced my body to that feeling of euphoria at this young age, I was forever afterwards searching for something much better. Smoking cigarettes may not be a sin to death, but it surely will lead a young man to much worse than a cigarette. I believe that smoking is a gateway for Satan to come into a man's life and entice him to do much more worse. So, do I believe that cigarette smoking is a sin to death? Yes I do, because it almost caused me my life. In the Holy Book of 1 Corinthians chapter 3, verse 17-18 it is written, "Know ye not that ye are the temple of God, and that the Spirit of God dwelleth in you? If any man def ile the temple of God, him shall God destroy; for the temple of God is Holy, which temple ye are.

Also in the Holy Book of Romans chapter 12, verses 1-2 and it is written, *"I beseech you therefore, breathren, by the mercies of God, that ye present your bodies a living sacrif ice, holy, acceptable unto God, which is your reasonable service. And be not conformed to this*

world: but be transformed by the renewing of your mind, the ye may
prove what is the good, and acceptable, and perfect, will of God."

I still smoke cigarettes as of today, but I am confident that God will remove this defect of my character just as he remove the others. I believe the reason that smoking cigarettes is so dangerous, is that of the deception of the device Satan uses to entice a man to much worse than smoking. One more thing my friend, the "Not only that the farmers need the income to feed their family" part is all about greed my friend. Farming tobacco is a Hugh business and the farmer knows it reaps more money than that of corn. Today I will say this with confidence to the farmers, "If you don't want your own children to be lead away from God's Will or reap the consequences of enticing a young man to his death, then quit farmer tobacco and grow something worthy." -Pause-

Now, let me sum up the matter of Self will. I wrote earlier that Self Will is more complex than any other Will, because we have the choice or willingness. We battle not only the spiritual wickedness, but also we as mankind battle our own lust and desires, which is of the flesh. I know for a fact I was deceived much of my life and suffered greatly the consequences of the deception. Today I can say with confidence that I try to the best of all my strengths live a normal life and it wasn't anything I had to work for. Salvation by the hope and belief that I had in me with all honesty at the time when I called on God to save me from the horrors and misery was my first step of living a normal life.

At that very moment when I trusted God for my Life, he was just and faithful to save me from destruction. All the defects of character that I had put on during my self will living were flying out the window of my heart, like flies from a fly swap. But it took time for God to remove these things and today he is willing to remove them as long as I am willing to allow him to do so. Now these defects of character took me almost 30years to put on, so I'm patient with God my Father to discern and examine my heart daily and cast these defects out of my life. I had so many defects of characters that there were times that I didn't even think God could help me, but my friend, today he is the Defect Character Terminator in my life and there is no other besides him. As long as I am willing to do his Will and keep my mind on God, he is able to remove the defects of character from my life. In the Holy Book of Ephesians chapter3, verse 20-21 and it is written, *"Now unto him that is able to do exceeding abundantly above all that we ask or think, according to the power that worketh in us, Unto him be glory in the church by Christ Jesus throughout all ages, world without end. Amen. "*

Now, let me just share a few simple defects of character that I had put on during my past self will living. Remember my friend, that these are just examples, even though they truly happened in my life. During these times of my life was when I was finally getting the understanding of my defects of character that I didn't even know I had, cursing being one also. I was asking God to examine my heart and remove these defects from my life. This first example of a defect of character is called my *compulsive behaviors*. One evening as I and my wife were settling in for the night, I asked my wife if she would get me a snack and something to drink. Before I go any further, I will say that I do suffer with the acid reflux disease. So, my wife jumps from the bed and before she got to the door I said, "Only bring me a small piece of cake and ½ of a glass of milk, ok?"

She goes to the kitchen and here the refrigerator open and close and then I heard as if she may had cut me a piece of cake and I thought nothing else of the matter. My friend, when she came through the door she had ½ of the whole cake and ½ a gallon of milk, no kidding. I said this as she came through the door, "What is this world are you doing. I only wanted a little cake and a little milk and you brought all of it." She said, "Well I didn't know. I thought that you or I may want some of it later and I wouldn't have to get up." and I said this, 'Well that good that you did that I may want a little more than I thought too." My friend I can't believe that I ate the whole thing in less than a wink of an eye. Later, I was hurting so greatly from my acid reflux, I almost went to the hospital.

Today I know it was because of the compulsive behavior I had put on during my life. I would go for weeks without eating and when I did eat I would eat the whole thing to make up for what I hadn't ate. In my past life I would live by compulsive behaviors, somewhat spontaneous at the spare of the moment without rationalizing of anything. But today, when it comes to eating, I know where my limit is and I'm careful of what I put in my body. My addition to alcohol and drugs was also a sign of the compulsive behaviors. When I used, I used until I ended in the hospital or at another rehabilitation center.

Now, here is another example in simplicity of another defect of character and it is called *dependency*. One evening during the summer season, I was lying in bed and somewhat warm. I had a remote control fan that I depended on for a long time. I depended on the remote, because using the remote I wouldn't have to get out of bed to turn the fan on or off. I thought this was one of the greatest inventions of mankind, no kidding. Nevertheless this evening I couldn't find the remote and I went somewhat hysterical, no kidding. I jump from the bed, looked under the bed, went to the den, to the kitchen, to the bathroom and then I just gave up on finding the remote.

I even accused my wife from hiding the remote form me, no kidding. It's somewhat comical now, but at that time, that remote was more important than reading the Bible to me, no kidding. This remote was like my buddy and I didn't want my buddy missing. Nevertheless, I just laid back on the bed, defeated from finding the remote and reached over inches from my headboard and just turned the fan on manually. And as soon as I reached inches away from the bed to turn the fan on, the remote comes out from under my pillow and falls on the floor. Somewhat comical isn't it? But really, this is an example of a defect of character that I had put on during my past living. I would get so dependant upon something and when I couldn't get it, I would go crazy and even start blaming others for the problems. My friend I didn't even know that their was such a thing as this type of dependency. I knew in my past I depended on someone like a preacher to help me with a personal problem, but soon found out he was just as bad off as I would be and then I would be quick to judge him. I would quit depending on the Man of God. Self Will, will put on defects of character in a man's life. But today I know that the Defect of Character Terminator is quick and swift to remove these things from my life and I just keep my heart and mind on him to do so for me. I also accept that I cant work to remove these defects and I wait patiently living a normal or consistent life in God's Will. I understand today that living a normal life in Jesus Christ, will I ever keep these things from entering my front door of my heart.

I also know with confidence that doing God's Will in my life can only remove them and keep them from entering back in. Therefore, self will is a road of destruction for any man. I believe that a man can be lifted up in his life with riches and fame and much knowledge and wisdom. But, I also know that none of these things are possible or would matter, if it wasn't for Jesus Christ fulfilling these things on the Cross of Calvary. It isn't about who or what you are in this life; for God isn't a respecter of persons.

What will matter at the end of your last breath on this earth and when your work is finished is this; "Have I lifted Jesus Christ up and did I follow God's Will to the best I could." In simplicity my friend, God's Will not Self Will. If a man would want the riches and inheritance of God's Will and the glorious garment of righteousness, the man must stop just thinking about it and he must start doing it.

Before I end these writings of, "Self Will a Road to Destruction," I desire to leave a comforting word with you. The following is all about the Will of God and how we as mankind could know and do such a Will. I have great confidence in using parables to give a man to help the man grasp onto the Word of Life. I will and have used many parables in my life. Almost every understanding that Jesus Christ has given mankind was as parables. He would look around in reality and find something, such as a sparrow, a grape vine and many others and explain God's Will in the parable. Every word that came out of Jesus Christ's mouth was Life for mankind or the Will of God for mankind.

Today I know that I must have the complete Word of God in my life, before I can paraphrase God's Word, because there is Life and death in the tongue. Remember, mankind lives within the sinful nature and Self-Will can take the Life out of all things and then it would be death. God doesn't need us to play boggle or scramble his written Word. When we are in self will our sinful nature can scramble or confuse the Word of God. If we are in self will the sinful nature of self-will can kill the Life that is in our words. But, if we receive God's Word and have his Teacher and Comforter, which is the Holy Ghost in us, then there is Life. I tell you my friend there is no other way to understand God's Word of Life, except by the teaching of the Holy Ghost; for the Holy Ghost is the one and only Witness of God to mankind. Please let me share what I know to be the truth of this matter today.

Jesus Christ mentioned many times that after he would arise and go back to the Father of Life, then the Father would send the Holy Ghost is his name to a man that believes. The Holy Ghost would Teach and Comfort the man in all matters (John chapter 14). When a man believes and receives his Only Begotten Son completely into his Life, God is faithful to send the Comforter into the Life of that man. This Comforter will be for confirmation that the man is walking and being taught the matter of Life.

In my past Life, I would think that when I read these scriptures about the promise of the Comforter (Holy Ghost) that he was there to comfort me in my tribulations or trials only, but that is only somewhat of the purpose of the promise of the comforter. Today, I know what the word comfort means, and here are just a few of the means of the comforter: To ease, to avenge, to console, to repent. The holy Ghost is not only sent to a man's life in the name of Jesus Christ to comfort a man during trouble times, he is there for avenging, repentance, understanding and confirmation of God's Word in a man's Life. The Holy Ghost is the Keeper of our souls while we are walking in the Will of the Father. Wow! The Holy Ghost is my teacher, my body guard, my discipline and my hope, all in one great and powerful package as a gift from God wrapped within God's Will with a scarlet bow and all I have to do, is unwrap it and loose it. I will say this also; the Holy Ghost is the understanding of Life. Today as I walk in God's Will the Holy Ghost is quickly to console me in God's Word and then he eases my Life by confirming what he teaches me and that my friend, is a Great Comfort. When I'm discerning that I'm being shown a great vision or revelation in my life, the Comforter is there quickly to ease my understanding and to confirm this understanding and I am comforted.

I don't anymore question "if," I am doing God's Will or Not, because the Holy Ghost is on me, in me and around me confirming my every move, and that my friend, is a great comfort. I have the understanding today that I must stand firmly in what God's Written Word is and not a paraphrased spoken word from man only. I still desire to hear preachers and ministers of the Gospel of Christ, but I'm also on the look out for man's will and how Satan can use anyone to change just one word as it is written and change the whole matter from Life to death. Jesus Christ even left for us understanding of this matter in the book of Matthew Chapter 16, verse 6. He knew about man's will and it wasn't to pleasant. We must be on the look out for the leaven in man's words and always check and search God's Word for confirmation.

Now, I had just turned 15 years of age and my destructive living is way out of hand. I remember riding in the passenger car with an older man driving; he was 32 years of age and had been smoking and drinking heavy all day. We were traveling approximately 45mph through town and I remember looking up at him and saying, "I think you'll on the wrong street", and the driver said, "Hell, I know where I'm at! " Suddenly everything stopped!! Crash!!! The driver thought we were on a different street, where a Railroad Crossing was and he was going to jump the railroad crossing, like the Dukes of Hazard, but we were not on that street, we were one street over and we ran straight into an embankment at 45mph,no kidding. I remember almost flying through the windshield of that vehicle. If it wasn't for me throwing my arm up to stop myself from flying out that windshield and my torso hitting the dash, I probably would be dead today or would I?I remember seeing the hood and motor almost flying through the front windshield. I remember glancing over at the driver and his face was splattered with blood and his nose was as big as a large red delicious apple. I was numb, stunned and hurting from my shoulders down and I was bleeding somewhat from my elbow. He reached for me, grabbed me by my shirt and said, "Let's go boy!".

We left the vehicle and stumbled to a nearby bar, just a few blocks away from the accident. As of today I have not seen this man who was driving the vehicle not ever again.

There at the bar, I seen a man I knew for along time and he took me and the driver to where we wanted to go. *Later, that man, who took me and the driver away, was killed in a one car accident from drunk driving.* As of today, I still suffer from major pain in my body from that particular car wreck. I know today, it was *the consequences of rebellion against my parents and God.* Still today I feel the pain from that touch of *God's chastisements* and it is a reminder to me, never fight against God, but fight for God and I never want to go though any chastisements like that ever again. This was only the beginning of God's Rod upon me to straighten me up and get me back on the right course. Satan had enticed me and I lusted for those things and then my lust turn to sin and I was facing the big whole. At the time, I didn't know God was trying to discipline me, I only thought we had made a mistake and crashed and began to be proud of surviving it.

I and the driver should of had been killed in that crash and It's Ironic now that I look back and remembered what I said to the driver, *"I think you'll on the wrong street"*. We were on the wrong street alright, we were on the wrong street of life and that wrong street liked to had killed me and the driver. That was a wake up chance for me to get on the right street and back in the Will of God as a child, but life kept revolving around my self will pleasures and without understanding of Life. I still continued to use drugs and alcohol and live by my self rebellious will and I was living a course straight to destruction.

Now there is one particular incident that happened during this time of my life. This incident effected my life, and my entire family's life at this time. I have mention several times about a particular brother that I loved very much and we were very close. This brother we have lost at this time. His appointed time was called or maybe he rushed his time, I will never know. I have mention how Satan tried to killed me and my family all throughout our lives, because of us being chosen as his people. Nevertheless this particular brother that we have lost was involved in an motorcycle accident when I was 15 going on 16. This accident almost killed him. He liked to had lost his right leg and broke many bones and dislocated his shoulders. I will never forget the day that his girlfriend came to my parents and was hysterical and told my father and mother about the accident. He was in an area the cars were not suppose to be in and came around a curve traveling at a high rate of speed and hit a car head on. It was a dark time in my family's life. We thought we were going to loose my brother at this time, but through plastic surgeries and quick medic procedures, my brother pulled out of it. He stayed in the hospital for about 6 months. His right leg was the worse injury. From his knee, to his ankle bone the meat was pulled away, but the doctors saved his leg and my brother later recovered greatly from the accident. The reason I am writing about this particular incident is to let you know how my brother got addicted to hard drugs. My brother stayed in pain for years and he was on very strong pain medicines. He did get addicted to hard drugs and that I believe was the reason this thorn became his death later in life. He was drinking beer and liquor just as I was during this time, but I don't think he was doing the hard drugs, such as heroin, but later, heroin was the death of his body.

Now, at the age of 16 I was so out of control, only God could help me now. My parents turn me over to God and the church and they all were praying for me night and day. My parents prayed every night and day for me and had no choice, but to give my life over to God and to the church of Christ Jesus. I would always tell them, "Daddy, Mother, I'm sorry and I promise I want do this no more." There comes a time that we need God to help us through trouble times and my parents knew this. I was beginning to be involved in illegal activities and I was place on probation for being evolved in a particular incident. I had been detained several times by Law Enforcement for being involved in illegal acts, like drug procession. I was beginning to quit school and when I would go to school, I would not listen to the teachers and would get in many fights and would not do the programs at school.

I was high almost every day that I remember, and I felt as if I couldn't go to school not being high, because I just didn't think I could fit into school. I didn't go back to church and didn't want anything to do with it during this time, because I began not to trust no one. I would only go to school, because I thought I could get drugs and girls and earthly things to meet my pleasures. I hardly passed ever a grade, but by the skin of my teeth that I could remember. I would never study and thought I knew everything more than my teachers and every one else around me. I was disciplined by school officials many times.

I don't remember much from the 8th grade to the 10th grade, because of being so high on drugs, but I do remember this incident. One day my Mother and Father took a chance and let me use their new ford vehicle to go to school. I told them I would go to school, if I could drive there and back because I didn't want to ride the school bus anymore, but my intents of my heart was another way of partying and being accepted by my friends and girls from school. I didn't go to school that day. I took another friend with me and we went on a ram page.

I took my Mothers car and used it for four wheeling at a riding club near my home. After the partying was over or lets say my friend left me, I was stuck to face my Mother and Father again. I had been taking valium, codeine, smoking pot and drinking very heavy and the car was in a mess. I thought to myself that I had to get out of this situation no matter what, so I came up with a crafty plan and it went like this: "I will take the vehicle and flip it into a tobacco field and then I will try to convince my parents that something ran out in front of me and made me to wreck the vehicle." So, I took the vehicle traveling approximately 40 mph to a nearby tobacco field that I knew about. I had never tried crashing a vehicle on purpose before and I didn't know how fast I should go, but I knew the damage that could be caused by 45mph and I didn't want that. I left the road toward a nearby tobacco field, and everything stopped suddenly. Crash!!! The vehicle did not flip and I was thrown around in that car like a rag doll at 40mph. I was thrown over to the passenger's side and was somewhat knocked out by the force and my head hit the side panel and my head also knocked out the passenger's window. I don't remember much more during this time, because I was somewhat knocked out. I do remember someone's voice and it was calling my name, asking where I was and if I was Ok; for he was a cousin of mine. I do remember somehow, my cousin came to the passenger side and he and a friend that was with him, pulled me from the vehicle and rushed me to the nearby hospital.

I will say that this was my second suicide attempt. Also, my Cousin soon after was killed in a car crash below his parents traveling at a high rate of speed approx 100mph. I was told he was forced off the road by the police officer that was chasing him around a curve. I took the death of my cousin very badly and held anger and resentments of this matter in my heart for a long time until I found out the truth of the whole matter later.

It was a shut casket funeral and I didn't go, because at the time I just couldn't handle deaths to good and thought it was normal for people to just die, if it is there time. I loved my cousin and he was a friend of mine that would always be there when I needed something. But later, I had to accept the death, because he was no longer there when I needed him. It is ironic that he was the one which found me at the accident and rescued me from the vehicle and rushed me to the hospital and I missed him very much. He and my Brother that has died recently were best friends and I looked up at them as my big brothers and they took care of me, when I couldn't take care of myself. They would let me hang around them every where they went, except when they feared the safety of my well being or they just didn't want me to know what they were doing.

So, I was released from the hospital in the care of my parents and had suffered from a concussion and bruises. After being released from the hospital to the care of my parents we headed home, I thought. I had forgotten about the vehicle and what I had done; for I thought, because of the suffering I was in that my parents would take me home and talk about it tomorrow. But, I wasn't headed home and it was time to face the consequences of my self will act. As we kept traveling toward home, I noticed Blue Lights flashing and Orange lights flashing just in the near distance and soon began to sense, It was where I had wrecked and the wrecker service and Highway Patrol was on the scene. I thought nothing much about it during this time, because I thought that my injuries and going to the hospital was enough for one night and my parents would feel badly for me and carry me home.

So, my father pulls behind the Highway Patrol Car and a large man with great stature came forth from the patrol car, throwing a large brim hat upon his head and I got fearful and my knees began to shake and I thought I was going to jail for sure this time and my parents could not save me from going.

As the Trooper approached the car that we were sitting in, my father gets out and meets the Trooper and I gently rolled my window down to try to listen. I could not hear what they were saying, except my father as he turn and looked toward me and said to this State Trooper, "He is in the back seat!" Then I seen the Trooper walk toward our vehicle and he opened the back door where I was sitting and when he opened the door, it suddenly opened as if he was mad at me and said to me, "Boy!! Do you know what you have done? "There was a pause as the Trooper began to shake his head in disbelief and I gulp a breath then he said, "You have destroyed your parents vehicle and almost killed yourself! What is wrong with you Boy?!" I heard my mother in the front seat crying softly. I didn't know what to say to the Trooper and I thought at that time, he was going to pull me out of that vehicle and beat me with his own belt or something worse. I couldn't answer the Trooper, I was beginning to fear him and I didn't want to go to jail. The Trooper said again something like this, "Boy! Are you listening to me?" I got the courage up and nodded my head in the "YES" response and then he said this, "Boy! I am not going to carry you away to jail this time, but If you ever do this again, I will put you there and your parents will not be able to save you!!.. pause and then he said, Boy! You need to straighten up! Do you here me?" Again, there was a pause and I nodded in the "Yes" position. Then the officer said this as he looked straight into my eyes, "I'm going to release you to the care of your parents and you best listen and do what they ask from you! Boy! Do you understand?" Again, I nodded my head at the "YES" response and took another gulp of breath. He shut the door suddenly and I watched him as he was walking away shaking his head as if he was in disbelief and I will say at this time I thought not much about the matter, except I didn't need to wreck my parent's car again and meet up with this Trooper. My father finally entered the vehicle for he was tending to the wrecker service and all the other problems I created from my own self will act. We went home and I went to bed thinking about what had happened.

After this incident, I began to slow down on using drugs and rebellion, but it didn't last for long. Even though, I was knocked hard on my head from the accident and a great authority was in my face speaking, I still didn't understand and listen.

Later, after a few months had past one evening during my self will living, my parents had gotten the vehicle repaired that I had destroyed. The insurance company did not claim the vehicle a complete total from my incident and my parents had to pay out of their pocket, much of the repairs to the vehicle and it was a lot and they suffered for it. I was somehow doing a little bit better by this time and I guess I was afraid of running into that State Trooper again.

No really, that may had been some of the reason, but I really wanted to do better for my parents at the time and thought I could do better with the help from myself. My parents were beginning to trust me a little bit and I ask my parents one weekend, if I could use the vehicle to pick up my girlfriend and go out to eat and to my surprise they agreed, but gave me a few restrictions. I went straight to an acquaintance home and got zombilized and blasted. I was so out of control, drinking wine, smoking pot and popping valiums. I drove and picked up my girlfriend and we never made it to dinner. I continually to get blasted all night and I had to park the vehicle in a nearby parking lot. My girlfriend was scare that I was going to wreck or worse kill us in a bad accident and was somewhat getting hysterical. My brother (The brother I just have lost) and his girlfriend found me in the parking lot and my brother came to the car and told me to go home, because I should had been home hours ago. I physically started fighting with my brother and cursed at his friend. I reach inside and pulled my friend out of the car and she also became an enemy to me at this time. I had so much anger in me, that I literally beat the windshield out of my Mothers vehicle with my bare hands.

At this time, I was so out of control with anger, that smashing glass, was all I remember and after this incident, I really damaged my shoulder very seriously this time. Knock! Knock! I think someone is at my door again. When I finally came to and calmed down, I thought of what just had happened, but it was to late the damage was done. I drove the battered vehicle home and when I drove up in the yard my father was waiting for me standing near the rear of his van and he looked very saddened. I remembered him saying something like this," Son, what have you done? Get out of the car and get in my Van now!" So, I did accordingly as he asked. He went inside the house for a few minutes and I stayed in his van and then he finally came out of the home and we left. My father said nothing to me as we began to enter the interstate and I would glance at him and he looked somewhat saddened. I knew we were heading out of town, but I had no idea what my father was up to or where we were going. As I was glancing over to my father, I noticed he was very sad and he began to cry softly, like he was in grief. I finally got the courage up and ask my father, "Daddy what's wrong? There was still silence. "Where are we going?" He looked at me with tears slowly coming from his eyes and said, "Son, I love you very much and so does your Mother. We can't help you, so we are going to get help for you. We have no choice Son; for we have tried the best we can to show you the way, but you don't understand. We don't want to loose you son and where I'm caring you, they can help you and us before it's too late." My father started crying even more and that was the first time, I had ever seen my father cry. I began to feel very bad at what I had put my family though at this time and I was thinking in my mind, what could I say or do to make them feel better.

For some reason, it seemed like every time I would face the consequences of my rebellious self will, I would feel sorry (repent) and try to get a little better and try to come out of the problems, but this time there was no getting out.

I was finally looking in the glass at my self and sensing that the consequences of my actions were manifesting, but it was too late to make it better for myself and my family. I knew at that moment, sitting in that van, that my father was in control and I had no choice, but to go where he took me. My parents were determined to get me help no matter what the costs where. We headed toward our destination and he said, "Son may God save you and keep you. I'm carrying you to a hospital and they will help you. Your mother and I have been working on this for sometime and they said to bring you to them, now! They will help you with your problems and I will be praying for you." When he had said this, my heart dropped and I felt like my parents had given up on me and was beginning to feel rejected again, but they had not given up on me; for they were suffering with and for me. As we pulled into the hospitals parking lot, my father hugged me and started to cry again. We entered the Hospital and there stood about 4 staff members from this hospital, waiting for me; for they were expecting me. My father hugged me again and said, "We love you Son. Pease let these people help you get better, Son!" At that time, I realized I was being Hospitalized and began to think that there wasn't much wrong with me. I was thinking and saying things like, "Yes! I made a mistake, but putting me into a hospital, that's not the way out. I will do better and I don't need to be put into any hospital. I'm not sick! Give me one more chance and I will do better." I did not understand at this time the seriousness of the course I was taking, that it would be death soon at this very young age, but my parents did and they could not bare it anymore.

As I was standing there in disbelief, one staff member said, "Come with me son and I will show you around." I said, "OK." I thought at that time, I would be staying for a few days or so and it would be ok to look around and maybe it would make my parents feel better. As we walked through this large double door, I heard it "click, click and lock" behind us and this large man said to me with a stern voice, "Son, we are going to help you.

Don't be scared, son; for there are others here also that we are helping and you will get to know them." I didn't know what to say accept, *"Where is my father? I don't need to be here!"* The large man said nothing and we continually to walk straight and as we entered thru another double door, the same happen, "click, click, and lock". I knew at that time, I wasn't leaving from that place by my self. I noticed down the corridor there were other teenagers there, playing and looking to see who I was. I began to sense I wasn't alone in this hospital and the large man was right and I was there to stay for a long time. *I was confined to that hospital for over one year.* I was just turning 18 years of age when I was released back to the care of my parents. During my institutionalization at this hospital, I began to grow a little in my spirit. I was going back to school there at the hospital and began to make friends again, in the hospital. The staff became my father and mother and the other youth became my brothers and sisters. I began to miss my real family very much and it saddened me greatly. My parents would come and visit once and a while when they could and I do remember my oldest sister visiting once, during this time. I began to miss my family very much and would cry in privately for them for a while.

As time passed there at this hospital, I began to sense and accept that the staff was there for me, to lean on during this long time away from home and became my new family. There was a staff member I do remember, that would come into my room occasionally to massage my bad shoulder. The Doctor of Medicine told me, after I was x-rayed and examined, that my shoulder was in a mess, but surgery would not be good for me at this time. He said, because I was so young, my shoulder would properly heal somewhat and surgery might would cause more damage. Well, it has healed somewhat today, but I still can't throw a ball with this side of my body very well and I have great pains sometimes with it.

I suffer from severe bursitis and tendonitis as of today in this shoulder and it is a reminder to me of my rebellion against God and my parents during this young age.

There were other staff members that I took to very closely at this hospital, but there were some that I hope never work at a place like that again. There was one time I remember that a staff member asked me if I wanted to get out for a while. The staff was the only way of leaving with permission. I said, "Of course I want to get out for a while!" So, we left that hospital and you would never believe where he took me, a Strip Bar full of alcohol and self-will.

Yes, that's right, a strip bar, full of naked girls and alcohol. I thought I was on top of the world with a staff carrying me to a Strip Bar. I was only 16 at this time and this was the first time I had ever been to a Strip Bar. I just couldn't believe it. He was drinking beer and I had to drink soda, root beer I believe. He did manage to slip me one beer, because he didn't want me to get drunk. After we were leaving, he told me not to tell anybody or he would not do this again for me and handed me some chewing gum and I never told anyone, except you now. After this, I could sense that this man wasn't where he needed to be.

There were times we would be in the lounge at the hospital, where all us youth would watch TV, and he would say, "Turn off the lights girls and boys." Occasionally another youth would come in and turn the lights on and there would be young girls on him doing things I will not mention and he and everyone in the room would say, "Turn the lights off stupid!" At first I liked him because of what he let me do, but after time, I began not to like him, because I didn't want what he was trying to give. In this hospital, it was like a family to me and I felt he was violating those rights. We lived together for a long time and girls would sneak into boy's rooms and boys would sneak into girl's rooms and I don't have to say much more.

The youth that were there with me at this hospital, were not only there for drugs, some were foster children being dumped from one family to another, some had sexual problems, some had medical problems and some where there because their parents where dead or in jail and I became like a big brother to some of them. Some of these children had no choice, but to be there or be on the streets with nothing. This is where I began to understand myself; for it was spending time with the orphans and foster children, that I began to appreciate my family and what they had done for me. These children had no families and it saddened me a lot. Life here on earth had just dumped them on the streets and left these children alone and had no parents to care for them, but most all of them were happy and I do remember one in particular. He was a small blond headed boy about 3 years younger than I and he had very fair skin. He was always happy, singing songs and melodies from his heart. Some of the other youth would make fun of him and tell him to quit singing that stupid mess, but he kept a singing. Sometimes as he would sing, he would cry at the same time, because of some of the others making fun of him, until all the others would leave the room or I would come into their mist. If, any child had a reason to be sad, he did; for he was an orphan without no earthly family and He would always tell me and others, "I have Jesus and his love in my heart." I began to watch over him and to become attached to him and started to think in my heart, "If he could be this happy dealing with what life had thrown at him, to be sure I can" and I wanted to find this happiness he had. It took a long time for me to start understanding one thing in life and that is, If you don't have God in your life, you are alone and if you have God in your life, you have all things your heart desires, even if you are left alone him on earth.

So, as I was still living in this hospital, I was walking like a child without understanding of life, but something was beginning to grow inside of me. Since I had been drug free now for almost 6 months, I was beginning to feel and sense again and my spirit was coming alive and beginning to grow somewhat. So, as time passed I began to follow the program, but had my guard up for the wolf in lamb's clothing. I was finally beginning to sense a little about my life in a perspective and started to know right from wrong in my life and began to think on this matter. I was confined to a hospital for help and refuge from drugs, alcohol, rebellion and even death, but Satan and man's self will was still trying to entice me to rebel against God, even during this time of my life. At the hospital, we didn't go to church and I don't think I read the Holy Bible, except maybe one time, when I was there. Sometimes, if I remember correctly, there would be a minister that would come in and talk with us children and share with us stories about Jesus Christ. It was a program of finding our self and this program didn't force nothing on us; for we had to live the way we chose, but there were still discipline there. There was much good that came forth from this experience, but also some bad experiences and I lived in this hospital for over 1 year.

CHAPTER THREE

FORGIVENESS BY GRACE.

AT THE AGE OF 17, NEARING THE AGE of 18, I was beginning to be discharge from the hospital. I was fearful of the change that was going to take place. The staff and the operation of this program became my life, and I didn't what to go back out and have to face my past again. I liked the way I was living and thought, "Why should I have to change it?" I knew that I had to go back to the same school; and continue my classes where I had problems at before time.

I had to go back to the same neighbor hood where I had so many problems in. I would have to face all the ones who had hurt me emotionally and physically. I really didn't want to leave this hospital, because I knew I was beginning to learn about Life somewhat and was beginning to grow in my spirit man. But, I also thought at the time, people may look at me in a different way since I wasn't on drugs anymore; and had grown up some, physically and spiritually. So, I lifted my head up and from somewhere, got the strength to press forward with this great change in my life; and I was discharged to the care of my parents.

After my discharge from the hospital, I did go back to the same school from earlier and to my surprise, the school officials had set me back one grade. I began to feel humiliation again and felt as if I didn't belong at this school. It was suppose to be my senior year in high school and I felt as if I would just quit school. But, instead I led my classmates to think I was still a senior, no kidding. This all changed one day as my classmates were getting their senior pictures taking for the school album. I do remember that I was standing in the shadow, watching and was very sadden. One of my classmates came up to me and said, "What's wrong? Be happy. Isn't it exciting that we are getting our pictures taking today?" This classmate that had come up to me was a beautiful girl that I liked very much, before I went to the hospital. Before I had went to the hospital, I felt embarrassed to ask her out, because of my drug use and felt ashamed of the matter. Nevertheless I said to her, "Yes it is." I just didn't have the courage to tell this friend of mine, I will not be graduating with you. The way the classes were set up then, most all juniors and seniors could take some of the same courses and were in the same classrooms. Most all my former classmates thought, even though I had been away, I was back and I was still in the senior year. This feeling of humiliation lit the fuse of the bomb of my heart and I was beginning to hold angry and resentments against the school officials for holding me back in school. My past was flaming up from the fiery deep well in my heart again.

I went home that day and went straight to someone's home and got high and nothing else mattered at this time.

I had met a beautiful Spanish-American girl in the hospital and we began a relationship there. I do remember the time that I was to meet her parents, and she was to meet my parents. We set a day and it was a Friday night. My mother's sister or my aunt carried me to their home, which was, approximately 28 miles away from my home. My aunt was going to take care of some business in this city and pick me back up later that evening. But, she didn't come back at the time she had said she would, and the girl's father said this, "He isn't staying here! I will carry him home. Where do you stay?" When I told him where I stayed, he was somewhat surprise, but he took me home anyway. Later that evening, my aunt did go by their home to pick me up.

Well, me and this girl where determined to stay together and I do remember coming home from school on a Friday and I was going to spend the weekend with her and some of her friends. So, after this situation happened at school the day of the picture taking, I was ready to get away with this young girl that I grew to Love somewhat. So, later I went with my girlfriend who I met in the hospital and her friends and we went out of town that weekend and stayed blasted. So, guess what? I had begun my course of destruction again, but I will say, this was the only way I knew at the time to numb my pains and feelings I had deep within my heart; for I was still without understanding of the matter. All of the anger and resentments deep down in my heart from the past, began to flare again. I dropped out of school and refused to go back and was getting high everyday.

Later, me and this girl (Spanish girl) broke our relationship apart and I began to see my girlfriend from the past. Let me say this also, during our relationship it was lust, but today I love her in a very special way. I love her for coming in my life when I felt alone; and I also love her soul.

She planted a seed in my life, just as all the others that have came across my path. I will always love her for her soul and life.

Not long after I started to use again, I was out of control again and my parents committed me back into the hospital for 45 days; for this was the number of days ordered by the Court Judge as I stood before him. So, there I was again in the same hospital and I became worse and worse. The anger and resentments was the culprits. I would fight almost every day against the staff and the other youth that were there for no reason, but I know today it was because of all the anger and resentments I had hidden and suppressed deep within the dark doors of my heart. I remembered being strapped down to the bed many times, because I was a threat to others and myself days and nights. But, after a few weeks had past, my anger was beginning to ease. I started to listen to the counselor and my doctor. They were very concerned about me and I began to sense and trust somewhat that they wanted to help me and I began to accept their help.

This time at the hospital, things were a little bit different. I began to trust and to be a little more honest with the staff and they were beginning to help me much more. There were a few new faces on the staff board and the wolf in lamb's clothing was gone this time. My Doctor this time in the hospital was a Spanish man of origin. This Spanish Doctor brought spiritual music to my life and taught me to play the guitar some and would share interesting stories with me of his life. He began to minister to me with music and I began to like this a lot. It soothed my soul and I was beginning to feel better things about life.

During this hard time of trying to find Life and letting go of my past, I still was without understanding, but I continually to press forward with the help of this doctor and the hospital staff.

Today, I know why that Doctor wanted to play that beautiful music for me. He would pick that 12 sting classical guitar like an angel with a harp, very softly for me. He would sit in my little room, at the foot of my bed and he would play every time he would come and check up on me. He knew that what I needed was not psychiatric drugs or anything as such at the time, but for my soul and spirit to calm and be at peace. He knew that I had been hurt and I was a very angry child, because of my past. All the music I had been listening during my past living was heavy metal, rock and roll, but, this music, change my look on the matter of music. As he would play this spiritual music, I will call it, my spirit and soul would feel a peace like never before, except at church when I was a little child. I got addicted to this spiritual music, literally. After this understanding of music and how it can affect your life, I started to seek after this soothing music to sooth my mind and spirit. He knew at this time, my spirit and soul was in anguish and I was suffering badly. He knew how to come into my life and share that there are better things in life, than horrors and pains. This doctor was a great help in my life and I know the staff thought I was crazy at times, but they didn't know what my problems were, because I wasn't honest with them before. I was not honest with them at all while I was there for the year and I only told them what I wanted to tell them. I kept the anger and resentments still deep within in my heart for revenge.

Now, this time at the hospital when I was committed, I would blame the hospital staff for my turning to drugs again, but later understood somewhat that it wasn't their fault for my problems. Even though, bad things had happened there the first time while I was being treated, these matters were not all the blame.

I began to understand somewhat at this time that my angers and resentments where coming from somewhere much deeper and darker within my heart. It was all the matters that had used me and abused me for eight agonizing years in my childhood and I felt that my childhood had been robbed from that which I deserved growing up as a child and I felt as if I was worthless. For today I know for It was all the anger and resentments I had built up in my heart against all those who had hurt me and I had hidden them crafty within the dark rooms of my heart and I would always think, "When I get older, I will repay them for what they have done to me."

So, later after I had calmed down and began to understand this matter somewhat, my 45 days was drawing near and I was feeling much better about facing life on its terms. I studied and worked hard to get my GED while I was there 45 days; for this was something the Staff knew I needed to do and I thank them. So I went back home with my parents and family. My oldest twin brothers and my oldest sister where married now and wasn't living at home and there were just a few of us left in the home and things weren't as stressful for my parents.

At the age of 18, I had been out of the hospital 2 or 3 months and I had gotten a job in communications installing Cable television transmission lines. I had to get a job, because I didn't want to stay in the house all the time and I wanted an income to buy things again on my own and also wanted to feel more responsible; for I was beginning not to be dependant upon my parents. I was beginning to read the Bible again and go back to church and had a better understanding of my life, somewhat. This company was laying the cable in front of my parent's home one day and I thought to my self this; "What a great chance to get a job. God has given me a Job and has sent it to my front door." So, this was an opportunity for me to ask for a job and I asked them and they did hire me as a crew helper.

I thought at the time, I was much stronger now than I was a year ago and was able to handle a job for sure. My perception of life was a little bit clearer and I was beginning to sense and feel things better.

Like I said before I had joined back with the girlfriend that I once knew from high school. We became very close and she was to me the only person I could trust in the whole world, besides my parents at this time. After I had worked on this job for sometime, I was making good money and doing somewhat better. I wasn't using much, but things got worse for my life later.

I know the job didn't lead me back to my horrors over again for it was because, I had anger and resentment still in my heart. I still hid the anger and resentments deep within me and they still flared like a furnace. I began to get much more crafty at suppressing these things within the deep closets of my heart and I was still without understanding of life on its terms. I noticed every day I would show up on the job site most everyone that I worked with was using drugs or was near drunk from the night before. Occasionally one of the older men, which was my foreman, would make remarks to me and tempt me as we would eat lunch together by saying things like this, "Me and your girlfriend had a good time last night." And another older man, which I will call my friend for now, would say this to the other man, "Want you shut up and leave him alone. You need to quit messing with him like that." You know, this friend that stood up for me that day was right, that man should had not messed with me like that. When this man said this to me, I didn't know what to say or do. I wanted to take my knife I had at the time and stick it deep into his eye or into his throat, no kidding. But I didn't want to kill him, I began to want to make him suffer greatly somehow. I didn't know why is this world someone that I thought was a friend to me would try to tear my heart out. Guess What? I started to get angry and hold resentments in my heart against this man greatly.

I didn't know if it was the truth or not what he had said to me, but maybe it was the truth and all of the doors of my heart started to open again and then I held murder in my heart. I started using drugs and drinking again with my co-workers heavy. I wanted this job because of the training and income it was providing for me and I would think this, "No one knows my past and I'm much better at controlling the drugs and alcohol and because they do them too, maybe I can fit into their life, but then things began to get hot again. I and one of my co-workers became friends and we would get blasted after work every day. He wasn't from around my parts of the country and I would get us the drugs.

Later, my friend just disappeared from the job site and I ask the foreman on the job site, where he was and then my Forman told me, *"He killed himself by jumping off a bridge near his home last week."* This younger boy that committed suicide and the foreman that said those things earlier to me, were cousins. This hurt me in my heart and later, I quit this job.

I do remember another man in particular during this same time. I was driving around in town and I was drinking and smoking pot during this day; for I wasn't working at this time. I saw a man cross the street and he waved me down like he knew me. So, I turned around and drove to where he was standing and as I rolled my drivers window down and asked this man if he needed something he said, "Would you please give me a ride to my room." At first, I didn't know if I should trust this man or not, but the fear left me as I looked into his eyes and seen the desperation and somewhat like tears.

Nevertheless I chose to carry him to his room which wasn't but 1 mile from where we had met. As we where there at his room which was a small 1 room at a motel there in town, He said "Boy want you come in for just a minute and we will talk. I need someone to help me and to talk to me". I began not to have any fear whatsoever from this man.

It was if God had sent a messenger to me to tell me something, but I will say this man was fearful to look upon when I first looked at him. He was I believe to be in his 40 years of age, had shoulder graying black hair, as if it had not been groomed, a beard and mustache also graying, his eyes where light blue, like the sky and watery and his clothes were somewhat dirty and I could smell alcohol from him strongly. I agreed to walk in with him to his room for a moment and I noticed as we started to enter his room, the door was already opened about a 1/4 the way and I asked him, "Do you think someone is in there?" and he said looking at me with a grin, "Why would there be? If their is someone in there, it would be bad for them, for there is nothing but bad things in this room, son." And we laughed somewhat. I entered the room very slowly with him and as he walked in, he laid on the bed as if he was exhausted and began to cry softly. I look around in this room and there was nothing but a bed, a nightstand and it was filled with empty liquor bottles and mason jars. I remember seeing, no food or any such things in this room, just liquor bottles and mason jars. There were liquor bottles everywhere that I looked and the room was cluttered and smelled like a brewery. This man was a serious alcoholic and I thought to myself, "He ought to be dead, if he drank all that liquor." So, I pretended not to think much of it and as he was sitting up in bed and I was still standing, because there wasn't a chair to sit in, we began to talk about things. I did finally ask him if he had drunk all that liquor and he said to me, "I sure did and I'm not proud of it. I'm dying son and its just time against me now. Son don't you ever start drinking like I drink, unless you want to die." I will never forget the words that came out of that man's hurting heart as he said this to me.

After that day, I remember going over and checking on him and he looked somewhat better. He had shaved somewhat and had cleaned up and I hardly recognized him, but he was drunk of course and I remember saying," where are you going? You look good!".

Then he asked me to take him across town to pick up some clothes that someone had for him and to eat supper with this person. So we left his room and I took him to this house and I set in the car for about 30 minutes drinking my beer. I insisted on staying in my vehicle and then I took him back to his little cluttered room. I noticed he had a large container of a clear liquid as he came from this house and I ask him, "What's that?" He said to me as he began to cry and then laugh at the same time, "It's my life boy!" And he began to softly cry somewhat and then he said again, "No really its moonshine." and laughed. He had a whole gallon of boot legged liquor. As we got back to the room he started to drink that like a thirsty camel and he drank almost ¼ of that gallon, before he came up for air. He ask me if I wanted some and he handed it to me and I smelled of it and refused to drink it and he laughed as if he knew I wasn't going to drink it. I can still smell that awful smell just thinking about it. I did drink this crap later in life, which I will share later. It was the awfulness mess I had ever smelled in my life and It smelled like a rotten dead possum. Only a country boy would know what that smells like and it isn't too pleasant. We began to laugh and he would drink that moonshine and I would be drinking my beer. That man's eyes began to grow as he felt that I was a friend to him.

So, I left afterwards and we had built a friendship that didn't last long, maybe 3 weeks. I would go to his room about twice a week, to check on him to see if he needed anything. One day I went to check on him and I noticed there was a 1qt mason jar sitting on his table with just a small amount of clear liquid left in the bottom. He was passed out on his stomach in bed, but his door would always be ¼ the way opened, as if he was expecting someone to show up there. I picked the jar up and smelled of it, but to my surprise it was not moonshine, it was rubbing alcohol. I tried to wake my friend and he finally mumbled some words and he looked up at me from his bed as if he had been crying and said, "Son, Please go Home!"

I left out the room concerned about his welfare, but I felt he didn't want my help or even to talk to me at this time.

A couple days later, I never got the chance to see this man again. He was found in an old Coca-Cola van body near his room, *dead and frozen from alcohol poisoning*. This incident hurt me deep within my heart again and I began to blame myself and God for not helping him.

After the death of this man, I began to drink and to use drugs again heavy. But, today I know why this man was sent to me; for in his desperate time of life, he was crying out for help. I truly believe today, that when he seen me, he thought that he had the chance at helping someone to stop using and he had the chance, at maybe helping someone before it was too late and by doing something good like this, he could then say within himself, he did something good in life and would feel inside his heart, good about that. He knew he was dying from using and he didn't want me to die like that. God did send this man to my life and everything he said to me during this time, I still remember. The last words he said to me quickens my spirit today. "Son, Please go Home!" That was the last words his spirit spoke to me. God wanted me to go home and the home was God. Truly, I really believe this today, but at the time when I had met this man, I was still without understanding and chances, choices, and changes where compounding my anger and resentments in my little heart. Later in life, I learned he was related to me by marriage, but he and I didn't know this at the time when we met; for I found it out later when one of my family members mentioned his name after his death. I also want to mentioned that his brother also recently died from alcoholism.

At the age of 19, I was out of control again and my using was worst than before times. My friend the following writings will somewhat explain why I went from worse, to much more worse during this time of my life. I had been clean for over a year, but now, things went worse than the beginning. In the Holy Book of Luke, chapter11, verses 21-26 it is written, *"When a strong man armed keepeth his palace, his goods are in peace: But when a stronger than he shall come upon him, and overcome him, he taketh from him all his armour wherein he trusted, and divided his spoils. He that is not with me is against me: and he that gathered not with me scattered. When the unclean spirit is gone out of a man, he walketh through dry places, seeking rest; and finding none, he saith, I will return unto my house whence I came out. And when he cometh, he findeth it swept and garnished. Then goeth he, and taketh to him seven other spirits more wicked than himself; and they enter in, and dwell there: and the last state of that man is worse than the first."*

I do remember having some troubles with my girlfriend. Her parents didn't want their daughter around me and she was not wanting to see me anymore and I had no reason whatsoever, why they felt this way towards me. I later found out from my girlfriend, that the matter was because of an abortion, which I will share more later. I thought to myself, I will just go over to their home and find out about this matter, but first I needed to get high and drunk. I took my car and lost control of it in their front yard and uprooted several of Pine trees that were planted beside there drive. I lost control of my tongue and called those people everything I could think of at the time. They called the Law to me and they arrested me and threw my butt into jail.

Now, when I was in jail, I was so angry that I was screaming from the top of my voice to start a fight, so that, maybe an officer would just shoot me, no kidding.

I do remember as I was angry and out of control, a State Trooper came into the area where I was at and stood there with a stern eye, just looking at me. I started yelling at him, as if he had killed my child and went toward him through the bars and he looked at me with a stern eye and "SLAP", yes, he slapped the crap right out of my mouth. He told me to calm down or something worse was going to happen. At the time I didn't care if he would had shot me, but I guess the "SLAP" to my right cheek calmed me down.

As I calmed down and looked around and seen the jail bars, I knew there was nothing that I could do for this matter in the shape I was in. I began to cry within myself and held all this anger in my heart and fell asleep in the jail cell. I will say, The Trooper did only what he had to do, because I was so hysterical over this matter and I wanted to just die. He didn't know my past and he didn't know my problems which led me to this anger at this time or did he? But, the Power of Authority that he had been given, he used it to the best of his ability and controlled it to try to calm me down and I respected it at the time.

So the next morning, I felt so humiliated and had come to my senses somewhat and thought I probably made a Jack Ass out of myself last night and I wanted to apologize to all that were in the jail area, especially the State Trooper. I ask the officers that were releasing me where the State Trooper was and they said, they didn't no a State Trooper was even there.

As I left the jail walking, for the law had impounded my vehicle at a local garage, my right molar tooth was in agony and it felt loose, like it was trying to come out of socket, no kidding. As I was walking down the street, holding my right jaw, I knew I had to walk right by a Dentist office there in town and said to myself, "I wonder if the dentist could pull this tooth and let me pay him later." I'm telling you, it was hurting very badly at this time.

So I went into this dentist office and waited, until they called me to the dentist room and as the dentist was pulling my tooth, I was thinking this, "Please let him pull it before he finds out I don't have any money to pay him" After he had pulled my tooth, I told him that I didn't have any money and I would be back to pay him and to my surprise he said, "Son, just pay me when you can." and I did pay him later. So I walk to the garage and the owner to my surprise, did the same for me and I did paid him later. It was if everybody knew what I had been through that night and knew I didn't have any money, but wanted to help me. Even the State Trooper when he slapped me wanted to help me, but

I just didn't understand. Oh Yes! I still don't know how I got out of a DWI that night, because I did break the law by drinking and driving and wrecking a vehicle. I guess it was the "SLAP" on my right cheek or maybe the Trooper could had been an Angel, but who ever he was, I thank him for the "SLAP" upon my face, no kidding.

So, after I got my battered vehicle out of the garage, I drove home to my parents and thought on this matter for awhile and stopped seeing my girlfriend for a while. I was still without understanding and I continued to drink heavy and do drugs and held all these things in my heart and didn't share these matters with anyone.

Later, soon after that incident, I remembered riding a nearby town with a friend I had just met and we were drinking and had been snorting and smoking pot that day. I left the town because I knew the town coppers were on the prowl and I didn't want to get caught drinking and driving, so I headed to the country. I traveled down a familiar road and came to an intersection and began to laugh and feel the power of the large car I was driving, it was an old 1972 Ford Ltd Brougham, the same vehicle that I had wreck earlier. It had a powerful motor under the hood and my friend wanted to feel the power of this car, so I let him feel it.

I put my foot heavy upon the gas pedal and then the vehicle began to sling around in circles, smoking the tires and making noise and we were laughing and enjoying the ride.

As I stopped and headed back toward the town, I noticed there was a vehicle flying up on my rear, like a speeding bullet. As I reached the town limit it happened, the blue light came on and I pulled over to a parking lot and this State Trooper pulled over toward me and blocked me in where I couldn't move. He came forth out of his vehicle like his pants were on fire and I was thinking, "I hope it isn't that Trooper I had met earlier in my life." He came to my window and said, "Boy! Get out!" I got out and he said again," What do you think you are doing, Boy!? Get into my passenger's seat of my vehicle, Now!" So, I got into his vehicle and we left faster than a speeding bullet right straight to jail and I had no get out of jail free card this time. I didn't say a word to him as we headed to jail except, "May I smoke a cigarette?" and his answer was, "No!" I began to sense I had no control over this matter and what the Trooper had told me in the past was coming true. I was charged and received *my first DWI at the age of 19 and spent 24hrs in jail.* I went to court over this matter and received another 48hours in the county jail and had lost my driving privilege for 1 year. I later found out, the State Trooper that had arrested me, lived in the house across from where I was drawing donuts with my vehicle.

Later my girlfriend and I was seeing each other again behind her parents backs and became pregnant. I thought at this time, "My God! This isn't a good time to be pregnant, especially with no drivers license." and then we moved into my parents home for awhile and there is a lot more to this matter that is not appropriate to mention for now. She was about 3 months pregnant with my child and I had no drivers license and my parents took it upon them to help care for her and myself at this time. My brother, whom has recently died, helped me get a job where he was working, which was a printing company. I took the job in the printing business as a machine operator helper; when I would show up for work.

I was given a driving privilege to drive to work and home only and I was caught several times driving with licenses revoked. I lost my diving privilege for another two years.

Later, she and I got married at a Church with a private wedding and moved to a mobile home of one of my cousin's that was for rent. We stayed there for awhile, until I became out of control again. I believe thinking of this may had set it off. You see, I and my wife had become pregnant, before we had this child that was born at this time, while we were just dating. We made a decision upon our self to have an *abortion on our on.* I also knew that she had another abortion before this particular one that I had mentioned before without my consent and that was some of the angry and resentment I had toward her and her family. I was thinking night and day about this matter and what they had done to me and I was going to pay them back, but of course I was without any understanding of life at this time. I remember this time very well and I thought if any one kills my child, it will be me, no kidding, I really thought this. As we headed to the Capital City to commit this murder I remember coming to an intersection in the middle of the city where we were going to have this abortion and there seem as if a large number of cars came up on me from the rear, all of a sudden. It was if they were trying to box me in where I couldn't move.

I couldn't turn into any other lane, because of the on coming traffic and I looked up and seen a sign that read, No U- Turn. I looked out of my side mirror and seen a very tall man about 6 car lengths behind me getting out of his car, standing beside the drivers door half opened. I heard him yell out something and it seemed as if he was looking straight into my eyes. I rolled my drivers window down and leaned my left ear to the window as I was watching him in my side mirror, but I still could not understand what he was saying. So, I put the car in park and slowly open the door with just my left foot on the pavement and he yelled at me, as if he was extremely mad at me and said," You can't do that!" He yelled this several times and then he slowly enter his vehicle.

But today, I know God was trying to intervene in my life from me committing this murder of this unborn child. But at that time, I thought nothing of it and closed the door and went my way. I thought the man wanted to cause trouble, because I was in a No-U turn lane and I just avoided the matter. So, as I was determined to commit this murder, I got lost in the city and there was a city cop sitting at a nearby store. I got out of my vehicle and asked him, "where is this abortion clinic?" He looked at me and his head and mouth dropped, but didn't say a word for a moment and then he looked up at me from his driver's seat and said, *"Follow me."* He said nothing else and led us to the slaughter house, which wasn't but a few blocks away from where the man was yelling at me. Again today, I know what those words were meant for me then at that moment, "You can't do that!" and "Follow Me." God was trying again to intervene in my life to keep me from committing this awful sin of murder. God was trying to tell me not to commit this murder and to follow his principle, *"Thou Shall Not Commit Murder"*, but I thought nothing about this matter at the time and we reached the clinic and the murder took place. My girlfriend came out crying and I began to cry like a baby. My friend, we were not crying for joy, we were crying because we knew it wasn't right and we had just killed a child, willingly. I felt inside my heart at that moment, as if I was a dead man for sure and now, I had put this lady in the same position. Later, both my life and her life began to grow from worse to the worst at this time in our relationship. There were a lot of suffering and pains from this relationship that I can't mention in words, but I will say all the sufferings were of self will and there wasn't no joy in it. I now know today that the relationship we had was not built on Love; for it was built on Lust and Self Will pleasures. Oh yes! May I please, share with you a few things what I know today about Lusting and Loving? I will say this first, I believe every man has a wife and every woman has a husband. God doesn't bring forth a man without a wife and vice versa. I thought during my younger days I loved girls, but looking back on the things, I know that the only thing I loved was the lust for them.

All the relationships I had gone through before I met my Godly Gift, which is my wife today, was lust and not love; for I had not the understanding of love at this time. I had one thing on my mind and I don't have to say anything else, but I will say it was all for self will pleasures. I know that sounds ugly, but it is the truth and I know today any action out of self will, is ugly.

I believe if I was walking in God's Will back in my youth, I would had not suffered the consequences of lust and then lust, after it had conceived, sin and after sin, death. Before I go any further, let me please share a principle from God's Word on this matter. In the Book of James , Chapter 1, verses 12-16, *"Blessed in the man that endureth temptation: for when he is tried, he shall receive the crown of life, which the Lord hath promised to them that love him. Let no man say when he is tempted, I am tempted of God: for God cannot be tempted with evil, neither tempteth he any man: But every man is tempted, when he is drawn away of his own lust, and enticed. Then when lust hath conceived, it bringeth forth sin: and sin, when it is finished, bringeth forth death. Do not err, my beloved brethren."*

Today I do know that the murders (Abortions) were the consequences of my lust and self will pleasures and after lust had manifested into sin, then sin brought forth death. I now know the difference between Love and Lust today and it did cost innocent blood for me to understand it. God did forgive me at the spare of my breath for this murder and I will share that in just a moment. God has laid something heavy on my heart concerning Abortions and I must share this with you.

First I will tell you I am Pro Life and not Pro Death. I love and cherish all things under heaven which God has made for us as a testimony of him.

In the Book of Genesis 1:26-27, *"And God said, Let us make man in our image, after our likeness: and let them have dominion over the f ish of the sea, and over the fowl of the air, and over the cattle, and over all the earth, and over every creeping thing that creepeth upon the earth. So God created man in his own image, in the image of God created he him; male and female created he them."* God created man in his Image, as a spirit and soul and blood, which contains Life.

God is a Spirit and I believe every embryo deserves to live, so that they too get the chance and live the Will of God and sense and grow in God's Loving Grace, so that they too can know our Creator and Spiritual Father more closely with understanding. God is the Creator of life, the Giver of life and the Taker of life. I believe when an Abortion takes place in any life, the man that commits the abortion, is held responsible in God's eyes of Murder. The reason I believe this is, God creates our spirit and it can't die: for he made us into his image. Will God destroy himself?

I believe when we commit an Abortion, we are in our self will and are saying to God, "I don't want this life and I'm going to destroy it", but remember, the blood cries out and the spirit can not die. What God creates doesn't go back to him void and when he creates a life or let's say a spirit and the blood, then it will not go back to him void; for that spirit will live. But if we snuff the life out of an unborn child then does it go back to God Void, without anything? I don't think so. Yes, I believe an unborn child has a spirit and contains the blood of Life , no matter how long the pregnancy is and I believe that if you commit murder in any way by snuffing out the life from an unborn child, then that spirit wonders to another pregnancy. I believe that the body (the blood) is destroyed during an abortion, but the void spirit wonders off to find another body, but you will not know it or where it goes or who it grows to be; for it is like a wind.

The spirit that God creates will live and grow and have the chance to know his Amazing Grace here on earth and have a chance at Eternal Life. Now I'm only talking unborn children, Infants and children; for they have not yet experienced the Love and Grace of God. A man that has had the chance of Life here on earth is a different topic, so please don't get lost in what the point is.

When I committed the awful murder (Abortion), I honestly believe the spirit of that child went forward to another pregnancy across the earth and It is Alive and well today somewhere, but I am not the father. I have not begotten it and it doesn't know me and I don't know it. My blood (life) isn't in it, because I destroy its body and blood (life). Nothing goes back to God Void and this spirit will grow up in the flesh and learn of the Great I AM, The God of The Living, and Creator of Life in another place on this earth. But, I want get a chance to see it grow up in God's Loving Grace, because I wasn't worthy of bringing a life into this world.

Today, I think it is Ironic that my wife today is barren and we can't have children, but If God finds us worthy, I will be responsible for another life. I know today a life is worth more than the universe and God holds us all responsible for its care; for all life is Gods and it is given to us as a blessing and gift. I believe as soon as the embryo made blood, it had life and I had no right to snuff it out, because life is in the blood and the blood is alive. It is written in the Holy Book of Genesis 4, Adam the first man and Eve the first women had two children and their names were Cain and Abel. As time passed both brought an offering to God, Cain brought fruit from the ground and Abel brought forth an offering of his flock and the fat from it, but God didn't respect Cain's offering and I wonder why? I would think there was no blood in it and God is Life.

As time passed Cain and Abel where talking in a field and Cain rose up against Abel and slew him. God said unto Cain, Where is Abel thy brother? And Cain said to God, I know not: Am I my brother's keeper? And God said to Cain, What hast thou done? The voice of thy brother's blood crieth unto me from the ground. Remember, God knows when man snuffs life out of the blood; for the blood cries out to him and there are consequences, if we don't honestly go to God and seek his forgiveness for shedding his blood.

Now, after we had married(my first wife) and we had the child, she was a very healthy little baby girl and I loved this child and was proud of her, but I missed the opportunity to be with her for a long time. I would leave the mother and child at home and go out and get blasted every weekend. I believe that I remember the reason I couldn't bear staying there in that home, with this child and mother. It wasn't because I didn't care for this child or the mother, it was because of this:

We were home one day at this time and my wife was in the bedroom and the child was in the bassinet in the living room and I was near the bassinet watching television. I thought I heard the child say something, but I knew she is too young to be talking at 3 months of age. But, I got up from the sofa anyway and slowly walked over to her and the child looked as if she was asleep. I got a little bit closer, inches from the child's face, and what happened next put a fear in me that I had never experienced before. I saw as if that child opened her eyes wide and looked straight at me in my eyes and spoke with a stern child's voice and said, *"Am I worth it!?"* It was if I was dead. I couldn't say a word. I ran out of that house into the back yard, as if I just had seen the Exorcist and yelled, "God please forgive me!" I knew at that moment deep within my heart that I had done something against God and God only and this would for ever haunt my heart.

I began to completely go out of control with my drugging and drinking and would not tell anyone this matter, because I knew they would think I was crazy and they would not had believed me, anyway. I began to stay away from home and leave my wife at this time and daughter to their self. I just could not bear looking into a child's eyes again for a long time and was literally scared to. We tried to make the marriage work, but it just wasn't working. We try to change our environment and had bought a Mobile home below my parents from a minister of the gospel of Christ. We lived there for just a week or so and then later divorced. We divorced after 6 months of marriage, due to my heavy drinking, cocaine use and self will pleasures. My life was clean and my temple when I first got out of the hospital, but Satan came back and brought forth 7 more devils even much stronger than I.

Yes, I will take the blame for the problems, even though, some could take responsibility for much of the problems, I will take it all, because I think this; if I wasn't doing drugs and drinking and living self will pleasures and had put God in my life first, I properly would have been accepted much better or would I? The family of this lady and the mother of my child was trying everything under heaven to keep this child from seeing me.

At the time, remembering the abortion, this child meant my life to me and it was killing me inside thinking on the matter, *"Am I Worth It"*. This was the beginning again of more angry and more resentments raging deep within my heart and I started to go into, major depression. This family would try anything to put me in jail or cause me to get angry and out of control and do something I should not do.

I do remember several occasions, the mistress of this family would see me on the streets and stop, look at me, until I seen her and then she would stick up her middle finger at me as if she was taunting me.

I will share with you in these writings about *God's Finger of Hope* later, but I will tell you, this finger she would hold up, wasn't a finger of Hope, it meant to destroy me. But, somehow I always took it out on myself in drinking and using drugs. I knew what the finger was all about and it wasn't what you think. I will share with you, about a good finger pointing to me from God in my life later in the writings, but this finger pointing, had no profit for me, except to destroy me. This lady wanted me to do something bad, so that I would be found as a bad person or worse and go to jail, but for some reason, I never fell for that gesture toward me and always tried to look away. Even at the times, I knew she had the understanding that I was not going to take a gun and go to their house and kill all of them at one time, but I will say, I did think on that matter. That my friend, became a course straight to the Big Hole for me and I was still without understanding of these matters. I was walking the streets as a full blown alcoholic and drug addict again.

During this time, my parents and that child were the only hope that I thought I had. I had lost my job and could not keep a job, because of drinking and drugging all night. I also began to go back into major depression. I would manage to work a couple of trade jobs, like painting, carpentry, sheetrock and anything that I could do. Most of these jobs I would get, I could use on the job at least smoke pot, snort some lines or pop some pills and didn't require drug testing. No matter who tried to help me or where I was at this time, the anger and resentments were in my heart and times got worse and worse and all I could think about was my child and what life had thrown at me. It was a fire burning deep in my heart and I was about to do something about it. I was then and I am still a man, that never wants to hurt anyone and if I have, it wasn't because I did it willingly. In my past life, I always hurt myself before hurting anyone else out of self will angry. I always turned to drugs and alcohol to numb me from my pains. As this progressed, I made a mistake and went to the mother of my child's home and she was living also with her parents.

I knocked on the door and she seen me. I said, "All I want is to see is my daughter". She began to laugh at me and I reached to open the screen door, I don't know for clarity and really don't care, I think I put my hand accidentally though the screen of the porch door, a tear 3 inches long, maybe 4 inches at the most. I was not trying to hurt no one.

I was reaching and begging for her to hold up this child for me to just glance at her and for her to see me, but the mother of my child, threatened me and said, "I will call the law if you don't leave." and then she started to laughed at me and went back into the house.

At this moment, I felt a rejection that destroyed me inside. Someone who I thought loved me, had turned against me. I held down my head and began to cry within myself and left her and didn't want to cause any trouble at all. Later the next day or so, I had a summoned to court. I was being charge for tearing down a complete screen door. I promise, that never happened, if it happened someone else did it. But today, I know who did it and am very thankful of his help. The wind maybe had blown it down or did God do it to help me at the time? I will say today this with *gratitude*, Thank you for helping me.

So, I went to court and they put a restraining order on me from their premises, but it was not the restraining order that hurt me. While we were in court, this family's lawyer was saying all but good things about me to the judge and all I could do was cry and listen as they were spilling their bellies out to the judge. I didn't think I was as bad as this lawyer was speaking me to be and it hurt me within very badly and I was hoping the judge wouldn't believe this crap coming from this lawyers trap. I thought this; "If, he did believe all this crap this lawyer was saying about me, this Judge would order me to a firing squad, immediately!" I had no lawyer and really at the time, I just didn't think that I needed one and If I thought that I needed one, I couldn't had afforded one.

My family insisted to help, but I refused their help on this matter and left it to the Judge; for I had told them, "Let God handle this matter the way he needs to handle it and every thing will be fine." They made me feel worthless and hurt me very bad and I started to understand somewhat at that moment what this family's intent was and it was to try to destroy me. I truly believe that they didn't care if I would just die and fall off the earth surface and never be heard from again. But today I know their intent and the reason behind their intents. They just wanted me out of their daughter's life and my life didn't matter much to them. They were willing to keep me away from their family at any cost, even my life. I can't say with confidence that their intent was to destroy me, but it wasn't to bring hope to me.

Now, as this lawyer was spilling his belly out, this Judge said, "I've heard enough. There is something more to this matter, than I know." He looked at me and said with a calm voice, "Son you need some help. I'm ordering you to an Alcohol and Drug Rehabilitation Center and also 2 years probation and the man to your right, will help you." KNOCK, KNOCK", someone is knocking again. And the Judge was honest that day, there was more to this matter than he knew and he wanted the truth, but I was unable to speak and set over to his left, in a jury chair waiting my next order. I will also mention this, there was a beautiful young lady sitting there two chairs to my left where I was sitting, I believe making notes for a paper and I had sit beside her as the bailiff pointed to where I should sit. I was very upset and couldn't help my self from crying. This Lady did look over at me, as if she didn't want no one to see her talking to me and said with a very soft, calm voice, "Its going to be ok, just be strong." Those words from this lady strengthened me that day and I got the courage up and held my head up and was ready to go. I don't know who she was, but I think she must had been an Angel sent from God to help me that day and I will never forget her.

So a few days later, I had my order sent to me from my probation officer for 45 days in a state funded rehabilitation center and *off I go to an Institution again at the age of 19*. Looking back at what the judge said and ordered for me to do, I realized he wanted to help me. He didn't care at the time what people were saying about me; for he knew something more than they did in his heart. All I needed at the time was help and not discouragement. I was so lost again and I needed some direction. Suicide and Worse were on top of my list to do at this early time of my Life. Today, I say to this Judge, "Thank You for helping me when I couldn't help myself." If I could see him today, I would hug him and kiss him upon his cheek. He also put me on probation, because I believe he knew in his heart that I needed some guidance in my life. So I went to the rehab center and there I started my first spiritual awakening. They did have church services and I started to read the Bible for the first time in 10 years that I remembered. I do remember a young man that was there for drugs, enticed me to do drugs while I was there in rehab and It was black beauties (speed) and pot. We would sneak and smoke a joint once and awhile, no kidding. They never drug tested me in this rehab and we knew this, actually looking back in all my rehab visits, they didn't drug test me, except when I was committed in. I was trying to do good while at this rehab, but all I wanted to do was get better and see my child and had to accept the fact that I wasn't going to see my child when I got out.

When I was released from this rehab center, I went back and stayed with my parents. I also was on probation and my probation officer was a good friend to me. He would be there in a flash if he knew I really needed him. He was more like a big brother than a probation officer and today we are still good friends, even though he knows the things I have done, he is always there to listen.

Today I thank God, and That Judge, for ordering me to the Rehabilitation Center and the two years probation. Today I know this with confidence, If it wasn't for the order, I probably would have never met this man and you may not be reading these writings now. I thank you both, God my Father and the Judge my friend for helping me when I couldn't even help myself during this terrible time of my life.

As time passed on now at the age of 20, I still continually to use drugs and drink, but not as heavy and too was living still by my self will understanding and was finding ways of hiding my using much better. My Uncle, one of my father's older brothers gave me a job after I got out of Rehab. He didn't have to, but he knew I was in need and my probation officer insisted that I went back to work. My uncle moved me near him in the Capital City, 35 miles away from my parents to a motel and paid me to help him in the Drywall Business he had. My uncle was well respected and known for his word and business here in the capital city and was a very busy man. My uncle was the first from my family to take me under his wings to help me. My probation officer at this time would carry me there on Monday mornings and I would stay in that motel day after day. I would go to my parents and wash my clothes once in awhile, and that was all I did for nearly 1 year.

My Uncle was a workaholic and he must have thought that working me from when the rooster crowed, until the wee hours of the night would tire me, where I didn't want to drink or do drugs. I wasn't doing many drugs at this time, but I was still sneaking and hiding on his job smoking pot and drinking heavy at night in the motel. I hid my using from my probation officer and my uncle for months very crafty, until one morning after a walk in the capital city that night, my uncle with saddened eyes looked over at me as we where going to a job site in his vehicle and said, "Son, what did you do, get drunk last night?". He must have smelled the liquor on my body from going out to some bars that evening and I will never forget that evening and the following weeks either.

Please let me share this with you. I had come to my motel room one evening after work, my uncle dropped me off. After my uncle would dropped me off from work, I would sneak across the highway and get wine or beer and set and drink and smoke alone in my room. One evening I heard some voices outside of my door and I looked out my window and their stood two young boys standing and looking at my door and talking to each other. These two boys were about 4-6 years younger than I was at the time. So I was very curious and open my door and ask them, "Are you looking for someone" and the oldest said," this is my little brother and we stay over there in the woods and we where just trying to find something" and again I had to ask , "What are you looking for? Maybe I can help you find it." and the older boy said, "We where just looking for some money. Sometimes people will drop money and we find it." I didn't know what to think at this time, when they told me they were staying in the woods and were looking for money, but I was thinking to myself, to be sure these boys aren't homeless. So I said to these boys, "Where did you say you stayed at?" and about that same time a old pick up truck pulls into the motel parking lot with two other boys and they pulled right to my door. They get out and ask the two boys that where standing with me this, "Did you ask him yet?" I knew at this moment those two younger boys were sent from these older boys to ask me for money and then the older boy that got out of the drivers seat said to me this; "These are my younger brothers and that is my other brother in the truck and we stay over in the woods and seen you the other day and thought maybe you could help us." And then I said to them," What do you need, Money? and he said, "Yes sir! And we will pay it back to you later". Again I didn't know what to believe at this time, so this is what I did. I gave them 10 dollars and ask them this, "Why are you staying in the woods? Do you have a house over there? Then the older boy which was about 18 years of age said, "No, Sir. We live in my truck behind those trees over there. We don't have a home and we cant talk about it right now, we got to go. Come on boys!"

About 1 hour later, they pull up to my door again and tooted their horn to my surprise. I opened the door and it was getting somewhat very cold outside, and they all got out and huddled at my doorway and the older boy said, "Can my little brothers stay with you tonight, because its going to get cold and I don't want them out here to get sick." Man, I felt liked I had been shot in the heart by a sniper. I thought about just telling them to get lost, but for some reason I said, "Yes. it will be ok, but they need to be gone early before I go to work."

So, we agreed and they where left to my care. I asked them if they had eating and they said, "No." I had some food in the room that I was snacking on during the week and they ate it all in about 10 minutes. We were there not saying much, but watching TV. The younger boy fell asleep on my bed and I didn't think much of the matter, except I was helping the boys through the night, out of the cold for it was very cold this night. Later about the time I was figuring out where I was going to sleep that night, the other boy crawls in my bed also and I started to feel a compassion for them, then I knew the bed wasn't my choice. As I was about to get comfortable into my chair the truck pulls up again and they knocked on my door and I let them in. To my surprised the older boy had a bottle of whiskey that had not been opened and he said, "We thought we would come over and stay with you too, but I brought us something that I know you like." He was right and myself and the older boy drank that bottle and then I said,

"Are you able to drive?" And he said "yes! I've been driving since I was 6." and we laughed. So I said "Do you know where any bars are?" and to my surprised he knew not only where a bar was, but the owner was his best friend, is what he told me.

So, me and this older boy and his younger brother got into this old beat up, rusty truck and with down town at 11:30pm that evening, drunk. We went straight to the bar and we drank and shot pool until about 2:30am that morning and I paid the bill and was broke; for that was my eating money for the week. So we left and headed to the motel and I knew I had to go to work and get them boys out of my bed and get some sleep. When we got to the motel room the older boy jump into my bed with the other two boys and fell asleep. The other boy was in my chair and I just fell asleep on the floor. About 5:30am these boys were up and they left my room in a hurry. I knew it was 5:30am, because of my watch ticking in my ear as I laid on the floor. I got up and watched them pull away from the motel and then I crawled into my bed and slept for about 30 minutes. Then when I began to sleep, I heard a horn and a hard knock on my door; for it was my uncle ready to go to work. I got up out of bed and went to his vehicle and got into it and we left, but not far. That's when he knew I was drunk and carried me back to my room for the day.

That evening the boys were back and I wasn't ready too play anymore. I told them to go back to the woods and die there to never come back around me again. The reason I suddenly felt this way is because my uncle told me that there were boys robbing people around that area. He told me this as he was carrying me back to my room that day. I had told him I had been up with some friends late, trying to make an excuses for being drunk that is. Then he ask, "What friends? What friends would be there with you, this far from home? Who did you let stay with you last night?" And I told him it was a homeless family and he laughed and then he told me about this group of young boys robbing people and that they may be linked to the robberies. At that time I knew there intent was to keep a check on me, until I got some money and rob me or worse, but thank God, my uncle was there for me at this time and gave me a little understanding of the matter.

I guess the reason I'm writing this is to let you know, if you are not in the spirit or sensing things in it's true perspective, then you could be in danger. Satan will use anyone that allows them to use them for his unrighteous work and that work is to destroy you. I never seen these boys again after I got angry with them and told them to get lost. They had seen me at my worse that day and maybe I scared them away, because the way I got angry with them, showed them and myself that I didn't care if I died or they died. I truly believe today these boys where trying to rob me or worse and thought it was a joy ride for them at the time. I became a little defensive while I stayed at that room after this incident and I stayed on my guard, watching for the enemy.

As time passed, I worked with my uncle for almost 8 months, until I would lie up in the motel drunk or passed out. I do remember on several occasions that I would not answer the knock from him in the morning for being so passed out and would make excuses the next morning. That job ended, not because my uncle gave up on me and fired me, it ended because, I didn't want my uncle to see me at my worse and I chose to end the job and to go back home. My uncle never did fire me or get angry with me; for he just let me freely go and I believe he must have thought he had not helped me. I always looked up at my uncle as a close friend and I loved him very much. *My uncle dies from Cancer a couple years later.* That was a blow to me again and I thought for a long time, that I was the blame for hurting him. He was my father's brother and he went out the way to help me and all I did for him was burden him. He did not have to help me during this time of my life, but he loved me and didn't want to see me suffering. He was like a father away from home to me and I never said, Thank You to his face. I took this death very bad and began to seek psychiatry again and was put on drugs to help cope with this death. I did go to his funeral and as I was looking into the casket, I was in disbelief that the body I was looking at, was my uncle.

He looked as if he was a 100 years of age, white snow hair, nearly bald and didn't weigh nothing from the treatments of cancer; for he was only 54 at the time. I thought for a long time that it wasn't him and someone was playing a joke on me, but reality hit me later, as I would need him and he wasn't there. Later in life, my earthly father was given a few things from my uncles widowed wife and my father gave me something. It's ironic that I'm wearing it today as I'm writing these words, no kidding. It is an olive green corduroy field coat and I still today, wear it for the testimony of him; for he was good to me.

After a few months had past after leaving my uncles job, I tried to stop using on my own and had quit taking the psychiatry drugs. I began to go to church and gave myself to the best I understood to God and was converted. My parents and church members still today, remember that day when I surrendered my Life to God and Jesus Christ and they still say today when I would see one of them, "You looked as if you were floating and your face was as bright as a light." God did save me from this misery and horror at this time, but I was still without understanding of life.

God was taking this used and abused little child back unto his Loving Arms and it was wonderful and I was beginning to sense life again as a new born child. During this time of my Life, I was beginning to really seek God for all that I could get to understand life as a child again. I didn't want to live the way I had been living in my past childhood and I was beginning to feel Gods spirit upon me, but all that I could think about at this time was my child and what that family had tried to do to me and all the others that had abused me as a child. And now I was feeling alone and desperate, wanting and I did begin to drink heavy and to use drugs again. I do remember very clearly one afternoon as I was at my parents in the bedroom and I was so depressed and was so hopeless again. I felt like I was a lost cause and I didn't feel much like living anymore.

All I could think about during this time was the abortions, the molestations, the anger and resentments, the loneliness and the emptiness from my heart and then I was beginning to enter major depression again. I had not worked in months. I didn't want to get out of bed and, except to walk outside to smoke. Sometimes, I would walk the streets to get some liquor or drugs. I wanted to end these sufferings, but had no understanding of how. I was thinking that I was making everyone around me to suffer and I did not want that anymore and I also didn't want to live anymore. So, this is what happened:

YOU ARE FORGIVEN

One Saturday afternoon, My parents were not home and I was alone in there house and I knew my father had a single shot rifle in the closest. I stumbled to the closet crying in agony and reached for it and took it to the back bedroom with me. I was beginning to cry from without and within very much. I was shaken and I wanted to kill myself and end this worthless life I thought I was living. I took the rifle and loaded it with a 22 cartridge and cocked the rifle and put in under my throat and closed my eyes and began to squeeze the trigger, but something amazing happened. It was if time had stopped and I seen this bright light as my eyes were closed and heard a deep powerful voice and it said to me, "You are Forgiven". This voice melted me as wax when it spoke to me and was a voice of Power, Love, Life and Understanding, without any doubt. I had never experienced this Power before, except a few weeks earlier, when I got converted at church, where I did experience a touch of God's Power and Love for me. At first I thought I was dead, but I slowly opened my eyes and seen the rifle lying on the floor in front of me. I could not move for a moment and I felt, I was as a dead man. I felt a love that man could never give; for God had intervene and saved me at near giving up on life and to be consumed by the Big Hole. He saved me from this act, when I could not save my self. God had forgiven me for all the dirty things I had ever done to him. He forgave me right there in my parents home with no one else around, except Him and me. There in the room, I was just looking at the floor on my knees crying and thanking God for forgiven me. I was beginning to understand forgiveness and love and what it is all about. That understanding is all I needed at the time, but at the time, I still didn't understand it. After a few moments I thought had past, I finally got up of my knees and got some strength back into my body and went to my parents kitchen to get some water, I noticed that almost 4hours had past and thought on this matter and told no one.

Now, looking back what God had done for me at that time, today I know the matter was just the beginning of understanding of forgiveness. I thought I understood what God had done for me at that time of my life, but I really did not understand the whole matter, until later in life. It was a great feeling of peace and serenity for sure at the time, but I still did not understand when he said, *"You Are Forgiven"*. Let me now share my understanding of this matter with you. When God said to me with that Loving voice, *"You are forgiven"*, I would have never thought that the God of all Living would have forgiven me or had anything to do with me for the sin I had committed, especially like murdering an unborn child.

At this time of my Life, I didn't know what forgiveness was and I didn't even know I had done anything wrong to God, but maybe the killing of the unborn child. I thought, if any forgiveness was to take place, it was those people in the past life time that needed to ask me for forgiveness too. After all, they were the ones who had hurt me and I wasn't sensing or feeling that I needed to seek forgiveness at this time, except from God. But now I know, that the intervention from God in my life at the spare of my breath was for the matter of understanding, forgiveness.

Now, God knew I was ignorant from understanding forgiveness and I needed forgiven from my trespasses against Him first, in order for me to begin to forgive them whom had trespassed against me. I had wondered away from God as a child and had forgotten his love. I had lost the little understanding that I had of him at the time. I had committed great sin and was deeply ashamed of who I was. I had broken everyone of God's Ten Commandments at this young age and I was living a dead course and was without understanding of true life. I had asked God several times to help me forgive those people from my past, but I just did not know how to forgive.

In order for me to even attempt to try to forgive anyone in my past, I had to receive the understanding of forgiveness, and God, did just that! God spoke the Life of forgiveness into my spirit man that day; for

God's Word is Life and I will forever praise him and meditate on that principle of forgiveness for the rest of my life. When I was converted and had surrender my life to God and His Christ earlier, God already knew what I needed. I felt the forgiveness from the Almighty God and it was an experience I will never forget. As of today, I'm still growing in the understanding of forgiveness. I've also learned forgiveness is a life and a gift, not something that you work for, if we will only ask for it and desire it with a true heart you can receive it without going through horrors and near death experiences. I will also say, "Don't tempt the Lord thy God." I will share much more on Tempting God later in the writings.

In the Holy Bible, Christ left the greatest example of how to receive forgiveness. In the Book of Matthew Chapter 6, verses 7-13 reads, *"After this manner therefore pray ye: Our Father which art in heaven, Hallowed be thy name. Thy kingdom come. Thy Will be done in earth, as it is in Heaven. Gives us this day our daily bread. And forgive us our debts, as we forgive our debtors. Lead us not into temptation, but deliver us from evil: For thine is the kingdom, and the power, and the glory, for ever. Amen."*

I do know today, if a man is without understanding of forgiveness, this man must go to God and receive understanding of forgiveness, before he can forgive anyone in his life. God forgave me when I was dead in my sins; for He sent his Son Jesus Christ to die on the cross, so that, I could receive forgiveness. When we can come to the understanding of forgiveness, then we can begin to forgive others and receive the complete package of God's forgiveness and I will share more on this forgiveness later as I got the understanding.

In my past life, I did not know how to fix my life and neither did I have understanding of forgiveness at this time. I know for today, if I am without understanding of something, it would be best for me to seek understanding of the matter. For an example: If I was at work and I had to repair something, lets say a robot, and didn't know how to fix the robot and tried to fix the robot, then it probably would never get fixed or I could cause more damage to the robot. But, if I had a diagram and understood how to fix it and had experience with fixing robots, my chances of repairing the robot would be much greater.

Today; I know where to go for an understanding; for I must ask it from my Father God who made me. At this time, I was seeking understanding of forgiveness, and God, whom is always faithful was there, at the breath of my life, to show and give it to me.

Now, at the ages of 21-22, I was beginning to get somewhat better after this Divine experience, but still didn't have understanding of the Matter. I knew God had forgiven me and to me at the time, that was all that mattered to me. I was coming out of my major depression at this time and things were beginning to get somewhat better. I had got another job at this time and my grandfather, my mother's father, helped me get my Drivers License back. My grandfather was staying with my parents and he was always there for me when I needed something. My grandfather also was an alcoholic and I remember times we would drink many days together and have great times together during this time, I thought. My grandfather was a minister; for he was called to the ministry, but his addition to alcohol hindered him from preaching during his later years here on earth and I began to loved this man more than anything. When I didn't have any money he would let me wash his cars, help him fix mowers and small engines and get me small jobs around town to make a dollar or two and he was one of the best small engine mechanics, I had ever known.

My grandfather would take a mower that had been sitting out in the elements for years, rusty and looked somewhat ready for the still wagon and he would say to me, "Son, this mower will come alive!" Soon after, I would notice he would have that mower, purring like a kitten. My grandfather also helped me set up a hearing at the DMV office and they let me get my license back a little earlier than I thought. *My grandfather later died at the age of 84 due to pneumonia.* Again this death hit me hard during this time; for he was like a father to me and would help me with anything. I could talk to him like a close friend and now he wasn't there for me either.

After my grandfather's death, I was working and doing fairly well for about 3 or 4 months. At the time I knew that God had place something inside me and it was trying to come out, but I didn't know that it was the Life of Forgiveness. My grandfather and I would talk sometimes alone and he would tell me always, "Son, you have got to forgive them people and let God take care it." At the time I was trying to forgive a lot of people for what they had done to me as a child, but I just couldn't forgive some. This unforgiving heart of mine led me straight back to heavy drinking and doing drugs again. God had showed me that he forgave me, but I still could not forgive others and would always think this, "How could I forgive some and not all?". Today, I know I was still without understanding of forgiveness, but God was ready and had intervene in my life to teach me what forgiveness was all about. In my past life, I never wanted to live by the sinful nature, such as, envying, Adultery, Fornications, Dishonesty, Distrust, murder, angers and resentments that came from deep from within my heart. I wanted to get rid of this life once and for all. I was tried of people treating me the way they were treating me. I was tried of be so ashamed and depressed, but I was without understanding of Life. All I could think about during this time was, I missed my child and what those people had done to me in the past. Chances, Choices and Change kept compounded my angers and resentments and I started to use drugs and alcohol heavy again.

During about this same season of my life, I remember during this time my mother's oldest brother moved into a mobile home a stone throw from my parents. He was a full blown alcoholic and stayed drunk every day that I could remember. This man would work every day and would never miss a day of work from staying up all night. I could not understand how a man could drink from the morning to the late hours of the night and still be able to work a full days labor, every day. I would be at his house every chance I could get, to see if he was at work and he would be gone and at work. I loved him also very much and he took care of me when I couldn't take care of myself and I could talk to him about things and he would always give his ear to me and listen and give me advice, just like his father would do for me. He also helped me get a job with him during this time, it was in the painting business. I really enjoyed spending time with my uncle and he became like a father and a buddy to me. He was a type of man that would give you his shirt and shoes if you needed it, but if he found out you didn't need it, he would be angry at you. I remember going fishing with him quite often at the local ponds. This man liked to fish! I thought at this time it was the only source of food that he enjoyed eating. His father loved fish in the same way and I learned a lot about fishing from these two men. My uncle later in life had quit drinking and to everyone's surprise no one could believe it. This was the word that was always said around the town and throughout my family, "Do you know Buddy has quit drinking?." *My uncle later dies also from pneumonia at the age of 67.* This death was also a blow to me and I never told him how much I loved him and appreciated what he had done for me. Before his death and after he had quit drinking, which I thought was a miracle, I do remember he wanted me to go fishing with him one day. I had quit drinking as much and doing drugs, but continually to smoke pot and drink beer some. I do remember going fishing with him one day and I will never forget it and this was the effect:

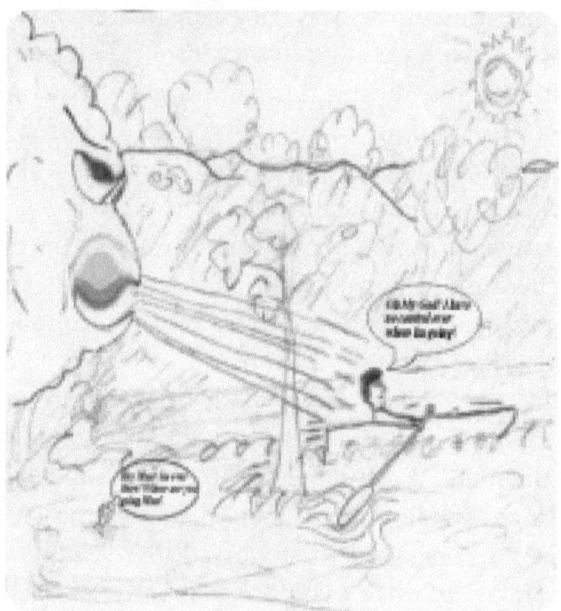

A GREAT LESSON OF FISHING

My Uncle and I went to a large pond, at least 15-20 acres and I had decided to rent a boat on my on, so that my uncle could fish where he would liked, and I could fish where I would like. My uncle was somewhat very private about certain spots in this pond and he knew where the abundance was. He wasn't really looking for the Large one, but he would had like it, if he did catch the record sized fish. My uncle was only interested in filling that 5-gal bucket up with fish, but I will say, he did catch a 3 3/4 lb crappy fish from this pond at one time. He didn't really like large fish, but he loved fish ready at size for the frying pan.

So off he goes in this two man boat, which was a small pontoon and off I go with this larger boat with only one long paddle. I was watching my uncle drag lining the pond and it was if he would pull a fish up every minute. So I thought to myself this, "Man! I need to find out what he is fishing with. I think that is what I need to do, because I haven't caught nothing and he is filling up that bucket he's got fast as lighting."

So, I took my very long paddle, of course my uncle had a motor and propeller on his little boat, and I started paddling toward him, but I never made it to him. A east wind came up and the pond became like the sea shore, it was rough. I couldn't move that boat one millimeter and began to paddle until my arms tired and just gave up the fight. I'm telling you, it was if the wind had taken control of my boat and began to carry me away and there was nothing I could do or anyone else to stop it from happening. I looked toward my uncle and seen my uncle look over toward me from his little boat, but there was nothing he could do for me. I seen him head for the shore, get out of his boat and was standing there for a minute watching me. Then the high wind caught me and took me and the boat around that pond for about 1/2 hour. I had no control of the steering of that boat and it seemed as if I was traveling at or near 25 knots. There were times I thought I was going to drown, because I had no floatation device with me. The wind had finally taken me to the edge of this pond and I would take my paddle and try to slow the boat down by sticking the paddle into the tree line. I also thought of jumping from the boat onto the shore, but it was too far away and I didn't know how deep the waters were and also thought, if my paddle would break, I would be up the creek without a paddle. So, I quit that and just went with the flow of the water and wind and sit down lowly inside the boat and held on for dear life and began to enjoy the scenery.

After the wind had carried me around the pond as it will, I ended up about 150 feet from the edge, back near my uncle. Then just as fast as the wind came in, it left and stopped blowing there where I was at. I finally had control of the boat and began to paddle in desperation towards my uncle who was on the shoreline of the pond, still looking at me. The wind had blown my uncles tent down and there were limbs all over the place. I reached the shoreline and jump to it and was relieved and then it began to rain very hard and it was starting to lightening and thunder greatly. We put the tent up quickly and as we were sitting in the tent, my uncle looks over to me with those half rim black glasses and said to me as if he wanted an explanation, "Boy! What took you so long? I was waiting for you to come in before it started to rain." I just couldn't believe that was all he said. Then I said, "What took me so long!!? You didn't see what was happening to me? I couldn't come in for the wind had taken control and I couldn't get to the shore!" He laugh somewhat and said, "The wind? What in this world are you talking about, boy? I thought you were looking for the big ones. Right there! Where you were at! There has been record size bass caught, boy." I began to sense that he really didn't know what had just happened with me and that boat. I looked down at his bucket and it was full of pan size fish and I didn't even catch a minnow. Later after the storm had passed, I didn't fish no more that day from a boat and watched my uncle from the shore catching fish like they were jumping from the water straight into that bucket.

Later on after the sun began to shine again, men were pouring into the waters of this pond. Some had large and fast boats with large motors and some had small motors and small boats, but my eye caught a man putting his small wooden, one man boat into the waters without a motor. This boat was so small, I began to laugh inside and was thinking, "If he did catch a big fish where in the world would he put it, on his shoulders or around his neck?"

As I watched this man with this little wooden boat about 4' long and began to enter into the water, I noticed he had two small wooden paddles about 1 foot long in each hand and I began to giggle somewhat within myself. I was watching this man in amazement, as he would paddle and head toward one spot very easily and quietly and guess where he started to fish at? Yes, the same spot where the wind had left me earlier, after the wind had ceased, about 150 feet out.

So, I just quit my fishing from the shore and took my fishing rod and line in and laid it to the side and began to watch this man fish in amazement and then, I just could not believe it! This man had already caught a large 4 pound bass in less than 10 minutes and I also saw where he put the fish, and that my friend is a fisherman secret, I cannot tell at this time. No just kidding. He had a fish line he pulled from the right side of his little boat from the waters and hooked the fish onto it. I watched him for 30 minutes as he continually caught large bass. I watched him as he turn the boat and headed back toward the shore where I was standing. After he had reach the shore, he reached down beside his boat and pulled up his fish line, as if he had a whale on it. This man had at least 5 large mouth 4-7 pound bass on the fish line and I just couldn't believe it. I had to ask him," Sir. How in this world, did you catch all those fish in less than an hour?" He was a small man and some what rugged looking and he looked over at me as he was holding the fish in his right hand and giggled somewhat and said, "Son, you larn by exparience. I know aftar it had wrained ware to go. I's always cum to dis dar spot after a rain starm." Then I also had to ask this man why he quit fishing when things were so good and I said, "Sir, those are some beautiful fish, but why did you quit fishing when you where catching so many?" He looked up at me as if I was crazy, but began to smile and giggle again and said, "Son, I's gots all dat Is neds far one dar day. Now, I's most go dar home and cleans them dar fishes far Is will be havins these dar fishes far suppa tonite ands Is has enuff far dis dar day and tomar, ands ifs I don't has enuff, I's will be backs.

Dares plenta of fishes in dat dare pond." Oh! My friend I guess he was talking somewhat in the deep south language, so, let me interpret what he said. When I ask him how he had caught so many fish in less than 1/2hr, he said to me, "Son, you learn by experience. I knew after it had rained where to go. I have always came to this spot after a rain storm." Then I also had to ask this man why he quit fishing when things were so good and I said, "Son, I have caught all that I need for one day. Now, I must go home and prepare these fish for supper tonight. I have enough of fish for one day and enough for tomorrow, but if it is not enough, I will be back, because there are plenty of fish in that pond." Then he left and I never caught one fish that day and watch everyone else as they would catch fish, but I learned a lot from that day about fishing.

Today, I know what happened at that fishing pond and I still today draw strength from that experience I had at that fishing pond with my Uncle. I still today have not received all the understanding of that fishing lesson, such as, why he would go to that fishing spot after a rain storm? But, I'm sure it will be revealed soon. I did have one thing on my mind, to catch the largest gill fish known to man. I was trying to empress my uncle and anyone else and show them a thing about fishing, but I was taught a great lesson about fishing. That wind had taken control of my will and my life and It had taken me around that pond, as if it was showing me the world and the pond was full of fish, but because I had a one track mind and was still living by self will, I couldn't catch one fish.

Today I know I must go where the spirit leads me, in order to catch fish and have the right bait, tackle and understanding of fishing. I also know today its not about the big one, it is about understanding of fishing, how many you catch and how you catch them. In the book of Matthew chapter 4, verses 18-19, *"And Jesus, walking by the sea of Galilee, saw two brethren, Simon called Peter, and Andrew his brother, casting a net into the sea: for they were fishers. And he saith to them, Follow me, and I will make you fishers of men."* Today I still like to go fishing for gill fish and eating gill fish, but I know the lesson that I was taught that day with my dear uncle, at that fishing hole, wasn't about fish with gills. Mankind is suffering and dying and going to Eternal Death today and I must follow the Spirit of God where he leads me to help catch these men before its too late. I don't spend my life on this matter, because there is so many other matters that count.

I will say this with confidence, I know it is God's Will for each of us to help another man from drowning in this world of self will. I am willing to go where the Spirit carries me and I don't think on the matter, I just go and do it. When God leads me to a man he gives me the right bait and fishing tools to help and I wouldn't want it any other way. I have tried to catch men on my own in the past, but I will say, because I was without understanding of fishing, it caused more damage to them and me. Let me please share one more point with you concerning this matter. After the resurrection of Jesus Christ from the grave, he showed himself to the disciples and told them of this great lesson of fishing in the Gospel of John, Chapter 21. If you would, please read it sometime soon. If I learned anything that my grandfather and my uncle would give to me, it was fishing. I never fish much in my life until my grandfather showed up in my life. Today fishing is my greatest exploration and I also like to eat fish greatly. They laid the foundation and I am just building upon the rock today.

I have a large picture hanging in the living area of my home today of a Sea Shore with fishing boats that my grandfather gave to me. He gave it to me years before the Great Fishing Lesson Revelation and before my Uncle even came into the picture, but I know that he left it for one particular reason, fishing. I miss them greatly both, but I hope to see them on the other side of the Jordan.

I do remember another fellow that came into my life during this time and was a close friend to someone in my family. He was in his upper 30's of age and was a serious alcoholic and drug addict. I was still drinking and using drugs and so was he and I was still without understanding of Life. So, I remember walking to my aunts and he was there one day by himself drunk and crying like a baby as he met me at the door and I asked him, "What is wrong, Buddy?" He said, "My dog is sick and I'm going to have to put her down." My mouth dropped to my feet and I thought the way he was crying that he just lost his mother. I had no idea what he was talking about and why he would be so sad about a dog. But, today I believe he was in grief of his long time companion; for this dog was the only thing he could trust in the whole wide world and it was dying, but I will say this man was very lonely in his heart. Then he ask me, as he continued to cry, "Will you please go with me to get my dog?" I didn't know what to say looking at a grown man crying over a sick dog, but I agreed to ride with him to his home and to be with him at this time. We stopped at a couple liquor joints on the way and he and I were getting pretty drunk.

So, we eventually ended up at his mothers house where this dog was suppose to be and he got out of the vehicle and started whistling for this dog. I began to think he was crazy, until I notice a gray looking dog coming from around the house with its head low. He reached down and put his arms around this dog and fell to his knees and began to yell and cry like a baby again. I was really beginning to think he was crazy and I needed to straighten up and be on the look out. He stood up and took the dog and put it in the back seat and then he went inside the house and came out with a rifle and put the rifle into the back seat with the dog and we left.

We went to a secluded place on a nearby river shore and he took the rifle out and propped it upon a nearby tree and started the crying and yelling again.

He looked at me through the side window as he began to calm down somewhat and said, "You best stay in the car. I've got to do something and I don't want you to see it." He may as well been talking to the tree with his gun, because I was watching his every move. He opened the back door again and left it opened and began to cry again very loud. He whistle for the dog and I seen to my left, the dog slowly leaving the vehicle with its head hung low and went to him. I watch as he hugged the dog and took the gun, put it to the dog's head and shot that dog.

I jumped to the roof of that vehicle as the round went off and I began to sense at this time, he was telling me the truth about his intent for this dog. I didn't take my eyes off him not one second for I thought, he may turn that gun on me and put me down and I don't want that. He began to quite down somewhat from the crying and called me to him. I slowly opened the passenger's door and got out and stood beside the vehicle and said, "Is your dog dead, Buddy?" and he said, "Yes. Come and help me put her away." I walked over to him and he handed me the gun and then I was relieved. Later, we became close friends after this, but it didn't last for long. He was found at his mothers in a shed with a rope around his neck and *He had committed suicide*. When I was told of his death, it hit me pretty hard and afterwards, I began to use even more and remember lying in the woods many nights crying and hiding from everyone to just stay away from me. I would pray in desperation, "God please send me someone that cares for me and understands me. Please God! Help me understand what I need to do. Please God send me someone, for I'm lonely."

Today I know why God had sent this man into my life, even though of other suspicions. Not only was this man lonely, but I was also lonely and needed something to fill the void spirit, that I had at the time. I was empty and void of God's Love for me and God again was knocking at my door.

The first suicide attempt I had suffered through was led from being lonely and fear, but now God had shown me again the consequences of this matter. God was saying through this man's desperate cry, "I'm Lonely and Void". At this time, I had put my trust in everything else, except God, and all had felled me, but at the time, I still didn't hear and listen with my heart what God was trying to do or say to me.

Later after the death of this man, my ex-wife started to bring my daughter over to my parents. I soon found out as she spoke, it wasn't she wanted the child to be with me, she only wanted money in support for the child. I knew at this time that I had a responsibility to her on this matter and I was willing to pay anything: for we had not been to court over this matter yet. I didn't want no fighting and I surely didn't want to go to court anymore and I just wanted peace and this trouble out of my life at this time. But, I did want to see this child and she knew I wanted to see this child and that was how I began to see my child, once in awhile, by paying my way with money, on her terms. I didn't have a full time job at this time, but like I said earlier, I would find trade jobs to get some income to meet my needs. I wanted to help with bringing this child up, but I felt as if it was on her terms. I just could not let go of the anger and resentments from these certain people of my past that had hurt me so bad. I thought I would never forgive them and thought they did not deserve forgiveness from me or God. Thinking on my terms headed me back to the Big Hole again. I was wondering around and away from God again; and I was still without understanding and living by my rebellious self will.

CHAPTER FOUR

WRESTLING WITH GOD.

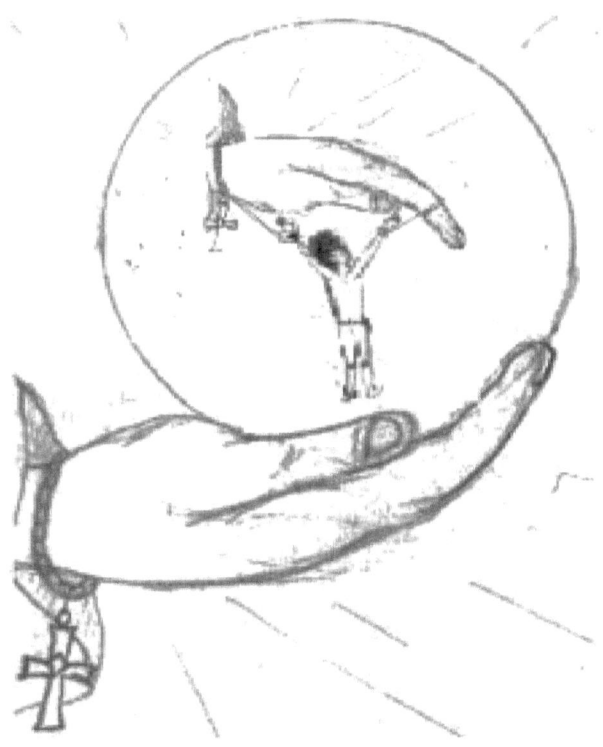

During this time of my life, I was battling with my self and God for better things for my profit. I wanted to do good and to have the good things of life with a passion, but I just didn't know what I needed. I knew I needed a friend or someone that I could trust, such as a wife. I felt like every girl that I would meet was not the one that I needed. Either they were too young or they too were on drugs or something else would happen to break our relationship apart. I did meet one girl and we started a relationship. Her father was a minister and at first, I thought we were meant for each other.

But, as time passed I somewhat called the relationship off, because of my drinking and drug using. I didn't want her to end up in a relationship with me, knowing my past. I thought if she knew my past, she would run like a jack rabbit from me anyway.

So, I somewhat called the relationship off and she looked at me as if I was crazy, but she really didn't understand the reason. Later we accepted the breakup and there I was alone again. I will say this also, today I am grateful that I called the relationship off, because she is well and has a family with children. I love her today in a different way than I loved her during those days. I love her for coming into my life and sharing with me, that God, would soon give me a wife. I love her deeply and all those that came across my path. May God bless each of you with all things your heart desires.

I continued to press forward for a friend during this time and I felt as if I was Jacob wrestling with God for the promise land, no kidding. I was so lonely and I needed someone in my life at all cost by this time. I laid in the bed day after day praying for a friend, or someone that I could trust besides my own parents. I was beginning again to go into a depressed state of mind, but I still pressed forward.

Now, I remember walking to my aunts, my mother's sister, one evening just to get away. My aunt was always good to me and tried, like all my other family, to keep me alive; for she was like a big sister to me and still today. I would go to visit her to get away and have someone to talk to and cry upon her shoulder. She was about the only person in the world I trusted at this time and I felt as if she understood my problems, besides my parents. I had been drinking all day and the journey was about 4 miles. I walked to my aunts with my bottle in one hand all the way. People would stop and ask if I needed a ride, but I would respond, "No! I don't need no ride! Please just leave me alone!"

I had began again to put a wall up from any people who wanted to help me, because I didn't trust no one, not even the church. I didn't want anything from anyone and I just wanting everyone to leave me alone and get out of my life. I thought at this time, I couldn't even trust an Angel, if it appeared if front of me in all its glory, but I had not forgotten what God did for me earlier; for it was still burning like a candle inside my heart and would not go out.

As I reach my aunts house I knocked on the door, but she wasn't home. In desperation I walked over to my aunts neighbor's home where she usually visits and knocked on there door. I remember a young lady answering the door and said, "No she isn't here, but come on in here. She will be back in just a few minutes. You can wait here for her, OK? She has left for the store before it closes. She usually goes to the store for us." I entered the home and my mouth dropped to the floor. I had to step over people passed out from drinking and using. These people were strung out like rag dolls all over this place. As I entered the house, I stepped over a few people and set at the table in their dining area and I took one little gulp of liquor, left in my bottle that I had brought with me. One strange fellow kept glancing over at me, as he would drink and then he said to me, "Boy there's plenty in the fridge and the cooler over dare." You know, for some earthly reason, I didn't want to drink anymore that night. I wanted to actually get straight and keep my eyes opened in this house.

My aunt on my mother's side didn't drink and if she did, I never knew it and was thinking to myself, "Why in this world would my aunt have anything to do with these people?" Later, I found out she would always help her neighbors to keep them for getting into trouble or from getting a DWI and believe me, these folks needed help. My aunt never showed up while I'm there at this house, either.

As I glanced over to my right side, I saw a figure come out of the bedroom. It was a very beautiful lady and she looked somewhat saddened, as if she had been crying. My friend, when I seen this lady, my mouth dropped to the floor. She looked like the Angel by the Fence grown up, no kidding. I felt something I had not felt for a long time and that was compassion. As I looked at this lady and this lady looked at me, we both began to speak at the same time. We both felt as if we knew each other at that very moment and it was if we were magnets and where being pulled together. I soon found out that she was married and one of the men on the floor passed out, was her husband. I also found out she was upset, because she didn't want to keep living the way she was living.

As we began to talk, something else amazing happened. This very lady that was sitting beside me, I remembered seeing her when I was younger and thought she was beautiful and would of like to had her as my friend, but I just could not figure out where I had seen her. As we were talking there alone in the kitchen, while every one else had passed out like rag dolls, we begin to ask each other, if I and her was kin to this person or that person. As I told her a few names of my kin folks, she became silent like a mouse, put her head down lowly and I began to sense, she knew something that I didn't know. Then she lifted her head up and looked at me with those beautiful eyes and said, "Your aunt is my mother's sister." That's right! This lady setting beside me had the same uncle and aunt that I had due to marriage and we both were amazed that we where together. Her mother's sister married my father's brother and I knew then, where I had seen her in the past time. I remember the time I had seen her while I was a child, as she would look at me with those big beautiful eyes and smile at me and giggle, as if she liked me, but at that time I was very shy and ashamed at things that I had done already in my life and thought she would not like me and would not smile at me, if she knew what things I had done in my childhood.

As time went on and time was getting late that evening, I told her I had to leave, but I hope to see her again and told her she didn't deserve living the way she was living and she said too, "Neither do you." She asks me if I was walking and I said, "I have no choice and I don't have Insurance on my car, neither can I afford it at this time." She wasn't drinking that evening and insisted on caring me home. I was very happy for her help and the way she would speak to me. I was sensing that she really cared for me and I began to trust her somewhat. I also found out that my friend was born exactly 9 months before me. She was born the same year during Easter and I was born during the same year on Christmas day, no kidding.

Now at this time, a few months had passed since I had seen this lady and was desiring to see her and she shows up at my parent's home, as if she felt my spirit call for her. My mother told me there was a young lady out side that wanted to speak to me and I thought at the time, it was my ex-wife. But it wasn't, for the lady I had just met weeks earlier was outside waiting for me and I ran to her with joy. I sat in her vehicle and she was very sad and looked as if she was crying and I said to her, "What is wrong? Did somebody hurt you!?" She said, "I've been hurt my whole life and I just left my husband and I needed someone to talk to." We talked a few minutes and I told her I would be there, if she needed me and for her not to hesitate to come and get me if she needed me. We comforted each other that evening and this comforting, was what she and I had been looking and seeking for so long, a friend and someone to lean on that would be still and listen with there heart. So as time went on, I and this lady began a relationship that could not be destroyed. I started to feel love again and not lust. I started to feel and sense life much better; for I was beginning to sense God answered my prayer. He sent someone to me, not the way I thought he would send the person to me, but this lady was definitely sent from God into my life and just on time.

Later, my friend, the lady, was living near her ½ brother in a camper by herself. Her brother had gave her a place on his property just a stone toss away. I moved in with her and we knew we were meant for each other. Her husband wasn't too happy with this. Every now and then we would have a love note from him on our camper door and I guessed it was a love note to my friend, because what it read wasn't love for me. I bought my first shotgun at this time and I meant to use it. My friend had already registered and bought her a 38 colt police special for her protection. That was the way we lived for quite some time, in fear that we would have to use force or do something worse to protects us. For me, I really didn't care at the time if I was killed or worse and there wasn't anyone going to hurt my friend. I began to take the responsibility of keeping her away from this fellow at any cost. *Later in life this man (my friend's ex-husband) was killed in a one vehicle accident from drunk driving.* My wife was saddened because he had died and I was there for her with open arms. She didn't go to the funeral, because she had to work, but she did go see his family and they were comforted by seeing her.

As time went on, I began to work and hold down a job and I had come out of my depression; for this lady gave me some much needed hope on life. She was also working and had always held down a job, since she was 15years of age and was very responsible and prudent. We still continued to live is this camper on her brother's property and I will tell you this; if you are in True Love, you will live anywhere. We didn't have running hot water for quite some time and we used a garden hose to wash with during the cold season, no kidding. We were living at the edge of a forest at this time and every now and then, we would have to clean the lamps from the little green tree frogs that would sacrifice their lives every night. Every now and then as we would sit and watch a movie, we would hear something like this; Buzzz! ~ Zappp!

It would be a little green frog caught by the lamps on the campers walls and electrocuted to death, because some had no shades or bulbs on them and would be just the light socket with power on them. Today I know the point of the little green frogs sacrifices and I will share it with you later, concerning this matter of creations suffering and sacrifices for mankind.

There were nights my friend, while living near this forest in this camper, I would jump out of bed, grab my shotgun, and open the door real slowly and say, "If anybody is out there, I will kill you!", then I would shoot the shotgun from the door entrance into the air several times. Sometimes, there would be sounds like someone was walking on the roof of that camper in the night, but soon would find out, it wasn't a man; for it would be possums or raccoons. At first little things like this bothered us, but later we were laughing and beginning to be joyful in our relationship we had. We began working hard and trying hard to better ourselves together. We were bringing in income, not much, but enough to meet our needs. We would spend the money left over from paying the little bills we had and go to the beach almost every weekend. I was still drinking and smoking pot at this time, but not the heavy drugs from the past. I was thinking it was Ok and we were happier than we had been in a long time and we knew this and life was much better, but I was still without of understanding of Life. We loved each other more than anything and we would always tell each other, as long as we had each other, we would live in a shoe if, we had to. Material things didn't matter to us then and today still don't matter. We had true love for each other then and still today and that my friend was all we needed at the time, I thought, but that wasn't all we needed.

Later at the ages of 24-25 after the Divorces, me and my friend were later married. I knew at this time that we must start to establish a home for our selves. I also knew that I needed to grow up some and start working and finding a real job and such things as that.

I did get a good paying production job in manufacturing of mobile homes and I learned how to put a home together in less than a day. Looking back I know why and for what reason, I had got this job. God was making another point in my life and I was beginning to sense this matter, but I was still without understanding of a normal life. I continued to live without understanding and by my self will and I was drinking almost every night and using drugs every day. My wife would sometimes drink with me during this time on the weekends, but she would refuse to use the heavy drugs. My wife already knew what drugs and alcohol had done to her life and she didn't want that anymore and I didn't force this matter on my wife in anyway. I would always leave the home to use the heavy drugs and hide this from my wife, but later I found out her family was destroyed because of alcoholism. Her childhood was taken from her when she was a small child and her mother and father had divorce at the age of 13 and were put on the streets to find shelter. She came from a broken home and I was beginning to feel for her at this time.

As she was beginning to share her childhood past with me, I began to sense that I could be some hope for her and she knew that we loved each other and she wanted everything to work out between us. The relationship she had just came out of, was an abusive relationship and she had found someone that would not abuse her and she like that very much.

Even though I was using drugs and drinking heavy, I thought I wasn't abusing this lady. I would think: if only I don't use the heavy drugs, she will be Ok. But, looking back in the past, I was abusing her and myself. Even though I knew God had answered my desperate cry for help and had sent me a prudent wife, a Godly gift, I was still without understanding of this matter. Please let me share with you what I now know concerning a wife.

In the Holy Book of Genesis Chapter 2, verses 21-25 in reads, ***"And the Lord God caused a deep sleep to fall upon Adam, and he slept: and he took one of his ribs, and closed up the flesh instead thereof; And the rib, which the Lord God had taken from man, made he a woman, and brought her unto the man. And Adam said, This is now*** *bone of my bones, and flesh of my flesh: she shall be called Woman, because she was taken out of Man. Therefore shall a man leave his father and his mother, and shall cleave unto his wife: and they shall be one flesh. And they were both naked, the man and his wife, and were not ashamed."*

Today, I do understand this matter of marriage and the understanding goes like this: My first wife and I had to get married, because we didn't want people to think badly of us; for my first wife was pregnant before our marriage. My friend, I will tell you this truth today, getting married to fulfill your self will pleasures want hold a true marriage together for life. God ordained Adam a Woman, lets say a wife, and Adam knew that this woman was flesh of his flesh and bones of his bones and when he suffered, she also suffered. They both were of one flesh and all things were giving to both, from God.

They also were not ashamed of their nakedness; for they were not in sin. The Word of God clearly states that a man shall leave his father and mother and cleave to his wife and they shall be one flesh. Both myself and my wife know today that we did leave our mothers and fathers for each other and we did become one flesh. Fathers and Mothers now cant come between us, unless we fall into self will again and then the marriage could divorce.

Self will, will destroy that of what God has given you, if you let it. Living the life of the sinful nature will eventually destroy everything that God has given to you.

In the Book of Proverbs Chapter 18, verse 22, reads **"Whosoever f indeth a wife f indeth a good thing, and obtaineth favor of the Lord."** God loves marriage, because he ordained it from the beginning for man and that is the way he favors it. When God sent my wife to me at this time, I knew that we were ordained and it was in God's favor for us to get married and she also knew this too. God's Word reads in **Proverbs 19:14, "House and riches are the inheritance of fathers: and a prudent wife is from the Lord."** I continually to thank God for bringing my dear wife to me today and will forever thank him; for she is life for me and remember all things that God gives, is Life.

When my wife and I were yet still young in our relationship of marriage, we both were without understanding of what True Life was. We had the understanding of the difference of Lust and Love and knew our relationship was built on Love and not Lust and that we had found each other and to us, that was all that mattered at the time, but we were without understanding and now we were going to learn about life as a team, in this world. My wife at the time was very prudent and still today and I don't every recall a day of work she missed due to her using or my using. She never got drunk and never used any drugs. She quit her smoking almost immediately when we met. She would drink mixed drinks occasionally with me on the weekends, but soon quit that also. She had been responsible and working since the age of 14. She had already married at the age of 15 then divorced at this age of 17 and then remarried soon after, into the relationship we have already discussed. She knew that she had to make it and be responsible already at a very young age of life. This lady at this young age, had already put up a defense up from life, but was trying to live it to the best she understood it. This lady was a grown adult, married and divorced, when I met her. She knew what I was going through and continually to help me with my problems. For many years I was never honest with my wife about my past and still hid this from her hoping she would never find out.

I would watch as she would live a normal life, but I thought I could never live a normal life. I continued to hold onto all the angry and resentments in my little heart; for I just didn't know how to let go and let God. I didn't want her to feel sorry for me and I didn't want her to know that my childhood had been taken from me as a child and I thought always, if she knew my childhood was worst than hers, then she would not have no hope in our relationship. I knew she didn't deserve to share that much burden when she had so many problems of her own. At the time I thought I had found someone that finally understood me to the best she could and that is all I wanted at that time. I also would always grasp onto to this; I knew within my heart that God had sent this gift to me. I was willing to hold onto to this gift that God had given to me at all cost, even if I could live a normal life. I thought, if she ever found out my true past, it would hurt her and she would give up and leave me and I didn't want that to happen.

As time passed by, I was beginning to sense somewhat, that I had to change the way I was living before she found out about the true me (my past). I did stop using the heavy drugs as much, but continued to smoke pot and drink heavy at this time. But, from somewhere deep within my life, I didn't want to use and I didn't have the understanding to quit my using for it was still liken a thorn in my flesh. I continued to try to live a normal life with the consistence of trying to quit using drugs and alcohol. I do want to share one more incident while we where still staying there at this camper in the forest.

I remember during this time, one evening after work; for it was a Friday afternoon, me and a family friend started to drink heavy and we worked together at this Mobile Home factory. This man was also a mature alcoholic at this time and had been in several wrecks and lost his driving privileges for a long time. He was about 10 years older than I was at the time and we went to his home and got drunk off Bacardi Rum and Wild Turkey whisky. We drank from that afternoon until the following mourning without stopping.

But I will say that I did slow down on my drinking because of this: It was winter and it was about 10 degrees F outdoors and we wanted to go out and do something for both of us loved the outdoors. We decided to go Raccoon hunting at 2:30am in the mourning with the outside temperature at or near 10 degrees F and on top of that, drunk as a spinning top. He got his shotgun and handed me a 12 gauge shotgun and off we go into the wilderness at 2:30am. We were stopping once and awhile and would take a couple of gulps of liquor we had with us and then kept moving and shinning our flashlights into trees for Raccoons.

Now, we got somewhat lost and my friend said to me, "The only way I know to get back now, is to find the railway trusses and cross them and then I will know where we are." So, we kept moving until he seen the Bridge and we started to move faster toward the trusses. As he went ahead of me without any difficult, I was beginning to stumble and I didn't think I would be able to make it across the bridge and I told him to go ahead, because it may take me a while longer to get across. He left me and moved across the trusses as if he wasn't drunk, but me, I was taking baby steps one foot at a time and then something happened. I fell off the trusses straight down and as I was falling, I was praying quickly in my heart, "God please save meeeeeeeee!" I fell 20' straight down onto my back. My legs from my knees down to my feet, landed into the frozen stream that was somewhat flowing. It was if time had slowed down and then I heard a noise that went like this, "BLOOP!" it was my shot gun. It stuck into the ground barrel first, approximately 12" from my head, no kidding. I just laid there with my legs in the cold flowing creek, because my breath was knock out of me. I began to thank God in my heart that the gun didn't hit me in my head and go off. I was wondering if the gun was loaded, but later found out at my friend's home that the gun was loaded.

So, as I was laying there with my breath knock out of me I heard a voice far away, but I couldn't move and I was stunned by the fall and the thought of the gun beside my head. I heard my friend calling out to me and asking, "Where are You?, Where are you?" I finally got some breath back and called out to him and he came down the side of the bridge and he couldn't believe that I had falling and said, "What are you doing down here? I didn't know where you were." and then I said to him with a meek angry voice, "No, I thought I would just lay in this frozen creek, as cold as it is and freeze to death!" And then I told him that I had falling and he helped me up, looked at me and then glancing up to the top of the trusses and then to where I landed and he was amazed. Then he helped me up the side of the bridge and I always ask this question to myself, "It would had taken me an hour to cross those trusses as drunk as I was, if I had made it, but it didn't take 5 minutes to go up the side of that bridge. Why didn't we do that the start with?"

Nevertheless, as I was walking, my legs were frozen as ice blocks and my friend would say to me every now and then as if he was giving me strength to keep going, "We are almost there buddy, come on, we are almost there." I got to his home and the sun was beginning to rise. I looked at the gun and then he looked at it and took it from me and ejected the cartridges out slowly and said with a grin, "It will take me a day to get the mud out of the barrel. Its Ok, the gun is not damaged." And then he and I giggled together somewhat. But, then I said to him with a very serious tone of voice, "You know that I should had been killed tonight. The fall didn't kill me, but the gun should of killed me." And then we giggled and then I left and went home. I said this to myself as I left my friends home, "I want go with him Raccoon hunting drunk anymore."

Today, I thank God that I didn't die that night in my sin, but by the Grace of God I was spare for another chance at life. Today I know what the fall was about, "Where are You?"; for I was away from God and this knock again, was trying to get me back to God. I know today I was in sin and God was knocking on my door again, but I continued to live still by my self will pleasures and was still without understanding of life. I continued to drink and use drugs heavy at this time. My friend and his Wife and family have moved away to another town and are doing well and I was told, that he has quit drinking.

After this incident, my wife and I were doing somewhat well financially and we moved from the camper in the forest and moved to a little house that was for rent in town to better ourselves. While here at this little house, I do remember loosing control one evening and my wife began to see me, for who I really was. I had been put on Antibuse, which is a drug to help me quit drinking. I was put on this drug, Antibuse, because of another car accident earlier and the hospital that I was seen at, requested a psychiatrist to review me.

Later the next week, I went to this psychiatrist and he found out some of my history and requested I be put on it, also some other psychiatric drugs for anxiety and depression. At the time, I thought I was going back to rehab, but for some reason I missed this chance. I accepted the request and started taking the drug Antibuse the following day. Oh yes! I will say, I only accepted it, because I knew it would ease my wife's concern for my heavy drinking. So the next day, I took one of the antibuse pills and guess what? I chased it down with some beer and after a while, I wasn't feeling so good. I didn't only drink on it, but I had been out all day doing cocaine and abusing my psychiatric drugs. I went berserk and went into an anger fit and was out of control and almost overdosed. The ambulance and the paramedics had to come and restrained me to the stretcher.

I was blaming the Doctor and my wife for insisting me to go on the drug, Antibuse. My wife knew that I had been drinking, but she didn't know about the cocaine and others drugs, until the following day when she was told by the doctors.

Later as I calmed down, with the help of the hospital drugs, I knew as my wife was standing there with tears in her eyes, that she had seen one of my worst sides of my life. I began to know that she knew that I had more problems than I had been sharing with her. I began to make excuses and telling her a few of my past problems to comfort her and I was hoping she wouldn't think I was crazy and leave me. These excuses led to another part of my life, which was, denying that I had any problems with drugs and alcohol. But, I felt as if God was weighing me and I was being disciplined for the lying or denial by God. During this time of my life I felt as if everything that I would do it would be wrong. I felt as if God had me on a string and was playing me as a "Yo- Yo," no kidding. Not that he was playing games, but as if he was weighing me to see how much Truth and Grace I professed to have in my life.

Now, I will quickly share with you some very important points throughout my life. These next ten years was the beginning of the most important points God was trying to show me, as I was still living by self will and without understand of his Will for me. Before I continue on the my life during this time, let me please share with you what God has revealed to me concerning the following writings. Please listen with your heart to what God is saying in the writings of his Holy Word. In Hebrews Chapter 12, verses 5-11, *"And ye have forgotten the exhortation which speaketh unto you as unto children, My son, despise not the chastening of the Lord, nor faint when thou art rebuked of him: For whom the Lord loveth he chasteneth, and scourgeth every son whom he recieveth. If ye endure chastening, God dealeth with you as with sons; for what son is he whom the father chasteneth not?*

But if ye be without chastisement, whereof all are partakers, then are ye bastards, and not sons. Furthermore we have had fathers of the flesh which corrected us, and we gave them reverence: shall we not much rather be in subjection unto the Father of spirits and live? For they verily for a few days chastened us after their own pleasures; but he for our prof it, that we might be partakers of his holiness. Now no chastening for the present seemth to be joyous, but grievous: nevertheless afterward it yieldeth the peaceable fruit of righteousness unto them which are exercised thereby."

Wow! Now, that was a lot to take in, wasn't it? Looking back as a rebellious child and when my father in the flesh would discipline me, I would rebel even more so, against the chastening. Also looking back when I was reaching adult hood and during my young adult hood, my father in the flesh could no longer discipline me, but now, it would be God's turn. But, I still didn't understand that it was God doing the disciplining at the time and I would always blame others and keep it within my heart as resentments. I was always thinking with my massive brain, rather than, with my heart and thought I had been through enough of suffering from my past childhood and I wasn't about to be chastised anymore by any man, or God. I had forgotten again what God had done for me at the age of 20 and how he forgave me and saved me at the last of my breath from death.

Before the suicide attempt, I had giving honestly to the best I knew how, my will to God and I had forgotten this matter now at this time. Today I do know this; When I honestly did turned my will over to the care of God as I understood him at the time and I was seeking understanding of his Will for me at this time, it was at that very moment I became a son of his; for he doesn't forget. I was not only a son of my earthly father, but now The Big Daddy, the Father of Life had intervened and he meant business.

He would discipline me, if it meant breaking ever bone in my body, no kidding. I had forgotten the exhortation (advice) that God had shared with me earlier during my first spiritual awakening at the age of 20. He forgave me and he meant for me to forgive others.

Looking back at the advice from God, now I understand what he meant. Even though God had forgiven me, I would not forgive others and that wasn't too nice at this time. It is like this: God had forgiven me for all that I had done against him, but I wouldn't forgive others.

I also know today, if I don't forgive others, then I am not forgiven completely and God's Will cannot work in my Life, but God was showing me at this time to forgive others first and then he could perfectly forgive me. I know today, If I don't forgive others, then God can't work though me to show me, His Perfected Will for me. Remember, God's Will is perfect. If we have any self will in our lives, then God's Perfect Will can not work in us. Where self will is, God's Perfection doesn't dwell.

At this time of my life, I was still rebelling against anyone that would rebuke or try to chastise me. I still could not forgive all those people whom had hurt me in the past and I was still without understanding. You will begin to see through the following writings it wasn't man, but God who was doing the exercising of chastisements in my life.

As time passed during the ages of 26-27, my wife and I moved back to the property that we were living on during our season. We stayed there in the mobile home 10 years and began to make a home for ourselves. Her brother had bought a house in town and his family had moved there. We had the opportunity to better our self and move into this newly single wide mobile home. So we did and we began to have more responsibilities and life was getting better though our eyes.

I had left the Mobile Home business and got a job back into Communications at this time and thought nothing else on this matter. I know for today, God was trying to communicate to me once more at this time of my life, but I was still without understanding and living by self will pleasures.

This neighborhood we moved into was known for its bootlegs, drugs and crimes. Almost every weekend there would be rumors of someone being shot or stabbed or worse in the local clubs that were just a stone toss from our home. I became very defensive on this matter and there are a lot of things I will not mention, because it isn't the point. I will say this; I was not afraid one bit, even though, I would continue to buy different guns and self defense weapons and invent things from my own understanding and skills. I'll tell you the truth, sometimes I would just sit in the shadows armed and get drunk and just hope someone would come across my path, so that, I could release a little bit of my hearts desires upon them. My self will even sometimes would go out into the darkness of the neighborhood to temp someone to give me a right to do something wrong. Again like I had mention before, I wasn't afraid of death and most people that I knew, would had never known that. My defense had been up since I was but a little child and this neighborhood was just a small challenge in my life. Death at this time wasn't a thought of suicide, but carelessness.

Today I know that living that way was suicide and even much worse. I didn't want to commit suicide, because of the hope I had before when God Intervened in my life and had said to me, "You are forgiven". I did have somewhat the understanding that suicide was murder. But now at this time of my life, I was finding other ways that was manipulating in the same sense of suicide and was not so obvious.

So, as chances past, I was still without understanding and wasn't forgiven anyone for the hurt from the past and as time went on, chances, choices and change were compounded a fire within my heart and things grew worse and worse in my life. After about a year staying there in this mobile home, the worse seemed to had happened to my wife and I. *My wife's father was found in his apartment dead, from alcoholism.* He had been dead several days during the middle of the hot summer months and I, my wife and her sister had to go and identify his body. We went to the morgue where his body was laid and when we went in where he laid, neither of us could not recognize him. My wife and her sister went a little closer toward this body and began to cry with extreme grief and said, "It is daddy!" They left the room hysterical, but I stayed back and looked at his body in disbelief. I just did know how they could had recognized him in that much decomposing, but later I knew how they did recognized him. I stood there and looked at this body and knew I didn't want to end up like this and thought my wife doesn't deserve me using anymore. I began to feel the grief somewhat and walk calmly to the care of my wife and her sister. Knock, Knock someone is at my door again. I really didn't want to live this way and now, I have a wife that God had sent to me as a gift and she was in desperate need for me. Looking back at this time of my life, this incident was an attempt and a slap upon my face to awake me from my sleep, but I was without understanding of the matter.

After the death of my wife's father, while living there on my wife's bothers property, her sister and her boyfriend and two sons moved near us. My wife's sister's boyfriend at this time was 2 years younger than I and a Spanish man of origin. We would drink together quite often, but he would never get drunk as I would begin to get, because of the children and he loved them and my sister-in-law very much. I will say this, during this time of my life, I had built up such a tolerance of alcohol, where 6 beers would get a man drunk, it would take me 24 beers to get to a point that I would think to myself, maybe I've had enough.

Most of the time I wouldn't stop drinking until I would throw my gut up or get very sick. I cant remember passing out much during this time of my life, I would only get very sick.

So, as I began to see he was stopping his drinking then I would leave and walk home and I would want him to think this; "I could stop drinking too." He knew when he had enough, but me, I would leave his home and go to my home or the woods and drink until sunrise. I do remember the first time my self will came out during this time. I and my wife's sister's boyfriend was drinking one evening and I thought he said an awful thing about my wife's sister. But today I know, that he said nothing out of evil toward my sister-in-law. It was my thinking and the angers and resentments that was puffing up from my imagination and I let these thoughts entered deep within my heart. I began to yell at him, cursed him and told him to never speak like that to her again and he looked at me as if he thought I was crazy. Well, I left with the anger inside of me raging like a fire and I went home and started blabbering this crap to my wife.

Well, I will say this also, after my wife's father died her sister had divorced from a very abusive relationship and had just met this Spanish Man. I really was very defensive for my wife and her sister and her children at this time and loved them very much and didn't want nobody hurting them anymore, especially those children. Today, looking back at this time of my life, now I know that it was all the angry and resentments from my past I had stored in my mind and it was starting to rise and boil again in my life and again to enter into my heart. Remember this my friend, It isn't what enters a man's mouth that defiles a man, it is what comes out of a man's mouth that defiles a man (Matthew 15:10-11) and at this time of my life, I didn't have much control of my mouth or my life.

So, after I blabbered this crap to my wife, she wanted to go and check on the kids and her sister. As we where pulling down the path to their home, they where pulling out to go somewhere. I jump out of my passenger side of the vehicle and I started at this fellow and threaten him and enticed him to come forth to me, so that we would fight and what happened next, happened extremely fast. He did get out of their vehicle and he did come toward me and as he was coming toward me, I took the passengers door and kicked it toward him to knock him into the ditch. I walked toward him to make sure he got the message, but he jumped up out of that ditch like a jack rabbit and latched onto me like a snapping turtle between my legs, no kidding. I started to yell to get this crazy man off me and began to beat him in the face and head, but like I said, he was latched on me like a snapping turtle and he was not going to let me go until the sun rose the next day, no kidding. It was so painful, I actually begged him to release me and he did. We slowly got up off the ground and we looked at each other and didn't say a word. But, it was if he was saying to me without speaking a word this; *"Do you want some more?"* I will say this man was smaller than I was and I did have the advantage over him, I thought. Well, I didn't want anymore of his medicine and I felt humiliated and I slowly got into my wife's vehicle and I was bleeding seriously from my mid section. My dear wife was hysterical and again she was seeing another side of me that she didn't know of. She couldn't believe what just happened, but for me, it was normal and all I was thinking about was this; "Now, I have a reason to do what I want to do", and that my friend, I will not mention, but it wasn't a good thought. So my wife took me to the hospital and even the ER nurses and Doctors could not believe where I was bleeding from. I heard a lot of laughing that night at the hospital, but for me, it only made things worse again and I began to feel really humiliated. I made an excuse and told the doctor that I had jumped a barbed wire fence and it caught me.

So after I was taken care of at the hospital, we went home. As I and my wife was driving into the yard, the headlights of the vehicle reflected another scene of the consequences of my actions. This Spanish Man had shot out the front windows of our home with a firearm. I knew he had a gun then and he didn't want to make any mud pies with me. I thought and said to my wife, as she was still hysterical and I was trying to calm her down, "What do I need to do?" After I ask this question, my dear wife calmed down somewhat.

As we where just sitting there in the vehicle looking at the glass scattered on the ground, I had a thought and said, "Take me to the Sheriff's office and I will report his actions in case I have to use force." We went to the sheriff's office and requested some help on this matter. A large man approximately 6 ft and 5 inches tall and weighed at least 300 lbs, came forth from his office and presented himself as the Sheriff 's Major and said to me, "I'm the Sheriff's Major. What can I help you with?" I looked up to him and I told him what had happened and I wanted to see the magistrate and put this man in jail! As I was spilling my belly out, he looked down at me somewhat as if I was crazy. And then the Sheriff's Major said to me with a stern voice, "Boy! You listen to me. I'll go and talk to this man and just to let you know, the magistrate will not listen to a drunk, anyhow." That was another blow to me in my heart and again I felt humiliated. I thought at that time, "This man just called me a drunk!" I was thinking about starting a fight with him then, but I did mange to keep my trap shut; for I did not want him to beat me or carry me to jail and I and my wife had already been through enough for one evening. He really made me angry at that time and I held this anger in my heart toward him for a long time. Oh yes! Let me share this with you, "The truth will set you free, but first it will piss you off, if you don't have understanding of the matter." And that is not written in God's Word my friend, it's just from me and forgive me my friend for my strong language, but it is the truth.

The truth did piss me off that night, but I had no choice, but to do what this Major requested. So, we went to my wife's sister's home and the Major pulled around us with his vehicle and got out of his vehicle and told me to stay in the vehicle and for me not to get out. He then asked, "Is that him sitting in the car?" And I said, "Yes, Sir." I watched as the Major walked calmly to the vehicle and my wife's sister's boyfriend was just sitting and looking at the steering wheel. The Major approached him and shined a flashlight into his vehicle and he did not move one hair and he just continued to look at the steering wheel without movement. I watched as the Major ask for the gun and he gave it to him without any confrontation. My wife's sister came out of the home as she seen the officer standing beside their vehicle with the gun. I watched and seen the Spanish man's head move toward his chest and I didn't know what was going on, but I was thinking for the worse at the time. The Major said something to my sister-in-law and he handed the gun to her and she went back into the house with the gun and I just couldn't believe the Major didn't take the gun with him. The Major left the Spanish man just sitting there in the car and calmly walk toward us and said to me as he tap on my window, "He said he was sorry and didn't mean to hurt you and said you hurt him. That boy is in that vehicle hurt and crying, not because he is weak, but because you hurt him and he had to bring out a bad side of himself. He didn't say that, but I know that is what he meant when I was talking to him. Now! You need to just stay away from him for a while and he said he was sorry and didn't want this to happen. When things get better, boy you best ask him to forgive you, so he will forgive you."

My friend, I will never forget that incident and I believe that was the first time I ever wanted to ask for forgiveness from somebody in my life that quickly. It really was another knock on my door to break this self will I was living in before it killed me or worse.

When I looked back into this past incident in my life, I now know God had put me into a position of forgiveness again. But at this time of my life, I was still without understanding and living by self will and now I had drawn blood again and it was crying out to God in desperation. I was beginning to sense that God was trying to tell me something important again at this time. But at this time, I was thinking this man had hurt me and he needed to ask me for forgiveness and I kept the anger from this incident in my heart for awhile and just stayed away from him.

Later, I was beginning to understand somewhat that God had put me into a position that I had to ask for forgiveness, and had no choice, or, suffer more consequences, such as, not seeing my nephews, loosing my dear wife, my sister-in-law mad at me and many other matters. I had no choice, but to ask of forgiveness to be forgiven. It's somewhat ironic isn't it? God was going to teach me forgiveness, if it cost me my blood and I didn't want that and I began to sense just a little bit of this matter. I did finally ask this man to forgive me in somewhat of a stubborn way, but it was as if I was made to do it and had no choice. But at this time, I had no choice and I did ask this man to forgive me. After I ask this man to forgive me, he was there with opened arms and then to my surprise, he asked me for forgiveness. Then I said to him, "You don't have to ask forgiveness from me, It was all my fault, not yours." But he continued to ask me to forgive him and I forgave him, for what I didn't know at the time, maybe for shooting out my windows?

At this time, I was still without understanding of this matter of forgiveness and continually to drink and do drugs, but this man did know about forgiveness and I will say as I got to know this man later in life, I knew he left his family because of forgiveness and I didn't know anything about his life at the time of the incident.

It seem to me at the time, as if God had sent an Angel into my life to show me hand to hand what forgiveness was all about and I will tell you today, it is a fearful thing to fall into the hand of the Living

God. I know what God was doing in my life at this time and he meant business and not to just for us to hold hands together. He was showing me that forgiveness is Life or Death and I have a choice, live or die and at the time, I wanted to live. The knocking of God upon my life was beginning to loosing the lock of self will on my door, but my self will had it locked and secured from the knocking and still wouldn't let God in. But, soon I found that I would open the door just little bit to slow the knocking down on my life, I thought.

After this incident, the Spanish man and I became very close and are still today. Today, I see him as my spiritual brother and love him very much. He has helped my sister-in-law bring up those children and they are good boys today and are doing great. This man suffered for me that day, because of my unforgiving heart and I will always ask forgiveness from him in my deeds and my love and I will show him every time I see him throughout my living, because I know that is God's Will for me in my life. For Now, please let me share with you another God's Principle on Forgiveness that has been reveal to me on this matter today. It is the greatest example of Forgiveness known to man, if we will believe it, receive it and do it in our life, then God's Will can be made perfect in our lives and there is no other way. In the Holy Book of Luke, Chapter 23 verse 34 Jesus Christ said to God the Father as he was suffering on the cross for us. As you read this, discern with you heart what man had done to him by crucified him on the cross for doing God's Will. Remember, Christ was without sin and even the Romans had recognized this matter at the time, but man still requested the death of Jesus Christ's pure spotless blood. *"Then said Jesus, Father, forgive them; for they know not what they do. And they parted his raiment, and cast lots."*

Now, if any man that had ever deserve forgiveness from man, Jesus Christ would be the one and only. God and Jesus Christ knows that man is without forgiveness and Christ stood in the way to ask God for our forgiveness when man didn't know how to forgive. Christ Jesus was without sin and he knew God's Will for him throughout his short life here on earth in the flesh and that Will is ours, if we only believe it and do it to the end of our breath. Even as Jesus Christ was hanging on the Cross suffering for mankind, and was the first of mankind to receive the garment of righteousness, mankind still didn't understanding the truth of the Will of God.

Even at the death of the Will of God to be fulfilled for mankind's Salvation, mankind was casting lots for the Righteous Son of God's Raiment. Even at this time mankind thought they could bet on righteousness are work for the righteous raiment of Jesus Christ. But, my friend, just to let any man know, you can't work for or cast lots for the garment of righteousness. The only Way to be righteous before God is through Christ Jesus. Will ever a man be justified enough for a garment that is whiter than snow? Christ suffered the ignorance of forgiveness of mankind on the Cross. He left that example to show, no matter what man has done to you on this earth, we must forgive them in order for God's Perfect Will to manifest into our lives.

Forgiving not another man, even if he had done something as horrible as killing your son on a cross, is the same as sin to God. Looking into my past dead life and not forgiving others was definitely sin in my life. God had forgiven me for all that I had done to him in my life at this time and he had wipe my slate of trespasses clean, but I wouldn't forgive another man. Jesus Christ knew the importance of forgiveness, even when he was dying the death on the cross by man's hand and as he was dying on the Cross, he knew he must fulfill all righteousness of God's Will, for all God's Perfect Will to work in his Life. Jesus Christ was and still is the complete forgiveness for mankind. He lived forgiveness which is God's Will for man every day of his life while he was here on earth, even when he took his last breath and gave up the Ghost on the Cross. Oh yes! I cant forget this principle my friend. There is another great principle of forgiveness that is written in the Holy Book of Matthew Chapter 18, verses21-35 and please read it sometime, now if you like. As Christ was hanging on that cross with just a little breath of his spirit left in his body, he knew if he didn't forgive man for killing him, then God's Will would be no effect for you and me today. This principle also points out that the good fight of God's Will for us will last us until our very last breath. It isn't a one day fight, it is a life time fight, even until the season we give up our spirit back to the God of the Living. Jesus never said this; "Once saved, always saved." and If he did say this in the Word of God, I have not yet found it as of today. But, Jesus Christ did say this and it is written;

Matthew Chapter 24, verse 13, *"But he that shall endure unto the end, the same shall be saved."*

Oh yes! While I'm still on this subject, Beware of the leaven of the Pharisees that Jesus Christ warned us about. Please let me share this principle with you. In the Holy Book of Matthew Chapter 16, Christ explains in detail how we must beware of this matter. Please read it Now, if you like. I know for confidence today this; I will listen to the gospel of Jesus Christ, but if one quotation or even one letter of the alphabet or a number is moved or twisted from the scripture as it was written, I will not listen, neither receive it in my heart, and I 0will search the scripture for the truth and the Life. I will tell you there are men and Satan, twisting the very written word of God to entice you and I away from the truth that is written and today leading many astray and straight to the Fiery Hell not knowing they are doing it. There was many times during my living in the past when someone would do something to me and it wouldn't be their fault, it was much easier for me to forgive them, but if I ever thought they did it to me willingly, it wasn't so easy to forgive.

Today, I do know that I must forgive people for their trespasses always, so that God can completely forgive me of my trespasses and if I don't forgive others, it is sin in God's Eyes and God cant work through sin.

In my past living, I would live by this course, "Do unto others as they have done unto you". I tried really hard to live good and my life was crying out for God's help, in the understanding forgiveness. Then I read the principle as it is written in God's Word and it read like this, Matthew Chapter 6, verse12, *"And forgive us our debts as we forgive our debtors."* I believe what I had heard in my past life from a man was this, "Do unto others as you would have them to do unto you." You know as of today, I can't find this principle in God's Word either. The only principle close to it would be the one written in Matthew chapter 7, verse 12, *"Therefore all things whatsoever ye would that men should do to you, do ye even so to them: for this is the law and the prophets."* You see my friend, there is much more to this principle than meets the eye and we cannot afford to listen to God's Word paraphrased only.

My friend, We have to search the scripture and confirm the Word which is spoken to us, because Satan and man's will doesn't want God's Will in your and my Life and sometimes will speak only 1/2 truth, which is a lie and there is no Life in it and only destruction. I will share this with you as the scripture is written, *"Therefore all things whatsoever ye would that men should do to you,"*. <u>Therefore</u> is a big word and also <u>all things</u> is extremely big and we must not overlook what Jesus Christ said. I want to share one more principle with you. In the book of Revelation Chapter 22, verses 18-19, ***"For I testify unto every man that hearth the words of the prophecy of this book, If any man shall add unto these things, God shall add unto him the plagues that are written in this book:***

And if any man shall take away from the words of the book of this prophecy, God shall take away his part out of the book of Life, and out of the holy city, and from the things which are written in this book." In my past life, I would listen to any ministry and paraphrasing of God's Word, but today my friend, I cant afford to listen to paraphrasing of God's written Word only. If it isn't written letter by letter, word by word, sentence by sentence and so forth, as it is written in God's Book, then I will not receive it, for there is no Life in it. I believe when you paraphrase God's Word without understanding of God's Word, you are doing it by self will and self will pleasures.

Later during this time of my life I began not to think on life the way I had been thinking. I was beginning to think that maybe God was telling me that I must forgive all those people in my past, before he could work his will in my Life, but I just still didn't know how. But I will say this with confidence, God was trying to break the chain of self will in my life, so that, his Will would come alive for my life. I knew at this time that it was an easy burden to ask for forgiveness, but it was not an easy burden to forgive others from the hurt of my past. I just could not forgive those who had hurt me in my past and continually to live in that will of my life. I was starting to drink heavy and doing drugs again and it was getting worst and I will say, I was beginning to smoke cocaine for the first time in my life. I never ever would had thought that I would had smoked the least of all drugs, because I would always get the powder cocaine and thought the crack was for crack heads and not coke heads. When I first tried smoking cocaine, I knew that I had found another way of to numb my pains at that very moment. I knew that I now didn't have to wait for any type of medicines to work. All I have to do now is find me a crack rock, no kidding. This drug immediately put a fleshly hook deep into my heart and this particular drug bound me with chains for nearly 18 years. I will share many points about this street drug that almost caused me my life throughout the book later.

CHAPTER FIVE

A HIGH CALLING

During this time of my life, I was really trying to let go of my self will that I had lived for so many years, and, wanting and willing to let God's Will into my life completely. God was revealing great understanding of the True Life to me during this time of my life, but I will say, I didn't have the greater understanding until later in life. I had lived so many years with the Knock on my heart from God and now, I had opened wide my door of my heart and was letting God and his Son Jesus Christ into my heart, freely without knocking. But, I will say there would be times I would shut the door of my heart, because of not having understanding and God would knock again and again. I will say I did have somewhat of a understanding to let him in quickly, before the knocking would continue or get quite loud; for I didn't like the knocking, because it was greatly painful to my heart. When I felt that God was approaching at my door, I would jump and open my door quickly by calling him into my home, before I thought he would knock. I was beginning to sense things by my spirit and not by the thinking and by experiences of my fleshly brain mass. I was also beginning to understand one thing and that was, I wasn't my own and there was more to life than that of myself.

I was beginning to understand that all the discipline or chastisements were not from the State or other people, but someone was behind this matter. I was still blaming other people for things that would happen to me, such as, Knocks on the door of my heart.

I was beginning to understand that these chastisements were from a greater power than that of what I was thinking. I began to understand that the State wouldn't set a special agent just on my case, but I still had a doubt that maybe that was the case, no kidding. I was beginning to believe that I was special or something to that effect. I was starting to believe that while I was in the Hospital for the 1 year and more, that the government put a chip in my brain or ear, no kidding. I still have a doubt today of not believing that to be so, no kidding. I think I should be careful of what I'm writing now, because they maybe listening. Oh! That's right! They cant read my mind, so I will continue. Just kidding my friend, I think.

Nevertheless, while I lived in this community that my wife and I had moved to, I had met a man at this time in this neighbor hood and we became very close. We started to drink and use heavy together and soon found out this man was a very serious alcoholic. He didn't like drugs that much, but would use drugs, if he had the money to buy them. There is one point I would like to make about this relationship that we had together. This man was somewhat always crying when he got drunk and would tell me that life just isn't fair. I would always ask him why he thought this way, but he would never tell me. I thought at the time he had a bad childhood and left it at that. When he would get drunk, he would start to cry and he would always say that I was

Raphael and he was Donatella. He would always say things such as, we weren't fighting with things we couldn't see for we are fighting with evil principalities in high places. When he would say things like this, my believing I had a chip in my ear or brain became greater, no kidding. I even thought at one time that he was sent from them to tell me this.

But, I soon understood that he was sent into my life for sure, but not from man.

Every time I would see him beside the road walking and stumbling, of course he was drunk, he would be acting as if he was a Mutant Ninja Turtle, but I would laugh and blow the horn and go about my business. I thought this guy was crazy when I first met him, but soon found out that I was a good friend to him. This man really thought that we together could do something in this life to better it. I soon began to sense somewhat, that this man was trying to tell me something. Raphael and Donatella, he would say. I finally ask him, "Are you talking about the Mutant Ninja Turtles?" and he would start to cry much more and rap a song with there name in it to me, as if they were to save the world and he would start crying even more so.

He did tell me, that we have got to be like them Mutant Ninja Turtles in this Life, to be able to fight against evil. At the time, like I said before, I thought he was crazy, but today I know what he was trying to say to me. We must be like a fighter in this life on earth, fighting for the good and against evil and we must have the Whole armor of God about us, as a turtle has around his entire body. I truly believe that this man's desire was that of, he and all man would live a good life and not have to live such a evil life. I believe that this man was hurting deeply within his heart.

Today, I understand what this man was trying to tell me while his chance of life was still blooming. The Turtles represented a solider with armor and I tell you, we must be like a Mutant Ninja Turtle today and to be able to fight against the wiles of the devil. Please let me share with you what began to be reveal to me at about this time in my life, but at the time I didn't understanding. Today I do understanding what this man was wanting to say to me during this time of my life, and it is this: "Out on the Whole Armour of God My Friend!"

The following writings will explain the perception of this cry for battle in this man's life, and mine.

THE WHOLE ARMOUR OF GOD

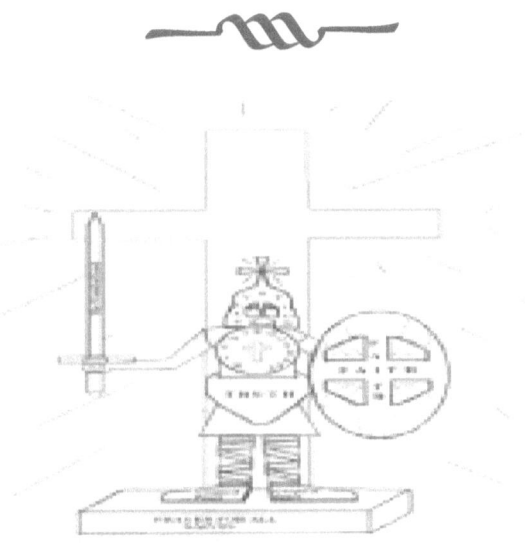

In the Holy Book of Ephesians, Chapter 6, verses 13-18, *"Finally my brethren, be strong in the Lord, and in the Power of his might. Put on the whole armour of God, that ye may be able to stand against the wiles of the devil. For we wrestle not against flesh and blood, but against principalities, against powers, against the rulers of the darkness of this world, against spiritual wickedness in high places. Wherefore take unto you the whole armour of God, that ye may be able to withstand in that evil day, and having done all, to stand. Stand therefore, having your loins girt about with truth, and having on the breastplate of righteousness; And your feet shod with the preparation of the gospel of peace;*

Above all, taking the shield of faith, wherewith ye shall be able to quench all the fiery darts of the wicked. And take the helmet of salvation, and the sword of the Spirit, which is the Word of God: Praying always with all prayer and supplication in the Spirit, and watching thereunto with all perseverance and supplication for all saints;"

Now, this man that I had met in my life may had looked crazy to some, but I took him to be my friend and very seriously. I did begin to understand what he was saying somewhat at the time. Like I have said before times, I don't believe in coincidences, I believe in chance and that the chance is for a specific reason. God did put this man in my life and even when I was without understanding of this matter, I knew that he was fighting a battle deep within his spirit. But at the time, I just didn't know how to help him, because I was fighting my own dragons. *I will say, this man did die later from liver cancer, the consequences of alcoholism and it hurt me in my heart.*

Today I know why God put that man into my life, but at the time, I was without understanding of the matter and I continually to live my life by self will pleasures. During this time in my life I had again totaled 2 vehicles and by the skin of my hair, wasn't found guilty of another DWI charge and wasn't killed in one of the accidents. I was charge on 1 count of Driving careless and reckless and lost my driving privileges for 1 year due to not submitting to a blood or breathe analyzer; for I was beginning the life again of suicide. There would be many nights and mornings I would awake in the ditch and the edge of the woods not knowing how I got there. There are many things today as I look back, not knowing how I survived through them. I can't go in details, because it doesn't matter, but I will say I thank God I'm alive today. But, Guess what? I told my wife in desperation I needed some help.

So, I and my wife took off like a flash of lightening and went to get help for me at the wee hours of the night. I committed myself to this Rehab, which was the very first time doing something good for myself like this and sought help at another Alcohol and Drug rehab center. I was 27 years of age and I was at the same hospital that I had been in earlier at 16-18 years of age, but of course in the adult unit. This was my fourth time in Rehab or the hospital for treatment from drugs, alcohol, depression, suicide thoughts and self will pleasures. I began to get somewhat honest and wanted the help from this hospital desperately. I knew at this time, I had to get help again from my drinking and drugging and most of all, I knew I needed help from God on these matters before something awful would happen to me or my dear wife. I was facing the Big hole again, looking in, deciding if I should just give up and fall in or turn and walk away. But as I was in the rehab center, I requested a minister to come and talk with me. Deep down within my heart, I knew it wasn't about all the drugs and alcohol, it was understanding and I was beginning to act like Jacob battling with God's Angel for that blessing of understanding.

Even though, God had knocked and knocked on my heart many times before, I was still without understanding. But, I was beginning to be somewhat tired of the knocking from God on my life and I thought that it would be in my favor, if I would let go and Let God and I did just that to the best I understood at the time. I was a very tired young man at this time of my life from living self will for so many years and I had the understanding that God was the one Knocking on my heart to come into me and to Love me and give me Life. So, I broke the lock of self will off my door and Opened my door widely and invited God into my heart and things began to get better.

Now, as I was getting well in Rehab, my spirit man (soul or replica body) was coming alive through me again. All I wanted at the time was to read and search God's Word for understanding of why I was going through so much suffering when I was doing the best that I could at the time. I was seeking God like a Hunter for his prey for answers to my life long problems. My spirit was so hungry for any thing of God, from the staff or this minister of God's Word. I was tired and weak from battling self will and wrestling with God for so many years and I knew I had to grow up, but I was still without understanding of this matter.

During this visit to Rehab, I began to have a spiritual awakening and I will say, it started at the rehab, but it really began after I went home to my wife. I had been drug free for this time 45 days and I was beginning to come alive and my perspective on life was different. My wife and I join a local church, the same church I went to as a child and my wife and I was baptized into the church a few months later.

At this time of my Life, I was willing to do whatsoever it took to stay from the horrors I had been living in for so many years. I had a peace again in my life and I thought at this time, what I must do in order for this peace in my life to continue. I knew I had to keep God in my life to live and I must keep a sober Mind and also stay in church to continue to grow in my spirit. I also knew this; I wanted my daughter in my life. So, my wife and I agreed that I had the right to have visitation rights to my daughter at this time. We found a Lawyer in this field and began the process of visitation.

At this time of my life, I would had never thought that it would had been so hard for me to see my child, but my wife and I pressed forward to have my daughter in my life to know me. The process began and I went to court over this matter and got visitation rights, for the price of child support, but I was willing to do anything to be with my daughter and I didn't think of the long process at the time for me to see my daughter.

As my wife and I began to grow somewhat in the spirit and mind, things began to work for us in our life with a greatness. I started to visit my daughter on the weekends and I had quit drinking and doing drugs. I felt that I had finally got my life back on the right course of life. I had not been this clean from drugs in a long time and it felt wonderful. My wife and I were happy and we where doing great and I was beginning to have a greater hope that I could now live a normal life.

But, as time passed, I noticed the mother of my child would not bring my daughter to see me. I thought at the time, "She was not wanting my child to see me again and she was up to the same crap from the past again. She got the child support order, so now, she would stop bringing my daughter to see me." I really thought this and it hurt me greatly. I knew she was trying anything in this world again to keep that child from me for some reason. I was doing great and would you know it, the past is at my door again knocking.

One day I came home from work and I had a summon to court from this women's lawyer. They where accusing me and my wife that my home was unfit for my daughters visits. I became outrage and through a terrible fit, but refused to do drugs or go back a drinking. I would think on the matter like this, "What in this world could had led this women to think of such a common thing to do to me again." and it was beginning to burn inside of me like a fire, but I pressed forward and waited.

Nevertheless, I went to court on her terms again and they accused that my daughter had gotten sick from my pets. I was raising quail and had a few full blooded Siamese cats and kittens and I would had never thought the outcome of this court order.

This judge ordered my child and her mother and myself for a psychiatric evaluation to determine if my daughter needed visitations rights to my home and also a few days later, found out that it was by request of her lawyer and herself. I just could not believe it and I started again to hold angry and resentments in my heart towards her and this matter. It was beginning to disturb my peace that I had received, but I agreed to the order and went to this psyche. I knew at the time this: I knew if I didn't go to this psyche, I would be in contempt of a court order and loose my visitation anyways, pretty crafty wasn't it? But, I will say with confidence, God knows all things. My child and her mother had already been to see this psyche days before I had went and I didn't know this, until I ask the psyche if she had been there already. I also knew that the mother of my child knew my past and so did her family and then I sensed within myself the intent again was to try to destroy me. I guess they taught I was going to this psyche and would get mad or worst and then this psyche would make notes and request my visitation rights to my child to cease, because I was an angry man, but that didn't happen.

While I was there at the interview of this psyche, I would say nothing and the psyche didn't know what to say to me, because I kept my trap shut. It was if God had shut my trap for a while and I also was thinking the psyche had the doctor degree and I didn't need to say nothing. I had nothing to say to this psyche, because I knew that I had no reason to be there the start with. I will say the outcome of this psyche notes were still not to pleasant at the time.

This psyche requested and order to the judge that I should remove my pets and quit drinking and my daughter wasn't old enough to bare seeing me at this time and her peeing on the bed at night was due to our visitations and requested my visitation rights to cease.

I will say, my daughter was around 9 or10 years of age at this time also. Oh yes! I do remember opening my trap one time during the visit and trying this psyche and requested that this psyche submit a request for me.

The request was this; "that my daughter needs to grow up and quit sleeping with her mother every night." Guess what? It was also in the order too. That request from this psyche was nothing but what we had said or asked and then I knew these people were at it again, destined to keep my child from seeing me. Oh Yes! I had already quit drinking and using before I went to this psyche too.

After a while, we went back to court for this order, per her lawyer and herself. There was another Judge and he denied the order and made a comment like this," Don't bring no more of this crap into my court room again."

I continued my visitations; for I had done nothing out of order from seeing my child and this Judge knew this. But, these people continued to put me under the microscope every chance they got and I knew this at the time, but I continually to keep myself on the right course and never gave up on the matter. I was also told by a good friend of the mother at the time, that the mother of my child was wanting to change my child's last name to her last name, but I kept going forward. I was at this time, living a more of a normal life. I assumed they thought that would bulge me to madness again also.

Before I go any further with the writings, please let me share with you something. In the Holy Book of Matthew Chapter 10, verses 37-39, Christ clearly states a principle for Life and it reads as written, *"He that loveth father or mother more than me is not worthy of me: and he that loveth son or daughter more than me is not worthy of me. He that taketh not his cross, and followeth after me is not worthy of me. He that f indeth his life shall lose it: and he that loseth his life for my sake shall f ind it."*

In my past dead life, I was putting all things first, before I would put God first and I had lost and suffered much. I will say this, there was one day that I did speak to the mother of my child and ask her why is she trying so hard to keep my daughter from me. This is what she said, "I thought that you wanted to fight for her."

I just couldn't understand those words from her at the time, because I didn't think I had to fight to see my daughter. At this time, I just began to quit my desiring to see my daughter, because I felt as if my daughter was a pull toy. I thought it was Pretty crafty on her part to keep my daughter from me, but I pressed forward in my new normal life. I was trying to do what I thought was right and honest to the best of my ability and understanding. I had been quit drinking and using now for about 6 months. I was really beginning to sense life on its terms and was getting much understanding of matters. I was beginning to make a list of all those who had hurt me in my past. I would pray and speak each name to God and ask God to forgive them and give me the forgiveness to forgive them and I wept many nights, until I knew in my spirit, that God gave me understanding and forgiveness. I did finally forgive all those people who had hurt and offended me as a child.

Later as my daughter turn 13 she again cease from coming over and it hurt me badly in my heart and I really didn't see much of her afterwards, until she got her drivers license.

At this time of my life, my child and I were just beginning to know each other and were getting very close, before she ceased from coming over to stay with me. I thought we had a good relationship building and she loved my wife very much also.

During times that my daughter wouldn't show up and her mother didn't have anymore excuses, I would call her mother and say, "You know you are in violation of the court order for the child not coming over to stay with me, don't you? You know I could carry you to court over this matter, don't you? I hope you have good reason for her not coming over, Do you?." And she would always say this time after time, "Well, she wanted to stay with a friend and I figured you wouldn't mind".

You know, after this incident, I began to give up on seeing my daughter, but I was still without understanding of the matter somewhat. One day we had gathered at my parents for Thanksgiving and I had called this women to bring my child over to my parents to see me and my parents. She finally showed up and I had something waiting for her; for it was forgiveness. I knew what I must do at this time, because of what God had revealed somewhat to me and my spirit was leading me to do this matter; for I knew Life was in it. So as they came, I met her at her vehicle and said this, "I know I've done some bad things in my life against God, you and my child, but God has forgiven me and I must ask forgiveness from you. It is time for me to lay the axe to the root and ask you, to forgive me." I couldn't believe what she said next. She looked at me as if I was crazy and said this, "Well. What are you asking for forgiveness from me for? Have you done anything wrong?"

At that time, I had honestly forgiven her and her family for all that they had done to me in the past and had wept much over this matter greatly. At the time, I was really hoping she would had said, "you are forgiven too." I just went my way and left it at that. After this incident I began to feel something coming from deep down within my heart. I had a peace over the matter and I knew that I had done what I was supposed to had done, which was, forgiveness. I felt a Joy and compassion in my spirit over the matter. I had finally ask her for forgiveness that day at my parents home, because I knew that God's Will could not begin to work in my life, if I didn't ask for forgiveness and forgive her with honestly. I began to suffer somewhat and just let my child go; for I knew in my spirit that this must be suffered for now, so that God's Will would manifest into my life. I was truly beginning to understand the gift of Forgiveness, but I will say, this teaching was a long and suffering road. I just didn't want the troubles anymore in my life and just let my daughter go. I thought at the time, "Well both are gone out of my life, maybe now I can live a much more normal life.

At least I want have to go to court anymore over this matter and if I did, it sure wouldn't be on my part. I've stayed on time with my child support and through court orders and tried my very best to have a relationship with my daughter, but there is nothing else I can do for this matter and *I must let go and Let God.*"

Now, I had to put this matter to rest and let go and let God and I will say that the suffering was not joyful for many years. I also know today, that the suffering was the consequences of my self will pleasures from the past and there was nothing that I could change in the past. I was beginning again to Trust God for who he was to the best of my understanding. I had now done something for the suffering for God's Will and not self will and it felt Joyful. I had finally trusted God for this matter and he rewarded me with the gift of forgiveness. At the time, I knew from deep down that this situation about my daughter was hindering my life and I had let go of my daughter for God to Work in my Life. When I ask her for forgiveness and surrendered this matter to God, then things got better and I began to have great compassion for this lady. I didn't have lust anymore for her; for now I was beginning to really love and have great compassion for her. I wanted deeply for her to feel the peace that I was experiencing at this time. I knew at the time that I had blamed her and her family for a lot of my problems, but now since I had forgiven all of these people and asked for forgiveness, God's Love was beginning to grow within my spirit.

When I trusted God for this one particular time of my life, It was at this very moment that God was ready to start working his perfected Will in my Life. You see, I never put my faith into action until this day and that day, I spoke life into my life; as I forgave and then God forgave me. I didn't understand that God was still working in my life for my profit and I was still without understanding of my life, but I pressed forward and still tried to live a normal life.

Later, I began to go to church on a weekly basis and then a every time the door opened basis. I continually to seek the understanding of God's Will for my Life. I began to be called to the ministry of the gospel of God's Word and started to work in the local church. My wife had been going to church for months, before I committed and was helping in the youth ministry and I would go in and help her sometimes. It was beginning to seem to me, I was living a normal life. I was determined to fight for understanding at any cost and I knew that God was telling me something, but I just could not put my finger on it. My life was so much more abundantly and my wife and myself, began to keep children all the time over at our home and tried to teach them a little about God's Will and Life in general.

It is also somewhat ironic looking back when I gave my daughter to God and just left the matter to him and that I didn't have my child over at my home much at all during this time, that I would have at least 6-10 children at my home most of the time and I loved them and still love them today. I also know today that my daughter that came from my loins, isn't my real daughter anymore, now she belongs to God; for I had given the matter to him. Looking back through all the years from when she was born to this day at her age of 22, I never had her and will never have her, because she wasn't mine the start with; for she is God's.

I do remember clearly the vision I had when she was just an infant in a bassinet, when I heard a voice from her and it said, "Am I Worth It." It took me 20 years to get the full understand of this matter. I know today it was all in the Words, "AM I WORTH IT." It wasn't my child speaking; for she was just a infant. It was the Spirit asking me a question, "AM I WORTH IT?" I could never put a question mark after this wording and today I know it was a question that God was asking; for it was this, "If He was worth it." God was asking me at this time, if I was willing to give up my daughter for him and today I can say with confidence, I did give her up for God.

But, I know this with great confidence today, she is now in God's Great Loving Hands. I'm just her father in the flesh and if she needs me today for any reason, I'm there waiting patiently for her. She and I know that I want get her to heaven, only following God's Will to her last breath will get her there and I have no control over that matter, except to pray for her always. I know Satan wants to sift her as wheat and to destroy her life, but I have given her to my God and have great hope in the matter today of his protection. God knew my heart and he also knew how to give me peace when I didn't know how to get peace during these times of suffering.

Today I know, God sent the other children to me and my wife and they where to me, as little lambs sent from God and I had a responsibility to help them learn about Life. They all would call me Uncle and my wife Aunt, when some where no kin to me. I love each of them as my own daughter and son. At this time of my Life, I was beginning to discern that God wanted me to do something for him and I was beginning to grow in my spirit quickly. I started to feel with my heart and spirit, that God wanted me to share the Hope I had in Him to this suffering World.

As time passed, my wife and I were dedicated to the Church and started a ministry together; for we knew this was God's Will for us deep within our spirit. The ministry started there at the church and later, I was elected to help in the Youth ministry with my wife. I was working in Communications at this time and was on call a lot and this Job was providing good income for me and my wife at this time. I will share with you now a vision I had when I was first called into the ministry of Jesus Christ. I had been clean now for a year or more and was beginning to understand God's Will for me in this Life and I was always praying and thanking God for the deliverance from my past and for giving me a chance at Life again, as a new born child.

God was revealing his Word to me and I was beginning to eat of it daily and I was growing stronger in my spirit and mind and looking at Life in a different perspective.

During this time of my Life, I was hungry (had a fervent passion) for what God could give me. I remember almost every night, I would fall asleep with the Word of God upon my chest and awake the next morning with the Word of God in my bed under my back.

One evening during this chance of my life, I do remember coming from church to my home after a great teaching of God's Word. I do remember that it was a time just before the Easter season. I'm confident the season was just before the Easter season, because of the preparedness of the Easter services around the communities and the teachings that night at church. The teachings that evening at church were on the resurrection of Jesus Christ. These teachings led me to have a greater passion and want for something of God. I honestly did not know what I needed, but I was desperate for God and Jesus Christ to build my Faith in them. I laid down that evening and had a visit. I call the following writings, "The Man in my Doorway."

THE MAN IN MY DOORWAY

Now, my wife and I came home from a church service one evening and I told her I wanted to pray alone with God in the other bedroom of our home. It seem as I was being led to do this alone without a understanding of why I needed to be alone with God. It seemed to me as if I was being led by the Spirit of God to do so. I was sitting up in bed with a lamp upon the headboard of my bed. I was reading God's Word and my wife was already asleep in the back bedroom. I do remember thinking somewhat this to myself at this time; "It smells sweet and good in here for some reason. I wonder where that smell is coming from. It surely smells familiar like something I've smelled before. I think I know where I smelled this at! It smells just like some Churches I've been in. Has someone been in my home while we were gone?" The smell was very sweet and much sweeter than a flower garden. The smell also had somewhat of a peppermint smell mixed with it. I began to breath this smell in amazement. I'm confident it was at this very moment that I began to get very sleepy and fell asleep.

I remember hearing and feeling something liken as if I was put into a Power Reactor Room. The sound and feeling would get stronger and stronger in and out through my complete being. It seem as if my body would move in and out in harmony with the power of this sound. I just laid in the bed thinking that it was all but just a dream, but, I couldn't awake from this dream. I felt as if I was tied down or something heavy had covered my complete body. I tried desperately to open my eyes and then I did opened my eyes barely. This was the only thing that I could do with my body was try to look with my eyes. It felt as if my whole complete body was somewhat dead, except my sense of sight. When

I did get my eyes to open somewhat, I was immediately amazed at what I was seeing. I tried to turn my head and move or get out of bed, because I was fearful of what I was seeing. But, my body became more as a dead man and I could not move my body at all. I was laying in bed horizontal with my head facing the doorway and I could not move.

I was fearful at first, but soon it was if Love had cast out the fear from my whole existence. There was a figure standing approximately 5' 11" high in my doorway and his likeness was as a man. His hair upon his head was white as snow and tall as if he had wore a tall and large crown upon it. It looked as if he had just took the crown off his head and his hair did move with the sound of the Power. This figure resembled a man's body with all that a man's body would have, such as a face, nose, lips, ears, eyes, hair, arms, hands, legs and even finger nails. But, his flesh was if it had light in it and it somewhat shined as mica or crystal gems with light coming from the inside out. He wore a very white garment that looked sleeveless and had no seams. I could see his arms from his shoulders to his hands. The garment went down from the top of his shoulders to the top of his knees.

His garment was whiter than snow and looked as if it had somewhat ruffles around his neck and there above his knees. His garment also moved with the Power of the sound. He wore golden bands with the width of them approximately 6" around the garment about his shoulder and his waist. The bands looked somewhat brilliant also as if they were polished. He was wearing on his feet like sandals that where made of shinning Gold. They strapped to his legs from the top of the sandals to the bottom of his knees without any knots as if they were not tied.

Now, I was as a dead man and I couldn't move my body: for the power of the sound had taken over my complete body. I just laid horizontal on the edge of the bed and watched this man with amazement and then, I felt a Love that my words cannot explain. It was if the power of this sound that I was feeling from within my complete body was the Love of God for the whole wide world and it had control over me. All that I could do was weep and my eyes were pouring with water as I just laid there watching him. I watched this man as if he was confirming that he was real.

He would slowly move just his head from left to right for me to see that he had ears. It was if he was confirming to me that he was for real and I wasn't dreaming. His eyes were like a small flame of fire and his lips were as the color of bright red blood. It seem as he would not look at me directly into my eyes as I laid on the bed as a dead man. He would somewhat just glace at me moving his head from left to right very slowly. I tried desperately to get up off the bed to just touch him. Every time that I would try to get off the bed I seen as if he moved his right foot backwards somewhat slowly as if he didn't want me to touch him. Then the heavy burden that held me down somewhat eased from my body. I did get the strength up and set up on the side of the bed. I tried to reach for him, but I fell from the bed immediately at his feet. When I was on my knees before him, I again became as a dead man that could not move. I could only move my head and look up to him and my eyes were running water as a water fall. It was if he had control and he gave me the strength to come forth from the bed. Then I set back to the edge of the bed and then he did glance into my eyes for a split second and it was if he had moved his right hand towards his waist slowly. He then moved his left hand near his right hand and it looked as if he wrote something down in the palm of his hand with his finger. He would somewhat glance at me as he was writing with his finger Then immediately after he had wrote in his palm looked straight into my eyes and he blew his breath upon me with gentleness. I fell backwards upon my bed as if I was dead as dead could be.

After I awoke, I was sitting up at the head of my bed in amazement. I couldn't move for a while and I had no strength in my body but just to set up in bed. I later got up from bed and I felt as a New Man. Later in life I would read many of God's Principles that would confirm many of God's servants that had seen this same familiar man in there visions and the Word of God confirmed this Man's Visit to me. I will not go in all details for now what I know of this vision.

But, I will say this with confidence; This was the beginning of my ministry in the Gospel of Jesus Christ. I couldn't say if it was Jesus Christ or Michael the Archangel of God at that time. But later in life, there was confirmation through God's Word revealed to me that this Man in my Doorway was in the likeness of the Son of the Living God.

After this vision, God's Will was becoming more clear to me and it was if I was enlightened on this matter. I was smoking cigarettes at this time and I had the understanding that smoking cigarettes was a hindrance to my ministry in the Gospel of Jesus Christ and for God's perfected Will to manifest in my Life and I remember clearly the day I quit smoking during this time of my life. I had smoked cigarettes at this time since I was 11years of age and never thought it was a hindrance from anything. As a young child, I would see Deacons of some churches sneak to the bathrooms at the churches, and I would catch them smoking cigarettes and they would somewhat try to hide the smoking from me. So, I always thought, if these men of God were smoking, then it is alright for me to smoke and still have a relationship with my God. My thinking this way was somewhat the truth, but not the whole truth, so my thinking must had been, a lie. You can have a relationship with God smoking cigarettes, but do you only want a little bit of God or do you want the Whole thing? I believe also that anything that you do to defile your body is a gateway for the enemy to come into your life.

So, I did have the understanding of this matter and I wanted the whole apple and not just a bite. I went forth one day during a call to the alter at church and I took my cigarettes out of my front pocket and threw them down upon the alter. I began to stomp upon them as if I wanted them dead and out of my Life. As some people were watching me and I would glace toward them stomping those cigarettes under my feet, and crying, I would say this,

"These things are the gateway to Hell! And they are a lie from the mouth of the father of lies, which is Satan himself and smoking cigarettes will get you there to Hell just as fast as committing an awful sin; for sin is sin!"

After Church service was over, I and my wife were leaving out the door and one of the elders in the church came up to me and hugged me and kissed me on the cheek and then said, "Son, what you said was not to nice. You shouldn't had said that here at the church." I was very saddened about this matter, but stood firm on my belief and then I said to the elder, "This is what I believe to be the truth. God doesn't want us to have anything in our lives to hinder us from all of his promises, and smoking, is a hindrance from God working completely in a man's life." And then the elder walked away from me slowly as if discourage somewhat. I was beginning to think at this time, "If this elder didn't like it, then I wonder how some of the others were feeling that I know smoked cigarettes." I counted this rebuked I call it, for joy that day and I did quit smoking for nearly 7 years, until later in life I began to smoke again and I will share the reason later in the writings.

Now at this time, I was totally drug free and had no hindrances from God working in my Life and things began to get somewhat better. I knew there were already judgments held against me in the hearts of some there at this church, but I pressed forward anyhow without a much more understanding of the matter. Please let me ask this question: "If smoking was good for a man, do you think Jesus Christ would had been smoking weed, grass, herbs or tobacco?" Well just to clear the matter up, Jesus Christ never smoked according to the scriptures written, maybe he knew that smoking was not good for the body of a man. I believe with confidence today this; God whom made our bodies, doesn't want any man to put in their body anything that could or would cause harm to their body, because he loves us and we are made in his Image."

I truly believe that it is not only the Spirit that a man is made in God's Image, but it is also the blood of Life that flows through a man's body and spiritual body that we are made in God's Image. It is written, 1Corinthians 4:16-17, *"Know ye not that ye are the temple of God, and that the Spirit of God dwelleth in you? If any man defile the temple of God, him shall God destroy; for the temple of God is holy, which temple ye are."* There is another great principle in the Holy Book of Romans chapter 12, verses 1-2 and it is written, *"I Beseech you therefore brethren, by the mercies of God, that ye presents your bodies a living sacrifices, holy and acceptable unto God, which is your reasonable service. And be not conformed to this world: but be ye transformed by the renewing of your mind, that ye may prove what is that good, and acceptable, and perfect, will of God."*

Now my friend, I'm not a perfect man and neither do I profess to be, but I do know that we must have a sound mind in this world or this world, will take you over like a consuming fire would take over a dry hay field. Smoking does defile the temple of the Lord, by destroying the body with its poisons. I do believe that maybe smoking isn't a sin to death, but, it surely will get you to heaven quicker.

Now, I ask this question, Did you create yourself or did God create you? I hope you agree with me, that God created you. If you agree with me that God made your body, do you think that maybe he wants to live in you? I would say with confidence, Yes he does! God doesn't want a man to smoke, because God doesn't want anything in our body to hinder him from living in us with Life and smoking destroys the blood in our bodies. I also can say today with confidence this; Not only is smoking harmful for a man's body, it can also tempt a man to do something worse to their body, if the man is weak in faith. I can say this also with confidence, smoking is a gateway for Satan to snake his way into a man's life for worse things to happen in a man's life, if the man is weak in faith.

I must ask this question, "Would I give a cigarette to a child and say, smoke this and live?" No, I would not and I hope you agree with me in one accord.

When I was at the church the time that I have mentioned and said this: "These things are the gateway to Hell! And they are a lie from the mouth of the father of lies, which is Satan himself and smoking cigarettes will get you there to Hell just as fast as committing an awful sin; for sin is sin!" I still today stand firmly on what I said with a great confidence. When the elder can to me and said to me that I shouldn't had said that at the church, again, I stand firmly in what I believe. If a man is weak in the faith and wanted to quit smoking, because he couldn't breath and was weak from smoking cigarettes for so long, Would I light a cigarette and blow the smoke into his nostrils?" No, I would not and I hope you agree with me in one accord. This is the point; I know from my past experiences that smoking led me to much worse things in my life, such as using again and why would I want to tell a man that is weak that cigarette smoking was good for him? In the Holy Book of 1Corinthians chapter 6, The apostle Paul explains these judgments in a man's life and I ask that you read it now. Also in the Holy Book of Matthew Chapter 7, Jesus Christ gives detail on this matter. I know today that smoking is bad for my body and it also can hinder me from specific works in my life.

When I was but a child at the age of 11, I started smoking cigarettes and the reasons I believe was this; First, finding cigarettes lit by the highways and I was tempted as a child and picked a lit cigarette up and tried one and got addicted to them. Second, I had seen some of the church elders smoking cigarettes and thought to myself later this;

"Cigarette smoking can't be that bad, if they are smoking." I started to smoke cigarettes when I was tempted at this early time of my life and have smoked cigarettes for almost 30 years. I did quit smoking during my first enlighten as I have mentioned before for almost 7 years, but later I started to smoke again, somewhat like a thorn in my flesh.

Even though, I know it is bad for my health and a hindrance for my life, I chose to start smoking and now I have gotten addicted to smoking again. I believe that this is the reason that I started back to smoking cigarettes again; I had quit smoking for about 7years during this season of my life and I was doing well with my life somewhat. I would stumble and fall sometimes such as drink alcohol, because I was weak and without true understanding of life, but I tried to stay straight on my course for the better at this time of my life. I didn't want to drink and use and was willing to live a good life during this season of my life. I was going to the psychiatrist for drugs at this time and I was on many different drugs. You will read more of this struggle during this time of my life, later. I had started a new job in the mapping industry this year of my life when I started to smoke again and I traveled by myself and stayed in different States and hotels for 1year. I remember that I didn't smoke this time much at all and I had struggled hard to do well with my life during this year. One day as I was traveling I thought this; "I want a cigarette. A cigarette want hurt me and I need something to help me relax while I'm traveling. Shoot! I haven't smoke for some time and my lungs and body feel ok. I will just smoke one when I need one and control it that way."

So, I stopped at a store and picked me up a pack of cigarettes. I opened the pack cigarettes in the parking lot of this store and lit one up and then inhaled it and it was as if I was 11 years old again saying this; "Boy it sure makes me cough, but it makes me feel good." About a week had past and I was beginning to smoke a pack a day again, one evening while I was at a hotel by my lonesome, I thought this, "Well no one would know if I go get me some beer and set in the tub in my room and drink it. I need to relax and beer will help me relax. I can set in the tub and drink me a few beers and smoke cigarettes and be relaxed. A couple of beers want hurt me and I will control it, because I'm stronger than before." So, guess what?

I went and got me a six pack of corona beer, and then I thought as I was getting the beer, "Well, I need some cigarettes, because I cant drink a beer without a cigarette and I don't want to give out of cigarettes after I know I've been drinking beer." My friend, that judgment and thinking almost cost me my physical life and eternal life later, no kidding. After that evening things went from worse to great worse for my life. I started drinking heavy and using drugs again and I continued to use for 6years after this evening of self will pleasures.

I will say this with confidence, Satan that deceiving serpent, knows a man's weaknesses or thorns. Smoking has always been a weakness in my flesh since I was but a child, and it was through this weakness, that serpent enticed me. Smoking to me is as a thorn in my flesh, a weakness that the devil knows and buffets me with daily. Satan knew all my weaknesses from when I was but a child and he knew if he could get me to start smoking again, then I would seek other avenues of pleasures and feelings and start using again and guess what, I did just that!

Today I can say with confidence; Cigarette smoking is a weakness in a man's life and Satan, if he can use the weaknesses for his strength over a man's life, he will do it! I will also say that I don't judge a man if he is smoking, because how can I judge unless I be judged. I'm not in control of any man's soul for only God himself has to power to give and take. But, I do know it is a weakness of the flesh in a man's life and that man should be extremely careful for the deceiver from entering through the gateway of smoking.

It is by the sinful nature of mankind that Satan can entice a man to do what that man is not willing to do. I will say this with confidence, smoking is somewhat like a thorn in my flesh. Cigarette smoking is the #1 killing of mankind's physical body, because of the poisons that are in the cigarettes. Smoking steals the oxygen from a man's life and causes great trouble in a man's physical health.

I believe that cigarette smoking is more addictive than any drug on man's market. I believe that Satan can use smoking to destroy a man's life, because Satan is a destroyer of life and he wants all mankind, believer or not to go to hell with him.

Now, during this time when the elder of the church railed me, I was already beginning to sense the persecution of a believer and by those

I thought were close to me. I was still much without understanding of God's Will for my life at this time. I knew also that people were perishing from the lack of understanding of God's Will and this was diffidently a act of not understanding God's Perfected Will. I forgave this elder in my heart and asked God to forgive them; for they no not what they do. I was beginning to feel the Power of Love for mankind and I will say, <u>it was not a controlling power;</u> for it was a Loving Power with mercy and grace and great compassion for mankind. I was beginning to be somewhat noticed in this church as a trouble maker, that's right, a trouble maker and I felt as if they didn't want me there to stir up any dirt, but I pressed forwards to the prize. At the time, I really didn't think much of these matters, but I did somewhat understand their intents and I will share with you much on this matter later.

At this time of my life, I would take these types of gestures and remarks, as a duck would with water. I would just let it roll off my back and continued to press forward and live a normal life. I do remember during this time how God would send many people into my life, even children and older men for ministry. I do remember an occasion or two that God would lead me to youth to give them hope on Life and they would come from the street and I would make my home, their home. I was beginning to have a understanding of what God's Will for my Life was and I pressed forward with the understanding of this matter and was working diligently with the youth in my church and on the streets from all different kinds of people. My wife would teach the younger children and I would work with the older youth.

We knew God's Will for us at this time; for we were happy and had great joy. We worked diligently with Love and dedication throughout this ministry there at this church to the best we could. I was still working in Communication at this time and I want to share with you another vision, soon after the Vision of the Man in my doorway. Remember as you read the following writings of this vision, I was making firm stands for God's Will in my life. My Life was growing with the blessing of God's Will and I was a new born child of God. I was living a normal and much more abundantly life and was somewhat on top of the mountain of my life: "A Vision Of Satan"

A VISION OF SATAN

One morning as I had left a meeting at work from where we would have these meetings every morning to organize the days work, I headed to my first service call for the day I would always tune the radio onto some good music and worship God there in the vehicle, as I would travel to my destination. As I was approaching a place void of houses, in a very wooded area that I would pass through sometimes to get too my service calls, it happened very quickly. I felt that my spirit was uneasy, as if I was in danger. I then sensed and seen with my eyes, a figure coming from no where and approached from my left side of my of my vehicle quickly to the front of my vehicle's windshield, looking straight into my eyes and the description of this figure is like this: He had somewhat a figure of a man. He wore a garment from the bottom of his neck to the bottom of his entire body and his garment looked somewhat dirty and gray and was without seams. He had no feet neither arms or hands, that I seen and the garment covered all of his body, as if he had no limbs. His skin was of a grayish color and wrinkled as a old dead man for many years, somewhat like a mummy. His hair was a shade lighter than that of his skin, but gray and as if it had not been groomed. His hair came from the sides of his head, above his ears only and looked somewhat thin as it went to about his shoulders straight. The top of his head was bald, but reflected no light and it was gray as his face. His eyes were set back into his forehead somewhat and were as dark as darkness can be defined. They were totally black and reflected no light. As he turned to his right towards me and fixed his eyes into my eyes through the front windshield, he opened his mouth which was the same color of his eyes and roared at me as if he wanted to kill me. When he did this roar, it was if time stopped and then he left as fast as he came, like the wind.

After seeing this Image, I was somewhat stunned and came to the stop sign, pulled over and thought on this matter, "Am I crazy or did I really just see what I saw." I did see this Image and it did stun me for a short time, but I continued to press forwards to my Job destination.

Today, I do know what this vision was all about. God allowed me to see with the eyes of my spirit this Image of Satan, to give me a better understanding of what I'm warring against; for at the time, I thought my battles where all because of other men only and my self will intents. I do know that Satan's intent was to discourage me from pressing on with my new life and he tried to put fear in me and to turn me back to my dead life and away from God's Will. I know today I'm really not only having little battles with my flesh to keep it under submission, but there is a enemy that wants me dead and that enemy is, Satan. Satan has many other names such as, Lucifer, the son of the morning, the morning star, that great serpent, the father of lies, the deceiver, the enemy, the adversary, the dragon, the falling one, the devil. I know today he is my enemy and neither does this enemy sleep; for he is a spirit. I now know, I'm not only fighting against flesh and self will of man, but against spiritual darkness. For in the Holy Book of Ephesians Chapter 6, verses 10-12, reads, ***"Finally my brethren, be strong in the Lord, and in the power of his might. Put on the whole armour*** *of God, that ye be able to stand against the wiles of the devil. For we wrestle not against flesh and blood, but against principalities, against powers, against the rulers of darkness of this world, against spiritual wickedness in high places. "* I tell you today with confidence, there is a spiritual enemy, which is Satan, and he would like it very much if all mankind would just go to the Hell with him. Satan has also a will for you and me and that my friend, is Death. I could spend eternally writing about God's Will and riches for mankind, but I will sum Satan's will for mankind in one word and that word again is, Death. I do understand Satan's will for mankind today, but I will say I was still without understanding of the matter at the time.

Please Let me share with you what I know today, concerning this filthy devil. Satan has only one intent and that my friend is to Kill and destroy mankind with the poison of his trap.

Even in the Holy Book of Genesis at the beginning, Satan enticed man to sin against God's Word and mankind did sin against God's Word and suffered greatly from the consequences of this sin. Not only did man suffer, but the whole creation suffered and I believe that was a dark day upon this earth. I have some understanding of this spiritual wickedness and would like to share it with you now. Satan was a great cherubim in God's Kingdom, but the will of his spirit rose up and wanted to be as God. God cast out this evil from heaven and made the evil a place here on earth; for the appointed time of Satan's consequences had not been manifested completely. I always asked the question, "Why in this world would God put the enemy where he just made man in his Image, on earth." Here is an understanding of this matter I have today: God made the heavens and the earth in the beginning and then cast that spirit upon the earth and appointed this spirit to eternal death. God cast this spirit out of heaven and made a place for him to dwell, until the appointed time of his eternal damnation. God's Will not Self will.

So, Satan was cast here to the earth as a testimony of his eternal damnation. Why do I think this? Because, God made the Sun and it is a eternal lake of fire and made a point to Satan, that this is his home soon. But, first God will rebuke him even more so, for rebelling against him. God cast him here on earth and out of the rebuke, Satan, now has to look at his destination everyday, which is the Lake of Fire. Satan knows without no doubt, he is going to this Lake of Fire, very soon. Man! God's rebuked is awesome isn't it? Not only does Satan know that the lake of fire is his eternal destination at the appointed time from God, he has to look at it every second. Satan is an angry spirit and he wants to carry all of mankind that God has made in his Image with him to the lake of fire. God gave mankind the gift of choice from the beginning and God made man as another rebuke to Satan. Remember, Satan was on the earth before man before God made the day from night and all the living things.

God said, Let us make man in our Image and God made man in his image. Remember the spirit and soul cannot be destroyed, but it can be tormented.

Now, God gave mankind a fleshly body and some would ask, "Why didn't God just make every body a spirit and then we never die the death of the body." Please follow me, the point is coming. Satan is a spirit and that spirit entered into a body of an serpent and deceived mankind and enticed mankind to Sin (rebel) against God's Word of Life. That serpent was also cursed for allowing the spirit of Satan to enter into its body and to entice man to sin, and this is the choice I'm talking about. I will say this now, It was not God's Will that mankind sinned against him, but like God said, *"Let us make man into our Image"*, he meant every word and his Word will not go back to him void or empty. Let me also clear this up, if I may? Your body is a temple of God. When God made our fleshly bodies he said, "It is Good." It wasn't the body or the Flesh that sinned in the garden for It was the sinful nature of Satan that enticed man to sin. Remember, man was without sin when God made man. That sinful nature was rebellion against God's Word. The same sinful nature that cast Satan from God's Face. If you could give Satan a permanent name, it would be Mr. Rebellious. Satan is without the understanding of God Perfect Will; for God is understanding and he was there as understanding, before he even thought to bring forth Lucifer into his kingdom. God is the beginning and the end and his time is Eternal and seems as if it takes a long time in our eyes for one word of God to manifest into existence.

For God's Word is written in the Holy Book of 2 Peter chapter 3, verse8, *"But, beloved be not ignorant of this one thing, that one day is with the Lord as a thousand years, and a thousand years as one day.*" Its somewhat like this: If I left the earth and went immediately to the Lord for one day and when I got back to the earth in the same day, I would be a thousand years old.

That would be just a day, just think of how old you would be, if you spent a thousand years with the Lord. Not only did God give us a choice to choose life or death in the beginning, but Satan was still there to entice mankind on earth. Satan has no power over life or death, he is only an enticer to death; for he has not the power over this matter. But, he is among the living to entice them away from God while his time is still waiting for eternal damnation. Satan's rebuke from God continues as God makes mankind into his image and now, Mankind has the power over Satan also through Christ Jesus. Boy! God's rebuke is awesome isn't it?

I'm confident today that Lucifer, that devil, is really mad at God and mankind now. We as mankind have a body (flesh) from the earth, we now have the choice to rebuke Satan or follow Satan. Why did God give mankind this Power of choice? Why didn't God just make man as a spirit and let mankind rebuke Satan as a spirit, rather than, giving us a body for choice? Remember, God speaks a living soul and spirit into life (existence) and this soul and spirit is void from understanding and it must grow in order to know the Father of its creation. Please follow me; for I'm almost there to the point. God creates a spirit and soul and the spirit and soul enters a man's body (an unborn child) and then the spiritual man will grow in wisdom of the creator and will get to know his amazing Grace, Love and Glory, if he follows God's Will. God gives a man a body with eyes, ears, a brain, a heart, hands, feet, nose, so that that man's spirit will use the body to grow into understanding of the Creator. I will say this with confidence, When God said let us make man in our image, he wasn't only talking the spirit my friend. Remember God made mankind a fleshly body and why did he make man a fleshly body? I will share much more later and expand on the body in the writings.

Now, I say this with confidence, it is because of the blood that flows through the veins of a man that gives man life. Blood contains all the life of a man and the blood is the witness of the man, follow me?

The blood contains Life and that Life of a man is also part of the Image of God. Like I've said, the spirit of a man is only a part of God's

Image, but the blood of a man contains also greatly the Image of God, which is Life. Its somewhat like going to school and being trained with hands on training.

So as a man grows in the spirit, if the man allows God's Spirit to teach him about the Creator and his creation and doesn't quench the Spirit of God, the man's spirit and Life will grow stronger and have the Power to rebuke that Devil from their Life. So God has given mankind the Power over Satan through his Son Jesus Christ (The Word of Life) and I will say today with confidence, that Satan is just a wolf in lamb's clothing trying to blow my house down and I looked at it, somewhat liken into the Three Little Pigs story book. Satan will huff and puff and try to blow your house down and will blow your house down if your house is built by hay stubble and not on a solid rock foundation and have the Corner Stone of Life laid as the solid foundation. I will also say, that the vision I had of this enemy looked as if he had no teeth either. I went to my fathers home during this same time that I was inserting this vision into these writings. I was sharing with him about the enemy not having any teeth, arms, hands, legs or feet and I asked him, "Daddy, you know that Satan's work was finished when he was drove out of heaven and when Jesus Christ defeated him at Calvary. But, would you know why Satan doesn't have any teeth to bite you with." My father then laughed somewhat and said, "There was an Older Minister in my day that I will always remember and he said this: The Devil may not be able to bite you, but he can sure gum you to death with his mouth."

I know today that my house may not be built by diamonds, but the Carpenter of Life has came and made my house firm with understanding of this matter and has set me upon the solid rock. The fight between good and evil is my good fight today and it is a good fight, because of understanding of the matter we have just read.

I know with confidence that Jesus Christ defeated Satan, which is death and ripped his work from him. I know with confidence that Jesus Christ ripped Satan's work from him at Calvary. Wars and crime, deaths and sufferings are the consequences of mankind's choice to fall into the sinful nature from the beginning. But, God has sent his Word into the earth, so that, we as mankind could have a 100% chance of having life on earth more abundantly and to enter Life everlasting: if only we follow God's Will. God loves mankind and all his creation and has given mankind the choice or willingness to Live eternal or Die eternal; for it is our choice or willingness and not God's or Satan's.

I do know Satan's work in God's kingdom is over and he is predestined to the Lake of Fire with all that follow him. Satan and his followers have been Judged and Sentence by God from the beginning to the end. Satan can entice a man to sin against God's Will, but he cant make man do anything. Have you every heard someone say, "The devil made me do it." That is a lie straight from the father of lies Satan himself and Satan can not make any man do anything, unless the man is willing to let him work in their life. Maybe if the man that would say such a thing had understanding, he would say this; "Satan enticed me to do wrong, but I made the choice to do wrong." But my friend, Satan is of ancient and his trap and roar is death and very enticing, so my friend, *"Be sober, be vigilant; because your adversary the devil, as a roaring lion, walketh about, seeking whom he may devour."* and also *"Submit yourselves therefore to God. resist the devil, and he will flee from you."* Please! Don't leave out the "Submit yourselves therefore to God" first! Because, if you don't have the Spirit of God on you, in you, around you, the Devil may destroy you with his dark trap and roar. I will say this, Satan doesn't sleep; for he is a spirit and he can sneak to your ears while you are sleeping and speak words of dea0th into your mind and trouble your heart greatly, if you do not have the Power of God looking over you while you sleep.

Satan and those that follow him are predestined for eternal death and Satan is in rage against mankind, because God has given mankind the Bread of Life and we have a Chance to enter Eternal Life and Life here on earth more abundantly. Therefore, Satan doesn't have choice or willingness, because he and his followers have already been sentence to Eternal Death. Satan is mankind's adversary and is not God's adversary; for God Judged and sentenced him and his followers to Eternal Death from the beginning. I will say this also, when a man sins, Satan did not make that man to sin. The man that sins, sins from his own sinful nature, because Satan can only open his trap and entice man to sin. But, a man that will sin, will be held accountable for the sin, if he does so.

In my past living, even after enlightens of God's Will for my Life, when things would go wrong I would immediately blame Satan, because I thought Satan was making me do the bad things in life or was causing the bad things to come into my life. But I will say this with confidence, Satan that devil has no more control over me, than I have control of God.

For I know today, Satan does entice and brings people and things in my life to hinder me from God working through my spirit, but he has no control over me and I know his enticements with confidence. I know today this with confidence; I wasn't in control of my life in my past dead life, because my self will intents had created the majority of the mess in my life, but at this time of the vision, I now had a understanding of the Devil. I was beginning to see myself for who I really was in true perceptiveness of this life and I knew that I had to take control and let God have me completely without any reservations. But, I still was without a greater understanding completely of God's Will for my life at this time.

I will say this now, While Eve was in the garden the serpent came to her; for Satan had entered the serpent and the serpent was more subtle (poisonous) than any beast of the field and enticed Eve to eat of the forbidden tree of good and evil. Satan didn't make Eve eat of the tree, but enticed her and told her 1/2 the truth, but Eve fell into the grip of the lie and man now had sinned against God's Will. I will now share an experience of how Satan can use the closes to you to try to come in your life and destroy you. Even when I thought I had the understanding of how this enemy was so deceiving, I didn't know squat. But, God's Spirit was quick to give to me the understanding and I use it liken into a Lock every second of my life today.

This particular time that I got this understanding was when I was doing everything from the strength that I had in me, to keep that enemy from my life. This particular time was about 14 years after this vision. I was going to church and listen to every word that my ears could hold of God's Word. I wasn't doing any drugs or dinking and my life was much more abundant and normal or more consistent. I was even back on my medicines and the medicines were helping me in my struggles daily. I didn't think I needed much more than that of what I had. But, I learned quickly again that my thoughts are not God's thoughts and

I guess his Spirit found a weak spot in my life at this time and it was this; I really didn't understanding the craftiness of Satan. I thought I knew all his devices, but I fell hard as this Devil tried again to destroy my life. There was a man that came in my life before I tried again to live a normal life. I and this man were doing the sinful nature thing at this time together. We began to talk, and I learned he was somewhat of my own family.

As we began to get to know each other, he told me that he was being evicted from his apartment. This man was a user and very weak. As we were talking during this time, I told him that I had an mobile home and he was welcomed to come and look at it, if he was needing a place. It didn't take him long to make his decision to come and stay there. I helped him move as his eviction day was near, to my mobile home. I will say this before I go any further with these writings. This man didn't want to live the way he was living, but he was bound by his sinful nature of living. This man and I would talk much about God and Jesus Christ. This man wanted desperately to live a normal life, as I did at the time. I do not blame or point my finger at this man for any reason, but I will say this with confidence, Satan used him to entice me away from God's Will. I love this man as Christ loved the whole world and I know it wasn't this man that cause any of my choices. I truly believe the reason I was enticed again to do something that I didn't want to do even though I made the choice to sin, was that of Satan.

So, as I was doing good and living a normal life, this man was still living on my property in the mobile home. I hadn't seen this man in about a month and it was time for him to pay rent. I didn't charge this man 1/3 of what I could charge a man for rent, because I thought the man needed help at the time. I had been clean for a moth at this time and I hadn't seen this man, but about 2 times during the entire month. The true reason I was avoiding him was I didn't want to be tempted if he was using. Not only not to be tempted, but also I wanted to walk what I was preaching to him at the time, follow me? Before that day that he was to pay me rent I had locked my gates, so that no one could come on my property. I didn't want to be disturbed and I surely didn't want to be tempted by Satan to do anything against God's Will. But, that Devil made it through the lock of my gate and enticed me away from God's Will, anyhow. I'm not at this time calling this man a devil, but Satan used this man to entice me away.

Satan knew I was still weak in my thorns of my flesh and Satan desired to destroy me, if he had to use someone as close as this to entice me. I thought at this time, I was much stronger and there wasn't anyway that this Devil could entice me away from God's Will, but I soon found out the craftiness of this devil. My friend, not only did he use this man to entice me, he enticed my wife to open the gate to let him in. Please let me explain myself: Before this time that this man was to pay me rent, I and my wife had already had one battle with this devil. About a few days before this time, Satan tried to come and sow discord between my wife and I and he almost did it. But, I exercised my faith and my gift of discernment and grabbed my wife's hand and went to God on the matter. With God's help, we defeated that devil and he fled like a dog with his tail between his legs.

At this time, Satan got mad and I'm sure he roared, even that much louder. He now had to find away into my life, if he had to use my wife or this man. This particular week this man jump my fence and came and knocked on my door. He told me he just wanted to talk to me. I didn't think much about it, except he shouldn't had jump my fence. I was much stronger at this time and thought I could deal with this situation. This man told me he was doing good and even had done no drugs and didn't want no drugs. When he began to talk in this way, I began to be unconcerned about him jumping over my fence.

Even though, I kept the gate locked, this man continually to jump my fence. One day as we were talking, I wanted to fence in my chickens that I had running free on my property. I didn't want to spend the time of cutting their wings and I asked him, if he could help me the next day when I got the material to do so and he was excited and answered yes. One other reason was that of, this man told me there was a Large hawk and a fox that tried to get my chickens. So, this man and I netting in the top of my small chicken farm and I was happy on the matter.

This day I and this man talked about God and Jesus Christ most of the time. Now the day that rent was due, my wife was home from work. I had my hands in a bowl of food preparing it for dinner. This man pulls up to my gate and blows the horn. I was quick to ask my wife to go get the rent, because I really didn't want to be tempted with the money. My wife was also quick to agree with me and went to the gate to get the rent money. But, all of a sudden I seen this man through the storm door running through my gate and yard. I stuck my head out the door and ask my wife, "What is wrong!?" The entire time that my wife went out the door, I had my eye out. My wife answered and said, "He said that he heard something trying to get the chickens." My friend, this was the moment that the enemy had the chance and came through my gate and enticed me away. It happened so quick, that my dear wife couldn't respond to it and neither could I. I thought I knew the craftiness of Satan, but again, what I knew wasn't what God wanted me to understand. Later that evening, I and this man were using together again, no kidding. Even this man had been telling me that a hawk and a fox was trying to get onto my property to kill my chickens and you would think maybe, that should had been a red flag or warning from God that the enemy was trying to get into my life. There was a hawk and fox trying to get onto my property to kill my chickens, but there was also a serpent trying to get into my life. A serpent, which is more subtle than any creation of the field, which is that devil, Satan.

Before, when I mentioned that my wife and I had defeated Satan and when we went to God in prayer, I had asked God to remove anything in my Life that could or would entice me away from his Will. I asked God to help me and protect me from the enemy, correct? Late that evening as this man and I were riding to use, we were stopped by the police. His vehicle was searched and our bodies were searched. I didn't have my wallet with me, because I wasn't driven. The police officers confirmed my identity, but when they confirmed his identity, they pulled him to the side and hand cuff this man, no kidding.

This man had a warrant against him for a probation violation. I drove his vehicle home to the mobile home and they drove him to jail. It is somewhat ironic isn't it. I will say this with confidence, if a man honestly wants to live a normal life and would ask God for something, that man best be sure what he ask of God, because God will do it and not the way that the man would think either.

The day after that all this had happed, I was laying in bed ashamed at what had happened as anyone would do, that did something they should of not done would feel. But, God was quick to give to me this understanding: Satan is much more crafty in his devices, than that of what I thought. I must be more diligent in my walk in life and have a better understanding that this enemy is wanting to kill me. God was quick to give me a word of greater understanding and it is this: In the Holy Book of 2Corinthians chapter 11, verses 13-15 it is written, *"For such are false apostles, deceitful workers, transforming themselves into the apostles of Christ. And no marvel; for Satan himself is transformed into an angel of light. Therefore it is no great thing if his ministers also be transformed as the ministers of righteousness; whose end shall be according to their works."* My friend this deception was the gap in my life that Satan entered. Believing and trusting in a man that would be willing to talk about God and Jesus Christ, that is. Today it is even more so for me not to trust my own wife, but I trust her more than even my own parents. My wife wasn't possessed by Satan that day as who would might think. When all happened so fast, she also trusted this man and let him in. I would had done the same, if I was at the gate holding the keys to my life. Since that happened, the only fox or hawk that comes on my property are animals.

Today, no man comes on my property without my first discerning the spirit of that man and knowing his fruit. The only man that I do somewhat trust with the keys to my property, is that of _, sorry cant tell you.

Not that I may think you are not trust worthy, but because of the sinful nature of mankind and the craftiness of that serpent. But I will tell you this, I don't live in fear like a man would judge me, by looking onto my property with locks on my gates and a 5 foot fence that covers every inch of my property boundaries. But, I live with the fear of God who can take both body and soul, and I trust only him with my life. I may look like a man in fear to some, but it isn't for the fear of them, it is just another way of protecting my life from the craftiness of Satan. If, Satan tries to get to me like he did that day, he best use another device. He will I'm sure try a different way to enter my life, but I will be watching and God will be watching as liken into the Angel with the Flaming Swords that watched the Garden of Eden to prevent Satan and sin from entering in.

My wife and I learned a great lesson that day and that lesson almost caused me my life again. But, God gave us a greater understanding that day and confirmed that he is protecting my life, if I would be willing for him to do so. Not only was God protecting me, he was also looking to see where my weaknesses was. God is looking for my weaknesses for my profit, but Satan is looking for my weaknesses to kill or destroy me. My friend I hope this enlighten your mind in the craftiness of this enemy and we can overcome any attack of this devil. I will end this understanding with these principles and I hope that you will bind them upon your heart forever. In the Holy Book of James chapter 4, verse 7 it is written, *"Submit yourselves therefore to God. Resist the devil, and he will flee from you."* Don't forget the "Submit yourselves therefore to God" first.

In the holy Book of Romans chapter 8, verses 37-39 it is written, "Nay, in all things we are more than conquerors through him that loved us.

For I am persuaded, neither death, nor life, nor angels, nor principalities, nor powers, nor things present, nor things to come, Nor height, nor dept, nor any other creature, shall be able to separate us from the love of God, which is in Christ Jesus our Lord." We can be much more a "Victor" in this life than a "Victim", if we are willing to let God live in our life and love us. One more principle my friend and this is a keeper. I have always been weak in this area and God had to intervene many times in my life to get me out of the mess.

When someone would come into my life, if I did discern if the man maybe of sinful in nature, I would still let the man into my life, because he talked about Jesus with me. But today, I will check references on a man, just like the government would check you out if you would apply for a job with them. In the Holy Book of Matthew chapter 7, verses 15-17 it Is written, *"Beware of false prophets, which come to you in sheep's clothing, but inwardly they are ravening wolves. Ye shall know them by their fruits. Do men gather grapes of thorns or figs of thistles?"*

CHAPTER SIX

WHAT GOD ARE YOU PREPARING FOR ME NOW?

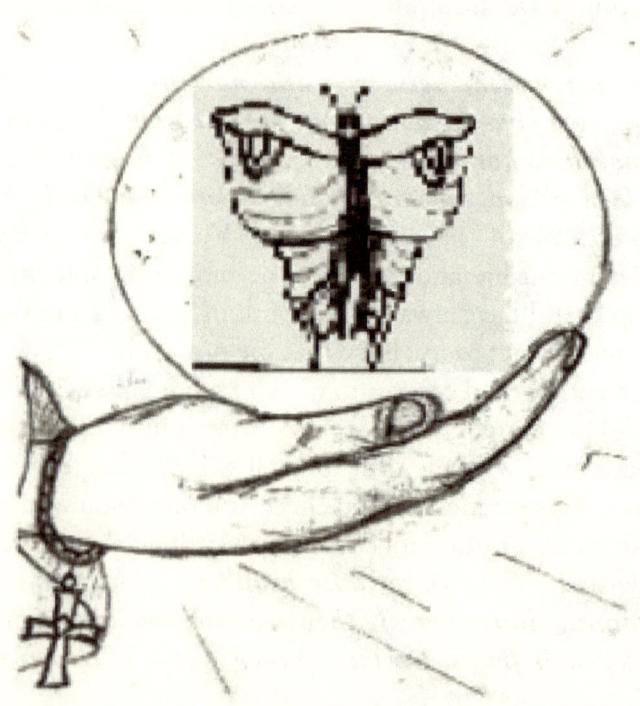

NOW, THIS CHAPTER IS THE BEGINNING OF MY true purpose, which is still today. I will share with you how God was preparing things for me to understand the purpose 18 year ago and more so, even when I was but a child. I was doing great at this time of my life, and thought perhaps, I was on the straight path of living a normal (consistent) life, but, let me first share with you the principle. In the

Holy Book of Ephesians Chapter 3, verses 1-21 explains my very words of what I desire to share with you; and please read this Chapter now if you will. Verses 1-12 is written, *"For this cause I Paul, the prisoner of Jesus Christ for you Gentiles, If he heard of the dispensation of the grace of God which is given to you-ward: How that by revelation he made known to me the mystery; (as I wrote afore in few words, Whereby, when ye read, ye may understand my knowledge in the mystery of Christ)*

Which in other ages was not made known unto the sons of men, as it is now revealed unto his holy apostles and prophets by the Spirit; That the Gentiles should be fellow-heirs, and of the same body and partakers of his promise in Christ by the gospel: Whereof I was made a minister, according to the gift of the grace of God given unto me by the effectual working of his power. Unto me, who am less than the least of all saints, is this grace given, that I should preach among the Gentiles the unsearchable riches of Christ; And to make all men see what is the fellowship of the mystery which from the beginning of the world hath been hid in God, who created all things by Christ Jesus: To the intent that now unto principalities and powers in heavenly places might be known by the church the manifold wisdom of God, Accordingly to the eternal purpose which he purposed in Christ Jesus our Lord: In whom we have boldness and access with confidence by the faith of him."

So, lets us continue to understand or begin to understand how God was beginning this ministry unto me by the grace of God. Now, I do remember clearly one evening as I came home from work and was extremely tired from working a lot of overtime. This time of my life, I was always searching and seeking God's Understanding of Life and panted after it as I do today; for I know with confidence it enlightens my Life. This particular evening it was late and my wife was at church and I was home alone. Home Alone? As I entered my home, I reached to my right side to put my keys on the nightstand, I began to panic, because the keys were not on my side. I thought at the time, "My God! Please help me find those keys." The keys that I had lost were to very important buildings, offices, customers boxes and vehicles keys. These keys I had for over 4 years on my side and was responsible for them and I felt very discourage; for I didn't know where I lost them. I had covered 3 counties that day and I thought it was a lost cause and it saddened me greatly.

I was afraid someone would find these keys and it would be trouble for the company that I was working for at the time. My personal spare vehicle keys were also with these keys and I had nothing to drive, except this large Service Line Truck that was from my company. Now, this truck was a gas hog and I had already been told by the company not to drive it earlier that week, unless of outages or on a work schedule maintenance. I was issued this truck for service on the main communication trunk lines and power outages. It had a large boom and bucket for 2 men to stand in while working.

So, I didn't know what to do at the time and I just decided that the keys were lost and I didn't have no way of finding them either, but I didn't give up. I thought that finding these keys would be liked finding a needle in a large cow's pasture and if I could go to look for them, I had nothing to drive except what I was told not to drive. I didn't know what to do at the time, my spare vehicle keys where with the lost ones, I didn't know where the keys where and if I did know where they were, I didn't have nothing to drive, except what I was told not to drive from my company. Like I said before, I had been all over 3 counties that day and I could had lost them anywhere and by now someone has probably found them and hidden them very crafty. I was very saddened. I wasn't sad because I felt that I would be reprimanded the next day, but I was saddened, because I felt like I lost something that was very important in my life; like a responsibility or something that I borrowed from another man and it was all he had. I just had to get these keys because I knew how important these keys where. I will say this, just 1of the keys where worth at least 150 thousand dollars, no kidding. And I had at least 10-15 keys like wise on this key chain.

I was so exhausted from working this day, because I had put in 13 hours this day and I just laid on the couch in silence praying that God would help me find these keys. It was if I had no choice, but to trust God to help me in this matter.

So, I prayed hard and didn't quit, until I was so tired I just collapsed and closed my eyes and went to sleep on the couch. But, something wonderful happened and I call this revelation, *"The Keys In The Moon's Light"*

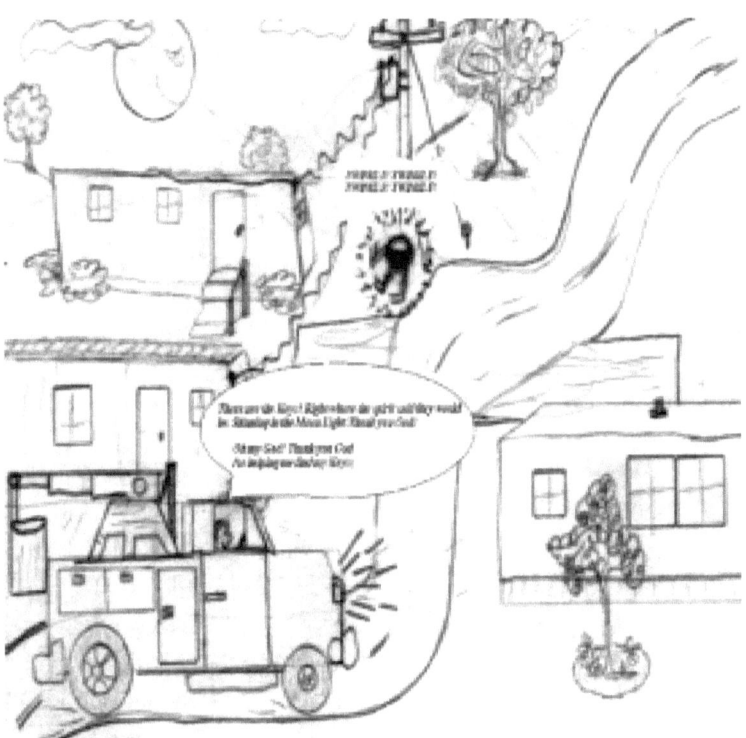

THE KEYS IN THE MOON'S LIGHT

As a was sleeping, a voice came into my spirit man and called me by my name and said, "____Go Now. Don't turn Back. Go Now! as the Spirit says. Go here and you will see the keys in the Moon Light shinning for you. Go Now! as the Spirit says, Go and don't turn back!." And then I said this out loud, "My God!" I jumped from my sleep as if someone stuck me with a hot poker straight into my belly button. I didn't have to put any clothes on; for I was already dressed to go. I didn't even think twice about the company saying ,"Don't drive that truck".

I grabbed the keys to that truck and took off like lighting. The voice didn't exactly speak to me with a loud audible voice where I was to go, it was if I was shown a picture in my mind, like a dream. I knew exactly where this area was, as it flash in my mind, when the spirit said, "Go Here".

At first when I was traveling to this destination, I had somewhat a doubt. But, I kept going forward as the Spirit said, "Go Now! and don't turn back" and I didn't turn back and I went faster towards the destination. When I was half the way to this destination, I had to stop and get gas, because the gas tank was about empty on this large truck I was driving. I knew when I went home that evening I had enough of gas to get to work and the store the next day where the company had an account at. I was away from that area and had to pay out of my pocket for the gas and I didn't think nothing of the matter. I had not turned back, but I had stopped and it was if, the Spirit of God was telling me continually to press forward quickly or the keys could be lost forever, no kidding.

So, I got my gas and took off like lightening again to this destination. Finally, I reached the destination and turn into the large mobile home park. The Spirit had shown me in the dream where the area was at. The Spirit showed me this mobile home park and said that the keys would be shinning in the Moon Light. There was a full moon that night and it was so bright that I really didn't need my headlights on. The Destination was 25 miles for my home at this time and I would had never believed it, if I wasn't seeing it for my self. As I took a curve in the Mobile Home Park, my eye caught a twinkle just about 150-200 ft away from my position at the time; for it was twinkling like a beacon light. As I got closer, there laid my keys at the bottom of a utility pole laying in some grass and it seemed as if God had hid them for me and it was if the Moon Light was shinning directly on these keys and they were shinning bright, so that I could see them. I began to cry somewhat out of relief, but I believe it came from the Love of God.

I had to set in the truck for just a few moments and I couldn't quit crying for joy, until I knew I must get back home; for my wife would be home by now.

Later, I went home and told my wife about the matter and told no one else. We both were very grateful and started praising God for his revelation. This is one understanding that I did get from this great work of the Holy Ghost and it was this: I must go were the Spirit leads and if I turn back, I will loose what is waiting for me. For it is written, *"And Jesus said unto him, No man, having put his hands to the plow, and looking back, is fit for the kingdom of God."*

Today that principle was one understanding that God wanted me to have at that time of my life. Yes, I was battling my flesh at this time and there were things that I was beginning to look back on to do, such as maybe drinking a beer or smoking a joint. But, I will say that I was without this great understanding at this time. I thought of the matter somewhat, but I thought God had just help me through another problem in my life at this time and I didn't think much about the matter, until later in life. "Don't Turn Back." I know that when I looked back and turned back from the enlightenment that God had shown me in my past life, my life turned from worse to much worse. Oh Yes! Remember Lot's Wife? But, today I say with confidence this; the plow is in my hand and I never look back; for I know looking back and dwelling in the past dead life led me to turn from God's Loving Grace and also led me to the big hole many times. My past is dead; and their is nothing worth looking and turning back to. Sure, I'm still in the my flesh and my mass of brain has experiences from my past, but I don't dwell in it; for I know it is all dead. I know this with confidence also, if I do lay the plow down, I don't have to leave it there. With Jesus Christ as my mediator and the Holy Ghost as my great help in times of troubles, I have hope. I just pick the plow up and start plowing again.

I will also say this with confidence; The moon light on my keys, as the light was twinkling was for another greater understanding that I have received today. It goes like this; "Twinkle, Twinkle, little star, how I wonder where you are?" Today I have a greater understanding that my life should be more than just a twinkle in this Life. During this time of my life when I received this great revelation, I was still without the full understanding of the revelation. I knew that God had interceded in my life during this time and had done a wonderful work in my life, but he wanted something greater for me. He made it clear through this revelation that I needed to go straight when his Spirit leads me to do so, without any hesitation; and for me not to judge with my brain mass and ask any questions, but to go straight and not to turn back as the Spirit leads. I was reminiscing on the twinkle, twinkle, there was another greater understanding that he wanted me to grasp onto. Now, in the Holy Book of Matthew chapter 5, verses 14-16 reads as written, *"Ye are the light of the world, A city that is set on a hill cannot be hid. Neither do men light a candle, and put it under a bushel, but on a candlestick; and it giveth light unto all that are in the house. Let your light so shine before men, that they may see your good works, and glorify your father which is in heaven."*

Today I do have a better understanding of the revelation. I do remember during this time of my life, I wasn't shining the light of Life the way that God wanted me to shine it. I would just do things when I wanted to do it and my good works wasn't manifesting into a greater light for men to see. During this time of my life, I did want all that I could do for good in my life, but I still hid my life and it wasn't shinning brightly. When someone would see me, I believe they would say this; "Was that a child of God or not?" Because, I quenched the fire of God from really working in my life during this time, I would only

Twinkle. God doesn't want any of his children to just twinkle as if his light was under a bushel.

God wants his children to walk as a fire on top of a candle for all men to see, so that it would draw men to God and God then would be Glorified.

Later during or about this same time of my life, I didn't turn back to my dead old life and I chose to plow on into a new beginning of a normal life, because I knew that the past was nothing but destruction. Sometimes I would look over my shoulder and there would be something calling me to turn away, but I didn't turn away at this time and continued to let go and let God in my Life to the best I could. Satan would always try to entice me with beautiful things, but I wanted God and I pressed forward at this time of my life. My spirit was growing somewhat and was getting stronger at this time.

I do remember another understanding that God reveal to me during this same time of my life. I remember asking God and searching for understanding of one thing at this time and it was an understanding of how men could treat other men badly and not suffer the consequences, immediately. I was also searching for a greater understanding of the call of ministry on my life. I knew God had called and chose me to do something in this life, but I just couldn't put my finger on it. I was somewhat frustrated without understanding of the matter and told no one, but continued to press forward in my new life. I was without much patience, but I had more patience in my life than I had ever before, when it came to God, but patience with men was still a different story.

So, I do remember coming from a church service one Sunday afternoon. It had been raining a little bit this Sunday morning and when I got home I was somewhat concerned in my heart at what I believed to had been said at church that morning. So, I asked God to please help me understand such a thought of a man's heart when I thought the man was a child of God and profess the Love of God to others.

It really frustrated me and I was desperate for an answer from God and God did give me a great understanding and I call this revelation, *"The Swallow-Tail Moth"*

THE SWALLOW- TAIL MOTH

I came home from a Sunday Church service this day and the Spirit of God was upon me. The Spirit drove (Led) me to the forest where I would always go and pray alone. I knew at this time God was going to show me something through his word. I reached for my Bible and my coat and went towards the door. My wife looked at me as if I was crazy and said, "You know that there is a thunder storm warning and I don't want you to be caught in it in those woods." Then I said to her, "I don't know where I'm going, but I do know what I must do for now and that is to go to the woods and seek God for understanding of this matter; for the spirit is leading me to do so." My wife looked at me and sighed somewhat and then kissed me and I left out the door.

Now, during this time of my life, I was beginning to experience what I call faith wisdom and would seek and pray for it continuously; for I knew that this type of wisdom out weighed any type of experienced wisdom and I wanted it with my whole heart. I knew that this type of wisdom kept me prepared and gave me the truth about life and it was the only wisdom I trusted; for I knew at the time that this wisdom only came from God and it gave me peace and understanding in my life. This Godly Wisdom was also what was making me strong in my Faith or walk with God and his Christ. At this time of my life, I was seeking wisdom and understanding from God about ministry, because at this time I was confident that God was calling me to the ministry and I wanted understanding of it greatly.

So, as I started to enter into the thick part of the woods, it began to rain and then it started to lightening all around me. The thunderstorm did come up suddenly and caught me by surprise, but I kept walking as if, I was supposed to be somewhere at a specific time. I was noticing that the lightening was hitting the top of the tall trees that where near me, but I kept walking as if, I was suppose to be somewhere at a specific time. The lightening didn't concern me much, but the thought of me just walking to a destination made it very interesting, because I knew that God had something preparing for me. I was discerning with no doubt, that I was being led by God's Spirit and was willing to go where the Spirit led me. As I entered deeper into the woods, the rain quit falling as fast as it started, somewhat like if you would turn a light switch on or off. But, now the lightening was somewhat getting closer and was continuously striking around me towards the ground.

I had some lighter sticks (kindle) that I had with me in order to start fires with. I pitched my tent and I made a fire here at this place that I ended up at deep into the forest. I felt as if I could go no deeper into the woods and felt as if I was getting somewhat tired and weak.

So after I had made the fire and pitched my tent, I began to pray to God, and I asked him this; "Lord, Why am I here? Lord Jesus, please show me what you want me to do, for I am willing Lord, just tell me Lord what you want me to do, so that, I will understand." I was lying under the tent and then I felt a power upon me somewhat like the Power of Love that I had experienced a while back from the man in my doorway revelation. It wasn't the sound, it was the Love part coming from deep in my spirit through me. And then as soon as I began to sense this great compassionate, agape Love, the Holy Spirit began to speak through my spirit and said to me, "Man, stand upon your feet." I stood upon my feet and then I started to sense the power of the sound and this awesome Love of God. I began to feel that same Power and sound that I felt with the vision of the man in my doorway. It was somewhat like a power reactor room and I felt it throughout my entire body. The Spirit opened my mouth and spoke through my body and it was as if I was rebuking the four corners of the earth, no kidding. This rebuke wasn't a condemnation type of rebuke either. This power rebuke was as if God was calling to all men from the whole wide world to come to him. Each time that I would turn to one side, the Spirit would speak with a powerful voice through me. I do remember somewhat the message from the Spirit of God and it went somewhat like this, *"Come unto me my children! Come unto me all ye that are heavy laden! Come unto me, your Creator and God! I am!"*

When I would speak through my mouth, a lightening bolt would strike the ground near me and I would feel the ground under my feet tremble as the lightening would strike it. After I had turned in all directions I felt the power stop suddenly, just as if, the Power was just turned off, like a light switch.

Now, I was very weak as a dead man after this powerful experience of the Anointing of the Holy Ghost. I laid down under the tent in amazement and thought on this matter.

After a while when I got some strength in my body I ask God, "Lord what does this mean? I don't understand Lord." And then the Spirit spoke through my spirit and said, *"I anoint whom I am pleased. I give power to whom I am pleased."* And then I began to think on this matter as I laid under the tent somewhat weak as a dead man. I began to open my Bible and the wind somewhat blew the Bible open to the Book of Jonah. I turned my body to become more comfortable to read this Book and then I turned my head and beheld something wonderful. I was looking at a beautiful lime-green swallow-tail moth about 4-5" long. I began to think this, "Out of all the places in these woods, there sits a beautiful lime-green swallow-tail moth on this tree, inches from my eyes." Then the Spirit spoke through my spirit again and said, "What do you see?" and then I answered and said, "A moth, a swallow-tail moth." And as soon as I said this, the moth opened and spread its wings to a fullness and I was amazed. The moth was inches away from my eyes and it had no fear of me whatsoever. The spots on this moths wings looked to me as if they were eyes, and they were looking straight into my eyes. Then, the Spirit of God began to minister to me concerning this matter and it went like this: The power he had shown through me, was giving at God's Will. When he turn the power off, it was again at God's Will. The understanding of that particular revelation was simply this; God gives and takes power according to His Will and I had no power over the matter.

Now, the moth represented many things. The moth's wings, as they looked like eyes upon them, represented God's eyes on who he chooses at his will and he knows where they are and what they are doing at all times, even when they sleep or hide; for the eyes of God are everywhere.

For it is written, *"The eyes of the Lord are upon the righteous, and his ears are open unto their cry."* (Psalms 34:15); *"Behold the eye of the Lord is upon them that fear him, upon them that hope in his mercy; To deliver their soul from death, and to keep them alive in famine."* (Psalms 33:18);

"The eyes of the Lord are in every place, beholding the evil and the good." (Proverbs 15:3)

The Moth also represents something that could be terrific. In the Holy Book of Matthew Chapter 6, verses 19-21 is written, *"Lay not up for yourselves treasures upon earth, where the moth and rust doth corrupt, and where thieves break through and steal: But lay up treasures in heaven, where neither moth nor rust doth corrupt, and where thieves do not break through nor steal: For where your treasure is, there will your heart be also."* Today, I will say this with confidence; the moth represented much more and I continually to get great understanding from this moth.

Now, the book of Jonah was an example of how I had tried to hide and run from God for many years, but now he is in control and he wants me to do something for him at his will and time, not my will and time. The Book of Jonah still reveals many understandings today for me, such as resentments, which I will share it with you later. When God calls a man to do a specific duty for him, he will not send you out without first training you and given you the understanding of the matter. Sometimes we think we maybe ready to take the world on, but the world takes us on and then we are in worse state than when we first began. Wait on the Lord and he will restore you and train you for the high calling of ministry, if you have been called to such a rewarding service. I will share much more of the Book of Jonah and the Understand as I see it today later throughout the writings.

During this time of my life, I knew that I had been called to the ministry, but I was still without understanding. God was beginning to work through me at this time and to show me His Will. But, sometimes I would run ahead thinking I had the understanding of God's Will and I would stumble, fall, and make wrong choices.

After I would make wrong choices I would suffer the consequences of my self will intents. At this time, I was comforted from this awesome revelation that day and always find comfort in it when the Spirit brings

A

it to my remembrance. I'm still today learning from the revelations, and receiving much more understanding. The Swallow-Tail Moth, The Anointed Power, The Book of Jonah was giving to me in lest than a few hours during that time, but that seed of Understanding that God had given me was eternally incorruptible and is still growing within me day by day. God is good and he is Life for us. But, I now know that I have got to have patience and wait for the complete Understanding of Life for God is in control and he is in control for my profit.

Later as time passed I was doing great and was beginning to receive understanding of matters from God. I submitted an application to a Local Bible college. I was accepted and I took courses in Pastoral Theology and Christian Education. I loved going back to School at this time, but I didn't pursue my diploma. I felt great at first when I went to college, but soon I sensed that it wasn't where I needed to be at the time. One of the reasons was that I needed to work, because of owing bills and I just could not work 10 hour days, six days a week and still go to school at night fulltime. I did this for awhile, but soon I was getting tired and I weighed the matter out. I knew that God wanted me to study his word and I knew that he wanted me out of debt for sure, but I also knew that I had to have patience and the job was my way of getting out of my debt.

So, I weighed the matter and studied God's Word at home and began to go to every church revival that I could go to. I was visiting all different churches and was learning great matters. It seem to me as if the Holy Ghost was leading me to different churches and showing me the different ministries of His Body. I will say during this time of my life, I learned a lot by the teaching of the Holy Ghost as he would lead me to different churches.

I had received my Local Minister License from our Headquarters and church at this time. I was appointed to a position in our church as the Youth Minister and I was joyful of the matter. God was training me up for his service and I knew at the time, that it was true. My wife and I had been given children to be with us most all the time. All these children were not my own. God had found me worthy for the care of these children, but God made it clear to me that I was responsible for these children at the time. I became as a big brother and father to these little children and loved them the same way. It was a burden, but I will say with confidence, the burden was light and I had great joy in the matter. Later I began to see through the eyes of God, somewhat, for the suffering of his creation and mankind. God had enlightened me in such a way, that I felt I wasn't looking at a man in there body anymore; for I was looking into their heart. After all the years that I had wrestled with man's intents, God had sent innocent children to my life and I had great joy in the matters. I will say, his burden was somewhat heavy at this time, but I and my wife pressed forward. I still felt as if something, such as understanding of His Will was still missing in my life.

Later during about this same time of my life, I had left the communication job and was working in an Textile Industry company as a Electro/Mechanical Technician. There was a man there at this job that became like a spiritual brother to me and we would talk sometimes about God and Christ in our life's. I was working at the Textile plant as an Electrician at this time and I was seeking God for a understanding of this matter and Guess what? I got the understanding through another vision.

A couple of days before I got this revelation, I had been working on a Machine that had been tripping (Overloading) a Main Power Breaker since, and, before I started working there at this plant. One day the breaker tripped and the Plant manager ask me to look at it and to see if I could fix it.

He knew that this machine was tripping the breaker every now and then, but now it was tripping every other hour. I found out what was causing the Main Breaker to Trip and repaired the matter, that day. The next day about 2 hours before quitting time, the plant manager comes to me and says that the machine is not tripping the breaker, but it seems as if it doesn't have any power now. The machine would take yarn and turn the yarn from this large creel onto a large cylinder and as the cylinder became somewhat 1/2 the way full, it would slow down and stop. I spent a couple hours on the matter and it was if I didn't have the understanding to fix it. I checked every thing known to my understanding of the machine, but it was if, something just didn't make no sense. The machine had the right voltage going to the Main Motor and the motor wasn't overloading, but it would just stop as the yarn would fill the cylinder. The matter just dazzled me.

About the time it was to go home that day, the plant manager came to me and said, "You did your best. We will call someone from-_-__---_ to come and help you with this matter in the morning. Go home and get you some rest." and I said, "Thanks-__-___. I thought I could fix it, but I'm really dazzled over this matter. Thanks again and I will see you in the morning."

So, I went home thinking of this matter, but just could not understand this: "Out of all the time I've been an electrician, I've never seen anything like this before. How can a motor have all the voltage it needed, but had no power to run. I fell asleep that night and I got my understanding of this matter and I call this revelation, *There Is No Power*"

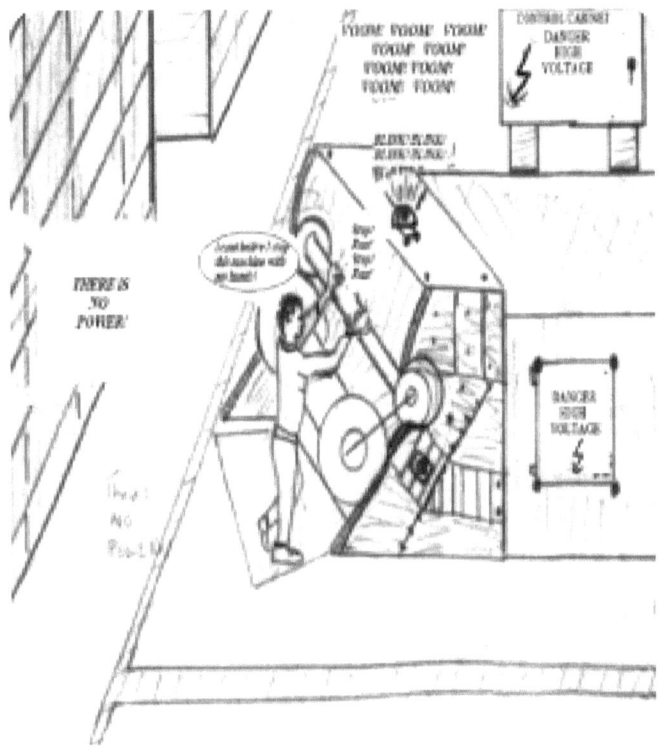

THERE IS NO POWER

I had a revelation, whether out of the body or not, I will say with confidence though, it seem as if I was in the spirit. I was standing at the entrance door of the plant and it was night time and there wasn't a soul there in the plant.

I heard a sound as if, a machine was running fast inside the plant. I thought to myself, "Who in this world is in there working. I don't see any cars." I opened the entrance door to the plant and the noise of the machine got louder. I walked into the plant and seen the machine that I had been working on early that day running fast, with no yarn on the cylinder. I thought someone was working on it. So, I walk around in the plant and found no one. I walk back to the machine and stood in front of it as it was running faster and faster. I put my hands forth and grabbed the top cylinder and the machine stop suddenly. I thought, "Now, that is crazy. That machine should had broken my arms off. I cant believe I stopped this machine with my hands." I stopped the machine again and again as if, I was confirming that it had no power. Then, from over my right shoulder, I heard a powerful voice that melted me like wax. It was the same voice I had heard in my past life and I knew who it was. The voice said, *"There is no Power."* The voice put a reverence into my soul as a fear of God. This voice was like a sound of great power with Love and it melted me as it did when it said to me in my past, *"You are forgiven."* It was the same voice and I knew no man had that type of understanding and Power. After the voice, I was as a dead man in this plant and I just stood there looking at this machine. Then I got the strength and look over my right shoulder to see if anyone was there, but there wasn't no one.

The next morning I went to work and was confident in what I had been given through this revelation. I walked to the machine and with a small electronic screw driver only, made one adjustment and it was fixed, no kidding. Not only was God trying to give me understanding of Power at this time of my life, but he also gave me the understanding how to fix this machine in the spirit. It took me 5 seconds to fix this machine the next morning, no kidding. The plant manager and the special project official came to me as I was telling the operators they could run the machine now. The plant manger and the other official were looking at me and this machine and then the Plant manager said to me, "Is it fixed?" I said with a smile upon my face with confidence, "Yes Sir. I just looked over the matter yesterday. God reveal it to me in a dream last night." Then the plant manager giggle and said, "That is good, but we have already called _--__-- and he should be here at anytime. Did you really fix it?" I said again, "Yes, Sir and I am confident with the matter; for God has reveal this matter to me in a dream last night." And then he would giggle as he was happy and went about his daily Plant routines.

Now, the other official that was standing beside us said to me, as I thought he doubted me, "I wish God would show me things like that in my dreams." and about that time the man they had called to help me on this matter walks through the door with a tool box. He had traveled from another part of the State to come and help with the matter. He looks at the machine, and then looks at us and says, "Well, it looks like I can go back home now. I guess you have fixed it, right?" and this official said to this man, "We think it is fixed? God showed him how to fix it last night, in a dream.", and then they laughed and giggled. But, I didn't feel within my spirit man though as if, they were laughing at me, because I knew that they had to believe something. It was if, they were laughing for joy and I would giggle with them when they would ask me over and over again, "Who showed you how to fix it?" and we would giggle and I would say, "Gooooood God."

At this time, it really didn't concern me what they believed, but I was really hoping that they believed me and perhaps they did. I can say with confidence that God had intervened in my Life for my profit at this time, but I was without much understanding of the matter. So, the official left me and this professional machine mechanic alone and he asked me what I had found out to be the problem. In my past life, when things like this would happen in my life, I wouldn't tell no one. I kept it all in my little heart, but if someone would ask me, I would tell them.

So, I told him what I had done and he was amazed that a electrician in my statue would know such a matter, no kidding. He had done this type of special work for nearly 30 years and I was only 5 years into being an Industrial electrician. I tell you today, God can do it, when I cant do it. This man became a good friend to me and he believed me somewhat in this matter and I also believe that the other two men believed also later.

This vision was another great enlightenment into understanding, but for some reason, I still didn't get it at the time. I came to believe that God wanted me to have power over Satan and his followers and I must use this power that he had given me at all cost. But, I would find out the hard way again, what I thought, isn't what God intended for me at the time. God was trying still to break the hard subsoil of my heart for understanding of the matter, ministry. I had some understanding, but some is not good enough when Lives are at stake. It took nearly 15 years for me to understand this vision, no kidding. For today, I know what this vision was for and it goes like this: First, I must explain what I believe to be the right definition of Power. Power is What? The Power to be in control of things? The Power to have authority over things? Or, could it be Power of Knowledge or the Power of Understanding Knowledge and Putting the Knowledge into Action? One more question my friend. Could Power mean, Power over Life or Death? Power is all of the above and much more. _Power_: 1.) possession of control, authority, or influence over others. 2.)ability to act or produce an effect.

During this time of my life when I had this revelation, I was only living what I thought to be this best I could understand. Here are a few things that I remember doing during this time of my life. I was staying clean, going to church, teaching the Word of God, Preaching the Word of God, praying and praising God for all things, searching for understanding from God, getting understanding from God, reading and studying God's Word every minute that I could get.

I was making firm stands towards what I knew was the truth of God's Word. I was rebuking Satan by the Power of God's Word when he would come into my ear and whisper enticements. I was living better than I had ever lived since I was a child in God's Will. I was called as a Minister of the Gospel. I was suffering for what I believed to be the Truth of God's Word. Now, I bet you are now thinking I was a Hero, somewhat like Super Man, hey? At the time I was thinking the same. I was really living good and a good normal life at this time and doing everything that I thought I should be doing of following God's Will, but I was still without understanding of the Power of God.

In my past dead life, I always had what I call the Power of Authority on my back continuously and I thought that this Power was giving from God to those for the authority and control over my Life and they would use their Authority for their profit. But, today I know that Power is all the above and not one being lost from the effect. For God is the Power of all Creation and has the Power to Give and Take from the Creation. God is the Power Reactor of Life. During this time of my Life, I will say that I still did not have the Power of God's Will in my life. God had giving me some great understanding, but I wasn't using what he was giving and then there was no effect. I was reading God's Word every day and night and it was filling my mind, my spirit and I was stronger and growing much in God's Will. I was enlightened more at this time than I had ever been in my life and I was counting it for Joy, but I was at a point that I had stopped growing somewhat in my spirit. I began to sense that I was still missing something and I just could not understand the matter. I was happy the way I was living; for I, my wife, my family, others and surely God was happy for me and I thought this must be what God wanted for me at the time. I was using the Power of God's Word over Satan and surely over self will; for I wasn't seeking self will pleasures at this time and I could sense Satan on a fly's eyelash coming towards me a mile away.

I had all this understanding that God had reveal to me, but I kept it to myself, because I thought that God didn't want me to share it with anybody; for I thought it was all about me and no one else, no kidding. I held all this understanding that God had given me under my belt and would only use it, if I needed to do so.

I really thought at the time that I was chosen to the ministry of the Gospel of Christ for one particular special calling and maybe I was. But, I thought that I was special and I didn't want no one to get what I knew, because it took me my whole life to get it, and I sure wasn't going to just give it away. What does that sound like my friend? You guessed right, if you said, "Self Will." Or, if you would had said selfish, it would had been the same. I was being given something and I wasn't giving nothing in return, so I had no effect; for I had no power at the time. I'm not talking about going out in the highways and byways and using the Power of Authority to grasp a sinner by his right ear and drag him to the alter. I'm talking about the Power of God, which is Life. God had already showed me a touch of his might and power throughout my whole life at this time, but I was still without the understanding of His Power. Surely I would talk about Jesus Christ and God to others, if the chance came to me, but I didn't have much effect on others. Surely I knew God called me and had confidence that I was chosen for the Ministry, but I would always think like this: I had to learn the hard way, they must learn the hard way too. My friend, I will say that isn't power, that is self will and there is no effect in life, thinking that way. Let me ask this question. Do you think that Jesus Christ thought the way I thought, while he was here in the flesh? Surely he didn't think that way; for he gave us all things on the cross of Calvary. This was the Power that he had been given from the Father God of Life. Jesus Christ had understanding and he was The Understanding for mankind.

Today I know with confidence this; *It isn't what you know in this life, it is what you do with what you know.* The Power that Jesus Christ proclaimed that he had when he said this, ***"Therefore doth my Father love me, because I lay down my life, that I might take it again. No man taketh it from me, but I lay it down of myself. I have power to lay it down, and I have power to take it again. This commandment have I received of my Father."*** The reason of the confidence and the power Jesus Christ had was that of, no other than, the Power of Understanding of God's Will for him. Jesus Christ has the complete package of the Understanding of God's Will for himself and mankind and that my friend is the Power of God the Father. At first during these times of my life, I thought I had the complete package of the Power of God, but my friend, I didn't have squat. I didn't even have the power of understanding of how to resurrect an ant and definitely not my self. Comparing what I thought I knew was a vapor compared to what God wanted me to know at the time. I thought that I had the understanding of the Power of God, but today I know that I only had been given the understanding of how to understand, no kidding. In order for me to understand something of God, first God had to show me what understanding was. All of the visions and Revelations that God had sent my way was for understanding of understanding, because I was without understanding, follow me? But I can say with confidence, I believe that I do have a little bit of understanding. I can say for starts, that I do have understanding of understanding. Please let me share what I believe to be the truth of understanding. What is understanding? First, <u>Understanding is The Power Reactor of Life.</u> All Life revolves around understanding; for it is of God. I will say also that understanding is the Intelligence of God. Psalms 147:5 reads, **"Great is our Lord, and of great power; his understanding is infinite."** and Proverbs 3:19 reads, **"The Lord by wisdom hath founded the earth; by understanding hath he established the heavens."** All existence of life that you could imagine and more beyond your imagination were made by understanding.

I can look back into my past at these times and see the seed of understanding from the Lord in my Life manifesting as he would enlighten me with understanding. Still today the visions and revelations that he had given me in my past are still coming alive in my Life today.

At the times when I received a revelation or vision from God, I thought I understood the matter, but today I can say with confidence, I'm still beginning to understand the completeness of them. This I will say, God was wanting me to understand this Power and he wanted to give it to me, but first I had to understand it, before it could start to manifest (grow or work) into my life. I now know the true reason why I didn't understand more clearly God's Will for my life at these times. It was because, I was still trying to live by my own understanding and self will. But today I can see much more clearly God's Understanding, because I have let go of my self will and let God's Will grow into my life. God's Will is the Understanding of Life. Living in his Will and keeping his commandments to the best I understand, is much more abundant than before in my past life. In the Holy Book of Psalms it is written, *"The fear of the Lord is the beginning of wisdom: a good understanding have all they that do his commandments: his praise endureth for ever."* (Psalms 111:10). I could spend eternity writing of this matter, but I know with confidence that God's Will is mankind's Power of understanding the gift of Life.

During this time of my life, I was desperate for God's Will in my life and I was panting after it like a thirsty animal in the dry desert. I would teach Sunday; for I was also appointed as a Mid Adult Sunday School Teacher at this time, and also I was the Youth Minister at this Church and I thought that this was the Power that God was giving me. Today I know it was just a drop in the Ocean compared to what God wanted me to have at the time. I also know that, the Power God gives to a man, isn't just for the man for it is for all things.

Now, I worked on this job for several years until later, I left this job for another. I will say at this time of my life, I did give up this job because of the lack of understanding. Let me share this with you before I go into a new point in my life. When I was working at this job, I was making stands in what I believed in to be the truth of Life. When I first started this job, things seemed to be going great in my life. But after awhile, things didn't seem to be so great, especially at this this job. I didn't like much of what I would hear from other people on the job, such as, the cursing, the sexual talking, the gossiping talk and such like. It grieved me deep within my heart, but I tried to pressed forward in this new life that I had found. I would try to shut my ears to people at this job as they would curse God, talk about there nights out on the town during the weekends, and the gossiping concerning others. It seemed as if the more I tried to shut this crap out of my life, the more it was beginning to happen. I was trying to live a good, honest and God fearing life and I was thinking that I just didn't need to be at this job anymore. One day I was in the canteen and I just had walk in for a break from my duties and there was a newly employee there in the canteen. This man was cursing worse than if he was possessed by Satan himself. The words are not appropriate to mention. So, as I was listened to this filthy language for he wasn't but about 4 feet from me and was speaking loudly as if he wanted me to hear it, I stood still, turned to him and said, "Listen. There are others in this canteen. Will you please respect others and hold that cursing or at least go outside." This man's mouth dropped and he looked at me as if I was crazy. I turned from him and got my soda out of the soda machine and then he said to me with a deceptive voice as one would taunt, "What are you going to do, tell on me?". I didn't know what to say, but this, "No. I not going to tell on you, because you have told on your self." and I just stood still glancing at him somewhat. He started to laugh and curse more, then he left the canteen. It wasn't but about a few minutes and then I was called to the Plant manager's office.

There was a man in the office that I had a great relationship with. This man asked if I was ok and I said, "Mr.-_--___, I'm well, but I just don't know how long I can hold out here at this job." He looked at me as if he was discourage, but had hope and said this, "You look stressed. You shouldn't let things like that bother you. You and I know both that we have a great hope and some just don't understand it. I have been there and done that. I even take medicine that helps me cope with matters today and it does help me. If I give you some, would you try it and see if it helps with your trials?" At the time when this friend of mine said that he had some medicine and it was coming from his mouth, I trusted him and I said, "Sure. I will try one."

So, he told me not to take but a half of this tablet and it would help me. But from deep inside my spirit, It was if my spirit was crying out within me, "Trust God and don't take the drug." I knew deep down that I didn't need to take any drug; for I was a recovery drug addict at this time. I had been completely clean for almost 4 years and life was so much more better. I had even quit smoking at this time of my life and was totally drug free. But, I chose to take the medicine and about 15 or 20 minutes later, I was calm and laughing and felt loose. I felt as if I had drank a six pack of corona beers. I started to think this, "Man! I like that. I need to get my hands on some of that. At least I feel better and it cant be so bad; for my friend is a Christian man and he takes them." So, as time passed I would go to him, when I would come up with an good excuse and get me a few of these feel good pills and then, I was addicted. My manipulative behavior began to grow in me and I wanted these drugs badly. I went to him one day and ask, "What Doctor do you go to? I need to go to this Doctor, because he is a medical and psychiatrist and I need them both. He can not only help me with my physical body, but he can also help me with my spiritual body." I began to manipulated this man to get these drugs. I will say that this man didn't know my past and I hold nothing against this man.

I still today love him very much in my heart, but I haven't seen him since the Plant has closed its doors. That was at least 11 years ago. This man only knew what I had allowed him to know at this job. We would talk alone sometimes, but if the conversion got close to my past, I would turn the subject or make an excuse and walk away. I'm sure that this man knew that I was a recovery alcoholic, because we would talk about that, but he didn't know that I was also a recovery drug addict. This man was also a recovering alcoholic and we would talk about that matter sometimes, but he didn't know my story at the time.

So, after I had asked him what doctor he went to he said, "Well, he is a medical doctor, but he is a psychiatrist also. I've been going to him for years and he is a swell guy. He is a Christian also. If I give you his number will you call him, so that, he will help you?" I grabbed the number and said to him, "Thank you very much for being here for me. I really needed something to help me through my troubles." I felt great burdens during this time of my life and this medicine had changed the way I was thinking. I knew that I had to do something about the way I was beginning to act in my life, because I thought these sufferings, such as this incident at work, had threaten my peace that I had with God and his Son Jesus Christ at this time. I knew what I believed was the truth and I would make stands in what I believed to be the truth. But I will say, I was without understanding of the matters at this time and the consequences that soon would manifest in my life. About two days later, there was a New Plant Supervisor on the job site. I had not been to the doctor at this time and I didn't have any feel good drugs in my pocket. This day someone was cursing at another person with angry and I went to this New Supervisor and said to him, "Is there anything in the manual that prohibits abusive language?" This man looked at me with very stern eyes and as if I was crazy and said to me, "If you come to me about this matter again, me and you are going to have problems."

I didn't say another word to this man and left from his presence and walked away. I never went back to this job.

CHAPTER SEVEN

ENDURANCE.

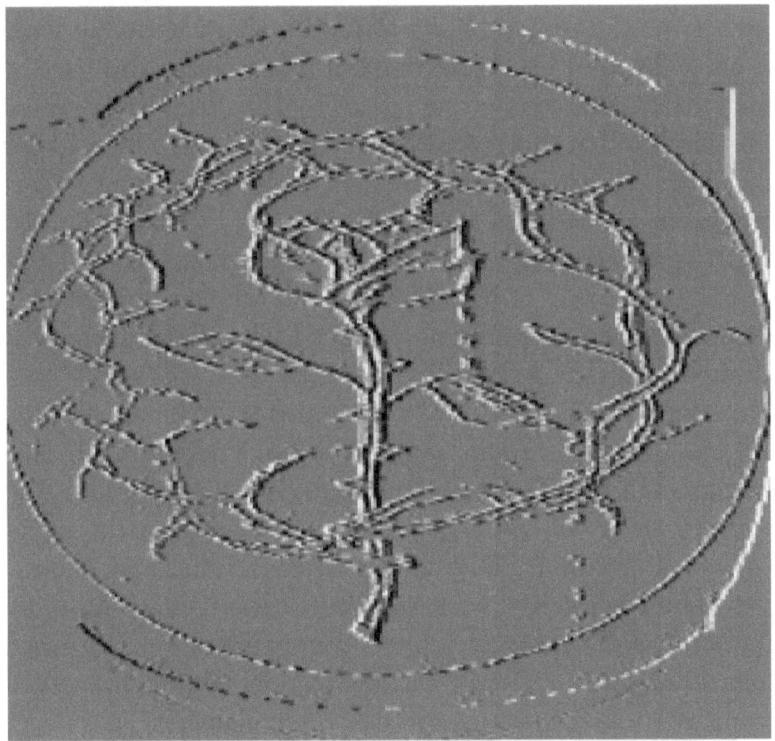

Before I took the mind altering drug that you have read about in the previous chapter, and I somewhat got addicted to it, God was revealing something to me at the time. I was studying the Holy Book of Job at the time and I thought I had an understanding of trials, temptations and tribulations. But my friend, I didn't have squat at this time.

Now, I started to write a Book 15 years ago on the matters, but after I took this drug it was if, my understandings had vanished away. I started to write the writings, because I thought at the time I could use them in the youth ministry that God had bless me greatly with. When my life was restored back to God this last time and was greatly resurrected from my past dead life and became a new born child of God, I found the writings that I attempted to write over 15 years ago. The writings were hidden on an old slave hard drive that I had stored away in a folder hidden in other folders. I really don't know how this hard drive survived during these times. I believe maybe God hid it for this right time of my life.

Its somewhat Ironic also knowing that when I found these writings, I wanted to write again and it was this time, that I started to with this book. My wife and I had moved several times during this time of my life and we had thrown many things away. This hard drive was hidden in some clothes that was stored in an container and when I installed it on another computer, I found the writings hidden in a folder that had no reason to be in that folder. Just like every thing else in my Life during this great resurrection from my past dead life, God had restored it to me again. I began to start with the following writings many years ago as God was revealing suffering to me. I never finished the writings and thought that they were lost.

But, when I had a desire of writing this book it was if, God was putting the puzzle of my life together again. I added much more to the writings as I would get the true understanding of what God was revealing to me. I will ask as you read the following writings, please keep this on your mind, "Why do I go through sufferings? I know that you will read duplicates of what you have already read, but my friend, have patience with me for the point is coming soon. When I found the writings, I had titled it, "Trials and Tribulation." But today, I titled the following as, *"What Sufferings are You Talking About?"*

WHAT SUFFERING ARE YOU TALKING ABOUT?

For today Being a Spiritual Man; for I am a Spiritual Being, is a glorious and much more of a abundant life. But, life as I see it, can become a little bit hot and cause the impurities of my life to rise and fester to a boil and cause some discomforts which in return may cause me to ask the big question, *Why God am I going through so much suffering?*

Well, just to let you know, that is a very common and sober question to ask. I know I have asked that question many a times, until I got an understanding of the matter. The answer wasn't really what I had hoped for, but as I became more aware of the sufferings in my life and began to understand this matter, I accepted God's answer to my life's long question. In the Holy Book of God's Word (God's Will for Mankind and all of his creation) 1Peter chapter 4, verses 12-13, Peter wrote to the church concerning that very question that we ask ourselves as a child of God. Peter writes to the children of God and it is written, ***"Beloved, think it not strange concerning the fiery trial which is to try you, as though some strange thing happened unto you: But rejoice, inasmuch as ye are partakers of Christ's sufferings; that, when his glory shall be revealed, ye maybe glad also with exceeding joy."***

We that are Changed and are walking as a New Creature in God's Will, will suffer with God and Jesus Christ. We will have to take up our own cross and carry it to the hill of Golgotha were we must lay our life on the line, just like Jesus Christ did for mankind and creation. No, we don't have to be nailed to the cross or shed any of our sinful blood, because Christ shed his innocent blood for us. Even if we did shed our blood, it would not be accepted. All we have to do is take up our cross and follow God's Will for our Life and bear the sufferings, not in the physical body only, but in the mind and spiritual body also.

What does it mean to suffer for God and Christ or to become partakers of his sufferings? Well, before I can attempt to answer that question, I must tell you what suffering means. To suffer doesn't only mean that you may think you are physically dying or suffering from pains of consequences of self will. The word suffer means; to submit to something or to endure something, to bear up under something. When I am speaking of suffering for God and Christ, I am merely speaking that we are submitting our Will and our life over to the Will of God and his Son Christ and that we will bare some of the same burdens that Christ bore for mankind and creation. Suffering also means to endure something, such as, humility. I will expand on thorns of the flesh later. In the Holy Book of Matthew Chapter 16, verse 24, Jesus Christ clearly leaves mankind the principle that must be followed, *"Then said Jesus to his disciples, If any man will come after me, let him deny himself, and take up his cross, and follow me."* Christ commands that we take up our own cross.

Also in Matthew Chapter 10, verse 38, *"And he that taketh not his cross, and followed after me, is not worthy of me."* We must take up our on cross and follow Christ, if we want to live much abundantly on earth and have Life Everlasting.

The Greatest example of totally submitting our will over to God's Will, is that of, Jesus Christ. Jesus Christ knew he would be Crucified on a Tree and suffer greatly for the Whole Wide World when he said, as he was in agony in the garden, *"Father, if thou be willing, remove this cup from me: nevertheless not my will, but thine, be done."* Jesus Christ knew that he was to suffer for all of mankind, but he stayed the course, even until his death, on the tree at Calvary. We will have to go through trials and tribulations for God and Christ, if we have giving our will and life to them. But, we have got to go through these sufferings to grow in the spirit and to attain that perfect understanding of his Will for us. God and Christ suffered for the whole world, because he loves us so much. The God of Life suffered greatly for Mankind; for God suffered his only begotten Son and all creation for mankind. God's Son Jesus Christ suffered, or lets say, he bore the sins and sorrows of the whole world and mankind. In the Holy Book of St. John Chapter 3, verse 16 it is written *"For God so Loved the World, that he gave his only begotten Son, that whosoever believeth in him should not perish but have everlasting life."* WOW! Now, that is Love. Have every asked this question, "What is God's Will for me?". This verse reveals it to us, Life Everlasting. Life Everlasting is what he wants for you, me and the whole wide world.

Now, Christ suffered the greatest suffering that any man had or will ever suffer, because he loves us and he wants us in heaven with him and the Father for ever and ever. Not only does he have great passion for this mission for mankind to reunion with him in heaven, he also wants us to have life here on earth, much more abundantly. Christ not only suffered for mankind only, but the Whole Wide World, including all of God's Creation. Yes, Jesus Christ suffered on the Cross of Calvary for all of God's Creation, so that, his creation could be restored back as it was from the beginning before man had fallen into sin. Today I can say with confidence, I do know what it means to suffer for and with Christ, but nothing to be compared of the suffering Christ did for mankind and creation on the tree; for he suffered not only for mankind, but for all of His Creation.

Oh Yes! Please let me share this with you. In my past life, I took living creatures, such as, Pigs, Cows, goats, chickens, and all creatures likewise, like I would drink a glass of water. I never thought that these animals suffered in such a way that made me not want to eat them. Please follow me for the point is coming.

Before my Resurrection from the dead life that I was living, I had been given a touch of this suffering somewhat one day and I was very burden. I was somewhat better and had stop doing drugs and drinking. I was trying to do good, but I was still without understanding of God's Will for my life at this time. I was without a job at this time and was searching for something new for my life, hoping it would help me get much better and I was blessed with a different job. When I started to work at this job for the first day, the owner told me that someone would be in later, to help with our duties. When this man showed up, he was a friend from my local church that I knew closely. He was an older gentleman and was a deacon at this church and he was like a brother to me when I was going to church.

During this time of my life, I knew that God was knocking on the door of my heart to go back to church, but I thought that I was an unworthy man at this time. So, when this man showed up at work, this made me happy within my spirit. This friend and myself worked together everyday and had a great time. I will say, I was searching for understanding of God's Will for my life at this time and I had prayed unto God to help me get a good job. He was faithful in doing so. I was suffering to do better, but soon found out that the suffering I was going through was counted as fly dung. So as time past, as I began to learn the functions of the duties there at this job, I thought that I had found the job I had been looking for. But, the job just didn't work out for me at this time. I believe it was because of not having the true understanding of this job. I had the skills by all means to do my duties at 100%, but I just couldn't bare the burden. So, I was working at this new job as a Butcher's helper and I got this understanding of the suffering of God's Creation and it went like this:

THE BUTCHER'S SHOP

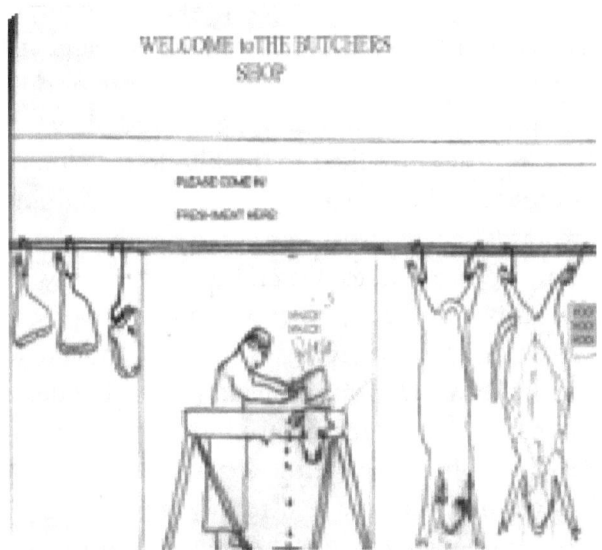

During my experience as a butcher helper, I would come into this shop everyday and there would be animals being killed by the dozens, like a production line. Everyday I could hear the screams from the animals, as they were killed.

At this shop, we only killed hoofed foot animals. I would open the cooler up everyday and there would be many animal carcasses hanging from hooks from a roll track from the ceiling. The animals would be killed on what was called the kill floor and then dressed and rolled into this cooler. My duty was to help get the carcasses from the cooler to the packing room.

The packing room was where we cut the meat or grind the meat and then pack it into boxes. I was a butcher's helper on this job and the experienced butchers would throw entire carcasses on top of these large steel tables and we would then cut the carcasses into steaks, pork chops, hams, shoulders, grind hamburger or sausage and many other special orders. We would use long sharp knifes, large electric saws and other tools to cut through the carcass's flesh and bones, like butter.

After we would cut the meats or grind the meats, we would then pack the meats into boxes and roll the boxes into large freezers waiting for the right customers. My duties continued on this job for about 3months and I believe it was for this very reason:

There was a day in particular that I will never forget. I walked into the shop area and there hung a large bull cow and it had already been skinned and dressed out. I didn't pay no attention to it; for it was normal for animals to be just hanging around. As we took a break that day from our duties, I walked to the kill floor to look around and to see the procedure of how these animals were killed and dressed. I looked over towards where there was a very large vat with extremely hot water and my heart began to flutter. I seen a large sow hog, flipping and flopping in this large vat, as if it was on a rotisserie. The eyes of this animal were closed and I new it was for meat now without mercy, with no doubt. As I walked around this kill floor, I ended back at this large bull cow that was just hanging around. I looked at this bull cow and it's eyes where opened and then I seen as if this bull cow started to cry, no kidding. It looked to me as if tears were flowing from this Big Bull's eyes. I left immediately from the presence of this bull cow and went outside to smoke a cigarette. My heart began to feel as if it was enlarging and pressing on my sternum bone. I had never felt such a great burden as I did that day for animals. I felt in my spirit as if that bull cow said to me in a voice within my spirit, *"I suffered for you."*

Today, I know what that touch of suffering was for at that time. God and His Christ was suffering for me and they wanted me back into their Will, before it was to late. It was just a knock on my heart to let God's Love into my heart, so that, he could show me that he loved me and that his creation was suffering for me also. God and Christ and all of God's Creation is suffering because of man's sin, since the time that man had sinned in the Garden of Eden. Christ Jesus suffered greatly on the cross of Calvary for all of God's Creation. But, I refused the knock on my heart from God at this time and I ran from this job and God. I believe it was because I didn't have the true understanding of this matter, until later in Life.

After I left this job, I began using drugs worse than I had ever used, no kidding. I had no insurance, and no medications. I was trying to numb myself from every pain that I could even think of, especially this touch of suffering that was revealed to me. This burden was too great for me to handle at this time of my life, but I'm not God and I cant judge the timing of any understanding revealed. God had blessed me with this job for one reason and one reason only. God wanting me to understand the suffering of his creation and how He and His Son Jesus Christ suffers for the Whole Wide Whole.

Today, since I have the understanding of this matter, things are not the same. In my past life, I would just go and eat a piece of cow flesh or pig flesh or chicken flesh and wouldn't think much about it. But today, I know that God suffered his creation for mankind and today before I eat any animal flesh, I ask Grace. Not only do I ask Grace, I also Thank God for the blood sacrifice that he has suffered for me to eat. Please follow me, the point is coming.

In the beginning from the Garden of Eden to this very day, mankind has sinned. When Adam and Eve sinned against God's Will in the beginning there had to be a blood sacrifice.

God's Creation became the blood sacrifice, such as, sheep, cows, goats and all that contains much blood. Not only did God require a sacrifice, but it had to have blood and much blood; for the blood contains Life. God required a blood sacrifice throughout the Old Testament Times. Why did God require a blood sacrifice? Today I know this with confidence, that blood has life and it cries out to God. When Adam and Eve had sinned in the beginning, God made coats of skins and covered them both. The only way now for Adam and Eve to have a relationship with God was by a blood sacrifice, but first God had to know where they were. When Adam and Eve had sinned, God came in the cool of the day and said, *"Where art thou?"*. Adam and Eve was hiding from God, because of sin. Sin had already separated man from God at this moment and now God had to ask, *"Where art thou?"*

In the Holy Book of Isaiah Chapters 59-66, verses 1-clearly states the hope of salvation and division from God, because of sin, **"BEHOLD, the Lord's hand is not shortened, that it cannot save; neither his ear heavy, that it cannot hear: But your iniquities have separated between you and your God, and your sins have hid his face from you, that he will not hear."** Sin separates God from man and the only way for a man to have a relationship with God is through a blood sacrifice. The blood cries out to God and lets him know where the man is. Remember Cain and Abel's Sacrifice, as they presented them to God? Which sacrificed did God find favor in? If you Guessed the blood sacrifice of Abel, then you are well. But, Cain was very wroth, and his countenance fell. *"And the Lord said unto Cain, Why art thou wroth? and why is thy countenance fallen? If thou doest well, shalt thou not be accepted? and if thou doest not well, sin lieth at the door. And unto thee shall be his desire, and thou shalt rule over him."* God was giving Cain a choice at this time and the choice was this: "Give me a blood sacrifice and do well or fall into sin."

But, as we keep reading in this book of Genesis chapter 4, Cain chose the wrong way and got angry with his little brother Abel, and slew him. *"And the Lord said unto Cain, Where is Abel thy brother? And he said, I know not: Am I my brother's keeper? And he said, What hast thou done? the voice of thy brother's blood crieth unto me from the ground. And now art thou cursed from the earth, which hath opened her mouth to receive thy brother's blood from thy hand; When thou tillest the ground, it shall not henceforth yield unto thee her strength; a fugitive and a vagabond shalt thou be in the earth."* My friend, there is life in the blood and God knows where every atom that makes it up is, at every moment. There is not one drop of blood shed on this earth that God doesn't know about and we as mankind are responsible for every drop that we shed. Oh The blood, The blood! Now, Cain had a choice to do well, but he chose by his own self will to follow sin and he suffered greatly the consequences for the matter. I will say today with confidence, there is a blood that covers all sin that is more precious and more purer than bullocks and any other creature; for it is the blood of Jesus Christ, the Son of the Living God.

As for the Old Testament times, there was a command from God for a blood sacrifice for sins, such as, bullocks. But, as you continually to read and study the Old Testament, there are prophesies throughout it that proclaimed that there would soon come a Ultimate Sacrifice for all of Man and his Creation. And there would never be a need for another blood sacrifice again. Mankind and creation would be restored back to God as In the beginning, by this one particular blood sacrifice.

Today I understand that Christ Jesus was the ultimate Sacrifice for mankind and creation. I know that if I'm covered by his blood, then God knows where I am and hears me. If I'm not covered by the blood, then God doesn't know where I am and neither would he hear me and I would be in danger of the consequence, such as, death.

Remember the Lord's Pass Over in the Book of Exodus, chapter 12, and the consequences of all those that were living, that were not covered by the blood of the lamb on the door post? When a man is covered by the blood of Jesus Christ (The Lamb of God), his blood cries out to God and says this to The Father of Life; "This man is covered by my blood. Father, Pass death by this man." Now that isn't written, but I truly believe that when a man is in God's Will, having the Blood of Christ spread around his doorpost of his Life, then that man will not suffer eternal death.

I believe today and say this with confidence, if a man hopes in God to save him from the misery and horrors and believes Christ Jesus for a resurrection from death in his life and trust them to do so, then Christ dips his cloth into his blood and covers that man. But, a man can be drawn away by the lust of their flesh and enticed to sin by Satan, and would be in danger of Hell's Tormenting Fire. But, if that man will believe again and ask Jesus Christ to cover him by his blood, he is faithful to cover the man again. It would be as if the man crucified Christ afresh to received the blood. But, Jesus Christ is Standing still and ready, waiting with all patience and understanding. Lets sing this song together, will you? *What can wash away my sin? Nothing but the blood of Jesus; What can make me whole again? Nothing but the blood of Jesus. Oh! precious is the flow That makes me white as snow; No other fount I know, Nothing but the blood of Jesus.* I know today that God's Word is a Blood Bath for mankind to wash in, if a man will only wash in the precious blood and let it completely wash him whiter than snow.

I know today that God has bless mankind with animals to eat, but there will come a day when all is fulfilled and we will not need to eat the flesh of God's Creation anymore. Jesus Christ has fulfilled all things and soon we will know.

But for now, we must eat of Christ (HIS WORD) daily and be covered by his pure blood and it is good to eat of God's creation; for he has cleaned and suffered all things for us to eat. In the Holy Book of Acts, chapter 10, verses 9-15, Peter, one of Jesus Christ's Disciple and Now an Apostle to the Church, had a vision. The vision was for Peter to understand that all manner of Four footed beasts, wild beasts, creeping things and fowls of the earth had already been cleansed for mankind to eat of. Peter didn't want to eat of these things, because he thought that only these things were excepted by the people of foreign nations. Not only did God show Peter that all things have been suffered for mankind to eat, but also he isn't a respecter of another man. Please read this Book sometime soon.

Now, in the Holy Book of Romans, chapter 8, verses 18-23, reads as written, *"For I reckon that the suffering of this present time are not worthy to be compared to the glory which shall be revealed in us. For the earnest expectation of the creature waiteth for the manifestation of the sons of God. For the creature was made subject to vanity, not willingly, but by reason of him who hath subjected the same hope, Because the creature itself also shall be delivered from the bondage of corruption into the glorious liberty of the children of God. For we know that the whole creation groaneth and travaileth in pain together until now. And not only they, but ourselves also, which have the f irstfruits of the Spirit, even we ourselves groan within ourselves, waiting for the adoption, to wit, the redemption of our body."* I know today and will say with confidence, God's Creation is good. Since Jesus Christ came and suffered on the cross of Calvary and gave mankind the Greater Hope in the resurrection, God's creation is Well. Before Jesus Christ came to this earth, his creation and mankind groaned within their selves for the hope that we would be restored back to the relationship with God, as it was in the beginning.

But, since Jesus Christ has giving mankind the hope now, the Creation is Well also. It is like this: During the Old times, lets say before Jesus Christ came to this earth, mankind and creation was lost in sin and groaned within the spirit to be delivered from sin. The creation was suffering greatly because of mankind not understanding sin. Jesus

Christ gave man the understanding of sin, but not only understanding of sin, but instructions how to live a life without sin.

So, now as mankind gets more understanding of how to live without sin, then the creation is better off, follow me? At the time I was at the job as a Butcher helper, I was without understanding of this matter and I got scared and ran and hid from God. When God showed this suffering to me, I just couldn't bare it, because I was without understanding of suffering. I believe when I asked God for a job, I added something in my request and it went like this, "Father God. Please help me get a good job. I don't want to suffer anymore from not getting a good job. Please God help me get a job, so that, I want suffer anymore." So, God gave me a job, but he didn't want me to suffer either. So, he just touched me with a small drop of his suffering and today I count my suffering as fly dung. I just can't imagine the suffering that God and Jesus Christ has done for mankind and the creation for thousands of years.

When I received the drop in the ocean of the suffering God and Christ has done for mankind, it is to much to imagine and to great a burden for a man to bare. Today when I eat a nice T-Bone steak or go to the grocery store and see all the suffering God has done for mankind, I almost go in tears knowing that God has suffered greatly for me.

Today I can eat good and I eat well and I like all types of meat, but I will say this, I don't kill the flesh of God's Creation just for sport. I am not saying, that there is anything wrong about the Sport of Hunting, but if we are hunting creatures just to fulfill our own self will pleasures, such as, not eating what you kill or not giving it to someone in need, then that animals blood will be required on that man's hands, no kidding. I believe it would be the same as murder. I enjoy still today to hunt, but I want just go out on a killing spree to get the big one. Today I still like to hunt rabbits and I desire sometimes for the game taste. But, if I do go hunting, I will only kill what I know I will eat and quickly ask God's Grace for the meat. We as mankind have a responsibility to keep what God has giving us, speaking of all his Creation. I now know today that Butchers have a great burden on there hearts, because they must supply man meat to eat. I believe that butchering animals is one of the most important jobs on the face of the earth today, because of being held accountable for the blood sacrifices.

I couldn't do it everyday, because of the great burden that I have today of this understanding. But I will say, when or if I do go deer hunting, rabbit hunting or someone brings me some game to dress, I'm happy for the blessing of the animals suffering.

I thank God for every piece of meat that I eat and for his great suffering for me and I don't waste not one part of the animal. I know and understand this today, when blood hits the ground and the blood cries out to God, God wants an answer for the sacrifice of His blood. It's somewhat like the Secretary of Treasury of the United States having to keep account for every dollar spent by the government. God is keeping account of every drop of blood shed on this earth and when we as mankind stand before him after the earthly death, mankind will have to account for every drop of blood that was shed. I could spend eternally writing about the blood, but I hope that what I have shared with you has giving you an understanding of how God, Jesus Christ and His Creation has suffered for mankind, greatly.

Today when I'm suffering, I can always go to the Cross of Calvary, that same Cross that Jesus bleed and suffered greatly for you, me and the Whole Wide World and get strength from the cross. Going to the cross, following the cross and keeping my eye on the cross, gets me through my sufferings. I know today I must carry my own cross, even to the end of the world. The Greatest example of a Trial of Faith and Temptation came from Jesus Christ for us to learn from. In God's Holy Bible the example starts in Matthew Chapter 3 where John the Baptist was sent from God to call all people to repentance and I ask you to please read it. In the 15 verse of Chapter 3 of Matthew, Jesus Christ told John the Baptist and the World, that he must suffer the baptism of the flesh to fulfill all righteousness. Even though, Jesus Christ was without sin and was a Divine Creature as a God-Man, he was still born into the sinful nature of mankind in the flesh. But, he was still willing to suffer for righteousness at the Baptism, at river of Jordan, even though he was without sin.

Now, in Chapter 4 of Matthew, God's Word clearly states the trials we will go through for our faith in him, as we give our will over to the care of his Will. Jesus Christ, a man without sin, was baptized to fulfill all righteousness of God's commandment and to leave the example for mankind to follow. God does command that we be baptized of water for the remission of our sins, after we give our will and life over to him. It is a renewal of Life and a public confession of our Faith in God and it is to me the first step of carrying our own cross. For God's Word clearly states, if we deny him, he will deny us. After Jesus was Baptized by water he was led up to the wilderness.

The wilderness always makes me think of the wild side of my living of all the temptations, lust and self will pleasures that I went through as I lived in the wilderness of life for nearly 28 years. But, I wasn't like Christ, I did give into Satan's Temptations and it was not good; for I suffered the consequences of self will.

So, Jesus was in the wilderness to be Tempted of Satan, but Christ Jesus was without sin. Remember this one thing about Jesus Christ as he was here on the earth; He was man and suffered as any man would had suffered in the flesh. God tempts no man. A man is tempted when he is drawn away from God by his own desires and lust of the things of this world. There is a night and day difference between being Tempted and Tried; for God Tries and Satan Tempts. Jesus Christ wasn't being tried in the wilderness, he was being tempted. Jesus Christ had to fulfill this matter; for all things of the Old Covenant to be fulfilled. Jesus Christ knew that he had to fulfill all righteousness while he was on this earth in the flesh, so that, this would leave for mankind an understanding that we can also defeat Satan's Temptations, as we are enticed to leave God's perfected Will for us. You can see as I have written that word "as", because I know with confident every man will be tempted and It isn't a matter of "If" it is a matter of "When". Jesus Christ was not being tempted because of leaving God's Will; for *Jesus Christ is God's Will for mankind.*

Jesus Christ went through and suffered the Temptation to leave us this greatest example, so that, when we are being tempted by that old serpent the devil, we will know what to do and I ask, will you please read Chapter 4 of Matthew sometime soon? Please, let me ask these questions. Why did God send his only begotten Son to this sinful world and Why would Christ Jesus even want to come to this sinful world and suffer for us? I believe this would be the answer, with great confidence. God had already repented that he had made mankind, because of the great fall into sin, the great rebellion against his word. I believe that sooner or later God was going to destroy mankind from the earth. He had already sent the Great Flood and only allowed a hand full of his creation to survive. Mankind was still rebellion against him and he was about to destroy mankind from off the face of his glorious creation, but someone stood in the gap and said," Father we have made them in our image.

Father, please have mercy on man and send me to the earth, so that, mankind would have an example to follow. And then Father, if they do not follow the example that I will leave for them, let it be the individuals choice to Live or Die." At this time, Mankind had the Laws to follow and knew what sin was, but mankind didn't have a Perfected Will to follow.

So, God sent his only begotten Son to the earth for us to follow. This is the only chance mankind has today to live much more abundantly on earth and to live life eternally. God and his only Begotten Son suffered greatly for mankind and all his creation, so that, a man could now have the choice to Live. In the Holy Book of Mark Chapter 8, verses 36-37, it is written, *"For what shall it profit a man, if he shall gain the whole world, and lose his soul? Or what shall a man give in exchange for his soul?"* Christ asked this question so that mankind could ponder on those words, because Christ knew the severity on mankind's existence. Christ ask this question, because he wanted mankind to understand that this life on earth is not a pleasure party, but Life or Death.

Like I have written before, "Life here is like boot camp. Training for a journey." God's Word clearly shows us what we must do when that old serpent Satan tries to tempt us and draw us from God's Perfect Will. Here is a big Key to unlock this matter. Christ used the sword of God, which is God's Word. Christ defeated Satan with the Word (Sword) of His Mouth, God's Word and Will for Him and the whole wide world. One more note to remember, *Satan is not God's adversary, he is Man's Adversary; for God has already judged and sentenced Satan.* There is a paradox of the word "Tempt" in the Old Testament and the New Testament. In the Old Testament, the Word is written that God Tempted Abraham. If, we would go back during the time of the Old Testament, the word "Tempt" doesn't define itself the same as the word "Tempt" in the New testament. In the Old Testament times the word "Tempt is defined as a trial.

In the New Testament times the word "Tempt" is defined as being enticed. Remember, God tempts NO Man. A man is tempted when he is enticed and drawn away from God by his own lust.

Now, I want to share something with you that happened to me during a Time I had giving my Life over to the care of God as I understood Him at a time. It was the second spiritual Awakening I had experience when I tried to do the right thing, which was, give my will to God. It was when I came out of a Drug and Alcohol Rehabilitation, which was, my forth time in Rehab. I made a choice to try God the second Time. As you have read before in the Apathetical Man, this was my second chance at life, but as I remember, it didn't last long. At the time I received this vision, I was truly trying to do what I thought was right in the eyes of God. I was seeking help from God and seeking understanding for his Will in my Life, but he showed me my weakness in this vision. I will say that it took a long time after this vision to come to an understanding of what God was showing me at that time. It took nearly 17 years later. I Can't tell you why it took so long for me to come to a better understanding of this vision, but I will also say that maybe it was for patience. For today, I know what the Vision was for and the vision has been restored by God and Christ in my life and I call this vision: *"The Glorious Cross"*

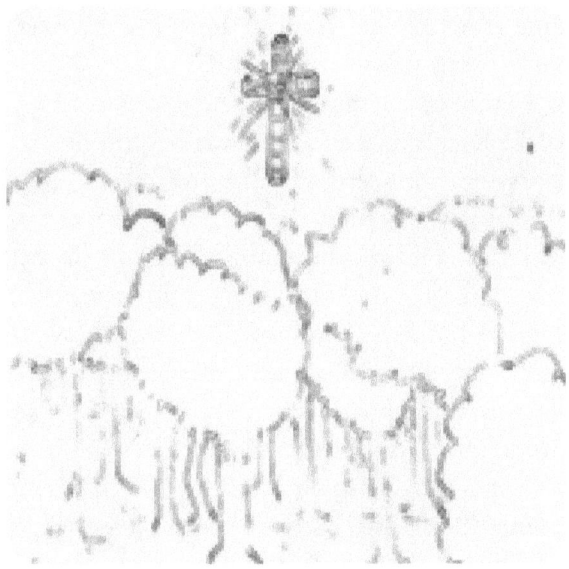

THE GLORIOUS CROSS

I was home seeking understanding of God's Will for me and reading God's Word. The Spirit of God moved on me. It had been raining early this morning and the windows and blinds where closed in the house. I was going through some troubled times of my life. The Spirit of God moved on me and pressed me, to open the blinds. It felt as time had slowed down. Somewhat like slow motion, in a stillness. I did according to what the Spirit was telling me through my spirit to do, not in a voice, but speaking through my mind. The Spirit was telling me to Open My Blinds and to Open My Window.

So, I did according to the Spirit's Will. There was a refreshing breeze that came through the window there where I was at. The wind was blowing gently and was very peaceful.

There was a stillness in the room and I was reading God's Word in the Book of Ezekiel, Chapter 16. I was beginning to read Chapter 17 of this book when the spirit of God pressed me again to look out the window. The Wind was nice, the rain had stopped; for it had been raining all night and early morning and the Sun was shinning bright. Then the Spirit spoke through my spirit and it was if it melted me and said," *What Do You See?*" I looked out the window and all I could see was the forest, the thick woods and trees. And I spoke and said in response to the Spirit of God, "I see Trees. Tall trees, small trees, green trees, barren trees, faded trees. All I see are trees." And the Spirit said again to me, *"Look Closer. What do You See?"* I tried to understand, but all I could see where Trees and I asked, "Lord Please help me! For I can only see Trees." Then, I thought of my Binoculars, that were laying six feet on a table from me. I searched the area through my Binoculars and there it was; A Cross, so beautiful my words could never explain in fullness. It was floating above the tree tops. It shine so bright from the center and from Top to Bottom, Left to Right. Its colors were brilliant and shinning as polished gems and the colors were Red, Blue and Brilliantly White. The center looked liked a shinning White Diamond and shined so bight, I could barely keep my eyes upon it. But, my eyes were fastened to it and I could not look away. When I would move just a little bit, the Cross would disappear. When I would drop the binoculars a little, the cross would disappear. I kept my eyes on it and I could not move as my eyes began to run with water.

As I was looking at the Cross, I was praying within my spirit, "God Please Help Me Keep My Eyes on the Cross; for It Is Beautiful!" It moved from left to right very slowly, but was still hard to look upon and follow it. My eyes were beginning to burn and water with extreme agony. I began to close my eyes, because of the burning sensation. I kept asking God to help me keep my eyes on the Cross.

My eyes became sore and dim, and I shut them. I had looked at the Cross as long as I possibly could. When I opened my eyes, I looked for the Cross and it was gone. Then the Spirit of God spoke to me again and said, *"What have you Seen?"* And I said," A Cross, A Glorious Cross." And then the Spirit began to minister to me the importance of keeping my eye on the Cross of Jesus Christ. The Spirit gave me the understanding of the importance of keeping my eyes on the Cross and following the Cross, no matter what happens in life. Keeping my eyes on the Cross and Following the Cross, until my eyes grow dim and I lay this old body down. He also revealed the Colors I had seen from the Cross. The Red Colors represented the Blood of Christ that he had shed for me and the Whole Wide World. The blue colors represented all the suffering and sorrows he bore for the whole wide world. The Center, like a brilliant diamond, is rewards for those who follow the Cross until the end. I must keep my eye on the center of the Cross, which is Christ and my reward, life everlasting.

The Cross is not something to be ashamed of; for The Cross is something to be grateful for, it is a Glorious Cross full of Life and rewards. It is full of God's Glory, Love, Mercy, and it is brilliantly shinning for the whole wide world to look upon, If only we will look for the Cross. I thank God every breath I make for his Son Jesus Christ going to the Cross of Calvary, where we can draw strength for our every need. Today when I go through a trial or tribulation, I can now look at the cross and see the sufferings Christ suffered for me. Then the trials become nothing compared to what Christ went through on cavalry. When I endure a trial and I overcome it through Christ, I am joyful and I have that blessed joy, because I have overcome the world through Christ my Lord. With out Christ I can not over come any trial or tribulations. Jesus Christ said in the gospel of John, chapter 16, verse 33 saying, *"These things I have spoken unto you, that in me ye might have peace. In the world ye shall have tribulation: but be of good cheer ; I have overcome the world."*

Now that says it all. Jesus Christ has overcame the world and I can draw near to him and also overcome the worlds trials and tribulations when it knocks on my door. Christ Jesus came to the World, so that, mankind could have a 100% understanding of how to live life here on earth much more abundantly and enter the Eternal Kingdom of his Father.

Now, let me share another great understanding that has been giving to me and I have great passion to share it with you. In the Holy Book of 2Corinthians, Chapter 12, verses 6-10, it is written by the Apostle Paul, *"For though I would desire to glory, I shall not be a fool; for I will say the truth: but now I forbear, lest any man should think of me above that which he seeth me to be, or that he heareth of me. And lest I should be exalted above measure through the abundance of the revelations, there was given me a thorn in the flesh, the messenger of Satan to buffet me, lest I should be exalted above measure. For this thing I besought the Lord thrice, that it might depart from me. And he said unto me, MY GRACE IS SUFFICIENT FOR THEE: FOR MY STRENGHT IS MADE PERFECT IN WEAKNESS. Most gladly therefore will I rather glory in my infirmities, that the power of Christ may rest upon me. Therefore I take pleasure in infirmities, in reproaches, in necessities, in persecutions, in distresses for Christ's sake: for when I am weak, then am I strong."* There is one extremely important word that I want you and I to grasp onto and that word is, "THORN". It has taken me many longsuffering years to understand this word, and today I can say this with confidence; The word "Thorn" doesn't only mean a prickly thing, such as, a rose's thorn. The word

"Thorn" also means something that causes great suffering. For examples: A Bi-Polar disease is a fleshly thorn. Osteo-arthuritis, Bursitis, Cancer, Heart Disease, Lung Disease are also thorns. Smoking, Alcohol, Drugs, Sex Additions, and such like, are also thorns in the flesh.

Some thorns have eased in my life, such as, alcohol and drug use, but, there are other thorns that have surfaced since these particular thorns has eased. I'm not going in details, because there are many. Since I was but a child, I was introduced or lets say, enticed to drugs, but I never desired to do these things. But, once I was introduced to the drugs, my flesh's chemistry changed.

These thorns embedded within my flesh is somewhat like, if you had a bad heart within your chest. The Doctor would tell me that I can't live without my heart, but he could help me with the symptoms, follow me? I know that I have to live with my heart in order for my blood to pump within my body and without it, I would die. I also know I can't ask a surgeon to remove my heart, but the surgeon may be able to help me live better with the bad heart. So, I learn to live with it and most of all, Accept that I have a bad heart. Please follow me for the point is coming. I now ask this question, "Can a Doctor remove this thorn, such as, addition from a man's life?" My answer would be certainly not. I maybe able to be delivered from one symptom of the thorn, but certainly not the thorn itself. Just like if you had a bad heart, you just learn to live with it. These maybe thorns within my flesh, but they were placed there by a divinity. These thorns are not something that you can just pluck out, like a rose's thorn. If these divine thorns could be remove, only the Great Surgeon, God Himself, would be the one and only that could remove them. Let me just clear this up also. I'm not saying that God got me addicted to drugs by any means or he gave me a Bi-Polar Disease. When I was a child and really didn't know any better about drugs, God used these situations to teach me about him and to draw closer to him. Like I said before, it has taken 30 years for me to understand what suffering means. These thorns were placed in my life, so that, I would never boast myself above which I am. They were placed there, so that, I would never say things like this; *"I don't need God or anyone. I can live the way that I want to."*

My friend, I thank God my Father for giving me the understanding that I can't even breath without Him. When things are going well in my life or lets say, I'm on top of my mountain, it is at this very moment that the thorn of my flesh knocks me back to the valley. It is here in the valley that I become closer to my Lord Jesus Christ and my Father God. Sometimes I get so far from God with my self, that God has to remind me that I cant even breath without Him, follow me? I see my life as a roller coaster. I have my ups and I have my downs. I'm not saying that I'm unstable, but that is just the way it is with my life. I can be on top of my mountain one day and the next day, the mountain is on me.

Let me just share this with you also my friend; Why are there mountains and valleys in a mans life? Why can't a man just stay on top of his mountain or just stay in the valley of his life? My friend, I truly believe it may be this very reason; The Top of the mountain is the Highest place a man can get without any mechanical devices, unless you are a eagle. The Valley is the lowest place a man can get, unless you are a mole in a hole, follow me? If a man would stay on top of the mountain his whole life, then that man wouldn't understand what living in the valley is like. If a man would stay in the valley his whole life, then that man wouldn't understand what living on top of a mountain would be like, correct? If I stay on top of my mountain of my life every day then I would probably say things like this; *"What's wrong with that man! Why is he going through so much. My life is great. I don't know why that man is going through such trouble. He is asking for help all the time and praying. Shoot! I don't ask nobody for nothing and I don't have to even pray."* And if I stayed in the valley my whole life, I would probably say things like this; *"Oh God, Please help me get back on top Lord. Will someone please help me today. I know now what people go through when they are going through troubles. Thank you Lord for helping me through this valley of my life dear God.* I also ask this question; Which way does water flow? If you would say downhill, then I would say you guessed correctly.

When I'm on top of my mountain of life, it seems that I get somewhat dehydrated. So, where do I go to get water again? The Valley.

It is here in the valley that I draw the living water. It is here in the valley that I draw my strength. For when I'm weak, God is strong. Jesus Christ said that he was the living water and if we would drink from him, we would thirst no more. It is here in the Valley that I draw closer to God and Jesus Christ and then I become strong again. In the

Holy Book of God it is written in the Psalms chapter 23, verse 4, ***"Yea though I walk through the valley of the shadow of death, I will fear no evil: for thou art with me; thy rod and thy staff they comfort me."*** God has never left me nor forsaken me. He is always there with open arms waiting patiently for me to come back, when I had left him. God is a jealous God when it comes to his children. He doesn't want his children to far from him. When I'm on top of the mountain of my life, it is here that I'm most vulnerable to things. I may get to far from God my Father, and may think I don't need him anymore. When I would think this way, God would use his Rod and comfort me. He would knock me back into the valley where he could talk to me again. It's good to be on top of your mountain, but don't forget God. God will remind a man if he is a child of his this one thing; that he can't even breath without him. So, God uses my thorns to get my attention when I'm walking away from him. God didn't want me to have thorns in my flesh, but he uses the thorns, so that, he gets my attention again. Some may judge me and say to me that these additions aren't thorns, but sin.

Again my friend, don't judge me, unless you be judge by what you judge. I ask this question, *"What is Sin?"* The best definition I found was in the Holy Book of God, James Chapter 4, verse17, ***"Therefore to him that knoweth to do good, and doeth it not, to him it is sin."***

If these thorns were sin, then why would I continuously pray and seek God to deliver me from all the thorns which suffers me so? I don't have pleasure in these thorns and neither do I lust after these thorns.

During many times that I was in Rehabilitation Centers and Hospitals, I would ask others if they enjoy doing drugs. 90% of all that I have asked would tell me that they wished God would take the addition away, so that, they could live a normal life without drugs. Being in the hospital or Rehab center would be a flag to me or telling me that they didn't want to suffer with addition, wouldn't it? I remember certain times that people would tell me that they committed their self to the Hospital, because the addition was to great and they didn't want to start using again and die. Being in the Hospital would tell me that they wanted help on how to live with the addition. Before I got this understanding, I would commit myself to a rehab center, because I thought the Doctors could deliver me from the additions. But, today I know they can only help a man to live with the addition.

Now, there is something else that I want to share with you now. The Apostle Paul wrote also in that scripture this; *"And lest I should be exalted above measure through the abundance of the revelations, there was given me a thorn in the flesh, <u>the messenger of Satan to buffet me, lest I should be exalted above measure."</u>* Satan knows my weakness and he is forever trying to buffet me by my thorns. It is here in my flesh that Satan knows my weakness and it is here that he tempts me more and more. But, since I understand my weakness, I'm always trying to be on guard and watching and discerning when he is trying to buffet me to do wrong. He comes at me by many different devices to lure and entice me away from God's Loving Grace, but God makes away for me to escape.

In the Holy Book of 1Corinthians 10:13 it is written, **"There hath no temptation taken you but such is common to man: but God is faithful, who will not suffer you to be tempted above that ye are able; but will with the temptation also make a way to escape, that ye may be able to bear it."** There has not been one time when I have suffered by the thorns of my flesh, God hasn't made away out of the suffering for me. God is Faithful to deliver you from the temptation and suffering of your thorns.

I will say this with confidence, if a man desires the thorns of his flesh and lust after the things of his thorns, then it is at this time that God may shut the door of escape for that man and that man may be endanger of destruction. One way out of the Temptations today is that of writing, reading, studying, meditating in God's Holy Word and to sum it entirely up, I try earnestly to keep my mind on Jesus Christ and God. One day as I was suffering greatly with a particular thorn, I prayed earnestly to God my Father and ask him to please take this thorn from me, but his answer was the same, *"MY GRACE IS SUFFIENT FOR THEE"*. I wasn't satisfied with his answer, so this is the answer he gave me, *"GIVE YOUR LIFE AWAY"*. Oh yes! Let me please share with you this understanding of what I believe to be the truth about thorns today. In the Book of Genesis Chapter3, verses 17-19, it is written, **"And unto Adam he said, Because thou hast hearkened unto the voice of thy wife, and hast eaten of the tree, of which I commanded thee, saying, Thou shalt not eat of it: cursed is the ground for thy sake; in sorrow shalt thou eat of it all the days of thy life; Thorns and thistles** *shall it bring forth to thee; and thou shalt eat the herb of the field; In the sweat of thy face shalt thou eat bread, till thou return unto the ground; for out of it wast thou taken: for dust thou art, and dust shalt thou return.* "Thorns and Thistles the Creator has said man shall reap. That grieves me deeply just reading, does it you?

It gives me great sorrow just knowing that mankind will forever reap thorns and thistles or until we have laid our bodies back to the dust that it was taken from. I believe truly that in the beginning of Adam and Eve in the Garden of Eden, mankind didn't till the ground and neither did they reap thorns and thistles. Man didn't even have to till the ground for food. Mankind in the beginning didn't have arthritis, bursitis, additions or suffer in anyway. Mankind in the beginning just walked and talked with the Father of Life and he supplied all things for them. But, mankind had rebelled against the Maker's very words and now mankind suffers. We may have to suffer with thorns of the flesh, but we have hope.

Since Jesus Christ came to this earth and suffered for mankind, we can now rejoice in the sufferings. That's Right! Rejoice! No, I do not run the streets and shout to people that I'm not suffering anymore, because my friend, I suffer daily. But, Christ Jesus makes the suffering much more easy for me to bear, daily. Looking to the Cross of Calvary where Jesus was crucified gives me great strength. Looking at his head with the thorns that pierced him, I know today he has crucified the thorns of the flesh also. By the blood of his head, my thorns have been crucified through Jesus Christ my Lord and I will forever praise his wonderful name for this. Christ made away for me to escape my thorns daily. Like I've mentioned before when I prayed and asked God many times to take away my sufferings, he gave me my answer my friend, and it was this; *"GIVE YOUR LIFE AWAY."* For it is written in God's Holy Word, *"For whosoever will save his life shall lose it: and whosoever will lose his life for my sake shall find it. For what is a man profited, if he shall gain the whole world, and lose his own soul? Or What shall a man give in exchange for his soul?"* So, I did just that and you have my life in your hand this very moment. This book is my way out of my suffering and when I'm writing, my mind is always on God and his Son Jesus Christ and Satan just flees away.

Today when I'm suffering with a thorn, I know where I get my strength. I read The Word of God and pray, meditate earnestly within it and go out and share my life with someone that is also suffering. His Grace is sufficient for me, and it is here in his Grace, that I become strong and overcome my thorns through Christ Jesus. I never at any time think that the thorn has been remove, because I know from experience when I think like this, I suffer much more greatly from the thorns. I know my thorns will forever be embedded within my life, but I've learned how to live with them and most of all, I've accepted them. The AA and NA prayer states as follows:

> *"God Grant Me The Serenity*
> *To Accept The Things I Cannot Change,*
> *Courage To Change The Things I Can,*
> *And The Wisdom To Know The Difference."*

Jesus Christ said that we will go through trials and tribulations and believe this, your faith in God and Jesus Christ will be tried and you will be also tempted. It isn't a matter of "IF" you will be tried or tempted, it is a matter of "WHEN." Christ suffered on the cross and overcame the world, but why must we suffer and have to go through trials and tribulations? This is another common and sober question to ask ourselves. Why do we, if we have giving our will and life over to God and his Son Jesus Christ, have to go through more trials and tribulations? One might would say this, "This is the reason why I gave myself to God and Christ, so that, I would not have to go through so much suffering. I hoped for more peace and more of a good life, but I have more sufferings now than I did before." But my dear friend, if we think this way we will miss the truth and be without understanding of trials and tribulations. We must get the full understanding of Trials and Tribulation in our life, before we can have a Life. We have to begin to define the words of trial and tribulation and work our faith in the matter for understanding. Please, let me share with you what I believe to be the Truth of this Matter.

First, what is a Trial? Great question! *Trial means, testing your trustworthiness.* There are God's Trials and Man's Trials. If we would say or believe that we have faith in something, such as patience, then we are tested in what we believe to be the truth of the matter of our faith in patience and that is a trial of your faith, which is God's Trials. God will test your faith, but that doesn't mean if we fail the test, we don't have faith in God. God will test our faith to show us and work through us to make our faith in him stronger and to have a greater understanding of the matter.

Remember always, God is the rewarded of our Faith in him. If we are found worthy through the testing or trial of our faith in God, then he will reward us with more faith. "The more faith we have, the more trials we get?" It isn't numbers with God, more or less isn't the matter, it is if we pass the test that really matters. But, I believe this; if you and I don't pass the testing of our faith, then God will continually testing it until we make an A+ for our profit and his Glory. "Well, if we don't pass the test the first time, how are we going to pass it the next time?" Good Question! If we believe in God for all that he is, then we must believe in his Word and Will for us, without doubts of not one word he has giving us. We must believe he is able to train us up to where we must be in our faith in him. God is able to do for us what we cannot do for ourselves. He made us, did he not? We have his Holy Ghost, which is, the *Comforter* to guide us through this life.

If we are of him, then God will send the Comforter and he will show us all things needed to pass the test of our faith. If we are willing to let the Comforter in us, and work through us, to teach us what God's Perfect Will is for us, then we begin to understand God's Will for our life. We begin to have much more hope and begin to trust God for the care of our life here and eternal life. With the Comforter as my Trainer, life here on earth gets much more better. The more that we have understanding in the Faith we have in God, the more chances are that we will pass the Trials of our faith.

But, it is a good trial and I rather be tried by God than Man, any day. God's trial is for life everlasting and is for our own profit, because God wants to give us his riches through Christ Jesus.

Remember this my friend, unbelievers will not go through a trial from God, they will only face judgment after death and tribulations here on earth. God's Trials are for the Believers only. I know today when my faith is being tested, that God is finding me worthy and not worthless; for Gods trials are merciful and gracious. Looking at what was written by the Apostle Peter above from the Holy Book of 1 Peter, chapter 4, verses 12-13, God's spirit told Peter to write it to us to give us understanding of the fiery trails that we will go through, if we our God's children. God's trials are not because we have done something wrong, like stealing from another man or even not having the Faith of Noah. Even though, I want the faith of Noah.

God's trials are for True Justice; for to find a man worthy for what He has for them. I believe when I started trusting God and His Son Jesus Christ for my life, then I was tried to see if I was worthy of God's riches he had for me, but I'm not talking finances only here. God's riches would be that of, Love, peace, mercy, wisdom, joy, faith, understanding, patience, and many more.

So, God tried me to find me worthy of his blessings and I can now say for today, through my testing of my faith in him, I'm found worthy and Justified and have received some of these rewards of my faith in him.

Before I gave my will and life over to God's Will, I was heading a course of destruction and eternal death; for I was without understanding of the matter. Today, God can bless me with understanding, and the others things I need for my Life here on earth and my journey Home when I drop this old fleshly body to the dust it came from.

Now, if I'm tried by man, then I must of done something wrong and I'm facing the Court Judge. There isn't much joy in that, is it? There is something different today in my life than it was when I was out and about in the world in my self will; for I do have more Peace, Love, Joy and understanding in my life today. I don't have to worry if I'll be arrested by man for doing something wrong or have to suffer for something I should had not done.

I've found a *Key to the Kingdom* and that key is Faith in God and his Son Jesus Christ and they haven't never left me nor forsaken me. This key is not anything that I had worked for, it was giving to me when I first to believe God and his Son, Jesus Christ to save me from death. Sure my faith is stronger to day than early in life for one reason only, because I try to exercise it daily. It was my choice when I walked away from God's Will in my Life and let self-will lead me to the horrors and even the big hole time after time. But, God was always at the center of the crossroad, where I left him, ready and waiting for me to ask him to intervene in my troubles and to save me at near my last breath. He always makes a way where I thought there was no way. Thank you God, my Father and my Lord Jesus Christ for being so faithful. Sometimes when I'm tested, I truly don't know if I'm going to pass the test of faith or not and sometimes don't even understanding that I'm being tested by God. I also think that I don't understand enough about God's Will for me to pass the test of my faith. But, my Hope in God and Jesus Christ is always there like a straight line, panting for His riches. I will say this, if a man has truly given their life over to the care of God and His Christ, that man will be tried. God doesn't want a man to just be saved only; for he wants them to have much more than salvation at the moment, because salvation alone cant get a man to eternal life.

In Matthew Chapter10 verse 22, Jesus Christ clearly states this as it is written, ***"And ye shall be hated of all men for my name's sake: but he that endureth to the end shall be saved."*** Please let me explain this matter. Yes! God and His Christ will save a man at the spare of his breath when he are calls out to them to save him from the horrors and misery that he is living. If God and his Christ just saved me from my horrors and just left me there still facing the Big Hole of death, then I still wouldn't have much hope, except to continually to ask God to save me. When a man is saved from his horrors and misery at the time, God wants to keep him from the horrors for ever. If salvation was only what God wanted to give mankind, then the Death and Resurrection of Jesus Christ would had been in vain. God wants to Bless a man for the keeping of his soul for ever and ever and that is the reason Christ came and was crucified and resurrected from the grave.

Being converted and being saved are two different words and we must never confuse the two. When we first call on God to deliver us from the pains and horrors of this life, we become converted. When we completely give our all and all, such as, our total life to God until the last breath we take on this earth, then I can say that we are saved. Being converted is the first step of entering life or the beginning of life. Being saved is the end of this life and have enter into rest, life everlasting.

Before in the Old Testament Times, the Prophets, Kings, Judges, and High Priest were the only way to received a Blessing from God. But since Jesus Christ came to earth to fulfill all righteousness and split the Vail in the Holy of Holies, all men can now come to the Father through His Christ and receive his eternal life saving blessings.

Christ made a way for all mankind to come boldly to God's Throne, individually. But, God will not bless a man if that man is without understanding of the blessing. I can say with confidence today this; if, I ask God for more peace in my life, as an example, I will be tried for the blessing of peace.

God will not just throw a dog a bone once in awhile because the dog just wants to play with the bone. If a man has any self will intent for the blessing of God, then that man will be tried and have to understand the blessing before that man is given the blessing, follow me? God gives man the blessing for Life. When God is ready to bless a certain man, this man will have to understand this one thing; all of God's Blessings are for his Glory and that man's profit for life eternal. Remember, God's blessings will not go back to him void. My friend, also remember this; when you ask for a blessing from God, be prepared for the trial of your life, no kidding.

Today, I know who has the power to resurrect a man from a dead man walking to a son of the Living God. It is mentioned time after time that God is Faithful to his people and he will never leave us or forsake us. The Lord is always on time, even when we sleep, the Lord is protecting and guiding us. I'm not writing to try to lead you to think that I know the answers for this matter, because believe me, I don't know jack squat! But I do know what I believe on in this matter. God's Will is the Way, The Truth and The Life, if only we will follow it. God and his Son Jesus Christ has all the answers. I'm sharing with you what the God of Life and His Son Christ Jesus did for me. God's Will, resurrected me from a Dead Man Walking, to now, a son of the Living God. I'm only a child of God. I'm still growing and need milk, but I rather have meat. I do know this with confidence, if you are a repented, converted and a willing child of God, you are being tried, cleaned, sanctified for God's Kingdom.

The word tells us in Revelation chapter 21:6-8, *"And he said unto me, It is done. I am Alpha and Omega, the beginning and the end. I will give unto him that is athirst of the fountain of the water of life freely. He that overcometh shall inherit all things; and I will be his God, and he shall be my son.*

But the fearful, and unbelieving, and the abominable, and murderers, and whoremongers, and sorcerers, and idolaters, and all liars, shall have their part in the lake of f ire which burneth with f ire and brimstone: which is the second death."

In Revelation chapter 22:12-15 the scripture reads alike. What the scripture is telling you and I, is that, sin will not be present in Heaven. Those that are sons and daughters of God through his Son Jesus Christ, we have become heirs to his kingdom and much more, whosoever that overcomes this world, shall inherit all things in this Life and the Life to come. In the Holy Book of Matthew Chapter 19, Jesus Christ gives this promise; It is written, *"And everyone that hath forsaken houses, or brethren, or sisters, or fathers, or mother, or wife, or children, or lands, for my sake, shall receive an hundredfold, and shall inherit everlasting life. But many that are f irst shall be last; and the last shall be f irst."* It doesn't matter if you give a glass of water to someone in the name of Jesus Christ, you want loose your reward.

Now lets read about *Tribulations.* First, what does tribulation mean? Again, great Question! Tribulation is defined as pressure, afflictions, trouble. In Romans 8:14-18 the apostle Paul wrote, *"For as many as are led by the Spirit of God, they are the sons of God. For ye have not received the spirit of bondage again to fear (of the world); but ye have received the Spirit of adoption, whereby we cry, Abba, Father. The Spirit itself beareth witness with our spirit, that we are the children of God: And if children, then heirs; heirs of God, and joint-heirs with Christ; if so be that we suffer with him, that we may be also glorif ied together. For I reckon that the sufferings of this present time are not worthy to be compared with the glory which shall be revealed to us."*

Now, that scripture sums it all up! The sufferings we go through here on earth is as a grain of sand on the ocean's shore compared to the glory that will be revealed in us when we lay these old fleshly bodies back to the dust where it came from.

Tribulations comes to every creature under heaven, rich or poor, lost or saved, it doesn't matter who you are, Tribulation will find you. Tribulations would be that such as, natural catastrophes, wars, sickness, prisons, a death in the family or even something as simple of dropping an anvil on your big toe. Oh yes! Let me not forget to add *Deception.* Deception is one of the biggest of all the devices of Satan. For Satan, that old deceiver, the devil, is like a roaring lion, walking about, seeking whom he may devour. The more my life changes for the good, it seems as if I have more tribulations, but the difference today from yesterday is that I'm getting the understanding of how to respond to a Tribulation. Before in my past dead life, I did not know what a tribulation was and definitely, I did not know how to respond to a tribulation that would arise in my life like the wind.

In my past, I would almost always responded to a tribulation as if some man was trying me and the world was ending. I would blamed others for the problems in my past life and start to get angry within myself and it made my life even that much more miserable. I responded by my own self-will compulsive behaviors, such as, running to the beer store, my drug dealer and even Doctors, to get drugs to hid behind and numb my pain. Now, I'm not saying that it is wrong for any man to seek counsel. Seeking counsel is one of the best efforts that a man could make, if he needs to do so.

In my past life, I did not go to the psychiatrist for counsel only; I went because I wanted the drugs to numb me from the pains of my life at the time. Drugs was a faster way of numbing these pains and the horrors that I was living. Counseling just wasn't fast enough for me. One of my Psychiatrist insisted one time that I really needed counseling, but I didn't want counseling and refused honest counseling; for I only wanted the drugs, because the drugs worked to numb my sufferings faster. I had another Doctor tell me one time that I needed God back in my life, but again, the only thing I really wanted was to get totally *Zombilized*, totally numbed from my sufferings. *Deception* led me to this act of compulsion, because I thought that the drugs would help me better, than a man. Drugs had always numb me my whole life and when I would go to a Doctor, that was all I desired. I didn't trust no man at this time and I wasn't about to start. But, the enemy, Satan, would deceive me to believe that nothing was worth trying, unless I could put my finger on it, such as, a drug to numb me. Satan knows if he could keep me on the drugs, then later I would start drinking heavy, doing illegal drugs and then possibly go back into depression and kill myself.

My friend, if you every get a chance to have counseling from a Professional Doctor, talk with him and share your life with him, so that, the Doctor will understand how he may help you. If a man were to seek counseling, that man must be honest with the Doctor and there is no other way. If you only tell him half of what you want to tell him, he will only be able to give you 50% of the help you need. Remember, God can't help a man if the man is in the way. Two heads are better than one and when two are gather together, you both get stronger. Self-will or the sinful nature of this world will divide anything, and it will also stir up confusion. Remember, Satan doesn't want any man to get well, he only wants to keep you in bondage and even worse, kill you.

Today, I'm much more stronger than before, because of God being first in my life and understanding what God's Will is for me and the whole wide world. Remember the scripture(John 16:33) mentioned before? When Christ told us we would have tribulations?

Well, we need to put it in our safe deposit box of our heart, for a keeper. Perhaps you have already said this to you self." I didn't think I would ever in my Life see that happen." My friend, Get ready! The longer we are here on earth, the more we will see and hear rumors of great Tribulations never known to man before. Christ said it would happen and trust him, it will. Knowing God's Will for us is our peace through tribulations. Knowing it is going to happen and knowing where to go when it comes to us is where we can draw strength and peace in times of troubles. Here is another Key. Would you like to have a Key? I can only share this key with you it is not mine to give away, but you are welcomed to use it, if you choose to do so. Tribulations and Trials come like the wind and If you know its coming, then you can be prepared for it. But, if you don't know or don't believe it is coming then you don't get prepared for it. If you are not prepared for a storm of your life you will suffer much more greatly.

It's not about the Trial or Tribulation that comes to us, but it is how we respond to it in our life. Understanding of God's Will for me and the Whole Wide World is the Key to Understanding of this matter, faith. Did it unlock any thing? I hope it did. I believe the Key to Trials and Tribulations is having a solid foundation laid from God's Will for our Life. When I know and understand what God's Will for my Life is then I know where my hope, joy, peace and most of all, my patience is. I know it is hard when we go through a Trial or Tribulation, but how do we respond to it? Responding is the sum of the matter.

When Tribulation comes in our life, do we run to the beer store, to the drug dealer, to the Doctors or even fly off the handle? I'm not talking about seeking counsel. Seeking counsel can lead to better things, but know where you faith and hope is. Its all about Understanding that perfect Will of God for us that keeps us from more calamity. I know, it works for me.

If we have a solid foundation of understanding Trials and Tribulations then we are watching for it, rather than, flying off the handle when it comes to us and blaming others for it. When we have true understanding of Trials and Tribulations, then we know how to respond to it.

In Proverbs chapter 24, verse 3, reads as written, *"Through Wisdom is an house builded; and by understanding it is established."* King Solomon was one of the wisest men to ever live here on the earth and he knew what God's Will for him was. Lets see, you use Carpenters, Masonry, Electricians and many more skilled wise fellows, but they only build the house, they do not Establish the home. There is a great difference between a house and a Home. A house is the Building and the Home is the Establishment and by understanding is the House Established. If, we establish our home from understanding of God's Perfect Will, then I can say for sure, that is a blessed Home. I want my home established by understanding of God's Will for my Life and then my Home is much better. I hope this helped, it sure help me. Please keep asking and searching for understanding (God's Will) and God will give it to you by the faith you have in him to do so. God rewards those who love him and seek him. There is nothing down here on earth that can ever compare to what God has for us. The sufferings we go thru here on earth is like vapors in the wind. If we are led by God's Spirit and the Comforter witnesses God's perfect Will to us, then we will have a greater confidence of the promises that we have through Jesus Christ. Now in 1 Peter 3:17 it is written, *"For it is better, if the will of God be so, that ye suffer for Well doing, than for evil doing."* That simple. The man that suffers for doing something sinful has no joy, but the man that suffers for God's Will has peace and joy. This is somewhat like having two men charged with a crime. One did the crime and the other did not. They Go to court and the man that did the crime would be found guilty and sentence for punishment, but the other man that had done no crime was set free.

Now you tell me which man would be rejoicing, even though he was tried? We that have given our will and life over to God, will still go through trials and tribulations, but make sure you are going thru them for God and Jesus Christ and not because you have sinned.

God will allow burdens to be placed on your Heart, and sometimes it may even fill as if you are going through a trial and tribulation, but God knows how Much weight you can carry. In 1 Peter 4:14-16 it is written, *"If ye be reproached for the name Of Christ, happy are ye; for the Spirit of Glory and of God resteth upon you: on their part he is Evil spoken of, but on your part he is glorified. But let none of you suffer as a murderer, or as a Thief, or as an evildoer, or as a busybody in other men's matters. Yet if any man suffer as a Christian, let him not be ashamed; but let him glorify God on this behalf."* Again, the word tells us to rejoice in our tribulations through God and Christ Jesus. In 1 Peter Chapter 4 the 17 verse it is written, "For the time has Come that judgment must begin at the house of God: and if it first begin at us, what shall the end Be of them that obey not the gospel of God?" Yes judgment will start as you give your life and will to God and Jesus Christ.

Oh yes! May I clear one thing up? Today I'm not a sinner, I'm a converted sinner, it is somewhat like a recovering drug addict and I still make mistakes. When a sinner gives themselves to God and his Son, Jesus Christ and totally submits his life in their trust, then God tries and justifies that sinner and makes him a new creature and all things become new to the sinner. I know it did for me.

Now, what is this judgment Peter is talking about, starting first at the church. You see, man has a choice, man can obey or he can disobey it is his choice. Oh yes, again! Please let me share one other matter with you. Satan, that serpent, the devil, the deceiver of mankind, can not make no man do any thing.

We are lead away by our on lust and temptations when we walk away from God's Will. Satan will tempt or try to entice you to sin, not make you sin. If you do something right or wrong, you do it by your own choice. Remember, choice is a gift from God. Please while we are on this subject of sin, I will ask you this; "What is sin?" The greatest definition of sin is written in the Holy Book of James chapter4, verse 17 and reads as written, ***"Therefore to him that knoweth to do good, and doeth it not, to him it is sin."*** There is no other defined word, as this word sin, found in this verse of James. If we obey, we get rewarded and if we disobey, we get punished or lets say disciplined. That was the case in my father's house everyday of my childhood when I would rebel against him or my mother.

Therefore, Satan can not make a man do anything, unless the man allows it. Have you ever heard the lie "The devil made me do it". Now! That is a lie right straight from the father of lies, Satan himself. The devil has no more control of your life than I have control of the weather. It is just not true. Again, Satan can entice you and try to lure you away from God's Will. The enemy, Satan, is as a roaring lion, walking about seeking whom he may devour or destroy. It is by choice a man goes out into the street and starts using drugs again. It is by choice that a man goes to the ABC store or any store and gets alcohol to drink. It is by choice that a man would watch pornography, or worse, exposed his body to it. It is by choice that a man rebels against God's Will. I could keep on and on, but I will stop here.

The point is; The sinful nature of mankind hinders a man from doing what he needs to do that is right in God's Eyes. But, It is by choice that a sinner is still a sinner, but we have the Spirit praying with us for the suffering of the world.

Jesus Christ came to set the captive free and whom the Son sets free is free indeed. There is something greater that I would like for you to grasp onto and it is this:

Why did Jesus Christ come to this sinful world and want to freely give his live for the payment of the sinful nature of mankind? I truly believe this to be the answer: Christ came, so that, we would have life much more abundantly in this sinful world. He also came to give the greatest gift of all Love for mankind. He knew that mankind's nature was to sin and that the enemy was always on a man's back to get him to rebel against God's Will. Jesus Christ went straight to the Abyss of Hell and ripped the Doors off Hell's gates and set men free, such as, Moses, Abraham, Elijah. This was the promise being fulfilled by Jesus Christ. God's Christ defeated Satan, and took the keys of death straight from that devils hands. I believe that battle was somewhat like a Lion (Christ) on a rat (Satan) and there wasn't much of a battle. Christ defeated death and rose up the third day to leave mankind the promise of, "If we would follow him, we would be raised from death to live Eternal." Not only did he leave us the Keys to The Kingdom of God, but also that he defeated death.

During the time, while Jesus Christ was walking the earth as the son of man, mankind was without the full understanding of, "What was causing mankind to be led away and be bound by Satan?" Mankind had the laws, but were still without the full understanding of God's Will and were perishing from the lack of understanding.

From the fall of man in the Garden of Eden by one man, Adam, to the crucifixion of one man, Jesus Christ, these times were all ordained and appointed from the foundations of the earth. The Word of God tells us this in the Holy Book of 1Corinthians chapter15, verses 21-22. It is written, ***"For since by man came death, by man came also the resurrection of the dead. For as in Adam all die, even so in Christ shall all be made alive;"*** Please keep reading the points are coming.

When we are saved by Grace, we are judged by God and are found justified before him by Jesus Christ, and only by Christ are we found justified, if we believe Grace to save us. We art not saved from this sinful nature of mankind from any work that we may do. It is entirely by faith that we are saved and by the Grace of God that we are found justified. One may ask at this time, "Where do I get faith?"

Oh yes! Please let me sing this song from my heart for you. *"I will call on the Lord to set me free, I will call on the Lord to Deliver me, I will call on the Lord through his Grace indeed, from the Pains of death and misery, From the pains of death and misery."* If I could sing a song of faith to you such as this song, I must of believe in what I believed to be truth, correct? I wasn't there when they crucified Jesus, and neither was I there when he rose from the dead. But, I believe God, because of his word. When I believe God for who he is and a rewarded to those who believe, then he is faithful to give me faith. The more I believe in his Word the much more faith he gives me by his Spirit.

As a child of God, I have already being judged and tried to receive salvation through my faith I have in Christ Jesus, but for sinners they are not justified neither are they sons of God and neither are they tried by God. I told a fellow child of God once this; "I Thank God that I had already been judged and it did not hurt a bit." But, my trials were just beginning, because I was a converted sinner and now I've been justified through faith in believing in God and his Son Jesus Christ. Now, God and Jesus Christ Is Lord of my life and Savior of my soul, but there are still impurities in my life that God is still Working on. These impurities in my life I will call for now, are my *Defects of Character.* These defects are somewhat like aphids on a vegetable plant. Your can wash the aphids, poison the aphids, but the aphids will still come back every now and then. You would ask; "Where do these aphids keep coming from? I thought I got rid of them, but they keep coming back."

It doesn't matter how many times you would poison the aphids or wash your vegetable plants, these aphids still would show up in the vegetable garden.

Defects of Character maybe things, such as, cursing, compulsive behaviors, or getting angry much easily, when things would go bad suddenly and it would be at this time that you would be ashamed of what you had said or done and then you would ask yourself, "Where did that come from?" My friend, I can tell you these things are defects of character, but getting to the point of the matter is that of, the sinful nature of mankind. Out of the heart proceed evil intents. As long as we are in the flesh, these things will forever want to dominate your life. But, we have a greater hope now, since Jesus Christ defeated all these things at the Cross of Calvary. These defects of character can be removed just like a Gardener would remove the aphids from his garden.

I would like to share with you this understanding; If aphids where to invade your garden, try planting flowers in your garden and the flowers will draw even more than aphids. The flowers would draw to them other insects that would eat away the aphids, no kidding, it really works.

Today the only way that you can remove defects of character from your life, is to let the great Husbandmen (God and his Son Jesus Christ) in your life and grow them in your heart, so that, they will cast out the defects and keep them from coming back. My friend, my past experiences led me to believe in this matter greatly and I know there is no other way. I still today have defects of character in my heart, but I'm willing to let the Great Husbandmen in my life and they are forever removing these sinful natures from my heart. There is something else that I would like to share with you now.

In the Holy Book of Matthew chapter 15, verses 16-20 it is written, *"And Jesus said, Are ye also yet without understanding? Do not ye yet understand, that whatsoever entereth in the mouth goeth into the belly, and is cast out into the draught? But those things which proceed out of the mouth come forth from the heart; and they def ile the man. For out of the heart proceed evil thoughts, murders, adulteries, fornications, thefts, false witness, blasphemies: These are the things which def ile a man: but to eat with unwashen hands def ileth not a man. "* As long as I am willing to let God and His Son Jesus Christ to abode in my heart, these things such as defects of character, are forever being chained and cast out of my life.

Like I mentioned earlier, I still today may have some defects, but nothing to be compared to my past dead life. God and his Son is the light of my life and God's Word is searching my heart daily looking for those things which would defile me. Therefore, I know today that I must become a perfect treasure in the mighty Kingdom of God. There is no room for any defects of character in my Life, more so, in God's Kingdom; but, God is forever removing them from my life. Let me go a little deeper if I may. I gave my life to God and his Son, Jesus Christ at the altar (the place where you give your life to God and his Son Christ) and when I made the choice to live a much more life than that of what I was living, they were faithful to come and abode in my life. When I gave my life to the Great Husbandmen, it was at that very moment that I was Judged by God, and was found not guilty, because Jesus Christ stood in for me at the altar and found me worthy of receiving him honestly into my heart. Jesus Christ is like a mediator or advocate. He pleaded his precious Blood on my soul to the Father of Life, God. Please follow the point is coming. So, *I was found justified* by my faith in the Only begotten Son of God, Jesus Christ, *but not completely purified.* So, the Lord is still today working on me to remove all of the impurities or lets say, defects of character I have put on during my world living in the past.

Like a Potter with his clay, God is to me; for God molds me in his fashion as a perfect treasure set aside for his Kingdom. I am liken into clay in a potters hand, being God as the potter. The potter is always pounding me, squeezing me, watering me, putting in the fire and such like, to get the impurities out of my life. In my past life when these things would happen, I would blame God, my family and even a stranger for the discomforts. But today, I know with a greater confidence, I will not enter the Kingdom of God without these sinful natures removed from my life. The Lord urges the sinner to try him. In Revelation 3:18 Christ urges us to try him. *"I counsel thee to buy of me gold tried in the fire, that thou mayest be rich; and white raiment, that thou mayest be clothed, and that the shame of the nakedness do not appear; and anoint thine eyes with eyeslave, that thou mayest see."*

My friend, take this chance and make the right choice and try letting Jesus Christ work in your life to remove the defects of character and he will be faithful in doing so. He did it for me and is still doing it in my life today. Remember this my friend: On the Great Judgment Day, all sinners and unbelievers will appear before God to be judged and Jesus Christ will not be there as their mediator. For it is written in Hebrews 9:27, *"And it is appointed unto men once to die, but after this the judgment."* This judgment is for the unbelievers and all those who deny the Power of God's Will to live in their hearts. The sons and daughters or children of God will not have to face this Great Judgment, because if you have been justified by Jesus Christ, there is no need for another judgment, follow me?. Yes!

We will have to go through sufferings, trials and tribulations, but our judgment is over. Only the sinners and unbelievers will be present during the Great Throne Judgment, where the word tells us they will die the second death and be cast into the lake of fire. Thank You Lord for saving my soul from the Great Throne of Judgment. God, you are a righteous God, faithful and true are your ways.

As a child of God and a joint-heir to life everlasting through Jesus Christ, we will go through trials and tribulations while we are here still on earth. When we go through a trial it is for our own good to make us wiser, stronger, and purer. These trials are also for the need to remove the defects of character from a believers life. Sometimes we go through trials not knowing what the trial is, but God knows. I will now share with you a story from the Holy Bible of one incredible Trial and Tribulation God's people went through in the Old Testament. My friend I know the following writings are long, but be patient with me for the point is near. It is for us as an example of how Trials happen and How God intervenes to save us from it ever hurting us. Open your heart and let God's Spirit witness to you as you read forward: In the Book of Daniel we are told of a story where three men were thrown in a furnace but wasn't consumed neither did any smell of fire or smoke kindle upon them. In the first chapter of Daniel, we read about the captivity and the fall of Jerusalem under the reign of Jehoiakim king of Judah. This was prophesied by the prophet Jeremiah and is found in the Holy Book of Jeremiah chapter 21.Judah did fall into the hands of the Babylonians and under the hand of King Nebuchadnezzar.

Now, King Nebuchadnezzar needed a few men from Judah skilled, well-favored, cunning in knowledge, and understanding in science, so that they could be taught the cultures and tongue of the Chaldeans. That was King Nebuchadnezzar's plan. There were four men found through out Judah and their names were Daniel, Hananiah, Mishael, and Azariah. However, King Nebucadnezzar didn't like their names, so he had them changed. Stick with me, this could get very long and hot. So, their names are now Belteshazzar (Daniel), the second was Shadrach (Hananiah), the third was Meshach (Mishael), and the fourth Abednego (Azariah). These names were probably Chaldean and it was easier to call them by the King. These four men grew in favor of the King (Nebuchadnezzar) and were found ten times wiser than all his magicians, and astrologers throughout the land.

Later, King Nebucadnezzar was having some very disturbing dreams and he call for all his wise men, such men like the magicians, sorcerer to interpret his dream. He also could not remember his dream. He made a decree that the wise men in all the lands that he possessed, should interpret his dream or be killed, including the four wise men of Judah. When Daniel heard this decree, it troubled him deeply and he began to ask the King for some time, so he could fulfill the Kings inquire. Daniel went to his three companions Shadrach, Meshach and Abedego and started praying for God's mercy and wisdom. Now that is one way to get a man to pray if his life is in danger, isn't it?

However, these three men were before God always praying for the needs of God's people. Then in Daniel chapter 2, verses 19-23 it reads, *"Then was the secret revealed unto Daniel in a night vision. Then Daniel blessed the God of heaven. Daniel answered and said, Blessed be the name of God for ever and ever: for wisdom and might are his: and changeth the times and the seasons: he removeth kings, and he setteth up kings: he giveth wisdom unto the wise, and knowledge to them that know understanding: he revealeth the deep and secret things: he knoweth what is in the darkness, and the light dwelleth with him, I thank thee and praise thee, O thou God of my fathers, who has given me wisdom and might, and has made known unto me now what we desired of thee: for thou hast now made known unto us the King's matter."* My friend, God is always on time even at your last breath. God has never failed me nor forsaken me ever in my life when I have called on him to save me from my misery and horrors. If any time I thought God wasn't around, it was the time I want around God and I didn't trust him to do so. Nevertheless, Daniel did interpret the King's dream and the King recognized the sovereign God of Daniel for just a moment. The Barbarian King realized for a moment that there really was a God of the Judah people and fell before Daniel and worshipped Daniel.

However, if I was that King, I think I probably would be asking much more questions about the God of Daniel.

Nevertheless, the King recognized that Daniel was worthy of honor and was given gifts and to rule the whole providence of Babylon. The king also made Daniel the chief over all the wise men in the lands. Daniel doesn't forget his companions though. He requested that Shadrach, Meshach, and Abednego be set over all the affairs of the providence of Babylon. Daniel knew that it was also their prayers that were heard from God, and Daniel was not about to take all the credit.

Now, in Daniel chapter 3, there is something awful that has happened. King Nebuchadnezzar has made a graven image of gold and there was a loud cry to all the people, and he made this decree, *"To you it is commanded, O people, nations, and languages. That at the time ye hear the sound of the cornet, flute, sackbut, psaltery, dulcimer, and all kinds of music, ye fall down and worship the golden image that Nebuchadnezzar, the King, hath set up: and whosoever falleth not down and worshipeth shall the same hour be cast into the midst of a burning fiery furnace".* Now, this decree would be very hard to resist, because it is written; all kinds of music. Anytime the people heard any music, they had to fall to their knees and worship this image. There wasn't any music played, except music to fall down to and worship that graven image. Nevertheless, the people did fall down and worship as the King decreed. However, this was just another fiery trial for the people of God. There were some that did not fall down to worship the image and that made the King very angry and furious. Some of the men of the Land went to the King and told him that Shadrach, Meshach, and Abednego did not fall and worship the image. So, these three men were called and were set before the King to give reason why they would not worship the graven image. Now this is a trial of life or death.

The time had come for the great question; "Will you worship the graven image or Will you die?" My friend, look closely at the words that came out of the mouth's of God's children. It is written in Daniel 3:16-18; *"O Nebuchadnezzar, we are not careful to answer thee in this matter. If it be so, our God whom we serve is able to deliver us from the burning fiery furnace, and he will deliver us out of thine hand, O King. But if not, be it known unto thee, O king, that we will not serve thy gods, nor worship the golden image which thou hast set up."* Now I will say this is faith and trust in God. These men knew they were in good hands, no matter what the out come was, like facing death. This answer made the King very angry, and he told his servants to heat the furnace seven more times hotter than usually. The furnace was so hot, it consumed the king's servants that had bound the children of God. Then the three children fell bound into the mist of the fiery furnace. But, the King shouted and said, *"Did we not cast three men into the mist of the fire?"* His servants reply was, *"yes we did".* And the king said, *"Lo, I see four men loose, walking in the midst of the fire, and they have no hurt; and the form of the forth is like the <u>Son of God.</u>"* God is always on time, like this great example as The Son of God walking through the fire with the children of God. Now, that is faithfulness.

When we are going through are troubles, and our own fiery trials, don't ever forget that the Son of God will keep us, even through the fire, if you believe him to do so. So, then the King came near to the mouth of the burning fiery furnace, and spoke and said to God's children, *"ye servants of the most high God, come forth, and come hither".* Shadrach, Meshach and Abednego came forth out of the fiery furnace and the fire had no power over these men. It reads in Daniel 3:27, *"And the princes, governors, and captains, and the King 's counselors, being gathered together, saw these men, upon whose bodies the fire had no power, nor was a hair singed, neither were their coats changed, nor the smell of fire had passed on them."*

Thank you Lord Jesus, for being with me through all my fiery trials and tribulations, because I do know that you are with me, no matter where I am or what I'm going through. I pray that God will bless you and will strengthen your faith and trust in him. Remember, no matter how hot the trial you are going though, trust God and his Son Jesus Christ for your life. Put all your faith and trust in them and they will deliver you from the flames of the fire.

Looking back when I was beginning to understand somewhat about God's Will for my life, I did not have much patience and I prayed to God <u>continually</u> to give me patience, but what I remember getting was a lot of trials. I was forever praying for something that I wanted, but really didn't understand what I needed. I was without much patience and I wanted it then and now. I wanted it then and now; for I did not have much patience at all, follow me?.

Today I say with confidence that when I thought I had understanding of a matter, such as, the gift of patience, I was without understanding. *Patience! What is Patience?* I will say this with confidence, Patience is the anchor of our everlasting Life. Reminiscing back in my life, I thought that I had patience and I did somewhat, but today, I know patience is a Life and not something that you can get over night. Sure you can get just a touch of patience, but your patience will be tried for the rest of your breath here on earth. Patience! Patience! How I've long for thee, To keep me safe for eternally. Patience is bearing pains and suffering calmly without complaint. Christ Jesus was the greatest example of Patience for mankind; for Christ Jesus knew every moment in his life here on earth, in the flesh, that he would be crucified. But, he also knew he would rise again, so that, mankind could get understanding of the gift of Life Everlasting and to be able to make the choice of living a life on this earth, much more abundantly. Jesus Christ knew that he must endure to the end for mankind's lack of understanding.

If he didn't endure God's Will to his last breath, then mankind would still be lost in only the laws of sin and we as mankind would be still under the curse of the Laws. As Jesus Christ was hanging upon his own cross, he said, *"It is Finished!"* Jesus Christ bored all the sinful nature of mankind upon his flesh on his own cross with the patience from his Father, God. He finished his course that he was sent to do with great patience. He will forever be mankind's greatest example of patience. In God's Holy Word in the Book of Luke chapter 21, verse 19, Jesus Christ gives us the importance of patience, *"In your patience possess ye your souls." How can man receive answer of the reward of patience from God, if the man cant wait for the answer from God?*

I know when I wanted patience in my past, I would only get trials and tribulations and suffer much more. But, today with the understanding of patience, I know that it keeps me safe in the arms of God the Father, if I continue to walk in his Will. I also understand that patience doesn't come over night and Patience is a life's virtual and it is the keeper of my soul. I will say this with a greater confidence: when I truly gave my life over to the care of God through faith in his Son Jesus Christ, patience immediately was beginning to work in my life. Looking back when God had saved me from the horrors and miseries I was living in, God knew that I first needed patience, because I was void of patience. As long as I am willing to let God and his Son, Jesus Christ, abode in my heart, patience will forever be an effect in my life. I hope that these words have given you a insight on Sufferings and why we must go through them and the key to unlock any doors that maybe closed, because of unanswered questions concerning Sufferings. We will fight the greatest fight of all for the rest of our lives, if we have given our will over to God and His Christ. But at the end, we can say this; I have fought the good fight and now I can enter rest forever and forever. I heard a man share this one day, *It isn't the things we do that we regret, it is the things that we don't do, that we regret.*

It is not how fast you run the race, but making it over the finish line and what's waiting for you, that counts. For it is written; ***"But many that are first shall be last; and the last shall be first."***

CHAPTER EIGHT

ACCEPTANCE

S O, LATER I LEFT THE JOB AT THIS Textile Industrious plant and was seeking another job. I had the number to this Psychiatrist that was given to me from my friend, before I had left the Textile Industrious job. I chose to go to this doctor, because I was beginning to go into major depression and began to have great moods swings. *The Psychiatrist diagnosed me with Major Depression, OCD and Bi-Polar*

disease. This diagnose of the Bi-Polar Disease was to great for me to bear, but I tried to accept it and continued on my way. I had other Doctors in my past to try to diagnose me with this disease, but I wouldn't allow it to happen and just quit going back to the doctors. But, this particular Doctor, I began to draw comfort from and I began to tell him things of my life and we became friends. I came to understand that this Doctor wanted to help me, and for me to get better.

The Doctor prescribed many medicines for this and when I started to take this medicine, I began to think that I had lost my trust in God again. I would think things like this: "If, I got to keep taken these drugs, then I'll never be able to walk with God the way that I've Walked with him in the past. If People find out about my illness and judge me, it want be good for them or me."

So, I started taken medicine for my Bi-Polar disease, Anxiety and Major Depression during this time and I started somewhat accepting that I had a illness. The medications did make me feel somewhat better, but it limited me from what I really wanted to do.

Now, I was still going to Church, but I had resigned my duties as the Youth pastor at this particular church, because I felt I just couldn't do the service that I once did. I felt that I had let the church down and God, because I was beginning to do drugs again. I was still going to the same church that I was a teacher and youth pastor at one time, but I started to visit different churches. I started to think that things wouldn't be the same now at this church, since I resigned from my duties there and especially being diagnosed with a Bi-Polar disease. I told no one about my sickness. The only people that knew my sickness was my Doctors and my Wife. I thought that people were judging me and it became to much for me to bare. At this time, I was beginning to think that other people didn't want me to preach. So, I began a ministry with my wife and we started to go out to nursing homes and senior citizen homes, singing and ministering the gospel.

Later, I finally got another job at a Nursing Home in the Maintenance Department. I was still alcohol free, and street drug free, but the thorns in my flesh were beginning to buffet me greatly again. I felt like I just couldn't face people at church, because they would say things like this; "Son! You got to trust God. He will deliver you from this illness."

But, I knew deep within my heart that this illness was progressing and it became a thorn within my flesh.

I do remember a time that I was suffering with a particular thorn and went to a revival. I was seeking God for everything his Word would promise and I was again desperate for away out of this particular suffering. I knew at this time for me to live, I must seek and find the complete understanding of God's Will for my life. I would exhaust myself by reading and listening to God's Word every night. Sometimes I would awake in the middle of the night to find a lump under my back and it would be my Bible. I would go to Churches and Revivals every chance I had and seek a Word from God for this matter.

So, I do remember going to a Revival at a local church and I found something that I didn't go for to get, but afterwards, I was grateful. It was a Pentecostal Church and as the Evangelist was preaching it seemed to me that he looked straight into my eyes and said, "If you want what God has, come now and stand here. I say, if you want what God has, come now and stand here." He kept saying this over and over, until I noticed a few older white headed fellows got up and went where this Evangelist asked them to stand. Then, they started to pray together and after a few moments, set down and the Evangelist said again, "God wants to show his Love and Power! If you want what God has, come now and stand here!" He continued to preach these same words over and over, but no one else went to him. At this time, I felt my heart jump and it began to pound, as if I just ran a 1 mile sprint. Then I felt an awesome power on and in me, somewhat like I had experienced before. It was the time God had said to me with that awesome and powerful voice, *"You are Forgiven"*. I began to weep and it felt as if the love of the all mighty God was upon my heart telling me to go and stand in that spot.

Things began to seem as if I could not hear anything or anyone, even the evangelist. It was if, I was going deaf and blind, no kidding. My heart kept pounding and I got up and it was if, I floated to this spot. The Evangelist laid his hands upon my head and it happened; for I was in the Spirit of the Almighty God. The Spirit of God took over my body and I began to speak in an unknown tongue. It was if my body was dead and my spirit man took over. I can't remember exactly how the tongue went, but it was angelical. Then as I was speaking this unknown tongue, I began to hear the Evangelist interpreting the language and I and this Evangelist was in one accord. Every time I felt the Spirit come from my belly and speak this tongue, the Evangelist would interpret it every time. I cant remember what I was saying exactly during this out of the body experience, but my ears where still opened to the words of the Evangelist and he would interpret the language that I was speaking in these words, *"Praise the Lamb of God! Praise the Lamb of God! Praise the Lamb of God! Praise the Lamb of God!"* I will say to, during this time of being in the Glory of God's Spirit, I would try to open my eyes and the entire room looked very smoky. I couldn't see clearly as it look like smoke was surrounding me and the entire congregation. I do remember a great sound as like to a power reactor. I felt as if I had left my body and I was inside some type of Power Reactor full of smoke. This sound and feeling was in the same likeness that I had experienced during my vision of the man in my doorway earlier.

After a while I was still in the spirit and It seem I didn't know where I was at, maybe in heaven. I began to slow on my tongue and the Evangelist somewhat put his hand upon the top of my head and the speaking began to ease and also the sound and feeling of power. I opened my eyes and the room was still somewhat smoky and my eyes were pouring with water. I knew at this moment that this is what I had been searching for all my life, The Love of God and his Power of Love. It was an awesome experience.

After things settled a bit, I walked towards my seat where I felt that I had floated from and a white headed man stood up and spoke to me in my ear and said this, "We here at this church needed that. Thank you for being obedient to God's Call." At the time he spoke this to me I didn't understand what his words to me meant, but later God revealed it to me. God had led me to this Church, because it needed edified. It was nothing that I did , it was all because of being obedient to his call and not being ashamed. God wanted to confirm to me that I was standing in what I believe to be the truth and he worked through me to give others the strength to stand in what they believed. I know for a fact that sometimes a man can get so rapped up in the things of this world and their ears begin to deafen from God's Words. God used me that evening and I count it a pearl in my life.

Later, I would be asked to preach at different churches. I thought at the time that God had showed me my calling, and it was preaching the Gospel of Jesus Christ with no doubt. During this same time of my life, I would hear other Preachers quote this scripture from the Holy Bible, as I would visit their congregation, *"For many are called, but few are chosen."* Many are called to repentance and Salvation, but there will be just a few that are chosen as God's sons and daughters. These that are chosen, are them that do the Father's Will.

Later I started to preach every week at different churches and even nursing homes on a regular basis. I continued to preach and minister the Gospel at nursing homes, Senior Citizen Homes for almost 4 years. I also still pressed forward with the ministry for the youth, which was called, Key Ministries. When I wasn't preaching somewhere I would go out in the town and find youth walking the road way and share the Hope of Christ with them. This work in the ministry seemed natural to me, as if I had done this my whole life.

I was still taking my medicines for the Bi- Polar Disease and Depression and later I started to abuse this medicines because things began to get stressful and burdensome on in my life. I believe this may have been the contributor to my stress.

In my past experiences as a child, I would see members of congregations doing things that I will not mention, but it wasn't good. One pastor even accused me of doing drugs and that my friend, led me to detour from my preaching. I was beginning to have anger in my heart toward people and then my life went down again. I had great burdens on my heart at this time and I just couldn't accept what this man had said to me. I was taking drugs at this time, which was, my medications. I began to be buffeted by my thorns of my flesh greatly again. The sinful nature of mankind was pounding my heart greatly. At this time, I was really hurt badly within my heart and felt persecuted by my own friend that I trusted in. I felt as a man that I trusted dearly with my life, had just judged me and condemned me to death, because of a few problems I had in my personal life. I felt as if he had had just ripped my heart out of my chest, no kidding. I began to think that some at this particular church was judging me and really didn't want me there. I really wanted to walk into this church with a gun and shoot this man, because I felt he shouldn't had said this to me. Somehow this preacher found out that I was taking medicines and he used this against me to try me. But my friend, I had been tried my whole life and now, men of God where even buffeting me and I didn't want to accept it. I began to deny that God had chosen me to the ministry and much more so, that I had an Illness. I began to go back into depression again and I started to have some bad thoughts. I tried to shake it off, but it was like fleas on a dog, the more I shook, the more I had fleas. I stopped preaching and going to church, but I tried to live normal, because I knew it was better than that of my past dead life.

Later, I began to think that I could minister to people outside the church and that is what I did. I remember one occasion that I had went to a families friend's Son's Home, because I knew that this young man and his wife were having troubles. One Sunday I drove to his home in town and knocked on his door. His wife came to the door and she said, "He's not here." I told her that I would be back that evening and if I didn't make it back, tell him that I love him and I needed to talk to him and she said, "Ok!" I never made it back to his home and neither did I get to talk to him again. Two days after I went to their home, he shot his wife in the face with a shotgun and put the gun to his throat and committed suicide. He was a young man and I knew his family very well. I went to their home and sat in my car and couldn't stop weeping for their lost. I was one of the pallbearers and helped bury this young man.

After this incident, my life began to hit bottom very fast and I began to doubt about my calling and I shun from God. I blamed myself for a long time and would always say this; "If I just went back that evening, he would still be alive." I started questioning God again, losing my trust and denying the call upon my life as a messen0ger of God's Word. I would always say things like this within my heart, "Why God? Why? Why do you put people in my life and then take them away? Why?" I would go to the Hospital where the wife was as I got the chance. She stayed in intensive care for a very long time. I could barely recognize this young lady, because half of her face was missing. I and my wife would weep much as we watched her laying in the bed, barely alive. Every chance I and my wife would get, we would go and visit her. I would hold her hand and pray for her to get well. She eventually got well and went home.

At this time of my life, I began to start clamming up again, somewhat like a mute. The thorns of my flesh were starting to buffet me greatly again and I was losing the Great Hope that I had been enlightened with. Satan was whispering doubts and great discouraging words into my mind. These things were to great for me to bare and it happened again. I was beginning to have suicide thoughts again and I didn't feel like living much anymore. I began to think that all that I had done for the church and God was in vain. I thought that every thing I was doing was coming from my own understanding, and I really didn't understand God's Will for my life and this was causing my sufferings. I also stopped taking my medications, because I thought that the medications were hindering me from doing God's Work. I left the job at the nursing home and started to let things eat at my heart. I began to doubt my calling to the call of the Gospel. I would think this, "I never had any problems until I started to take this medicine. These medicines are the reason I'm having so much trouble and I'm being punished for taking them. Taking these medicines is the same as saying, "I don't trust God!"

So, I stopped taking my medications and Later, I started to drink alcohol heavy again. Not only did I start drinking alcohol, I started doing street drugs heavy. I fell away from the church and when I fell this time, I fell hard to lowest part of the valley. I stopped going out to the nursing homes and Senior Citizen Homes to minister and ministering and singing the gospel. It was if, I just gave up on God. I stopped going to church on a regular basis and thought this; if God wanted to give me a word, I didn't want any other man telling me. God would have to speak to me with his voice, before I believe anything.

Later after the incident with the pastor, I left the job at this particular Nursing Home that I was a Maintenance Man and was out of work for several weeks. I started to drink alcohol heavy again, because I needed something to numb me from the suffering and the pains of my self will thoughts. I couldn't sleep well at all during this time again and I would only take my medications for insomnia. I was beginning to have nightmares that kept me from sleeping again. I quit taking my other medications for my Bi-Polar, because I would think things like this; Well, If I do take the medications, isn't that the same as doing drugs or drinking? I would think this over and over again, until I just refused and denied that I even had a Bi-Polar Disease. Like I've said before, it was hard for me to accept that I had to live with a Bi-Polar disease, so I made an excuse and I stopped accepting it.

After I started drinking again, I started to do street drugs again. I wouldn't do the street drugs as heavy as I would drink alcohol, but if it came to me I would do them. I became very depressed again and sometimes didn't want to get out of bed. I became as a mole in a hole and just refused to come out of the house. Before I go any further, please let me share something with you. As you read the following writings, you may sense the way that I was feeling during these horrible times of my life, but my friend, don't feel for me, feel with me. The following writings where put together like a puzzle in my life as God revealed the understanding to me and the Title of the following writings is, *"A Mole in a Hole."* Enjoy.

A MOLE IN A HOLE

Today I know with confidence that my life is much more abundant than my past dead life, since I have been given the Greater Hope. I can say this today; "I am who I am and I know who I Am is. I know who I am, rather than, asking within myself, Who am I? When I would go into my depressed state of mind, I wasn't concerned of the matter, "Who I Am", or more so, who I was or what I was. I didn't care if I lived to see another sunset or sunrise, no kidding. The days became my own Dark Abyss.

The sunshine would put fear in me and made me feel as if I just didn't belong on this earth. There were times that I actually thought that I was a Vampire or some nocturnal animal. I even gave myself a screen name, which was, "The Night Owl." I didn't want to go outside when people, such as my family, would come to me and say, "It is a beautiful Day! Its warm outside and the Sun is shinning bright. Lets go out and do some fishing or something. Lets not let this beautiful day pass before we get out and do something." And I would say this; "Leave me alone and go about your own business. Please!"

Things of the physical, neither things of the Spiritual, would matter much to me. I had medications on my night stand for the depression, but I wouldn't take them, because I didn't care if I face tomorrow or not. I would think within myself this, "if I did take my medicines, I just couldn't be normal. The World isn't normal, why even try to be normal? And I've tried to be normal many times, but I never succeeded in being normal."

During these times, I would rather just stay in my own Dark Abyss where I felt more secured, because there, I would be by myself and wouldn't have to try to be normal. I began to become as a *Mole in a Hole.* Yes, that's right, A mole in a hole. A mole can be defined as a simple bump upon your face, but the mole that I'm talking about is an animal. This particular animal is a burrowing animal. It spends his entire life digging deep beneath the earth's surface. This animal has no external ears, and has pin sized eyes and is almost totally blind. Its stays his entire life underground and makes his way though the earth's surface with his two front feet. This animal is one of the most disabled animals that I can think of, but it survives.

If, I could be transformed into an animal as I would go into my depressed state of mind, this animal is what I probably would be like. I'm somewhat like a mole when I would go into my depression with maybe a little badger mixed. I would begin digging deeper away from others, blind from wanting to see the sunshine and deaf from the sounds of someone trying to help me. I would stay away from the outside world, digging deeper within my own Dark Abyss trying to survive day by day. I would dig deeper and deeper into my own Abyss when others would try to help me. I would just shut my ears and my eyes as they would try to approach me and dig deeper and deeper away from them.

Depression came to me, I didn't go out into the world looking for it. When I was but a child, I was exposed to some traumatic times in my life. I started to clam up and be depressed at a very young age. I was already a child that was extremely shy and sometimes ashamed of my self for just being alive. As a young child at the age of 10, I was already a depressed child. Things that others had done to me and the things that just happen in life, came to me as the wind would blow through the tree tops, unexpected. Sometimes I would even blame my self for the bad times that came my way, even though, I had nothing to do with any of them. I felt ashamed and had great self-pity for myself, as I thought that these bad things had been my fault. Even when I knew that it wasn't my fault, these terrible times still kept compounding my early depression. I was diagnosed with manic depression at the age of 16. Like a Mole in its Hole, I lived for nearly 28 years. I did get out once and awhile and try to live a normal life and did succeed many times, but it seem as soon as I tried to live a normal life, I was right back into my own dark Abyss and just gave up on trying to be normal.

People would let me down as I put my trust in them to help me and then I began to trust no one.

During my entire life I have always tried to trust another man for things in my life. It seemed to me the more that I trusted another man, the more the man would let me down. These times of my life when people would let me down, I became angry as a Badger as if you tried to pull him from his den. Over and Over I would still try to trust a man, but it was the same, a total let down. There were times that this discouragement would make me dig, even more so, deeper within my depressed state of mind. I started to think within myself that their wasn't a man on the face of the earth that I trusted. As I would dig deeper within my depression, I would always ask God this; *"God? Is there not a man on the earth that you could send to my life that I can trust? Why God do people let me down so much?"* Well, here is the answer that he gave me; *"No son there is not!"* I just couldn't believe that there wasn't one man on this whole earth that I could put my trust in. I had thought that I had always been a man that you could trust in, but looking back through my life, that just wasn't true. The reason it wasn't true, was because I couldn't even trust in my self at times. I thought I was a trust worthy man and everyone else should treat me the same way, but I was let down time after time. Please Follow me the point is coming. First, God made it clear that I didn't need to trust man, but only Him.

Since I was but a child, I had put my trust in some people for my life and that made my God jealous. I'm only talking about adult hood here, not as an infant. Sure my life was in the hands of my mother and father as a young child, but still they couldn't save me or resurrect me from the dead, if I had died. Yes! My God is a jealous God and I should had not put no other thing, even a man, before I had put my trust in him. God doesn't want 99.9% of trust from a man, he wants the whole thing, 100%. God made it clear to me, if I trusted a man for my life, then it was the same as saying to him, "I don't trust you God." Not given God your 100% trust for your life would be the same as throwing a dog a bone every now and then.

Time after time, God has tried to get that understanding through my thick Brain mass. In my past life, I lived a life without any type of feelings, except, if I would hit my finger with a hammer. I had no trust for no man and I had lost my hope in God. I wasn't totally honest with God or myself. I was *denying* anything that came my way, unless someone sent me a certified check through the mail. I was beginning to blame others for all my problems. I was beginning to be somewhat angry much of the time again. Not only was I somewhat angry, I had fear of my life or not being able to be consistent in living a normal life. I lived in shame most of the time, because of my past experiences and was fearful that someone would talk about me. I had lost my trust in God, because I had sinned and I just couldn't face God nor Man. I felt like a total let down and I was tired of trying to live a normal life and then, BAM!!!! The normal would be over. My life would explode into a disaster. But, the true understanding that I have today of not living a much more abundant life during these times of my life, is this; I'm still in the flesh and in the sinful world. The sinful nature within me was not completely eradicated. I trusted in my own understanding and would puff up imaginations continually that wasn't truthful or not consistent with God's Will. Satan knew my weaknesses and I thought I understood his devices, but soon found out he knew more about God than I would had ever dreamed. Satan used my weaknesses and used them against me. He buffeted me greatly until I became weak and just gave up, without the True understanding of God's Will for my Life. When I fell or turn back into the easy sinful nature of mankind, I began fulfilling the lust of my flesh, rather than, walking in the Spirit of God.

Therefore after all this had happened, which happened very quickly, I was ashamed of myself and I tried to hide from God and Man. I began to lose my spiritual hope and I will say, I did lose the Hope. When I lost my spiritual Hope, I lost my faith also. When I lost my faith or wavered from my faith, I stopped trusting God for my Life.

This sinful nature of mankind, such as not trusting God or Not being honest, A.K.A. Rebellion, carried me deeper into my own Dark Abyss. The more I was willing to live back in this sinful nature, the more I would be denied and the more I would deny. I became more and more depressed and suicide was always on my mind. I thought that I trusted God and knew him, but I just didn't understand him. *Trust! How can a man trust God, if the man doesn't understand him?* My friend, You don't trust him! Let me just clear this up quickly.

Trusting and Revering something are two different understandings. I revere my Superiors, such as my Country and it's Government that are charged over me, but I don't trust them with my Eternal Soul, follow me? Can the Government save my soul from Hell? Is the Government the Judge over my Eternal Soul? But, I deeply revere the government as I would God.

During some of these times of my life, I didn't even trust my own wife, no kidding. I would say things like this; "I will cook my own dinner dear, because I don't know if you are poisoning me or not. You may be the one causing all my problems." My friend, I can say for today this with great confidence; God sent this women to my life and she has become part of my life. She became flesh of my flesh and bones of my bones and I love her with all my heart. My wife has always stuck it out with me and suffered for me almost my whole life. Distrust led me deeper into my own dark abyss. Not having the true understanding of trust led to all the other sinful nature of my living. Dishonesty led me to Distrust; Not being honest with my wife, led me to the distrust of my wife, follow me. Shoot! To be honest with you now, I didn't even trust myself. If any one was causing the problems, it was I and I only that we suffered greatly.

Today I know why I didn't trust God, it was because I didn't understand him or his Will for my Life. I was leaning on my own understanding and soon found out my understanding wasn't his understanding.

It was that simple my friend, trusting in what I believed wasn't the answer. I soon found out also that Trusting in God's Word was the answer. Here is just an example only: I may think this; *God knows my needs and he knows I need a new vehicle to get to work. So, I know I will get it tomorrow.* But, tomorrow came and the new car didn't. Instead I got a ride to work from a co-worker that live just a few minutes from my home. I would ride with him everyday for almost a year and my new car, didn't come either. I would say this again, *God knows my needs and he knows I need a new vehicle to get to work. So, I know its coming soon, because I trust him to do so.* But, the man that was given me a ride to work, pulls up on a new vehicle of his own one morning and sports it around in my driveway. The man would say this to me, as I would envy his new car; "How do you like my new car? Its nice isn't it. Oh yes! When are you going to sell your old vehicle and get yourself a new vehicle." It would be at this time that I would just give up on my trust in God. I would go to town and get parts to fix my own old vehicle and start driven it back to work, just to stay away from the co-worker with the new vehicle. But, it seemed as I would do such things as this there would be something just tugging continuous at my heart. I would fall to my knees in my home and cry out to God and say this; "Dear God, Have mercy on me. Forgive me Lord for not trusting you. I know Lord you do know my every need, because you made me. Be patient with me Lord for I'm still trying to Trust you with my whole life. Please God forgive me."

About the time I would say this to God, God would say this to me, *"Son, my child, have patience with me. I'm still waiting for your vehicle to come off the Production Line. You are my child and I want the best for you, so I special order your vehicle and when its finished, I will tell you where to pick it up and the Old vehicle that you've just got to run, I'm sending a missionary to pick it up. Give it to him and charge him nothing"* And I would be disobedient of what God has told me. The missionary came by and I thought this," I don't understand why God would tell me that.

I wouldn't have a vehicle again to drive to work and not only would I not have a vehicle, I would have to call my co-worker and ask him for a ride to work." So, I said this to the missionary, "I cant give you the vehicle right now, because I would be without a vehicle. Didn't God tell you to come and get it after I got my new vehicle?" And the missionary would say this, "Well, No. You must know God better than I do, because God didn't tell me to come by and pick any vehicle up. I just seen the "FOR FREE" sign in its window." And then it would hit me, I had put the wrong signs in the wrong place. That must had been why nobody wanted those old tires I set beside the road for free. I had put the "FOR SALE" sign near the tires and the "FOR FREE" sign in my vehicle window, what a dummy.

So, the missionary stands and looks at me as if I was not a man of my word. I would be quick to think this; "I've got no choice but to trust God now." So, I give the vehicle away to the missionary and he drives the vehicle away for free, waving his hand and saying, "Thank you very much for the free vehicle. God will Bless you Mr." I'm stunned at what just happen and begin to go to the house to my call my co-worker to pick me up the next morning. But, before I reach the phone, it rings. I answer the phone and there is a Car Dealer on the phone telling me that I had just won the raffle. I paid for one raffle ticket 3 months ago and forgot about it and the ticket was still in my Bible, where I had left it. The car dealer tells me where to pick up my new vehicle and congratulates me. Strange, but comical hey?

Now, that was only an example, but I will say that things would happen in my life just the way that I wrote the example. But there were many times that I would give up on God and just quit trusting him for something in my life. I would try to fix the problem with my own understanding and soon find out my understanding wasn't what God had for me. Sometimes a man will give up on trusting God, because of trusting in their own understanding and then their Life becomes much more destructive than before.

Therefore, since I was calling out to him from a honest heart for help on the matter, he was faithful to teach me about trust. It took me nearly 28 years to come to a confidence on the matter of trust and I will share this with you in just a moment. In the Holy Book of Isaiah chapter 26, verse 3-4 it is written, *"Thou wilt keep him in perfect peace, whose mind is stayed on thee: because he trusteth in thee. Trust ye in the Lord forever: for in the Lord JEHOVAH is everlasting strength."* The man that keeps his mind on the Lord at all times will have much more peace and trust in God.

As I got older and somewhat began to understand my depression and got medications for my illness, I would again and again try to live a normal life. I really didn't understand what a normal life was, but maybe, just to do good. When I tried to live good, I would fall every time and then I would just quit trying to live a normal life. Trying to live a normal life was a fearful time of my life, because I would always think that someone was talking about me. I would always think that people would say things like this and would spread rumors about me, *"Look at him. He thinks he is some kind of good man. I know the time that he did this or he did that. He is no more a Christian than I am a snail."* I wished I was Bruce Almighty at that time, because he would had been a snail. When I would sense any of this persecution, I would run quickly back to my mole hole and hide. I would become even more so depressed, and then I would get right ugly and show my teeth.

Sometimes, because of the anger being so pressed inside me, I would transform from a humble Mole to an aggressive Badger, right before their eyes. If I ever felt threaten or corner in any way, the Badger would come out from within me and people would run from me, as if I was nipping at their behinds. I would show my teeth and threaten them as they would run from me and they would call me "Crazy." It would be at this time, that I would be ashamed of what I had done and crawl back into my Mole Hole.

During some of these times, I would try to live normal, but gave up quickly on the matter of normal. I believe the true reason for given up on living a normal life, was because of this one thing, of not understanding normal. Now, I ask this question my friend, *"What is a Normal Life?"* Is a normal life having all the money your heart would desire? Is a normal life living prideful and saying, "I'm glad I'm not like him!"? Is a normal Life saying, "I can live the way I want to live." Or could a normal life be as simple, as living an Obedient Life? If you guessed that the last question to be the truth, then you are well my friend. Living a Obedient Life is living a normal life. Obedience is the Key to Living an Normal Life. Please follow me for the point is near.

Like the Mole, I am sure it has it's good days and it's bad days. Sometimes it will burrow deeper or further into the earth looking for something good for him, such as, food. There were times that the only way that I would eat was if my wife would cook and bring it to me near my nose to smell how good the food was, but I would just turn to the side and refuse to eat.

Like I've mentioned before, If someone kept nudging me and tried to touch me, it would be at this time I would transform into an aggressive Badger and show my teeth. I would become angry and all the resentments would start to flare at this time. Even my wife would shut the door to the bedroom where I would lay for days and walk away with the delicious food. She would always wrap the food and put it upon the stove top as if she knew I would come to it later, like a dog that was hungry. When I knew she was asleep, I would manage to crawl from my nest and creep to the kitchen and engulf the delicious food.

A mole is somewhat liken to me, as a man that is in his own prison. The Mole survives in this prison day by day and it manages to survive, without much hope. In my depressed times of my life, it was like living in my own prison.

Surrounded by the same things day after day, I became comfortable in my own prison and I didn't want no other man trying to trap me or entice me away from my comfortable nest. The things that I was exposed to in my early childhood, led to depression and depression became my way of feeling fearless. Speaking of the Mole, it wouldn't matter how many times that you would pull a mole from his hole, it would always dig deeper into the earth's surface and hide in another place from you. It is the Mole's Natural Instinct to dig and if you took the shovels that it has from its front parts, it would possibly die. Taken the shovels from a Mole would be in the same likeness as taken your head off your shoulders. A mole can't live without it's shovels and neither can a man live without his head. It's just the way creatures are made, hey?

In my depressed times, it didn't matter how many times that I would come out of my hole, I would always crawl back into my hole, where I felt safe and secured. If, a mole's natural instinct is to dig deep and live in a hole, I'm sure he knows how to escape from any predator that would try to eat him. I believe this is the way he survives: First, he digs deep into the earths surface. Second, he makes a nest deep into the earth's surface. Third, he digs many different tunnels in many different directions. Forth, he leaves his smell around in each tunnel. I have sat back and watched a hound dog as he would try to trap a mole, but the hound never got the mole, just a dirty nose. The hound would dig fiercely as if he was mad that he couldn't get the mole. The hound would bark and bark at the mole holes, as if he knew that the mole had escape from him. It was very comical really. Later the hound just gave up and walked away defeated. As the hound was digging in every tunnel that the mole had made, the mole was resting in it's nest deep within the earth surface, somewhat giggling at the hounds defeat. Just as the mole would hide in it's nest deep within the earth's surface, my depression carried me deep into my nest where I felt safe and secured.

My depression kept me trap in my own little nest where I would lay and laugh at those that tried to trap me with their enticing words or devices. I would stay in my dark hole for many days at a time not wanting nothing.

This Dark Abyss that I would stay in, day after day somewhat relieved me from reality and the pains that tried to ponder through my mind. But, I will say this with confidence, deep down from somewhere within my heart I didn't want to live that way. I really wanted to live a normal life, as I would see others live. These dark times of my life gave me understanding of one great thing and it was this; I had a minister to tell me one day, "If it wasn't for the dark threads woven into a blanket, the blanket wouldn't be as beautiful." These words from this minister opened a door within my heart and I began to see a little light within my own Abyss.

In my depressed states that I would go through, the depression was for a season and I would pray unto God to help me out of this dark Abyss. I knew if I didn't get help I was surely going to die one way or the other. I also know this with confidence," A man with understanding is a man with great sorrows." It seemed to me when God would send someone, such as a minister to my life, I would go deeper into my depression. It wasn't anything that the minister would say, it was the understanding that I would get as the Minister would share the Word of God with me. As the Word of God would shine into my life, it was extremely bright and the light would over shadow my darkness and I would try to dig deeper into my dark Abyss and hide from the light. This bright light would shine into my dark Abyss and it would try to break the chains that bound me within, such as, shame, self-pity, Resentments, Dishonesty, and Fearlessness.

It would be at this time when I felt the Word of God as a Bright Light shinning into my dark closets of my heart, I would become much more ashamed of my life. It would be at these times that I would give up trying to be normal, because I would think it was too much for me to bear.

But as the Light kept shinning into my life, things began to get much more better. The light was an intent of goodness to bring me back to life again. This Light, which is the Word of God, is a Lamp upon my feet a Light into my path today. The Word revealed itself as Love, Compassion, an Avenger, Truth and Grace. The Word of God gave me a greater hope than I ever had before. This hope gave me Life and today, I live! I also know this with a greater confidence, I'm not a mole in a Hole, but a child of the Living God. This Light or The Word of God, broke the chains of bondage from Rebellion which led me to all of my depressed life. Sure I still today go through some depressed states of mind, but nothing compared to my past life without this Greater Hope.

This greater hope helps me through my troubled times and I know today that I can now live normal. Oh yes! This word "normal" that I'm talking about, isn't the normal of the wanting of the things of this world. The Norm that I'm talking about is and only this; Living a consistent, honest, grateful and forgiving life. Living a normal life before all mankind and most of all, my God and his Son Jesus Christ, is the hope and joy for any man. I was told once by a man this; "A blank memory is a sign of a clear conscience." I really don't know why I threw that at you, but I thought I needed it also.

Today, depression is still a thorn of my flesh and I still take medications for it, but since I have been given the Great Hope of Salvation and Eternal Life my life is much more abundant than the past. Today, I not only survive day by day, but I live day by day. Today I live and fight the good fight of my faith that I have in the promises of God, such as, Eternal Life and a Life much more Abundantly here on earth. These things are spiritual, such as Faith, and it was these things that I didn't have the understanding of during my past. It was these things that I would always ask myself, Who I am? It was these things that kept coming from deep within my spirit man wanting to grow with understanding of the Great Creator.

By the chains of the sinful nature of mankind, such as, rebellions, resentments, distrust, dishonesty and self-pity, had bound my spirit man. It was my spirit man that was crying out to the Father of Lights every day and night, "Abba, Father." My spirit man wanted to live, but the sinful nature of my life wanted to die before my time.

Therefore, today I live and its not I that live, but he that lives in me, is why I live. All the rebellions, such as, resentments, self-pity, dishonesty, distrust and such like, have been broken away from my life and now today, these things live in their own Dark Abyss and are bound by their own sinful chains. But today I live in the Light and here in the light, I like it much more better. In the Holy Book of Isaiah chapter 61, verse 1-3 reads as written, ***"The Spirit of God is upon me; because the Lord has anointed me to preach good tidings unto the*** *meek; he hath sent me to bind up the brokenhearted, to proclaim liberty to the captives, and the opening of the prison to them that are bound; To proclaim the acceptable year of the Lord, and the day of vengeance of our God; to comfort all that mourn; To appoint unto them that mourn in Zion, to give them beauty for ashes, the oil of joy for mourning, the garment of praise for the spirit of heaviness; that they might be called the trees of righteousness, the planting of the Lord, that he might be glorified.*"Today, God's only begotten Son Jesus Christ holds all the things mentioned above in the palm of his hand waiting patiently to give to any man that is willing to ask for it. Christ is ready to set any man free, from their own sinful nature or prison and it is written, *"Who the Son sets free, is free indeed!"*

Now, my wife and I were still living in the Mobile Home that we had lived in for nearly 12 years. One day the Landlord came to us and said, "I'm raising your rent. You can afford $50.00 more a month can't you?" and I said this, "Of course we can. If we are willing to pay you more, then we don't have to stay here. We can find a better place to stay! If we are able to pay that, then we will move."

I was still without a job and no one else knew this, except my wife. My wife started to ask me questions like, "You don't even have a job. How do think we can move and afford any more than what we are paying now." Boy! that was the kicker for me and I said, "I'm getting another job. I don't want to stay around in this area anymore. This place is driving me crazy. I want to leave here, if I have to live in a old boot. I've paid the same rent for almost 12 years and now they want more. I'm going to make a point. Besides I have already got a call and I'm going for a interview next week." It so happened, that a first cousin had moved from his home near my parents and family and had ask me, if I wanted to rent the Home. I hadn't discussed this with my wife, because I thought that maybe she didn't want to move from where we were living, but I was going to move just to make a point.

Later the next week, I went to the Job Interview and got the job. When I was working at the First Nursing Home, I made a lot of good friends. People respected me and I respected most all of them. My supervisor was a great man and he was like a big brother to me. This man was a retired Veteran of the Naval Forces and was a Nuclear Submarine Mechanic. This man showed me a lot of different ways to stop a water leak, no kidding. Really, it was if God had put this man in my life to help me on my way and I respected him as if he was a man of God or much more as a brethren. One day as I was suffering because of some things at work, he put his arms around me and said, "Come on. Lets go talk. Things can't be that bad and if they are, you know that I will help you." We did go and set and talk and he said this to me, "You got to let go and quit letting little things get to you. You are a good man and you deserve more for yourself than letting little things like this brother you. It's just not worth it. You will be fine, but you got to let go."

During this time at this particular job, the company that I was working for, was a contractor to maintain the Maintenance and Cleaning of the Nursing Home. The entire time that I worked there I didn't feel too secure at this place, but continued with my job with all diligence that I had. The Administrator that was there at this time was a very loving, compassionate woman. She would come to me sometimes and just talk to me about life or I could go to her and talk. I really had a lot of respect for this lady. I really loved working there at this job, and some became as close as my own family to me. I got close to a lot of the residents and would pray with them a lot. Some of the residents would ask for me to come to them and just talk about life in general.

Now, I do remember one particular day that I responded to an emergency at the nursing home. I was always on the alert for anything that could or would harm the residents. It was if God had put me in this place to look over the residents and protect them from harm. Most of the residents at this Home couldn't get out of bed, because of being so sick. So, this particular day, I heard the Fire Alarm go off. I ran straight to the fire alarm panel to see where the problem was at. A couple of CNAs where yelling and I heard them, and I grabbed a fire extinguisher and ran to where they were standing. I looked into the room where they where standing and there was a fire starting in a bed next to a women who couldn't move from her neck down. I ran into the room and extinguished the fire and demanded that the CNAs remove the women before she suffocated. I helped get the women out of the room in the hallway to fresh air. Later, the Administrator found out that the resident that was residing in the same room with the paralyzed woman, had set the mattress on fire on purpose. This woman told the

Administrator that she didn't like the other woman. This woman who set the fire, was a mental patient and should had never been in this convalescent home. The Administrator served papers on this woman and she left to be committed into a mental hospital.

Now, I seen a lot deaths there and throughout my life by this time and I thought this," My whole life has consisted of dying people. God, am I the Death Angel?" I was really beginning to think this at this time, but I also thought this; "If I am the death angel, I must be doing something right for God. Working at a Nursing home must be the right job for me at this time."

Later at this particular job at the Nursing Home, I got some bad news. The Administrator that I had got close to, was leaving. I and this lady were friends and I just couldn't accept that she was going to leave. I had told her once that if she ever left, I was leaving too. She would always tell me this; "These people need you. They need someone to watch over them. Thank you for being concerned, but you need to stay here. You are a good friend and I would feel better knowing that you were still here, if I were to leave." Her family had been in the HealthCare business a long time and she was leaving to help her family with their businesses. She also just had a newborn baby and she wanted to stay home to care for it. This really broke my heart when I found out she was leaving, because I felt as if she was the one and only, that kept this Nursing Home going. She was the only one that I really trusted there.

So, she left and there was another Administrator Hired for the job. I also found out later that this particular Nursing Home was having some financial problems and weren't paying the company that I was working for, as promised. I got discouraged and things began to be somewhat hot under my collar. I remember the time that I quit this job: My Supervisor had went on vacation for two weeks and he had left another man in charge over the operation of the company that I was working with. I really thought that my Supervisor knew that the company was going to pack up and leave and he just couldn't tell me this. When I thought this about my supervisor knowing these things and wouldn't tell me, I lost my trust in him also.

So, one day as I was doing my duties, one of my co-workers came to me and told me something that the New Administrator had said about the company that I was working for. It made me somewhat angry and I went to her and asked her if this was true. She told me this; "What is your problem! That is not any of your business." Boy! Just the tone of her voice made me extremely mad. I released a little bit of my feeling to her and I then was fired from this Job by the Charge person of my company. I was so angry that I cursed the Administrator and my Charge person, and then I left and never went back. I was so discouraged about this matter, that I wanted to track this lady down and give her some more of my feelings. Again the sinful nature of this world was beginning to buffet me greatly. So, I was without a job again.

During this same time, my Landlord came to me and my wife and told us that we had to pay more rent. There I was without a job and the Landlord was asking for more rent. My Landlord didn't know that I had no job at this time and really, I didn't want the Landlord to know. We had already paid the rent and the next rent was almost due.

One day as I was home by myself, I prayed to God and asked him to help me with this situation. A few days past and I got a call from a friend there at the nursing home that I once worked at. She was a RN and also a great friend. She called me and told me that she had heard about what had happened and there was someone at another nursing home that needed a Maintenance Man, badly. This RN would go from Nursing Home to Nursing Home helping others. She worked Independently on her own and she was considered to me, as someone that was always watching others backs, somewhat like an angel. It surprised me when she called me, but not that I would get a call about a job. So, I went to this other Nursing Home and met the Administrator and he and I became friends. He gave me the job with a significant pay raise. So, I told my wife when she got home from work that day, that I had a job.

She was very happy for me and excited. Then I told her about my cousin that wanted me to rent his Home. She agreed with me and we began to pack our belongings and one week later, left from her brothers Mobile home that we had live in for almost 12 years. The rent for my cousin's Home was $150.00 more than we were paying, but we didn't care, we wanted to move. My wife was ready to leave this area also, because she knew the troubles that I had been through in this place. I was drinking some at this time, but not doing illegal drugs. I had quit my medications, except the meds to help my depression and insomnia.

Again, I started a new job at another Nursing Home and began to make other friends. The Administrator became a good friend to me and he called on me many times. I was hired as the Maintenance Director and Hazard Communication Director. During this time here, I began to get close to the residents and employees of this facility, as if they were my own family. I stopped drinking again, because I didn't want the friends that I had just found, find out about my past or any of my past issues. There was one resident that became as liken into me as my own grand mother. She was a white headed very dedicated Christian lady that encouraged me every time I went to sit with her. We would talk about the Lord and then she would read scriptures to me. I really began to love this lady with all my heart. There were others that I began to get attach to, but soon found out this wasn't a real good idea. Some of the people that I began to get attached to would die in their sleep and I would get the bad news as I would come to work the next day. It began to be a burden on my heart, but I just stayed the course, because I knew that God wanted me there for some reason. It wasn't a feeling that I trusted my life upon, but I just went by my gut feeling. I began to train the personnel there at this Nursing Home in the Safety and Hazard Communication program. This part of the job was a learning process for me as well as for the others.

One day I was discouraged about this particular job and the Administrator said to me, "You need to quit taking this part of your job so seriously." I didn't quite understand what he meant, because I thought the welfare and safety of the residents were just as important as the Maintenance job. I have always been the type of man that when I was hired to do a particular job, I would do it with all my strength no matter how non-important someone may have thought it was.

I do remember one particular day as I was making my rounds, as I would do every day, I walked to the dinning area where the residents would go and eat. I somewhat stood in the shadow and watched as some of the residents tried to eat. But, some were so sick, they couldn't even pick up their utensils to eat with, and I began to weep somewhat within myself. Most of the residents had to have an CNA (Certified Nurse's Assistant) to help feed them. This particular day as I was standing in the shadow, I seen something that made me angry inside my heart. I watched as a helpless resident was sitting at the dinning table and she was unable to eat. Then I couldn't believe what I saw next. I seen an CNA take a spoon, and start slapping this elderly sick resident in her face. I knew this wasn't a good technique to get any human to eat, especially a helpless elder that couldn't even open her mouth to eat. This incident made me very angry inside and I almost lost it. I wanted to take my hand and start slapping the CNA's face, no kidding. But, I control myself and I walk calmly away from where I was standing, and went straight to the Administrator's office. I knocked on his door and he asked me to enter. He look up at me and ask if everything was ok. Then I asked him this question, "I know that your CNAs use different techniques that they were trained to do so, in order to get someone to eat, if they need to eat. But, do they have a technique of hitting a resident on the face continuously with a large spoon to get them to eat."

The Administrator looked at me as if I was crazy and said, "Do What?"

He stood up as if he was very surprised and insisted that I and him walk the corridors and point out this particular CNA to him. So, we walked around the facility corridor by corridor as if we were just making our rounds, and then this particular CNA came from a resident room. I pointing in a way that he knew that this was the CAN and he calmly said this, "Thank You. I will take care of the rest." I never seen this CNA at this Nursing Home again while I was working there.

Later, these particular things began to eat at my heart in such a way that I was on the look out for any such acts toward another person. The job became burdensome on my heart and I was beginning to think this, "If I did see someone hurt another resident at the nursing home, I don't know if I could control myself as I did the last time." I began to hold a little anger in my heart toward certain CNAs there at the nursing home and the job didn't feel to me as it did when I first started. I do remember this: One day I went to a resident's room, where I would go and talk to her (The White Headed Christian Lady) and we began to talk and she told me that she knew some of my family. We talk a bit and then she said this, "Son, are you happy? You don't seem to be as happy as you used to be. Is there something wrong? I know that you are leaving, but just trust God with all your needs and he will supply." I just couldn't tell her the problem, but I did say this; "Well, I've got some issues I'm dealing with right now, but I know that God will work it out." She said, "Son, you said the right thing. I know that God loves you and he has a call on your life. I knew that when I first met you. But son, put all your trust in God and not just a little and all things will be fine."

At this time, my wife and I were starting to find another place to live. We wanted some Land that we could someday build a house on. My wife and I were beginning to be financially blessed and we were saving for that particular reason. Later, I talked to this friend of mine again in the nursing home (The White Headed Christian Lady) and before I could say anything she said this; "Have you found any land yet?" I didn't know what to think, because at the time, I haven't told any one about me looking for land, except my wife and my wife surely didn't know this woman. So, I said this; "No Ma. But I'm still looking for the right place. I'm trusting God to put me where I need to be. If I do find a piece of property, I want to stay there the rest of my life, without moving again. I want to make it my permanent home. I'm tired of moving from place to place." The lady said this and only this; "Son, keep looking, because it is there waiting for you. Just keep Looking. Don't give up. God will bless you." I then hugged her neck and I told her that I loved her and left the room and went about my business. What is so ironic about the last conversation that I had with this lady, is this; It seemed that she knew more about me than my own mother and father. She knew that I wasn't happy and I was going to leave the job. She also knew that I was looking for a piece of land to settle on. It seemed to me at this time that this sweet lady was getting information from God himself about me and I truly believed that. This lady cared for me and I truly believed that she loved me without any condition, which I will call an agape love, an unconditional love. I also know that this lady loved everyone the same way.

As a few weeks had past here at this job and I was with a cousin and we were riding not to far from my parents place. We rode down this particular street and a sign jump out at me as if it wanted to come through the windshield. I rode this street several times a week and never did I see this sign before this particular day. The sign read, "FOR SALE".

I told my cousin to stop the truck and he did and I got the phone number and the same day called the owner of the property. This property was just a stone throw down from my Parent's Home and it at one time belong to my family many years ago. I remember running barefoot through this piece of property when I was but a child and at that time, it was but a corn field. But, at this time it was a commercial piece of property being used as a Mobile Home Park. It was a small park with only 4 mobile homes. So, a couple of days later as I was at work, I went to see my friend (The White Headed Christian Lady) and told her the good news. She hugged my neck and said to me, "Son, God will give your hearts desire, if only you trust him with your whole heart." But, she also wanted to know if I was going to leave the job and I told her I wasn't sure.

Later, after my wife and I closed on the property, we began to think that maybe that wasn't the right thing to do. I was beginning to doubt myself and God again, because of this: This property that we had just purchased was known for drugs, alcohol and other sinful natures of man. It was surrounded by alcoholics and drugs addicts. But, I knew that this property was once owned by my family and I felt within my heart deep down, that it was for me. This property was on a hill and was set at a T-Intersection; either you would go left or right that is.

At the time, I wasn't concerned about whom or what was living around me, all that I cared for was I needed a place to settle on and these things weren't going to scare me away. The place that I had just moved from for almost 12 years, was worse than this. Plus, I will be nearer to my family.

Well, we moved into one of the Mobile Homes, after I gutted it and repaired it, and it left 2 mobile homes for the taken. My youngest brother needed a place to stay and his family came, and stayed in one of the other Mobile Homes. Then a young couple that I used to minister to, that were members of the youth ministry, needed a place to stay. So, I let them stay there in the other Mobile Home and then the Homes were full. What is so Ironic is this: I didn't really have the money to move from the beginning, but afterwards, I had tenants paying my mortgage, no kidding. This was changing my thinking about, "maybe it wasn't a good choice to purchase this property."

Even though things were starting to work out for myself and my wife at this time financially, the thorns of my flesh began to buffet me greatly. One day, I started to use alcohol again. I not only started to drink, but I also started to use drugs again. When I started using again, I felt ashamed of my self and I knew that I couldn't face my friends at the Nursing Home. When I went back to work, I shun from all the residents and even the employees and submitted my 2 week resignation to the Administrator. He was discourage and said this, "I don't quite understand this. Why do you want to leave? You are the best Maintenance Man I have ever seen. Is it something that I can help you with to keep you from leaving?" and I said, "No Sir. I have issues that I need to deal with and I can't deal with them and give you my 100% service and more so, these people need someone here everyday. I already have another job interview closer to home. I need to be closer to home and I've got to get off from being on call duties 24-7." The Administrator accepted my resignation, but was somewhat discouraged.

So I left this job, not only because of job issues, but I left this job because I was ashamed at what I had done. I had been somewhat clean and living a consistent life or normal life for so long, but now I was so depressed and ashamed at what I had done. During this time of my life, I had been clean for almost 7 years, no kidding. Everyone respected me as a minister of the Gospel of Jesus Christ and now not only had I let people down, I had let God down.

During the 7 years of Sobriety, I was on my medications and took them as prescribed, but it seemed to me that when I quit them, things got worse.

Like I said before, I couldn't accept that I had a Bi-Polar disease and also couldn't accept that I had to take medications for the rest of my life. I would always think this; "Taken these drugs is the same as using. If I'm going to be drug free, then I can't take the prescription drugs. To me it is the same as taken drugs. A drug is a drug isn't it? If I do take these medications, then it is the same as saying, "I don't trust God to deliver me from my sufferings." I was beginning to deny that I had a illness and started blaming the medications for my problems, follow me? At this time, I truly did something that I really didn't want to do and that was, to start using drugs again. I started the manipulative way of living by self-will and I just quit walking in God's Will and it became disastrous for me.

After I started to use again, it was if things got worse and worse for me. But, I did manage to change my thinking and then I tried again to live a normal life. Later, I began to go back to church again. I always knew that when I went to church, I could draw strength from others with the same faith like I had. I knew from past experience that staying in Church gave me hope and it was much easier for me to live a normal life. I finally stopped using illegal drugs, because I knew that I had to find another job. I was still somewhat drinking, but not heavy and I was trying to stop on my own.

Later, I did get another job at an Industrial Plant. My wife had been working at this same Industrial Plant for almost 2 years and I thought that it would be good for both of us to be working at the same place. The Part of the Plant that I worked in was the Old Part and the Part my Wife work in was the Newest Technical Part. My job at this plant didn't last long because of this; I was on the Night shift from 7:00pm-7:00am.

Now, there is one particular incident that I do remember quite well. One night as I was working I had to go to the bathroom. As I was coming out the bathroom I began to see a young man running and somewhat yelling. I didn't know what was going own and there was not any other person near him at the time. I seen him grab some rags and fall to the floor and then I knew something bad was wrong with this young man. I ran as fast as I could to this man and he was going hysterical. I sat down beside this young man and held him in my arms and tried to calm him down. He kept telling me that he had just lost his hand in one of the machines. I continued to calm him down and then others began to come to us. I told the first person to call 911 and Code Red over the Load Speaker for the night Emergency response team. It wasn't a great burden for me, but it hurt me in my heart, because I knew that this young man was hurt severely. Later after a few days, I talked to his brother and he told me that he had lost all of his fingers from the palm up. I began to think that this job wasn't for me or my wife. Some of the Older men that were about to retire from this plant that worked in my department were also missing a few fingers, no kidding.

At this time I started to see things like this and I began wanting my wife and I out of that place before one of us lost our fingers or worse. There were already issues with the near retirees there at the plant, because of the New Ownership of the Plant. The Plant had just been bought by another Corporation and I didn't think the near retirees liked that action. There were several nights that I would go into work and some of these retirees would just leave and go out side, late at night, and leave me alone to run the whole section of this department.

One night I got somewhat angry and went looking for this particular man that was supposed to had been helping me run the line. I finally found him and others outside smoking, as if he was already retired for the evening.

I ask him if he was going to help me, or what do I need to do to keep this section going and he said, "You are the new man, you figure it out. I don't care how you run it. I used to run it by myself." Boy! I looked at him and said this," Run it your_ -_-_self dick!" I got my bag and walked right out the door at about 2:30am that mourning and never went back. My wife later left her job there at the Plant also, because they were shutting down the new section she worked in. They had already laid off some of the workers in my wife's department and I guess my wife thought she was next. My wife got another great job later and still today is working the same job. She has been with this job for many years.

Later for me, after other jobs that just didn't work out, I did eventually get another job working back in the communication field. I had stopped drinking and doing illegal drugs entirely on my own and things began to work out better for me. I was beginning to get strong again and come out of my mole hole. I began to go to church again on a regular basis and was beginning to have much more peace in my life. I hadn't been back to my doctor, because I had no Insurance and I thought this; "Well I've made it this far without medicines, maybe, I can make it even further without them." I thought that I had found the best job I had ever had before. The only people I reported to were nearly 1600 miles away and if things job of my life. The pay was great and I was my own boss, somewhat. were well, we didn't talk much. They would call me if they needed me to do something, but they trusted me to do the job that I was hired to do and I did it well. I was hired in the Communication Industry as a Field Mapper, but the main job was to Quality Check (QC) Contractors that were mapping the Industry. Sometimes I would have 10 crews going in 5 different States and it was a great job to keep up with them. It was a traveling job and I would travel around the southeast USA from the States of Alabama to West Virginia. I would stay gone from home weeks at a time, sometimes more.

Like I mentioned before, During this time, I had stopped taken my medications again, because I had no Insurance. Today I know with confidence, stopping my medications like that, as I did most of the time without Insurance, was somewhat suicidal for me. Most of the times that I did stop my medications, were the times that I had no Medical Insurance. I just couldn't afford those expensive drugs, so I would just quit taken them. I had quit taken my medications for about 6 months at this time, because I was changing jobs.

So, I had this great job that I was blessed with, right back into the Communication Industry. I was traveling and meeting many people in different States. Not only did this job give me the opportunity to get out and meet people, it was as if I wanted to stick it in the other jobs face. Let me explain: This Industry was the first job that I had every work in. I felt comfortable in this job and this company gave me the opportunity to get back into this field again. I knew most of all the technical terms and I was much more advanced in the field than other co-workers. But there was one thing that would always try to come into my thoughts every day. In one of my last jobs that I was in this same Industry, I quit that job because of the manager. I didn't hold no grudge against this man, but this man now was working for the same company that had hired the company I was working for as contractors. Both companies where large and had Billions in assets. When I quit the job that I and this man previously worked together at, I felt that he was some of the reason why I had to quit. Please follow the point is coming. So, now I was working again as a contractor for the company that I had quit. Somewhat Ironic isn't it.

When I began to understand the job much more, I would think about this particular incident always. I would think things like this; I will show them that I am better than, they think I am. I will meet every body I can with this company and someday, maybe my company will buy out their company and I will be that managers boss." No kidding, I would really think this. When I was traveling, I passed through a town that I was told this manager was living in at this time. I even stopped at phones booths and took the phones book to look up his name. But, I never found it. So, I just continued on my way. It wasn't a thought of revenge, it was a thought of pride. I just wanting this man to know, I was working for his company and I was much more better off. Sounds like pride to me, doesn't it you? Well, I somewhat just let that thought flow from my heart, until I decided to just forget it and get on with my life. I continued to do my job and did it well, until later I resigned from this job, because of this: I had been with this company now for almost a year. I had been clean from alcohol and drugs now for about a year. I wasn't taken any medications for my Bi-Polar or depression during this time. I was clean as a whistle. But, there was one thorn that I was always struggling with and it was the Lust of sex, no kidding. This thorn is a great, deep thorn in my flesh and even though I was clean from drugs and alcohol, this particular thorn would always be there to buffet me greatly. This job somewhat kept me from doing drugs or drinking alcohol, because of the dangers of my job duties and the perfection it required. But this particular thorn, I could hide this from others much more easier.

At this time no one thought I had a drug, alcohol problem or much more a mental illness. I hid these things from everyone. I would act as if I never had any problem. I do remember one occasion that the company's chief officers came to meet with me and meet the next day with the clients. The day that they came I was ready to meet them. I had every thing in order and I wanted to make my first impression. One of the men wanting to go out and eat and ask if I knew where a fine place around town to eat was. I told him I did. When we left from the Hotel he asked if I knew where a certain food restaurant was and I told him I did. So, we rode and rode and rode until one of the men said, "Just go there. Shoot I'm hungry and tired of just riding. I thought you knew where the restaurant was." I felt like crawling under the front seat of the vehicle like a worm.

I had forgotten where this restaurant was, but was driving around looking for it as If it was there. Anyway, we went to a Mexican Restaurant and began to order. The men from the office ordered their food and a beer a piece.

So, it was my turn to order and I ordered also a beer, but I had to say, "add a lime please." I felt in my spirit at that very moment that I just maybe getting my self in trouble, but I also thought that these two office men just ordered beer too and they had no right to judge me for drinking a beer with them. We got our food and beer and they drank their beers like thirsty camels, one after another, but, I sip on my one beer like a little baby with a bottle. They asked me if I wanted another beer and I said this, "No sir. I'm Driving and I don't drink that much. I don't really like alcohol." One of the men looked at me as if I was crazy and said, "Hell, if you don't like alcohol why did you order it. You could have had a coke or an Ice tea." Again I felt like crawling under my seat like a worm. After we had ate and drank, we left and just rode the scenery some and went back to the Hotel. I began to get to know these men and I began to know that what I thought wasn't what they thought, follow me? These men were just as I was, a man. These men were not angels sent from on high to check on me. They where they for company business and I judged the wrong way. These two men were good men and I began to get to know them and they began to know me. The man that was over my position did tell me the next day this," Don't try to hard, relax. Its just a job. We aren't here to tell you what you have or what you haven't done, we just wanted to meet you. You are a good guy and I believe we picked a good man to do this job, Thank you."

Later as time passed on this job, I began to feel something, like a want, coming from my flesh. The sub-contractors that were under my watch were always going out and getting drunk or high. I smelled the odor of alcohol almost everyday on their breath or from their rooms as we would meet in the mourning. This feeling of want form my flesh kept getting stronger and stronger.

So, one evening as I was alone in my Hotel room, I thought that I just needed to take the advice from my superior and relax some. I thought this: "I could lay in some hot water in the tub and drink a couple of beers to relax and no one would know it." My friend, that thought enter into my heart and I did just that. That one thought led me back down to a road of destruction. I went to a store in another town and bought me a six-pack of beer. I didn't stop at the beer, because I also need cigarettes. I just couldn't drink beer without smoking cigarettes, follow me?

As time passed I was smoking and drinking everyday. I wouldn't drink while working, but I just couldn't wait to get drunk. Later I was working in a different area and I went to another motel to stay. I was beginning to drink heavy at this time, almost a case of beer every other night. I was also starting to drive while drinking alcohol. I knew that this wasn't good and I had to do something. I will say this, the area that I was driving was on and near the Appalachian Mountains and driving drunk on these roads at night was suicidal. There were a couple of times that I had to stop and thank God that I didn't go off the edge of a mountain, no kidding. One day as I was headed back to my room at this little motel in a cove in the Appalachian Mountains, I noticed a Large Billboard that I had not noticed before, nearly 1 mile from the motel. The billboard read, "PREPARE TO MEET THY GOD", no kidding. The only way to get to the cove and the motel was to drive by this large billboard. As of today it is still there, but I haven't been back there since this time.

During this time, I was drinking and starting to go out to many bars around these areas. I would drive up, down and through these mountains almost zombilized. Not only was the alcohol buffeting me, the lust of sex was also buffeting me. I would be gone weeks at a time from home and these lustful thoughts kept pounding day by day. I had many opportunities to be with girls from the Universities or just go pickup a women off the streets, but somehow I managed not to get that deep in my sinful nature.

There were times I would be at a bar and a beautiful girl or women would come to me and rub my shoulder and I would be quick to say, "I'm Married." and the women or girl would say, "Oh! I didn't know. I'm sorry."

There was a particular time that I remember very well. There was a bar that was near a Large University and all the students would come to this place and listen to the live music and get drunk. One evening I thought that I would just go in and listen to the music and drink a few beers. I walked in and there wasn't a seat in the house except at a table where two beautiful blond headed girls were sitting. I ask if I could sit with them and they insisted that I sit with them. I ordered a couple of beers and we drank. I order more beer and we drank. I ordered more beer and we drank. I began to order pitchers of beer on drank. About this time when I ordered the last pitcher, I thought, there were loud noises coming into the bar as it would sound of many drunk people. It was these two girls friends and they circle us at the table as if we were going to sing together. There were some of them boys that I knew weren't old enough to drink. Some were vomiting on the floor and under the tables. It was just horrible. I stopped buying any beer, but beer kept showing up on the table like magic.

One of the girls, which I will call the guardian girl, said to me, "I'm sorry for my friends. I've told them about drinking like that, but they just want listen to me." This girl was older, but not much older than about 22 years of age. I will say this with confidence, she looked like Brittany Spear's twin Sister. I looked at her and said this, "You know? God has told me my whole life I shouldn't drink alcohol, but look at me now. I don't want to drink, but it could be worse. I could be strung out of drugs." She looked at me and said this again, "You are a good looking man and I believe you too be very smart also. You have a lot going for yourself. You will be fine. What are you doing in a place like this anyway?"

About that time, one of the boys vomited on the table and this girl stood up and demanded them to get back to campus and away from there and this girl really meant business. I was thinking that it was all a plan for them to get beer from me, but that wasn't it at all. She seem to me as if she was their guardian, no kidding. Those kids started leaving the bar and it settle somewhat from the yelling and noise from those kids. After it had settle, the other blond headed girl had call a taxi and said to the other guardian girl, "The taxi will be here in just a few moments. Lets go outside and wait for it." The guardian girl said, "No. You go out and wait and let me know when it is here." So, the other girl walks out the bar and I never see her again. Please follow me the point is coming. It was I and the guardian girl now only left at the table. We set there listen to the Live Band and then she said this to me, "I seen the girl put her hands on her shoulders. Did that offend you?" I said, "No. It didn't offend me, but I knew that her intents wasn't just to put her hand on my shoulder." We laughed together and then she said, "You said you were married. I bet she is a wonderful women. She is blessed to have someone like you. You could have had any girl in here, but you were faithful to your wife, even when she isn't here with you. I have a fiancé out there and I'm hoping he is as faithful to me as you are with your wife." And this is what I said, "You are a very beautiful girl and I'm blessed for meeting you. If he isn't faithful, you want know it, because God will hide it from you and you will be bless with someone good. But, we will hope that he is faithful." And about that time the other girl comes in and tells her that the taxi was waiting. This girl left from my presences and I never seen her again. The very points are these: God was sending people into my life at this very moment warning me about the dangers that were ahead of me. I was beginning to drink heavy and the Lust of my flesh was buffeting me so and I was beginning again to live a destructive life. I will call this girl an angel in my life and I will forever thank God for sending her into my life at that time.

Later I was still drinking, but I knew deep down that I had to put an end to this before I killed myself or worse. One evening I decided to travel home and surprise my wife. It was our anniversary and I wanted to get home that day before and surprise her, but I didn't make it home. The reason was this: I had left from the Appalachian area at this time and was staying in another town and hotel. I had already been drinking earlier that day and was somewhat disoriented. I left this town and I started traveling home. As I came to the next City I began to think again. This City was very large and it was known for its murders and high crimes every day. So, as I neared this city I thought this, "I bet I can find some drugs in this town. There is drugs everywhere, that I've been told." You want believe what happened to me next.

As I was in this city I turned into a neighborhood. When I traveled not too deep into the neighborhood, I seen people standing and drinking and partying. I was deep into a Hood without doubt, but I continued on my mission. As I cruised nearer to this party, I stopped and a young man comes to my window. I didn't ask if he had drugs, but I asked if anything was going on, any parties or whatsoever. He asked me what did I need, and I told him that I was looking for. It was cocaine or crack. He said drive around the corner and park, someone will meet you. So, I pulled around the corner and parked and a young girl comes to my passenger window. I roll the window down and she said, "What do you need?" I told her what I wanted and she said she had it and ask me if she could sit down. I was getting a little desperate now and I wanted to get out of that area.

So, I let the girl set down and what she wanted to give me wasn't cocaine. I ask her this, "What in the world is such a pretty girl like you doing stuff like this?" She was somewhat humble and said to me, "I just needed enough of money to get my hair done. I'll do anything you want if you want to." You know, that just destroyed my mission of getting cocaine.

Nevertheless I said this to her, "How much money do you need to get your hair done?" and she said to me, "Maybe $10.00, but I can do something for you if you like." Then I said, "Here is $10.00 and please use it to get your hair done, OK." She looked amazed as I gave her the 10 bucks and said thank you to me over and over. She got out of my car and left from my presence. A few minutes passed and I drove off deeper into this neighborhood. I park the vehicle that I was driving a couple of blocks from where I was sitting, because I didn't want to get a ticket from drinking and driving, neither did I want another girl wanting money. I sat there in the vehicle for a few moments and then I got out of my vehicle and started to walk into this neighborhood. Just as I was walking deeper into this area, from out of no where, someone grabbed me by my hand and said, "What is your problem?! You shouldn't be walking around here by yourself! Someone could rob you or kill you. Come On!" This somebody was a woman, much older than the first, and older than I was at the time. She said, "What are you doing out here like this, are you crazy?" I finally said this to her as she was leading much deeper into the neighborhood by my wrist now, "I just thought I would take a walk and I didn't want to get a ticket from drinking."

During times like this as I would drink alcohol, I was somewhat fearless. I wasn't afraid of much anything. I always looked at this time as a challenge of my life and a reason for the time in my life. But looking back at the times when I would drink alcohol, it was these times that I was suicidal. My mind was blank and my judgments and the sense of discernment was impaired. As we kept walking deeper into the hood, she carried me to an apartment and she knock on the door. The resident came to the door and slammed the door in her face. At that time, I was beginning to sober up somewhat. I turned from her to walk away and then she said, "Wait just a minute. He's just drunk. He does that every time. He's got what you are looking for." When she said this, I began to sober up even more so.

Then the door opens and the women whispered something in the man's ear and then we entered the apartment. I know what you are probably thinking about now my friend, but be patient. You haven't heard the best yet.

So, this women and man began to smoke cocaine and then they wanted me to smoke it in front of them, so they could see me smoke it. I guess they were thinking I was an drug agent or something. I was a drug agent alright, looking for drugs to use. Anyway we set there and smoked dope for a few moments and they were drinking liquor like thirsty camels. After I refused to drink, I believe it was at this time that the resident ask us to leave. The resident and this women must had something going on that they didn't want me to hear, because they would always whisper into each others ears. I will say that this woman was very diligent in helping me find cocaine. It was if my mission became her mission. I began to get somewhat more sober and I began to walk back to my vehicle to get out of that place. She refused to let me walk alone and I thought that it was a good gesture at the time.

Later we ended back at my vehicle and she said, "If I could get some money I can get the best you every had." So, I knew I could get some money and I let her into the vehicle and we drove not far from where we were. She insisted that I come with her to the door of this home. So, I got out and walked with her to the door of this home. The resident came to the door and let us in, without any whisper or cursing. We walk through the house following this man and we walked down to a basement floor of the home. When I came into the room, it was very cloudy with smoke. As I kept walking, I was ask to sit down at a large round table where there were maybe 5 or 6 other people besides me and the other two. There was some smoking going on in this place and they weren't smoking cigarettes. The woman ask if I had the money and I said, "I've got some, but not much." She and the resident started whispering and then I knew it was something they didn't want me to hear.

They asked me how much cash did I have and I told them. When I told them how much cash I had on me at the time, everyone that sat around the table fixed their eyes on me and their mouths dropped. I had almost $300.00 in cash. The reason I told them about the cash, because by now, if they had me where they were going to kill me, the money didn't matter much to me at this point. The tenant looked around at everyone there sitting and said this to me, "How are you doing. There is not one person going to hurt you and if they try, they will have to come through me."

So, we continued on with the cash I had and he and the girl would guard me to the ATM many times that night. At one time he asked for my keys and I thought for sure my life was over. He said that he didn't want my vehicle in the front where it was at. So I ask if he would show me out and I would move it to where he would like. He sat back in the chair and somewhat shook his head in the NO, NO, NO, gesture. He got my keys and gave the keys to another man that was there and that man took my car are pulled it to back of the home where it couldn't be seen from the road. At this time I knew I was kidnapped for sure. There wasn't really anything that I could do, except go crazy. I just continued on with the party and then this man, the tenant, sat beside me. He introduced himself to me and I introduced myself to him. He kept saying things like this, "If you are working a sting, you have nothing on me." I finally convinced this man that I made a mistake, but I thank him and this woman for getting me off the streets for the night. This man's mouth dropped and then he said this, "What are you some kind of crazy preacher?" and then he began to laugh and the others began to giggle somewhat also. I did tell him I had been in the ministry, but I didn't have to explain much more. As we were sitting there and smoking, this man pulls a Bible from under his chair, no kidding. And this is what he said to me, "I was called to the ministry also, but the difference between me and you is that I'm still in the ministry no matter what happens in my life. I fall, I get up, I fall, I get up and that's my story.

I just keep living man, because I have no choice but to live. Hell! I don't want to die, I want to live." At this time I was really beginning to think it was now closer than before and I was waiting now for the gun to be put to my head, no kidding. But, for some reason things changed and all the others had left and it was just me the woman and the Strange Preacher (The man tenant). This man and I talk about God until the next day and then I thought, "Oh my God! I've got to go. It is my anniversary." It was already in the late evening the next day, no kidding. About the time I said this, another man came down the stairs and called the woman away. Then the strange preacher told me that I needed to go. He also said this, "I know you will be back in 3 days. So, I'll see you then"

I finally left this city and this home and I was so relieved. Thoughts were pounding my heart, such as, I could had been killed. Why wasn't I killed. They had me where they could had killed me. After awhile from staying up all night and the next day, I began get sleepy and I could barely keep my eyes opened. My destination was about 70 miles from home at this point. I made it home, but me and my wife didn't celebrate our anniversary, because I slept for almost 2 days. I told her I had to work when I got to were I could speak to her and I began to get somewhat depressed about what I had done. Not only was it about me lying to her, I had spent nearly $1000.00 that night and had once again started to use drugs. She became saddened about the incident, but was also relieved at the same time, that I wasn't murdered. The night that I left the Hotel was a Thursday night. The night that I got home was a late Friday night. Our anniversary was that Friday. I know what you are thinking about now my friend, but be patient. It wasn't a good thing I did that night by any means, but I will say, it was a Life's Lesson. This lesson almost caused my life and I thank God every time it comes to my remembrance, that my life was spared once more. I did go through the City that third day as the Strange Preacher had prophesied, but I kept traveling on.

I want to Thank that Woman and the Strange Preacher, for taken me off the streets that night and hiding me from all the destruction that could had happen to me. It was an expensive lesson, but like I mentioned before, it could had been my life.

Later I would resign from this job, because of drinking and doing drugs again. I knew sooner or later I would get a DWI or worse, get killed. I began to go into somewhat liken into a mole hole (my depressed state of mind) and I become very ashamed of what I had done. It seems to me when I would do these terrible things, I would go and hide in a hole. It would be this time I would be so ashamed and all that I wanted was, just to die. It would be at this time that I would call out to God, "God please save me! Help me God!" God was faithful in saving my life again from death.

During this same time I started to go back to my Doctor again, and I started to take my medications as prescribed. I started to go to church again and I was determined to stay normal. I still didn't want to accept that I had to take these medicines for the rest of my life, but it was sure better than, living like I was living. So, I again tried to accept my Illness again and began to stop using illegal drugs, but continued to drink alcohol. I was trying my best to live a normal life and did it to the best I could understand at the time. One evening as I was preparing to travel the next day, I began to hurt all over my body, as I would much of the time without taken my medicines. I asked my wife to carry me to the Hospital.

There at the Hospital they checked me for hours in the emergency room and was amazed at the pain I was complaining about. They gave me a shot to calm me down and to lower my blood pressure and it did help. Later, after blood and other examinations, the Doctor had diagnosed me with *Fibromyalgia*, a rare illness of the muscles and joints of the body.

For a very long time since I was a teenager, I would hurt and have soreness all over my body, but continued on with my life without a diagnose. I guess I didn't want to know what the problem was and I was fearful that it could be something worse than I thought. But, this particular time of my life I had no choice but to get help on the matter. I also knew that these pains were contributing to my using of alcohol and drugs to relive me from the pains of my body. I never told any one about these pains, except my wife. I would awake some nights screaming to the top of my voice, with cramps in my arms and legs, continuously, since we had been together. It would be at these times that I hurt so badly in my body that I would run to the liquor store or a drug dealer. The Doctor told me that this was rare and that it wasn't too common among young men of my age.

So, they gave me medicines and I went home with the diagnosis. This diagnosis was another thorn in my flesh. But, I was glad finally that I had a diagnosis for the chronic pains of my body. So, I was taken my Medicines for my mental Illness and now I was taken medicines for this illness of my body. I later went to my Doctor had been going to for years and he reworked my medicines, so that, the medicines he prescribed, would also treat the fibromyalgia symptoms. These medicines began to help me greatly and I continued to take them for awhile. I returned to work at the Communication job and did my job much more greatly. But, deep down I still had fear within my heart that I would get myself in trouble from my drinking. I was taken a lot of medicines and drinking at the same time. At the time, It was hard for me to accept my mental illness, more so, there was another illness that I had to live with for the rest of my life.

Later I decided that I needed to quit this job traveling and find something closer to home to keep me off the roads and I did just that. I found another job closer to home and I gave my 2 week notice there at this job.

As I was talking to one of the officers in the Companies Human Resource's department a man said something to me that I pondered on quite some time within my mind. He said this; "I know this job is stressful and Hoped that you could had worked longer for us. Are you drinking again?" And I told him the truth, that I was drinking again. Here is the pondering part; I know I've had alcohol issues my whole life, but this man, whom I've never met and is 1600 miles away, had just asked me, "Are you drinking again?" There again, it was if God was whispering things in people ears without me knowing. They accepted my resignation and I left this job with a broken heart. This was the best job that I had ever had in my life and I had just let go, because I rebelled against living a normal life. I left this job, because of a one night pleasure party in my sinful nature man. I left this job, because I was ashamed of myself and more so, I just couldn't tell these people that had been so good to me, what the real problems were. I just couldn't let them find out about all my problems, because I thought, if they did find out the problems in my life, they would had fired me anyways. I had been blessed with this job greatly and it was gone, just as quick as I got it, in a flash. It broke my heart greatly, but I continued to press forward.

Later I started my new job. It was in the Skilled Trade Industry. I was continually to drink and take my medications and hide my illnesses from this company. I thought this as I continued on this job, "If they knew my problems and my illnesses, they would fire me in a second." I did manage to hide this from them for a couple of years, until the problems again became too great. When these things began too surface was about the same time the Two World Trade Centers and the Pentagon were bombed. I began to buy guns and act like a Hero during these times. I began to drink and go out in public, hoping, I would find someone doing something to hurt another man, no kidding. It was that same feeling, as long before, when I had just moved into a bad neighborhood and would stand in the shadows hoping I could release some of anger upon them, no kidding.

I would take my guns deep into the woods and a gravel pit, where I was living and target practice. I would pack myself with an assault rifle, heavy rifle, and a hand gun. I would put my fatigues upon my body and go to the woods. The noises from the guns was if a war was going on in my own back yard, no kidding.

During this time that the World Trade Centers and the Pentagon were bombed, somewhat gave me another chance of releasing some of my deep anger from my heart. I wanted to join the service and hoped that they would assign me to go on an assassin mission to kill those suckers who were responsible for such an awful act of murder upon innocent people. But at the time I was much too old to join the service. So, I thought that I could just be like an National Guardsman without any commander and just kept my eyes open for the enemy here on my own land. I began to drink somewhat heavy again, but pressed forward and was still wanting and hoping, that someday I would have my chance at those dogs.

Later, I did calm somewhat on my drinking and not long after the bombings of the World Trade Centers, something else awful happened. Early the next year, I *lost my older brother to a drug overdose.* Before I go any further about this incident, let me share this with you; The day before we got the awful news of my brother death, I had pulled my back at home. I went out on a Sunday after noon to rearrange some bolts and hardware in boxes in my shed. The back of the Home was fenced in, because we had a couple of small dogs, a Chihuahua and a Dachshund. I picked up a box of the hardware and tried to go through the gate, but the dachshund tried to run out at the same time. I twisted my torso and closed the gate quickly. When I twisted my torso, I felt something pull within my back, but I didn't pay much attention it, because it just didn't hurt. My back was already damaged from my past injuries, so I thought nothing about it. Later it started to swell somewhat.

I didn't go to the doctor and called into work Monday morning and told them that I pulled my back, but I would be in the next day. The medicines that I was taken for my illnesses had numb me somewhat from the pain of the injury. Monday evening I got the strength up and went to my parents just to see them.

Deep down within my body, I knew I had hurt my back worse than I thought, but I tried to deny the pain I was going through. Well, while I was there at my parents the phone rung, as it does almost every hour at my parents and I thought nothing about, until I noticed my father's mouth drop. Then I heard him yell out, "My son!? What are you talking about? My Son! And then I saw my mother come from the left side of where I was standing and she began to cry out loud, "My Son!? What's wrong with my Son? Oh my God! My Son!. I knew that my mother felt within her spirit that my brother was dead. My father calmed down somewhat and listened to the instructions over the phone by the Medical Examiner where my brother's body was lying. I took the phone from my father and started calling my brothers and sisters and they were there in a flash. Everyone's faces, look as if they knew something was awfully wrong and were weeping greatly. My father and my two Oldest brothers left to where my brother laid. My wife and I stayed with my mother until the rest of my family started to come to my parents home. I was beginning at this time not only hurting in my back, but grieving in my heart greatly, because I knew he was gone.

A few weeks before my brother died, I went to my parents and he was lying on the couch, somewhat like someone on a hang over. Before I awoke him, I noticed that there was large whelps and bruises near his middle arm area. I awoke him and said, "What in this world is wrong with your arms?" He said to me slowly and somewhat blurred, "I got into a hornets nest and they stung me." I said this, "My God. Too be sure you are not running dope again."

He didn't say anything else and fell back to sleep. When my father got the call, I knew deep down within my heart, that my brother was dead. I tried to stay calm and after the rest of my family came in, my back was beginning to hurt so bad I couldn't even stand upon my feet. I told my wife that I had to go home and lay down, before I passed out. So, we went home that evening.

It is Tuesday now, a day after my brother's death and two days after I had pulled my back. Everyone was to meet at my parents this day and prepare for my brothers funeral. I didn't make it to my parents until later that evening. By this time, I could barely walk, no kidding. I had my wife to go get me a walker from my parents. I walked into my parents with a walker in both hands that Tuesday. I stayed as long as I could and I had to leave, because of the pain. I had plan to go to the doctor the next day and guess what? I did make it to a doctor. It's Wednesday morning now, 3 days after my injury and two days after my brother's death. This particular morning, I awoke and never got a word out my mouth. My back went into spasms and my Wife had to call the Ambulance to me. I was in so great of enscusiating pain. It felt as if someone had a large knife and would take the knife and dig and turn it deep into my spine about every 5 minutes, no kidding. The paramedics got me stable with medicines in the Ambulance, until they could get me to the Hospital. When I got to the hospital the spasms continued for hours and my blood pressure was out the roof. They infused me with strong inflammation fluids and my spasms eased somewhat and I began to get stable again. I was admitted to the Hospital for four days. What is so Ironic about this incident is this; I never got to see my brother again. I didn't get a chance to go to the Wake or his funeral.

During the time of my brothers wake, people would come to the hospital and visit me also. It was a very strange time in my life. I felt like I was the one that died and began to think that it was all just a bad dream. Oh yes! Let me tell you this also and it's somewhat comical really.

I thought maybe you would like to giggle just a bit at this time, I sure do. When I was admitted to the Hospital you would never guess where they put me in a room at, The Labor Ward. That's right, in the labor ward where women have babies, no Kidding. I was in so much pain and screaming, I guess they didn't know what the deep problem was. So, I guess they thought maybe I was having a baby. Maybe I was having a baby or maybe I was being reborn at this time.

So, after these terrible times at these chances, things began to calm somewhat. My back got somewhat better after months of physical therapy and rest and then I went back to work. I was doing much better and again trying to live a normal life. I continued to live a normal life until something else happened. I had slowed on my drinking and was on my medications as prescribed and going back to church occasionally. My life was beginning to grow again and I was beginning to be much more happy and also my dear wife was much more happier. I would go to my parents and comfort them almost everyday. My parents were suffering extremely much for the lost of their son and my brother. I bought my mother a book which was, *"When the Bough Breaks-Forever After The Death Of A Son Or Daughter"*, written by Judith R. Bernstein, Ph.D. My mother would weep everyday after my brothers death and began to go deeply in depression. I would ask her day after day if she had read the book and she would tell me, "Yes son. I'm still trying to read it." and then she would start crying. I wouldn't disturb her in the grieving as she would leave the room and go back to the bedroom and shut the door. I'm not certain that she ever read the book, but I know that she tried.

During times like this, such as my brother's death or a close friend's death, I was numbed from grieving, because of so many in my life. But, I just couldn't had imagined if it had been my child, how much more would I had grieved.

Grieving during this time of my life, wasn't a grief as some would grieve. I knew that I had just lost my brother to the sinful nature of mankind, but I also knew that he loved God and believed in Jesus Christ, much so. My brother and I would talk sometime when I had the chance to talk with him and he would cry and suffer for his children and would always say that he wished things were much better in this World and his own life. He had 3 children at this time and his youngest child was just getting to understand life somewhat. His oldest child, which is a young adult female, is married now and has had a new born child. The youngest child, which is a male, is being fostered by his

Uncle and Aunt on his mother's side of her family at this time. But, the mother may sometime in the near future get back custody of my nephew. Life goes on, hey?

Today, I keep my mind on my brother sitting in Heaven preparing the time for his family to come. This particular brother was more than a brother to me, he was also one of my closest friends. Me and this brother were only 2 years of age difference. We had grown up together like two peas in a pod, but the sinful nature of mankind had separated us as we got older and older. I miss my brother greatly, but I know also his rewards on earth are done and his life is no longing in the care of this world. It grieves me deeply in my heart always about seeing my brother, but I know also, I have to wait and I don't need to rush things. The death of my brother was liken until a "*SLAP*" upon my face. This *slap* quickened me to reality and it made me understand again that this life isn't a self-will living party. This slap woke me, somewhat from a sleep, and I understood much clearly, that this life it is a matter of Life or Death. Not only did it again make me understand reality, it also made me understand that I needed to change my mind in the way I was thinking.

At this time, I had slowed, even more so, on my drinking and tried much more to live a normal life. It wasn't a matter of not wanting to die the way that my brother died, it was a matter of not putting my parents through anymore grief. My friend, have you every heard this saying; "*When it Rains, It Pours!*"? As time passed, after the death of my brother, my family and parents were trying to live with the great loss. It was an agonizing grief for my parents, such as, the following times for our family gatherings and there was an empty place at the dinning table.

CHAPTER NINE

A CALL FOR CHANGE

DURING THIS TIME, I WAS BEGINNING TO DRINK heavy again. There were many times I would call into work and call in sick from being so hung over or depressed where I couldn't get out of bed. I was still taken my medicines for my other illness, but I also began to slow on taken them as prescribed.

Now, I had 2 rental mobile homes on my property at this time and 1 was empty and 1 was vacated. In one of the Homes lived a young couple. The young man I knew from when he was but in diapers, and his parents are great friends of my parents, myself and my wife. His father was an elder in the church and is one of the most good men that I had ever met. This young man was a teenager in my youth ministry many years before, but at this time, he and his wife were on drugs and drank like whales.

During this time, most all of the teenagers that were in my youth ministry were either married or had moved away. There were a few that still hung out around town together and other places partying. I began to see these young people every now and then, but hid my drinking from them. I was a professor at this time at hiding things like this and it wasn't to hard to do. The hardest times of hiding anything was when I tried to hide things from my wife, follow me? That I just gave up on many years ago, because I didn't want to hide anything from my wife.

There was particular evening that this young man and his wife were partying at the mobile home and I thought that I would just walk over and visit them, as a guest. I did walk over and I began to party with them, no kidding. I started smoking weed with them and drinking heavy. So, later it wasn't abnormal for me and this young man to party together with his friends.

Now, there was one other young man in particular that was in the youth ministry many years before that I will never forget. I would see him ride by my property, but would never stop and talk to me. During the youth ministry he was the toughest all the rest to reason with.

Later not long after my young party friend and I became drinking buddies, I asked him if he had seen this particular boy and he told me where he was hanging out. He told me that this boy was hanging with some bike riders at a local riding club. One day as I was standing near my gate on my property, I seen him flash by on his vehicle like lightening. I waved to him, because I just wanted to talk with him, but, he kept going. About a week later, I would never get a chance to see this young man again. He was killed late one evening in a one car accident not but 1 mile from my home.

I just couldn't believe it at the time that there was another death and someone that I had great compassion for was dead. I went to the funeral at the church he had went to, which was the same church the youth ministry was organized. I was also one of his pallbearers. I set in the church and this was this first death that I couldn't hold my exposure. I whelped like a child for many days and I went into a major depressed state of mind. I had been through a lot of suffering before this time, but this time it felt as if I lost a son. I was beginning to think this; "All that I had showed this young kids and told these young kids wasn't worth the effort. I wished I never came into their lives. These kids are suffering because I'm not living up to what I preached to them and they see me as a hypocrite. I'm lesser than a dog!" My friend this was a great tragedy in my life, because even though this young man didn't come from my loins, I loved him as my own son. This young boy reminded me as myself when I was his age, struggling to understand. I will say this, I was beginning to understand what the grieving was all about now.

Now after the death of this young man, I stayed in a depressed state of mind for months. I continued to work, but I was calling in continually at this time for sick days. I would stay home and drink until sundown and weep much of the day. Even when times where good, I would just sigh from deep within my heart.

Later, I began to strengthen in my body and spirit man and I finally quit drinking. I began to take my medications as prescribed again and I somewhat started to get my life together. I also started going back to church again. I was once again trying to live a normal life, but something happened. One day, after several months had past after the death of this young man, I was out mowing grass. I started to smell something and you wouldn't believe what it smelled like. It smelled just like crack cocaine, no-kidding. I had been clean now for almost 6 months and I was getting much stronger day by the day. I was also taken my medications on a regular basis. I don't think I had missed one day of work during this entire time that I was clean and taking my medications. This smell kept getting stronger and I stopped mowing and just set there under a wax myrtle tree as if, I was trying to determined what I was smelling, was real. Then not only did I start to smell this odor, I began to somewhat taste it in my mouth, no kidding. About that same time I thought this; "Well a little want hurt. Plus, these medicines that I'm taken are just as bad as doing drugs. These medications are causing this!" I cut the mower off, got into my vehicle and guess what? If you guess that I went to get a crack rock, then you are well. That is exactly what I did and I continued on this binge, until this happened in my life:

One evening as I was on my binge, I started having chest pains at home and the pains became more frequent, somewhat like if you would ring out a wet rag once in awhile. I told my wife this, "Carry me to the hospital. I think I may be having a heart attack or stroke. Carry me to the best hospital in the Capital City." She carried me to a Hospital in the Capital City that was known for Heart Care.

So, I went to the hospital and they admitted me into the emergency area of the Heart Center. They checked my blood pressure and it was extremely high, so they needed to bring my blood pressure down. A nurse came in and told me that the shot they were going to administer to me would help calm me down and bring my blood pressure down. They were right, it did bring my blood pressure down and I die on the table there where I was laying. I don't remember nothing, except total darkness. I seen no light and neither heard any sounds, it was if I was in a Dark Abyss, waiting for something. This medicine they administered to me reacted on my body and literally killed me. The Doctors must had work on me for quite some time, because I did come back to the light within a hour. When I came back to feel the pains of my body, I remember screaming this; "Please Don't do that to me anymore! Please don't do that to me anymore!" I remember coming to somewhat, and hearing a small voice in the distant saying, "Mr., Mr., We lost you, we lost you. Mr., Mr., can you hear me? We have stop the medicine and it will calm down in a few moments." That was all I remember as my body was beginning to come alive again. They had placed Life Packs upon my body to contract my heart to help get it too function again. It was one of the most excruciating pains I had every felt. It felt as if my body was being sandwich between two Buffaloes every other minute. I had no strength to move.

At first, I was fearful to open my eyes, because I was thinking that maybe I was in Hell, no kidding. But, as I got the strength to open my eyes, I started to see some dim light through my eyelids. I kept feeling someone on my right side, rubbing my hand and I began to think that it was my wife.

After I finally open my eyes somewhat, everything seem to look smoky, somewhat like a fog. I was still determined to open my eyes and I began to see people walking around me. I couldn't make the faces or genders, but I knew they were human silhouettes.

I still couldn't hear much, but I began to get my senses back. I looked up to my right side, with eyes barely opened, and I was hoping my wife was there beside me. But, it wasn't my wife holding my hand, it was the Hospital's Chaplain. When I seen the chaplain, I began to weep somewhat, because I knew it wasn't too good. I still kept looking for my wife and I fixed my eyes on her as she was weeping, standing behind the Chaplain. Not only was my wife there, my parents were also there, weeping near the foot of the bed where I was laying. When I began to get my senses back and began to see these things, I knew that something had happen that just wasn't good. I must had been out for over 1 hour, because my parents lived 1 hour away from the hospital. Then I heard that voice again that I heard as I was coming too saying, "Mr. We lost you. Mr. we lost you. You'll ok now. Can you hear me?" I remember nodding my head in the yes gesture. I laid there in the emergency room for hours and then they admitted me into a room there at the hospital.

Now, I stayed in the hospital for evaluation and for a heart specialist to check my heart for several days. I remember what this heart specialist said to me also, after the examinations. He said this to me, "I don't know what caused the problem, but it certainly wasn't your heart. You have a good looking heart and I don't see anything wrong there. What ever the problem may be, you need to get more help with it." During this particular incident, I wrote some poetry and it is called,

THE ABYSS

I close my eyes from this world around me, only to see the darkness deep within me. I fall deeper within the doors of my heart and find the Abyss that compasses me about. No endings or searching of its infinite passages, as the darkness covers my total existence. I'm consumed with the darkness as a cloak that would wrap about me. I seem to feel safe in my own Abyss, but soon find out, I'm not sensing any of this. As the Fire Consumes and the Waters give Life, there's no searching of such things in my own dead life. But, Oh Lord you are always with me, even during the dark times of my Life. Your light shines within me and shows me the way, even in the valley of death. You hold the night and day in the palm of thy hand, Oh lord how long will it be before I can stand. Oh Lord, bring me now to thy Light, so I may live in your glorious sight."

Now, at this time I knew that this Doctor was telling me the truth. I thought that it may had been my heart, but it was all the things that I had done to my body. My friend, here is the reason why I had almost lost my life there at this hospital. I was suicidal and I was at the time hoping I would die. But looking back, if I didn't want to die, I made the wrong choice of hospitals to go to. This hospital was one of the Best known Heart Centers in the USA. Before I ever went to the hospital I was thinking this; "I know I'm on drugs heavy, but if I could just go to a hospital and get some help with these drugs, then maybe I can get back living normal again. They will give me medicines and I will quit this crap." My friend, not being honest with the Doctors as I was admitted to the Emergency room almost caused me to lose my life. I thought that I could quit the drugs on my own and hide it, but my thinking almost killed me. I didn't tell them the real reason why my blood pressure was so high. But I know the truth, If I would had told them that I was on cocaine heavy, they may not had gave me the shot that put me out. But, No! All I wanted was more drugs. I knew that if I went to this hospital with high blood pressure, they would certainly give me a shot and then I could tell then my problem, follow me? This kind of thinking almost killed me and I learned a very Life's Lesson there. The lesson is this; _Be honest with the Doctors, so that they can help you, rather than, kill you!_ I don't blame no one at the hospital, even if it may had been their fault, because sooner or later it was going to happen anyway.

My friend, that lesson I just couldn't comprehend at the time and I continued to use drugs, until I became suicidal. I totally quit my medications at this time and was again denying that I even had a Bi-Polar disease. I became so depressed at what was and had happen in my life and things around me just didn't matter anymore. But, my dear wife stood in and begged me to get help. She told me how much she loved me and my family loved me and they or her just couldn't bare another lose. So, I went and got help at a Hospital in the Capital city for my Illness and addiction. I was admitted and stay there for almost 14 days.

So, I went and got help at a Hospital in the Capital city for my Illness and addiction. I was admitted and stay there for almost 14 days. After I left this Hospital I was again getting stronger and I was again back on my medications as prescribed. I was again getting stronger and I was again back on my medications as prescribed. I did get somewhat better, but my friend I was beginning to deny again my Illness. I thought that I had accepted this illness early in my life, but I began to understand that I had deny it all the time.

I began to understand that my whole life had consisted of this deception and I would hide so great, even from my self. People would tell me that I was in denial, but I lent my ear to them as a duck with water on it's back. At this time I knew that I had an addition problem and had accepted this thorn many years ago. But, a Bi-Polar Disease? Now this was something that I couldn't believe that I had and I thought that is was because of all the different chemicals that I introduced to my body over the years and it wasn't a mental illness, but only a physical illness and I was able to solve this problem myself by not doing drugs or drinking alcohol.

After many episodes of depression, suicidal thoughts, mood changes, paranoids, and compulsive behaviors, I was beginning to accept what the Doctors had been telling me the whole time, was the truth. I had the understanding at this time, not only now would I have to be on the look out for the enemy, Satan, but also I had to be on the look out for myself. Accepting this Illness wasn't as hard to accept than that of what I thought, especially after time and time of the symptoms would arise. I never believed before this time that it was a problem with myself and I would always blame others for the failures of my life during this time. There at this Hospital I accepted this illness after Doctor and Doctor diagnosed me with the illness. I did start taking medications again and now I thought that this Illness was under control. I began to work and stay somewhat normal for a year.

Later I fell again. I didn't want to take all those medicines everyday and it wasn't long after I quit the medications I started to use again. I went on a drug binge and went completely out of control. I began to get suicidal again and worse. At this time, I again tried to accept my Illness, but I was blaming my Illness on my addition. I deceived my self from the truth of both. I thought that I wasn't going to live with both addition and a Bi-Polar disease and I didn't care if I would just die. I tried to control my Bi-Polar illness by another illness, which was addiction.

I convinced my self that the Bi-Polar was a symptom of my addiction and I could control my Bi- Polar by my additions. My friend, my life became disastrous and extremely deadly for what I believed to be the truth of my illnesses. I continued on this path of destruction for awhile, until, I began so bad off that I was committed to a hospital again. After a time at the hospital the Doctors requested me to a Rehabilitation Center again. There at the Hospital, the Doctors again tried to change my mind of what I believed to be the truth of my Bi-Polar disease and they did just that. They stabilized me back on my medications again and I was much better. It is somewhat strange of how I would be convinced one day and accept my Bi-Polar illness and the next day, I would deny it and blame my problems on other things.

When I left this particular Hospital I was doing great and becoming stronger by the second. I went to the Rehabilitation Center and stayed as long as I could. The Insurance I had at the time with the company that I worked with, wouldn't pay for all the time I needed at the Rehab center. But, it wasn't long that I started to use again. I started to blame the Insurance company for not understanding the sever-ness of my need of help and also, I blamed the counselors at the Rehab Center for not concentrating more on me. Not that I wanted all the attention, but it was if the Rehab was a fight for yourself experience. There wasn't one time I was counseled one on one about anything. Even when we were in group sessions the subject would be on what was going on in our life's that day. Most of the crap that I would sit in listen to was something like," Johnny and I had sex in the shower and were caught and we cant be near each other anymore. I think that is wrong and I don't know how to deal with it." My friend, I would set back and listen to crap after crap and decided that I needed to get the crap out of there and get some real help or I was going to die. I believe that the anger I had in me, that I didn't know I even had in me, was beginning to come to the surface of my mouth at this time.

This anger that I had toward this Rehab Center lead me even deeper into my own abyss. I knew at this time that I couldn't even trust a Doctor for the help I needed, with any problem in my life. I blamed the whole world at this time for my problems.

So, I thought that I could control my own problems. I started to use again and quit taking my medicines, because I lost the trust I had in the Doctors. I also quit going to my personnel Doctor I had been going to for years. I had quit drinking alcohol all together during this time, but I was using cocaine every weekend. I thought I could control my using by only doing it when I was suffering. My friend it was course straight to hell in my life. I will continue with that hell in just a moment, but first there is something I would like to share.

During about this time, the rental mobile home on my property was vacant once more. I really didn't want to rent it out to no one again, because of the problems I had before. I also knew I was using at this time and I didn't want no one to get into any of my business, follow me? One day my nephew came by my home and talked to me about renting the home. He was discourage and wanted to leave from his mother's home greatly. My brother and his mother had divorced around 12 years before this time and he was staying with his mother. This particular nephew I loved as if he was my only begotten son. When he was younger I would always take him deer hunting with me and fishing. When he got older he loved to fish and deer hunt. He also raised Walkers hounds and loved his dogs as I loved my animals. He would always talk to me about his hounds of how he was training them to hunt with him and of how smart they were. Every time I think about my nephew today, I think of how much he loved God and nature. He was an outdoors man and loved every thing that God had made for our use on this earth.

So, he wanted to move to my mobile home and get away from his mother. I don't know the true reason what was causing him to want to leave his home that greatly, but I knew his mother was also a user and drank alcohol like a fish would drink water. I believe also she was doing drugs. My nephew had a girlfriend at this time that he had met over the internet. They were of the same age, but she had been out in the world, much more than my nephew. My nephew wanted to get out of his mother's home and get somewhat more responsible, because of this relationship. Even though that may had been the problem at the time, but deep down in my heart, I knew he just wanted to be on his own and out of his mother's home. He would tell me that he needed to leave his mother, because he didn't like what she was doing and didn't want to be around what she was doing. My Nephew was 23 years of age at this time. So, when he asked me about renting the mobile home, I was quick to respond and said, "Yes! Of course you can stay there son. But you have got to behave and no loud music, bla, bla ,bla." I wanted my nephew there, because I knew he was going through a lot of troubled times in his life at this time. My brother would talk to me, when he got a chance to talk to me, about my nephew.

My brother would always tell me that he didn't want his son to end up like our brother did, dead. I felt a deep compassion and love for that boy as if he was my own son. He knew he could depend on me and trust me for what I would tell him. My nephew was also Bi-Polar and he look up to me as a good friend that he could depend on. I always knew my nephew had something mentally wrong with his life, because of his slow character as a child in his thinking and of the hospitalizations of his past. My nephew look up to me in that way of trust, but I looked up to him, because of his physical stature. He was 6' 5" and wore a 16" shoe and weighed around 300lbs. He was always a big boy in the body, but was somewhat like a child in his heart and just as gentle as a rose petal.

So, later my nephew and his girlfriend move into my rental home. My nephew began to get very sickly with excruciating pain from his back. He had a tumor growing on his spine, since he was but a small child. The Doctors in the past didn't think that it would grow much. He went to a special Doctor and they set him up immediately for a major back surgery. The Doctors removed this tumor and it was the size of a baseball from his spine, no kidding. I believe that this boy was suffering greatly and I also believe the pain from the tumor on his spine was the true reason he would use.

After the surgery, he was disable for quite some time and I would watch over him much. He didn't work, except maybe around his other Uncle's property that is a large piece of land, with horses and cows. My nephew had been drawing Disability since he was young from his mental illness. My nephew was a very depressed child at this time and was battling many dragons in his life I'm sure. He began to get better and was telling me that his back felt better, even though, he wasn't healed completely. My nephew grieved me within my heart, because I knew and felt the burdens of this young man's life. He knew that I was concerned for him and he would always say this, "Uncle. Its Ok. Don't worry about me, Ill be ok. I'm just going through some bad times right now. I will get better, I promise."

I remember about this very time of my nephews surgery I had gotten a Large Blood Hound from a Animal Shelter. I was setting and talking to a friend at the shelter when a man came in with this Large Hound on a lease. He wanted to give her up and I just couldn't believe that someone with such a beautiful animal, would want to just give it up. But later, I knew why and will share it in just moment. I asked the man what her name was and he was quick to tell me her name was, "Shelby." So, I took the Hound home with me that day and it was somewhat strange. This hound howled somewhat like it was talking to me and licked my face, with the slobber of course, and it was if she was thanking me for saving her life.

So, I carried this Large Hound home with me that day and I let her loose on my property that was completely fenced in. This hound was happy for a new home and I and this hound became buddies. This blood hound was somewhat aggressive toward anything or any person near my gate or own my property. I remember clearly the time as my nephew was somewhat better and he went outside and I seen him standing near my fence. I had told my nephew earlier not to try to come on the property with out me or stick his hands over the fence either, because I knew that the blood hound would bite. This particular day, I seen as if my nephew was about to stick his hand over the fence and I shouted at him not to do it. But my nephew said this, "Ah. Uncle, she want bite me. She's a good little dog." About that moment he did stick his hand over the fence and that hound gashed a wound in his hand about 2" long and 1' deep. I said, "I said not to do it. Are you Ok? I believe you need stitches." My nephew looked at me as he held his hand tightly with his other hand to keep it from bleeding as bad and said, 'Uncle it isn't that bad. I will be Ok. Don't worry about it Uncle. The medicines I'm on I cant feel it anyway. Have you got a band aid?" And then he giggled somewhat. My friend, he needed more than a band aid. I cleaned the wound and bandaged it with gauze and medical tape. I will never forget the laugh from my nephew that day when the dog bit him. I believe I would had scream, but he laughed and said, "She didn't mean to bite me. She accidentally bit me." and again he would giggle and laugh.

I remember one occasion as she bit the hind side of a telephone man's foot as he was walking up my steps to check my phone service. She also hemmed in my neighbor under my neighbor's carport and my neighbor had to call my wife at work to come and get her. This hound was somewhat intelligent and trained my other hound how to climb a 5' chain link fence.

This hound would get out from my property and I couldn't find no where he could get out. Then one day I seen the female blood hound and my other hound near the fence. I seen my male hound jump straight up as a jack rabbit would from a hole, right on the top of the fence. He was perched like a bird and looked left and right and then jump to the other side. Not only was that amazing, this male hound was on the out side of the fence digging, while the female blood hound was on the inside digging.

I truly believe the female, which was full blooded, train my mixed hound to jump to the other side and help her escape from the property, no kidding. They were like a team, determined to escape from a prison. I finally had to chain the female up.

This female, full blooded hound, would look at me with those saggy eyes and lowly ears as if she knew she was going to get me back for chaining her up. I would also say this to her as she somewhat gave me the eyes, "You best not look at me that way and don't you even think I'm letting you off that chain. If you ever do what you have done again, I will carry you back from where I got you. Do you here me?!" I'm not kidding, this hound seemed to me as if she was a English teacher or a professor in the language, except without glasses and she knew every word that I was saying. When I would say this to her she would somewhat look down with those saggy eyes and pout and wine all night.

Later it seemed to me as if this Large hound was getting Larger. I said to my wife, "We need to quit feeding her as much. Look how big she's getting!" Then my wife said this to me, "Are you crazy. You didn't only bring this hound home with you, you also brought her whole family home. She's pregnant stupid." That right, she was pregnant and that was the reason the man carried her to the pound. We helped raise 11 puppies from this Hound and it was a joy, burdensome, but a joy.

Later about the same time as my nephew found another place to stay with his girlfriend, I had no choice, but to carry this Blood Hound back to the pound, no kidding. She was breaking every chain I would out around her neck, unless the other hound had a pair of bolts cutters, and she would dig out my property and hem my neighbors in their yards. It really hurt me, but I had no choice. But I did give her the chance to have her babies and they all got a good home. I also believe she got another home and she was adopted from the pound. I'm sure she's somewhere given another man the understanding that she gave me at the time she was in my life, positive.

Now, during this time of my life, I was doing somewhat better. I had stop using drugs as much, but began to drink again. My nephew and his girlfriend had moved from my property to a house about 3 miles away. The male hound at this time, I had no control of keeping him inside the property, so I just let him be. Not long after, he was killed by a vehicle and it broke my heart. I remember the very night that it happened. I was using drugs this night and was standing out side, somewhat zombilized. I knew that my hound, whose name was "Chomper" wasn't on the property, but I didn't think nothing about it, because he would do this all the time. This time that I was using outside, I heard something just down the road, as if someone threw a steel chain in a bed of a truck. I thought someone had wreck, but I didn't think nothing else about it. The next mourning, which was a Saturday, my younger brother and my father delivered the body of my hound.

That evening before I got the body, I felt deep within me that Chomper was dead, but I just didn't want to go and see the reality and the consequence of my sin. I know things happen, but I knew that I loved my drugs more than I loved my buddy, Chomper. I know if I hadn't been doing drugs and wasn't zombilized during these times, I would had found away to keep him from danger, but I just let him be and he died for me.

When I had an animal, such as "Chomper" my beloved hound, "Spirit" my first loved Chihuahua, "Shorty" my beloved Dachshund and "Shelby" my educated beloved hound, I would love them as Christ loved me. I treated them as I would want another man to treat me. I really loved these animals with great compassion. I believe it is because I know they suffer just in the same likeness as a man suffers, spiritually and physically, no kidding. I had Chomper for 8 years at this time.

Now, I remember the very day of how "Chomper" came into my life. All my animals came in my life in a special way, but Chomper I will expand on. I believe the reason I'm expanded on Chomper's entrance in my life, is that he gave his life for me to receive another understanding from God. I know that you maybe thinking I'm crazy at this time, but feel with me my friend for the point is coming.

During this time that "Chomper" came into my life was 8 years earlier. I was doing great and living a normal life. It was the Easter season and my wife and I went to my sister's church to visit for the Easter service. As we left the church we were traveling toward home when I noticed something small in the middle on the road. I thought maybe it was a wild dead animal, but when I got closer I noticed it was a puppy. I thought the puppy had been ran over, but when I stopped and got out of my vehicle, and then touched this puppy, he stood up and wagged his tail and licked my pant leg. He was so beautiful and I felt in my spirit that it wasn't no coincidence that this animal was just lying in the middle of a road waiting for me. I took the puppy into my arms and went to a house that was near where I found the puppy. When I pull into the yard, I knew where the puppy came from. The man had puppies coming out from everywhere you could imagine. I knocked on the door and a ruggy looking young man came to the door with no shirt or shoes on. I ask him if this was his puppy and he said, "Yes sir. I believe that is one of them. Do you want him?

Sir, you can have more than one, I got plenty. "and I was quick to say," No. I would like to have only this one, because he was waiting for me in the road. "and we both giggled together. Then this man said quickly, "Wait! Let me worm him first. I wouldn't want him to die of any worms." and I thanked him for the worm treatment and the gift of the animal. I raised this puppy as if he was my own son, no kidding. I had another before him and his name was "Spirit". I had to put him down because of a bad heart and this puppy came into my life about two weeks after, I had to put my beloved "Spirit" down. I believe the reason I'm writing of these animals is that my nephew loved his animals in the same way as I loved my animals. My nephew treated his hounds just like if they were his only friends.

My friend, later about the same time that "Chomper" was killed, my family got some horrible news. *My nephew had accidentally died from a drug overdose.* It was a greater slap upon my face, than that of, my hound dying. I went to my brothers side as he went into a hysterical state of mind. I went with him and comforted him as we went and identified his precious son's body at the morgue. As the Hospital attendant opened the cooler where my nephew laid, my brother completely lost since of reality. I was calm somewhat and tried to comfort my suffering brother. All the worse that he every thought would happen, had happened and it was laying right before his eyes in reality. My nephew was lying on a steel gurney as if he was asleep with his shirt open. He had no cover to cover his body and my Brother began to blame everything and everyone he could fix his eyes upon.

My friend, it was a horrible time in my families life again. We had just lost another of our children to this awful sinful world.

At this time my friend, after the death of my nephew, things began to come out of my heart that I didn't really know that existed. I went into a depressed and suicidal state of mind. I was using worse than I had every used in my life. Day after day, night after night, I stayed numb from reality.

I didn't want nothing to happen like this in my life again and I wanted to die. I was tired of seeing so much death in my life and I just didn't want to live in this world any longer. I was sick and tired of trying to live a normal life and then fall and then something from God would Slap me in the face to awake me from my sleep. I started to blame God for all my suffering and wished he would take my life every day. I didn't want God or my family in my life anymore. I was thinking now that this life was all about survival and not living. I lost all hope that I had at the time in a split second. I began to think that nothing matter to me anymore and I hated this world deeply within my heart. I was asking God please destroy us before we destroy ourselves. "Why are you God allowing this to happen?!! Why God?! Why?! Why don't you just kill me and get me out of this stinking filthy world, before I get myself out of it.!? I began to go into the worse state of depression I had every experienced. I began to use everyday and I eventually had to resign from my job, because of using. I would be stopped by law enforcement many times and searched for drugs. I was spending money that wasn't even my own. My addiction got a hold on me and I was now in the worse state that I had ever been in my entire life. I stayed on this drug binge for one whole year, using everyday. I was so numb from reality my family even began to prepare for my death, no kidding. I had lost so much weight that my eyes were sinking back into my forehead. I wasn't working from using. My family didn't want to see me this way, so I stayed away from them. My wife had even given up hope and she also was preparing for my death. My wife cried almost every day pleading for me to get help.

During this time, I was working at a Manufacturing Plant that Specialized in Truck Body building. I was an Industrial Electrician that specialized in special projects for the owner. I will say this; God Won the Battle of my Life! God will Win ever time my friend, no matter how much you kick against the pricks. God will Win with no doubt!

It was a learning chance in my Life and this job was a great lesson. I had struggled my whole life to finally get to this pint of my life with understand of Reality. At this time I was confident of the word Reality, but I had a greater hope in the things from God than the things of this World. I knew if I didn't change my way of living I would had been dead and lost forever. Like I said I really didn't understand reality in it's trueness, but I pressed forward for the understanding. One day as I was using I looked into the mirror and for a second seen myself as a dead man. I looked closer and seen that I had age in this little time, much more than I had age in 10 years. I looked even closer and I fell to my knees and prayed out loud to God to help me. There was something coming out deep within that I didn't know was there. This something was reality of a hole of survival kicking in. I prayed and pleaded with God to help me get out of this death that I was living. The hope of survival was my only hope, but it gave me enough of hope to look at myself in the mirror for one second. My friend, I wept the whole day before God pleading for salvation. I knew I was dying and it wasn't a matter of "IF" it was a matter of just "When". When I seen myself in the glass, I was ashamed of my self, but I really didn't want to die. I was just bound by the thorns and the chains of my addictions and I needed God to help me. I had no choice at this time to call on God again, unless I would die.

So, I began to get back on my medication for my mental illness and other Illnesses and tried to stop using on my own. I did mange to stop using for a chance and I got another job, but I continued using some. I did good for about 6 months, but then I fell hard.

Later, there was a particular day when my wife came home from work, I held her in my arms and said, "I'm Sorry, carry me to the hospital now!" We couldn't go at that moment so we agreed to go the next day. The next day I was admitted to the hospital again and this time, I was confident I would get help. I knew at this time if I don't get help, I would surely die soon.

When I was being admitted into the hospital, their was man that can in to the room where my wife and I were sitting. I was beginning to deny again and I wanted to leave the hospital and was getting somewhat irate. This man said this to me, "You best set down and calm down, because if you don't commit yourself voluntary, I will commit you involuntary. You are not leaving this hospital in the condition you are in." My friend when this man said this to me, it was if my own father would say such as he loved me. I felt the love and compassion of this man and then I stared to sense again the truth of my condition. This hospital was for detoxification and Mental Illnesses. I will say it took me almost 14 days to get my sense of reality back functioning again. I remember the Doctors coming into my room several times at night checking my blood pressure, because it wouldn't register by the nurse.

Later, after I began to get well at the Hospital and my medications stable, the Doctors requested me to go back to the Rehabilitation Center for more treatment and I did. Now, I want to share something with you that came to my mind as a revelation of something great. I will say I started getting the revelations at the Hospital and the Treatment Center, but later it manifested into a greater revelation of understanding. I call these writings, *"What Hope?"*

WHAT HOPE?

It seemed like every time I found myself at, or, near the Big Hole, I would be desperate for something or someone to help me, turn me and deliver me, from facing the hole. When I speak of the Hole, I'm speaking of void, emptiness or even death. I would be so desperate at these times that my compulsive reactions from my own self will thoughts, would be even more devastating. I didn't know how to ask for help and I definitely didn't know what to ask for, during these times of desperation. I remember crying out, "God!

Please help me or kill me! I was so far from God in my self will and sin, I thought God would never hear me, but I cried out for him louder and louder within myself; for I wanted the horrors to stop. I thought the only thing left for me to do, was to survive just for that day. I had no hope for tomorrow and sometimes for that day. I had no Hope in God, myself or others at these times and trusted no one for my Life. The only hope that I did have, was the Hope of Survival, I will call it for now. I knew I was in a terrible mess and I didn't think there was any hope for me; for all that I had trusted in, had vanished away. The hope of survival came from somewhere that I just could not put my finger on during these desperate times. I really didn't want to physically die, but I thought to myself, "if I have to keep living the way I'm living, death would be just for me; for I was suffering, others were suffering and all creatures were suffering for me."

I believe that every creature that breaths under heaven has the hope of survival embedded into their spiritual being, even animals. What is Hope? Hope is to desire with expectation of fulfillment. When we hope for something, we began to desire for it and expect that it will happen in our life. Hope isn't Faith, but the beginning process of Faith in something; for faith is in the Will of Hope, as a reward. In the Holy Book of Romans, Chapter 8, verses 24-25 reads as written, *"For we are saved by hope: but hope that is seen is not hope: for what a man seeth, why doth he yet hope for? But if we hope that we see not, then do we with patience wait for it."* This Hope of Survival is there waiting patiently within our spirits, until we reach a point in our life, that death is drawing us to complete obliteration.

I know this hope was for me to survive for another day and to give me a hope for a chance once more, to better my life. But, the last time of my desperation, I really didn't want to live anymore; for the hope of survival wasn't even helping me at this time.

I thought at the time, if I hadn't changed by now, after all that God and others had done for me in the past, then I wasn't going to change, and I was beginning to give up on this life. But, God's Word came to me like the wind and reads in Ecclesiastes chapter 9, verse 4-5, *"For to him that is joined to the living there is hope: for a living dog is better than a dead lion. For the living know that they shall die: but the dead know not anything, neither have they any more reward; for the memory of them is forgotten."* Because I was still alive physically, I still had hope and this hope, wasn't giving up so easy for me. I will say this with confidence, as long as you and I are still alive, there is hope and I believe also that this hope can not be destroyed; for it is a gift from God. But, this hope can be over looked, refused or sensed at times of desperation and cause a man to be drawn into the big hole of death, if a man is without understanding of this hope. This Hope is always there in our spirit, patiently fighting for life, and as long as the living are here on earth, this hope will always be there within us. This hope came to us from God and It is embedded into our spirit, which cannot die. It is there for Life and for change from facing the hole before our time. It is one more chance of living and not dying the death. Looking back through my desperations and wanting, this hope pointed me into a different direction than I was living, rather than survival for the day.

Today, I can say I have a better Hope than that of just the Hope of Survival and that my friend, is the Hope in God and His Son Jesus Christ. This hope of survival pointed me to heaven and God, and I reacted on it in desperation, knowing it had to be better than, facing the Ultimate Big Hole. Once God intervened into my Life, it was up to me to grab hold onto it for dear life, and I did just that. I believe you have this hope, even if you don't believe in God, the Creator of all Living. This Hope of Survival points a man to God as our Creator and is the only Hope in desperation or facing the Big Hole.

At the time of my desperation, I knew that this hope came from deep within my spirit man crying out, "Please Hear me God! Help Me! Please Lord! Save me from the horrors!" and this hope pointing me to God as my only Hope, at the time.

Sometimes when I was facing the big hole, I felt in my heart that I was an unworthy man to receive anything from God and would not cry out to him; for I didn't believe he would hear my desperate cry. I was being lead by self will pleasures and acting on compulsive behaviors from the past experiences that I had stored in my mind; for I had lost my understanding of the Great Hope. My spiritual man was leaving my body; for I had quench the Spirit of God from my life and my body was dying. I was living by my past experiences from my mind that I had stored in it and my heart was only pumping life through my veins to keep me alive, second by second. But, I didn't want to live the way I was living and I would think, that there had to be a better way of living. I had lost all that had been given to me for understanding of Hope from the past and this Great Hope that I once had in God and his Son Jesus Christ, had vanished away from my heart.

There wasn't any of the Ten Commandments that I had not broken at this time and looking back, seeing the faces of my precious Wife, Father and Mother, Family and Church and all those who were suffering for me, even my little Chihuahuas, flashing like a photo book in my mind, I was killing them. I was surely tearing there hearts out and they were dying spiritually for me, but I was without understanding of the matter at this time again. While I was in Drug Rehabilitation for the last time, these images in my mind gave me some hope. I knew within my spirit that I must do something to change, because I knew at the time, it wasn't all about me; for others were also suffering and dying for me. It was if their spirits were crying out to me, "LIVE!LIVE!LIVE! We Love you and we don't want you to die."

These photos in my mind would pop up in my sleep, as I was in groups and even eating meals and all the faces of my loved ones would have tears flowing down their faces, even my Chihuahuas and I would start to cry within my heart, very much.

I know today with confidence that it was God's Spirit showing me that I had much to change for and He didn't want me to die either and wanted me to have Life; for I had much to live for and had hope. So, I began wanting and was willing to change for the better and stood still and let Go and began to Let God into my life again and began to hope on this matter. As I started to believe in this Hope again, I began to put my hope in God and his Son Jesus Christ. At this very time, a few of us men were talking about past experiences and a very compassionate Spanish man was among us. We were in the same group, but never talked much together.

At this time, I was beginning to come out of my turtle shell and was searching for God and anything that would help me get better and well. At the Rehab Center, I had even over heard this question concerning me, "Is he a Mute?" I didn't say nothing and didn't want to talk to no one; for I just listened and didn't trust no one for my life. But, this Spanish Man came up to me and ask me very softly with gentleness and compassion in his voice and said, "How are you? My name is --_____. I have something that you need to read. It is a little book, but I feel within my spirit that it might be something that you need at this time. Will you read it, if I go and get it for you?" and I felt this mans love for me and I said as I was still crying within my spirit, "Yes, I'm Willing." So, he went to fetch this little book for me and brought it to me. When I seen the little book, I began to have a Joy within my spirit and I began to giggle. The name of the little book was, "Who Moved My Cheese". I read this book and I got an answer of one of my battles that I was struggling with at this time. This little book gave me insight within my darkened heart and then I was ready to face the big battles.

I do remember as I was trying to read this little book that I went into a room to be alone and there was a younger man sitting. I would go into this room and play music on the guitar from my heart. This young man had the community guitar and handed it to me and said, "Will you play me something that is dark?" and I responded by saying, "Dark! I only play from my heart. You don't need to be listening to dark music!" and then the young man said to me with a very soft compassionate voice, "I've been listening to you play from the hallway and it sounded dark from inside your heart and I felt it and it was very touching to me. Dark, really doesn't mean Evil, but could be a dark time in someone's life." I didn't know what to say, but I began to believe that this young man knew more than I thought he knew and then I said to him, "I remember being in Church one day and a Minister was preaching on the Dark Times in a man's life. He would say that the dark times was like a dark thread woven into a covering, and if it wasn't for the dark threads, the covering would not be as beautiful." And then I played the guitar as I was in a darken time of my life for this young man. Me and this young man began to feel the pains of dark times in our lives and began to minister to each other. God had sent another person into my life at this very moment to give me understanding that the dark times are not all evil; for they are for understanding and we will go through them, but not stay in them. "Do you imagine that it perhaps was a dark time on the earth when Jesus was crucified on the cross of Calvary?"

So after me and this young man that I had just met went about our own, I began to read the Little Book, "Who Moved My Cheese?" This little book was all about change and it was if God sent this Spanish Man into my Life also at that very moment of my life. Please read this Little book sometime, if you get the chance, *"Who moved my cheese?"*

I will say this book didn't give me the great hope I was searching for, but it definitely helped change the way I was thinking at the time.

I will always thank God and these two men for listened to there spirit and sharing with me this understanding.

There was another word giving to me at this time and It reads like this, ***"For by Grace are ye saved through Faith; and that not of yourself: It is the gift of God: Not of works, lest any man should boast."*** Grace, being defined, means Favor and it was by God's Grace that I was saved from the Horrors and facing the Big Hole. I put my Hope in God and His Son Jesus Christ and they were Faithful to bring me to the judgment seat at their feet, once more and they found me at the seat of judgment before them, worthy to live. But, why would God favor someone like me, who was not worthy of receiving his Grace or the air I was breathing? I believe it was because I called on him, when I cried out "God please help Me! Lord! Please save me!". When cried out and I said, "God" something miraculous happened. Grace is where our Hope lives and we are all his creation and his children, because He created us in his image as a spiritual man. All mankind and creation are under his Umbrella of Grace.

Now, In the Holy Book of Lamentations, Chapter 3, gives a perfect writing for all mankind that have every experience Grief and the point of No Hope. It also writes the relief from these experiences and gives great hope. It reads as written, *"I am the man that hath seen affliction by the rod of his wrath. He hath led me, and brought me into darkness, but not into light. Surely against me has he turned; he turneth his hand against me all the day. My flesh and my skin has he made old: he had broken my bones. He hath builded against me, and compassed me with gall and travail. He had set me in the dark places, as they that be dead of old. He had hedged me about, that I cannot get out: he hath made my chain heavy. Also when I cry and shout, he shutteth out my prayer. He hath enclosed my ways with hewn stone, he had made my paths crooked. He was unto me as a bear lying in wait, and as a Lion in secret places.*

He hath turn aside my ways, and pulled me into pieces: he had made me desolate. He hath bent his bow, and set me a mark for his arrow. He hath caused the arrows of his quiver to enter into my reins. I was a derision to all my people; and their song all day. He hath f illed me with bitterness, he had made me drunken with wormwood. He hath also broken my teeth with gravel stones, he hath covered me with ashes. And thou hast removed my soul far off from peace: I forgot prosperity. And I said, My strength and my hope is perished from the Lord: Remembering mine affliction and my misery, the wormwood and the gall. This I recall to my mind, therefore have I hope. It is of the Lord's Mercies that we are not consumed, because his compassions fail not. They are new every morning: great is thy faithfulness. The Lord is my portion, saith my soul; therefore will I hope in him. The Lord is good unto them that wait for him, to the soul that seeketh him. It is good that a man should both hope and quietly wait for the Salvation of the Lord. It is good for a man that he bear the yoke in his youth. He sitteth alone and keepeth silence, because he hath borne it upon him. He putteth his mouth in the dust; if so be there may be hope. He giveth his cheek to him that smiteth him: he is filled full of reproach. For the Lord will not cast off for ever. But though he cause grief, yet will he have compassion according to the multitude of his mercies. For he doeth not afflict willingly nor grieve the children of men. To crush under his feet all the prisoners of the earth, To turn aside the right of a man before the face of the most High, To subvert a man in his cause, the Lord approveth not. Who is he that saith, and it cometh to pass, when the Lord commandeth it not? Out of the mouth of the most High proceedeth not evil and good? Wherefore doth a living man complain, a man for the punishment of his sins? Let us search and try our ways, and turn again to the Lord. Let us lift up our heart with our hands unto God in the heavens.

We have transgressed and rebelled: thou hast not pardoned. Thou hast covered with anger, and persecuted us: thou hast slain, thou hast not pitied. Thou hast covered thyself with a cloud, that our prayer should not pass through. Thou hast made us as the off scouring and refuse in the midst of the people. All of our enemies have opened their mouths against us. Fear and a snare is come upon us, desolation and destruction. Mine eye runneth down with rivers of water for the destruction of the daughter of my people. Mine eye trickleth down, and ceaseth not, without any intermission, Till the Lord look down, and behold heaven. Mine enemies chased me sore, like a bird, without cause. They cut off my life in the dungeon, and cast a stone upon me. Waters flowed over mine head; then I said, I am cut off. I called upon thy name, O Lord, out of the low dungeon. Thou hast heard my voice: hide not thine ear at my breathing, at my cry. Thou drewest near in the day that I called upon thee: thou saidst, Fear not. O Lord, thou hast pleaded the causes of my soul; thou hast redeemed my life. O Lord, thou hast seen my wrong; judge thou my cause. Thou hast seen all their vengeance and all their imaginations against me. Thou hast heard their reproach, O Lord, and all their imaginations against me; The lips of those who rose up against me, and their devices against me all the day. Behold their sitting down, and their rising up; I am their music. Render unto them a recompence, O Lord, according to the work of their hands. Persecute and destroy them in anger from under the heavens of the Lord.

I know God doesn't want to loose any of his children or to destroy his marvelous creation, but if only they will do his Will. Today I can say with confidence, the hope of survival that I thought I had, was that of God's Loving Grace for all mankind and his creation.

The hope that I had at desperate times when I was facing the big hole was my spirit calling out from within, "LIVE!LIVE!LIVE by GRACE!" I call the hope, the Hope of Survival, but I know today, it was by God's Loving Grace for all mankind, that I didn't die the ultimate death. Today I know that it wasn't the Hope of survival that would deter me from the big hole; for it was my Hope of God and by his Grace found me worthy to live.

When I was without, empty and void, I almost fell into and was facing the Big hole many times, but by the Grace of God, it never consumed me. It seemed as if I had a choice each time that I would face the Big hole, such as, fall in or walk away. I always went back in the same direction from where I was just Living in, Horror and miseries. I thought, going back could be no worse than falling into the Big Hole. But, at times there where thoughts of just falling in and being consumed by the Big Hole and just end all the horror I was living at the time. I really never wanted to die, but the Horror was to much for me to take and I just wanted for the horrors to stop. I always tried to do the best that I could under circumstances, but I know the good intents were not enough; for I was without understanding.

Today, I do understand that there is nothing that I have control of concerning God's Loving Grace, except, live in it freely; for it is a gift from God for all mankind and his creation. I really wanted to live a good life during these desperate times of my life, but my self will had taking me over and I had lost the Hope that I once had.

The last time that I was facing the Big Hole, I had a vision. I was in a Rehabilitation Center at this time and I was trying to let go and let God. This vision I titled, *"God's Finger of Hope."*

The Apathetical Man

GOD'S FINGER OF HOPE

I was in a Rehab Center and had been clean from illegal drugs for about 3 weeks. In this dream, it seemed to me as if there was a Finger pointing at me from a big hole, as if it was a grave. There when I seen the finger point at me, I thought the finger was pointing back to the direction I just came from. I respond quickly and tried to run back into the Horrors and misery, but soon I turn and was facing the Hole again. Then, this finger reached toward me and touched me and the touch, got my attention! I felt something that I hadn't felt since I was but a child.

I felt a touch of Peace, Love, Understanding. I stood there facing the Big Hole for a few more moments and I was like a dead man in my dream and I couldn't move. I watch as the Finger pointed at me and then, slowly pointed up toward heaven. In the dream, I never stood still long enough to see the Finger point toward Heaven, because I was running back and forth from the Big Hole; for I was without understanding of the matter. I would see the finger point in the same direction I had just come from and would think, going back, had to be better than falling into the big hole. But this time, after seeing the finger point toward heaven and it touched me, it quickened my spirit and I knew at that moment that I needed Hope in God and His Christ, much more than, only the hope of Grace.

When the Finger of Hope touched me, I opened my eyes to see it point toward heaven and God and then I knew in my spirit, that I needed the Hope of God, rather than, the Hope of Grace only. The Hope of Grace only got me from the Hole, but the touch from God's Finger of Hope, keeps me from and out of the Big Hole. We all need to be touched by God's Finger of Hope, to bring us to, where he wants us to be, in His Will. My self-will pleasures carried me to the Big Hole many times and the Hope of Grace saved me from falling into the big hole many times, but now I know, doing Gods Will keeps me from the Big Hole, if only I do God's Will. When I seen the Finger of Hope pointing toward God, I knew at that second what I had to do. I had to Hope and believe in God, to save me from the Hole and the Horror I was living. Once I started Hoping and believing God was able to save me at this time, God responded with a Miracle, *Resurrection!* I began to come alive again and began to sense things better and I was being restored; for I was being Resurrected from my spiritual death. Here is the Point: For by Grace we are saved from the Big Hole, if we believe it to do so, but Grace cant keep a man from going back to the Big Hole over and over again.

God's Grace is like an Umbrella over his creation, but if Grace alone could save a man eternally, when he would cry out in desperation to God, then the Death and Resurrection of his Son Jesus Christ on the cross of Calvary would be no effect today for all mankind. Sure we are all under God's Grace, but there is more than just God's Grace. I Thank God every second of my Life for his Grace for me and all mankind and that he doesn't just come down from his throne with anger and destroy all of his creation like he did in the Book of Genesis.

Remember Noah's Ark? But today we are under his Umbrella of Grace. Today, I now know that the finger I seen in my dream was God's Finger of Grace. There is much more than just having hope in his Grace, but I will say, it is a start at the first step in faith in God; for it is our Hope that we find favor in God's Eyes like Noah. Grace is a gift for all mankind and his creation. God's Grace is there for man's choice and we cant work for it; for it is a gift from God to mankind and for all creation. Grace alone doesn't save a man from Mortality or Immortality and by just thinking, "Well, I'm saved by God's Loving Grace forever!" That is a truth, but only half the truth; for that isn't the way it is writing in God's Word. In God's Word, Matthew chapter 24, verse 13 reads, ***"But he that shall endure to the end, the same shall be saved."*** God's Grace, if we call on it, can save a man from dying the death eternally at that moment of desperation. Remember the Malefactors that were crucified with Jesus at Calvary?

Today I know that I don't want to be paying the consequences self will pleasures by hanging on a cross and then have to start believing in Jesus Christ to save me from the death. But I will say this, the malefactor that believed Jesus was Lord, did go with Jesus Christ to paradise that day, because he believed that Jesus was Lord. I don't want to wait to believe in Christ when I'm laying on my death bed any more. I want what God and his Son Jesus Christ wants to give me now, while I'm Alive.

Sure the malefactor went to paradise with the Lord that day, but you can have paradise in your life as you live here on earth today, but if only a man will follow God's Will. Today I know that God's Finger of Grace kept me from falling into the Big Hole, time after time, but I also know doing God's Will keeps a me from going back to the Big Hole.

At the time I had this vision, I had already called on God and by his Grace and his faithfulness of his promise, I was saved from the Big Hole, but God didn't leave me just having the Hope of his Grace; for now he was showing me the Way to Life Everlasting and Life on earth much more abundantly. Grace is there in the Hope of Life, waiting patiently for a man to call on it; if the man calls on it. After a man accepts and believes in God's Loving Grace to save him from the horror at the time, then God is able to work through that man to show him the Way to Life everlasting and there is no other way. The touch from God's Finger of Hope (*His Loving Grace*) began a Stepping Process from the Horrors and self will pleasures I was living for so long, to Peace and Understanding of Life. Peace and understanding of Life and that is what I had always wanted since I was but a child and back into the Loving Arms of God my Father. When I called on God, he heard my cry. Yes! The God of Creation, The God of Existence, heard this old worthless sinner, not worthy to breathe the air he made and had been sentence to death from my own self will choices. When I called out his name in desperation, God found favor (Grace) in me and reached down and took me in his arms and said with a Loving, compassionate voice through my spirit, "My child, son, where have you Been?" God, already knew me when I was created; for he created my spirit, but it was up to me to call on Him and doing so, God rewarded me with faith. I put my mustard seed size of faith that I had at the time, into action.

Yes, this old filthy sinner called on him, crying like a child in desperate need from within my desperate spirit. When I cried out to God, this was the beginning of my Resurrection and Spiritual Awakening.

In God's Word, it clearly showed me my course I was taking and a new course I am taking today. It is written and reads, Ephesians Chapter 2, verse 1-7, *"And you has he quickened, who were dead in trespasses and sins; Wherein in time past you walked according to the course of this world, according to the prince of the power of the air, the spirit that now worketh in the children of disobedience: Among whom also we all had our conversation in times past in the Lusts of the Flesh, fulfilling the desires of the flesh and the mind; and were by nature the children of wrath, even as others. But, GOD, who is rich in mercy, for his great Love wherewith he loved us, Even when we were dead in sins, hath quickened us together with Christ, (by Grace ye are saved;) And hath raised us up together, and made us sit together in heavenly places in Christ Jesus: That in the ages to come might shew the exceeding riches of his Grace in his kindness toward us through Christ Jesus."*

I started hoping and believing in God for who he was and then I put my faith in Him into Action! I had to believe Him and His Will for the saving of my life and I began to come ALIVE again, like a new born child and I began to grow stronger in my spirit and my mind. My mind had to be renewed from the past and the Spirit of God was working through my spirit and shinning the Light of Life into the dark crevices of my Heart. God's Spirit was somewhat like a searching Light, searching for bugs hidden deep within dark hidden places of my heart.

After I had the vision of the Finger of Hope, it seem to me as if every day when I would get honest with my self and God and God's Searching light would shine deep into my heart, there would be a dragon to come out of these dark hidden places within my life at this time and they would want to battle me and we did battle. I did defeat these dragons, but there was a greater dragon that just did not want to give up.

I searched the Bible and prayed every night to God asking, "Please God! Help me with this battle; for it is to great for me to battle." The battle was definitely a Self Will intent, but I just didn't have the understanding of the matter at that time. I was battling something that

I had battled my whole life and it was a great battle. In my past life I would had just gave up and start using to numb me from the pains of this battle, but at this time I knew that I had to defeat this great battle in order for me to live or I was going to die with no doubt. During my past life, when I was weak and I wanted to battle this great battle of self will, things would come into my life and make the battle worse than it was in reality. I know today that Satan knows when a man wants to do the right thing for their life and sends his spirits of evil upon that man to make him to quit the battle and makes it much more easier for a man to just give up on Life. But, God is faithful and just and reveal a greater understanding to me in a dream. I call this revelation, *"A Battle of a Great Dragon"*

A BATTLE OF A GREAT DRAGON

In my dream there was a dragon that looked similar to a T-Rex dinosaur and he was hunting me, as if he wanted to eat me alive. He would hide in the edge of the woods and be waiting for me, as I would attempt to go out side. I was always on a look out for this Dragon and knew it wanted to kill me. When I would attempt to open the door and to walk outside, I could here him start pounding his feet and breathing hard and making a roar, as if he knew where I was, every moment and he would race toward me, to eat me alive and I would shut the door and hide in the building and watch this dragon looking into the windows, as if he wanted to kill me. But, I had an understanding in this matter in the dream, that this old dragon didn't know of.

After I knew he went back to the edge of the woods, I stuck my head out the door and I spoke out to the dragon; for I knew he was listening to me and then I said with a stern voice with power, "Today! The battle is over between you and me! And you will be chained down and you will become my pet!" So, I got on the telephone and called the Arm Forces of the United States and told them that there was a Large Dragon loose and it was trying to kill me. As soon as I told them this, they were outside with Helicopters and Armed soldiers. These soldiers battled this dragon for me and they took control of this beast and they chained it down to the earth, with concrete, large steel beams and steel chains. The dragon was furious and was putting up a great fight and was bleeding somewhat from different places of his body. But, when they chained him down to the earth, this dragon became as a little puppy and began to sniffle as if it was saddened and then he cried out and tears flowed from his eyes softly.

I finally walked outside where this dragon was chained down and came close to it and I wasn't afraid of him anymore. Then I spoke to it and said, "You are my pet now and you will do as I say" and the little dragon shook his head gently as he was confirming, "Yes Sir!", to me. I reached out and put my hand upon his head and started to pet him like a puppy and the dragon became under my control and bowed his head down, but I left him chained down to the earth and then I woke up from my sleep, thinking of this matter. The dream was because I was battling intents after intents of my flesh, in my life, at this time. I had defeated a lot of past intents of my heart during this great Resurrection of my spirit, but this intent I was battling at this time, I didn't know how to deal with him and was afraid of it. I will say that these great dragon was my self will.

After this dream, I knew what I had to do in order to defeat this self will intent in my life; for it was a big battle, I thought. I knew that I must call on help for this matter, and I did. I asked God to help me with this battle and he made it easy for me, by saying through my spirit, "Son, Seek Counsel." I really didn't know at this time, who I should ask, because the Doctor had just changed my psychiatric drugs to better ones and I didn't think that he could help me. I was on psychiatric drugs for 15 years, but deep down within my spirit, I knew that I didn't want them and I didn't need them; for they were reservations for my using. I knew that I had manipulated to get these drugs for so long, without understanding of the consequences. I didn't even know that I was manipulating for these strong drugs, until this time at the Rehab Center. I would always have a reservation of drugs legally, if I couldn't get drugs Illegally. I knew from my past and would always think, 'Well, I'm already on drugs, another drug want hurt." and I would start using again and again, after past Rehab and Treatment visits. I was also so scared that I would go through more emotional withdrawals and physical withdrawals, because I had been on these powerful drugs for 15 years.

I really didn't want to let go of this power I had of getting legal drugs when I wanted them, but I came to my senses, as I was beginning to get stronger in my spirit. I knew at this time that for me to get well, I had to let go and get honest and I did just that.

One day while I was battling this great dragon within myself we had our group meeting. My counselor was our group leader this day and he arranged the group accordingly from 1st time treatment, to Most time treatments and guess who was on the end for the most treatment cares? yes! yours truly, me. I stood up and said to my counselor, "This isn't right! you shouldn't rail people like this! You are just pointing people out for your own pleasure!" and then I got somewhat angry in my heart towards my counselor. And then he turned and looked at me and said to me with a very soft, compassionate voice, "Please, just give me a chance, because I know that something good is going to come forth from this group to day, for all of us. Please just calm down and give me a chance. Will you?" So, I set back down and then my counselor asked the young boy that was there at the Treatment Center for his first time, a question like this, "What are you looking for, out of this treatment?" And the young boy said, "I want to do better and quit doing drugs. But you know, I really don't know what I need." So, he asked this question to each person there, as he would go around in the circle from the 1st time treatments to the most treatments. Every one had an different answer and would say things like this, "Well, I want to live better for my children.", "I want this treatment to help me with my depression, so that, I don't have to take medicines anymore.", "I want this treatment to give me tools to use in my life, out there in the world.", "I want to have a good life and a family and be normal like everyone else.". The answers kept getting better, as the ones with the most treatments were asked the question, until I was the only one left without answering and it was my turn to respond to the question. I was battling this dragon and no one knew anything about it.

I just sat there for a few seconds thinking if I should just leave out of the group, because I didn't know what to say. Then my counselor looked at me with compassion and said with a soft voice, as he called me by my name and asked me this question, "_____-_. What are you looking for out of this treatment?" and then I felt in my spirit a great Love and it was if my thoughts had just vanished away and I couldn't say anything and I began to be very saddened and burden and began to cry from within and without my heart, in front of all that were there and then I said, as I looked up into my counselors eyes, "I don't know. I really don't know what I need. I do know, that I don't want to die and if

I don't find out what I need, I'm going to die". And then my counselor looked at the entire group and then back at me and said, "Well done. Great answer." The finger of God was beginning to touch me at this time, but I was without understanding of the matter.

So, I fought this dragon in my heart for several days, until I just wanted to give up and requested to be discharge from this hospital by a AMA order. Oh yes! Let me share something with you my friend, what I know of this matter today. It seemed to me in my past life when things like this battle would progress in my life, that this would be the time that I would just give up and say, "It just isn't worth the battle." and I would give up, without getting the blessing of understanding and fall back into the horrors and would be facing the Big Hole again and again. For today, I know and have a great understanding that when things looked gloomy and without reach for our life and seems to hard to get, it is that time that we must not give up, but stand and if that is all we can do at the time is to stand. Stand in what we believe! Stand! And wait on the promise of the understanding, because if you just give up, you will not receive what you are looking for or you will battle the matter for a long time without understanding. *"And Moses said unto the people, Fear ye not, stand still, and see the salvation of the Lord, which he will shew to you to-day: for the Egyptians whom ye have seen to-day, ye shall see them again no more forever."*

We must stand still before God and watch his salvation of his people when that is all we can do, but to Stand!

At this time of my life, I had no choice, but to stand and wait on salvation for my life; for I knew it was Life or Death. Today, I know that I must press forward without any doubt or hesitation, because I know it is a matter of Life or Death for my life, and I have to ask this question, "Is your Life worth just giving up on?" I can answer this question for you with confidence and my answer is, Nooooooooo! Your Life and My life and all mankind are worth, much more than, the Universe and all that it contains. I remember a great story, in God's Holy Word, concerning a battle of Life and Death, that always comes to my remembrance concerning this matter. Every time a battle comes up in my life I begin to think of Jacob and God's Angel wrestling for the blessing of the promise from God, but I really didn't have the understanding of the matter, until I read the entire story in God's Holy

Word. I would always think that I had to wrestle with God to get what he has promised for my Life, but I tell you with confidence my friend, that isn't the matter. In my past life, I did wrestle with God, but it wasn't for the promises for my life, it was because I had the lock of self will on the door of my heart and would not let God into my heart and I suffered from locking my door greatly.

Today I have the scares in my body and mind from the "Knocks of God". The Knocks from God didn't cause the suffering, self will caused the sufferings. God only knocked on my heart to come in so that, I wouldn't suffer from the consequences of the Lock of self will. Oh yes! Since it is appropriate to say at this time, If God is Knocking on your heart, then your door must be Locked. But today I can say with confidence, God very seldom has to knock on my door; for the lock of my self will is broken and God and His Christ and Holy Ghost comes into my heart freely as they Will; for I let go and Let God. If I receive a promise by his word, I stand still and wait on it with hope and patience, which is my faith.

In God's Word in the Holy Book of Genesis, Chapters 27- 33, explains clearly, a battle between a man that took a blessing by the intents of self will from another man, the consequences of this action and the faithfulness of the blessing. Please read it sometime, soon.

So after I requested an AMA order there at the Treatment Center, my counselor called for me and asked me what the problem was and he said to me, "Please, Give me and the Doctors a chance to help you." But, I said to him as I was suffering and crying, "You cant help me with this problem, because you don't understand!". Then he shut the door and said, "Will you please share with me the problem, so that, I can understand?" Then as I told him my problem, he insisted for me not to quit my psychiatric drugs, because he thought that I really needed them; for I was crying and was depressed somewhat and was saying things that concerned him, such as, "If I don't get help with this problem, I know that I will go back out into this world, start using again and die, no doubt." My counselor continually to try to explain the need for me to continue my medications and would continue to tell me that, "if you don't take your meds, you probably will die or go back to using anyway. Thinking this way is symptoms of your mental disease. You really need to take your meds." When he kept saying these things to me, I got somewhat worse and said this to him, "You See! You cant help me with this dragon I'm battling! I want to leave, now. If you don't sign a AMA, then I will just leave on my own!" My counselor said to me, "Don't give up and leave. There's got to be an answer. I tell you what, let me go talk to the Doctor about this matter and you sit here, until I get back, Please!."

So, I set there in my counselors room for about 30 minutes crying and was thinking of suicide, no kidding, because I knew that I had to quit these drugs before I went home or I would be worse than when I went to this rehab and knew death wasn't a choice, but definite.

This battle was larger for me to handle on my own and I knew that the Doctor had to write an order for me to stop using these meds, because I knew that I just could not quit them at one time on my own. I knew at this time that the withdraws would harm me or kill me and I was so scare of what I would go through, if I quit them at one time and knew in my heart, that I must quit them now. I knew that I had to quit these drugs now at the drug rehabilitation center and under the care of a Doctor. I knew that the Insurance company only approved 21 days there at the Treatment Center and I didn't have much time to get the help I needed. I had already been through detoxification from cocaine at another hospital, for 14 days, before I went to this Treatment Center and I was going through mental and physical withdrawals still at this time.

During my detoxification from cocaine at the other hospital, there were times that the Medical Doctor would be called into my room, because there was not much of a pulse and thought that I was dying; for my blood pressure was leaving me or crashing very low. It was over a week before I could even get out of bed and function properly, no kidding. I thought at this time at the Treatment Center, that it would be too much for my body to go through at one time, withdrawing mentally and physically from cocaine and my psychiatric drugs all at one time and I thought, I would die for sure, but I also thought, that if I didn't quit all these drugs, I would die anyway.

So, I weighed out this matter for several days, until I decided that if I die the death trying to do what I knew was right, then I rather die knowing this, than dying doing drugs again and going through the Horrors over again.

There was a time during this battle that I left walking from this Treatment Center to call someone to come and get me and just give up on life. I will say I was also having suicide thoughts at this time.

The battles were greatly burdensome on my heart and I really thought for sure no one could help me with these problems. But, these people never gave up on me and insisted to me, that I needed to stay and give them a chance to help me and at least try. I remember one time that I did sneak away from the surveillance of the cameras, leaving walking at the night hours to go to a phone and call my drug dealer or an acquaintance at this time and offer $500.00 cash to just come and get me and carry me home, because I didn't think these people could help me. I also left with suicide thoughts, such as walking to the ocean and just falling into it and drowning, no kidding. Sometimes I would try to make the staff mad at me, so that they would just kick me out from the Treatment center, so that, if I was kicked out, then it wouldn't be my fault for given up, but it wasn't working. But, this particular time that I left looking for a phone, one of the staff members came looking for me and when he found me, he rolled the window down from his vehicle, glancing at a photo that he had in his hand for ID confirmation of me, and said to me, as he called me by my name with a very compassionate voice, "_____-_ What are you doing?" And I said to him, as I would begin to cry softly within my heart for desperate help, "I'm looking for a phone to call someone to carry me home." and then he said to me, still with that compassionate voice," Come with me and I will carry you home and to a phone. Please come with me." He did carry me home, straight back to the Treatment Center and when I got there, he led me to the canteen and brought me food and left me there to myself, thinking to myself on this matter. I began to understand at this moment that I had to trust these people to help me or I was going to die.

Oh yes! I will say this, I never found a phone that night either. I had wondered away from the Treatment Center for over a mile into the city. After the battle was victorious and the staff began to trust me again, I went out for a haircut. As I would glace out the window of the vehicle where I had walked that night, there were phones every 100 ft and they were everywhere.

I knew at this time, my eyes were blind from the phones that night. I began to Praise and Thank God, that my eyes where blind from finding a phone or maybe you would not be reading these writings now.

So the next day is when my counselor and I met. My counselor came back into the room where I was waiting and shut the door and said to me, as if he had Hope, "The Doctor wants to help you and said for you to go to him, now." I went to the Doctors office down the corridor and I sit there in a chair and he looked at me and said, "I'm willing to get you off this medicine, but you will have to stay for me to watch your condition. Are you willing to Stay?" I didn't hesitate and said, Yes, Sir!" So, he wrote the order for me to stop using these medicine. I had to wean off the medicines for a few days, but I was willing to do anything to get off these drugs; for I knew I didn't have much time left at this Treatment Center. As I was walking out the door of my Doctors office, he said to me with somewhat like a serious voice, "If you start acting stupid, I will put you back on these medicines." and I said , "No, problem. I understand." and we both giggled. I knew at this time, that I didn't need any drugs and I was extremely happy at that moment and I had defeated a major dragon in my life. So during this time in my life, Gods spirit was washing my mind like a washer machine. His spirit was purging my Mind to clean it from my past with His will. The hope gave me the serenity I had panted for so many years as a young child. I knew then the Horror was over!

Once I started believing God, for his Will in my Life, He started rewarding me with Faith; for Faith is the Action of all of our Beliefs and Hopes and if we are found worthy for more faith in our life, God will reward us with more.

In Hebrews Chapter 11, verse 1 clearly defines what Faith is for it is written, ***"Now faith is the substance of things hoped for, the evidence of things not seen."***

When you put your Hopes and Beliefs in something, you began to have faith in it. Just for an example: "If you had a Key and you hoped it would start you car, believe it would start your car and even had faith that the key would start your car, but if you do not put your Key in the ignition set and turn the key, then I would say your faith is dead. But if you do put you key in the ignition and turn it and your car starts and runs, then I would say you have Faith and Works in that key". This is how faith works. You can't have faith without action or works and you can't have works without faith. You got to have both Works and Faith for Faith to work in and about your and my Life. So, I hoped in God to save me from the past Horrors and made a stand and stood still and watched and God brought salvation to my life at that moment. I began to believe that God was my only hope and then I began to believe again, that God was the only answer to my hope. I began to put my hope and belief in him by giving my will and life over to him and now, God shows me what His Will is for me by rewarding me with Faith. Remember, you cannot work for Faith itself; for You must have all three elements (Hope, Beliefs, Works) in place for faith to work in your life. In God's Word, in the book of James he clearly explains in detail about faith and works and Please read it sometime soon.

Today God rewards me with much more Faith and How is that so? I begin to trust God and I begin to do his Will in my life. God points me in directions and paths I need to follow and rewards me with more faith. I put my Faith into action when I do his Will, such as, reading and studying his Word, praying always, going to church, sharing hope with someone at the right time and most of all stay standing in God's Presence by rejecting the evil things that come up in my life. Something else happened when I completely surrendered to God and His Christ. I was happier than I had ever been in my Life, but what made me even happier, my family and others around me, began to be much happier. I never knew the misery and horrors I was putting my family through, until I seen how much happier they are today.

I have found what I needed and it wasn't nothing I had to work for; for It is God's Will and His Grace that saved me and keeps me. We must change for ourselves and for others, so that we can give the Hope as a open book for those that are suffering to read. I truly believe, the best Book to read, is the one that walks it. I never knew how much suffering my wife, family and others were going through, just because they Loved me very much. We must change for the better and be transformed to a new Life in order to receive and give Hope for Life.

In God's Word it clearly again states, what we must do to change, Romans chapter 12,verse 1-2, *"I beseech you therefore brethren, by the mercies of God, that ye present your Bodies a Living Sacrif ice, holy, acceptable unto God, which is your reasonable service. And be not conformed to this world; but be ye Transformed by the renewing of your Mind, that ye may prove what is that good, and acceptable, and perfect Will of God."* I could have not renewed my mind and spirit by myself. Only God could have restore my mind back to sanity and resurrect me from the death I was facing. Please Trust God; for He is able and His Will is the only answer for mankind. I now know the Truth and the Truth has set me free from all the Horrors, I once lived in for a long time. I now know where I've been, where I'm at today, and where I'm going, after I shed this fleshly body back to the dust it came from. I have a new straight course now, where I was walking in a maze in my past dead life, and that was the Big Hole, death. Please let me ask you this question. Have you every wished or hoped that you could be reborn as a new born child, but knew what you know as a grown adult? I can say with confidence today, that you can; for it is the miracle of Resurrection. My body didn't enter into my mother's womb again and start over as a embryo, but my spirit was reborn as a new born child. I feel the sufferings of my body because of past experiences but my spirit is rejoicing in the Hope that I have in God and his Christ second by second for Resurrecting me from death.

My life has been transformed from death to life and I wouldn't have it no other way. It is like starting over again in Life, but I kept the wisdom of my past experiences and wisdom from God that he had blessed me with and my spirit grows in stature every moment by moment to learn of his Loving Grace. I now desire for the things of God and his Rewards through his Son Jesus Christ and my life is much more abundant today, than before, in my past dead life. Thank you God and Christ Jesus, for Resurrecting me from and keeping from, the Big Hole and given me a Chance at Life again, as a new born child.

CHAPTER TEN

IT JUST DOESN'T MAKE NO SENSE!

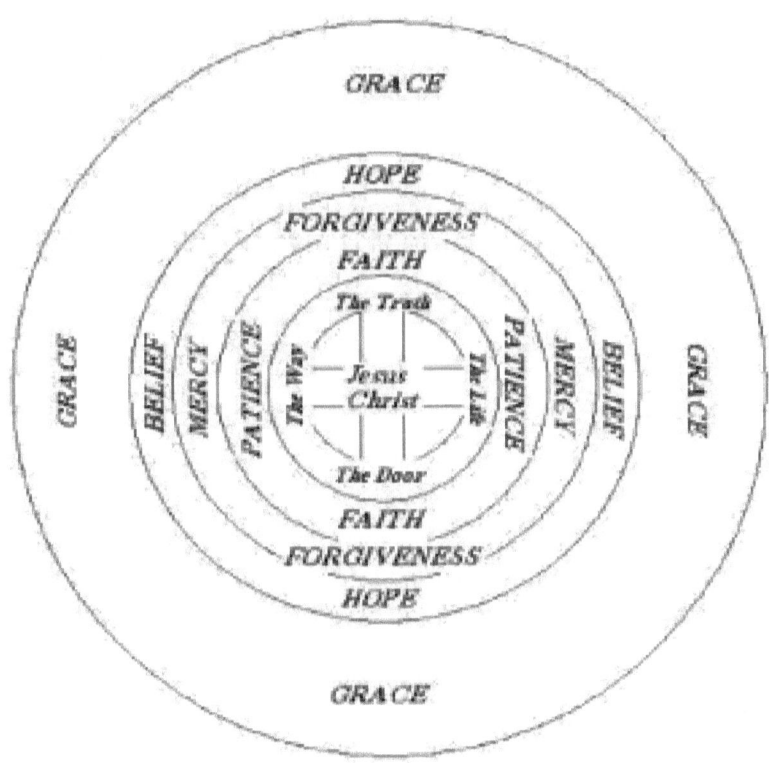

AFTER I HAD LEFT THIS REHAB CENTER, I felt like a new creator, no kidding. I know the Doctors and counselors help me greater this time than the last, but I will give the credit to the ones who were in the Rehab Center for Treatment.

Now, after a few months had past, I was doing great, but things just still didn't make no sense to me. I was clean and wasn't on any drugs at this time and I was beginning a grieving process that I had stuffed deep within my heart for many years. The deaths of all those before me in my life and even my animals that I lost during my using, I was just now beginning to sense the grieving of them. The personnel at the job I was working, had somewhat, given up on me, but they gave me another chance to work at the Industrial Plant. I was praying and praying continuously to stay living a normal life. I was once beginning to feel again within my spirit man and this world around me I thought its seemed like a dream that I just couldn't awake from. I was working with drug uses and alcoholics at this work place, and I knew it was just time for me to leave this job. While I was here at this job during the last days, the Spirit of God revealed something wonderful to me and now I will share it with you. It is called, "It just Doesn't Make No Sense!"

IT JUST DOESN'T MAKE NO SENSE!

"But, beloved, be not ignorant of this one thing, that one day is with the Lord as a thousand years, and a thousand years as one day. The Lord is not slack concerning his promise, as some count slackness; but is longsuffering to us-ward, not willing that any should perish, but that all should come to repentance.; Nevertheless we, accordingly to his promise, look for new heavens and a new earth, wherein dwelleth righteousness."

(2Peter 3:8-9;13).

My friend, what is the True Reality of Life? Let me pause before I ask these other life changing questions. -Pause- Have you ever felt deep within yourself that maybe you just didn't belong here on this earth? Or Have you felt from somewhere deep within yourself that you came from a different world? Have you ever thought that there had to be another World beyond this World? Have you ever dream about a different world and felt as if you where there in the spirit, soul and body? Have you ever thought that everything in this Life on earth just doesn't make no sense?

The Last, but not least of the questions my friend, "What is the true reality of Life?"

My friend, I have a greater confidence today in all things, much more than in my past life. I have confidence that this Universe is infinite and I'm confident there is life out there beyond our Imaginations. ***"But as it is written, Eye hath not seen, nor ear heard, neither have entered into the heart of man, the things which God hath prepared for them that love him." (1Corinthians 2:9).*** I also have greater confidence that every thing done under the heavens has purpose. This life on earth seems to me as only a dream that vanishes away in the night at the wink of my eye. Sometimes, I wish that I could just awake from this dream, but then what? Will Eternity be the True Reality of Life? I will not be hasty in want to awake from this dream. So, I must press forward in my dream, until I am confident with the understanding of the Truth of Reality of Life. I will press forward in this Life, even if it takes until my Life is called to Eternity. Will I know then the Truth of Life, even at that appointed time of my life? Or Will I just awake into just another dream?

During dark seasons of my life I would stopped all my medications for my mental illnesses. I had no jobs or insurance and I would fall back into dependency of illegal drugs. During these dark seasons of my life, everything that I would try to do, to live a normal life, just vanished away into darkness right before my eyes. My life just didn't make no sense to me during these dark times. The word "nothing" barely made any sense to me, much more, the things around me. During these dark seasons of my life there was one thing that did make sense in my life and it was my breath. Knowing that I was still breathing and death had not call my name made all the sense to me and that was sufficient enough for me to live for another day. I was so ashamed of my self during these dark times, because of failure and fear. I would go and hide and dig deeper away from this life into my mole hole.

I was given up on trying to understand my life, much more, the Life that tried to engulf me.

Even after failure after failure, I tried earnestly to live a normal life and struggled greatly, until I couldn't struggle no more. I would call out to God and cry to him for understandings, but nothing would make any sense to me. I was beginning to believe that I was even cursed for the sins and I was doomed for Hell. I thought during these times that God had seared my mind or turn my mind reprobate from understand Life. I would even think that the God that I trusted in with my whole life, wouldn't even listen to me. I would stop calling out to God during these times, because I thought he had forsaken me, because of all my sins. I would think this greatly because of what God had shown me and given me before times and how I would just give up on this Life and throw the great Hope that he had given once before, to the dogs.

During these dark times of my life, suicide was definitely on my mind continuously. But, I just didn't want to shoot myself in the head. So, I would come up with much more crafty ways of suicide, such as an overdose of cocaine or even a Doctor to put me to sleep with a needle. I would think that I would be better off on the other side of Life than living in this life that made no sense.

Now, during this time of these writings, "It just doesn't make no sense!", I was jobless, I had no medications for my mental illnesses and my physical body was beginning to buffet me greatly. I had no choice at this time to depend on a man to help me with my illnesses or I would had just gave up. The pride that I once had, was no longer a matter, because I had to humble myself and ask for help or die.

One of the State Hospitals covered me with a charity fund and these folks help me get my medications and the healthcare for many of my conditions.

I was beginning to make sense again of this life, but God had already prepared an understanding for me long ago. It wasn't that God let me go through the misery and horrors to make me understand what he was about to give me, but I will say this with confidence, it was for an appointed time in my life to received such and awesome gift from God. I felt as if, I was back into God The Father's Loving Grace and Arms. I was again trying to live a normal life, and this time, I was ready for battle. I began to seek God fervently and revering every word I could get from him. I kept my mind on the Spiritual things of God and refused the foolishness of this physical life. I began to go back to church again at this time and was desperate for the understanding of Reality. After I began to get well somewhat in mind, body and spirit, I got the understandings of the Dark seasons of my life that just didn't make no sense and this is where it started:

Early One fall night, I walked outside my home and looked up to the sky. The sky was clear and the stars were twinkling quit beautifully. It was somewhat cool and crisp and sounds where forever bouncing from my eardrums. I could here the children laughing in the near distance as they were playing outside, perhaps, bouncing upon a trampoline. There were a few dogs barking in the far distance, as if they too, were excited about the seasons approaching, or, maybe they were just barking at the new moon that was above the horizon. I could hear the sound of steel chains dropping upon a truck bed in the far distance, perhaps, a farmer getting ready to harvest his crop the next day. I could hear the soft sounds of wind chimes in the far distance, as if, there was a small breeze where they were hung.

When all these things where happening I was alone and I asked myself from the depth of my inner man, "Is this Reality or is this just a dream?" During this time alone and thinking of God's Wonderful Works and seeing with my eyes and hearing with my ears everything around me, It just seem too surreal. I really thought I was dreaming, no kidding.

It was a peace that only God could give to a man and I didn't want to be hasty in awaking from this dream. But I did of course, because my wife came out the door and said, "Dear! Are you out here? Why are you out here alone? Everyone is ready to eat. Come inside and eat."

This season was near the Thanksgiving Holiday and it was one of the most beautiful nights that a man could ask for. It brings to me the remembrance of the smell of Sweet potato and Pumpkin pies baking in the oven. Turkey and dressing and a fresh pork ham ready for the pickings. Cranberry Sauce, Candied Yams, Coconut Raisin Cakes and many other marvelous delicious eats, but the one most important of all, my family getting together at my parents home. It was, and still is today, about the Love that we share for one another at the dinning tables. Laughing and even weeping, eating and drinking together and being most merry. Laughing and giggling as we would share stories of our past childhood. Seeing my Brothers and my Sisters with their families and their children that are now adults with their own children. Seeing my Father and Mother's faces as their great grand children, crawling upon their laps saying, "Mama, Papa I love you." The time of year to give thanks to all of those that made it possible, such as our Nation, our forefathers and our soldiers for such a fellowship of goodness and freedom. I will forever thank my God the Father and his Son Jesus Christ for the suffering they have done for me and the Whole Wide World. I will forever thank God and his Christ for given mankind the Grace to live, in freedom.

God and his Christ suffers greatly for all their creation, so that, mankind could have a chance to live life and life much more abundantly on this earth. I know this with a greater confidence; if it wasn't for all of those that have laid their life's down for freedom, I truly would have no chance to live a life, in freedom. If it wasn't for them, I would be surely dead in the darkness of my own Abyss, waiting and wanting, with no sense of any existence.

Today I have the understanding that Freedom is not free. Even the Salvation of your soul, a price was paid in Blood.

This one particular evening, I was also pondering my own heart about who I am. I looked toward God's marvelous heavens and I felt as a micro-organism compared to the infinite of his marvelous, enormous works. I will share with you a insert on "Who I am" later in the writings. I began to understand that God had placed me here with great purpose. I began to feel within my spiritual man that I was bound and pressed by my own earthly body on this earth. I began to understand that there was, much more than, just my fleshly body and this world. I began to understand that my fleshly body had me bound by the gravity of this great and marvelous earth. I looked toward the stars and began to think this; "If, I could just drop my fleshly body and sore through the heavens as an eagle to the furthest star that my fleshly eyes could see, what would I see?" After I thought these things within my spirit man, I began to understand clearly this; "I am truly not who I think I am." I began to feel within my spirit man the trueness of who I truly am. My spirit man confirmed himself of who I truly am in less than a minute. My sprit man confirmed that I was only an foreigner from a great distant land. Again and Again the thought of this kept going through my mind; "This Life on Earth is only Boot Camp. Training for a great journey Home."

As I was pondering on that thought through my mind, the Spirit of God began to show me something even much more marvelous and it was this: As a Joint-Heir through God's Son, Jesus Christ, I will be in God's Glorious Kingdom one day and will be able to see the stars one by one. In the Holy Book of John 8: 23, it is written, ***"And he said unto them, Ye are from beneath; I am from above: Ye are from this World; I am not of this World."*** Jesus Christ clearly stated that he is from another world and my friend, I believe him with all my spirit, soul and body. The Word of God also gives this promise for those that are willing to follow his Son, Jesus Christ to the end.

In the Holy Book of Romans 8:14-18 it is written, *"For as many as are led by the Spirit of God, they are the sons of God. For ye have not received the spirit of bondage again to fear; but ye have received the spirit of adoption, whereby we cry, Ab'-ba, Father. The Spirit itself beareth witness with our spirit, that we are the sons of God: and if children, then heirs; heirs of God, and joint-heirs with Christ; if so be that we suffer with him, that we may be also glorified together. For I reckon that the sufferings of this present time are not worthy to be compared with the glory which shall be revealed in us."*

Now, as mankind on this earth, we are bound by our earthly bodies and the physical properties of this earth, such as, gravity. The physical properties limits are abilities to do really what our spirit man wants us to do, such as, maybe soaring like an eagle to the furthest star that our eyes can see. We as mankind are always looking to the physical where the eye can see, the ear can hear and the fingers can touch. Perhaps, if it isn't in the physical where we can see, hear, smell, taste, and touch, we just don't care for it.

Speaking of myself, there has been many days in my life that if I couldn't put my finger on it, I just didn't care for it. It would be in these seasons that I would go into a depressed state of mind. This would be the true reason; I wanted something then and now where I could see it with my eyes and grab a hold of it with my hand for keeps and did not get it. Before I got any understand of reality in its trueness, I didn't even want to hear about the spiritual things, such as a preacher preaching the Gospel. I didn't want to wait for nothing.

During these seasons of my past life, I would try to go to church and hear the preaching of the Gospel. Sometimes I was hoping I could get something from the preacher, right then and now, to help me in my physical life.

I would watch men and women and even children, singing loud, clap their hands, raise their hands as in want, speaking in strange languages, running up and down the corridors. I would even see some of the elder women shaking their heads and their hair would come loose from their tops. I would giggle somewhat inside thinking, "this isn't reality. This is foolishness." One of the elder women with her hair flying in the wind, weeping and laughing at the same time would look at me in tears and say this; "God is good isn't he son!? Praise God! Trust him son. He will give you you're answer." Then I would giggle even more so within and without. But, later in my life, I began to understand the true foolishness wasn't what I thought; it was my thinking.

As a intelligent being in the flesh, we as mankind are forever seeing with our eyes, hearing with our ears, smelling with our noses, tasting with our mouths, and feeling with our finger tips. Perhaps, as we begin to sense these matters in our physical body we have no doubt or we would have confidence in these senses as the true reality of life. We began to trust in these physical senses as we use them in our daily lives. But, I'm confident that some would still look into a glass or a mirror and ask this question within themselves, "Who am I? It is appropriated at this time to insert the Who I Am. Enjoy!

WHO I AM, OR, WHO AM I?

Today, I believe the most weakness of mankind is not knowing the Truth. This weakness would be the same as spiritual ignorance. I'm confident that mankind is intelligent in the physical, but is mankind full of the truth of wisdom and Knowledge of God; the God that made him and All things? One question that I am confident that a man would try to shun from answering is this one: What am I or Who am I? Surely we can say are names, but do we really truly know who and what we are?

"I yam what I yam, because I yam what I yam!" No, I am not Pop-Eye the Sailor Man, nor, a sweet potato writing this book. But, if there was truly a Pop-Eyed Sailor Man that said the, "I yam what I yam", then he and I are on the same path of believing who we truly yam. Matter of a fact, and just for an example, lets use Pop-Eye the Sailor Man. When Pop-Eye eats his Spinach he becomes stronger correct?

But, does the Spinach change his physical or spiritual body? If you guess his physical body then you are correct. Now, this is just an example and don't think I pounding on Pop-Eye as he would pound on Brutus. But, as pop-eye eats his spinach, you would see his physical body change, but what about his spiritual body, does it change? Yes! He also becomes more witty and smarter. So, does the body have to get food to grow strong, so that, the spirit man can grow strong? No! Now, since I hope I got your attention, let me explain. We as mankind have three parts to our life, which are, the body, the soul, and the spirit. Just because a man would be as big as a hippo, doesn't mean that his replica eternal soul is the same size. Your soul doesn't grow on spinach, but spiritual food, which is given from above or God. If, a man would be as big as a hippo, but doesn't know God as who he is, I believe that his Soul would be the size of an ant.

So, how do we grow in the spirit man? Great question! My friend, there is only one way to grow in the spirit man; and it is to know God for who he is and follow him. If this life were all I knew, I would be a man most miserable, even if I was the size of a hippo. I will never know who I am or what I truly am, until, I know "He whom had made me." Once I began to know the Creator of All things, then these things become my spiritual meat for my Soul to grow, follow me? It is written in the Holy Book of Matthew 6:33, *"But seek ye first the kingdom of God, and his righteousness; and all these things shall be added unto you."*

So, I believe it would be appropriate first to let you know a few things I know concerning the Creator of All things. First his name is "I AM." I AM in Hebrew tongue means, existence. God is the Existence of All things and without him there would be nothing. I AM has given his ALL and ALL to mankind to know him. Just look into the mirror my friend, and see what God has done. Just look to the Stars my friend, and see what God has done. Everything that has life is a miracle in itself, by the Handiwork of the Great I am. Here are just a few of who God is:

I Am is my Heavenly Father.

I Am is my God. I Am is my Life.

I AM is my existence.

I AM is the first, the last and the beginning and the end.

I Am is Love unconditional.

I Am is the Bread of Life.

I AM is the Living Water.

I AM is the Light of the World.

I AM is the Word of Life.

I AM is the Door of His Sheep.

I AM is the Good Shepherd.

I AM is the Resurrection and the Life.

I AM is the Way, the Truth and the Life.

IAM is the True Vine.

I am is the Alpha and Omega.

I Am is a Consuming Fire.

By this time, I hope you know Who I AM is. I never have to ask the question, Who am I? Because I know the Great I AM, and today, I know who I am. Now let me just share with you what the Great I am has done for me in a few simple words. I Am spoke me into existence for Life. I Am is my heavenly Father and supplies my every need. I Am breathed into my nostrils the breath of Life as a infant, and gave me an eternal Soul. I Am gave me eyes to see all his glory. I Am gave me ears to hear his voice calling me to his side. I Am gave me a mouth to praise and talk to him. I Am gave me arms and hands to touch his wonderful handiwork. I Am gave me legs and feet to walk with him. I Am gave me a mind and heart to Love him and feel his Love for me. So, I am forever thankful for knowing the Great I am, and now, I know who I am and my purpose here in the physical body. In the Holy Book of Ecclesiastes 12:13-14 it is written, ***"Let us here the conclusion of the matter: Fear God and keep his commandments: for this is the whole duty of man. For God shall bring every work into judgment, with secret thing, whether it be good, or whether it be evil."***

Even though our fleshly body would be reflecting an Image in the glass we would still have doubt of who we really are. I am confident some would just walk away from the greatest question of reality in hast and continue as the same man in this life, with no answer. I'm also confident that a man may ask this question within, "I can see with my eyes, hear with my ears, feel and touch with my hands everything that is among me on this earth, but I truly don't know who or what I really am. Even though, I'm looking into the Mirror, I don't know who I am."

As a man, I can smell things, such as a sweet apple pie baking in the oven, the sweetness of a fresh rose, the freshness in the air after a great rain storm and the perfumes that I would spray upon my body.

I can hear things, such as the beautiful voices of the song birds in the yard, children laughing as they would play, the marvelous orchestras playing their instruments, the voice of one calling your name. I can touch things, such as the dew upon a roses petal, a new born baby's face, a book, and even a snow flake that falls from heaven. Even though, I have these senses, there is something greater coming from deep within my spirit man that I just can not put my finger upon. This feeling that I get from deep within my heart is somewhat like the wind. I can see the effect of the wind, but I just cant see where it comes from or where it goes. I know the wind is there, because I see the effect that it has on the leaves in the tree tops and the pressure that it causes upon my fleshly body.

As a man and an intelligent being such as you and I are, if I couldn't grasp hold onto it in the physical in my past life, I didn't think that it would be much effect in my life. This thinking is somewhat liken unto this question, "What good would it be for me to catch the wind?" In my past dead life, the material things of this life became my gods, such as drugs, alcohol, money, sex, and many other material things. I began to trust in the things of this world, much more, than I trusted the Creator that made me. Like I mentioned before, when I couldn't get what I wanted then and now, I just didn't want it. This kind of living led me to a road of destruction and also bound my spirit man from growing in the knowledge and wisdom of what Life was and the True reality. Thinking that those things of the spiritual were foolishness, led me straight to a course of destruction and almost my death before my appointed time of the Creator.

Today, I have a better understanding of what all of the physical senses are for and it is this; To grow in the Love and Grace of the Almighty God, the Creator of all Life. These physical senses are given, so that I will have a chance to grow in the spirit man (soul) and to get to know the Creator much more abundantly, day by day.

My Life is filled much more with Gratitude toward God and his Son, Jesus Christ for the understanding of these physical senses. As we take these physical senses and learn from the experiences (understandings) of this life on earth, these experiences are stored in the spiritual man's mind. As we begin to store these experiences in our spiritual man's mind these experiences began to manifest and enter into the heart (the complete intent of a man, either they are good or evil) of a man. After these experiences have entered into the heart of a man, they are then manifested into intents of a man's daily life. As these intents are manifested in and out of a man's life on this earth, they become the fruit of that man's life or labor. I truly believe this matter with my whole heart, mind and body. If, perhaps God didn't give mankind the physical senses would there be any reason for mankind to exist, or more so, for anything to exist? It is here in and by the physical senses we begin too understand who and what we are and also to grow in the Grace of God much more abundantly.

It is by the physical sense of sight that we can see a sweet potato pie sitting and cooling on the window seal. It is by the physical sense of smell that we can smell the sweet potato pie and desire to eat of it. It is the physical sense of taste when we do eat of the pie and then we would say this, "Thank you God for the Sweet Potato Pie." The more we learn with our senses, the more we grow in our spirit, if the experiences are either good or evil. There is a truth of growing in the spirit man and it is this: If, a man lives this life and binds up the spirit man from learning about God, I'm confident that man would be low in statue of the wisdom of God. The man's spirit would also be void of God. The man that quenches the spirit man from growing in the wisdom of the Creator is greatly dark and void of God within his complete life, spiritual and physical. I also believe if a man isn't willing to grow in the wisdom of the Creator then that man's spiritual soul is in danger of eternal torment. If a man that would close his eyes and die the earthly death, what then?

In the Holy Book of Hebrew 9:27-28 it is written, **"And as it is appointed unto men once to die, but after this the judgment. So Christ was once offered to bear the sins of many; and unto them that look for him shall he appear the second time without sin unto salvation."**

Today, I believe with a greater confidence that man will be judged and measured accordingly of how much of the Love of God that he has in his life, before and after the appointed time of his death of this life. If the man would be void of the Love of God then he would be also void of the Eternal Creator that made him the Creator would refuse him. Only darkness would compass him and he want know nothing, not even the darkness that has engulfed him. After he waits in the darkness then he would be judged by the Creator. The Creator would search his life by his Word (Jesus Christ) and when the Creator would find him void of his Word, he will say, "I never knew you. Depart from me that work iniquity and be cast into the Eternal Lake of Fire." Now I believe this with confidence also: The man that is mature in God and has lived a life full of the understanding of God would have a much more greater hope and the Love of God. God's Love would dwell within and without his complete life. If a man endures this life and follows God's Will until his appointed time is called, I'm confident that man will pass the judgment and the darkness of the second death and enter through the straight gate of God's Glorious Kingdom. Remember the Passover? (Exodus chapter 12.)A man that is mature of God in all obedience to his Will, I'm confident he will awake from his dream into the True Reality. This man will find himself in the arms of his savior, Jesus Christ. Christ will say to him, "Well done, thou good and faithful servant: thou hast been faithful over a few things, I will make thee ruler over many things: enter thou into the joy of the Lord." Here in paradise will this man live in the Love of the Father, forever and forever. He would had entered the straight gate of Heaven and receive his reward, which is Life Everlasting.

He will eat of the Tree of Life and live eternity in the Love of the Father and his Christ, Jesus Christ.

Again these physical senses are given to a man, so that he would grow and mature in the understanding of the Creator and his Son, Jesus Christ. In the Holy Book of Matthew 7:20 is written, **"Wherefore by their fruits ye shall know them."** Throughout my life, I have discerned, not judged, many spirits, even the spirits of men. As I would try the spirits of man there were some that was immature in the knowledge of God's Word or unskillful. But, these people loved the Lord with all their heart and were very obedient for the promise of eternal life. There have been some that had great knowledge of the Word of God as if they had written the Word themselves. But they weren't obedient and didn't have the faith of a maggot. There were some that knew the Word of God and could quote many scriptures from the Bible, profess the faith before your face and were also somewhat obedient to the promise all together. But, when a trial or tribulation came their way, they would go crazy and would lose hope. There would be some that couldn't quote the Lord's prayer, if the Word of God was laying in their lap, but they where faithful and obedient and put all their life in the Trust in God for their complete Life. When a trail or tribulation would come their way, they would say, "Ah! This tribulation will pass me by. Jesus Christ said it would come and I've been waiting for it. I trust my God with all my life. My God will see me through, as he has always!" These people would be just as calm as little babes with a bottle.

There has been children that came in my life, one in particular that I remember. This child was maybe 10 years of age, but had the understanding of who God was as if he was a Saint of maturity, no kidding. This child grabbed my hand at a church service, that I was a guest at one Sunday morning, and I felt the Awesome Love of God within this child's life. He would hold my hand and dance and sing and weep and laugh and then he said to me,

"Trust God with your whole heart Mr. and God will be your Help in all your troubles." I couldn't believe it, but I accepted that this child had just prophesied to me. I was definitely going through some troubled times and I knew that no other man knew this, except my wife and she surely didn't know the people there. I will never forget it or that child. My friend, listen, it doesn't matter how much you know or how little you know or how old you are. What matters is if you have the Light or Love of God and the understanding of God's Perfect Will in your life at your appointed time. In the Holy Book of Matthew 7:21-23, clearly comes alive fervently, about not doing God's Will. It is written, **"Not every one that saith unto me, Lord, Lord, shall enter into the Kingdom of heaven; but he that doeth the will of my Father which is in heaven. Many will say to me in that day, Lord, Lord, have we not prophesied in thy name? And in thy name cast out devils? And in thy name done many wonderful works? And then I will profess unto them, I never knew you: depart from me that work iniquity."**

If you are a child of God then you are a child of God indeed and there is no respect of persons with God. Children grow at different rates, some grow slow and some grow fast. It doesn't matter how many scriptures that you can quote from the Word of God and my friend that is great, but does God live in your life and are you laboring for the promise?

At the end of your race on this earth, it will not matter how old you are or how much wisdom you would have of the things of this world, what will matter is this; Having the Word of God, which is the Will of God working in your spiritual man. In the Holy Book

Ecclesiastes12:13-14 it Is written, "Lets us hear the conclusion of the whole matter: Fear God, and keep his commandments: for this is the whole duty of man. For God shall bring every work into judgment, with every secret thing, whether it be good, or whether it be evil."

Therefore, It is the physical senses of this life on earth that are given to mankind, so that we would have a chance to grow in God's Loving Grace. The more we are willing to grow in God's Loving Grace the more he and his Son Jesus Christ comes into our life and dwells. The more that a man is willing to let God and his Will dwell within him, the more spiritual understanding of wisdom and patience he would have in his spiritual man. The more we would believe in God and his Son, Jesus Christ, the more Hope we have for Life. The more hope a man has in God and his Word, the more patience he would have in this life and he wait for the promise. Hope is the willingness of a man to grow in his Understanding within his spirit man. Hope holds all the elements of understanding. Hope is having confidence in Living a normal life. For it is written in God's Word, **"For we are saved by hope: but hope that is seen is not hope: for what a man seeth, why doth he yet hope for? But if we hope that we see not, then do we with patience wait for it."** The much more Hope a man would have, the much more of a normal and abundant life he can live. Hoping in something that we cant put our finger upon in the physical sense, takes something greater than that of a physical man's understanding. If, a man would have hope in something that he couldn't put his finger on, it will become Faith in their life. Where would I get faith in something that I can't see? That is a great question my friend and here is the answer. The much more a man would believe and have hope in something the more he would have faith in it, correct?. But how can a man have faith in something that he cant see? Great question my friend and here is the answer. Faith is given to every man severally accordingly by the Spirit of God. Faith is a spiritual gift given to man for confidence in the life on earth, so that the man would have patience, peace and understanding of God's Perfect Will for mankind. Every man under the heavens are given a portion of faith.

In the Holy Book of Luke 17:5-6 and it is written, **"And the apostles said unto the Lord, Increase our faith. And the Lord said, If ye had faith of a grain of mustard seed, ye might say unto this** sycamine tree, Be thou plucked up by the root, and be thou planted in the sea; and it should obey you." In the Holy Book of Romans 12:3 and it is written, "For I say, through the grace given unto me, to every man that is among you, not to think of himself more highly than he ought to think; but to think soberly, according as God halt dealt to every man the measure of faith."

Therefore, spiritual faith only comes from God and it is a gift by his Spirit. We could have lesser than a measure of faith the size of a grain of a mustard seed and if we are willing to exercise the gift within our spiritual man, it would surely grow into a Oak tree. The more faith we have in something, the much more of patience we would wait for it. It is here in Faith that a man is willing to grow and get to know God for who he is and have a much more chance of growing within his spiritual man. Not only is it a chance to grow stronger in the spiritual man it is also a much more greater chance of living an much more of an abundant life on this earth. The much more spiritual faith a man would have and the much more understanding a man will have of the Creator and if, he endures to the end he will inherit the things of God's Glorious Kingdom through his Son, Jesus Christ. I look at spiritual faith as this; The more a man is willing to exercise the gift of faith in God in their life the much more of a patient life he will live on this earth and he would be counted much more worthy of the promise of Eternal Life.

The physical senses, such as sight, we can see with our eyes the marvelous works of this universe and search on how the universe was made, correct? But I have got to ask this question, "Where would you search for the answer on how the universe was made?" Would you go to the Library and search books on astrology?

Would you go to the physicist and ask him if he knew how the universe was made? Or, would you just give up and quit trying to understand how the universe was made? Would you think it just didn't matter in your life or it just didn't make no sense? My friend, I can give you one way that I have a greater confidence of how to ask how the universe was made and it is as simple as this; "Ask God." He made it didn't he? If you believe that God made the universe, then you are well. When we start asking and believing in something that we cant see, then we begin to grow in the spirit man and this growth is called,

"Faith." My friend bare with me I have just a few more question to stir the mind up somewhat. Were you there in the beginning when God made the Universe? If you said no, then how would you believe that he made the universe, if you were not there? If you said yes, I would like it greatly to meet you. This question and answer is the measure of faith given to every man under the heavens to be exercised within their spiritual man.

Now, mankind has also spiritual senses. Did you sense that? WOW! Mankind shouldn't have any more excuses, correct? The only thing now that a man would need is that of the Will of God be written on paper for the eyes to see. WOW! God's Will is already written on paper and we have been reading it all throughout the writings of this book. I hope you have been sensing these spiritual things of God by now. These spiritual senses are always wanting more of the spiritual things, just like the physical senses are wanting more of the physical things. Just as a man would stand in front of a mirror and the mirror would reflect the image of that man, the man in the mirror is only a replica of the true man in the mirror. As the man would still stand in front of the mirror, he begins to sense the image in the mirror. In similarity as the physical senses, we as mankind have a spiritual senses as well. We can not see the spiritual senses with the physical eye, but we know it is there, with no doubt. The Spirit of God gives a man gifts accordingly as he will.

There is one gift that I would like to expand on somewhat. The spiritual man has a sense, which I believe every man needs to exercise. This spiritual sense is called Discernment, and it is there waiting patiently for the physical man to feed it everyday, so that it may grow and become of great statue. Have you heard the saying, "Go by your Gut Feeling!"? This "Go by your Gut feeling" is a great example of how a man would exercise the spiritual gifts in his inward man to grow with the Spiritual Gift of Discernment. This spiritual sense is explained in the Holy Book of Matthew 16:1-4 and I ask that you read it now, if you like. This spiritual sense is given at God's Will accordingly. There are other Spiritual gifts by the selfsame Spirit and are also given to man severally accordingly to God's Will. I believe every man under the heavens should pray for the Spiritual Gifts it to be exercised within their spirit man. I truly believe that God gives every man these spiritual senses and gifts as they are willing to give much more of their life to him.

There is one question that I have asked people in my past and present life. When I would ask this question, they would look at me as if I was some kind of nut. But, sense you cant see me with your physical eyes at this very moment, I will ask it. Ready? Here it is.-_- So, what was your answer? Oh! Forgive me. That didn't make much sense did it? I thought that you could read my mind from where you are now. The senses just don't work that way. Please let me explain. One of my greatest failures in life has been that very thought. I would think that God would read my mind and I didn't have to do anything, but just let him read my mind.

My friend, if you can sense any of this, please sense this one thing: God does know your thoughts and intents before you can wink your eye, but he also gave us senses to grow in him, such as the physical senses and the spiritual senses.

At this time it is appropriate for me to now share with you an understanding of the spiritual gifts. I ask you not to think in no way that I'm trying to lead you to believe I have the answers to all the gifts.

But, I know what I know and I would very much like to share these spiritual gifts with you at this very moment. I know the importance of this gifts in my life for the keeping of my Life here on earth and the life to come. The following writings are called, "Heavenly Treasures."

HEAVENLY TREASURES

"Lay not up for yourselves treasures upon earth, where the moth and rust doth corrupt, and where thieves break through and steal: but lay up for yourselves treasures in heaven, where neither moth nor rust doth corrupt, and where thieves do not break through nor steal: For where your treasure is, there will your heart be also." (Matthew 6:19-21) "But my God shall supply all your need according to his riches in glory by Christ Jesus."

(Philippians 4:19)

Today and always and the days to come, I'm confident that God supplies all my needs, "<u>All</u> my needs", spiritual and the physical accordingly to his Will through Christ Jesus.

The physical things are such like, food and water, clothing, shelter from the elements, a great wife, a great husband, children, family, friends, pets and livestock, finances, land, a good job, skills to do the good job, good body health and many more. The good spiritual things of God would be peace, joy, thanksgiving, longsuffering, meekness, gentleness, goodness, faith, patience, love, charity and many more. These good spiritual things that I have just mentioned are not gifts by the Spirit of God, but are good fruits in a man's life that is doing Gods Will.

Before I continue with the Heavenly Treasures let me just clear the mind of the differences of all the spiritual things of God I have just mentioned. <u>First, there are Spiritual Gifts.</u> These Spiritual Gifts by the Spirit of God are given to mankind, so that the man that is willing to do God's Will could produce the good spiritual fruits within and without his complete life here on this earth. Not only are they for the man's profit here on earth, but also for the keeping of his soul eternity. Second, there are Spiritual Fruits (intents manifested in a man's life whether the intents are good or evil). There are good fruits of a man's life and there are evil fruits of a man's life. Last, there are rewards that Christ holds in the palm of his hand waiting patiently to give to every man accordingly as he will. I have confidence one reward is Salvation. Another would be Righteousness (Justification) before God the Father through Christ. Then there are other rewards, such as Faith, Hope, Wisdom, Knowledge, Endurance and Love and the greatest is Life Everlasting. I'm confident that there lays in Christ's hand many more rewards beyond my imagination, but these are the rewards I'm familiar with and I will share them with you.

Now, lets exercise our minds first on the fruits of a man's life. Exercise What? **"For bodily exercise profited little: but godliness is profitable unto all things, having promise of the life that now is, and that which is to come." (1 Timothy 4:8).** The difference between the Fruits of the spirit and Gifts by the Spirit is this:

The fruits of the spirit is the man's intent, where as, the Gifts by the Spirit are only exercised by the Spirit of God accordingly at his Will for mankind's profit and the edification of the Body of Christ. I will say this with confidence; a man will not produce the good spiritual fruits in his life, if the man isn't doing God's Will.

The way a man can start to produce the goods fruits is that of, no other than, letting go of his life and letting God exercising the gifts by his Spirit through his life. How can God help a man, if the man stands in the way? One great way to let God exercise the gift of Faith in his life is through prayer. For an example: "A man that professes that he has faith should indeed exercise the Gift of faith. If a man believes in prayer then he will pray much. If a man doesn't believe in prayer he would not pray and the Gift of Faith would be suppressed or bound in that man's life. If the man that wouldn't exercise the gift of faith through prayer he would not be producing much of good fruits of the spirit, such as love, joy, gentleness, goodness and such like. If a man believes in prayer and prays continually, I'm confident that God would exercise the gift of Faith by his Spirit and reward the man with a good fruit of the spirit If the man continues to exercise the gift of Faith in his life.

I'm confident that God will exercise other gifts by his Spirit for the man and the man will produce much more good fruits in his life." My friend, It's all about letting go of yourself and letting God's Spirit work through your complete life.

Since we are on the subject of prayer, I would like to share this with you. In the Holy Book of James 5:13-16 it is written, **"Is any among you afflicted? Let him pray. Is any merry? Let him sing psalms. Is any sick among you? Let him call for the elders of the church; and let them pray over him, anointing him with oil in the name of the Lord: And the prayer of faith shall save the sick, and the Lord shall raise him up; and if he had committed sins, they shall be forgiven him.**

Confess your faults one to another, and pray one for another, that ye may be healed. The effectual fervent prayer of a righteous man availeth much." Remember Elijah? If a man isn't doing God's Will or worse, doesn't believe in God for who he is, the man will only reap the fruit from the seeds he has sown of his flesh in his life. Not only that my friend, the awful thought of just knowing these things of this world would be his only rewards in this life and the True Life to come. If these things of this world was my only hope, I would be a man most miserable.

In the Holy Book of Galatians 6:7-8 and it is written, **"Be not deceived; God is not mocked: for whatsoever a man soweth, that shall he reap. For he that soweth to his flesh reap corruption; but he that soweth to the Spirit shall of the Spirit reap life everlasting."** "Mary, Mary quite contrary how does your garden growing?" The following principles will explain the life of corruption of sowing to the flesh and the good life in sowing to the spirit. These principles will explain the good fruits of the spirit and the fruits of the flesh (sinful nature). The fruits of the spirit and the fruits of flesh are the products from the seeds sown in a man's life. In the Holy Book of Galatians 5:16-23 and it is written, **"This I say then, Walk in the Spirit, and ye shall not fulfil the lust of the flesh. For the flesh lusteth against the Spirit, and the Spirit against the flesh: and these are contrary the one to the other: so that ye cannot do the things ye would. But if ye be led of the Spirit, ye are not under the law. Now the works of the flesh are manifest, which are these; Adultery, fornication,** uncleanness, lasciviousness, Idolatry, witchcraft, hatred, variance, emulations, wrath, strife, seditions, heresies, Envyings, murders, drunkenness, revellings, and such like: of the which I tell you before, as I have also told you in time past, that they which do such things shall not inherit the kingdom of God.

But the fruit of the Spirit is love, joy, peace, longsuffering, gentleness, goodness, faith, meekness, temperance: against such there is no law. And they that are Christ's have crucified the flesh with the afflictions and lusts."

Now, we have the fruits of the flesh and fruits of the spirit laid out before our eyes and I hope we now know the difference between the two. I will expand much more in the writings later. In the Holy Book of Matthew 7:15-16 it is written, **"Beware of false prophets, which come to you in sheep's clothing, but inwardly they are ravening wolves. Ye shall know them by their fruits. Do men gather grapes of thorns, or figs of thistles?"** In the same chapter of Matthew, Jesus Christ explains more about identifying those that are walking in the lust of the flesh, rather than, walking in the Spirit and please read it sometime soon. We have laid the fruits of the lust of the flesh and the fruits of walking in the Spirit clearly before our eyes to see on the table. Plainly on paper we see them with our eyes, so that we can read and learn from them and make a willing choice to choose to walk either by the lust of the flesh or by the Spirit. We know now the consequences of fulfilling the lust of the flesh and the Life of walking in the Spirit. Again, these good spiritual fruits that we have just read about of walking in the Spirit are not the Gifts of the Spirit and are only the good fruits of a man's life from walking in the Spirit by Obedience. There is not in anyway that a man can produce the good fruits of the Spirit in their life, except to walk in the Spirit of God.

Therefore, the good fruits of the Spirit are manifested in a man's life whom are exercising the Gifts by the Spirit in their Life. I have laid the fruits again and referenced them in the Bad fruit column and the Good fruit column:

Bad Fruits of the Flesh	Good Fruits of the Spirit
Adultery, fornication, uncleanness, Idolatry, witchcraft, hatred, variance, emulations, strife, seditions, heresies, Envyings, murders, drunkenness, revellings, and such like:	Love, Joy, Peace, Longsuffering, Gentleness, Goodness, Faith, Meekness, Temperature: against such theree is no law

If, a man is willing to be Obedient of those few things from God he is able to give many and "All Things" to a man, such as the Spiritual Gifts by the Spirit of God. If only a man is willing to "let go" and "let God" work in his life, then the good fruits of the Spirit of God will manifest in the man's life. The man will not only produce the good fruits of the Spirit, but he will also receive spiritual rewards from Christ.

In this world today, I don't hear much at all about things of these spiritual treasures, unless I'm setting on a pew at church, reading the Word of God or perhaps fellowshipping with the brethren. Perhaps, I have heard something of spiritual treasures, such as watching a Movie, but it would be most always something imagined from the mind of a man or worse, Satan. The following scripture will clearly lay out the gifts by the Spirit to produce the good fruits of the Spirit in a man's Life. These Spiritual Gifts are not only for producing an effect of godliness in a man's life here on this earth, but they are the keepers of a man's soul. In the Holy Book of 1Corinthians Chapter 12, clearly lays the foundation of the understanding of the spiritual Gifts of the Spirit. If you like, please read these entire chapter sometime soon, if you are willing. I just want to point out and expand somewhat on the gifts, so that we can see the gifts with the eyes somewhat in the written Word of God.

In the verses of 7-11 the Word of God clearly gives us the names of the Spiritual Gifts and it is written, **"But the manifestation of the Spirit is given to every man to profit withal. For to one is given by the Spirit <u>the word of wisdom</u>; to another <u>the word of knowledge</u> by the same Spirit; To another <u>faith</u> by the same Spirit; to another <u>the gifts of healing</u> by the same Spirit; To another <u>the working of miracles</u>; to another <u>prophecy</u>; to another <u>discerning of spirits</u>; to another <u>divers kinds of tongues</u>; to another the <u>interpretation of</u>**

tongues: But all these worketh that one and the selfsame Spirit, dividing to every man severally as he will."

Therefore, it is God's Will for <u>every man</u> under the heavens to have the Gifts of the Spirit. My friend remember this fervently; God can and will do anything he wants to do. God is not a respecter of no man. The reason a man would need these gifts would be that of no other than, for the man's profit and the man's life to spiritually grow in his Amazing Love. These heavenly gifts are to keep a man rooted and secured in God's Will, so that he could have a life on this earth much more abundantly and have a chance to enter into Life Everlasting, which is, the Greatest Reward of God and his Son, Jesus Christ for mankind. You have read throughout the writings of this book that I believe greatly in the Holy Ghost and the Power of his effect in my life. I also believe it is by the Holy Ghost that a man receives and exercises the gifts by the Spirit.

In the principle that we have just read (1Corinthians 12:7-11), we have learned that there are 9 gifts mentioned. I believe these gifts are the keeper of a man's life and another Great Key to Eternal Life. It is an importance at this time of the writings for me to share what I believe to be the truth of these gifts. Listen my friend, I believe in a lot of things, but I will say this with confidence;

I don't believe that I have any control of these gifts, much less than, I would have the strength to hold the Enormous Fiery Sun in the palm of my hand. These gifts are only given to a man for that man's profit, "accordingly as God's Will by his Spirit" and only by God are they given to a man. But, I know that God is Willing to give mankind these gifts with a great passion. In the Holy Book of Romans 11:29 it is written, **"For the gifts and the calling of God are without repentance."**

Now, listen closely with your heart my friend, and hear what the Spirit is saying to you and I at this very moment. "God is not a respecter of man. God gives power to whom he choose at his Will. If a man isn't willing to allow the Spirit of God to work in his Life or refuses to do God's Will he will make a jack ass talk, no kidding." Let me explain. In the following scripture you are about to read is about a jack ass talking to a man of God that got in the Way of God. This man of God refused to do God's Will and God used a Jack Ass, yes a Jack Ass to speak, to get a man's attention. God can and will do anything he wants my friend. In the Holy Book of Numbers 22:28 it is written, **"And the Lord opened the mouth of the ass, and she said unto Balaam, What have I done unto thee, that thou hast smitten me three times?"** That isn't the only thing that the Jack Ass said either as you would read the entire scripture. I know it seems somewhat comical, but it is the truth. There is a greater understanding of that scripture that lies deeper from only the Jack Ass speaking. I understand that it is somewhat more easy to focus on the Jack Ass speaking with a man's voice, but there is something greater in that scripture. I have a greater confidence today that God's Spirit is working in every living being of the face of this earth. One way of looking at that truth is that of this; God is Life and all Life has the Spirit of God working in it. All of existence was made by the Great Creator, God. I believe with a great confidence that if a man isn't willing, God is and will forever be.

Perhaps, every man under the heavens would quench God's Spirit from working in their Life all at one time, I honestly believe the animals and stones would start talking and start allowing God's Spirit to work through them.

I believe also the greatest of mankind's weakness is that of limiting the Effect of God's Spirit in this World and the World to come. "This weakness is of the flesh is, doubt. Doubt is the opposite of Faith." Doubt can bind a man spirit so tight that I believe it is a possibility he would die the death before his appointed time. Just as the Jack Ass spoke to the Man of God with a man's voice, would be enough to make someone doubt, hey? The Power behind that scripture also packs a punch into my life from the Power of God's Spirit wanting to Work in my Life. It took a Jack Ass to give a man the understanding If a man isn't willing to allow God's Spirit to work in his Life he will use something foolish to confound the wise.

In the Holy book of Luke 19:37-40 it is written, **"And when he was come nigh, even now at the descent of the mount of Olives, the whole multitude of the disciples began to rejoice and praise God with a loud voice for all the mighty works that they had seen; Saying, blessed be the King that cometh in the name of the Lord: peace in heaven, and glory in the highest. And some of the Pharisees from among the multitude said unto him, Master, rebuke thy disciples. And he answered and said unto them, I tell you that,**

if these should hold their peace, the stones would immediately cry out." My friend, if a gift has worked in your life and you have gifts and rewards of peace, joy or thanksgiving in your heart, don't let the stones praise God much more than you.

I know and have confidence that these gifts are exercise by the Spirit of God in a man's life to strengthen that man's life in God's Will, if the man is willing to let go and let God. I believe and have a greater confidence today that God is willing to give these Spiritual Gifts to every man.

God doesn't change his mind about the calling of man to repentance and to give every man the Gifts by his Spirit to be exercised for the man's profit. I believe these Spiritual Gifts are given to all mankind for all mankind's profit. Let me now explain **"For the gifts and the calling of God are without repentance."** I do not believe one certain man had a dream one evening and just decide to become a Medical Surgeon and say this that morning, "I think I will cut my friends heart out to look at it to see what's causing his mini strokes. I think I could do it well." I do not believe the Apostle Peter had a dream one night and the next day decided, "I believe I will start building a Church. I think people need that stuff. Besides Jesus Christ wanted us to build him a Church anyway." The last but not least, I do not believe that God said, "I think I will make a man and all creation, because I don't have anything else to do. I have the understanding. What am I saying? I am Understanding. That is what I will do today."

My friend, I know that sounded somewhat out of place, but there is a point. Lets just reflect some on what God has done for mankind. I will just hit on a few, because I don't understand God in completeness. I am only a man. I just know what I know. Who could exhaust the Understanding of God? I will now list just a few of what God has done for mankind by the Gifts of the Spirit. Governments, Sciences and Technologies, Hospitals (HealthCare), Rehabilitation Centers, Agricultures, Languages, Writing, Missionary, AA and NA help groups, Veterinary Hospitals and Clinics (lets not leave out our little ones) and the greatest the Body of Christ Jesus (The Church). I could spend eternity writing on those few pieces of God's Understandings. The point is this; God is working his Gifts right before our eyes this very second, in and throughout Eternity. If it wasn't for the Gifts by the Spirit of God working for mankind's profit we would be as a vapor in the wind. Since the time of Adam and Eve the Spirit of God work in mankind's life.

All of the Wisdoms, Knowledge's, Languages, Prophecies, Healings, Miracles and Faith were founded from the foundations of existence by the Gifts by the Spirit of God. We as mankind may think we are smart and intelligent, which we are, but we are only building onto the present from the past of what mankind had laid before times. God works his Gifts by his Spirit throughout this World ever second of a man's life, even when you are sleeping or worse, dead.

We as mankind live today as a man in a race for a prize. We race, but we don't understand the prize. We race, but we don't know the true reason. But, we race. I believe that mankind's biggest enemy is time. Remember my friend, God holds chance and not time in his hand. I'm confident that God doesn't where a Rolex watch or Holds a Calendar in his hand. But he has a eye watch over all his creation and he works even when we are without understanding of the prize of what we labor for. **"Labor not for the meat which perish, but for that meat which endureth unto everlasting life, which the Son of man shall give unto you: for him hath God the Father sealed."** God's gifts and calling are without repentance. Even though God's Spirit works the Gifts in the Universal and Eternal Arena, such as those things we have just read; God's Spirit also works in the Individual Arena. All is God and God is All. All things Work for the Glory of the Great I am, the God of Creation. All of his Handy Works are God's Testimony to mankind that he is Alive and he is "Big". God is so big, he can live in the heart of a man. I know my friend, the saying should be more like this; "God is so big, yet he is so small, he can live in the heart of a man." But my friend, I don't limit my God. God is not small. Let me try to be a little "bigger" in what I'm trying to say here.

In the Holy Book of John 14:37-38 it is written, **"Philip saith unto him, Lord, shew us the Father, and it sufficeth us. Jesus saith unto him, Have I been so long time with you, and yet hast thou not known me, Philip? He that hath seen me hath seen the Father; and how sayest thou then, Shew us the Father? Believest thou not that I am in the Father, and the Father in me? The words that I speak unto you I speak not of myself: but the Father that dwelleth in me, he** doeth the works. Believe me that I am in the Father, and the Father in me: or else believe me for the very works' sake. Verily, Verily, I say unto you, He that believeth on me, the works that I do shall he do also; and greater works than these shall he do; because I go unto my Father."

Today when I read this great principle I set my mind on the greatness of God the Father. God's Body is the Total Existence that surrounds you. I believe that this Great Universe that we live in is only one Atom in God's Great Body. Perhaps this Universe is one Atom in God's Enormous Body then we as mankind are in the Body of God. If we are in his Great Body then he is in All Bodies that we could ever think or ever Imagine. -Pause- Simply put; If you believe that you are in God's Works and you believe you are in his Great Body, then God is in you.

Now, I believe God's gifts work in the individual man's life as well as the Universal and Eternal. God's gifts work in a man's life somewhat like this; If, you would be trusted with a few hundred dollars from a friend and you would by chance loose the hundred dollars the other man perhaps wouldn't favor you with holding his money thereafter. But, maybe later the man may give you another chance, because he loves you and knows that loosing the money, wasn't your true intent. This next time that you would hold his money you would use the money and invest (exercise) the money to make more money and the money becomes much more abundant, right before your very eyes.

When the man comes and ask for the only amount of his money that he had asked you to hold for him you would have his money, also, much more than you had before times. Not only would you have more than you had not labored for, the man continues to trust you with his money. As you would continue to exercise his money you become somewhat liken into a Bank Reserve for the other man. That was only an example of what I believe of how God's Spirit gives to an individual man the gifts of the Spirit accordingly at his will. God's Spirit gives a man a gift and if he isn't faithful in the one gift, he may loose that particular gift and have a less chance of getting any other gift from God. One way of loosing such a gift is that of not "exercising" the gift or using, working the gift. God will try a man of what he has given the man, such as the Gifts of the Spirit.

I believe every man that receives a gift by the Spirit will be tried by God in exercising of the gift. I believe the Spiritual gift that is given most to mankind is the Gift of Faith, not saying that the Gift of Faith is any less important than the other gifts by the Spirit. But, the gift of faith is exercised, more so, for a man's profit. I believe every man under the heavens has a measure of faith given to them from God at their birth. I believe when a man start to believe God for who he is in truth and spirit, this measure of faith begins to grow when a man gives his life to God for a new birth in Christ Jesus. Let me give these examples to help explain these exercises with the gift of Faith in my life. This first example was a time I had to go to the Doctor's office, 65 miles away from my home. As we got to the Doctor's Office, I noticed we had a flat tire on the rear passenger side. I didn't fret not one bit, because I knew I had the emergency tire in the trunk of the car. After I visited my Doctor, I came out ready and I change the flat tire with the emergency tire. I will say this was a time that I was also being treated for severe bursitis in my right shoulder and the pain was great. My shoulder started to hurt somewhat after changing the tires, but I didn't fret.

We left the Doctors office and I had to drive to the main pharmacy to get my medications approximately 2 miles away. As we were traveling along the busy streets of this city, the emergency tire went flat, no kidding. My wife and I were then beginning to get somewhat anxious, but we didn't fret.

As we pulled into the parking deck and got the parking ticket we drove just a few feet and there was an empty space close to the entrance of the parking deck and we parked the vehicle quickly, before the space was taken. My wife and I just sat there in amazement for a few moments and then I said this to my dear wife, "What are the chances that you would have a flat tire, switch the flat tire with a spare tire and then the spare tire would go flat in minutes?" and then my wife said this, "Slim!" My wife and I didn't fret and we began to pray much more and asking God with our mouths to help us understand these chances in our life at that time. After we had prayed we got the reward of patience and peace. We got out of the vehicle and I stood there just looking at this spare flat tire, somewhat shaking my head in amazement.

About the time we were beginning to walk away from the vehicle, to the shuttle bus, a tow truck from a service station came cruising right beside us. I waved somewhat to get the drivers attention and he stopped. I asked the driver this, "Sir. You would never believe the problem I have. Can you help me?" and I told him the problem. This is what the driver of the Tow Truck from a service station that I would think fixed tires, said to me, "I don't know anyone that would come out to fix a flat tire this late. I don't have a air tank on the truck either. If you cant get no one else to help you, call me. I tell you what. Let me tow the vehicle that I've come for and I will be back and bring a tank and pump your tire up." At that time the driver of the tow truck gives me his company card and he leaves quickly. My wife and I began to have a little more hope in this situation, but something still was pulling at my heart as if I didn't believe he would be back.

So, my wife and I sat in the vehicle for almost 45 minutes and then I decided that we would go on ahead to the pharmacy and get my medicines filled. We took the little shuttle bus there at the hospital to the main pharmacy. It took about 3 minutes from the vehicle to the main pharmacy and hospital lobby. I said to my wife, "I would call him from the lobby of the Hospital and check on the status. They have a courteous phone. I don't need no change, because the number isn't long distance." So, I called the number on the card that the driver had given me. A man answers and I spoke with a different man. I told him the situation and then he told me to hang on the phone line and he would ask the driver by Radio about the status of my situation. I heard the conversations somewhat over the phone and this is what the man on the phone told me, "Ok Sir. He said that he just pumped your tire up. Now, we close in just a bit and you need to get the car here before we close to fix the tires." I told him this, "Yes Sir. I know it is getting late and Thank you Sir. I will be there as soon as possible. I'm almost done here at the pharmacy."

After we had completed our business at the Hospital my wife and I started walking back to the vehicle hoping that the Emergency tire was fixed. We somewhat walked fast to the vehicle, so that I could drive it to the Service Station before it closed. I knew we had to be hasty to get to service station, because of the attendant on the phone had told me that they would be closed soon. I knew that I was too far to drive home with an emergency tire only, but we didn't fret. When we reached the vehicle, the emergency tire was still flat, no kidding. We were still stuck there with no tire to ride on and it was getting late. I began to feel something coming from deep within my flesh at this time. I began to doubt that the man had ever pumped my tire up and thought these people had just lied to me. Yes, I thought that those people had lied to me over just a flat tire.

I thought all these men wanted was to Tow my vehicle to their Service Station and charge me much more money, which I didn't have at the time. That feeling of doubt that was coming from deep from within my flesh, began manifest into anger. This anger tried to grab me by my heart and give me a heart attack. At that moment this is what I said to my dear wife, "Get in the car dear. I will drive this car if the rim goes out in a flaming fire ball. Just pray that the rubber will stay on the rim dear. If I do make it to another service station, I will drive to their station, cruise around their station with a smile upon my face and maybe I will blow my horn continuously and wave good bye." I left the parking deck and I drove that vehicle with a flat tire 2 miles in the middle of a large city, in the heavy traffic hour, with my flashers on the blink, at night. Cars were honking their horns, flashing their lights, speeding around me as if bats from the darkness of hell wanting me to get out of their way or they would eat me There was one time that I was almost ran me off the road by some maniac, but I did not fret. I just ignored them and continued on with my journey to a service station to get my tire fixed.

The driver of the Tow truck had told me, during our conversation, that his station was about 3 miles down the road from where we were at off the busy highway. I drove the car until I thought I seen the station and turn into the parking lot off the main highway, but it wasn't the service station it was a Kangaroo Store. I drove around the parking lot with the flat tire going bump, bump, bump, bump, and people were looking and laughing somewhat from where they were getting gas at the Store. I said to my wife "Well at least we have made it this far dear. God please let them have a air compressor. They have got to have an air compressor." I looked and drove around the store twice and couldn't find an Air compressor at this store. I thought that was one of the strangest things, because I always seen air compressors at these types of stores in recent towns. About the time I was driving out the parking lot of this store back on the busy highway, I noticed a small hose hiding somewhat behind a Car Vacuum Cleaner.

My wife and I gave ourselves the "High Five" and we were beginning to be exceedingly happy. I got the coins from my wife and began to shake somewhat as I was putting the coins into the Air Compressor switch. I guess I was shaking from the joy of knowing I would pump this tire up and we could make it either home or at least to a service station before it got too late. My friend, that never happened. The tire was so flat that it was almost off the rim and the tire would not hold any air. Immediately, I felt that same feeling I felt before getting stronger from within my flesh. I looked at the flat tire and I almost gave up and I said this to my dear wife, "I'm going in that store and call a Taxi and we are going to get the hell out of this city." That feeling again was anger growing stronger and stronger and now it was coming out of my flesh. This anger wanting me to do what wasn't right or good in my life. When I look at my dear wife setting there in the passenger car somewhat amazed, I began to understand that it wasn't all about me. I began to weep somewhat within and without. This weeping wasn't because I wasn't near home or I thought someone had done me wrong. This weeping was of defeat and I felt defeated and humiliated. When I seen my wife's eyes with somewhat tears in them, because of my frustration, I knew I had to change my way of thinking. The weeping change from defeat to compassionate Love that I felt of my wife and I didn't want her to be in that mess that we were in. I had no choice again, but to call on God for help. I cried out to God holding my wife's hand and I asked unto God somewhat this, "My God and My king and Lord of my Life. Please God help my wife and I with this problem. Forgive me for my doubt and my accusing another man for something they may had never meant to do. Father God forgive me for judging another man that I don't even know. Please God help us!" My friend, at that very moment I began to have peace again and I set in the car with my wife holding her hand and praying. About that same time I began to understand and discern that the serpent was tempting me again.

I knew that the chance wasn't a chance of man. I knew that I was being tried for something wonderful from God and that crafty serpent did not want me to get it. The Spirit of God exercised the gift of discernment the gift of Faith, the Word of Wisdom, the Word of Knowledge, Prophecy all at one time in my life at that one time.

When I had settle somewhat, my wife and I just sat in the vehicle keeping warm; for it was cold outside. I then began to feel within my spirit man the gift of Faith being exercised by the Spirit of God in my life. Then a light came on in my mind and I said this to my wife, "Dear, I wonder if that store has a tire repair kit. I will go in there and check. Be right back." I walked into this store and there was not much of nothing except soda, chips, paper products and such like. But, I still fixed my mind on trusting God no matter what happened and to keep the peace I had at the time at all cost.

When I began to believe God to help me, I felt a greater confidence within my heart and this confidence completely overpowered the anger and then I got a reward from God by his Spirit, which was peace. I walked near the counter and just to the side of the pay counter and somewhat hid were a few things that you would use on a vehicle, such as a fuse, battery terminals, window defogger and such. I kept hoping and believing and trusting in God that he was able. I continually to feel the gift of Faith being exercised within my life and I was getting stronger and, BAM!! There was the tire repair kit for $5.00. I didn't know at that time if I should had paid the store clerk or kissed her on the cheek, no kidding. But, I did pay her the price of the kit as I thanked her for having the repair kit. I walked to the vehicle where my wife that was patiently waiting for me raising my hand and waving the repair kit. I seen my wife somewhat clap her hands and I was well. My friend the funniest thing was that of the store clerk when she asked me this, "Hello sir. Is that all you need?" At the time I'm confident that this young lady thought that perhaps I was the happiest man that she had ever met.

I wept somewhat before her and said, "Yes sweet heart. This is all I need and thank you so much for being here when I needed you. I will not forget this Kangaroo store and may God Bless you and the company.

I began to giggle and smile with happiness upon my face as I walked out the door. As I walked out of the store I began to feel like a new man with a greater joy singing and praising God with melodies within and without. I took the Emergency tire off and fixed the main tire with the repair kit and installed the main tire and off we finally go toward home. As my wife and I started to drive off from the Kangaroo store we gave each other the High Five and thank God for his Faithfulness.

About this same time I began to feel the Spirit of God somewhat tugging at my heart. The Spirit didn't ask me in a audible voice, but it seem like God was asking me this, "What have you learned son?" The Spirit of God began to minister to me and I was sharing this understanding with my wife as we continued towards home. The Spirit gave me the Cake that night of the understanding of the matter, but I got much more understanding later which I will share with you in just a moment. This is what was ministered to me by the Spirit of God as my wife and I were traveling home. My Faith was being tried by God. Remember God doesn't try a man just for fun my friend, it was for my life. Not only was God trying me, Satan, that serpent, was at that same time of my life enticing me to sin through the weakness of my flesh. But, this time my wife and I had already put our Armour on and Mounted it upon our spirit man ready for battle. That enemy was trying to entice me to accuse and judge someone for something they had not done. That serpent tried to entice me to give up and do something awful, such as getting angry and go to the service station and accuse them of lying to me. He tried to use me to sow discord and strife among another man. He wanted desperately to accuse me of not being worthy of God's Love and the gift of Faith that God had given me.

But, my wife and I defeated that serpent when we trusted with our whole heart that God would take care of us, no matter what. We defeated that serpent by the Word of God when I discerned that he was trying to buffet us in our weakness. We used the Word of God on that serpent and said, "I shall love my God with all my heart, mind and soul. I shall love my neighbors as Christ loved me on the Tree of Calvary."

My friend, I learned greatly from that one particular trial of my faith that evening at the trip to the Doctor's Office. Today this understanding is a keeper in my mind, heart and soul. I exercised the gift of Faith that evening and didn't heed to that serpents poison. If, perhaps I had heeded to that serpents poison, I would had suffered for it greatly in the flesh, I'm sure. If, I had heeded to the flesh, that serpent would had been accusing me before God of not being worthy of the Gift of Faith. I'm confident that the serpent is rubbing his bald head at this time from the bruising from the bottom of my foot. But, I know his devices and I'm confident that the serpent will try to squeeze into my life by another way of weakness. I will say, I may have an axe or a hoe waiting for him the next time.

Just one more point my friend concerning the trip to the Doctor's Office. That following weekend after the day at the Doctor's Office my wife and I went to a local service station there at my home town to get the Emergency Tire Pumped up with air. After the kind service attendant pumped my Emergency tire up with air, I ask him how much did I owe him and this is what the attendant said to me, "Buddy, you don't owe me nothing for that." We giggled somewhat and then I said this to him, "No, sir. I want to pay you something. No body does nothing without getting something" I reach in my wallet and I had no bills, so I reached in my pocket and got the change (all the coins) that I had and gave him.45 cents. The attendant said this, "Sir, you didn't have to do that. I only put air in your tire. It was nothing, but thank you anyway." And then I said this to him, "Sir, air is something. Without air we would have nothing." Now here is the understanding and the point.

That day at the Doctor's Visit I learned a great lesson of something and it is this; Ready? "Something." That's right, just the word something. I learn that that day, if I didn't do something about nothing, then I would had done nothing and be still without nothing. But, that evening at the Doctor's Office I and my wife was determined to do something about nothing when we pressed forward to get the tire fixed on the vehicle. If, or perhaps we had not done something about nothing we would by chance be still sitting under the parking deck there at the Doctor's Office, follow me? Let me just share this with you. Have you every look up the word nothing in a dictionary? If you have, what did you find? If you would say you found something, then you are well. I thought, if I would look up the word nothing there would had been a dark abyss beside the word nothing, but I found something. Its really comical, but the word nothing is really a great understanding of something. My friend, there is nothing except total darkness. If, a man would do nothing then I would say, that man is in dead.

It is somewhat comical in a way as I reminisce into that day, but it was a serious time in our Lives. I look into that day as life or death, no kidding. Just let me throw this in too. Before I went to get the emergency tire pumped up at the service station I had went by and got some chicken feed for my little ones, my chickens of course, from the local feed store. I had only a twenty dollar bill at that time and that was all the cash I had on me at the time. When I bought the chicken feed I was given back the change, which was,.45 cent and a 10 dollar bill. I put both the bill and the change in my front pocket. When I went to the service station I knew that I had the 10 dollar bill and the. 45 cents. It didn't really concern me about the ten dollar bill, because I knew it wasn't worth 10 dollars to pump a tire up with air only. Plus, I thought my wife had a few 1 dollar bills, but later found out she didn't.

I will say this with confidence, if the service attendant would had ask me for 10 dollars, I would had gave my last 10 dollars to him to get air in that tire without any hesitation. So, my wife and I had to leave the service station and make a trip to another Doctor's appointment that Saturday mourning 30 miles away from home. After we left the Doctor's Office we were hungry for lunch. We pull into a McDonald's, one of my favorite eating establishments, and my wife said this, "I don't have any change. Just use the 10 dollars to buy our lunch and I will break the other bill later at Wal-Mart" another favorite hang out. When we got out of the car I checked my front pocket and guess what? If you guessed that the 10 dollar bill was missing, then you are correct. I just couldn't believe it. That serpent was beginning again to start his poison in our life again. That serpent never quits my friend. This is what my wife said as she patted me on my shoulder, "It's fine dear. We will go back to the station when we get back home and ask about the 10 dollar bill." and this is what I said, "No dear. I gave the money to you, didn't I?" And as soon as I said that, I seen the look in my wife's eyes as she thought I accused her of lying to me. I began to discern again that the serpent was at work. That serpent again was trying to sow a seed of discord among my wife and I. His device was for wanting me to accuse my wife of lying to me and sow discord, distrust and dishonesty in our life, in less than a wink of an eye. It happened suddenly, but I was still mounted with my Spiritual Armour and I drew the Sword on that serpent this time. That serpent was cut short and this is what I said, "No we will not go back to the service station either. It is gone dear. All is God's. If someone did pick the 10 bucks up, which I hope the Service Attendant did, I hope the 10 dollars will bless that man greatly and be a testimony in his life." I left it at that and kept my trust and my mind on God and his Son, Jesus Christ and again my wife and I were rewarded with peace.

Now, the other example was a time Satan tried to come into my mind and sow discord among my wife and I as you have read in the "Vision of Satan" insert. I was quick to discern the evil by the Spirit and quick to respond to the gift of discernment exercising within my spirit man and then I exercised my gift of Faith in God, as I submitted unto God for the answer. When I exercised my gift of discernment and resisted Satan, I was quick to receive an reward, which was peace. I will say this with confidence my friend, the battle still continues between my flesh and my spirit. That serpent is still today continually trying to find a weak spot in my flesh to slimmer his way in.

Therefore, the gifts are given to a man for his own profit. The gifts are given to man to keep him, to teach him, to discipline him and to secure him for God's promise and the greatest reward, which is of Eternal Life. The gifts are also given to a man, so that the man will have a life much more abundantly on this earth and to produce good fruit in his life. If a man doesn't let go and let God, he will only receive the rewards of his flesh. That serpent continual to try to sow his corruption in my life and marriage. Marriage between a man and a women is Holy before God and that serpent hates it with a fervent passion. That serpent wants to destroy the Holy Matrimony between a wife and husband greatly. The reason is, marriage is a gift from the Love of God for mankind right from his Loving Throne of Grace.

Today, I have a greater confidence in every written Word of God and his gifts by his Spirit with all my soul, spirit and body and I try to accept it in my heart continuously and keep those things on my mind. I have changed my way of thinking and let go and let God do for me through my spirit and through my mind. I can't even breath without him. I cant see the things of the spiritual and neither do I understand God in fullness. But, God is faithful in training me of his understandings by his written Word and Spiritual Gifts by his Spirit.

I have let go and let God work in my life and my life is much more abundant and fruitful with the good fruits of the spirit. I still today have my good days and my dark nights, but since I know who is in control of my life, I am well. Remember my friend, "This life is like Boot Camp, Training for a Journey." Mankind needs to respond to the High Calling which is Repentance and Salvation. We must have God's Will forever on our thoughts and minds, so that we would understand that Perfect Will of God and do it. Doing God's Will is the one and only way to produce the Spiritual fruits and receive the Spiritual rewards here on this earth, such as peace, patience, goodness, love.

Every man under the heavens are called, but not every man are chosen. In the Holy Book of Matthew 7:21 is written, **"Not every one that saith unto me, Lord, Lord, shall enter into the kingdom of heaven; but he that doeth the will of my Father which is in heaven."** These Spiritual gifts are God's Will for mankind. I believe if a man is without understand of something, such as the gifts of the Spirit then the man must ask for the understanding. The flesh is always wanting to do for pleasure, but the spirit is always wanting to do for the man's profit for life. I ask, Which do you desire? In the Holy Book of Isaiah 26:3 it is written, **"Thou wilt keep him in perfect peace, whose mind is stayed on thee: because he trusteth in thee."** When I began to discern that serpent, Satan, creeping near me when he tried to come between my life many times, I would be quick to submit myself to God and God was faithful in given me the reward of peace. If, by chance I would had not submitted my self to God, I would had been puffing up imaginations and thoughts from my understanding of what I thought the problems may had been. If this would had happened, then my wife and I possibly would not be together today and our prayers would had been hindered. I possibly would had suppressed my gift of Faith and my gift of discernment. I'm confident that the state of my life would had been much worse than before.

Not only that my friend, Satan would have a chance to accuse me before God of not trusting him with my whole life and that rotten maggot would be standing in the shadow laughing at me of my lost.

At this moment, I'm confident that you have exercise at least one of the gifts of the Spirit in your life. In the Holy Book of Hebrews 5:12-14 it is written, **"For when for the time ye ought to be teachers, ye** have need that one to teach you again which be the first oracles of God; and are become such as have need of milk, and not of strong meat. For every one that useth milk is unskillful in the word of righteousness: for he is a babe. But strong meat belonged to them that are of full age, even those who by reason of use have their senses exercised to discern both good and evil." Exercising the gifts that God's Spirit has given us as mankind will make the spirit man and mind much more stronger and we will grow in the Will of God much more greater. There is no other way my friend to grow in your spiritual man and the mind, than that of, exercising the gifts of the Spirit.

Now, lets look somewhat deeper into the Gift of Faith. For an example: If, I would believe that a key would crank my vehicle and it would carry me to town, but didn't stick the key into the ignition and turn the key, crank the vehicle, I would never make it to town, follow me? Exercising the gifts of the Spirit is in the same likeness as that example. If, I believed in Jesus Christ to save me from death, but refused to call on him and trust him to do so for me, I would be still dead in sin, misery and horrors of my life and stunted in my spirit man by my own understandings. If, I say I had faith in Jesus Christ and profess him Lord of my life, but didn't do God's Will, my faith in Jesus Christ would be still dead. A man without works is a man dead in faith indeed. A man that believes in prayer is a man that prays much, but a man that doesn't pray, doesn't believe in prayer. **"The Just shall live by faith."**

A man that has works and faith and exercises what he believes to be the truth of what he believes, would be well and live a life much more abundantly. How would a man exercise this gift of faith? <u>Do God's Will and Don't know it only.</u> Even Satan and his followers knows God and his Christ and they tremble at their name, but they don't do God's Will.

Remember this my friend, Satan has no will and neither does his followers. Satan has no will and the only thing he does know, is to kill and destroy. Satan has no Life and no chance of Life. Satan and his followers have been already Judged and Sentenced to eternal death by the Creator, God the Father. Just look at the Sun or Son my friend, and see the Will of God. God placed the Fiery Sun into orbit as another rebuke to Satan and his followers. They have to look to the Sun every second of their existence; knowing that the Lake of Fire will be their home at the appointed time of God. The Fiery Lake and Torment of Eternity awakes them at the appointed time. The Fiery Sun is an eternal testimony form God of the eternal torments where the thirst is not quenched for Satan and his followers. The Sun could be another eternal testimony such as the Son of God as the Light of the World and gives the Water of Life to all that come to him that thirst. Christ urges mankind to come unto the Light and take of the Water of Life freely. God's Testimonies that engulf mankind's life is for choice, do you want to Live or Die? I am confident today that mankind has no more excuses.

I believe every man under the heaven has been given a "measure of faith" in their life accordingly to God's Will. In the Holy Book of Romans 12:3 is written, **"For I say, through the grace given unto me, to every man that is among you, not to think of himself more highly than he ought to think; but to think soberly, accordingly as God hath dealt to every man the measure of faith."** I believe that God implants this "measure of faith" into the life of an embryo in the mother's wombs.

At this time in the mother's womb, I believe the measure of the faith couldn't be the size of a mustard seed or it could be the size of an acorn or even greater. I believe this "measure of faith" it is given in measure at God's Will for a specific purpose for a man in this life on earth. The more a man is willing to exercise this small mustard size seed of faith, the much more greater the Faith will grow within his inner man into a Tree planted by the waters. The more I began to seek reality, the much more my little seed of faith begins to grow within my inner man. The Father of Life, God, begins to teach me and get my attention of what the truth of reality is. I then begin to have a greater hope in the spiritual than the physical, if I am willing. Then the little mustard seed of faith from God begins to point me to his Words. If, I continue in God's Words and be a doer of His Will in this life to my last breath, I'm confident that I will make it through the gates of Paradise and take of the Tree of Life. My friend at the appointed time when I lay my flesh to the dust that I am made from, I'm confident I will awake and that will be true reality. When I finally began to get honest with God and myself and Let go of my life and let God into my Life, I again live a normal life, and this time, I am ready for battle. I will seek God fervently and revering every word I get from him. I will keep my mind on the Words of God at all cost. I will keep my mind on the Spiritual things of God and refused the evil that temps a man so.

Today my Race isn't for the prize that I set on the top of a mantle and gaze upon, or, all the Money that I could fan in my hand, all the Land I could own or the houses that I could own or even my Dear Loving Wife. Even though, all those things are good to have, but I pressed forward for the Eternal Prize which is, Life Everlasting. Today I know what I am Laboring for and I am at peace with it. Today, I know why mankind is in such hast and go by the appointed time of their clocks. I truly believe the true reason mankind is in such a hasty race is, because mankind knows from deep within their real man, the true reality is knocking at their door.

It isn't a matter of "IF" I will die the fleshly death it is a matter of just "WHEN. "I honestly try to the best of my ability to run my race of life with all my endurance, consistence and obedience before mankind and the Eternal God, which is the True Reality. I do not fret if I by chance do fall behind, for I have a Mediator that Stands in for me. This Mediator is always praying for me and pulling for me through my race on this earth and my mediator is the Eternal God's Only Begotten Son, Jesus Christ.

Today I do have greater sense of the physical and the of eternal. I do not question What or Who I am and I do not question What True Reality is. I just look into the mirror and smile at reality. Today I am forever thanking God for given me my senses.

CHAPTER ELEVEN

ENTER IN THE STRAIT GATE.

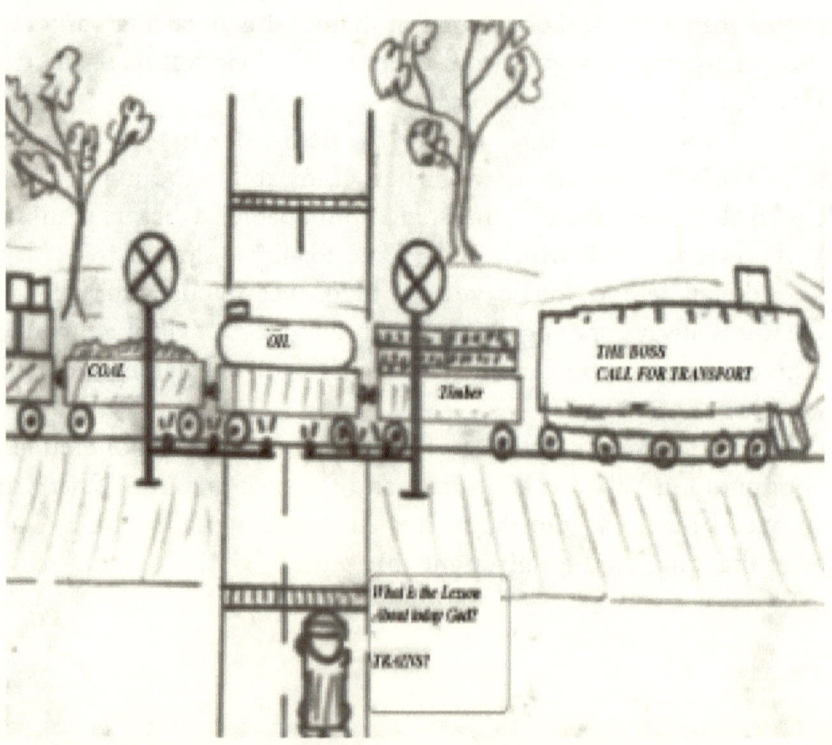

NOW, DURING THIS TIME OF MY LIFE I I was beginning to see Life in a different perspective. I was beginning to sense Life in a different way. Like I have mention in the previous chapters, I was drug free during this time, even from my medications. At first, I thought I was denying I had a Bi-Polar disease, because of doing so well, but soon found out the hard way, I was wrong. I had been off my medications for about 6 months at this time, but this thorn in my flesh was again beginning to buffet me. I had left the Manufacturing job at the Truck Body plant and later, found a job working as a Maintenance man at some disability apartments for the elderly.

Before I left the Manufacturing job, I was on my way to work one last day. I had a revelation at it is called "The Train Revelation." During this time, I again was asking, seeking, and knocking on God's Heart for everything I could get to keep me safe from drugs and alcohol; and as always he was faithful in given me this small, but powerful revelation.

In my past dead life, I thought I was running the course of Life the way I wanted to run it, was a right course, but that course would always lead me back to the Big Hole and the horrors time after time. I tried running the race of life the way I thought was right from my own self rebellious will and from my own understanding from the experiences of my own brain mass, but I would suffer greatly the consequences and have much burden for the matters. Please let me share a matter of burden through a revelation with you.

THE TRAIN REVELATION

After my Resurrection from the dead life, I was headed to work early one morning. I would always leave early in case of traffic or a Train crossing. So off to work I go and this morning was the first mourning a Train had crossed my path in a long time. God was revealing a lot of his principles to me at this time and I remember saying to my self within my heart this morning, as I watched the Crossing Arms come down, "Father God? What is the lesson about today, Trains?" and to my surprise, it was about Trains.

This train wasn't a passenger train, like an Amtrak that carried only people, it was a Industrious train that carried only merchandise and products, like cars, wood, chemicals, etc. As I watched in detail every movement of that train, it was if, I had God's Spirit with me educating me about each part and each movement of this train. It was somewhat like going to school again. The education that God had giving me this morning went like this: A train has an power engine and it pulls cars where it wants them to go, straight, without hesitation. The cars can't go anywhere without the power engine pulling it; for the cars don't have an power engine. The cars can be different and with different loads; for some where empty and some where full, some were small and some were large. The cars were all hooked to the engine by a yoke, and the first and last didn't much matter, because they where going straight where the engine took them, and they became one in my eyes. The engine had the power to take all the train cars without hesitations, straight forward to a destination.

So later that day and that night, all I could think about was this train and what the Spirit of God was teaching me, and then, I got the understanding of this matter later and it went like this: The power engine represented God and the cars represented men of all different makes and with all different loads. If we give our load and get hook up to God, then he will make are load easy. If, we are hooked up to God, he will carry us straight to are destination without hesitation, which is, Eternal Life.

In God's Holy Word, Matthew chapter 11, verses 28-30, "*Come unto me, all ye that labor and are heavy laden, and I will give you rest. Take my yoke upon you, and learn of me; for I am meek and lowly in heart: and ye shall f ind rest unto your souls. For my yoke is easy, and my burden is light.*" That is one part of the revelation God had revealed to me that day concerning the train and I was very thankful for the understanding.

There was another point that was reveal to me and it was of Power and I will share it with you, later in the writings.

Today I now know what real Living is all about, since God has took full control of my will and he has became my power engine, in my life. He has made his burden for me light, which is Life and I now know my rewards are not death, but Life. If, I will stay hooked to the power engine (His Holy Ghost), I will go where he leads me, Eternal Life.

The following writings came to me as I was pondering my Life one evening. The following writings are called, "The Mind of Christ."

THE MIND OF CHRIST

In the Holy Book of Romans 12:1-2 it is written, *"I beseech you therefore, brethren, by the mercies of God, that ye present your bodies a living sacrif ice, holy, acceptable unto God, which is your reasonable service. And be not conformed to this world: but be ye transformed by the renewing of you mind, that ye may prove what is that good, and acceptable, and perfect, will of God."*

One evening, after a Christmas Season had past, I remember greatly this day as I and my wife had stayed this evening with my parents. We would do this almost every year during the Christmas season. I never really thought to my self why I really wanted to stay at my parents, when my home was just a stone throw away from their home. I think it maybe that I just wanted to see if I could find all those delicious chocolates that my father will hide, like a squirrel would hide his nuts. The chocolates, the pies and cakes, the special candies and other delicious foods that my mother would prepare for the Celebration, may had played a part, but I know within my mind that we needed them as much and they needed us. My father and mother raised us children and there were a herd of us, eight to be exact; and today they sit at home just the two of them with a want of their children at home with them, cuddled together at the Christmas tree or upon their laps. The Christmas tree played an important part of my life while I was but a child, and still today plays a great part in the Celebration of Jesus Christ's Birth. The Christmas Tree would bring out something deep with in my spirit. It would give me a sense of Life that I groaned for throughout the year. I remember clearly as my parents couldn't afford to go to the Tree market and buy a tree, but my older brothers and my father would go out to the woods and bring in a fresh pine tree into the home. Just the smell of the fresh pine tree gave me a great sense of enlighten within my mind.

Not only the smell enlightened my mind, but just knowing that the tree was alive and standing in the home. I still today want a fresh tree in my home during the Christmas season, but today I have replaced it with an artificial tree and with a potpourri pine oil in a lamp.

This particular Christmas Season as my wife and I stayed with my parents, something greater was revealed to me and it was this; I was lying and resting on the couch with my mind on different things of the Christmas Season, and then a Light came on in my mind. I began to fix my eyes upon the Christmas Tree. The clear lights on the tree were shinning brightly and changed my mind at what I was thinking at the time. I began to look closer at the tree's lights and seen the ornaments hanging about the tree in their splendor, and then the Spirit of God came into my mind and talk to me. He revealed to me as Jesus Christ being the Tree of Life and the ornaments represented the rewards for those who are willing to do the Father's Will. Just as the Tree of Life in the Garden of Eden, Jesus Christ being that exact Tree of Life. Just as the Christmas Tree was shinning and decked with all the lights and ornaments, Christ is the Light of the World and has been deck with many Crowns. Just as the Christmas Tree was a sense of Life, Jesus Christ is the Way, the Truth and the Life. Just as the Christmas Tree had the ornaments hanging about it, Jesus Christ has the rewards for mankind hanging upon him. Just as the Christmas Tree was putting out a sweet smell for all to be drawn to it, Jesus Christ is a sweet Smell into the World and draws mankind to him.

Now, today I look at a Christmas Tree and I see no Tree of the Earth, but Jesus Christ as the Tree of Life. At the time, the Spirit of God enlightened my mind of this great revelation , but later taught me of much more about the Tree of Life. I will now share this Greater understanding of the Tree of Life and the eating of it to obtain the Mind of Christ.

Today and perhaps always, I have the enjoyment of having a real tree in my home, but I much rather have the Tree of Life growing within my heart and mind, everyday. Like I had mentioned before, Christmas has and will always play an important part of my Life as I grow, with the Life within me. I will always remember the excitement as the Christmas Season drew near. I remember when I was but a child many different things in particular about Christmas. Their were 10 in the home counting my parents and it wasn't any problem about cuddling during the cold nights of winter. The night before Christmas, my parents would ask my older brothers and sister for their Christmas stockings, so that Santa Claus could fill them. We little ones, my mother would pull our stockings from the drawer and when we seen them, our eyes would open wide with excitement, knowing and confirming Santa Claus would soon be there. There were 10 stockings that hung about the home of all the family, including my parents. They were hung at this time on a old oil burner heater that sat in the middle of our home and they were also hung on the doors. I still like to hang stockings on my door or near where I know that Santa Claus will fill it, no kidding. I still like waking in the cool of the morning with the hope that Santa filled my stocking with many different goodies, such as a tangerine and an orange, an apple, lots of nuts, hard candy and chocolates. I would also have something special that Santa would leave for me, such as a note telling me, that he loved me. I remember clearly as a child when my parents would tell us children, "You children need to go to sleep, because Santa Claus cant come down the Chimney with your gifts. If, he finds anyone of you peeping at him or at the gifts that his Helpers have already brought under the tree, he want come down the chimney.

You best not try to sneak and peep, because his helpers have eyes everywhere."

During the entire years of my childhood, I would anticipate the Day of Christmas day by day. My mother would tell me that Santa was watching me and if I wasn't good, he would bring me a bag of Switches and tell her to use them on me. When my mother told me this, I would straighten up like a Iron Board and shut my mouth with a little smile upon my face, as if I was being nice. I think it must had been that I believed in Santa Claus, much more than, I believed in the Easter Bunny. I believed that Santa Claus would have reindeers and soar through the heavens, much more than, I would believe a rabbit would hide eggs, much more, lay an egg. Maybe it was because my father raised rabbits and I never seen them have any eggs. Plus, my father raised chickens and my father would take the hen eggs and my father and some of the hens would fight and feathers would fly all over the place, no kidding. If, my father and a chicken hen would fight over an egg, how much more less chance that a rabbit would have of getting eggs from a hen or laying an egg. Now, the Easter Egg I did believe in as a child and today still like to hide them and find them and eat them.

Today, I have my own chickens just for that purpose, the eggs. I do raise maybe a handful of chickens and have one trained to set as I call out to it. When this particular chicken, which my wife has now named Blondie, comes up to me or I approach it, it will squat quickly as if it wants to lay an egg right before my eyes, no kidding. Now, the egg like I said before I went off into a different tangent, is a gift to mankind. The egg to me represents many things, if you would use your mind and imagine such things as this; First the egg represents a new born life. Second the egg represents bondage and captivity of our life here on this earth. Bound by our bodies we are held captive by our own flesh in this life, but if we continue to grow we can have victory and break the yokes of bondage in our life. Third, the egg also represents the resurrection of a man from his old dark creature life, to a new creature in the Light of God.

My friend, Easter is no more important than Christmas and vise versa, but the Christmas Season I was drawn much more to it. Santa Claus was a good part of my life as a child in the way of teaching me somewhat about Obedience. I would try to be obedient to my parents and others all throughout the year. I would see Santa Clauses in parades, on Television playing music, driving cars and even smoking cigarettes while driving a motorcycle down the interstate. I would even see Santa Claus sometimes as I would go to church! I would see Santa Claus in so many places and doing so many things that I would ask my mother this; "Santa is doing to much mama. I don't think that he will be able to come and visit us this year, will he?" My mother would try to comfort me and say, "They are just Santa's Helpers son and they are keeping an good eye on you and all the children of the World. His helpers are everywhere and they tell Santa Claus, if you are good or bad, so you best be good." There were times I would see Santa Claus at a retail store and my mother would tell me, "Go set on his lap and tell him what you want special for Christmas." When my mother would tell me this, I would look at this strange looking man and say something like this;

"He isn't small like the real Santa Claus and neither does he have a real beard. He don't have the reindeers with him either. Oh No! He must be one of Santa's helpers." And then I would run and hide from him. As I would see so many Santa Claus, I would straightened up in my seat immediately and shut my mouth. I would even hide from the Santa Claus's helpers, hoping that they couldn't see me do anything wrong, but somehow they would always find out. Just using the imagination of my mind and I guess it's the child coming out of me again, when I think of Christmas.

My friend, I don't set my mind to believe that Christmas is any more important than Easter, but since I was but a child, Christmas brings a want from deep within my life. Wanting for something like a gift or maybe a love that is unconditional. A hug perhaps and a gentle kiss upon my cheek from my mother as she would ask me, "Are you hungry son? I love you son and I am so happy to see you. Have you lost some weight!? There is some coconut raisin cake ready for you to eat." A hug and a word as my father looks at me with the eyes of a Wiseman and says, "We love you Son and so does Jesus." Maybe a gift from my daughter and a card that reads, "There are moments in my Life that I will remember, but the greatest, is this day with you Daddy: Merry Christmas Daddy. I love you!" Christmas has been and will always play a much greater part in my developing as a normal living man. Christmas has and always will bring out the child within me.

During this time of season, to me it is a greater hope of Life. It's a time of season to rejoice in Life and know that we have a chance for Life to be born within us. The Christmas season has always been a time that I anticipate, as a child would want candy or a toy from a store. I know today, if it wasn't for the birth of Christ, I wouldn't have any of the things that I have just mentioned. If Christ wasn't incarnated into Flesh and entered into the womb of his mother, Mary, I couldn't have any life. If it wasn't for the Greatest Gift from God that he gave mankind, I would have no life at all.

In the Holy Book of John Chapter 3:16 it is written, ***"For God so loved the world, that he gave his only begotten Son, that whosoever believeth in him should not perish, but have everlasting life."*** If it wasn't for the Obedience of Jesus Christ suffering for God's Will for mankind from his Birth to his Death on the Tree of Calvary, I would be still lost and void with no conscience of Life. If it wasn't for Christmas I would be certainly lost in my own dark abyss. Remember this my friend and store it in your mind; *Christmas is the beginning of Life, where Easter is the Fulfillment of Life. If it wasn't for Christmas, there would be no Easter.* Please follow for the points are growing within, but the points are not mature right yet. Therefore, be patient in the mind.

Now, I will begin to share with you *how I failed* many times in my life from growing in my mind and spirit of my past dead life. I also will share with you *how I know not to fail as much* in my life and grow much more in my spirit and mind. Please remember this my friend and store it in your mind as you read the following writings: *Failing in one place of life is an experience, but to continue to fail in Life, is ignorance.* Also this much greater Principle from the Holy Book of Romans chapter 8, verse 27-28 and it is written, **"And he that searcheth the hearts knoweth what is the mind of the Spirit, because he maketh intercession for the saints according to the will of God. And we know that all things work together for good to them that love God, to them who are the called according to his purpose."**

There is one particular evening that I and my wife were beginning to settled down for the night. I was already in bed with the Bible reading some principles. I began to discern within my spirit that something was wrong or just not right. I just couldn't understanding what could had been making me feel so uneasy.

Then I began to get somewhat frustrated and began to think this: I just couldn't believe all that God has given me that I couldn't figure out what the problem was. It wasn't the fact I was discerning something wrong or not right, it was the fact that I just didn't know what the problem was. I began to get much more frustrated and desperate for the solution to the problem.

So, the first physical matter that I fixed my eyes upon was my dear wife and I said this to my wife, "What have you done? I know that something is wrong and don't you even try to hide it from me. I know that you have done something wrong, so just be honest with me and I will forgive you." About that time I wished I had never said that to my wife. She looked at me as if she wanted to use me as a punching bag, no kidding.

Then my wife said this, "What in the World are you talking about saying, What have I done? My question is what have you done? You are the one asking the question, so you must be the problem. I haven't done anything wrong that I know of and I'm certainly not hiding anything from you. Be honest with me!? You are my best friend and my life, I wouldn't do anything to you or us and especially hide anything from you. That is the strangest thing you have ever said to me and you have said some strange things. You need to check yourself. I love you and I surely wouldn't hide anything from you. You have always trusted me and I have always trusted you. What in this World would make you say something like that!?" After my wife got the last word out, I began to feel like a worm and I wanted to crawl away and hide, no kidding. I did feel badly of how I accused and began to puff up things in my mind of what I thought she had done to me and us, but I did something about it. I grabbed my wife's hand and we began to pray for the understanding and as always, God was faithful when we called upon him.

When I began to understand that something else was wrong and it wasn't my wife, a light came on in my mind. It was an understanding that I would had never thought that I didn't have. After my wife and I began to pray, the Spirit of God began enlightening my mind. The Spirit of God was revealing a gift and sense to me with a greater understanding and the gift, *Discernment*. I knew about the sense of discernment for a long time, but I never knew how to use it. I always thought that discernment came naturally, somewhat like a fish knows to swim in water, but the Spirit of God was quick to enlighten me of the truth. I was enlightened by the truth that discernment is a gift and if I didn't use it, I would loose it. I always knew from deep within my heart that this gift was there, but I thought wrong when I thought that it came naturally and it would show me the problem. Its somewhat like a fish knows that he needs to swim in water, but if he never gets in the water and swims, then the fish would die.

Like I said, I knew I had the gift of discernment, but I never knew how to use it and because I didn't know how to use this gift, I was quick to puff up imaginations from my own thoughts, follow me? But, this time I was quick and I did something with the gift of discernment. When I grabbed my wife's hand and we began to seek God for the answer, I finally knew how to use the gift. The reason I had failed so many times in my past when I thought I was sensing something wrong and then be quick to judged something wrong, was the fact I did not know how to use the gift of discernment. This sense and gift of discernment does come spiritually to a man, if he has the gift, somewhat like a fish knows to swim, but if a man is ignorant from how to use it, he will be quick in judging something that he would fix his physical eyes upon.

Now, when I began to sense something wrong or just not right, the gift of discernment started to work immediately with no doubt. The gift of discernment is given to a man to discern right from wrong and has no respect of any man. The gift isn't given to a man for him to discern and then be quick to judge, it is given only for the discerning of right from wrong. The gift of discernment is given to a man to discern good from evil. This sense is in the same likeness as the Angel holding the Flaming Swords that kept Adam and Eve from the Garden of Eden after they had sinned. The Angel was placed there to keep evil from entering back into the garden and I have confidence the Angel doesn't respect no man.

Reminiscing into my past life, God would always try me for the gifts that he wanted me to have. During my past dead life, my life, was almost always destructive from not allowing or quenching God's Spirit to give me the confidence that I needed in the gifts. I guess I thought that every time that I had ever asked God for something, my life began to have great suffering and I just didn't want that. I thought that I had what I needed and I was Ok with what I had, but soon learn again, my thoughts were not God's thoughts.

I believe the only time that I remember that God had not tried me was at the time he saved me when I was near committing suicide at the age of 19. At this time as you have already read in the Apathetical Man, God intervened and said this to me with an audible voice that melted me, "You Are Forgiven." God didn't try me, but he had justified me when I had given my life to him a few months before the suicide attempt. God justified me when I believe in him as I understood him at the time. When I honestly gave my life to the Lord at the age of 19 he was faithful and just to save me and keep me safe from death, as long as I believed him to do so. At that time of my life, God didn't try me, but it was just the beginning of my life as a child of God. I thought I understood forgiveness at the time, but I couldn't even forgive myself and God the One and Only had to intervene and give me the understanding of forgiveness. I will say this also, I didn't get the complete details on forgiveness until 12 years later, no kidding. God knew at the time what I needed, such as forgiveness, but it would take me 12 years to know how to use the gift of forgiveness.

Today, nearly 25 years after that incident, I'm still growing in forgiveness. After I honestly gave my life to the Lord at the age of 19, I became a child of his. God would now become my Spiritual Father who would discipline me, teach me, keep me, and save me from death. God not only became my Spiritual Father, but my Good Shepherd also. God would discipline me, if he had to use mankind to battle me hand to hand for me to get the understanding. Sometimes I would be so rebellious that God would even cause my own blood to be shed. When I would see my own blood, it would be at this moment that I would call out to God and repent my self back into his Will. God has sent many people, creatures and things my way to teach, discipline, keep, and save me from death during my entire life, but I will say this; If I had been just a little more Obedient in my Life, I may not had went through so much suffering for rebellion.

The time that I had mentioned before, about my wife and I on the subject of discernment, is an example of how I would be quick to lean on my own understandings and then suffer for being ignorant from the true understanding of what God wanted for me. I would quenched the Spirit of God, because of judging another man or creature with my flesh.

Now, during this time that my wife and I was having this trouble in our season, I did discern something evil in my life. The gift of discernment was working perfect, because it discerned evil from good. But, I thought it would remove the evil from my life, if it came to me and I would not have to be concerned with it.

My friend, I have a greater understanding in the matter today. Life isn't all about what you know, it is also about what you do with what you know about life and this will determine the way you live your life. The greater understanding was that the gift of discernment was working perfect, but it was waiting patiently for me to respond to it. I did get the understanding after I submitted my will for God's Will and it was this; The gift and sense of discernment was discerning evil, which is, Satan. The gift was just letting me know that the enemy was near my camp. That devil was trying his best to sow the seeds of destruction in our Life. He was attempting to sow the evil seeds of distrust, dishonesty, discord in our life and I almost let him get away with it, again. But, because I responded to the gift and sense of discernment and grabbed my wife's hand and fell to our knees and prayed out to God with our mouths and not our thoughts, I defeated that Devil by the Word of God. When God enlightened me with this understanding, the Spirit quickened me with what I needed to do with the gift and I said this out loud as I was holding my wife's hand, "Satan! It is written, Thou shalt not tempt the Lord thy God. Satan! It is written, Thou shalt not live by bread alone, but by ever word that proceeds out the mouth of God. Get behind me Satan!" When I began to say this with my mouth out loud, I began to sense peace and that evil feeling, just fled away.

Please follow my friend, the points are near. Please let me share this principle with you.

In the Holy Book of James Chapter 4, verse 7-8 reads as written, *"Submit yourselves therefore to God. Resist the devil, and he will flee from you. Draw nigh to God, and he will draw nigh to you."* James also writes in Chapter 1, verse 22-25 and it is written, *"But be ye doers of the word and not hearers only, deceiving your own selves. For if any be a hearer of the word, and not a doer, he is like unto a man beholding his natural face in a glass: For he behold himself, and goeth his way, and straightway fretted what manner of man he was."* My friend, these are powerful principles written, so that we today as mankind would have the understanding of what to do with the spiritual gifts that God has given mankind. Like I said many times throughout this book: It isn't all about what you know in this Life, it is also what you do with what you know that will determine the way a man will live his life.

During this time of my Life I was again trying to live a normal life, but I was determined much more this time and I had a greater understanding of the Will of God. I was drug free and obedient as I could possibly be at this time. I had committed my Life back to the Trust of God and I and my wife where doing much better in the spirit.

My wife was so much happier and I had found, serenity. Not only was I reading and listening to God's Word, I was beginning to do God's Word in my life. I thought I had all of my spiritual Armour about my body, but that devil almost found a gap within my helmet of Salvation. He tried to sow the evil seeds into my mind and cause great discord in our life. He knew that he just couldn't come and knock on my door and say, "We're here! Its time to party! Lets us come in and we will give you your hearts desire and after that, I will give you a tour of Hell. Are you ready to ride?" That devil knew he couldn't buffet me with my thorns of the flesh at this time, because he knew that I was not going to fall for those devices. So, what does the this devil try to do?

He tries to get into my mind and plant discord among my wife and I. He knows that my wife is flesh of my flesh and bones of my bones and he would try anything to break that which God had given us apart. I've always been somewhat fearful of this and that fear I held deep within my heart. This type of fear almost cause my Life, no kidding. Why would this fear almost cause my life? It was this; In my past, if I knew that Satan was trying to pull my wife and I apart, I would be quick to give up trying to live a normal life and go back to my dead life. What!!? I would had much rather to do drugs and stay drunk and not go to church and not live a good life, than to loose my wife. So, this fear of loosing my wife was a fear that I did not want to face. I had already been through 1 divorce and it wasn't good and I just knew I wouldn't survive through another. I do know this with a greater confidence; *Those things that I hide deep in my heart, are not because I want to save them. It's because I fear them, and I just don't want to face them.* I also know that these fears will lead to much more worse things, such as anger, resentments and bitterness. So, that devil knew if he could cause discord among us, then our prayers would had been hindered. Later it was possible that we may had separated and my wife and I would had been miserable and possibly gave up or worse. That devil, Satan, is spiritual and he has a soul and he has no flesh. It is in the spiritual man that he will try to enter.

It is in the Mind that that devil will sow his evil seeds and whisper deceit. Satan can enter another creature or man and use them against you also. But, Satan can in no way be incarnated into the flesh, because he has no power to do so. It is by deceit through the mind that Satan comes into a man and sows discord among the brethren. Satan is continuously trying to sow his evil seeds, somewhat liken unto the story of "Johnny Apple Seed" who goes around the Whole Earth and plants apple seeds. But, Satan isn't planting no apple seeds my friend, and neither does he rest from his labor. The seeds of Satan are only for growing in death and that is about the simplest way I can explain it.

His seeds, are nothing but destruction and Death. Today Satan is defeated by and through, Jesus Christ, which is, The Seed of Righteousness, The Seed of Glory, The Seed of Life.

Now, let me just clear this up real quickly. I said that Satan has no flesh and can only enter the mind to sow deceit, but I will also say that Satan can buffet a man by his flesh, such as a man's thorns. I believe totally on this one fact and be careful my friend and be patient. Satan has been given a lot of credit for things of this world, but there is one thing he want get no credit from me about which is, my flesh. I have been told many times that Satan gave a man cancer or Satan killed that man in a wreck or Satan did this or that. Satan has no power to give or take Life. It isn't Satan that is killing mankind, it is the sinful nature of mankind that is killing mankind. Today, I can say this with honesty; The only fear that I fear today, is that of my flesh, which is, my self will or sinful nature. ***"Submit yourselves therefore to God. Resist the devil, and he will flee from you. Draw nigh to God, and he will draw nigh to you."*** If, only a man would set his mind on that matter and do God's Will and not Self Will would he ever understand God's Will.

My friend I have written earlier in the book about the Spiritual Armour. There is one piece that I just want to expand on somewhat and it is the Helmet of Salvation. A Helmet is the protection that would cover the entire head. The Helmet's main purpose I believe, is to protect a soldier from a brain injury. If a soldier would get a brain injury, that soldier what be brain dead or die from the wound. Their are different helmets in this World, such as a soldier's helmet that he would wear into battle. I just want to ask this question and then I will continue. Would you ever think that a soldier on the front line of a war, would ever take his helmet off during battle? No. So why if we have given our life to God as we understood him at the time to save us from death take our helmet of salvation off and lay it to the side. I guess this would be the answer:

"I'm saved and God will protect me now and I don't need to wear my helmet no more." Just to let anyone that would like to know, we as mankind are still at war and will always forever be at war until that devil, Satan, is bound and chained and cast into the Lake of Fire. And if a man that has been given the gift of Salvation would take his Helmet off at any time, he would be just as vulnerable for a mind injury in the same likeness as the soldier would get a brain injury. As long as the enemy is there I will be mounted up with my Armour and if I do sleep and a piece may try to fall from my body, I have set my mind that God will protect me at that very moment and let me know where my weakness is. But, until I do sleep or rest, I will be ready for battle and I will have my helmet of Salvation protecting my mind from the fiery darts that Satan fires continuously at me. Just one more little note. When you receive something from God and you don't use it, be careful that you don't loose it. Satan knew that he couldn't get to me with his darts in any other way, but through my mind. If it had been in my past, he would had probably caught me off guard and I would have had my Helmet of Salvation off from about my mind. This time I may have had my helmet on, but it must had not been mounted correctly and Satan almost got a poisonous dart into my mind. But, my spirit was quick to respond to the God's Spirit's gift of discernment and I remounted my helmet.

Now, when the darts are flying, they began to bounce off my helmet as if you would throw a rubber ball against a concrete wall. Not only did I submit myself to God, I resisted that devil by the Word of God. Let me please ask you this question; "Do you think that Satan knows God's Will?" My friend, Satan knows not any will, except his own and let me define his will in one word, Death. If Satan knew God's Will do you ever think he would had enticed mankind to murder Jesus Christ on a tree? No, I don't believe he would had ever crucified God's Will on the Tree for mankind. Satan is ignorant from God's Will, but is extremely crafty in his own will.

> So my friend, "Humble yourselves therefore under the mighty hand of God, that he may exalt you in due time: Casting all your care upon him; for he careth for you. Be sober, be vigilant; because your adversary the devil, as a roaring lion, walketh about, seeking whom he may devour.

Whom resist steadfast in the faith, knowing that the same afflictions are accomplished in your brethren that are in the world. But the God of all grace, who hath called us unto his eternal glory by Christ Jesus, after that ye suffered a while, make you perfect, stablish, strengthen, settle you. To him be glory and dominion for ever and ever. Amen."

(1Peter 5:6-11)

I have share a few things to get our mind stirred up somewhat and now I ask this wanting question; "How can a man grow in the spirit man and become stronger in the his mind?" My friend, only obedience will get you there. Being obedience would be a flag to me that the man is well and seeking the good things of life. Obedience in all your ways can lead to greater rewards. If a man is willing to give his complete life to God as he understands him at the time, without holding or hiding any sinful intent in their heart, God is faithful to save him from death, destruction, misery, and horrors of his life. If a man is Obedient in the one gift of Salvation, then God is faithful to reward him with much more others.

Today, I try to the best I possibly can to living a normal life or obedient life and have my good times and my bad times. Now this normal life that I'm talking about isn't making it to church when the doors are open, so that I would want to know what Miss Piggy or Kermit the frog had for dinning last night. I'm talking total Obedience of God's Will in my life.

The physical life of a man is like a vapor compared to Eternity and I don't have room in my life today for non-sense or foolishness. I know today that this life isn't about baking cakes or flying a kite, even though that still is good to do. But, I know today that this life is all about the choice of Life or Death and it is extremely serious. If, I could ask some willing questions to a man, these are the ones I would ask: Are you willing to die for the cause of what you believe in? --Pause-- Oh! This is the other. Are you willing to give up all that you have for the cause of what you believe in? --Pause-- Oh! These are surely hard concrete questions and your response to them, is your answer of Obedience. Whatever your answer maybe, don't fret my friend. The way that I would answer these questions would be is in this way: I would use the Word of God.

In the Holy Book of Matthew chapter 6, verses 21;33-34 it is written, *"For where your treasure is, there will your heart be also. But seek ye f irst the kingdom of God, and his righteousness; and all these things shall be added unto you. Take therefore no thought for the morrow: for the morrow shall take thought for the things of itself. Suff icient unto the day is the evil thereof."* My friend, I ran like a mouse from an Elephant fight when these questions were asked to me in the past.

I thought I would give my all and all to God and but would soon understand I wasn't willing to give my life to him. When I refused and held things from God, I lost them quickly. Later I had the understanding that God wanted the whole apple and not just a bite of my life every now and then.

When I finally got stronger in my mind and spirit, I did honestly submit my self totally and honestly to God and I die daily for the cause of God's Love to manifest into my Life. When I did give my all and all to God, he was faithful and he now gives me all the things I need in this life without not one piece missing.

Today, he supplies all my needs, physical where the eyes can see and spiritual where my soul finds peace. When I truly began to seek God for his righteousness, he was faithful and just to give me the understanding of his righteousness by his Spirit, accordingly to his Will. *"For where your treasure is, there will your heart be also."* My friend, the way a man grows in the mind and his spirit is where the man holds his treasure.

Now, lets stir the mind up some more and get to know it much better, ok? The Mind. What is the Mind? I believe that the mind is the gateway to the spiritual. I believe the mind stores the man's complete intent of his life, rather they be good or evil. I believe it is here in the mind that a man dreams, fantasies, and imagines. I believe it is here in the mind that the enemy can enter into and lead a man by his sinful lust. It is here in the mind that the enemy will deceive a man to believe in his own understanding and then the man would be void and empty of God the Creator and be lead by his own sinful lust. The enemy, which is Satan, can enter into the mind of the man's dreams, imaginations and fantasies. When I was but a child, I would remember dreaming many times and awake screaming to the top of my voice, because of the horror that I had just dreamed. But, it seemed as if I kept my mind on the things of God, he would reveal things to me which I would later get the true understandings. In my past there would be someone that had done something to me that I felt was wrong. I would fix my mind on something like this; "I wish I could become a Dragon and fly over that man's house and spit fire upon it." Exercising our minds in this way will lead to destruction my friend. I did imagine and fantasize in these vain and sinful ways, but God would be swift to discipline me for the disobedience. He would chastise me many times, until I would get the point and submit myself to him with great repentance. Exercising your mind in this way would be the same as saying, "Hello. My name is Mr. Rebellious, A.K.A. the Evil Man, or The Devil"

During these times that I would exercise my mind to do evil, the enemy was in the shadow accusing and even laughing at me. The mind isn't meant for this type of growing. The mind is given, so that, a man would grow in the knowledge and Understanding of God's Promise and not Satan or self will desires. There is something greater that I would like to share with you and it is this; The mind is the gateway to the spiritual and it is here that a man will begin to exercise his life. It is here in the mind that the gifts that we have read about earlier, enter and are exercised by the Spirit of God, but the mind can not discern itself. Now the mind is the conscious of the soul, but it cannot use the gifts on it's own. The Spirit of God gives a man the gifts and the man must exercise the gifts, by the Spirit, to grow and mature in the Love of God. Let me explain quickly. If you believe in God, have you ever seen him.? If you believe in the Lord Jesus Christ and all that he did for mankind over 2 thousand years, were you there when they crucified him?-Pause-- I don't think you have met God face to Face, and neither were you there at the very moment when the crowd cried out and said, "Crucify Him!" But. somehow we believe anyway, if you are a believer that is, correct? This is the gift of faith that God gives a man when a man first believes in God for Salvation and deliverance from this World of pain and misery. The more we hear about God's Word, such as going to Church, hearing preaching of the Gospel, reading our Bibles, loving our brethren, praying for each other and our enemies, we at this time set our mind on God and Jesus Christ and are obedient to the Will of God. The much more that we are willing to let go and exercise what we believe to be the Way, the Truth, and the Life and let God's Will manifest into our life, the more faith we get. The more faith we get, the more trust we get. But, how can that be since we were not there and neither have we seen God face to Face, that we can still believe? This is how the Spirit of God exercises the gifts in our mind. The Spirit uses the spiritual gifts, if we are willing to let him, to teach and show us greater things than you could ever imagine from your own understandings.

The mind can not discern or examine itself. But, the Spirit of God will examine our life and search out the darkness and bring it to our remembrance. The much more a man is willing to do God's Will, the much more that God is willing to show himself to him by his Spirit. The more we are willing to do God's Will the more we exercise our faith in God, such as praying for others and reading and studying God's Word.

We can look into a mirror and see a bump upon the face and start judging if it would be a pimple, mole or cancer, but the mind can not examine itself. Therefore, the Spirit of God is the Great Examiner and he is quick to search the soul, spirit and body and revel these things to a man, rather they be good or evil. The Spirit of God is also swift and quick to call and bring a man to repentance and submission, but the Spirit is meek and Lowly and doesn't knock the door down. The Spirit is gentle and will only knock on a man's heart to let him in.

The Apostle Paul wrote this letter to the Ephesians and it is found in the 3rd chapter, verses 14-21, and it is written, ***"For this cause I bow my knees unto the Father of our Lord Jesus Christ, Of whom the whole family in heaven and earth are named, That he would grant you, according to the riches of his glory, to be strengthened with might by his Spirit in the inner man; That Christ may dwell in your hearts by faith; that ye, being rooted and grounded in love, May be able to comprehend with all saints what is the breadth, and length, and depth, and height; And to know the love of Christ, which passeth the knowledge, that ye might be filled with all the fulness of God. Now unto him that is able to do exceeding abundantly above all that we ask or think, according to the power that worketh in us,***

Unto him be glory in the church by Christ Jesus throughout the all ages, world without end. Amen."

Now, there is something that I would like greatly to share with you at this time, but first, let me ask this question; What happens to an infant that never got the chance to grow in the Grace and Truth of God and his Will? Are they judged by God and cast into Hell, because of being void of God's Love? First I will say this: It is written, *"A man that knoweth to do good and doeth it not, to him it is sin."* I am no Judge and neither do I want to be judged, but I will say this with confidence: A man that can not discern from his left or right knows no sin. The God Almighty an Just Judge and he has the power to give and the power to take. What about the creatures, do they know sin? Let me share with you now about a man that was taught of a great understanding of this matter. In the Holy Book of Jonah chapter 4, verse 11 it is written, *"And should not I spare Nineveh, that great city, wherein are more than six score thousand persons that cannot discern between their right hand and their left hand; and also the cattle?"* I believe the answer to those questions are laying patiently here in this book for a man to have.

Let me explain somewhat the understanding. Now, Jonah was called and chosen to do something for God, which was the Will of God. God chose Jonah and said to him, "Go to Nineveh and preach Repentance to the people." God never said he would kill and destroy the people, but he was giving them a chance to submit themselves to God's Will. But no, Jonah rebelled and ran and tried to hide from God. I believe it wasn't because he was afraid of going to Nineveh or that he was afraid of the call from God, it would be that Jonah had *resentments* and much *anger* for the people of Nineveh. I believe that Jonah thought he was much better than the people of Nineveh and it would had greatly pleased Jonah, if God would had just destroyed Nineveh off the face of the earth. So, because Jonah was a child of his or a seed of Abraham, God was swift to prepare something for him for a great understanding of his "Love" for mankind.

God prepared a great fish for Jonah and the fish swallowed Jonah and delivered Jonah straight to the front door of Nineveh. I bet after this preparation from God, Jonah changed his mind, would you think? Jonah did change his mind and went about the city preaching Repentance.

So, after the King heard that a man of God was at his doorsteps of his own land preaching repentance, the King cried out loud and put out a proclamation throughout Nineveh for all the people to repent and submit themselves to God. The people were obedient and submitted themselves to God. It is written that God then repented (changed his mind) of the evil (not good) what he was going to do toward Nineveh, because it pleased God that they repented. But no, Jonah got greatly displease and got angry at God, because God changed his mind. Jonah was so angry, that he wanted to die, no kidding. So, God prepares some other things for Jonah. God said to Jonah, **"Doest thou well to be angry?"** What a great truth of what God was asking Jonah was this question. God was asking Jonah if his life was well off to be angry. Not only was God given Jonah an understanding at the time, he was also given him the answer to his problem, which was anger and resentments against another man that he didn't even know. I believe that this anger that he held in his heart was all the resentments that he had against Nineveh by what he had heard by the physical of his ears. Jonah had puffed up in his own imaginations and was bound by his own thoughts that Nineveh wasn't worth Living on the face of the earth. Jonah was judging a Nation that he had never set foot upon and neither did he know any man there is this city. These thoughts that Jonah had were causing the grief he was experiencing.

It is amazing to know that God took one man and showed the Whole world the understanding of these great things. God is God and there is no other besides him. God is the Great Righteous Judge of all things. God is merciful and righteous to forgive us of our sins, if we are willing to repent. The best point was that of Jonah holding in the deep parts of his heart and mind, all the anger and resentments against a nation he had judged from his own understanding. God disciplined Jonah with great understandings and prepared for Jonah many things that he could feel and see with the physical eyes. Jonah may had never been to Nineveh before the day the great fish vomited him out on it's shore. Jonah had no part of building Nineveh or labor there, neither had any property there. But, because he was lead by his own understandings, Jonah suffered for the disobedience of not doing and knowing God's Will. The suffering was so great, that Jonah cried out to God asking him to take his Life. The anger that Jonah held in his heart was his only intent and it consumed his entire Life. My friend, God is the Righteous Judge.

Today, I must set my mind on the things of God and I try honestly not to judge any man. I have no worries of the things of tomorrow or dwell in my past dead life, because I live. I live not of myself, but because he lives in me, is why I live. God knows a man if the man knows God. God can not help a man, if the man stands in the way. If an infant would die before the fulfillment of its obedience, God would surely take it back, not because it was void of him, but God would have a passion to give it another chance at choice, so that it would grow in his Loving Grace. I'm talking only about the innocent here my friend, only them that are innocent. I do have thoughts on these things today, but I keep my mind on the real point and it is this; "How can I live a much more abundant Life here on earth and Enter into Life Everlasting?"

Doing the Will of God and not Knowing only the Will of God, is the answer to that question. Today these are my thoughts and I will always keep my mind on those things, because I do not want God to prepare something for me to change my mind, as he did Jonah. Let me just briefly share with you what God prepared for Jonah so that Jonah would understand his Love for mankind. *First* - God sent out a great wind in the sea for Jonah, to rock his boat.

Second -God prepared a great fish to swallow Jonah and vomit him on the doorsteps at the place he was running from. *Third* -God prepared a beautiful gourd for Jonah to comfort him and cover his head from the heat one day.

Fourth -God prepared a worm that came during the night that destroyed the beautiful gourd that comfort Jonah from the heat upon his bald head. *Finally* -God prepared a vehement east wind and the sun beat upon the head of Jonah that he fainted. My friend, I know that sounds comical, but it is serious for it was a matter of life or death for Jonah. God still today will prepare things for his disobedient children, but it is good for his children.

Today, I just don't want God to prepare anything for me to get an understanding like that, anymore. I just go where the Spirit leads me and I am willing to do whatsoever that God's Spirit leads me to do, even if I don't like what I was asked to do from God, because I don't want God to prepare something for me like he did Jonah, follow me? Could you ever imagine how Jonah must had felt, as he was in the belly of that great fish and then the fish vomited him out of it's mouth on Nineveh's sea shore. If, I would had seen this man vomited out of a great fish on a sea shore and then the man stood straight up and immediately started shouting, "Repent! For the Kingdom of God is at Hand!", I believe I would had changed my mind of thinking also, wouldn't you?

Now there is another principle that I want to share with you at this moment. In the Holy Book of 2Corinthians chapter10, verses 3-6 and it is written, *"For though we walk in the flesh, we do not war after the flesh: (For the weapons of our warfare are not carnal, but mighty through God to the pulling down of strong holds;) Casting down imaginations, and every high thing that exalteth itself against the knowledge of God, and bringing into captivity every thought to the obedience of Christ; And having in readiness to revenge all disobedience, when your obedience is fulfilled."* -Pause-- Oh God!How long is it going to take for my Obedience to be fulfilled? Oh Obedience, how I've long for thee! My friend, I sure wish I had that understanding during my past. Obedience was to me something I never understood. I thought that God saved me from near death and the rebellion that I once had would be a shadow of my past, but it just doesn't work that way my friend. How can a man be obedient to God's Will, if the man doesn't know what obedience is, much more, his Will?

Oh God, can I ever live an obedient life before you, living among a World that is greatly disobedient to your Love and Grace? Have you ever heard the saying, "Play with fire you will be burnt with the fire?" or perhaps, "Play with the swine and you will smell like the swine." And, "Eat with the chickens long enough, you will become like a chicken." Most of all my past life was surrounded and most all times, engulfed in disobedience. It wasn't that I wanted to be this way, but I truly did not know what obedience was.

I thought that obedience was that of when the teacher would ask someone to raise their hand in the classroom and I would raise my hand. When I would raise my hand the teacher would ask me for the answer and I would say, "I wasn't raising my hand because I have the answer, but I was raising my hand to tell you, I don't have the answer." Then the teacher would look at me with those eyes of discipline and say to me, "I said raise your hand, if you have the answer, not if you didn't have the answer. If you try to pull that again, I will send you to the principle's office." I guess I wasn't paying attention to what the teacher said, hey? Disobedience was somewhat like a joke as I would play on a friend during my past. But when the joke got out of hand, I would be then quick to repent that I had ever did it. The hand of the principle would slap me across my behind with a large wooden paddle and change my mind quickly. Sometimes the disobedience would even cause me to draw my own blood, because of not listening to the instructions of my parents. My parents would tell me something like this; "You can got out to play, but don't be climbing any trees." and I would fall out the tree and break my arm and crack my nose. When I seen the blood again and again I regretted that I didn't listen to my parents.

Disobedience has been my greatest downfalls of my life and also my greatest lessons. My parents disciplined me until they had no choice, but to get me help on the matter. They knew if I didn't get help, I would be killed or worse. So, my parents did get me help and I was admitted to a Hospital for almost 2 years at the age of 16. Not only did my parents turn me over to the care of a professional, but they also turn me over to God and left me at his feet. Its not that my parents didn't love me or care for me, but It was the fact that my parents did love me greatly and didn't want to loose me. I was very rebellious during my young years and was totally out of control sometimes. Somewhat like a wild animal that would get loose from the Zoo. The only way to get to the wild animal is to shoot it with a sleeping dart and cage him up. But, I did calm down after the rod of God was on my behind for many years and I began to submit my self to his care. During this time I would ask this question, "God, why did it take so long for you to tell me just to submit myself to you. I would had rather you told me that, than you disciplining me."

And then God would answer me quickly and say, "Son, I had to teach you what obedience is first, so that, you would listen to me. Son, can you hear me Now!?

STRAIGHT ARE THE GATES

"Enter ye in at the strait gate: for wide is the gate, and broad is the way, that leadeth to destruction, and many there be which go in thereat: Because strait is the gate, and narrow is the way, which leadeth unto Life, and few there be that find it." (Matthew 7, verses 13-14) "So the last shall be first, and the first last: for many be called, but few are chosen." (Matthew chapter 20, verse 16).

Living a normal life in my past life was something that I thought only the rich or those that had been called to do something specific for God's purpose. But today, I know that not to be the whole truth. Today, Living a normal life, would be the same as living a straight and consistent life in all things. I would say also, the simplest of a Normal Life would be that of Living a Obedient Life and not a rebellious Life.

My friend, I fell many times in my past life of not understanding this matter. I thought I understood normal, but my thoughts weren't God's thoughts. The following writings will help explain the "Strait Gates" somewhat more clearly as I share with you my belief of the truth of the meaning of the scripture above.

Before I start, let me just say that All mankind is called to Salvation, but there will be only a few that are chosen as his sons and daughters, follow me? This call from God is without repentance. God will never change his mind on the calling for mankind to live a straight life before him.

Now, this revelation was given to me after my Resurrection from my dead life into the Living, in Christ Jesus. It was a time that I was again seeking God for answers of his Loving Will for my life. He was faithful in leading me to a spot in a capital city 35 miles away from home.

Straight are the Gates came to me as I went with my father and mother one day during a visit to the hospital for my father's check up. While my father was in with the doctor, I went out side as if, I was drawn to do so. I walked around somewhat and then was drawn to a corner of a parking deck looking over to the main entrance of the hospital. I was leaning over the side somewhat looking around and then I felt my spirit starting to discern something, like I have felt many times as if, the Holy Ghost was trying to commune with me. So, I asked God this question: "Lord, What is the lesson about today, straightness?" I was watching traffic from all different directions around the hospital as they would go quickly to their destinations and then I felt within my spirit the answer, "Yes." I was standing upon a high parking deck at a hospital and it was revealed to me concerning the Strait Gates. The Spirit of God ministered to me, as a Father would talk to his own child to teaching the child the way to Life.

During this time of my Life, I had been resurrected from my past dead life and I had again enter into Life, and, living Life much more abundantly. God had restored me to where I was 15 years before when I had been chosen as a servant of the Gospel of Jesus Christ. Not only had he restored all things unto me again, I also began to have a greater understanding of what God had done for me throughout my life without doubt. But I still felt within my spirit man that something just wasn't clear of God's Will in my Life.

One day I went to a hospital with my parents for a check up on my father. He had chest pains and one doctor referred him to this special heart doctor at this particular hospital in the capital city. Let me say that this hospital's marquee was this; "THE POWER TO HEAL, THE PASSION FOR CARE." So we were there at this hospital and my father went in for examinations. I was drawn to go outside the waiting area and was drawn to a corner in the parking area.

This parking area was set high above the vehicle entrance to the hospital, and my eyes became fixed to this entrance. About this same time, it was if time was slowed down. And then, the Spirit Of God spoke through me and said, "Son, what do you see?" I responded by saying, "Cars. Many cars and the highways." The Spirit said again, "Look closer. What do you see?" When the Spirit said this, my eyes looked straight ahead and I noticed a one way street sign. But, I also noticed that there was four lanes. Two lanes going straight towards the City, and Two going straight from the City. When I kept looking at these signs, as the Spirit was pressing me to look, I noticed the sign (One Way) that pointed to the city was covered by a vine. The sign that led from the city was very visible, but the sign leading towards the city was covered where you couldn't see it, with a vine. And then the Spirit again said, "Son, What do you see?" And then I said Strait ways. One way from the City and one way from the city. Then the Spirit of God ask me this question, "Son, where are you going?" And then the Holy Ghost began ministering to me about this revelation and it goes like this; First there was four lanes and cars where going straight from the city and straight to the city. There were many cars going from the city, but just a few going towards the city.

There, where I was standing, I could see the turn off from the highway to the entrance of the hospital from the overlook. I noticed people turning into the Hospital coming from the city, and going toward the city. People would turn into the entrance from the city, and as they would leave, turn away from the city and head away from the city. Some people would turn into the Entrance and as they would leave, turn back toward the city. Some people were turning from the way from the city and then turning back towards the city. Some people would not turn into the entrance, but would make a U-Turn. If they where going toward the city, they would make a U-turn and turn away from the city. Some, if they were coming from the city, would make a U- turn and go toward the city.

Then the Spirit of God asked this, "Where are my people going? Straight is the way to Life. Why are they turning back?"

Now lets put this in simplicity. There was four lanes. Two lanes headed from the city and two lanes headed to the city. The sign that showed the one-way toward the city was covered by a vine, but the sign headed from the city was in plain sight. Cars where going in both directions and some where making U-turns, away and towards the city. Some were making turns into the entrance off the highway into the Hospital.

Now this is the way I interpreted this revelation; First people were turning into the Hospital Entrance for help or health care for their bodies and understandings. The Spirit of God made it clear to me that day, that this Hospital is under his power for healing. People are going to need help one day or another from a professional doctor, without doubt. But, when you get help which way do you go when you get the help. Do you continue your way toward Life (Towards the City) or do you give up, and head toward destruction (Away from the City). This Entrance was somewhat liken to a pit stop off the Straight Narrow way that leads to Life (The City). I also notice people making choices, and making U-turns. Some where turning from the City and some where turning towards the city. This represented people making their own decisions of Life or Death.

Now, like I said, the sign that lead towards the city was covered by a vine and the sign that lead away from the city was very visible. This covering represented the Narrow Way that leads to everlasting life and few there will be that find it. The visible sign represented the Broad Way to destruction and many there be that find it.

During my past dead life, I thought I knew understanding, but today I can say with confidence that I only began to understand what the meaning of the word understanding was at those times of my life. There were many times in my life that I was Obedient to the Spirit of God, and, there was many times that God had to knock on the door of my heart for me to let him in. There were many times that God had to prepare something for me, just as he did for Jonah to get my attention. Throughout my entire Life, I have asked God for wisdom and not the wisdom of a old man from the experiences by this life on earth. I prayed much for God to give me wisdom of his Grace and Love. I've always wanted and have panted after the Love of God. God has revealed many times to me either by dreams, visions, revelations the understanding of his Love for me and all his creation. He would use many things of this world, but he would many times reveal himself to me through his Spirit. Most of the times that I would get these things that I have just mentioned, were the times that I was vigilant in the Will of God and Doing his Will, rather than, just setting and waiting for him to do it for me. I have sought, asked, and knocked many times in my life for Wisdom from God and he has always been faithful in doing so for me.

Now, in the Holy Book of James chapter 2, verse 26 it is written, *"For as the body without the spirit be dead, so faith without works is dead also."* If, it wasn't for the works of my faith during times of trials, tribulation and temptations in my chances of life, my faith would had been dead and I would had been still confused or even void of God's Will. But, I exercised my faith by my works when I called on God and submitted my will to him and asked him for the answer. Growing in the mind and spirit is somewhat the same way as growing in the fleshly body. When I was but a child, I drank lots of milk to grow. Somewhat in the same likeness as a kid would suck upon it's mother's tit for milk. As we began to grow in the physical body, it soon requires more than, just milk.

Our bodies as a man, require food, water and exercise to make the body structure much stronger. A man may be able to survive in this world by food and water only, but if the man would not exercise the body by just laying in the bed asleep, he would be the same as a dead man. In the Holy Book of Deuteronomy chapter 8 the Word of God clearly lays the table of the spiritual bread before our eyes to witness. Please read this chapter soon if you are willing to do so.

In the Wilderness of Temptation, while Jesus was fasting and praying and exercising the Spiritual Gifts within his life by the Spirit of God, Satan, that serpent, came to him at his weakness and said, *"If thou be the Son of God, command that these stones be made bread."* But, Jesus was quick and defeated that serpent by the Sword of his Mouth and said, *"It is written, Man shall not live by bread alone, but by every word that proceeded out of the mouth of God."* (Matthew chapter 4).

Now, today I know that I'm not who I really see in the glass, for I know reality is my everlasting soul. Today, I know who I am and what I am, so, I must feed my soul also. If, I was to grow in my replica body, which is my soul, I will require much more than milk. My soul also requires meat just as my physical body requires meat. In the Holy Book of John chapter 6, verses 48;53-58 and it is written, *"I am that bread of life. Then Jesus said unto them, Verily, Verily, I say unto you, Except ye eat the flesh of the Son of man, and drink his blood, ye have no life in you. Whoso eateth my flesh, and drinketh my blood, hath eternal life; and I will raise him up at the last day. For my flesh is meat indeed, and my blood is drink indeed. He that eatheth my flesh, and drinketh my blood, dwelleth in me, and I in him. As the living Father hath sent me, and I live by the Father: so he that eatheth me, even he shall live by me. This is the bread which came down from heaven: not as your fathers did eat manna, and are dead: he that eatheth of this bread shall live for ever."*

There was a past President of the United States of America that once said to the Nation, "The only fear we have, is fear itself." There was a man that told me once this, "The things we do in this life are not the things we regret, it's the things in life we don't do, that we regret." My friend, today we can sit and do nothing about something, but until we do something about nothing, we have only done nothing." My friend, "The things we hide deep within our heart, are not because we want to save them, it's because we fear them and do not want to face them."

Today I can say this my friend with honesty, "The only fear I have today are not the things of this world, it is of myself." Today, I also know with confidence that there are differences in the word fear. Fear can be define in two different ways. First- Fear can be defined as something awful, bad, harmful and dangerous in a man's life.

Second- Fear can be defined as reverence to the Almighty God or an authority of supremacy, such as a Judge of the courts. In the Holy Book of Matthew chapter 10, verse 28 it is written, *"And fear not them which kill the body, but are not able to kill the soul: but rather fear him which is able to destroy both soul and body in Hell."* In the Holy Book of 1 John chapter 4 clearly lay out the perfection of the Love of God for mankind. In the 8-9 verses and the of this chapter it is written, *"He that loveth not knoweth not God; for God is love. In this was manifested the love of God toward us, because that God sent his only begotten Son into the world, that we might live through him."* And the 18th verse it is written, "There is no fear in love; but perfect love casteth out fear: because fear hath torment. He that feareth is not made perfect in love." Please read the Book of 1 John entirely sometime soon and it will give you a much clearer look into the Love of God.

Today I don't fear nothing of this world, but I fear God with my whole body, soul and spirit. Today I can say this with confidence; God has cast out the fear of the things of this world with his Love and his Love has cast out the darkness that once had me bound by my own understandings. If, we as mankind are not willing to let God work his Love in our Life, then we will miss the opportunity for Life. I truly believe that God has great passion for mankind to exercise his Love into a man's life. I believe that God is in the likeness of a spiritual Father or Mother that wants their children to grow in Love of them. I believe God is panting for a man to come to him and set upon his lap and laugh with him and be filled with joy of Life. If only a man is willing to let go and let God's Unconditional Love into their life, will they ever understand life or be filled with joy? Before I continue, let me please share just a little of what I understand today of God's Love. First, I will say this with confidence: if a man is willing to "let go" and "let God" exercise his Love in his life, this man would be free from the curse of the law. God's Love will break the chains of the curse of the law that so beseeches a man's life. In the Holy Word of God in the Book of Romans chapter 13, verse 9-10 it is written, *"For this, Thou shalt not commit adultery, Thou shalt not kill, Thou shalt not steal, Thou not not bear false witness, Thou shalt not covet; and if there be any other commandment, it is briefly comprehended in this saying, namely, Thou shalt love thy neighbor as thyself. Love worketh no ill to his neighbor: therefore love is the fulfilling of the law."*

My friend, God has many times tried to exercise his Will in my Life. There were many times that I did let go and let God's Will into my life and there were times that I rebelled from letting God exercise his Will in my life. I believe the truth of my rebellion in my past life was that of no other than, not having the understanding of the love of God in my heart. Since I was a child able to speak, I loved church and loved all things that I could get from church. Sometimes I didn't want to even go home and just cried when the time came to go home from that day at church.

Church was liken into a new world to me when I was a young child. I felt a love and a peace at church that no man could give and I panted for it continually as a child. The older I got, I began to stray away from the fold of the church. The truth behind this matter was that of no other than, lusting after the things of this world. I had lost my true love that I had as a child, which is, the Love of God for my life here and the eternal life to come. In the Holy Book of Revelation 2:4-5 it is written, *"Nevertheless I have somewhat against thee, because thou hast left thy first love. Remember therefore from whence thou art fallen, and repent, and do the first works; or else I will come unto quickly and will remove thy candlestick out of his place, except thou repent."*

After I grew into a young man, I thought I knew love, but soon found out it was lust for the things of this world. When I began to lust for the things of this world, I began to trust in the things of this world, much more than, God. The love that I once had in my little heart as a child of The Spiritual Father, God, was quenched from growing in my inner man and my outer man; from the lusting of the things of this world, more than, the Love of God.

I will say this with confidence, during these times of my life, I would still believed in, revered and loved God and Jesus Christ greatly and I did love people as I understood at the time. But, the lust of the things of this world were exercised much more than the Love of God in my life. The lust of the things of this world had bound me with the chains of the sinful nature of mankind. I began to be ashamed of myself and hide these things of the world in my heart. I would begin to lust much more for the things of this world, until the things of this world would cause great suffering in my life. The more I lusted for things of this world, the more it seemed to me that I would loose those things. Loosing those things of the world started another growing process in my heart.

My friend, it wasn't the Love of God growing. Those things that began to grow in my heart were anger, resentments, hatred, dishonesty and distrust. These sufferings became my own dark abyss. I would try to hide in this dark abyss for many years, but periodically a bright light would always seem to shine in my life. This bright light would make me shun away and dig deeper into my Mole Hole even more so. The More that God would shine his Light of Love into my heart, the much more I would try to dig deeper away from the brightness of the Life of his Love. It wasn't that I didn't want the Light of the Love of God in my Life; it was because I didn't understand God's Will for my life at these times. I was fearful to face the Light of his Love, because I just didn't understand his Will at the time.

Like I mentioned before, I honestly Loved God and others when I couldn't even love my self. I could love God and others, even when

I didn't understand God's Will for my life. During these dark times of my life, I could love God and others, but I didn't want God or others to love me. I thought that the love from God and from others was for wanting something from me. I felt unworthy at these time of my Life and would say things like this; "Why are you trying to Love me. What are you wanting from me? Go love someone else beside me and just leave me alone. I don't need no one loving me. I've seen the love in this world and it is all vanity and your love, I don't need. I don't need your love, but you need love. Why don't you ask God for his Love!? Get!"

During these times of my life, I knew with no doubt that the love of this world was conditional. All of my past sufferings, I would become more crafty in hiding them deeper in my little heart and the sufferings oppressed me greatly. I would run from everyone that would try to love me, even my own father and mother.

Even as one of my family members would come toward me as a child and tell me that they love me and then pinched me quickly on the cheek, I knew right then the only reason they said that they loved me, was to pinch my cheek and that made me more angry. Even during my dark times, from somewhere deep within my inner man, I knew that conditional love wasn't love and I just fled from it. I'm sure people in the past has said this to themselves about me, "Why want that child let me love him? or Why want that man let me and God love him?"

I look into my past life and see clearly many times that God wanting to manifest and exercised his Love within and without my life. These were also chances after chances the "Disciplining Rod of God" was being exercise directly into my life. I began submit my life somewhat to God and his Christ. I began seeking them for the understanding of God's Will and began to revere God and his Christ diligently for my life.

As I would give my life away, somewhat piece by piece, to God and his Christ, I was beginning to understand that God wanted to do something for me and I do something for him. This want from God and Christ wasn't a want of this world, it was a true want of compassion, a Love unconditional, and without repentance for my Life and my profit. I tried again to let go and let God into my heart earnestly. I truly didn't understand God's Will at this time in fullness, but I continued to be more willing to let go of the things of this world.

I was willing more so to "let go" than to have his "Discipline Rod" exercised continuously within my life. I started going back to church for the first time after 10 years of suffering from the long hand on God's Longsuffering for my life.

These 10 years of God's longsuffering hand exercised his "Disciplining Rod" upon my life. I was beginning to understand much more of his Will for me as he would exercise this great "Rod of Disciplining." I will also say that this was the same time that my wife's father died from alcoholism. I had lived out of the fold of the sheep of the pasture and God and his Christ for a long time. They loved me with a great passion and wanted back into my Life, before death called me before my time appointed. Death was beginning to call out to me from the reaper's voice and the darkness of death was somewhat beginning to overshadow me. I know with no doubt and with a greater confidence today how much God loved me then, now and the life to come. God would knock on my door, if it took breaking every bone in my body, no kidding God was taken everything that I had ever loved in this life away from me. God again was exercising his "Disciplining Rod" in my life to correct my path straight to the understanding of his Will with a great passion. Let me now share with you a greater understanding of how much God and his Christ Loved me throughout my life. I didn't know How much they care for my life and really didn't understand that God was the one Disciplining me. I would think the State or Government assigned an agent specifically to discipline me to submission unto God. But, I soon found out it wasn't any man doing the discipline, it was God and God alone.

When we call on God to save us from the chance that we call on him you might consider to count the cost first. "AM I WORTH IT?" would be a great place to start. Remember this my friend, and store it deeply within your mind, body and soul for your Life. God's Great Call for every man under the heavens to repentance is without repentance from him. Remember and it is written, *"For the gifts and calling of God are without repentance." (Romans 11:29)* God doesn't change his mind about repentance or the gifts he wants to exercise in the completeness of a man's life.**"Count the Cost?"**

If you call on God through his Christ to save you, with honestly, and not holding no self-will intent for pleasure in your heart, they are faithful to save you and keep you for this life and the Life to come. In the Holy Book of Luke chapter 14, verses 26-28;33 and it is written, *"If any man come tome and hate not his father, and his mother, and wife, and children, and brethren, and sisters, yea, and his own life also, he cannot be my disciple. And whosoever doth not bear his own cross, and come after me, cannot be my disciple. For which of you, intending to build a tower, sitteth not down first, and counteth the cost, whether he have sufficient to finish it?; So likewise, whosoever he be of you that forsaketh not all that he hath, he cannot be my disciple."* ***"Then said Jesus to those Jews which believed on him, If ye continue in my word, then are ye my disciples indeed; And ye shall know the truth, and the truth shall make you free."*** (John 8:31-32), -Pause.

I continued to seek God and his Christ diligently with all my life at this time. When I finally got honest and willing to let go of my life and let God into my life, God's only begotten Son, Jesus Christ, the great avenger, responded when I cried out to him, Abba, Father, immediately broke the chains of my bondage of ignorance of God's Perfect Will. The great avenger cast out the darkness of doubt from my heart and started shinning his Great Light of Love within the deepness and the hiding crevices of my heart. It was the same Love that I felt when I was but a small child, standing at the altar of God, panting for his Love. Today I understand this great matter of God's Will. When I'm speaking of "God's Will for me" it is the same as saying, "God's Love for me."

In the Holy Book of John 3:16 it is clearly written on paper about this Love that God has for me and the whole wide world and it is written, *"For God so loved the world that he gave his only begotten Son, that whosoever believeth on him should not perish, but have everlasting life."* I asked God many times what the purpose of his WILL was for my life.

It has taken many years, after I asked that question to God, to get an answer. His answer was this, "Am I worth it? Son, lets us reason together. Son, let me Love you. Son, give all your life to me, so that, I can love you and you can love me. Son, if you try to hide anything of this world in your life for yourself then I cant love you and my love cant live in you. I want you as a man liken into Adam in the beginning when I breathed my Life into his nostrils. Adam loved me and I love him and we were as a Father and a son in accord. You are my son and I want to Love you. I've given you all things beyond your imaginations for you to understanding my Love for you. I have suffered greatly my creation for you. I have suffered the greatest that I could suffer for you; my only begotten Son to bare your sufferings on a cross. My Will for you, is to Love you unconditional and there is no repentance of my Love for you. My Will for you, is that you may enter into my arms and I can love you as a Father would love his own child. I am Love and my only begotten Son, Jesus Christ, will show you my Love. Listen to my Son's instructions and follow him. Son, if you what I have compelled you to do by my Love for you we will live together in this life and the Life Everlasting to come. Come son and let go and let me love you as my own child." I didn't know what the truth of love was and neither could I let someone love me. I always thought in my past life that love was conditional. I thought in my past life this; if, someone said they loved me, they were only wanting something from me. When people at church would tell me they loved me, I would be quick think they were judging me and they wanted to help me or they would want me to do something for them.

It is by the Gifts of the Spirit of God that exercises God's Love within and without my life on this earth yesterday, today and the life to come. All of the gifts by the Spirit are for a man's profit and it is meant for one purpose, to manifest God's Love in a man's Life, so that, the man would know God much better and have a chance of the promise, which is Eternal Life.

I believe that God Love's for mankind is without repentance and there is nothing that can separate that Love. I will say this with confidence; The true reality of the rebellion in my past life, was that of fear. Not wanting to "let go" and "let God" exercise the gifts within my life and to give me the understanding of reality in it's trueness. This fear was that of no other than, hiding things deep within my heart and fearing them to come out. Honestly my friend, I feared God greatly and I gave up on wanting him to do anything in my life at times, but the fear of him was the wrong fear. When I began to allow God to exercise his gifts within my life, I began to understand that I could no longer hide things from God, either they be good or evil.

When God was working in my Life at times, when I honestly "let go" and would get out of his way, things happened in my life that amazed me. In the Holy Book of Proverbs chapter 1, verse 7 and it is written, ***"The fear of the Lord is the beginning of knowledge: but fools despise wisdom and instruction."*** These times were fearful and it was the right fear of God. I was fearful of the power or effect of God working or exercising gifts in my in my life. There were times that I was just weak in the flesh and Satan would try everything by the poison of his trap to destroy me or prove me unworthy, such as not being skillful in the Word of God. When we think of exercise, it is much easier to think of the body or flesh. But, we have got to understand this; *"we are not who we think we are and we are not what we think we are."*

I believe today that mankind is perplex between these two realities. I ask, "What is reality?" Is reality the things that we see with the physical eyes or is reality the things that are spiritual that cant be seen with the physical eyes? These perplexities has driven mankind from Life to Death, because of not understanding the matter of reality. I will say this with confidence; I know I'm not who I am, when I look into the glass. I know that there is something spiritual going on within my life because of the evidence of things not seen.

If, I would be willing to understand the perplexities of reality then I must start to look somewhere. So, I look in the mirror and I see my body. I want to start assuming what I'm looking with my physical eyes truly reality. Then, my memory reminds me of all the deaths, the miseries and horrors of this life on earth. I start weeping and hoping in something greater than that of, my physical body and my physical life. I begin to hope that this physical body and life just can't be true reality; there's got to be more than just misery, horrors and death in Life. I began to hope more that there is a different life than that of what I'm living. I'm not confident in what I'm hoping for or where the hope came from, but I still keep hoping in something much greater than that of this physical life. I begin to hope that something must be greater than living a life here on this earth only and waiting for my appointed time; when the "Reaper" calls my name from the depths of death. I begin to hope in something greater than just this life on earth. I began to question my self; Is this physical Life on this earth truly reality or is this Greater Hope of something spiritual, reality?

In his Word I find the truth in the scriptures, such as, *"Then said Jesus to those Jews which believed on him, If ye continue in my word, then are ye my disciples indeed; And ye shall know the truth, and the truth shall make you free."* (John 8:31-32) *"Heaven and earth shall pass away, but my words shall not pass away."* (Matthew chapter 24:35). This small seed of faith that God has given me packed an enormous punch deep into my heart.

Just thinking of the reality of when Jesus was in the flesh on this earth and the enormous examples that he has left for mankind, is it evident enough for one to believe in something greater for themselves? Is the Obedience of Jesus Christ from the birth to his death, and the evidence of his Words he has left for mankind for examples to follow today, be something greater to hope in, rather than, the things of this physical world? If perhaps that would not be evident enough to give a man hope in the spiritual eternity; then would the Death of Jesus Christ on the Cross of Calvary, and the Resurrection of Jesus Christ from the grave be evidence enough of the true reality beyond this life on earth?

Now what is reality? My friend, reality would be no less than this; "The Truth." In the Holy Book of One other principle my friend to exercise the mind. In the Holy Book of John chapter 4, verses 23-24 and it is written, *"But the hour cometh, and now is, when the true worshippers shall worship the Father in spirit and in truth: for the Father seeketh such to worship him. God is a Spirit: and they that worship him must worship him in spirit and truth."* Just a question my friend. If you are not a believe by chance, why would you worship anything? What is your profit in worshipping anything? If you are a believe in the Grace of God, why do you worship God? And what is your profit for worshipping the Father God? If by chance you are not a believer, you are perhaps worshipping your flesh or the things of this world. If you are a believer, I hope that you are worshipping the Father God in spirit and truth. Therefore again, what is reality? I will say this with confidence my friend; If this life was all that I had hope in, my life would be most miserable.

Today I know and believe with a greater confidence what reality is and it is this; My spiritual man or soul that can not die. I must be willing to keep my soul for Eternal Life and that is the profit that I labor for today. These things of this world are going to pass away and it isn't a matter of "IF" it is a matter of "When." So, are the things of this world the truth or are the things of the spiritual the truth? If I was a better in a game, I would put my chips on the table for the reality of the spiritual being the complete truth of Life. These things in the physical are for understanding and to grow in the spiritual man for the eternal purpose of reality. I must set my mind on the truth which is the Father God and worship him in spirit and truth for the keeping and saving of my soul from eternal death.

My body will be called to the grave at the appointed time and then, what?

If, I continue in God's Words and be a doer of His Will in this life to my last breath, I'm confident that I will make it through the gates of Paradise and take of the Tree of Life. My friend at the appointed time when I lay my flesh to the dust that I am made from, I'm confident I will awake and that will be reality. The following writings will help in a way to exercise the mind in reality. These Spiritual Gifts by the Spirit are given to mankind for that reality. If we miss the opportunity to use the Gifts by the Spirit of God, will we ever know the truth of reality? We have read about the bad fruits of the fleshly man and we have read about the good fruits produced by a man walking in the Spirit, but we have not read of how to walk in the spirit to produce good fruit, worthy for sacrifice before God.

Today I have a greater confidence why Jesus didn't give up in the garden of Gethsemane. It was because of the Love he had for God and mankind. While Jesus Christ was in the Flesh and he was in the garden of Gethsemane praying in the Spirit unto the Father he said this, *"O Father, if it be possible, let this cup pass from me: nevertheless not as I will, but as thou wilt."* That scripture has always been a thorn in my flesh for one reason, doubt. During my past life there were times that I would doubt that Jesus was the Christ and thought he was only a man, because I thought if he was the Son of God and if he knew that the Crucifixion was the greatest example he could leave for mankind, then Why would Jesus asked the Father God to take the death(this cup) from him. Since the time that I gave my life over to God for him to become my Spiritual Father, Faith was one of the greatest gifts he Worked in my Life.

Today, I much rather hold the Hand of that Great Angel and let him lead me, than have his large foot in my back. Today I much rather have the Spirit of God in me and be lead by him, than have his Spirit on me and binding me.

I was always somewhat like Jacob wrestling with the Angel of God in my past life. If, I didn't get it my way, I fought to get it, but God only wanted to give it to me as he had promised and today, I still suffer from the wrestling with the Angel of God in my past.

There were times that I felt as if the Angel didn't hit me on my hip with a rod like he did Jacob. I thought he had hit me with a steel 4x4 right across my back and head and was somewhat tenderizing me as you would do to a piece of tough meat. I believe today, if I didn't stop my rebellious sinful nature, he would had broken almost every bone in my body and beat me with the 4 x 4 into submission. My friend that isn't living, that is only misery and horrors and sufferings from living rebellious and fighting against God.

I have a greater confidence today that Jesus Christ and my Father God are my good shepherds. They don't use the rod on me like they did in my younger days and my life is much more peaceful and well. I have a better understanding of this; if, you are a child of God, you will be trained and disciplined, if you get out of the Shepherd's Hand. Sometimes it takes God to use his rod upon a man, but I will say this; A man that doesn't believe in God will not experience the Rod of God's Love in their life, because God isn't his Good Shepherd and God doesn't know the man. If, a man doesn't believe in God there would be no sense in teaching and discipline the man, would it? The man that doesn't know God and hasn't submitted their life into his hands will only know and live by his own understandings and these understandings will be that man's only rewards and discipline in this life and the life to come. In the Holy Book of Revelations chapter 22, verses 12-17 and it is written, *"And behold, I come quickly; and my reward is with me, to give every man accordingly as his work shall be. I am the Alpha and Omega, the beginning and the end, the first and the last. Blessed are they that do his commandments, that they may have right to the tree of life; and may enter in through the gates into the city.*

For without are dogs, and sorcerers, and whoremongers, and murderers, and idolaters, and whosoever loveth and maketh a lie. I Jesus have sent mine angel to testify unto you these things in the churches. I am the root and the offspring of David, and the bright and morning star. And the Spirit and the Bride say, Come. And let him that heareth say, Come. And let him that is athirst come. And whosoever will, let him take the water of life freely."

Now, what about a man that doesn't believe in God's Will or even God the Father? Then that man will grow in the sinful nature of his own understanding. His mind will stay on the things of this world and trust in the things of this world, much more than the things of God. The man that doesn't believe in God will believe in his own understandings from the wisdom he has stored in his own mind. The man that believes not in God and be willing to do his Will, will only puff up thoughts and fantasies and Imaginations of his own understandings and these things will enter the heart of that man. Again, the sinful nature of man's intents are these; Adultery, fornication, uncleanness, lasciviousness, idolatry, witchcraft, hatred, variance, emulations, wrath, strife, seditions, heresies, envying, murders, drunkenness, revelings and such like. My friend, even when I believed in God to save me from these evil sinful natures, I still walked somewhat in the sinful natures and I was in danger of complete torments many times in my past life.

These things that I have just mention were removed from me instantly when I believed God and his Son Jesus Christ to do so. I was changed in a twinkling of an eye from a old creature to a new creature. God had removed these things from me at that very moment, but later I fell back to the sinful nature of mankind by my own lust of the things of this world.

When I would fall, it was always worse than the first fall and Jesus clearly warns of this great fall in the Holy Book of Matthew chapter 12, verses 43-45 and it is written, *"When the unclean spirit is gone out of a man, he walketh through the dry places, seeking rest, and f indeth none. Then he saith, I will return into my house from whence I came out; and when he is come, he f indeth it empty, swept, and garnished. Then goeth he, and taketh with him seven other spirits more wicked than himself, and they enter in and dwell there: and the last state of that man is worse than the first. Even so shall it be also unto this wicked generation."*

Every time that I would fall, it felt as if an Great Angel had his foot upon my back and it began to get harder to get up, no kidding. But, I would always call on God and he would be faithful to deliver me from myself and the spirits that had me bound. Then the Great Angel would ease off my back and lift me up. All the scares of my fleshly body and the pains in my body that I feel today are from the falls that I suffered during my past life.

I believe that God Loved me as his own and he had to show me the truth of that matter, so that, the truth would set me free from that fleshly doubt. God was faithful and he is still today my strength and my high tower in the matter. Let me just share some points when God had revealed to me on the matter.

You have read many of the revelations and visions that I have been blessed with and my friend, I would not have any of these gifts, except that God's Spirit worked through my spirit to do this. The following are the few revelations and visions that you have and will read about, throughout this book. They are in no way exhausted, because each vision and revelation reveals and still today comes alive within my spiritual man to keep me, my eternal soul from destruction by the exercising of the Gifts by the Spirit.

Here are the few wisdoms that I have and will shared with you throughout this book. By no means again has God exhausted any such to me for they are still today revealing many matters in my life. These matters that I have and will share with you ,are given to me only by the Work of the Spirit of God in my Life:

1. **The Mutant Ninja Turtles**—*The Whole Armour for the Spiritual Man.*

2. **The Butcher's Shop**—*Suffering of his Creation for mankind.*

3. **The Glorious Cross**—*The reward and the Prize of the high calling of mankind.*

4. **The Keys in the Moonlight**—*Straightness in God's Will and Obedience and comfort in times of tribulations.*

5. **The Man in the Doorway**—*To strengthen my Faith in God and his Son, Jesus Christ and to be chosen to ministry of the Gospel of Jesus Christ.*

6. **The Swallow-Tail Moth**—*God's Sovereign over all things.*

7. **The Train Revelation**—*The need of my life staying hooked to God for the chance I here on this earth, so that I would have a greater chance to receive the promise of Eternal Life.*

8. **There's No Power**—*The need of the Holy Ghost to be effective in a man's life.*

9. **What Sufferings are you talking about?**—*The Suffering of mankind and the Suffering of God and his Christ for mankind.*

10. **White as Snow**—*The Righteousness of Christ and the just in Christ.*

11. **You are forgiven**—*The need of man to be forgiven from God and the need to forgive Others before God can forgive a man for their trespasses.*

12. **The Battle of the Great Dragon**—*The need to seek God in times of Troubles.*

13. **What Hope?**—*The need to hope in God than hope in the things of this World.*

14. **A Great Lesson of Fishing**—*The necessities of ministry and the tools for ministry to a lost world drowning in the sinful nature of mankind.*

15. **A Mole in a Hole**—*The Need of the Hope in God in a dark lost World.*

16. **A Vision of Satan**—*Building of my Faith and Knowing there is an enemy that I can't see with my physical eyes.*

17. **Self-Will a road to Destruction**—*The need of Letting go of Self-Will and Letting God's Will work in the spiritual man for the Keeping of my soul from destruction.*

18. **It just doesn't make no sense**—*The differences between the Physical and Spiritual Senses and The Truth of Reality.*

19. **Heavenly Treasures**—*The need to have Treasures in heaven than only treasures of this earth.*

20. **The Mind of Christ**—*The Obedience to God's Will through the Obedience in Doing God's Will to my last breath on this earth. So that I can receive the promise of Life Eternal.*

21. **Straight is the Gate**—*The need to stay straight in the Obedience of God's Will.*

22. **Who I am**—*The Confidence of the Truth of my Life in Christ Jesus.*

23. **Exercise What?**—*The importance of letting go and letting God work through our spirit man to give us confidence in this life and have confidence in the truth of the Life to come.*

Today, I have confidence that God and his Christ will keep my feet straight on the narrow way. We as mankind live today as a man in a race for a prize. We race, but we don't understand the prize. We race, but we don't know the true reason, but, we race. I believe that mankind's biggest enemy is time and time is our fear.

My friend, Keep your obedience and mind always on the Lord Jesus Christ that you will grow and have a mind of Christ, through your obedience and there is no other way my friend, if you want God's Will in your Life. *"Father take this cup from me nevertheless thy will be done."* As long as we are in the fleshly body, we will battle to do good. Let me leave this principle with you. In the Holy Book of 1 Peter chapter 4, verses 1-2 and it is written, ***"Forasmuch then as Christ hath suffered for us in the flesh, arm yourselves likewise with the same mind: for he that hath suffered in the flesh hath ceased from sin; That he no longer should live the rest of his time in the flesh to the lusts of men, but to the will of God."***

CHAPTER TWELVE

ANOTHER CHANCE AT LIFE

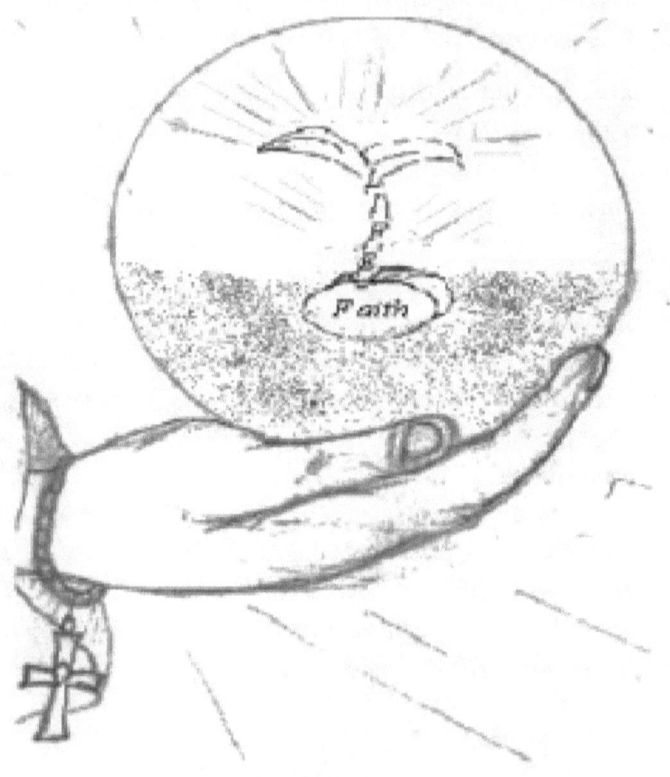

DURING THIS TIME OF MY LIFE, I WAS completely drug and alcohol free. It was if, God had taken these thorns from my flesh. I was back in Church and doing well and I felt as if, I was again living a normal life like I desired for many years. Things were beginning to make sense again of my purpose on this earth. God's Will was becoming much more clearly to me, daily. At this time, I depended on Church and my Faith to keep me clean, but later, my greatest thorn was buffeting me again which is, my mental Illness.

Now, I had left the Manufacturing job as mentioned in the previous chapters, and I was now working with a Property Management Company as a Maintenance Man overseeing Senior and Disability Apartments. There were 90 apartments total in a distant of 25 miles apart from my home. I was on call 24 hours a day, every week. I liked the "on call position", because it brought me to a being of more alertness and readiness. I had wore a pager for 11 years from other jobs, before the manufacturing of truck body's job and this particular job. Being on call 24/7 seemed like a part of me had came back to life again. There was one set of Apartments that brought back a remembrance of when I was ministering the Gospel of Christ to Senior Citizens and nursing homes nearly 14 years earlier. When I was hired with this particular company, I knew within my heart it was meant for me. One day as I was cleaning the Resident Meeting Area, near my office, I picked up one of the Bibles that was lying on a coffee table. I opened it up and to my surprise, it was a Bible I left there for the Seniors over 14 years before, no kidding. It had the Church and the youth group's marquee that I stamped upon its front cover.

Now, this was like a confirmation of this job to me, and I will never forget this job. But, I later left this job due to this; drugs and missed work days. I had no insurance during this time and I had no medications and really couldn't afford them. The reason I fell this time, was because I thought I could be strong on my own and battle this Mental illness and Addictions by myself. I would always think this; I going to quit soon, but, later found out these thorns were not the main problem. These thorns were still within my flesh and I let my guard down to the buffeting of Satan by my thorns. One other true reason is that I wanted to see if I could live without all those medications for my Mental Illness. I had not been on medicines for almost 6 months during this time, and thought, "if I could go that long without them, I could go even further." But my friend, I fell and fell hard this time. I also would think that I was ok and God would not allow nothing on me that I couldn't bare. My friend, that is the truth written, but it wasn't in my case. The reason was, I tempted God by thinking I was ok. Also I thought that I could be strong and battle these thorns and Satan's temptations without him. There is a principle you have already read once about A clean Swept House in the Holy Book of Luke chapter11, verses 21-26 and it is written, *"When a strong man armed keepeth his palace, his goods are in peace: But when a stronger than he shall come upon him, and overcome him, he taketh from him all his armour wherein he trusted, and divided his spoils. He that is not with me is against me: and he that gathered not with me scattered. When the unclean spirit is gone out of a man, he walketh through dry places, seeking rest; and f inding none, he saith, I will return unto my house whence I came out. And when he cometh, he f indeth it swept and garnished. Then goeth he, and taketh to him seven other spirits more wicked than himself; and they enter in, and dwell there: and the last state of that man is worse than the first."*

My friend, I was over powered by that strong man again and I made the choice to do what I should had not done. I remember clearly the place and the person Satan used to buffet me with these thorns. One day during this time, I was cleaning one of the vacant apartments and one of my long lost drug using friends stopped in for a visit. He knew I was trying to do well, but his thorn was buffeting him greater than myself. So, I thought I could be his friend and talk to him about life in general. He started talking about the past days and people and even Jesus. Before I go any further, let me share this little story with you: *There was a snake laying in the middle of a road one night. It was cold outside. I seen the snake lying in the road and I walked toward it. The snake stood his head up and spoke and said, "Mr. I am freezing. Will you put me in you coat ,so that, I can get warm. I am so cold I believe I might die." Then I said to the snake, "No! You will bite me!" Then the poor old snake that was shaking and cold said, "I promise I will not bite you, if you put me in your coat. I promise!" So I picked the cold snake up and put him in my coat and started walking and that snake bit me right on my belly and then crawled done my pant leg. I said to the snake, "You promised me that you wouldn't bite me!" and then the snake said, "I am a snake and you should had not believed me! Plus, I crawled in your shirt, not your coat"*

Now, after my acquaintance left from this apartment where I was working, I thought this, "Well one hit of cocaine want hurt me. It will help calm this thorn down from buffeting me. My friend, I left for lunch and went to one of my other acquaintance and there I was smoking drugs again, no kidding. I thought I was strong enough to stop using on my own. But, I continued to use drugs again for 6 months, until, I knew that I was facing the big hole, once more. I was without insurance, medications and no way out of this addiction this time. I began to loose my sense of reality again, until I finally look into the glass and the Spirit of God said this, "I am not a respecter of persons."

At first I thought that God was going to take my drug using friends from me, but soon found out, that it was me that he was telling me about. After all the Grace and Love God had shown to me, I again turn from him and was facing death again, no kidding. I seen myself either in jail or dead, and it wasn't a matter of "IF", it was a matter of just "When." I felt as if, I was tempting God and I became ashamed again.

In the Holy Book of Deuteronomy 6:16 it is written, *"Ye shall not tempt the Lord your God, as ye tempted him in Massah."* My friend, God intervened and showed me myself in the glass, tempting him, and the consequences. It was enough to turn me back to him. I surely didn't want to end up in jail, another institution, or worse, in Hell. This led to my depression and suicide adventures again.

My friend, again, God is not a respecter of persons. If you are a Saint and die in your sins, you are Hell bound. If you are a Preacher and die in your sins, you are Hell bound. This understanding came to me quick and I responded to it by changing my way of thinking. In the Holy Book of 1Peter chapter 4:17-19 it is written, *"For the time has come that judgment must begin at the house of God: and if it first begin at us, what shall the end be of them that obey not the gospel of God? And if the righteous scarcely be saved, where shall the ungodly and the sinner appear? Wherefore let them that suffer accordingly to the will of God commit the keeping of their souls to him in well-doing, as unto a faithful Creator."* Just because a man may know God and Jesus Christ and look righteous, and perhaps maybe righteous, doesn't mean he can tempt the Lord God. The righteous will die in his sin, just as a sinner.

Now, there is one more principle and I will get to the point. In the Holy Book of James chapter 4:7 it is written, *"Submit yourselves therefore to God. Resist the devil, and he will flee from you."*

Now, Satan came like the wind to destroy me at this time. He wanted me to loose this job, because I was doing well and ministering to the seniors. Out of all the places an old drug using friend would be staying, there he was staying at one of these apartments, and the apartment that I was cleaning was right beside the one he was staying at. Satan got me that day my friend, but he want get me that way again. Satan reminded me of the thorns and now he wished he never did. Satan reminds me somewhat like a porcupine with thorns. If you get too close to him, he will shoot one of his thorns into your flesh, and it want be too nice. So, I learned again the hard way about that porcupine, just stay away from him, and if he tries to come to you, Run!

Sometimes, such as the case I just mentioned, Satan will corner you and try to shoot those fiery darts into your mind, what would you do then? Well, I've learn to just shoot that devil with the word of my mouth, such as, _"Get thee Behind me Satan, For it is written, Thou shalt not tempt the Lord your God!_ My friend, shooting back at Satan really works. We as mankind have the power over that serpent, only if we use it. We have the Word of God, and it is Sharper than any two-edged sword, ready for battle, even if we sleep. We have the Authority in Jesus Christ Name to defeat that buzzard by the Words of Christ and the Father God.

Now, let me share with you the point that Quicken me to Life again from the course of death, that I was living. Hope and believing in God, got me saved from my horror, but God goes further than just saving a man from the horrors, if the man is willing to stay from the horrors. I had been saved many times from my horrors in the past, but like I said before, I would end up back at the Big Hole. I have shared many of God's Principles with you, haven't I? I know today with confidence that God's Words are Life for all those that are willing to received His Life into their Life; for God is Life.

In the Holy Book of Hebrews, Chapter 4, verse 12, reads as written, **_"For the word of God is quick, and powerful, and sharper than any two-edged sword, piercing even the dividing asunder of soul and spirit, and of the joints and marrow, and is a discerner of the thoughts and intents of the heart."_** The point is this: _The Two-Edged Sword, the Word of God._

Today I can have confidence in the Word of God and I know it is the Point of the Sword that keeps me safe from horrors in my Life. I have great hope in this matter and it keeps me safe and secure at all times. When Christ Jesus was here in the flesh, I believe it to be true that he never looked at a man for his outer appearance. He pierced through the mans' soul, spirit and to the bone marrow looking to see if the man had God, which is Life, in him. If the man didn't have God he would point it out by the Word of God, not his finger.

Now here is one way that God will continual to keep me, even though, I was in sin. It was all about the pruning of dead branches from my life and God was cutting them like straw in a huge fan. This Revelation came to me as I was outside gardening one day. I was cutting back some of my grapevine branches, and the Spirit of God was there quick to minister to me.

DISCIPLINE OR DISCIPLE

The son said to the father, "Why Father aren't these branches bearing fruit? Why can't I grow fruit like you want me too, Father? And the Father said to the son, "Son, It's all about training your branches too bear fruit. You have got too keep them pruned. You've got to cut away the dead branches and take away the branches that aren't bearing more fruit. Son, your vine needs disciplining. It has grown wild. Let me help you." Then the son said, "No father, don't cut it and kill it. This vine I planted of my own, and I want to see it grow and bear much fruit.

I don't want to see it bleed and hurt. Father, isn't there another way?" And the Father said, "Son if you don't let me discipline it and train it, it will grow wild and will not bear much fruit and worse, it possibly will choke itself to death." And the son said to the Father, "Father, please show me how to bear much more fruit at your will. Do it Father. I will suffer it for you."

Now, before I get started let me just say that cutting away, and taken away, are two different job task for a husbandman of a vineyard. Cutting away would be exactly as stated. You would cut the dead branches away and cast them into a fire. Now, the taken away are those branches that are trying to bear fruit, but are growing somewhat wild branches or little fruit. You would take away that particular branch and stake it or tie it to the side and prune it from the other branches, so that, it would be able to bare much more fruit.

In the Holy Book of John 15:1-8 it is written, ***"I AM the true vine, and my Father is the husbandman. Every branch in me that beareth not fruit he taketh away: and every branch that beareth*** *fruit, he purgeth it, that it may bring forth more fruit. Now ye are clean through the word which I have spoken unto you. Abide in me, and I in you. As the branch cannot bear fruit of itself, except it abide in the vine; no more can ye, except ye abide in me. I am the vine, ye are the branches: He that abideth in me, and I in him, the same bringeth forth much fruit: for without me ye can do nothing. If a man abide not in me, he is cast forth as a branch, and is withered; and men gather them, and cast them into the fire, and they are burned. If ye abide in me, and my words abide in you, ye shall ask what ye will, and it shall be done unto you. Herein is my Father glorified, that ye bear much fruit; so shall ye be my disciples."*

My friend look closely at what Jesus said in this scripture, *"Now ye are clean through the word which I have spoken unto you."* I believe that Jesus made it clearly for us to see with our eyes that very word that prunes the dead braches from our lives. My friend, it was this very verse that turn my thoughts back to godly thoughts. I started to read God's Word again and it cleaned (purged) my mind like a washer machine would wash clothes. Reading God's Word is somewhat liken into a Husbandman of a Vineyard, purging and cleaning his vines.

I look at God's word today as for discipline and discipleship. In the Holy Word of 2Timothy 4:16-17 and it is written, *"All scripture is given by inspiration of God, and is profitable for doctrine, for reproof, for correction, for instruction in righteousness: That the man of God may be perfect, thoroughly furnished unto all good works."* I also know how the good spiritual fruit is produced in a man's life much more abundantly. It is produce by receiving the Word and following the Word, until the appointed time is called to the grave. My friend, there is no other way under the heavens to produce the fruit of the Spirit in a man's life than that of knowing and following the Word of God. Reading and hearing the Word of God is like a purging or cleaning process, but following the Word is liken to fruit produced on a tree or vine.

In the Word of God, Jesus clearly states the seeds sown to produce fruit and how the seeds can be taken away or destroyed. In Luke Chapter 8:4-15 it is written, ***"And when much people were gathered together, and were come to him out of every city, he spake by a parable: A sower went out to sow his seed: and as he sowed, some fell by the way side; and it was trodden down, and the fowls of the air devoured it.***

And some fell upon a rock; and as soon as it sprung up, it withered away, because it lacked moisture. And some fell among thorns; and the thorns sprang up with it, and choked it.

And some fell on good ground, and sprang up, and bare fruit an hundredfold. And when he had said these things, he cried, He that hath ears to hear, let him hear. And his disciples asked him, saying, What might this parable be? And he said, Unto you it is given to know the mysteries of the kingdom of God: but to others in parables; that seeing they might not see, and hearing they might not understand. Now the parable is this: The seed is the word of God. Those by the way side are they that hear; then cometh the devil, and taketh away the word out of their hearts, lest they should believe and be saved. They on the rock are they, which, when they hear, receive the word with joy; and these have no root, which for a while believe, and in time of temptation fall away. And they which fell among thorns are they, which, when they have heard, go forth, and are choked with cares and riches and pleasures of this life, and bring no fruit to perfection. But that on good ground are they, which in an honest and good heart, having heard the word, keep it, and bring forth fruit with patience."

At one time or another my seed laid in every place to bare fruit, but today, it is rooted in good ground. Surely my thorns try to buffet me and the devil tries to take the word from me, but the more he tries, the much more my roots dig deeper into the Word of God. My friend, I know we have already expanded on the fruit of the Spirit and flesh, but lets look at them again. In the Holy Book of Galatians 5:16-23 and it is written, *"This I say then, Walk in the Spirit, and ye shall not fulfil the lust of the flesh. For the flesh lusteth against the Spirit, and the Spirit against the flesh: and these are contrary the one to the other: so that ye cannot do the things ye would. But if ye be led of the Spirit, ye are not under the law.*

Now the works of the flesh are manifest, which are these; Adultery, fornication, uncleanness, lasciviousness, Idolatry, witchcraft, hatred, variance, emulations, wrath, strife, seditions, heresies, Envyings, murders, drunkenness, revellings, and such like: of the which I tell you before, as I have also told you in time past, that they which do such things shall not inherit the kingdom *of God. <u>But the fruit of the Spirit is love, joy, peace, longsuffering, gentleness, goodness, faith, meekness, temperance: against such there is no law. And they that are Christ's have crucified the flesh with the afflictions and lusts.</u>"*

Now, during this time of using again, I felt unworthy as a dead worm. Suicide was on my mind continually, but, I just couldn't shoot myself, so, I was thinking of other ways, maybe overdosing or something in that field. My seed was lying in the thorns of my flesh during this time of my life, and I was ready to be cultivated. My thorns were so great, I bowed before God and pleaded for my Life and said, "God either take these thorns from me or take my life." This is what he said to me, "Give your life away, so you can have Life."

My friend, after those words from God, I made the choice to change my way of thinking. I finally gave my life away totally to God and his Christ and I didn't hold .1% back. God wants 100 percent and not 99.9%. Would you think that Christ came for 99 of the fold or 100 of the fold? I would say he came for his whole complete flock, 100%.

Like I said, I was jobless, I had spent all the money I had in savings, and my wife was struggling again to pay the bills. I had no Income coming in whatsoever. But, it seemed to me that once I gave my total life to God and his Christ, my cup began to overfill, no kidding. I was in church and we were managing to pay a little tithes and from there, God received my offering or my Living Sacrifice and he supplies my every need, daily.

Later, I had no choice but to seek help. My right shoulder, where I had no medications for nearly a year was beginning to be very agonizing. My budging discs in my lower back, my vision, my memory, my moods and depression was terrible. I had no choice but to seek help; and I did find help at the UNC Hospital. These people were concerned with my problems and they are today taking care of all my needs. I will forever be at their debt, because if, it wasn't for them helping me with my medications, my shoulder, my back and mental illnesses, I know I would be dead or lost in my thorns of my flesh. I was hospitalized for 6 days to get back on my medications. These people at this Hospital really cared for me and it was all from Charity; not wanting anything back except for me to get well. I will now recall the word to our minds in writings, *"charity."* These folks helped me get my medications and gave me the healthcare I needed for many of my conditions. I was beginning to make sense again of this life, but God had already prepared an understanding for me long ago. It wasn't that God let me go through the misery and horrors to make me understand what he was about to give me. But, I will say this with confidence, it was for an appointed time in my life to received such an awesome gift from God. I felt as if, I was back into the Father's Loving Grace and Arms. Before I go any further, I wrote some poetry about Charity while in this particular Hospital. The name of the poetry piece is "Charity." I wrote this in a dark time of my life when I had nothing, but this Hospital, which is, the UNC, helped me when I needed help. I Dedicate this Poetry to the UNC Hospital Staff and all their Clinician Staff.

CHARITY

Behold the Beauty of God's Love from his Longsuffering Hand from Above. His Love brought forth Charity, as a child comes forth from it's mother's womb. Charity sprang forth as the buds on an Oak tree during the spring season, as new life upon the branches. Charity is like the Sea shore waiting patiently to give itself away, grain by grain, without a end. Charity gives and never wants to receive, as the waters from the heavens gives to the earth in a dry season. As a hurricane furiously turns the Oceans, so does Charity turn a man's heart from wrath. As the snow covers the landscape, so does Charity cover a multitude of sins. If a man would have all things under the heavens and wouldn't have charity, he would only have, nothing.

When I finally gave my Life away, God gave me life and today, I am well. My thorns are still there within my flesh trying always to buffet me, but I find ways of escape. I never, ever think that theses thorns are gone, but I keep them somewhat in remission. Today I have found ways to Resist the Devil, by keeping my mind on the Godly things, and making firm stands when he tries to buffet me with my fleshly thorns. I find ways to ease my thorns by reading God's Word, crafts, gardening, going to Church, listening to good music, writing, visiting family and finding ways of "Charity" for another man that needs it.

Now, I would like to share with you a revelation of Righteousness. It was the winter season and I was traveling to get a part for a job from where I was working at this time. It had snowed somewhat that evening and also accumulated much ice on the roads. I was somewhat in a halt on an interstate and It started to snow again this morning. As I was sitting there in the vehicle, I began to watched closely at the snow, as it was falling from the heavens, and then the Holy Spirit came into my spirit and gave me this revelation.

I will say that it took me many years to received this understanding of the revelation and I'm confident today, it is all about righteousness. I call this revelation, *"White as Snow."*

WHITE AS SNOW

"Oh How I wish I could have a white Christmas!"; "I'm Dreaming of a White Christmas just Like the one I use to know." "Let it snow, let it snow, let it snow."; "Oh how beautiful and pure is the snow that falls from Heaven." A snowfall to me does make everything look beautiful, somewhat heavenly and glorious hiding and covering all that our eyes would see. The trees bowing down to the earth from the heavy snow, the kids playing and making snowmen, the snow cream that we would eat from it and the joy of a child coming out of our hearts as something like a miracle happened. But sometimes, a snowstorm can also be what we don't want, because of the discomforts it causes in our daily life. A snowstorm will bring out the child from the heart of a man, if the man is willing to let it come out that is. I believe that a snowstorm is a testimony from the God of Creation from his throne to mankind on the earth, reminding mankind of his love, mercy and grace.

Snow is also a testimony of how we as mankind liken into filthy rags can be changed before him and be as white as snow. Snow to me is God's Testimony of his righteousness, purer than a man can attempt to imagine. Whiter than anything your thoughts can imagine; for God is Righteousness and is without spot or blemish. I believe that snow is also a testimony to us as mankind that if we trust and love him with all our strengths, he will hid us and cover us and make our sins as white as snow. It is a testimony for all mankind, if we are willing to do God's Will, we can be covered by his righteousness and be whiter than snow. If we are willing to do his Will and not Our will and continue in his Will, then he is faithful to give to us a righteous garment whiter than snow.

In the Holy Book of Isaiah chapter 1, verses 18-20 and it is written, *"Come now, and let us reason together, saith the Lord: though your sins be as scarlet, they shall be as white as snow; though they be red as crimson, they shall be as wool. If ye be obedient, ye shall eat the good of the land: But if ye refuse and rebel, ye shall be devoured with the sword: for the mouth of the Lord hath spoken it."* The Lord pleads with a great passion to mankind daily for mankind to repent and change their sinful nature, so that, they can be prosperous and take on his righteousness. The Lord also pleads the consequences of not reasoning with him and rebellion against his word. God pleads the importance of being obedient to his Word throughout the existence of mankind. We as mankind only have one way to put on righteousness before God and that is no other than, through Jesus Christ his only begotten Son.

Just as Jesus Christ put on his cloak of righteousness, as he was obedient from his birth to his death, we as mankind must be willing to follow that example of righteousness. My friend, there is no other way to get the garment of righteousness, except through Jesus Christ. Jesus Christ was counted for all righteousness and is the first fruit of all righteousness. Even at the Jordan River as John the Baptist seen Jesus Christ as the Lamb of God without spot or blemish, Jesus said to John, *"Suffer it to be so now: for thus it becometh us to fulfill all righteousness."* I believe a man's profession of his Faith in Jesus Christ, as he would be baptized by water, is the beginning of righteousness to be fulfilled in that man's life. No my friend, we don't have to work for righteousness, but righteousness comes to a man as he does God's Will. Surely all things that are good are good, but there is only one way to receive the cloak of righteousness and that is, doing God's Will.

Now there are a few more scriptures that I would like to share. In the Holy Book of Daniel he had a vision and seen the Throne of God. Daniel chapter 7, verse 9 and it is written, *"I beheld till the Thrones were cast down, and the Ancient of days did sit, whose garment was white as snow, and the hair of his head like pure wool: his throne was like the f iery flame, and his wheels as burning f ire."* If you would read more about this vision of Daniel, you would understand the Power of this dream. Now, in the Holy Book of Mark chapter 9, verses 2-4 it is written, *"And after six days Jesus taketh with him Peter, and James, and John, and leadeth them up into an high mountain apart by themselves: and he was transfigured before them. And his raiment became shinning, exceeding white as snow; so as no fuller on earth can white them. And there appeared unto them Elias with Moses: and they were talking to Jesus."*

This scripture above is one of the most revealing of righteousness that you can imagine. Jesus Christ being transfigure into Righteousness right before a man's eyes. I believe this with great confidence; Jesus Christ transfigured right before the eyes of mankind, so that mankind could behold the righteousness of God. Jesus Christ transfigured on top of that mountain into righteousness and to leave for mankind the hope of receiving this exceedingly glorious raiment of righteousness, if only we will do God's Will.

So, *"Come now, and let us reason together, saith the Lord: though your sins be as scarlet, they shall be as white as snow; though they be red as crimson, they shall be as wool. If ye be obedient, ye shall eat the good of the land: But if ye refuse and rebel, ye shall be devoured with the sword: for the mouth of the Lord hath spoken it."*

My friend, I am a bruised reed that has been beaten and tossed about in this life for many years. I would had never known it to cease at the voice of God saying, "Give your Life away, so that, you can have Life." It took 30 years for me to understand one thing in this life and it is this; If I try to save my life with the things of this world, I will surely loose my life. God's call to repentance is without repentance. All the revelations and dreams and visions God had given me was for one purpose, Life for me. I have today found a key to the kingdom and it is this; "Give your Life Away to Jesus Christ 100% and he will give you much more than 100% back with Love unconditional.

Today I am a Ordained Minister of the Gospel of Jesus Christ and I will always be given my life away, until I receive my Eternal Prize, which is, Life. Being an Ordained Minister makes me no less or no more than still a man.

I still have my trials. But my friend, Life is well for me today, because of that one thing; "Give your Life away." It was that simple, and my life on this earth has great purpose and so does yours. No matter what you have done or who you are, God is and always will be

God. God will always be faithful and just to forgive us for our sins, if only we will called upon him to do so.

There was a time since I was ordained to the Ministry of Jesus Christ that I fell once, but my friend I was quick to respond back and get up on my knees to Jesus and ask for forgiveness. I am desperately trying to "plow on", even though, I still am buffeted with theses thorns of my flesh. There is a story I will share with you concerning my addictions and mental illness as I try desperately to live a good and clean life, and it goes like this:

There was a young rabbit that was prancing around a garden one day, somewhat desperate for food. The rabbit seen the garden, but there was also some fresh lettuce lying in a box not but a few feet from him. The rabbit thought to himself, "Out of all the places that lettuce would be, why is it lying in that box?" The rabbit looked at the beautiful garden and then back at the lettuce lying by itself in the box and said to himself again, "I think I will eat that lettuce and come back for the garden latter. Someone must know that I am desperate for food and has laid that lettuce in a box for me to eat. The garden will always be there, but that lettuce will not." So, the rabbit hopped into the box and that rabbit was never heard from again.

There was another young rabbit that was prancing around a garden one day, somewhat desperate for food. This rabbit also seen the garden, but there was also some fresh lettuce lying in a box not but a few feet from him. The rabbit thought to himself, "Out of all the places that lettuce would be, why is it lying in that box?"

The rabbit looked at the beautiful garden and then back at the lettuce lying by itself in the box and said to himself again, "I think I will eat that lettuce and come back for the garden latter. Someone must know that I am desperate for food and has laid that lettuce in a box for me to eat. The garden will always be there, but that lettuce will not." So, the rabbit hopped into the box and that rabbit was never heard from again also.

Now, there was a older rabbit that was prancing around a garden one day, somewhat desperate for food. The rabbit seen the garden, but there was also some fresh lettuce lying in a box, not but a few feet from him. The rabbit thought to himself, "Out of all the places that lettuce would be, why is it lying in that box?" The rabbit looked at the beautiful garden and then back at the lettuce lying by itself in the box and said to himself again, "Well, lettuce is great, but carrots are much more better. Someone must know that I am desperate for food and has laid that lettuce in a box for me to eat. The lettuce will always be there, but the carrots will not." I will eat of the garden and come back for the lettuce latter. So, the rabbit hopped into the garden and ate of the freshly growing carrots. After the rabbit was filled he happily hopped away back to his comfortable nest.

Later, the same older rabbit was prancing around the garden one day, somewhat desperate for food. The rabbit seen the garden, but there was also a fresh large carrot lying in a box, not but a few feet from him. The rabbit thought to himself, "Out of all the places that carrot would be, why is it lying in that box?" The rabbit looked at the beautiful garden and seen that there wasn't any carrots in the garden, then back at the tasty carrot lying by itself in the box and said to himself again, "Someone must know that I am desperate for food and has laid that carrot in a box for me to eat. The garden will always be there, but that carrot will not. I will eat the carrot and come back for the garden latter. So, the rabbit hopped into the box and that rabbit was never heard from again also.

Now my friend, things may look good from one perspective in life, but from another, it could be a trap. I have many times found out that the things that I desire the most, are not the things that I need, and they also maybe a trap to lure me away from the truth of Life. There has been many times that I chose the wrong things of this life and they were almost deadly for me. I have desire and have lusted for the things of this world more than the things of God, just because it was much easier to get. Just as the older rabbit knew that the garden would always be there, he chose to eat of the trap of his life anyway. Today, I try to eat from the garden of God and stay away from the traps of my lust and desires. I have been clean for quite some time now and it seems as if my thorn of addictions have eased somewhat, but I know they still exist within my flesh and I must be on the guard at all times.

Today, I am well for one reason, "I have given my life away." Before I end these writings I would like to share a dream that I had recently. It was a time after I had been ordained as a minister of the Gospel of Christ. The Dream is called, *"Iron Man."*

IRON MAN

As I was sleeping one night I had a dream. I dream that I was away in a far land somewhere unfamiliar. There was a Community Fair in play and I remember the rides and the children screaming in my dream from the fear of the rides. I remember smelling cotton candy and the flannel cakes cooking and all those things that go with a Community Fair. But, all of a sudden it seem as if all these things were attaching to my body, such as the cotton candy, sugars of all kinds. People were running and bumping me to the side, nearly knocking me down, as they were off to the fair in a hurry. Some would say, "If your not going, get out of my way!" I remember running away from the fair as fast as people were running toward the Fair.

I remember struggling as I ran and there were holes in the way filled with sticky cotton candy, clinging and somewhat holding me back. I would fall and get back up and continual to run away from this fair in desperation.

For some reason I didn't see the fair as a good thing, I seen it as a trap and I didn't want no part of it. As I finally got away in a distance I stood still and watch people being entangled into the cotton candy and all the traps of this fair. I stood still and wept and said to myself, "Dear God help me get away from this trap." About the time I finished my prayer in my dream, I felt a touch on my right shoulder. I turn my head away from the Fair and there stood a man that looked somewhat holy. He wore a white robe and looked like a normal man. He looked somewhat younger than I, but something just caught my thoughts. He looked somewhat angelical and I turn and he said to me, "Follow me and I will show you something much more amazing than the Fair."

So, he grabbed me by my hand and we somewhat floated down a low side of a brook and then to a place secluded from all the noise from the fair in a forest. I remember hearing a powerful sound, somewhat like a power reactor room. I and this angelical being ended up at a enormous furnace that had a great fire protruding forth from it. I and this being stood back somewhat, but there was another angelical being standing in front of this large flaming furnace. This particular man wore no robe, but just wore a white covering over his privates, somewhat like a skirt to his knees. I couldn't' see this man face, but he was built like a mountain. He had huge arms and built like a body builder. He had somewhat black thick hair and his skin was the color of crimson. He would not turn around, but just stood in front of this large furnace as if he was waiting for something. Then, the angelical being that brought me to this place, said to me, "Watch the man!" I fixed my eyes on this man and I couldn't believe what I was seeing. This man would walk into the furnace and stand there. His body would not burn, even the hairs on his head, but turn red as if you had put iron into a furnace. Then the man would backup and cool off.

This man did this three times and then the angelical being said to me, "Can you do that?" I was fearful and said, "Sir, I don't understand." and the angel said, "You will." I awoke from this dream immediately after those words.

Today, I somewhat do understand that dream and it goes like this; The furnace represents God. The fire represents the trials of a man's life here on earth. The sticky candies and the rides of the fair represent the things of this world and how a man can be wrapped up in it. The man in the fire, represents a man that is mature and has been fired in a furnace, or, has been tried time after time to become a vessel of honor before God. It's somewhat liken to making pottery and firing the pottery in a high temperature furnace to make the pottery into vessels of honor.

In the holy book of 2 Timothy 2:19-21 it is written, ***"Nevertheless the foundation of God standeth sure, having this seal, The Lord knoweth them that are his. And, Let every one that nameth the name of Christ depart from iniquity. But in a great house there are not only vessels of gold and of silver, but of wood and of earth; and some to honour, and some to dishonor. If a man therefore purge himself*** *from these, he shall be a vessel unto honour, sanctified, and meet for the master's use, and prepared unto every good work."*

My friend, God will not leave his children to burn in the furnace, but just for an appointed time, and then he makes away out of the furnace for his children. Before I end these writings, there is another revelation that was shown to me many years ago. This revelation was the beginning of my writing of this book, which was nearly 15 years ago. I explained earlier in Chapter 7 in the section or insert of "What Sufferings are you talking about?" of how I came to the writings. This part of the revelation came after Trials and tribulations, but these writings are just as important as the writings of Chapter 7. The name of the following writings are called, "The Fiery Furnace."

THE FIERY FURNACE

Let me just start by saying that a Boiler and Furnace works in the same manner to produce a product, after and during use, for special purposes. A boiler's product is for heating water only to specific temperatures and purifying for special uses, such as, climate control and cleaning Kitchen Utensils for eating and cooking or washing your body. A furnace is used in the same manner, but the product is somewhat different. A furnace's product is for heat and for using the extremely intense heat for cleaning, heat or evaporation of water molecules to purify a product, such as, climate control, burning heavy paint off iron and even cremation.

Both furnaces and boilers work in the same manner to produce a very extreme heat by fire, but the only difference, is that boilers, produce extreme hot water and furnaces only produce extreme heat. But, I'm sure that a boiler and furnace can be combined to produce both products at the same time. The point that I ask that you keep in mind as you read these writings is that, both furnaces and boilers use extreme heat, from fire, to produce a product. If I happen to change the word boiler to furnace or vise versa it will mean the same; for both uses fire to purify and to produce a product and that is the point of the matter. I will ask you now to Pray for the guidance of the Holy Ghost to lead you through the following writings. These writings will help in such a way to apply the Fire of Furnaces to the Trials of our spiritual life as we live here on earth; if you chose to do so. The following elements of a mechanical furnace are applied, so that, you and I can apply them to our daily life. The elements of a furnace that I will be referring to are: *The Furnace Body, The Fuel for the Furnace, The Fuel Pump, The Igniters,*

The Fire, The Water, The Blower or Fan, The Soot and at last, The Product from the Furnace.

I do ask as you read these following writings that you keep one question on your mind and that is, *Am I going through a trial, temptation or is it a season for tribulation?*

When this understanding came to me during this time of my life, I was without understanding of trials; for I thought I was being tempted by Satan and by Man's will only. After I received this understanding, I applied it to my life and then things became much more clearer to me. In my past life when I would go through a trial, sometimes I didn't know if it was a temptation, trial or tribulation, but today I can say that I know the difference between the three big Ts.

Trials, temptations and tribulations still come like the wind in my life today and I know with confidence they will always, until I take my last breath here on earth. Today I know the difference between being tried by God, tempted by Satan and the season for tribulations in my life.

Please let me again define these three matters into their true relations with simplicity: Trial- to test something's worthiness, such as, faith, patience. Tempt- to entice or to seduce to do wrong. Tribulation- suffering from oppression or persecution.

Even though, all three of these matters have different meanings, they three can be combined to test a man's worthiness. Please give your ear as I try to clear a paradox concerning, Temptation, Trial and Tribulation. Remember in the Holy Book of Genesis, chapter 22, how God tempted Abraham? Now I will say this, God's Tempt at this time for Abraham, wasn't for evil; for it was to try Abraham's faith in God, for the riches God had for him. Yes! The Holy Book uses Tempt in the first verse of this chapter, but tempt in the old testament meant to try a man's worthiness. Please follow me, the point is coming. God doesn't tempt a man to do evil, neither does a man need to tempt God with evil.

My friend let me say this first, "Don't tempt the Lord thy God." Here is an example of tempting God from that of the children as they were still in the wilderness of Sin.

They were without water and they chided (disapproval) to Moses and said, *"Wherefore is it this that thou hast brought us up out of Egypt, to kill us and our children and our cattle with thirst?* At the time during this great journey of God's People through the Wilderness of Understanding Sin, God's people had committed sin by tempting God, by those words. Even though God had sent a deliver for God's People from slavery and oppression under the Iron Rod of the Egyptian Ruler, they still didn't understand and tempted Moses and God by there unbelief. They were ready to stone Moses for delivering them from the bondage of the Pharaoh of Egypt and had already forgotten the miracles of what God had done for them. They may as well had said to Moses, "God is going to kill us by your hand Moses." They tempted God by there unbelief, nevertheless, God looked down and knew they were without understanding of Sin and provided water for them. But, later on in the Book of Exodus the people of God tempted Moses and God again. As Moses was on the mountain, getting the understanding of sin for God's people, the people of God began to worship a graven image. Moses had been away on top of the mountain for quite some time communing with God and God said go back to the people before I destroy them; for they are worshipping a graven image, but the deliverer (Moses) stood in the gap for the people and pleaded with God not to destroy them of the face of the earth. When the cats away, the mouse will play.

This should be a great example how we as mankind need God in our life every second that we breath. Moses was God's deliver for his people at this time and when Moses went away to commune with God the people chided within their selves saying, Is God with us or not? Later in the scriptures, God's people had to pay the price of their sin this time. Many where killed by the sword and the rest where plagued. I will say this today with confidence, if we do know to do right and choose to do wrong, we will be held accountable and suffer the consequences of our sin, not only ourselves, but every thing around us will suffer.

Here is a example of that matter today," ***Well I know that I shouldn't do this rock of cocaine, but one little hit will be OK and God will help me through it and keep me from getting hooked on it again.***" This thinking is like playing Russian roulette with your life. A man that tempts God in this way is really saying within himself, "I want to die rather than live." It is possible that a man would survive through this thinking, but it is also possible when the man takes the hit of cocaine, he has a stroke or dies the death in his sin and awakes at the judgment seat of the God Almighty. For it is also written in the Holy Book of James, chapter 1, verses 12-16, and the word reads, *"Blessed is the man that endureth temptation: for when he is tried, he shall receive the crown of life, which the Lord has promised to them that love him. Let no man say when he is tempted, I am tempted of God: for God cannot be tempted with evil, neither tempteth he any man: But every man is tempted, when he is drawn away of his own lust, and enticed. Then when lust hath conceived, it bringeth forth sin: and sin, when it is finished, bringeth forth death. Do not err, my beloved brethren."*

My friend, I will say this with confidence, God tempts no man. In the Old testament, Satan was allowed to tempt man by God to try the man's heart. Before Christ came and defeated death (SIN) and Satan at Calvary, Satan had the power from God to tempt an Honest and just man of God, such as Abraham or Job. But, since Christ defeated Satan and took that work from him, now, a child of God is not tempted by Satan, unless that child errs from the truth and is enticed by Satan to fall into sin. Christ defeated that old serpent and took his work from him, so that, we as a child of God will not suffer the temptations of Satan. We have been given the understanding how to put that old serpent under our feet. In the Old Testament, Satan would walk from going to and fro in the earth, and from walking up and down in it for one particular reason, to try a just man's heart of God; for mankind had no mediator between God and themselves at this time.

But as I mentioned above, Satan lost that power when Christ defeated him at Calvary.

Today I can say with confidence, that when I go through a trial, it is for my own good from God, and that old serpent, Satan, isn't the one that has control over me; for Christ gave mankind the Authority over Satan and the understanding of what to do when he opens that dark trap of his to entice me from God's Loving Will. When I know that I am going through a trial of God to find me worthy of his riches he wants me to have, it seems like that old serpent will try to crawl his way around from under my heel, up my body, around my neck and whisper in my ear to try to entice me away from God's blessing. But, I now know his devices. *"Get behind me Satan! For it is Written! Man shall not live by bread alone, but by every word that proceedeth out the mouth of God."* The word of God is the Power over that old serpent and I will say, if you don't know the word of God, he will try to entice you from God's Loving Will.

Remember Jesus Christ, as he went to the wilderness to be tempted by Satan 40 days and 40 nights? I had always asked myself, "Why did Jesus get tempted by Satan when he was the Will of God for mankind and was without sin?" Today I know why he had to fulfill all righteousness from the time he was baptized by water to his last breath. He had to go through everything that a man goes through, in order, for us to have understanding of all matters. When Christ was in the wilderness of temptation, he would always Stand and say this: "IT IS WRITTEN!" Christ left mankind the authority over Satan by the Word of God, which is a Two-Edged Sword from his Mouth. For it is written, *"Submit yourselves therefore to God. Resist the devil, and he will flee from you."* Have you every heard the saying, "Play with fire, get burnt with fire?" We as children of God must not tempt the Lord our God.

Now, Remember Job? Remember how God allowed Satan to try or test Job's faith and how Satan brought great travail to Job? Remember how Satan would go back and forth to God concerning Job, after Job would endure the trial? Satan always started with things that where around a man, like his farm, his flocks, and even his family. Then after the man would endure that trial, Satan would ask God to let him touch his body (flesh and bone) and bring great suffering to a man's body, such as, broils, opened wounds that would not heal and worms would come forth from these wounds. But, Job was tried by Satan, but he never cursed God and always Blessed the God of Creation.

After Job was tried by Satan and Endured the great trials of Satan, he was blessed afterwards with, more than, when he had begun. This Book of Job is a great example of how God wants to bless all mankind, if they will only do his Will and use the power of authority that Christ Jesus has left to all mankind over that old serpent, Lucifer. Remember, Satan has lost the power over mankind, but he can still open that dark trap of his and entice a man from God.

Today I can say with confidence, no matter how hot the trial seems to me or the suffering that I may be going through at the time, I stand still and I trust God and His Son Jesus Christ with my life and know

I have no choice, unless I want to die in sin. I put my faith in them, without any doubt and he does deliver me from the heat of the fiery indignations.

Today, because of understanding of trials, temptations and tribulations, I have much more peace and confidence in my life. Now I will share with you an understanding of how I apply my confidence of these matters in my life every day. I will also ask now, that you ask God to give you this little key of understanding in the name of his Son Jesus Christ. This understanding came to me nearly 15 years ago, but I was without understanding of the matter, until later in life.

Nearly 15 years ago as I was an Industrial Electro/Mechanic, God reveal to me as I was cleaning and servicing a Large Boiler at my job, a revelation of understanding of trials and why we as God's Children must go through them. Remember also and I will say this now, only God's Children will go through God's Loving and merciful Trials here on earth. The trials are because he loves his children and he wants them to understanding his Loving Will and that if we understand his perfect merciful Will we can have a 100% chance of living with him in paradise for ever and ever. But, those that don't believe or that are lost in sin, will not go through these trials. They will face the judgment after they die the appointed time of there death and face the second death which is the eternal fire.

Today I don't have much temptation, because I know Satan's devices and I know that I have been given the authority over this devil, by the Word of God. But, I still go through trials and tribulations today and know that I will always until my last breath.

At this time of my life, I was searching and seeking God for understanding of, "Why God, must I go through these trials? God, I know there not temptations, because I'm walking the best I can in your Will and you have shown me the power over temptation. Is it because I'm not doing your Will the way you want me to do it? or is it because you want to bless me with something? Please God give me understanding." I had been out of Rehabilitation this time around for almost 3 years and I was clean from using and wasn't taking any drugs whatsoever. My mind and spirit were stronger than ever before at this time of my life. God was answering many of my request to him in such ways like, revelations and visions. I will say that It was later in life when

I finally understood what God had done for me at this time. The reason is that, I began to use again and fell away from the enlightens of God's Understanding.

So, at this time of this revelation, I had worked on this job for several years as a Industrial Electrician/Mechanic. There was a large furnace that I had serviced for this entire time at this job. One particular day as I went into work, the plant manager came to me and asked that I look into finding the problem of the furnace shutting down at night. The furnace had been doing this for a while, but the Plant supervisor on the night shift would reset the furnace and start it up to run. I had serviced this furnace several times since I had been there and this problem was different than I had every experienced. I asked the questioned to myself, "Why in this world would the furnace shutdown just at night time and then run well during the day time while I'm here?" I will say this, that day for some reason, I had to trouble shoot almost every part of this furnace to find the bad part. The bad part was something to do with water and it was the last part I would had ever thought would had been bad. Surely I had the skills to service, repair, and run the furnace, but I didn't have the understanding that God was showing me something great at this time.

As I was servicing this furnace, it was as time had slowed down. After I had repaired this furnace from the bad part and had it purring like a kitten, I began to think that I was suffering this day from a trial, but I just couldn't understand why I was going through a trial when things were going so good for me at this time. I will say also that I was suffering, because of trials in my life at this time and the trials were somewhat like, trying to keep my trap shut from other peoples opinions or lifestyles. I battled these trials for quite some time, until I understood the matter of the understanding of trials later.

So, this particular day that I was working on this furnace, I was near my tool box on my knees and then I felt a power of love in me and around me. I began to look at each part of this Large Boiler and the Holy Ghost was on my shoulders teaching me about each part and its function, no kidding. It seemed to me as if time had slowed down and I was in slow motion. The Holy Ghost minister to me and then after work, I went home and began to think of this matter. The Holy Ghost lead me around this furnace and showed me every part and why it had to have every part in order to produce a purified product. After this happened at work, I began to ask the Holy Ghost to help me understand why he was showing me these furnace's functions. I thought at the time that God was just helping me trouble shoot the problem and understand how to fix the furnace quickly, if it should shut off again and not start. But, that was only a microscopic look at the true understanding that God wanted me to have at the time. Sure he help me fix the furnace that day, but he really was showing me a greater understanding.

So, I went home that night and I began to get my understanding. The Holy Ghost led me through many Books of God's Word for several days after this revelation and reveal the truth to me as I would submit myself under his teaching. I will say, I started nearly 15 years ago learning this understanding and today have became much more clearer on the matter.

Here is something that took me nearly 15 years to understand and it is as a key to my daily life, when trials, temptations or tribulations come like the wind into my life. The understanding came to me as I was learning every part of this furnace. With every element of this furnace, the Holy Ghost made a point for me to apply them to this understanding. Here is the following elements of a furnace with application for my life, on a simple level:

1. *The Furnace Body*
2. *The Fuel for the Furnace*
3. *The Fuel Pump*
4. *The Igniters*
5. *The Fire*
6. *The Blower or Fan*
7. *The Product from the Furnace*

1) THE FURNACE BODY:

What is a furnace body and how can I apply this information to my spiritual life? I first will have to explain to you that a furnace is always working to produce a product. All furnaces have thermostats or safety switches, which will act like a cut-off switch when the furnace reaches the desired temperature to produce a product. The furnace body is the complete machine that is made up of many other parts. How can I apply the furnace body to my life? Our fleshly body is an example of a furnace body. Our body temperature is regulated by glands that acts somewhat like a switch.If we get to hot, we begin to sweat and the sweat becomes our coolant. Our bodies needs maintenance just like a furnace needs maintenance.

We should take care of our bodies, because if you don't take care of it, it want take care of you.

At this job I was working, I would always keep the furnace body clean from dirt or chemicals, because I knew that dirt and chemicals can cause corrosion of the metal that makes up the furnace body. God made our bodies to last along time, but if you think about it, 70 years is a vapor compared to eternity. The body can only produce for a short period of time and we must take care of our bodies or we could have a disaster on our hands, Our physical bodies are in similarity just like a furnace's body, if, it is not took care of and maintained, it will break down.

I knew as I was cleaning the furnace body that dirt or chemicals could cause a leak and a breakdown of the body's metal. So, first I would hand wash the furnace down, with just soap and water and then after I knew it was clean, I would wipe it down with a machine oil to protect the metal from the elements. I would clean and wipe oil on every part of the furnace body accordingly and would try not to miss not one spot. I knew as I would maintain and keep this furnace cleaned and oiled down, that the furnace body was just as important as the flame and I would take care of it as if I knew, that if I didn't, it would break down and possibly explode.

Now, the soap and water. We know how to apply them to our life by washing our bodies, but what about the Oil? There are different oils for different purposes, such as, cooking oils made from plants or animals, petroleum oils such as, motor oils, gear oils, fuel oils, which will be covered later and anointing oils, such as, ointments that have different ingredients set aside for special purposes and I'm sure there are others. But I will say, this oil I used to wipe down the furnace, was a special oil for that particular reason. It was a plant oil that was made for wiping down metals to protect it from corrosion.

It was somewhat a water repellant, because we know what happens when metals such as raw iron comes in contact with water; it will rust and corrode away, correct? Oil is mention much in the Holy Bible for anointing of the body for a special purpose, such as sickness, death, prayer, commissions, and many more. Oil is also mention in the Holy Bible concerning commandments from God for anointing special parts of the Tabernacle, which was the place of the Ark of the Covenant, the Holies of Holies. This is the oil that I'm referring to as for the anointing of the Body for a special purpose. Please let me share with you now what God commanded Moses to do concerning this special oil. In the Holy Book of Exodus, Chapter 30, verses 22-33 reads as written, *"Moreover the Lord spake unto Moses, saying, Take thou also unto thee principle spices, of pure myrrh five hundred she-kels, and of sweet cinnamon half so much, even two hundred and fifty shekels, and of sweet calamus two hundred and fifty shekels, And of cassia five hundred she-kels, after the shekel of the sanctuary, and of oil olive an hin: And thou shalt make it an oil of holy ointment, and ointment compound after the art of the apothecary: it shall be an holy anointing oil. And thou shalt anoint the tabernacle of the congregation therewith, and the ark of the testimony, And the table and all his vessels, and the candlestick and his vessels, and the altar of incense, And the altar of burnt offering with all vessels, and the laver and his foot. And thou shalt sanctify them, that they may be most holy: whatsoever toucheth them shall be holy. And thou shalt anoint Aaron and his sons, and consecrate them, that they may minister unto me in the priest's office. And thou shalt speak unto the children of Israel, saying, This shall be an holy anointing oil unto me throughout your generations. Upon man's flesh shall it not be poured, neither shall ye make any other like it, after the composition of it: it is holy, and it shall be holy unto you.*

Whosoever compoundeth any like it, or whosoever putteth any of it upon a stranger, shall be cut off from his people." Boy! God really made a serious anointing oil here, didn't he?

Now, the tabernacle was just being established at this time and God was leading Moses in how to built and establish his dwelling place; for God is holy. This special holy oil that God had commanded Moses to compound for the tabernacle was compounded for a special purpose and God meant what he said about not using this oil for the special purpose he had commanded. It was not to be poured on a man's fleshly body, put upon a stranger and not to be replicated for any other purpose. If these commandments were broken, God said, they would be cut off from his people. Please follow me the point is coming.

God had commanded Moses to compound this special oil for his entire Tabernacle and didn't leave nothing out. This oil is an example of how we must anoint our bodies for the Lords service for he is holy. But God said not to pour this oil on a man's flesh! Ok, here is the point of these great anointing oil. In the old testament the only way that God would dwell in this tabernacle was if Moses anointed every part of the tabernacle with this oil, correct? But, I will say with confidence today, that, that special oil, was the prophecy of a greater anointing oil to come.

Today there is a greater anointing oil just like that of the tabernacle and that oil is, Christ Jesus. If we let the anointing of Christ on our life, which is his pure blood, and let it cover us from the soles of our feet to the top of our head not missing not one spot, the anointing of Christ will make our body holy, just like the tabernacle. God will only dwell where his Son's anointing blood is and if your body hasn't been anointed by the blood of Christ Jesus, then God will not dwell on it or in it; for God is holy and his Son Christ Jesus is holy.

And if a man tries to replicate Christ anointing or even tries to pour the anointing on an unbeliever, for his own pleasures, then that man will be cut off from God's people.

Now, how do I apply this to my life? Just as the tabernacle was a dwelling place for God to his people in the Old Testament, your body is like the tabernacle for God to dwell in. And if we don't anoint every part of our body by the anointing of the blood of Christ, we will be cut off from God's people. Like I mentioned before there are different oils for different purposes, but this anointing oil, Christ Blood, is the point of the matter. When Christ died on the cross of Calvary, for it is written, the veil of the temple was rent. What that meant, was that mankind now had away to dwell with God on an individual relation. In the Old testament days the only flesh that enter through the veil was the high priest for he was anointed to do so only. But, since Christ shed his blood for all mankind, now we as individuals can have a special anointing of the blood of Christ and have a personnel relationship with God. How wonderful it is!

Oh yes! In the Holy book of 1Corinthians Chapter 3, verses 16-17, the Apostle Paul wrote to the Corinthians at the time, but is also for us for understanding of our bodies today, for it is written, *"Know ye not that ye are the temple of God, and that the Spirit of God dwelleth in you? If any man defile the temple of God, him shall God destroy; for the temple of God is holy, which temple ye are."* Now, God's Word clearly states that we must do to keep our living bodies in well condition. Also in the Holy Book of Romans 12:1-2, the apostle Paul wrote, *"I Beseech you therefore, brethren, by the mercies of God, that you present your bodies a living sacrifice, holy, acceptable unto God, which is your reasonable service. And be not conformed to this world: but be ye transformed by the renewing of your mind, that ye may prove what is that good, and acceptable, and perfect, will of God."*

Our body structure is made up of many different elements, such as, the organs, bones, skin. Our flesh is like a shell and consist of all of our elements that should each be took care of and not abused or neglected. They're so many human bodies being corroded and consumed by Hell, because of allowing their bodies to the lust of the flesh. In the epistle to the Galatians apostle Paul wrote to them concerning the lust of the flesh and explained how we could avoid walking in the flesh and desiring the lust of the flesh. In Galatians 5:16-18 it reads, *"This I say then, Walk in the Spirit, and ye shall not fulfill the lust of the flesh. For the flesh lusteth against the Spirit, and the spirit against the flesh: and these are contrary the one to the other: so that ye cannot do the things that you would. But if ye be led of the Spirit, ye are not under the law (curse)."*

The human body is the most complex and greatest miracle in all God's creation. To be able to think and make decisions and choices. Therefore, Paul explains that there is a battle going on in our lives every day between the flesh and our spirit. Our flesh wanting after the world and our spirit wanting after God. Paul wrote if the spirit lead us then we are not under the law or curse. If we walk after the flesh and commit ourselves to the things of the world (self will pleasures) then we are still under the law and have not been set free. Jesus says, if he sets a man free then he is free indeed and then that man, is no longer under the laws of the curse. Jesus crucified the laws when he went to Calvary, so that, man could have victory over the lust of the flesh by submitting themselves to the spirit. Please at this time, say this prayer with me, if you want victory over your flesh and want to be lead by your spirit. "Thank You Lord for creating me that I can work and produce the way that you would have me to do here while I am on your earth. Lord now, I pray that you take my body and use it for your Kingdom and renew my mind, that I will know what your perfect will is for my life, in the name of The Father, The Son, and The Holy Ghost."

If a person is under the law, then he has to be judge by the law. If a person is walking in the Spirit of God then he can't be judged, because he is not under the law. This is like unto a man that while he was a sinner he got caught committing theft. He was brought before the judge and he was punished for the theft. He was placed on probation and he had to abide by the law unless he went to prison. Now, I can't see much joy in that, can you? However, the man gave himself to Christ totally committing himself and the Lord sets him free from sin and forgives him for all his trespasses. That doesn't mean that he would get off probation, but maybe, what it would mean, is that, Christ has forgave him for all his sins and has set his spirit free from the curse of the law. Now I can have a great fruit of joy in my life today, knowing Christ forgave me for all the sins I had committed in my lifetime.

Jesus said in St. John 8:31-32 *"If ye continue in my word, then ye are my disciples indeed; And ye shall know the truth, and the truth shall make you free."* In verse 34 he said, *"Verily, Verily, I say unto you, Whosoever committeth sin is the servant of sin."* If he walk under the Spirit then he will never want to commit another sin again, because the Spirit has not sin in it and is always giving and not taking. Jesus said in St John 8:36, *"If the Son therefore shall make you free, ye shall be free indeed."* As long as I am walking in the spirit, I have no desire to commit sin.

However, Satan will tempt or entice you, but remember whom the Son sets free is free indeed. It is our choice to either walk in the Spirit of God or not. I hope that you are walking in the spirit and if you are going through any trial, that it is only for the suffering of Christ; and that you have joy. Please take care of your body so it will take care of you. There is nothing that can be compared to the anointing blood of Jesus Christ, for it washes away all sin white as snow.

2.) THE FUEL FOR THE FURNACE.

I am going to start here by listing some fuels for the mechanical furnaces and fuels for the spiritual man. There are so many different fuels you can use to make a fire, but I am only going to expound on the ones that I am familiar with. I will also apply the working fuels to our spiritual life. Starting with mechanical fuels, there are many, such as, coal, oils, wood and gases, but there are others I'm sure. Remember, a furnace will not produce a product, if it does not have any fuel to produce fire. Every living creature under the sun that God has made, must have fuel to live, unless it is dead and then it is useless; for it produces no product. Like our bodies are to the furnace body, it has to have fuel to live and to produce a product. Depending on the type and the amount of fuel you use will effect the product that you will produce. If I only lived on water and unleavened bread then I would possibly perish to death or I would not have enough of strength in my body to produce a product. However, I know that I have got to have the right amount and the right types of food, to survive and also the right amount of water.

There are also spiritual fuels that act like the physical fuels. These fuels that affect our life are fleshly and spiritual; for we are flesh and bone and have a spirit. Our fleshly body must have food to eat and so does our spirit. Our spirit needs understanding to grow and mature, just like our flesh needs fruits, vegetables, meat and water to stay healthy. There are fuels that come from a man's brain and fleshly heart, which I will call the fleshly fuels, and there are Godly fuels that come from God for our spirit man to mature in understanding, which I will call the spiritual fuels, follow me? I will break these down and expound on each, so that, we can apply these to our spiritual life. There are fleshly fuels and Spiritual fuels for living and each different fuel determines the product that will be produced. In the Word of God, these fleshly fuels are listed.

Galatians chapter 5, verses 19-23 reads, ***"Now the works of the flesh are manifest, which are these; adultery, fornication, uncleanness, lasciviousness, idolatry, witchcraft, hatred, variance, emulations, wrath, strife, seditions, heresies, envyings, murders, drunkenness,*** *revellings, and such like: of the which I tell you before, as I have also told you in time past, that they which do such things shall not inherit the Kingdom of God."* Now that is a lot of worldly fleshly fuels that will eventually destroy the spiritual and physical body of a man, if he chooses to fuel his life with them. Paul said that they which do such things, shall not inherit the Kingdom of God. That must mean that our spiritual bodies, which are our souls, will be cast into the lake of fire, if we choose to fuel our fleshly body with such.

Now lets expound on these fuels of the fleshly body somewhat in simplicity, and make sure we are not fueling our life with any of these. Because, if you are like me, I do not want to miss out on the promise God has given to me concerning the Eternal Kingdom, and for sure, I don't want to go to the Lake of Fire that doesn't quench. So, lets get to the root of these fuels of the flesh. I will not expand of all these fuels of the flesh, but I will expand on the point of some fuels. Just keep this on your mind as you read the following, "All of these fuels are engulfed within the heart of mankind."

A.) Adultery.

What is adultery? It is sin and God hates sin. In the Holy Book of Exodus chapter 20, verse 14 reads, *"Thou shall not commit adultery"*. This is a commandment that God has given his people and we must obey it to its fullness. It isn't complex for it is simple for man to understand not to do it. Adultery today has become a every day thing in peoples lives and that is sad, very sad, because they really don't know that they are doing.

Today, adulteries are tearing good families apart and causing much sorrows for the children. Divorce today is like drinking water from a glass. I've even heard many times from the trap of some this, "Well, if our marriage doesn't work out, I'll find someone else." I'm telling you my friend, that is a set up for adultery. For it is written in the Holy Book of Matthew chapter 5, verses 31-32, *"It has been said, Whosoever shall put away his wife, let him give a writing of divorcement: But I say unto you, That whosoever shall put away his wife, saving for the cause of fornication, causeth her to commit adultery: and whosoever shall marry her that is divorced committeth adultery."* Marriage is a covenant between a Man, Woman and God. If a man leaves his wife to commit fornication (for another woman) he breaks the covenant not only between him and his wife, but God also.

Now, there is a difference of divorcements and we are not ignorant from the difference, but here are just a few examples: First, If a man and a woman get married and later in life one becomes converted over to God and the other is a non-believer and refuses to be converted to God, then that relationship is unequally yoked together and the converted has the right to write out an divorcement. Second, If a man and women were married for 50 years and one of them dies, then the other has the right for another mate and there wouldn't be a need for divorcement.

Marriage is for Life; for it is a covenant between a man and woman and God, but many are fallen away to the dark hole, because of adultery and fornications. Some are committing adulteries, such as, having affairs behind their spouses backs. Pornography is definitely the biggest problem today. There are two killers among our lives today that mankind is just waving like a banner to come to. There are many more, but these two are among the greatest killers to mankind. *First, Alcohol and drugs.*

Alcohol is killing our youth by the truck loads and I wonder why it is legal to just go to the store and reach into a cooler and get the loaded bottle and just drive off to death. Alcohol is a drug and it will alter the mind. I believe if a man is caught given a child alcohol or drugs, that man is guilty of murder, no kidding. As a great nation or this super power man calls it, we can go over to other nations and restore order, but we cant restore order in our own house? *Second, Pornography.*

I thought that we as mankind were civilized, but as I look at all the transgressions, such as, this filthy abomination of pornography, we as mankind our no more civilized than a dog. Remember Sodom and Gomorrah? I'll tell you today, I just cant believe the way man is living. Sometimes I believe that some of our leaders are enemies within our camp, killing the youth of this great nation, or, could they just be animals or perhaps a bunch of chickens plucking away. I was once addicted to pornography and it put a hook into my flesh that was worse than the drugs I was addicted to. What is wrong with mankind, I ask? Pornography is a killer and destroyer of man and marriage and is fueling the gates of Hell faster than darkness itself. I am very saddened for all the youth and young ladies that have defiled their life to porn.

After I came back to God from all my whoredoms, God was faithful and wipe my sins away by the blood of his Son Jesus Christ. Adultery is wiping out the families through out the earth, like a plague would wipe out entire cities and even countries. Adultery is defined in two different ways, one being; to voluntary engage in a relationship with another married man or woman other than their wife or husband. Jesus Christ said in the gospel of Matthew 5:27-28 *"Ye have heard that it was said by them of old time, Thou shall not commit adultery: But I say unto you, That whosoever looketh on a woman to lust after her hath committed adultery with her in his heart."* When Jesus was here on the earth in his body, he never respected any man over another.

He had eyes that pierced into the heart of man and not the outer appearance only. Jesus Christ still today pierces man's hearts and knows his need before he would ask. He knows who you are and what kind of product you are producing. In the Book of Proverbs 6:32 reads, *"But whoso committeth adultery with a woman lacketh understanding: he that doeth it destroyeth his own soul."* If you are producing adultery in your heart, then that is same as committing it in the physical body, no kidding.

Today, that filthy devil has tried many times to pierce my mind with the lust of a beautiful lady, but the Holy Ghost has always been there to convict me of that sin. Even if I had thought of such a sinful act. I know that the thorn of lust still exist within my flesh, but I also know the consequences of lusting and then sinning; for it would be death. I will say this, in my past dead life, not only was I addicted to drugs and alcohol, I was also addicted to porn. I was a very addictive addict. Like I have said before times, I had broken every 10 commandment that are written. I was a very adulterous man and I had one thing on my mind constantly and that was to fulfill my self will pleasures. I not only had committed sin of adultery in the flesh, but I had committed the sin of adultery, against God.

During these horrible times of my life, I had quenched the fuels of the spirit and was living by the fuels of the flesh. But, after I left my whoredoms and went back to God as a broken vessel, God was faithful and restored my life to a new born child. He wash me by the blood of his Son Jesus Christ and made me whole again. The blood of Christ washed my mind like a washing machine, with bleach, would do to a dirty white garment.

Before I went to God in desperation, porn and the images of porn was in my mind and flashing through my mind as if I was looking at it on the television or the internet all the time.

But, after Christ washed my entire body by the blood, that he has shed for all mankind, the only thing that flashes in my mind today is MORE of YOUR BLOOD LORD! Even when my brain throws up hidden images, the blood quickly washes it away, without hesitation. A man has a choice to respond to conviction and to repent of the sin they have committed, but I will say that many are loosing their lives, because of not repenting of the sin and not receiving God's true forgiveness.

When I began to fuel my flesh during these times of my life, my spirit was leaving my body. Sure, the Holy Ghost did convict me every time that I committed adultery, but like I said, I had quench the spirit and was living by the lust of my flesh and my spirit was beginning to leave my body and I was headed straight into eternal death. I also know this with confidence, If I would had die in my sin, then I would had awoke to the fire of hell, which doesn't quench. But, I chose to change and began to seek help to get off drugs and alcohol and then my spirit began to get stronger and then the conviction began. The word of God was like a bright light shinning into the dark hidden places of my soul, spirit and flesh. After the word had pierced through my soul and my spirit the miracle was beginning to happen. It started to pierce deep into my bones and to my marrow where the blood (life) is made. When the Word of God began to pierce my flesh it was battles after battles. The Word of God was like a bright light shinning into the dark hidden places of my hearts intents. Have you every shined a light into a dark place and seen bugs run? That was somewhat how it was working. The Word of God was chasing the bugs out of my flesh and as the Light would hit the bugs, they would melt away.

Remember, only God's people are convicted of sin; for the Spirit of God doesn't convict an unbeliever. The unbeliever will be lost forever into the abyss of void and emptiness which is, death.

But he that believes in the only begotten Son of God will have the Holy Ghost to convict him, if he chooses to commit sin. God's Word is convicting and is like unto a purifying fire. I believe that a believer that was once enlighten of the truth of God's Perfect Will can commit sin, but it is what he does with the conviction that determines his life.

It doesn't matter who you are; for you are still with a fleshly body and if you are lusting after something and then commit sin, then sin is sin. It doesn't matter if it was a little bit of sin, because sin is sin. Here is an example of a little bit of sin as a man would reason within himself, "Well, as long as I don't have sex and have a relationship with another women in real life, I guess pornography would be Ok, to just look at it every now and then." Again I say with confidence, sin is sin and a little leaven leavens the whole loaf. Christ said that even if we thought of the matter of adultery in our heart, it is the same as committing adultery in reality. And I tell you today my friend, I should know, been there, done that and suffered greatly for it.

It isn't written in God's Word that once saved always saved, but it is written that he that endures to the end will find life everlasting. I was enlighten and even was called and was chosen to the ministry 15 years ago, but I lusted after the things of this world and committed great sin. The sin that I was living was leading me straight to the big hole of emptiness and void and death was definite. If I had not heard of the hope in Christ Jesus and God the Father, I would had already been dead and lost to the big hole of emptiness and void. I chose to lust after my flesh and to fulfill my self will pleasures and I was headed straight to the gate of destruction.

I remember the very second that I chose to commit sin, after I was enlightened of God's Will. I was at work and had been clean for over three years, no kidding. God was revealing many things to me through the Holy Ghost and was enlighten me on his Perfect Will for me and the whole wide world. One day as I was at work, a close Christian friend of mine suggested that I take a pill. I was going through some trials during this time of my life and I went to him to talk about this matter. He told me that he had some medicine (a narcotic drug) that would help ease my burden. I thought coming from this man, it couldn't be bad. I chose to take this medicine and I began again lusting after this medicine. I asked him what Doctor he went to and he suggested that he would set me up an appointment to go see this doctor. When I did go see this doctor, I was back on psychiatric drugs again. I was on mind altering drugs which lasted for 15 years. It wasn't this man's fault, because he didn't know my past and I surely wasn't going to tell him of my past. But the point is I did chose to commit sin, because doing drugs was sin to me and God didn't want me to do drugs; for it quenched the Holy Spirit from teaching me his Perfect Will.

I was a full blown addict at 13 years of age and these three years of my life being clean and God in my life, was the beginning of a new life and I just threw it away for a stinking little pill not any bigger than a small pea. Was I enticed to do this? Yes! I was enticed and I chose to sin over life, but I will say I was without understanding at the time. By God's Loving Grace I can tell you this today. My friend, It doesn't matter who you are, converted or not; for God is not a respecter of man, that if you commit sin, death is the consequence, unless ye repent.

Adultery can also mean to apostatize. The word Adultery comes from a Hebrew prime root meaning to commit or to apostatize. Apostatize means the renunciation of a religious faith and also revolting and defection. What has apostasy have to do with adultery?

Israel defected and revolted from God many times according to his word. Nevertheless, he was always merciful to receive a repented heart and repented nation. Satan is busy today tempting Gods children to commit this awful abomination. If, Satan can cause a child of the King to commit this sin, then that child has defected from Gods loving Grace and is endangered of Hell Fire, unless he would repent and come back to Gods loving Arms. But, what about those who don't believe? I will say this with confidence today, there is a great fire ready and wanting them greatly.

This fuel of adultery is a fleshly sin and it can be completely abolished by walking in the Spirit of God. Have you defected from God like the Hebrew children did at mount Sinai? Have you committed an adulterous act in your heart? You will never be free from the burdens and trials of life, but you can be free and free in deed from this destructive sin. All you have to do is to repent with an honest heart and give your life to God and God will have his Son Jesus Christ to wash you whiter than snow and wipe all the sins away. Don't let this type of fuel tempt you for it is only temporary, but the Fire of Hell is eternity.

B.) Fornication.

What is fornication? Unlike the word adultery, fornication means to have sexual relationships between unmarried men and women. Let me explain, if a man had a girlfriend, but wasn't married to the women (girlfriend) and were having sexual relations with each other, this would be fornication. You don't have to be married to commit fornication? No, that would be adultery. There was fornication thought to be among the Corinthians during the new testament times of writings and the apostle Paul wrote to them, in concern for their salvation.

In the epistle of 1Corinthians chapter 5, verse1 reads, *"It is reported commonly that there is fornication among you, and such fornication as is not so much as named among the Gentiles, that one should have his father's wife."*

Now that was sick, wasn't it? Can you believe that someone in the church would commit such a perverted sin as this? Paul had heard that a son was having sexual relations with his father's wife. I bet that man rolled day and night in the grave, if he was dead. Apostle Paul said even the Gentiles had never had this problem or even heard of it. In verse 2 apostle Paul told them they were even proud to have let such a sin enter into the church. In verse 4 and 5 apostle Paul wrote that it would be best that the one that had committed this fornication be delivered into Satan and to be killed or destroyed, so that, his spiritual man may be saved in the day of the Lord.

However, fornication exists today just the same yesterday and I believe to be much worse. The saddest that I know of today is fornication among the youth, teenagers and even children. Children are getting pregnant every day and are being victimized also. They're having sexual relations at very young ages and don't understand the consequences that they soon will face.

Nevertheless, God has preserved children from this and there are some children that are brought up in God's Word and are keeping and preserving themselves for marriage. When I was but a young child in the fifth grade,11 or 12 years of age, the year after some dead man had taken the Ten Commandments from the Walls of the school houses, I would over hear many young boys and girls talking about sex. I'm not talking about wanting to experience sex, I'm talking that they had sex with each other.

Sex among our youth is very concerning especially when there is so many different plagues out there in the world today. There is also a staggering number of single women and men that commit fornication. There are so many men and women committing fornication and that every where you look, there are dating services to keep up with their sin. Yep, just call one up and find your type and even they will guarantee you the right date or your money back.

I bet the Gentiles didn't know about that one either.

I tell you with confidence today, God made every man a wife and every wife a husband and If you can't wait for your blessing of a spouse, please don't commit fornication. This fuel is fueling Hell faster than Satan himself. I got caught up in fornication when I was a younger man and believe me, I didn't know what I was getting into. It got the young lady pregnant and caused both of us terrifying troubles. We were both young and without a bit of adulthood or understanding of love and life. We were 19 years of age and had been committing fornication for many years. However, we didn't know that it was sin. As far as we were concerned, it was love. However it wasn't love it was a fuel for the flesh. We got married and had the child and I love her very much. The young lady and I got a divorce within 6 months of marriage. She went her way and I went my way.

I gave myself to the Lord in March of 1985 and one of my prayers was, "God please send me a wife. Someone that will love me and understand me." My prayer was answered in August of 1986. I met the lady that God had sent for me to be my wife. If I just would have waited for God, I would not have went through all the troubles I had went through. My wife and I have been married happily for 22 years as of 2007. Yes we have been through tribulations, trials and temptations, but I can say this with confidence, my wife and I are still together through all the Horrors and miseries. Thank you Lord for my Wife and forgive me Lord for my impatience.

Apostle Paul writes that there is a way to avoid fornication, 1 Corinthians 7:2 reads, *"Nevertheless, to avoid fornication, let every man have his own wife, and let every woman have her own husband."* That simple. Sex is a device that Satan will use to tempt and fuel your flesh for fornication. Don't let Satan fuel you with garbage such as, "You aren't married, so you can have any one your heart desires".

Remember, one of Satan's biggest devices, is that of, half the truth. Satan is some what enticing with his words, but you don't have to give in to him or the lust of the flesh. If the above sentence was near truth, it would had been like this, "You aren't married, so you can have any one your heart desires, but wait on the Lord for the blessing of your spouse". Call on God and draw nigh unto him and he will draw nigh unto you. If you don't have a spouse, call on God and pray that he send your blessing, because she or he is there waiting somewhere just like you. Don't give in to fortification for it will only bring sorrows from the sin that you sow. Try God and he will bless you with the blessing of your life for I know, he did for me when he answered my desperate prayer. It wasn't overnight express, but my wife and I came together like a plan. Where there is peace, God reigns. Please remember this Word from the Holy Book of Hebrews, chapter 13, verse 4, *"Marriage is honorable in all, and the bed undef iled: but whoremongers and adulterers God will judge."* Please don't let fornication fuel your life, because it will bring troubles and even destruction.

C.) Uncleanness.

What is uncleanness? Uncleanness comes from a prim root Hebrew word meaning to be defile, polluted. It also means, impurity, foul, demonic in Greek. I tell you there is a lot of pollution in the world today, so much, it probably would take forever to write about. However, I am only going to expound on what God says about uncleanness and try to apply it to our spiritual life. Uncleanness in the world today is another killer Satan has unloosed on the earth. In the Old Testament there are several incidents where uncleanness is considered as a person with leprosy. However, uncleanness also means demonic, without God or his Son Jesus Christ or his Spirit. In the book of 1 Thessalonians 4:1-7 it is written, *"Furthermore then we beseech you, brethren, and exhort you by the Lord Jesus Christ, that as ye have received of us how ye ought to walk and to please God, so ye would abound more and more. For ye know what commandment we gave you by the Lord Jesus.*

For this is the will of God, even your sanctification, that ye abstain from fornication: That everyone of you should know how to possess his vessel in sanctification and honor; Not in the lust of concupiscence, even as the Gentiles which know not God: That no man go beyond and defraud his brother in any matter: because that the Lord is the avenger of all such, as we also have forewarned you and testified. For God had not called us unto uncleanness, but unto holiness."

My friend, this uncleanness or impurity, is like a disease in this world and is infecting even some of God's Elect. Uncleanness comes from self-will pleasures of this world, such as, fornication. Uncleanness could be the capsule of all the fuels of the flesh. I believe that uncleanness is the total of all the works of the flesh in simple form. God has called and his call is without repentance. His call is for everyman to come to his holiness by his Spirit in the name of his Son Jesus Christ. Remember the Avenger of Uncleanness, which is, the Lord of Holies, Jesus Christ. Uncleanness is somewhat like a swine in the mud. But, just as the swine can be washed with water, so can a man be washed from uncleanness by the blood of Jesus and by the Holy Spirit.

D.) Lasciviousness

The word lasciviousness in simple form means; Lacking moral restraint. Today is this world, morals seem to be something that your elders or the old timers had only. Now I have seen morals standards taught at Church, but what about the millions of children not being taught the morals of Life? I tell you today my friend, it all comes down to the lack of teaching of moral standards in our public schools. I am confident the reason is that of the teachers not have good morals themselves. Every other day I see something on the news about a teacher being arrested for something immoral toward a child or their students. What in this world is wrong with our Education system.

I believe that the only way to get out of the terrible mess today in our public school is to have a moral test for the teachers themselves. If, they don't pass the moral test with an A+, then they should be fired or sent away.

The children are the most precious and important Creature walking this earth, and they need morals taught. I believe that teaching Morals would start at the blackboard of the Holy Word of God at home, but school would also be a great place. The Holy Book of Proverbs would be a great beginning of Moral teaching. I also believe the reason morals aren't taught is because of disciple techniques.

My friend, when I was young, the strap across my rear was a great lesson of moral teaching; and I will never forget it. In the Holy Book of Proverbs it states the importance and the reason for the strap across a child's rear. Now, I am only talking about a child reaching the right from wrong age, not an innocent infant. Proverbs 23: 13-14 and it is written, ***"Withhold not correction from the child: for if thou beastest him with a rod, he shall not die. Thou shalt beat him with the rod, and shalt deliver his soul from hell."*** I have heard people that would tell me that thet don't believe in the rod on a child's rear end. They would tell me that thet take away the video game or such. My friend, that isn't what the Word of God says and any parent that doesn't discipline their child will be accountable for their child's soul. This lascivious concept is spreading this nation like a fire would spread through a dry wheat field. I do not believe that the Government should be responsible for any law passed about the disciplining of our children, but somehow they are. I believe the greatest reason why there isn't much disciplining of children today is, because the parents are afraid of child abuse. If a blue mark upon a rebellious child's rear end can send a parent to jail for child abuse, then what? I guess the parent will not discipline the child and the child will miss the opportunity to remember the moral rod.

When I was young and these laws (child abuse) started to come into effect, my parents stop using the moral strap and I remember becoming even that much more rebellious, so what do we do? Well if you don't disciple the child, the State will; and the matter will become the State's responsibility. Then, if, the State doesn't discipline the child, the child will grow and God will use his Rod upon him. I will say today that God's Long Hand of Discipline, surely out weighs a man's hand of discipline.

E.) Idolatry

My friend, now we are getting to the meat of these fleshly fuels. Idolatry means exactly what it states,

Idol worshipping or Image worshipping. My friend I will say there is nothing wrong with sports, dancing, movies, if they are truth, and such, but we as mankind find ways of worshipping those things more than going to church and worshipping the Creator whom made us. I like NasCar and all types of car racing, Bowling, Football and such, but I wouldn't give a nickel for it over my God. If it wasn't for Jesus Christ, we wouldn't have the freedom to even worship God. What do you worship or whom do you worship?

I have heard many times this saying, "I worship the feet that that man walks." My friend, there is but one to worship, and it is the Creator God and his Son Jesus Christ. I tell you the truth, Idolizing a man is a abomination before God. It's Ok to like those things, but if you are worshipping those things more than God, you will be recompensed accordingly to your works, no kidding. In the Holy Book of Deuteronomy 6:5 it is written, *"And thou shalt love the Lord thy God with all thine heart, and with all thy soul, and with all thy might."* My friend, God is a jealous God over you and if you are worshipping something or someone more than him, he will avenge your works sooner or later. In the Holy Book of Matthew 6:24 it is written, *"No man can serve two master: for either he will hate the one , and love the other; or else he will hold to the one, and despise the other. Ye cannot serve God and mammon."*

F.) Witchcraft

Witchcraft is a lie right straight from Satan himself. Listen my friend, I don't need Harry Potter to get my mind to image. Witchcraft is the same as, magic, sorcery, voodoo, palm readings, superstitions, etc. Yes, come and get you palm read. My friend, there is only one man that I will let read my palms, and his hands are already red, by the blood that he shed on Calvary.

Have you ever drawled a cross on your front windshield of your vehicle as a black cat crossed in front of you. My question is, What in this world!? Witchcraft comes form a Greek Word, "pharmakeia" or "pharmacy." Simply put, "medicine." My friend Satan almost got me to believe in this crap when I was younger, but after I found out it was a lie, I fled from it. The only magic that is going to work in my life, will be by the miracles through God. I was watching a News channel one day and they did a special on a certain women. This women had cooked up something and called it snake oil. This women was around 90-100 years of age. She told the news correspondent that she found the recipe in her grandfather's Bible and cooked the recipe up. Now she claims it is a healing potion. She will not say with confidence that it is what gives her longevity, but she may as well. She laughs when someone ask her about this potion and then she says this, "I do it out of Christian Love." My friend, deceiving another human being in to believing that they can live longer by a potion stirred up, it ludicrous. God limited man's days; and if I was to bet, her days are number also. Some die young and some die old and that potion, is no more than eating a fish. Just as a palm reader would say, "Let me read your palm and see how long a life span you have." The palm reader reads the man's palm and says this, "You will live a long time and have great wisdom." The man walks out from this sorcerer, hoping this be true, but gets hit be a freight train and dies in a second.

My friend, we have got to believe the Word of God to be the Truth of "all things" and if, you are not a believer in the Word of God, at least try it, you may like it. My friend all these programs on television, such as, Harry Potter, King of the Rings, Be-Witched, and such are carrying deception like a fire through our youth. Some believe and Idolized this stuff and it is an abomination before God. My friend, if you have children, why take a chance on their life and feed their little souls a bunch of lies? Why not give them the truth, and see their lives and soul grow in he that made them? My friend just remember that one day they will be of an age of recognition. Think on this: When my child or whomever it may be, grows to maturity, will he respect me as a parent for teaching him a bunch of lies?

My God my friend! What is wrong with this world? Deception! Surely in the Old Testament days miracles happened, such as Elijah calling on God to send fire down from heaven. Moses asking God to depart the Red Sea, and my favorite, God's Complete Creation in Harmony. Just look into the mirror my friend, and ask yourself, "who do I believe, God or Mammon?"

There is a story in the Word of God about a man that turned to witchcraft, rather than, calling on God and he paid the price of his Life latter. It's about a King whose name was Saul and he rebelled against God's very Word. There was a prophet whose name was Samuel that was lead by God. God sent this prophet to Saul and the prophet said unto Saul, ***"For rebellion is as the sin of witchcraft, and stubbornness is as iniquity and idolatry. Because thou hast rejected the word of the Lord, he hath also rejected thee from being King. And Saul said unto Samuel, I have sinned: for I have transgressed the commandment of the Lord, and thy words: because I feared the people, and obeyed their voice.(1Samuel 15:23-24)"*** This King trusted the people of Israel more than he trusted God and God took this King's Kingship away. Later, this King dies in Battle.

Great Example of How we must trust God for our Life, rather than, people.

There is a eye opener written in the Holy Book of Revelations 21:7-8 and it is written, ***"He that overcometh shall inherit all things; and I will be his***

God and he shall be my son. But the fearful, and unbelievers, and the abominable, and murderers, and whoremongers, and sorcerers, and idolaters, and all liars, shall have their part in the lake of fire and brimstone: which is the second death."

G.) Hatred

In the Holy Book of Proverbs chapter 10 verses 12 and 18 it is written, *"Hatred stirreth up strifes: but love covereth all sins.; He that hideth hatred with lying lips, and he that uttered a slander, is a fool."* Hatred is to me the same thing as not forgiving your fellow man. Hated is a rebellion against God and man. Some may say, "I hate this government", but, what they are really saying is, "I hate God." If you would, please read Ecclesiastes chapter 9.

Hatred is also a great fuel of the flesh as it fuels people with different beliefs. I believe all the Wars that has cause millions of Lives, started by hatred of some sort. I also believe that hatred is just like murder within a man's heart.

Let me just say this one thing about hatred, and then I will continue to the next fuel of the flesh. Satan hates mankind and if any man has hatred in his heart, it is possible that man is being lead by Satan.

H.)Variance

Variance in simple form, means to break apart or faction. It also means contention or division. Have you ever heard this before from a man, "If I can't get it, he want get it." That type of thinking is discord, and there is plenty of this to going around among people, even in the Body of Christ. But, within the Body of Christ, it doesn't last long, because Jesus Christ takes care of variance himself, quickly.

I believe the greatest examples of Variances is that of Politics. Republicans and Democrats always having contention or debating among themselves. I've got to a point now in my life, that I'm going independent. It hurts me greatly to see political advertisements on television, on the news, or different places where the leaders of our nation are debating or contenting with each other. Why can't there be a single party and just let the people vote that way? Why not give the people what we need, rather than, fighting for a political position, where the same old same, always happens. Maybe one day there will be no more variance among our leaders, and love will be the vote. Please don't read me wrong my friend; I love the leaders of this great Nation of the USA, but to be sure there is another way without variance among our leaders.

My friend let me clear up something that Jesus said while walking this earth many years ago. In the Holy Book of Matthew Chapter 10 verses 34-35 and it is written, *"Think not that I have come to send peace on earth: I came not to send peace, but a sword. For I am come to set a man at variance against his father, and the daughter against her mother, and the daughter in law against her mother in law. And a man's foes shall be they of his own household."* Now that may sound contradicting or varying, but Jesus meant this: He has come to bring a sword and not peace. What he is saying is that the sword, which is the Word of God, will divide a father and son, a mother and daughter, and such. There will be some that believe on the Word of God and there will be some that don't believe in the same household. When a household has variance or lets say, the father believes in the Word of God, and his son doesn't believe, then there is variance or contention between the two, follow me?

The word variance is only mention in the word of God twice and we had already read them both. Now the word of God is explained in Hebrew 4:12 and it is written, *"For the Word of God is quick, and powerful, and sharper than any two-edged sword, piercing even to the dividing asunder of soul and spirit, and of the joints and marrow, and is a discerner of the thoughts and intents of the heart."*

I.) Emulations

Emulation can be defined in simplicity as Imitation or to eagerly to excel above what we really are. It also means jealousy. Now before I say what I am going to say about this particular fuel of their flesh, let me just say this; In this world today, mankind is good, but this fuel is definitely a monster in society. One great example is trying to be someone that your not. For examples: face lifts, lip puffs, breast implants, gender changes and I could keep going on, but, that is what I will leave for examples.

My friend, you are different than any other human on this earth and Why should you want to change that? Now, I understand if you were born with defects of the body and wanting to have surgeries to make your body more tolerable to face, but injections in the flesh just to look like someone else, or, because someone else did it, is ludicrous. I know of men of the age of 80 that dies their hair black. My friend, their faces are as wrinkled as the oceans waves during a hurricane, but yet their hair looks as if they where just born. I have to keep myself from rolling on the ground sometimes from laughter. I don't laugh at them, but that hair, and knowing the man is 80 yeas of age, and trying to look like an infant, I just can't help myself. Let me ask this question, Will it matter what you look like after you appointed time is called to the grave? If you answered No, then you are well. Why in this world does someone go through a surgery to look younger and spend thousands of dollars and the next day, is lying in a casket. Maybe not lying in a casket, but infected from the surgery and their face is disfigured.

Emulations is of the devil and if you think you can change the way you were made, then you are trying to imitate the devil. My friend, I know that is strong, but really, why not just live in truth and grace and be who you are. God isn't a respecter of persons and I am sure he doesn't care if you have ten fingers or twenty. I am confident that he doesn't look at the outer appearance of a man, but his heart.

Like I said, emulation also means jealousy. I am confident that Satan is jealous over God's sons and daughters, and he would like it very much if, they would change to the way he is, which is, jealousy. My friend, I keep one thing of my mind and it is definitely not a lip puff, it is my soul in the hands of God. Like I said, God isn't a respecter of person and he doesn't care if you live in an old boot, rather than, a mansion here on earth. What God does care about is if, you have his Love and Son Jesus within your heart. These things of this world are like a vapor, but your soul is eternal. Now, I ask this question, who are you imitating?

J.) Wrath

This will be the last fuel I will expand on; for I am confident the points have already been made. Before we hit on this fuel of the flesh, let me say that wrath, is the work of all the fuels. Wrath comes from adultery, fornication, uncleanness, lasciviousness, idolatry, witchcraft, hatred, variance, emulations, strife, seditions, heresies, envyings, murders, drunkenness, revellings, and such like of the which I tell you before, as I have also told you in time past, that they which do such things shall not inherit the Kingdom of God.

My friend, wrath is the product of all the fuels of the flesh. I believe that wrath in the capsule of all the works of the flesh. But, is in no way more or less than the other fuels of the flesh. Wrath when it comes to mankind, means, rage, madness, great anger. Wrath is the opposite of Love and Charity. Let me leave with you some principles concerning this monster of a fuel.

__Proverbs 14:29__- "He that is slow to wrath is of great understanding: but he that is hasty of spirit exalteth folly.

__Proverbs 15:1__- "A soft answer turneth away wrath: but grievous words stir up anger."

__Proverbs 15:18__- "A wrathful man stirreth up strife: but he that is slow to anger appeaseth strife."

__Proverbs 19:19__- "A man of great wrath shall suffer punishment: for if thou deliver him, yet thou must do it again."

__Proverbs 27:4__- Wrath is cruel, and anger is outrageous; but who is able to stand before envy?

3.) THE FUEL PUMP

The fuel pump is the heart of a furnace. It pumps the fuel to the igniters, and then the fire burns as long as there is fuel present. In a furnace or boiler, you can adjust the fuel rate on the fuel pump to allow the proper fuel for a particular flame size.

Now I am going to apply the fuel pump to a man's life. The fuel pump will be applied as the heart of a man and the fuel will be applied as the fruit, rather they be fleshly or spiritual. Now, the fuels, fuel the furnace through the fuel pump just as the heart pumps blood throughout a man's body. First let me share this principle with you and then I will continue. In the Holy Book of Proverbs 23:7 it is written, ***"For as he thinketh in his heart, so is he:"*** I have mentioned in the first part of the book about the heart and the blood, and the importance of keeping your mind on Godly things. I have also mentioned that the blood contains the life of a man. Now, the heart of a man is somewhat liken to a fuel pump on a furnace. The heart pumps blood through a man's body, just as the fuel pump pumps fuel to the furnace. Now, if I would change the fuel of a furnace to a different type fuel that the furnace is set up to run, the furnace wouldn't run or light. Just as a man's heart that pumps blood, if you don't have the right fuels, your body wouldn't light or produce light, follow me?

If perhaps, I thought of bad things all the time, then my blood would pick up those bad thoughts and carry those thoughts throughout my body and my body possibly would not feel too good, would it? But, if I thought of good things all the time, then my body would possibly feel better. "As a man thinks, so he is." If I was running a furnace on kerosene and put gasoline into the fuel tank, the furnace would possible explode and I also would not be feeling too great.

Your body needs the right thoughts pumping though the heart, just as the furnace needs the proper fuel pumping through the fuel pump. Lets use a good fuel for the next example. This good fuel will be faith. In the Holy Book of Hebrews 11:1 it is written, *"Now faith is the substance of things hoped for, the evidence of things not seen."* If I would keep my mind and heart on those things from faith, then faith is exercised within my life. I start to believe in things that I cant see, but know it be the truth, because of witnesses of what I believe to be the truth.

Once I start believing God's Word, as it is written, then my faith in believing God's Word is exercised and then these thoughts enter into my heart and throughout my complete life. If by chance I continue to believe and exercise the good fruit of faith in my life, then my life will shine, just as a fire gives off light, follow me? The more I exercise faith, the much more I will bare fruit, and my Life will shine as a bright light in this dark world. But, if I fuel my heart with a bad fruit such as, adultery, murder, hatred, then my life is dim and dark. For it is written in the Gospel of Luke 12:34, *"For where your treasure is, there will your heart be also."*

4.) THE IGNITERS

Now, we have covered some of the fuels of the flesh and spirit. We also know that a furnace can not burn without fuel. But, what causes the ignition of such fuels to ignite the fuels to become a flame or fire? In a furnace, there is a set or pair of igniters that spark, like a spark plug in a car would spark to ignite gasoline fumes. In a furnace, the igniters work in the same manner as a spark plug. I have worked on many furnaces that the igniters would try to ignite, even though, there was no fuel. I will try to apply the igniters to our bodies, just as I have applied the other components to our bodies.

The igniters working in a furnace, is in the likeness of our eyes and thoughts and senses. Our eyes is what catches light and all things around us, rather they be good or evil. Our senses are somewhat like to the igniters of a furnace. We respond by hearing and seeing or even touching, correct? When we see something or hear something our senses sends these messages to the brain and we respond by our brain function, rather it is good or evil. The igniters are the most, but not least important. If you don't have an ignition, a furnace will not light. Just as are bodies are, if you don't have something to impel your life, you will die. A man without a vision will perish. The eyes are the light of a mans life. In the Holy Book of Matthew 6:22-23 it is written, *"The light of the body is the eye: if therefore thine eye be single, thy whole body shall be full of light. But if thine eye be evil, thy whole body shall be full of darkness. If therefore the light that is in these be darkness, how great is that darkness!"* So, is your flame shining or are you just sparking?

5.) THE FIRE

Now we are getting to the meat of this matter, which is, the fire or flame and the water. My friend, I will not spend a lot of time on this matter, but I will get to the points. I could spend eternity writing about fire and water, but I don't have that much time here on this earth. I will share with you what I believe to be the truth of fire and water in a simple perspective.

Fire can be used to purify, heat and consume matter. Fire is also used for a sign or signals. Fire is a phenomenon that happens and really truly can not be explain. It is somewhat like water. As mankind we understand what fire is made of, but really, what is fire? Just as water, we as mankind know what water is made of, but truly, what is water? Fire and water work together and can be worked against each other's elements. Fire can destroy or move water and water can destroy fire or move fire. In a furnace, fire is used to purify water or to consume water from matter. For an example; A man's body contains 75% water and 25% dust. If you would cremate a man in a furnace, and the man weighed 180 lbs before the cremation, then after the cremation the body would weigh around 35lbs or less. If you would take a pot of water and boil the water away you would have only dust, if the water isn't 100% pure. But, if the water is 100% pure, you would have nothing left in the pot, follow me?

These two matters, fire and water, have always fascinated my imagination. The word fire comes from the Hebrew word, "aysk" meaning, fiery, burning, hot. Fire is mentioned many times throughout God's Word. I believe that there is a fire that will never be quenched. This fire is called Hell. Just to get started on this fire, I would like to share with you what Jesus Christ says about this unquenchable fire. I honestly believe there is a Hell that the fire is never quenched and I look at this Hell as I look at the sun of the Universe.

The sun is an enormous fire that grows day by day. Sometimes my imagination carries me to the likeness of the Sun, as it represents the fiery hell waiting for the rebellious children of this earth. I honestly believe that the sun is a testimony of God how he is a consuming fire and how this fire is waiting day by day for the rebellious children of the earth. Sometimes my imagination carries me to think that maybe, the sun is the lake of fire and is being fuel by the souls of many.

Now in the Holy Book of Mark 9:43-44 it is written, *"And if thy hand offend thee, cut it off: it is better for thee to enter life maimed, than having two hands to go into hell, into the fire that never shall be quenched: Where their worm dieth not, and the fire is not quenched."* My friend, this is serious, and Jesus Christ knows how serious Hell is, and he warned mankind many times about this fire that never shall be quenched. Hell is real. Just looked at the sun for God's Testimony. The sun is like a nucleolus of an atom and it feeds on itself and grows and grows enormously. I mentioned earlier in the writings that I believe that the sun is also a testimony for the rebellious children of the earth. I believe it is also a testimony for Satan and his followers he to look at every day, knowing with no doubt, he will be cast into it one day at the appointed time.

I believe that fire represents God. In the Holy Book of Hebrews 12:29 it is written, *"For our God is a consuming fire."* In the Holy Book of Genesis, fire is also revealed as God in the Burning Bush, as Moses looked upon it as God gives him his commission, which was, to deliver Israel from Egypt. God revealed himself as fire. I honestly believe that God is like a flame that burns not away, but he is.

The Holy Ghost is also represented as a fire in the Word of God. The Cloven Tongues of Fire which was seen on the disciples in the upper room as they were all filled with the Holy Ghost in Acts chapter 2. This power represented "Authority" of the Holy Ghost, as it manifested into the disciples lives.

Now, fire in the spiritual form represents trials also. In the Holy Book of 1 Peter 1:3-9 and it is written, ***"Blessed be the God and Father of our Lord Jesus Christ, which accordingly to his abundant mercy hath begotten us again unto a lively hope by the resurrection of Jesus Christ from the dead, To an inheritance incorruptible, and undef iled, and the fadeth not away, reserved in heaven for you, Who are kept by the power of God through faith unto salvation ready to be revealed in the last time. Wherein ye greatly rejoice, though now for a season, if need be, ye are in heaviness through manifold temptations: That the trial of your faith being much more precious than of gold that perisheth, though it be tried with f ire, might be found unto praise and honour and glory at the appearing of Jesus Christ: Whom having not seen, ye love; in whom, though now ye see him not, yet believing, ye rejoice with joy unspeakable and full of glory: Receiving the end of your faith, even the salvation of your souls."*** Also, 1 Peter 4:12-13 and it is written, ***"Beloved, think it not strange concerning the f iery trials which is to try you, as0 though some strange thing happened unto you: But rejoice, inasmuch as ye are partakers of Christ's suffering; that, when his glory shall be revealed, ye may be glad also with exceeding joy."***

I have mentioned many times throughout this book about trials and how they effect a man's life, but to sum the matter up is this; As a man that believes in Jesus Christ, he will be tried for an inheritance.

Just say that you where a great wealthy Millionaire, and perhaps you are, and you wanted to leave your inheritance to someone responsible and that you love greatly. Perhaps the one that you wanted to leave the inheritance to wasn't quite responsible to care for all you details of your will, so, what do you do? First you would either train him in your affairs or try him to see if he be worthy of you millions, follow me? Now, God is in the trying business my friend. It isn't temptation or any type of evil; it is strictly trials. God will try a man and fire the man in the furnace many times even at the man's appointed time to be found worthy of his riches. Only a believer in Jesus Christ will be tried. If this wasn't so, then what would the purpose be of the cross and the resurrection of Jesus Christ? So, what does God try? Your faith in him, and, his Son Jesus Christ. The above scriptures lay the foundation of the trials of you faith for your eternal soul.

If we say we love Jesus and the Father, our faith in them will be tried. In the Holy Book of Revelation, Jesus Christ urges man to try him. Not to tempt him, but to try his worthiness and faithfulness. In Revelation 3:18-22 it is written, *"I counsel thee to buy of me gold tried in the fire, that thou mayest be rich; and white raiment, that thou mayest be clotheth, and that the shame of thy nakedness do not appear; and anoint thine eyes with eye-slave, that thou mayest see. As many as I love, I rebuke and chasten: be zealous therefore, and repent. Behold I stand at the door, and knock: If any man hear my voice, and open the door, I will come into him, and will sup with him, and he with me. To him that overcometh will I grant to sit with me in my throne, even as I also overcame, and am set down with my Father in his throne. He that hath ear, let him hear what the Spirit saith unto the churches.*

6.) THE BLOWER OR FAN

The Blower or fan of a furnace is used for different reason and there are many types of fans and uses. I will expand on a few. First a fan can be used in a furnace to keep the temperature of the furnace at a desired temperature, by regulating the size of the flame. A fan also can be used to blow the heat through the furnace at a regulated speed for heated air outside of the furnace for particular reasons, such as heat for your home during the cold winters. Every furnace that I know of has a fan, either to regulate the flame or to use for carrying the heat to certain places from the flame.

In the old and ancient days, men would use a type of fan also to fan out chaff from grain. They would thresh the wheat, for an example, and then they would use large fans, somewhat like a leaf rake today, and throw the threshed grain into the air and the chaff would separate itself from the heavy grain. The grain would land in a pile before them and the chaff would be carried away from them by the air or wind. But today, because of wisdom and great technologies, grains are separated by machinery by enormous quantities.

There are particular scriptures in the Holy Word that tells that Jesus Christ holds this particular fan in his hand. John the Baptist proclaimed that Jesus Christ is the one that holds the fan and separates the wheat from the chaff. In the Holy Book of Matthew 3:7-12 it is written, *"But when he saw many of the Pharisees and Sadducees come to his baptism, he said to them, O generation of vipers, who hath warned you to flee from the wrath to come? Bring therefore fruits meet for repentance: And think not to say within yourselves, We have Abraham to our father: for I say unto you, that God is able of these stones to raise up children unto Abraham. And now the axe is laid unto the root of the trees: therefore every tree which bringeth not forth good fruit is hewn down, and cast into the f ire.*

I indeed baptize you with water unto repentance: but he that cometh after me is mightier than I, whose shoes I am not worthy to bear: he shall baptize you with the Holy Ghost, and with f ire: Whose fan is in his hand, and he will thoroughly purge his floor, and gather his wheat into the garner; but he will burn up the chaff with unquenchable f ire."

7.) THE PRODUCT FROM THE FURNACE

The product of a furnace could be many different things, such as, pottery, iron, steel, gold, silver, and even purified water. Spiritually speaking, I will be expanding on the product of water, since the furnace that I was working on at the time produce purified water. Spiritually, the water will represent your soul as the purified product of a furnace.

I remember almost every day I would check the water's purification of the large furnace that I was appointed too maintain. I would check the water level and also the purification out in the large plant are in humidity. I would take a humidity checker and check every foot of the plant floor area to see if the humidity was correct for production. If the humidity wasn't correct, I would open or close valves to the plant floor areas.

Now, of course water on the other hand is the opposite of fire. Water is a coolant for any vessel that is burning. There are times that I feel as if the fiery trials I am going through is going to burn me away, but it soon is quenched by living water. My faith may be tried, but the word of God and Jesus Words are refreshing to my life just as Ice water on a extremely hot day cools my body. When I read God's Word, it is like refreshing living water.

I ask this question. What happens to fire if you would pour a cup of water into the middle of it? Now I am only talking small fire here, like a camp fire, 3' in diameter with a top flame of 3' also.

On a simple note, the fire evaporates the water into the atmosphere and the fire where you poured the water, dissipates, correct? Well, I guess the truth would be that the fire also goes into the atmosphere in smoke or moisture also. The fire would also somewhat spread away from the water spot also. The point that I am trying to make is this; Where water is, fire cant be, and where fire is, water cant be. Looking at the camp fire size above, if we had the same measure of mass makeup that the fire makes up with water, the total fire would dissipate into the atmosphere, if we would pour the entire mass of water onto the fire, follow me? If we did this there would be no fire, but just moisture rising to the atmosphere. But why? Its all because of both compounds use oxygen to live. Fire has got to have oxygen to burn and water has got to have oxygen to live. But, oxygen molecules can not be destroyed, except by some type of nuclear explosion, just my theory my friend. And then there not really destroyed, just separated from it's orbit. I want go deeper into the water, because I am not a scientist in the matter, but I do know that water can't be destroyed; only moved. I also know that heat can't be destroyed, but only moved. The following will explain somewhat more.

Now in the beginning of creation it is written that the Spirit of God moved upon the waters. In the Holy Book of Genesis 1:1-9 it is written, ***"In the beginning God created the heaven and the earth. And the earth was without form, and void; and darkness was upon the face of the deep. And the Spirit of God moved upon the face of the waters. And God said, Let there be light: and there was light. And God saw the light, that it was good: and God divided the light from the darkness. And God called the light Day. And the darkness he called Night. And the evening and the morning were the first day. And God said let there be a firmament in the midst of the waters, and let it divide the waters from the waters. And God made the firmament, and divided the firmament from the waters which were*** *above the firmament: and it was so. And God called the firmament Heaven.*

And the evening and the morning were the second day. And God said, Let the waters under the heaven be gathered unto one place, and let the dry land appear: and it was so. And God called the dry land Earth; and the gathering together of the waters called he Seas: and God saw that it was good."

In the scriptures above it is written that God's Spirit moved upon the waters and then God said, "Let there be light." These scriptures gives in detail how God separated the heavens or waters by light, which is the Sun. I can imagine now the sun coming to life with fire and given off light into the dark abyss. This dark abyss that I am talking about was the waters. I honestly believe that the heavens are made of water. Just as a man would float in water on earth, a man can float around in the heavens. The further away you would get away from the earth's gravity's pull, a man would float around in the heavens like a float in the earth's waters. I honestly believe that the universe is made of water, and the heavens way beyond our universe, is made of water. I believe that this universe we live in is only 1 atom in Gods' great body and we are in God and God is in us. When God said, *"Let there be a f irmament in the midst of the waters, and let it divide the waters from the waters."*

There is the key to the eternal body of water. I honestly believe that the heavens above and all around about us was all water, before God separated the waters with the light or sun. I believe that the heavens were dark and void until God said, "Let there be light." It is Somewhat like if you took a pot on a hot burner and then dropped a drop of water in the pot and the water will scatter from the heat or the light of the hot burner, follow me? So when God said, *"Let there be light",* *the sun was made and the waters separated from the light. God also said, "Let there be a f irmament in the midst of the waters, and let it divide the waters from the waters.*

And God made the f irmament, and divided the f irmament from the waters which were above the f irmament: and it was so. And God called the f irmament Heaven. And the evening and the morning were the second day. And God said, Let the waters under the heaven be gathered unto one place, and let the dry land appear: and it was so. And God called the dry land Earth; and the gathering together of the waters called he Seas: and God saw that it was good." So, at the end of creation of the heavens, the earth, and the Seas, God saw that it was good. The above writings was only a touch of the phenomenon of water, but there is also more to the water than meets the eyes. It's written that God saw that is was all good and he called the gathering of the waters "he Seas." I believe it is written "he Seas" for one purpose, and it is this; God Sees that it was good. God saw the waters separate and he sees all things and all that he did at the time was good.

Spiritually speaking, water represents something even greater than the oceans or seas. I honestly believe that the soul is in the likeness of water. Like I have mention before in other chapters, if you could form a man out of water, then you would have a representation of what a soul of a man is like. There is physical water as we know of and there is also spiritual water that the eyes can't see. Most of all water on this earth today isn't 100% pure. The only way to get pure water is to distill the water and burn away the other elements from it. Pure water has no other elements in it, such as dirt, iron, calcium, etc. Now looking at it in a spiritual sense, water still has to be fired or burned off to get 100% purified water. If your soul is in the likeness of water, then it has to be tried in the furnace to produce 100% purification. Spiritually speaking your soul has to be tried in the fire also to be 100%. The things of this world can corrupt your soul, just as the things of the earth can corrupt water, follow me? So, how does your soul become 100% pure? There is only one way that your soul can be 100% purified and sanctified and that is through the trials of you faith.

Your faith in God and his Son Jesus Christ will be tried, but if it is something evil it will not be tried. All unbelievers will only be judged at the Great Judgment at there appointed time. Only Christians will be tried on this earth, so that, they will understand and walk a pure life before God. How are they tried? By the Holy Ghost or The Spirit of God. This purification is done by the work of the Holy Ghost and through the Word of God. The much more faith a man confesses, the much more trials he goes through? Yes. We have already read this scripture, but I will quote it again. *"For the time has come that judgment must begin at the house of God: and if it first begin at us, what shall the end be of them that obey not the gospel of God? And if the righteous scarcely be saved, where shall the ungodly and the sinner appear? Wherefore let them that suffer according to the Will of God commit the keeping of their souls to him in well-doing, as unto a faithful Creator (1Peter 4:17-19)."*

As I end these writings, please remember this one scripture. In Revelation 3:18-22 it is written, *"I counsel thee to buy of me gold tried in the f ire, that thou mayest be rich; and white raiment, that thou mayest be clotheth, and that the shame of thy nakedness do not appear; and anoint thine eyes with eye-slave, that thou mayest see. As many as I love, I rebuke and chasten: be zealous therefore, and repent. Behold I stand at the door, and knock: If any man hear my voice, and open the door, I will come into him, and will sup with him, and he with me. To him that overcometh will I grant to sit with me in my throne, even as I also overcame, and am set down with my Father in his throne. He that hath ear, let him hear what the Spirit saith unto the churches.* If, you could have anything in this world, what would you want? I hope that you want life much more abundantly here on earth and to receive eternal life everlasting. My friend, be good always, but the most important, don't give up.

Have Jesus Christ as your personal friend and he will show you the way, just as he has shown me for 30 years. Sometimes I look at myself as a Timex Watch; I take a licking, but I keep a ticking. These things of this world will pass away, but eternity is forever and forever. Trials, temptations, tribulation may still come like the wind in my life, but I continually to keep my eyes on the prize, which is eternal life. There is a story in the Word of God that I will now share with you. It's about a Rich Man and a Beggar named Lazarus. The story is found In the Holy Book of Luke chapter 16, verses 19-31; and I ask if you be willing to read it now. May God and his Christ richly Bless you with his Love and Grace forever and ever. Amen.

SCRIPTURE REFERENCES

Proverbs 3:5-6

"Trust in the Lord with all thine heart, and lean not unto thine own understanding."

Proverbs 1:7

"The fear of the Lord is the beginning of knowledge: but fools despise wisdom and instruction."

Ecclesiastes 9:4-6

"For to him that is joined to all the living there is hope: for a living dog is better than a dead lion. For the living know that they shall die: but the dead know not any thing, neither have they any more reward; for the memory of them is forgotten. Also their love, and their hatred, and their envy, is now perished; neither have they any more a portion for ever in any thing that is done under the sun."

Genesis 1:26

"And God said, Let us make man in our image, after our likeness: and let them have dominion over the fish of the sea, and over the fowl of the air, and over the cattle, and over all the earth, and over every creeping thing that creepeth upon the earth."

Genesis 2:7

"And the Lord God formed man of the dust of the ground, and breathed into his nostrils the breath of life; and man became a living soul."

John 3:1-6

"There was a man of the Pharisees, named Nicodemus, a ruler of the Jews: The same came to Jesus by night, and said unto him, Rabbi, we know that thou art a teacher come from God: for no man can do these miracles that thou doest, except God be with him. Jesus answered and said unto him, Verily, verily, I say unto thee, Except a man be born again, he cannot see the kingdom of God. Nicodemus saith unto him, How can a man be born when he is old? can he enter the second time into his mother's womb, and be born? Jesus answered, Verily, verily, I say unto thee, Except a man be born of water and of the Spirit, he cannot enter the kingdom of God. That which is born of the flesh is flesh; and that which is born of the Spirit is spirit."

Matthew 6:33

"Seek ye first The Kingdom of God and His Righteousness; and all these things shall be added unto you."

Hebrews 4:12

"For the Word of God is quick, and Powerful, and sharper than any two-edged sword, piercing even to the dividing asunder of Soul and Spirit, and of the joints and marrow, and is a discerner of the thoughts and intents of the heart."

Hebrews 11:6

"But without Faith it is impossible to please him: for he that cometh to God must Believe that he is, and that he is a rewarded of them that diligently seek him."

Proverbs 1:7

"The fear of the Lord is the beginning of knowledge: but fools despise wisdom and instruction."

Hebrews 11:1,

"Now faith is the substance of things hoped for, the evidence of things not seen".

Luke 23:32-43

"If thou be the Christ, save thyself and us. But, the other malefactor rebuked this malefactor and said to him, Dost not thou fear God, seeing thou art in the same condemnation?

And we indeed justly; for we received the due reward of our deeds: but this man hath done nothing amiss. And he said unto Jesus, Lord, remember me when thou comest into thy kingdom. And Jesus said unto him, Verily I say unto thee, To-day shalt thou be with me in paradise."

2 Corinthians 12:7-9

"And lest I should be exalted above measure through the abundance of the revelations, there was given a thorn in the flesh, the messenger of Satan to buffet me, lest I should be exalted above measure. For this thing I besought the Lord thrice, that it might depart from me. And He Said unto me, My grace is sufficient for thee: for my strength is made perfect in weakness. Most gladly therefore will I rather glory in my infirmities, that the power of Christ may rest upon me."

John 11:24-25

"Martha said unto him, I know that he shall rise again in the resurrection at the last day. Jesus said unto her, I am the resurrection, and the life: he that believeth in me, though he were dead, yet shall he live: And whosoever liveth and believeth in me shall never die. Believest thou this?

1 Corinthians 15:55-57

"O death, where is thy sting? O grave where is thy victory? The sting of death is sin; and the strength of sin is the law. But thanks be to God, which giveth us victory through our Lord Jesus Christ."

Proverbs 1:7

"The fear of the Lord is the beginning of knowledge: but fools despise wisdom and instruction."

Hebrews 12:1-2

"WHEREFORE seeing we also are compassed about with so great a cloud of witnesses, let us lay aside every weight, and the sin which

doth so easily beset us, and run with patience the race that is set before us, Looking unto Jesus the author and finisher of our faith; who for the joy that was set before him endured the cross, despising the shame, and is set down at the right hand of the throne of God."

John 14:23-26

"If a man love me, he will keep my words: and my Father will love him, and we will come unto him, and make our abode with him. He that loveth me not keepeth not my sayings: and the word which ye hear is not mine, but the Father's which sent me. These things have I spoken unto you, being yet present with you. But the Comforter, which is the Holy Ghost, whom the Father will send in my name, he shall teach you all things, and bring all things to your remembrance, whatsoever I have said unto you."

John 1:1-2

"In the beginning was the Word, and the Word was with God, and the Word was God. The same was in the beginning with God."

Matthew 5:17-18

"Think not that I am come to destroy the law, or the prophets: I am not come to destroy, but to fulfill. For verily I say unto you, Till heaven and earth pass, one jot or one tittle shall in no wise pass from the law, till all be fulfilled."

Matthew 8:1-4

"When he was come down from the mountain, great multitudes followed him. And, behold, there came a leper and worshipped him, saying, Lord, if thou wilt, thou canst make me clean. And Jesus put forth his hand, and touched him, saying, I will; be thou clean. And immediately his leprosy was cleansed.

And Jesus saith unto him, See thou tell no man; but go thy way, shew thyself to the priest, and offer the gift that Moses commanded, for a testimony unto them."

John 20:24-31

"Except I shall see in his hands the print of the nails and put my finger into the print of the nails and thrust my hand into his side, I will not believe." Later after all the disciples were together with

Thomas, Jesus came into them again. Jesus said to Thomas, "Reach hither thy finger, and behold my hands; and reach hither thy hand, and thrust it into my side: and be not faithless, but believing." And Thomas said unto the Lord, "My Lord and my God." Then Jesus said to Thomas, "Thomas, because thou hast seen me, thou hast believed: blessed are they that have not seen, and yet have believed."

John 14:26

"But the Comforter, which is the Holy Ghost, whom the Father will send in my name, he shall teach you all things, and bring all things to your remembrance, whatsoever I have said unto you."

Matthew 15:16-20

"And Jesus said, Are ye also yet without understanding? Do not ye understand, that whatsoever entereth in at the mouth goeth into the belly, and is cast out into the draught? But those things which proceed out of the mouth come forth from the heart; and they defile the man. For out of the heart proceed evil thoughts, murders, adulteries, fornications, thefts, false witness, blasphemies: These are the things that defile a man: but to eat with unclean hands defileth not a man."

John10:10

"The thief cometh not, but to steal, and to kill, and to destroy: I am come that they might have life, and that they might have it more abundantly."

Matthew 7:13-14

"Enter ye in at the strait gate: for wide is the gate, and broad is the way, that leadeth to destruction, and many there be which go in thereat: Because strait is the gate, and narrow is the way, which leadeth unto life, and few there be that find it."

Psalms 23

"The Lord is my Shepherd; I shall not want. He maketh me to lie down in green pastures: he leadeth me beside the still waters. He restoreth my soul: he leadeth me in the paths of righteousness for his name's sake. Yea, though I walk through the valley of the shadow

of death, I will fear no evil: for thou art with me; thy rod and thy staff they comfort me. Thou preparest a table before me in the presence of mine enemies: thou anointest my head with oil; my cup runneth over.

Surely goodness and mercy shall follow me all the days of my life: and I will dwell in the house of the Lord for ever."

Matthew16:24-26

"Then said Jesus unto his disciples, If any man will come after me, let him deny himself, and take up his cross, and follow me. For whosoever will save his life shall lose it: and whosoever will lose his life for my sake shall find it. For what is a man profited, if he shall gain the whole world, and lose his own soul? Or what shall a man give in exchange for his soul?"

II Timothy 4:7-8

"I have fought a good fight, I have finished my course, I have kept the faith: Henceforth there is laid up for me a crown of righteousness, which the Lord, the righteous judge, shall give me at that day: and not to me only, but unto all them also that love his appearing."

Matthew 10:37-38

"He that loveth father or mother more than me is not worthy of me: and he that loveth son or daughter more than me is not worthy of me. And he that taketh not his cross, and followeth after me is not worthy of me."

Hebrews 9:27

"And as it is appointed unto men once to die, but after this the judgment:"

Genesis 2:28

"And God blessed them and God said unto them, Be fruitful, and multiply, and replenish the earth, and subdue it:"

Genesis 2:7

"And the Lord God formed man of the dust of the ground, and breathed into his nostrils the breath of life; and man became a living soul."

Genesis 1:26

"And God said, Let us make man in our image, after our likeness: and let them have dominion over the fish of the sea, and over the fowl of the air, and over the cattle, and over all the earth, and over every creeping thing that creepeth upon the earth."

Jonah 4:11

"And should I spare Nineveh that great city, wherein are more than six score thousand persons that cannot discern from the right hand and their left hand; and also much cattle?"

Proverbs 22:6

"Train up a child in the way he should go; and when he is old, he will not depart from it."

Matthew 3:13-15

"Then cometh Jesus from Galilee to Jordan unto John, to be baptized of him. But John forbad him, saying, I have need to be baptized of thee, and comesth thou to me? And Jesus answering said unto him, Suffer it to be so now: for thus it becometh us to fulfil all righteousness. Then he suffered him."

Matthew 18:1-6

"At the same time came the disciples unto Jesus, saying, Who is the greatest in the kingdom of Heaven? And Jesus called a little child unto him, and set him in the midst of them, and said, Verily I say unto you, Except ye be converted, and become as little children, ye shall not enter into the kingdom of heaven. Whosoever therefore shall humble himself as this little child, the same is greatest in the kingdom of heaven. And whoso shall receive one such little child in my name receiveth me. But whoso shall offend one of these little ones which believe in me, it were better for him that a millstone were hanged about his neck, and that he were drowned in the depth of the sea."

Genesis chapter 3:16-19

"Unto the woman he said, I will greatly multiply thy sorrow and conception; in sorrow thou shalt bring forth children; and thy desire shall be to thy husband, and he shall rule over you. And

unto Adam he said, Because thou has hearkened unto the voice of thy wife, and hast eaten of the tree, of which I commanded thee, saying, Thou shalt not eat of it: cursed is the ground for thy sake; in sorrow shalt thou eat of it all the days of thy life; Thorns and thistles shall it bring forth to thee; and thou shalt eat the herb of the field; In thy sweat of thy face shalt thou eat bread, till thou return unto the ground; for out of it wast thou taken: for dust thou art, and unto dust shalt thou return."

Luke 7:37-50

"And, behold, a woman in the city, which was a sinner, when she knew that Jesus sat at meat in the Pharisee's house, brought an alabaster box of ointment, And stood at his feet behind him weeping, and began to wash his feet with tears, and did wipe them with the hairs of her head, and kissed his feet, and anointed them with the ointment. Now when the Pharisee which had bidden him saw it, he spake within himself, saying, This man, if he were a prophet, would had known and what manner of woman this is that toucheth him: for she is a sinner. And Jesus answering said unto him, Simon, I have somewhat to say unto thee. And he saith, Master, say on. There was a certain creditor which had two debtors: the one owed five hundred pence, and the other fifty. And when they had nothing to pay, he frankly forgave them both. Tell me therefore, which of them will love him most? Simon answered and said, I suppose that he, to whom he forgave most. And he said unto him, Thou hast rightly judged. And he turned to the woman, and said unto Simon, Seest thou this woman? I entered into thine house, thou gavest me no water for my feet: but she hath wiped them with the hairs of her head. Thou gavest me no kiss: but this woman since the time I came in hath not ceased to kiss my feet. My head with oil thou didst not anoint: but this woman hath anointed my feet with ointment. Wherefore I say unto thee, Her sins, which are many, are forgiven; for she loved much: but to whom little is forgiven, the same loveth little. And he saith unto her, Thy sins are forgiven."

Matthew 26:13

"Verily I say unto you, Wheresoever this gospel shall be preached in the whole world, there shall also this, that this woman hath done, be told for a memorial of her."

Mark Chapter 6

"A prophet is not without honor, but in his own country, and among his own kin, and in his own house." ;"And he called unto him the twelve, and began to send them forth by two by two; and gave them power over unclean spirits; <u>And commanded them that they should take nothing for their journey, save a staff only;</u> no scrip, no bread, no money in their purse: But be shod with sandals; and not put on two coats. And he said unto them, In what place soever ye enter into an house, there abide till ye depart from that place. And whosoever shall not receive you, nor hear you, when ye depart thence, shake off the dust under your feet for a testimony against them. Verily I say unto you, It shall be more tolerable for Sodom and Gomorrah in the day of judgment, than for that city."

Jeremiah 18:1-6

"The word which came to Jeremiah from the Lord, saying, Arise, and go down to the potter's house, and there I will cause thee to hear my words. Then I went down to the potter's house, and, behold, he wrought a work on the wheels. And the vessel that he made of clay was marred in the hand of the potter: So he made it again another vessel, as seemed good to the potter to make it. Then the word of the Lord came to me saying, O House of Israel, cannot I do with you as this potter? saith the Lord. Behold, as the clay is in the potter's hand, so are you in my hand, O house of Israel."

Matthew 20:16

"Many are called, but few are chosen." "Blessed are the peacemakers: for they shall be called the children of God."

Matthew 7:21

"Not every one that saith unto me, Lord, Lord, shall enter into the kingdom of heaven; but he that doeth the will of my Father which is in heaven. Many will say to me in that day, Lord, Lord, have we not prophesied in thy name? And in thy name have cast out

devils? And in thy name done many wonderful works? And then will I profess unto them, I never knew you: depart from me, ye that work iniquity."

Hebrews 11:1-3,

"Now faith is the substance of things hoped for, the evidence of things not seen. For by it the elders obtained a good report. Through faith we understand that the worlds were framed by the word of God, so that things which are seen were not made of things which do appear."

Matthew 7:21,

"Not every one that saith unto me, Lord, Lord, shall enter into the kingdom of heaven; but he that doeth the will of my Father which is in heaven. Many will say to me in that day, Lord, Lord, have we not prophesied in thy name? And in thy name have cast out devils? And in thy name done many wonderful works? And then will I profess unto them, I never knew you: depart from me, ye that work iniquity."

John 14:6,

"Jesus saith unto him, I am the way, the truth, and the life: no man cometh to the Father, but by me."

John 10:9

"I am the door: by me if any man enter in, he shall be saved, and shall go in and out, and find pasture."

Matthew 7:7-8,

"Ask, and it shall be given to you; seek, and ye shall find; knock and it shall be opened unto you: For every one that asketh recieiveth; and he that seeketh findeth; and to him that knocketh it shall be opened."

Matthew 6:24

"No man can serve two masters: for either he will hate the one, and love the other; or else he will hold to the one, and despise the other. Ye cannot serve God and mammon."

James 1:5-8

"If any of you lack wisdom, let him ask God, that giveth to all men liberally, and upbraided not; and it shall be given him. But let him ask in faith, nothing wavering. For he that wavereth is like a wave of the sea driven with the wind and tossed. For let not that man think he shall receive any thing of the Lord. A double-minded man is unstable in all his ways."

Genesis 2:16-17

"And the Lord commanded the man, saying, Of every tree of the garden thou mayest freely eat: But of the tree of the knowledge of good and evil, thou shalt not eat of it: for in the day that thou eatest thereof thou shalt surely die."

Genesis 3:4-6

"And the serpent said unto the woman, Ye shall not surely die: For God doth know that in the day ye eat thereof, then your eyes shall be opened, and ye shall be as gods, knowing good and evil. And when the woman saw that the tree was good for food, and that it was pleasant to the eyes, and a tree to be desired to make one wise, she took of the fruit thereof, and did eat, and gave also unto her husband with her; and he did eat."

Romans 3:23

"For all have sinned, and come short of the glory of God;"

Isaiah 64:6

"But we are all as an unclean thing, and all our righteousnesses are as filthy rags: and we all do fade as a leaf; and our iniquities, like the wind, have taken us away."

1 John 1:5-10,

"If we say that we have not sinned, we make him a liar, and his word is not in us."

1 Corinthians 3:17-18

"Know ye not that ye are the temple of God, and that the Spirit of God dwelleth in you? If any man defile the temple of God, him

shall God destroy; for the temple of God is Holy, which temple ye are.

Romans 12:1-2

"I beseech you therefore, breathren, by the mercies of God, that ye present your bodies a living sacrifice, holy, acceptable unto God, which is your reasonable service. And be not conformed to this world: but be transformed by the renewing of your mind, the ye may prove what is the good, and acceptable, and perfect, will of God."

Ephesians 3:20-21

"Now unto him that is able to do exceeding abundantly above all that we ask or think, according to the power that worketh in us, Unto him be glory in the church by Christ Jesus throughout all ages, world without end. Amen."

Luke 11:21-26

"When a strong man armed keepeth his palace, his goods are in peace: But when a stronger than he shall come upon him, and overcome him, he taketh from him all his armour wherein he trusted, and divided his spoils. He that is not with me is against me: and he that gathered not with me scattered. When the unclean spirit is gone out of a man, he walketh through dry places, seeking rest; and finding none, he saith, I will return unto my house whence I came out. And when he cometh, he findeth it swept and garnished. Then goeth he, and taketh to him seven other spirits more wicked than himself; and they enter in, and dwell there: and the last state of that man is worse than the first."

James 1:12-16

"Blessed in the man that endureth temptation: for when he is tried, he shall receive the crown of life, which the Lord hath promised to them that love him. Let no man say when he is tempted, I am tempted of God: for God cannot be tempted with evil, neither tempteth he any man: But every man is tempted, when he is drawn away of his own lust, and enticed. Then when lust hath conceived, it bringeth forth sin: and sin, when it is finished, bringeth forth death. Do not err, my beloved brethren."

Genesis 1:26-27

"And God said, Let us make man in our image, after our likeness: and let them have dominion over the fish of the sea, and over the fowl of the air, and over the cattle, and over all the earth, and over every creeping thing that creepeth upon the earth. So God created man in his own image, in the image of God created he him; male and female created he them."

Matthew 6:7-13

"After this manner therefore pray ye: Our Father which art in heaven, Hallowed be thy name. Thy kingdom come. Thy Will be done in earth, as it is in Heaven. Gives us this day our daily bread. And forgive us our debts, as we forgive our debtors. Lead us not into temptation, but deliver us from evil: For thine is the kingdom, and the power, and the glory, for ever. Amen."

Matthew 4:18-19

"And Jesus, walking by the sea of Galilee, saw two brethren, Simon called Peter, and Andrew his brother, casting a net into the sea: for they were fishers. And he saith to them, Follow me, and I will make you fishers of men."

Genesis 2:21-25

"And the Lord God caused a deep sleep to fall upon Adam, and he slept: and he took one of his ribs, and closed up the flesh instead thereof; And the rib, which the Lord God had taken from man, made he a woman, and brought her unto the man. And Adam said, This is now bone of my bones, and flesh of my flesh: she shall be called Woman, because she was taken out of Man. Therefore shall a man leave his father and his mother, and shall cleave unto his wife: and they shall be one flesh. And they were both naked, the man and his wife, and were not ashamed."

Proverbs 18:22

"Whosoever findeth a wife findeth a good thing, and obtaineth favor of the Lord."

Proverbs 19:14

"House and riches are the inheritance of fathers: and a prudent wife is from the Lord."

Hebrews 12:5-11

"And ye have forgotten the exhortation which speaketh unto you as unto children, My son, despise not the chastening of the Lord, nor faint when thou art rebuked of him: For whom the Lord loveth he chasteneth, and scourgeth every son whom he recieveth. If ye endure chastening, God dealeth with you as with sons; for what son is he whom the father chasteneth not? But if ye be without chastisement, whereof all are partakers, then are ye bastards, and not sons. Furthermore we have had fathers of the flesh which corrected us, and we gave them reverence: shall we not much rather be in subjection unto the Father of spirits and live? For they verily for a few days chastened us after their own pleasures; but he for our profit, that we might be partakers of his holiness. Now no chastening for the present seemth to be joyous, but grievous: nevertheless afterward it yieldeth the peaceable fruit of righteousness unto them which are exercised thereby."

Matthew 24:13

"But he that shall endure unto the end, the same shall be saved."

Matthew chapter 7:12

"Therefore all things whatsoever ye would that men should do to you, do ye even so to them: for this is the law and the prophets."

Revelation 22:18-19

"For I testify unto every man that hearth the words of the prophecy of this book, If any man shall add unto these things, God shall add unto him the plagues that are written in this book: And if any man shall take away from the words of the book of this prophecy, God shall take away his part out of the book of Life, and out of the holy city, and from the things which are written in this book."

Ephesians 6:13-18

"Finally my brethren, be strong in the Lord, and in the Power of his might. Put on the whole armour of God, that ye may be able

to stand against the wiles of the devil. For we wrestle not against flesh and blood, but against principalities, against powers, against the rulers of the darkness of this world, against spiritual wickedness in high places. Wherefore take unto you the whole armour of God, that ye may be able to withstand in that evil day, and having done all, to stand. Stand therefore, having your loins girt about with truth, and having on the breastplate of righteousness; And your feet shod with the preparation of the gospel of peace; Above all, taking the shield of faith, wherewith ye shall be able to quench all the fiery darts of the wicked. And take the helmet of salvation, and the sword of the Spirit, which is the Word of God: Praying always with all prayer and supplication in the Spirit, and watching thereunto with all perseverance and supplication for all saints;"

2 Peter 3:8

"But, beloved be not ignorant of this one thing, that one day is with the Lord as a thousand years, and a thousand years as one day."

1 Peter 5:8

"Be sober, be vigilant; because your adversary the devil, as a roaring lion, walketh about, seeking whom he may devour."

James 4:7

"Submit yourselves therefore to God. resist the devil, and he will flee from you."

2 Corinthians 11:13-15

"For such are false apostles, deceitful workers, transforming themselves into the apostles of Christ. And no marvel; for Satan himself is transformed into an angel of light. Therefore it is no great thing if his ministers also be transformed as the ministers of righteousness; whose end shall be according to their works."

Romans 8:37-39

"Nay, in all things we are more than conquerors through him that loved us. For I am persuaded, neither death, nor life, nor angels, nor principalities, nor powers, nor things present, nor things to come, Nor height, nor dept, nor any other creature, shall be able

to separate us from the love of God, which is in Christ Jesus our Lord."

Matthew 7:15-17

"Beware of false prophets, which come to you in sheep's clothing, but inwardly they are ravening wolves. Ye shall know them by their fruits. Do men gather grapes of thorns or figs of thistles?"

Ephesians 3:1-12

"For this cause I Paul, the prisoner of Jesus Christ for you Gentiles, If he heard of the dispensation of the grace of God which is given to you-ward: How that by revelation he made known to me the mystery; (as I wrote afore in few words, Whereby, when ye read, ye may understand my knowledge in the mystery of Christ) Which in other ages was not made known unto the sons of men, as it is now revealed unto his holy apostles and prophets by the Spirit; That the Gentiles should be fellow-heirs, and of the same body and partakers of his promise in Christ by the gospel: Whereof I was made a minister, according to the gift of the grace of God given unto me by the effectual working of his power. Unto me, who am less than the least of all saints, is this grace given, that I should preach among the Gentiles the unsearchable riches of Christ; And to make all men see what is the fellowship of the mystery which from the beginning of the world hath been hid in God, who created all things by Christ Jesus: To the intent that now unto principalities and powers in heavenly places might be known by the church the manifold wisdom of God, Accordingly to the eternal purpose which he purposed in Christ Jesus our Lord: In whom we have boldness and access with confidence by the faith of him."

Matthew 5:14-16

"Ye are the light of the world, A city that is set on a hill cannot be hid. Neither do men light a candle, and put it under a bushel, but on a candlestick; and it giveth light unto all that are in the house. Let your light so shine before men, that they may see your good works, and glorify your father which is in heaven."

Psalms 34:15

"The eyes of the Lord are upon the righteous, and his ears are open unto their cry."

Psalms 33:18

"Behold the eye of the Lord is upon them that fear him, upon them that hope in his mercy; To deliver their soul from death, and to keep them alive in famine."

Proverbs 15:3

"The eyes of the Lord are in every place, beholding the evil and the good."

Matthew 6:19-21

"Lay not up for yourselves treasures upon earth, where the moth and rust doth corrupt, and where thieves break through and steal: But lay up treasures in heaven, where neither moth nor rust doth corrupt, and where thieves do not break through nor steal: For where your treasure is, there will your heart be also."

John 10:18

"Therefore doth my Father love me, because I lay down my life, that I might take it again. No man taketh it from me, but I lay it down of myself. I have power to lay it down, and I have power to take it again. This commandment have I received of my Father."

Psalms 147:5

"Great is our Lord, and of great power; his understanding is infinite."

Proverbs 3:19

"The Lord by wisdom hath founded the earth; by understanding hath he established the heavens."

Psalms 111:10

"The fear of the Lord is the beginning of wisdom: a good understanding have all they that do his commandments: his praise endureth for ever."

1 Peter 4:12-13

"Beloved, think it not strange concerning the fiery trial which is to try you, as though some strange thing happened unto you: But rejoice, inasmuch as ye are partakers of Christ's sufferings; that, when his glory shall be revealed, ye maybe glad also with exceeding joy."

Matthew 16:24

"Then said Jesus to his disciples, If any man will come after me, let him deny himself, and take up his cross, and follow me."

Matthew 10:38

"And he that taketh not his cross, and followed after me, is not worthy of me."

John 3:16

"For God so Loved the World, that he gave his only begotten Son, that whosoever believeth in him should not perish but have everlasting life."

Isaiah 59:1

"BEHOLD, the Lord's hand is not shortened, that it cannot save; neither his ear heavy, that it cannot hear: But your iniquities have separated between you and your God, and your sins have hid his face from you, that he will not hear."

Romans 8:18-23

"For I reckon that the suffering of this present time are not worthy to be compared to the glory which shall be revealed in us. For the earnest expectation of the creature waiteth for the manifestation of the sons of God. For the creature was made subject to vanity, not willingly, but by reason of him who hath subjected the same hope, Because the creature itself also shall be delivered from the bondage of corruption into the glorious liberty of the children of God. For we know that the whole creation groaneth and travaileth in pain together until now. And not only they, but ourselves also, which have the firstfruits of the Spirit, even we ourselves groan within ourselves, waiting for the adoption, to wit, the redemption of our body."

John 16:33

"These things I have spoken unto you, that in me ye might have peace. In the world ye shall have tribulation: but be of good cheer; I have overcome the world."

2 Corinthians 12: 6-10

"For though I would desire to glory, I shall not be a fool; for I will say the truth: but now I forbear, lest any man should think of me above that which he seeth me to be, or that he heareth of me. And lest I should be exalted above measure through the abundance of the revelations, there was given me a thorn in the flesh, the messenger of Satan to buffet me, lest I should be exalted above measure. For this thing I besought the Lord thrice, that it might depart from me. And he said unto me, MY GRACE IS SUFFICIENT FOR THEE: FOR MY STRENGHT IS MADE PERFECT IN WEAKNESS. Most gladly therefore will I rather glory in my infirmities, that the power of Christ may rest upon me. Therefore I take pleasure in infirmities, in reproaches, in necessities, in persecutions, in distresses for Christ's sake: for when I am weak, then am I strong."

James 4:17

"Therefore to him that knoweth to do good, and doeth it not, to him it is sin."

1 Corinthians 10:13

"There hath no temptation taken you but such is common to man: but God is faithful, who will not suffer you to be tempted above that ye are able; but will with the temptation also make a way to escape, that ye may be able to bear it."

Genesis 3:17-19

"And unto Adam he said, Because thou hast hearkened unto the voice of thy wife, and hast eaten of the tree, of which I commanded thee, saying, Thou shalt not eat of it: cursed is the ground for thy sake; in sorrow shalt thou eat of it all the days of thy life; Thorns and thistles shall it bring forth to thee; and thou shalt eat the herb of the field; In the sweat of thy face shalt thou eat bread, till thou

return unto the ground; for out of it wast thou taken: for dust thou art, and dust shalt thou return."

Matthew 10:22

"And ye shall be hated of all men for my name's sake: but he that endureth to the end shall be saved."

Revelation 21:6-8

"And he said unto me, It is done. I am Alpha and Omega, the beginning and the end. I will give unto him that is athirst of the fountain of the water of life freely. <u>*He that overcometh shall inherit all things;*</u> *and I will be his God, and he shall be my son. But the fearful, and unbelieving, and the abominable, and murderers, and whoremongers, and sorcerers, and idolaters, and all liars, shall have their part in the lake of fire which burneth with fire and brimstone: which is the second death."*

Romans 8:14-18

"For as many as are led by the Spirit of God, they are the sons of God. For ye have not received the spirit of bondage again to fear (of the world); but ye have received the Spirit of adoption, whereby we cry, Abba, Father. The Spirit itself beareth witness with our spirit, that we are the children of God: And if children, then heirs; heirs of God, and joint-heirs with Christ; if so be that we suffer with him, that we may be also glorified together. For I reckon that the sufferings of this present time are not worthy to be compared with the glory which shall be revealed to us."

Proverbs 24:3

"Through Wisdom is an house builded; and by understanding it is established."

1 Peter 3:17

"For it is better, if the will of God be so, that ye suffer for Well doing, than for evil doing."

1 Peter 4:14-17

"If ye be reproached for the name Of Christ, happy are ye; for the Spirit of Glory and of God resteth upon you: on their part he is Evil spoken of, but on your part he is glorified. But let none of you suffer

as a murderer, or as a Thief, or as an evildoer, or as a busybody in other men's matters. Yet if any man suffer as a Christian, let him not be ashamed; but let him glorify God on this behalf. For the time has Come that judgment must begin at the house of God: and if it first begin at us, what shall the end Be of them that obey not the gospel of God?"

1 Corinthians 15:21-22

"For since by man came death, by man came also the resurrection of the dead. For as in Adam all die, even so in Christ shall all be made alive;"

Matthew 15:16-20

"And Jesus said, Are ye also yet without understanding? Do not ye yet understand, that whatsoever entereth in the mouth goeth into the belly, and is cast out into the draught? But those things which proceed out of the mouth come forth from the heart; and they defile the man. For out of the heart proceed evil thoughts, murders, adulteries, fornications, thefts, false witness, blasphemies: These are the things which defile a man: but to eat with unwashen hands defileth not a man."

Revelation 3:18

"I counsel thee to buy of me gold tried in the fire, that thou mayest be rich; and white raiment, that thou mayest be clothed, and that the shame of the nakedness do not appear; and anoint thine eyes with eyeslave, that thou mayest see."

Hebrews 9:27

"And it is appointed unto men once to die, but after this the judgment."

Luke 21:19

"In your patience possess ye your souls."

Isaiah 26:3-4

"Thou wilt keep him in perfect peace, whose mind is stayed on thee: because he trusteth in thee. Trust ye in the Lord forever: for in the Lord JEHOVAH is everlasting strength."

Isaiah 61:1-3

"The Spirit of God is upon me; because the Lord has anointed me to preach good tidings unto the meek; he hath sent me to bind up the brokenhearted, to proclaim liberty to the captives, and the opening of the prison to them that are bound; To proclaim the acceptable year of the Lord, and the day of vengeance of our God; to comfort all that mourn; To appoint unto them that mourn in Zion, to give them beauty for ashes, the oil of joy for mourning, the garment of praise for the spirit of heaviness; that they might be called the trees of righteousness, the planting of the Lord, that he might be glorified."

Romans 8:24-25

"For we are saved by hope: but hope that is seen is not hope: for what a man seeth, why doth he yet hope for? But if we hope that we see not, then do we with patience wait for it."

Ecclesiastes 9:4-5

"For to him that is joined to the living there is hope: for a living dog is better than a dead lion. For the living know that they shall die: but the dead know not anything, neither have they any more reward; for the memory of them is forgotten."

Lamentations 3

"I am the man that hath seen affliction by the rod of his wrath. He hath led me, and brought me into darkness, but not into light. Surely against me has he turned; he turneth his hand against me all the day. My flesh and my skin has he made old: he had broken my bones. He hath builded against me, and compassed me with gall and travail. He had set me in the dark places, as they that be dead of old. He had hedged me about, that I cannot get out: he hath made my chain heavy. Also when I cry and shout, he shutteth out my prayer. He hath enclosed my ways with hewn stone, he had made my paths crooked. He was unto me as a bear lying in wait, and as a Lion in secret places.

He hath turn aside my ways, and pulled me into pieces: he had made me desolate. He hath bent his bow, and set me a mark for his arrow. He hath caused the arrows of his quiver to enter into my reins. I was a derision to all my people; and their song all day. He hath filled me with bitterness, he had made me drunken with wormwood. He hath also broken my teeth with gravel stones, he hath covered me with ashes. And thou hast removed my soul far off from peace: I forgot prosperity. And I said, My strength and my hope is perished from the Lord: Remembering mine affliction and my misery, the wormwood and the gall. This I recall to my mind, therefore have I hope. It is of the Lord's Mercies that we are not consumed, because his compassions fail not. They are new every morning: great is thy faithfulness. The Lord is my portion, saith my soul; therefore will I hope in him. The Lord is good unto them that wait for him, to the soul that seeketh him. It is good that a man should both hope and quietly wait for the Salvation of the Lord. It is good for a man that he bear the yoke in his youth. He sitteth alone and keepeth silence, because he hath borne it upon him. He putteth his mouth in the dust; if so be there may be hope. He giveth his cheek to him that smiteth him: he is filled full of reproach. For the Lord will not cast off for ever. But though he cause grief, yet will he have compassion according to the multitude of his mercies. For he doeth not afflict willingly nor grieve the children of men. To crush under his feet all the prisoners of the earth, To turn aside the right of a man before the face of the most High, To subvert a man in his cause, the Lord approveth not. Who is he that saith, and it cometh to pass, when the Lord commandeth it not? Out of the mouth of the most High proceedeth not evil and good? Wherefore doth a living man complain, a man for the punishment of his sins? Let us search and try our ways, and turn again to the Lord. Let us lift up our heart with our hands unto God in the heavens. We have transgressed and rebelled: thou hast not pardoned. Thou hast covered with anger, and persecuted us: thou hast slain, thou hast not pitied. Thou hast covered thyself with a cloud, that our prayer should not pass through.

Thou hast made us as the off scouring and refuse in the midst of the people. All of our enemies have opened their mouths against us. Fear and a snare is come upon us, desolation and destruction. Mine eye runneth down with rivers of water for the destruction of the daughter of my people. Mine eye trickleth down, and ceaseth not, without any intermission, Till the Lord look down, and behold heaven. Mine enemies chased me sore, like a bird, without cause. They cut off my life in the dungeon, and cast a stone upon me. Waters flowed over mine head; then I said, I am cut off. I called upon thy name, O Lord, out of the low dungeon. Thou hast heard my voice: hide not thine ear at my breathing, at my cry. Thou drewest near in the day that I called upon thee: thou saidst, Fear not. O Lord, thou hast pleaded the causes of my soul; thou hast redeemed my life. O Lord, thou hast seen my wrong; judge thou my cause. Thou hast seen all their vengeance and all their imaginations against me. Thou hast heard their reproach, O Lord, and all their imaginations against me; The lips of those who rose up against me, and their devices against me all the day. Behold their sitting down, and their rising up; I am their music. Render unto them a recompence, O Lord, according to the work of their hands. Persecute and destroy them in anger from under the heavens of the Lord.

Ephesians 20:1-7

"And you has he quickened, who were dead in trespasses and sins; Wherein in time past you walked according to the course of this world, according to the prince of the power of the air, the spirit that now worketh in the children of disobedience: Among whom also we all had our conversation in times past in the Lusts of the Flesh, fulfilling the desires of the flesh and the mind; and were by nature the children of wrath, even as others. But, GOD, who is rich in mercy, for his great Love wherewith he loved us, Even when we were dead in sins, hath quickened us together with Christ, (by Grace ye are saved;) And hath raised us up together, and made us sit together in heavenly places in Christ Jesus: That in the ages to come might shew the exceeding riches of his Grace in his kindness toward us through Christ Jesus.

Hebrews 11:1

"Now faith is the substance of things hoped for, the evidence of things not seen."

2 Peter 3:8-9;13

"But, beloved, be not ignorant of this one thing, that one day is with the Lord as a thousand years, and a thousand years as one day. The Lord is not slack concerning his promise, as some count slackness; but is longsuffering to us-ward, not willing that any should perish, but that all should come to repentance.; Nevertheless we, accordingly to his promise, look for new heavens and a new earth, wherein dwelleth righteousness."

1 Corinthians 2:9

"But as it is written, Eye hath not seen, nor ear heard, neither have entered into the heart of man, the things which God hath prepared for them that love him."

John 8: 23

"And he said unto them, Ye are from beneath; I am from above: Ye are from this World; I am not of this World."

Romans 8:14-18

"For as many as are led by the Spirit of God, they are the sons of God. For ye have not received the spirit of bondage again to fear; but ye have received the spirit of adoption, whereby we cry, Ab'-ba, Father. The Spirit itself beareth witness with our spirit, that we are the sons of God: and if children, then heirs; heirs of God, and joint-heirs with Christ; if so be that we suffer with him, that we may be also glorified together. For I reckon that the sufferings of this present time are not worthy to be compared with the glory which shall be revealed in us."

Matthew 6:33

"But seek ye first the kingdom of God, and his righteousness; and all these things shall be added unto you."

Ecclesiastes 12:13-14

"Let us here the conclusion of the matter: Fear God and keep his commandments: for this is the whole duty of man. For God shall bring every work into judgment, with secret thing, whether it be good, or whether it be evil."

Matthew 7:20

"Wherefore by their fruits ye shall know them."

Matthew 7:21-23

"Not every one that saith unto me, Lord, Lord, shall enter into the Kingdom of heaven; but he that doeth the will of my Father which is in heaven. Many will say to me in that day, Lord, Lord, have we not prophesied in thy name? And in thy name cast out devils? And in thy name done many wonderful works? And then I will profess unto them, I never knew you: depart from me that work iniquity."

Luke 17:5-6

"And the apostles said unto the Lord, Increase our faith. And the Lord said, If ye had faith of a grain of mustard seed, ye might say unto this sycamine tree, Be thou plucked up by the root, and be thou planted in the sea; and it should obey you."

Romans 12:3

"For I say, through the grace given unto me, to every man that is among you, not to think of himself more highly than he ought to think; but to think soberly, according as God halt dealt to every man the measure of faith."

Philippians 4:19

"But my God shall supply all your need according to his riches in glory by Christ Jesus."

1 Timothy 4:8

"For bodily exercise profited little: but godliness is profitable unto all things, having promise of the life that now is, and that which is to come."

James 5:13-16

"Is any among you afflicted? Let him pray. Is any merry? Let him sing psalms. Is any sick among you? Let him call for the elders of the church; and let them pray over him, anointing him with oil in the name of the Lord: And the prayer of faith shall save the sick, and the Lord shall raise him up; and if he had committed sins, they shall be forgiven him. Confess your faults one to another, and pray

one for another, that ye may be healed. The effectual fervent prayer of a righteous man availeth much."

Galatians 6:7-8

"Be not deceived; God is not mocked: for whatsoever a man soweth, that shall he reap. For he that soweth to his flesh reap corruption; but he that soweth to the Spirit shall of the Spirit reap life everlasting."

Galatians 5:16-23

"This I say then, Walk in the Spirit, and ye shall not fulfil the lust of the flesh. For the flesh lusteth against the Spirit, and the Spirit against the flesh: and these are contrary the one to the other: so that ye cannot do the things ye would. But if ye be led of the Spirit, ye are not under the law. Now the works of the flesh are manifest, which are these; Adultery, fornication, uncleanness, lasciviousness, Idolatry, witchcraft, hatred, variance, emulations, wrath, strife, seditions, heresies, Envyings, murders, drunkenness, revellings, and such like: of the which I tell you before, as I have also told you in time past, that they which do such things shall not inherit the kingdom of God. _But the fruit of the Spirit is love, joy, peace, longsuffering, gentleness, goodness, faith, meekness, temperance: against such there is no law. And they that are Christ's have crucified the flesh with the afflictions and lusts._"

1 Corinthians 12:7-11

"But the manifestation of the Spirit is given to every man to profit withal. For to one is given by the Spirit _the word of wisdom;_ to another _the word of knowledge_ by the same Spirit; To another _faith_ by the same Spirit; to another _the gifts of healing_ by the same Spirit; To another _the working of miracles;_ to another _prophecy;_ to another _discerning of spirits;_ to another _divers kinds of tongues;_ to another the _interpretation of tongues:_ But all these worketh that one and the selfsame Spirit, _dividing to every man severally as he will._"

Romans 11:29

"For the gifts and the calling of God are without repentance."

Luke 19:37-40

"And when he was come nigh, even now at the descent of the mount of Olives, the whole multitude of the disciples began to rejoice and praise God with a loud voice for all the mighty works that they had seen; Saying, blessed be the King that cometh in the name of the Lord: peace in heaven, and glory in the highest. And some of the Pharisees from among the multitude said unto him, Master, rebuke thy disciples. And he answered and said unto them, I tell you that, if these should hold their peace, the stones would immediately cry out."

John 14:37-38

"Philip saith unto him, Lord, shew us the Father, and it sufficeth us. Jesus saith unto him, Have I been so long time with you, and yet hast thou not known me, Philip? He that hath seen me hath seen the Father; and how sayest thou then, Shew us the Father? Believest thou not that I am in the Father, and the Father in me?

The words that I speak unto you I speak not of myself: but the Father that dwelleth in me, he doeth the works. Believe me that I am in the Father, and the Father in me: or else believe me for the very works' sake. Verily, Verily, I say unto you, He that believeth on me, the works that I do shall he do also; and greater works than these shall he do; because I go unto my Father."

Hebrews 5:12-14

"For when for the time ye ought to be teachers, ye have need that one to teach you again which be the first oracles of God; and are become such as have need of milk, and not of strong meat. For every one that useth milk is unskillful in the word of righteousness: for he is a babe. But strong meat belonged to them that are of full age, even those who by reason of use have their senses exercised to discern both good and evil."

Romans 12:3

"For I say, through the grace given unto me, to every man that is among you, not to think of himself more highly than he ought to think; but to think soberly, accordingly as God hath dealt to every man the measure of faith."

Matthew 11:28-30

"Come unto me, all ye that labor and are heavy laden, and I will give you rest. Take my yoke upon you, and learn of me; for I am meek and lowly in heart: and ye shall find rest unto your souls. For my yoke is easy, and my burden is light."

Romans 8:27-28

"And he that searcheth the hearts knoweth what is the mind of the Spirit, because he maketh intercession for the saints according to the will of God. And we know that all things work together for good to them that love God, to them who are the called according to his purpose."

James 1: 22-25

"But be ye doers of the word and not hearers only, deceiving your own selves. For if any be a hearer of the word, and not a doer, he is like unto a man beholding his natural face in a glass: For he behold himself, and goeth his way, and straightway fretted what manner of man he was."

1 Peter 5:6-11

"Humble yourselves therefore under the mighty hand of God, that he may exalt you in due time: Casting all your care upon him; for he careth for you. Be sober, be vigilant; because your adversary the devil, as a roaring lion, walketh about, seeking whom he may devour. Whom resist steadfast in the faith, knowing that the same afflictions are accomplished in your brethren that are in the world. But the God of all grace, who hath called us unto his eternal glory by Christ Jesus, after that ye suffered a while, make you perfect, stablish, strengthen, settle you.

To him be glory and dominion for ever and ever. Amen."

Ephesians 3:14-21

"For this cause I bow my knees unto the Father of our Lord Jesus Christ, Of whom the whole family in heaven and earth are named, That he would grant you, according to the riches of his glory, to be strengthened with might by his Spirit in the inner man; That Christ may dwell in your hearts by faith; that ye, being rooted and

grounded in love, May be able to comprehend with all saints what is the breadth, and length, and depth, and height; And to know the love of Christ, which passeth the knowledge, that ye might be filled with all the fulness of God. Now unto him that is able to do exceeding abundantly above all that we ask or think, according to the power that worketh in us, Unto him be glory in the church by Christ Jesus throughout the all ages, world without end. Amen."

2Corinthians 10:3-6

"For though we walk in the flesh, we do not war after the flesh: (For the weapons of our warfare are not carnal, but mighty through God to the pulling down of strong holds;) Casting down imaginations, and every high thing that exalteth itself against the knowledge of God, and bringing into captivity every thought to the obedience of Christ; And having in readiness to revenge all disobedience, when your obedience is fulfilled."

Matthew 7, verses 13-14

"Enter ye in at the strait gate: for wide is the gate, and broad is the way, that leadeth to destruction, and many there be which go in thereat: Because strait is the gate, and narrow is the way, which leadeth unto Life, and few there be that find it."

Matthew 20:16

"So the last shall be first, and the first last: for many be called, but few are chosen."

Matthew chapter 4

"It is written, Man shall not live by bread alone, but by every word that proceeded out of the mouth of God."

John 6:48;53-58

"I am that bread of life. Then Jesus said unto them, Verily, Verily, I say unto you, Except ye eat the flesh of the Son of man, and drink his blood, ye have no life in you. Whoso eateth my flesh, and drinketh my blood, hath eternal life; and I will raise him up at the last day. For my flesh is meat indeed, and my blood is drink indeed. He that eateth my flesh, and drinketh my blood, dwelleth in me, and I in him. As the living Father hath sent me, and I live by the

Father: so he that eateth me, even he shall live by me. This is the bread which came down from heaven: not as your fathers did eat manna, and are dead: he that eateth of this bread shall live for ever."

Matthew 10:28

"And fear not them which kill the body, but are not able to kill the soul: but rather fear him which is able to destroy both soul and body in Hell."

1 John 4:8-9

"He that loveth not knoweth not God; for God is love. In this was manifested the love of God toward us, because that God sent his only begotten Son into the world, that we might live through him." And the 18th verse it is written, "There is no fear in love; but perfect love casteth out fear: because fear hath torment. He that feareth is not made perfect in love."

Luke 14:26-28;33

"If any man come to me and hate not his father, and his mother, and wife, and children, and brethren, and sisters, yea, and his own life also, he cannot be my disciple. And whosoever doth not bear his own cross, and come after me, cannot be my disciple. For which of you, intending to build a tower, sitteth not down first, and counteth the cost, whether he have sufficient to finish it?; So likewise, whosoever he be of you that forsaketh not all that he hath, he cannot be my disciple."

John 4:23-24

"But the hour cometh, and now is, when the true worshippers shall worship the Father in spirit and in truth: for the Father seeketh such to worship him. God is a Spirit: and they that worship him must worship him in spirit and truth."

Revelations 22:12-17

"And behold, I come quickly; and my reward is with me, to give every man accordingly as his work shall be. I am the Alpha and Omega, the beginning and the end, the first and the last. Blessed

are they that do his commandments, that they may have right to the tree of life; and may enter in through the gates into the city.

For without are dogs, and sorcerers, and whoremongers, and murderers, and idolaters, and whosoever loveth and maketh a lie. I Jesus have sent mine angel to testify unto you these things in the churches. I am the root and the offspring of David, and the bright and morning star. And the Spirit and the Bride say, Come. And let him that heareth say, Come. And let him that is athirst come. And whosoever will, let him take the water of life freely."

Matthew 12:43-45

"When the unclean spirit is gone out of a man, he walketh through the dry places, seeking rest, and findeth none. Then he saith, I will return into my house from whence I came out; and when he is come, he findeth it empty, swept, and garnished. Then goeth he, and taketh with him seven other spirits more wicked than himself, and they enter in and dwell there: and the last state of that man is worse than the first. Even so shall it be also unto this wicked generation."

1 Peter 4:1-2

"Forasmuch then as Christ hath suffered for us in the flesh, arm yourselves likewise with the same mind: for he that hath suffered in the flesh hath ceased from sin; That he no longer should live the rest of his time in the flesh to the lusts of men, but to the will of God."

Luke 11:21-26

"When a strong man armed keepeth his palace, his goods are in peace: But when a stronger than he shall come upon him, and overcome him, he taketh from him all his armour wherein he trusted, and divided his spoils. He that is not with me is against me: and he that gathered not with me scattered. When the unclean spirit is gone out of a man, he walketh through dry places, seeking rest; and finding none, he saith, I will return unto my house whence I came out. And when he cometh, he findeth it swept and garnished. Then goeth he, and taketh to him seven other spirits more wicked than himself; and they enter in, and dwell there: and the last state of that man is worse than the first."

1 Peter 4:17-19

"For the time has come that judgment must begin at the house of God: and if it first begin at us, what shall the end be of them that obey not the gospel of God? And if the righteous scarcely be saved, where shall the ungodly and the sinner appear? Wherefore let them that suffer accordingly to the will of God commit the keeping of their souls to him in well-doing, as unto a faithful Creator."

John 15:1-8

"I AM the true vine, and my Father is the husbandman. Every branch in me that beareth not fruit he taketh away: and every branch that beareth fruit, he purgeth it, that it may bring forth more fruit. Now ye are clean through the word which I have spoken unto you. Abide in me, and I in you. As the branch cannot bear fruit of itself, except it abide in the vine; no more can ye, except ye abide in me. I am the vine, ye are the branches: He that abideth in me, and I in him, the same bringeth forth much fruit: for without me ye can do nothing. If a man abide not in me, he is cast forth as a branch, and is withered; and men gather them, and cast them into the fire, and they are burned. If ye abide in me, and my words abide in you, ye shall ask what ye will, and it shall be done unto you. Herein is my Father glorified, that ye bear much fruit; so shall ye be my disciples."

Luke 8:4-15

"And when much people were gathered together, and were come to him out of every city, he spake by a parable: A sower went out to sow his seed: and as he sowed, some fell by the way side; and it was trodden down, and the fowls of the air devoured it. And some fell upon a rock; and as soon as it sprung up, it withered away, because it lacked moisture. And some fell among thorns;

And the thorns sprang up with it, and choked it. And some fell on good ground, and sprang up, and bare fruit an hundredfold. And when he had said these things, he cried, He that hath ears to hear, let him hear. And his disciples asked him, saying, What might this parable be?

And he said, Unto you it is given to know the mysteries of the kingdom of God: but to others in parables; that seeing they might not see, and hearing they might not understand. Now the parable is this: The seed is the word of God. Those by the way side are they that hear; then cometh the devil, and taketh away the word out of their hearts, lest they should believe and be saved. They on the rock are they, which, when they hear, receive the word with joy; and these have no root, which for a while believe, and in time of temptation fall away. And they which fell among thorns are they, which, when they have heard, go forth, and are choked with cares and riches and pleasures of this life, and bring no fruit to perfection. But that on good ground are they, which in an honest and good heart, having heard the word, keep it, and bring forth fruit with patience."

Galatians 5:16-23

"This I say then, Walk in the Spirit, and ye shall not fulfil the lust of the flesh. For the flesh lusteth against the Spirit, and the Spirit against the flesh: and these are contrary the one to the other: so that ye cannot do the things ye would. But if ye be led of the Spirit, ye are not under the law. Now the works of the flesh are manifest, which are these; Adultery, fornication, uncleanness, lasciviousness, Idolatry, witchcraft, hatred, variance, emulations, wrath, strife, seditions, heresies, Envyings, murders, drunkenness, revellings, and such like: of the which I tell you before, as I have also told you in time past, that they which do such things shall not inherit the kingdom of God. But the fruit of the Spirit is love, joy, peace, longsuffering, gentleness, goodness, faith, meekness, temperance: against such there is no law. And they that are Christ's have crucified the flesh with the afflictions and lusts."

Isaiah 1:18-20

"Come now, and let us reason together, saith the Lord: though your sins be as scarlet, they shall be as white as snow; though they be red as crimson, they shall be as wool. If ye be obedient, ye shall eat the good of the land: But if ye refuse and rebel, ye shall be devoured with the sword: for the mouth of the Lord hath spoken it."

2 Timothy 2:19-21

"Nevertheless the foundation of God standeth sure, having this seal, The Lord knoweth them that are his. And, Let every one that nameth the name of Christ depart from iniquity. But in a great house there are not only vessels of gold and of silver, but of wood and of earth; and some to honour, and some to dishonor. If a man therefore purge himself from these, he shall be a vessel unto honour, sanctified, and meet for the master's use, and prepared unto every good work."

James 1:12-16

"Blessed is the man that endureth temptation: for when he is tried, he shall receive the crown of life, which the Lord has promised to them that love him. Let no man say when he is tempted, I am tempted of God: for God cannot be tempted with evil, neither tempteth he any man: But every man is tempted, when he is drawn away of his own lust, and enticed. Then when lust hath conceived, it bringeth forth sin: and sin, when it is finished, bringeth forth death. Do not err, my beloved brethren."

Exodus 30:22-33

"Moreover the Lord spake unto Moses, saying, Take thou also unto thee principle spices, of pure myrrh five hundred she-kels, and of sweet cinnamon half so much, even two hundred and fifty shekels, and of sweet calamus two hundred and fifty shekels, And of cassia five hundred she-kels, after the shekel of the sanctuary, and of oil olive an hin: And thou shalt make it an oil of holy ointment, and ointment compound after the art of the apothecary: it shall be an holy anointing oil. And thou shalt anoint the tabernacle of the congregation therewith, and the ark of the testimony, And the table and all his vessels, and the candlestick and his vessels, and the altar of incense, And the altar of burnt offering with all vessels, and the laver and his foot. And thou shalt sanctify them, that they may be most holy: whatsoever toucheth them shall be holy. And thou shalt anoint Aaron and his sons, and consecrate them, that they may minister unto me in the priest's office. And thou shalt speak unto the children of Israel, saying, This shall be an holy anointing oil unto me throughout your generations. Upon man's

flesh shall it not be poured, neither shall ye make any other like it, after the composition of it: it is holy, and it shall be holy unto you. Whosoever compoundeth any like it, or whosoever putteth any of it upon a stranger, shall be cut of from his people."

Galatians 5:16-18

"This I say then, Walk in the Spirit, and ye shall not fulfill the lust of the flesh. For the flesh lusteth against the Spirit, and the spirit against the flesh: and these are contrary the one to the other: so that ye cannot do the things that you would. But if ye be led of the Spirit, ye are not under the law (curse)."

John 8:31-32;34;36

"If ye continue in my word, then ye are my disciples indeed; And ye shall know the truth, and the truth shall make you free."; "Verily, Verily, I say unto you, Whosoever committeth sin is the servant of sin."; "If the Son therefore shall make you free, ye shall be free indeed."

Galatians 5:19-23

"Now the works of the flesh are manifest, which are these; adultery, fornication, uncleanness, lasciviousness, idolatry, witchcraft, hatred, variance, emulations, wrath, strife, seditions, heresies, envyings, murders, drunkenness, revellings, and such like: of the which I tell you before, as I have also told you in time past, that they which do such things shall not inherit the Kingdom of God."

1 Thessalonians 4:1-7

"Furthermore then we beseech you, brethren, and exhort you by the Lord Jesus Christ, that as ye have received of us how ye ought to walk and to please God, so ye would abound more and more. For ye know what commandment we gave you by the Lord Jesus. For this is the will of God, even your sanctification, that ye abstain from fornication: That everyone of you should know how to possess his vessel in sanctification and honor; Not in the lust of concupiscence, even as the Gentiles which know not God: That no man go beyond and defraud his brother in any matter: because that the Lord is the avenger of all such, as we also have forewarned you and testified. For God had not called us unto uncleanness, but unto holiness."

Revelations 21:7-8

"He that overcometh shall inherit all things; and I will be his God and he shall be my son. But the fearful, and unbelievers, and the abominable, and murderers, and whoremongers, and sorcerers, and idolaters, and all liars, shall have their part in the lake of fire and brimstone: which is the second death."

Matthew 6:22-23

"The light of the body is the eye: if therefore thine eye be single, thy whole body shall be full of light. But if thine eye be evil, thy whole body shall be full of darkness. If therefore the light that is in these be darkness, how great is that darkness!"

Mark 9:43-44

"And if thy hand offend thee, cut it off: it is better for thee to enter life maimed, than having two hands to go into hell, into the fire that never shall be quenched: Where their worm dieth not, and the fire is not quenched."

1Peter 1:3-9

"Blessed be the God and Father of our Lord Jesus Christ, which accordingly to his abundant mercy hath begotten us again unto a lively hope by the resurrection of Jesus Christ from the dead, To an inheritance incorruptible, and undefiled, and the fadeth not away, reserved in heaven for you, Who are kept by the power of God through faith unto salvation ready to be revealed in the last time. Wherein ye greatly rejoice, though now for a season, if need be, ye are in heaviness through manifold temptations: That the trial of your faith being much more precious than of gold that perisheth, though it be tried with fire, might be found unto praise and honour and glory at the appearing of Jesus Christ: Whom having not seen, ye love; in whom, though now ye see him not, yet believing, ye rejoice with joy unspeakable and full of glory: Receiving the end of your faith, even the salvation of your souls."

Matthew 3:7-12

"But when he saw many of the Pharisees and Sadducees come to his baptism, he said to them, O generation of vipers, who hath warned you to flee from the wrath to come? Bring therefore fruits

meet for repentance: And think not to say within yourselves, We have Abraham to our father: for I say unto you, that God is able of these stones to raise up children unto Abraham. And now the axe is laid unto the root of the trees: therefore every tree which bringeth not forth good fruit is hewn down, and cast into the fire. I indeed baptize you with water unto repentance: but he that cometh after me is mightier than I, whose shoes I am not worthy to bear: he shall baptize you with the Holy Ghost, and with fire: Whose fan is in his hand, and he will thoroughly purge his floor, and gather his wheat into the garner; but he will burn up the chaff with unquenchable fire."